B

DATA ANALYSIS
A Model-Comparison Approach

Under the General Editorship of
Jerome Kagan
Harvard University

DATA ANALYSIS
A Model-Comparison Approach

Charles M. Judd

Gary H. McClelland

University of Colorado

 Harcourt Brace Jovanovich, Publishers

San Diego   New York   Chicago   Austin   Washington, D.C.
London   Sydney   Tokyo   Toronto

ISBN: 0-15-516765-0

Library of Congress Catalog Card Number: 88-82141

Printed in the United States of America

PREFACE

Goals and Assumptions

Statistics courses, textbooks, and software are usually organized in the same way that a cookbook is organized. Typically, various recipes are given in different chapters for different kinds of research designs or data structures. In fact, numerous statistics books include a chart at the beginning, pointing the reader to various chapters and ostensibly different statistical procedures, depending on what their data look like and the kinds of questions that they wish to answer. As a result, social and behavioral scientists, as consumers of statistics, typically organize their statistical knowledge in much the same way: "With this sort of data, I know to do this test. With that sort of data, I know to do that test."

This book has been written under the assumption that this sort of organization for statistical knowledge has distinct costs. To extend the cookbook analogy, cooks who rely on cookbooks don't know how to proceed when they wish to prepare a dish for which no recipe has been included. When students are confronted with data that do not fit nicely into one of the categories for which they have learned a statistical procedure, frustration and errors frequently occur. The student may proceed to use the wrong test, making inappropriate assumptions about the structure of the data in order to use a well-learned statistical procedure. We have encountered far too many students who have learned only orthogonal analysis of variance with equal sample sizes who bludgeon their data to fit the test they know well. We have also heard some of our colleagues moan that a given data analysis problem would be simple if only they had a particular specialized computer program that was available at their previous university.

A totally different sort of organization forms the basis of this book. Our focus is on how statistical procedures can be seen as tools for building and testing MODELs of DATA. A consistent framework is used throughout the book to develop a few powerful techniques for model building and statistical inference. This framework subsumes all of the different statistical recipes that are normally found in the cookbooks, but it does so in a totally integrated manner. As we build and test MODELs, we develop a consistent vocabulary to refer to our models and inference procedures. At each step, however, we clearly show the reader how our vocabulary and models can be translated back into the recipes of the old cookbooks.

We are convinced that this integrated framework represents a better way to learn and think about data analysis. Students who understand data analysis through our framework will be able to ask the questions of their data which they want to ask instead of the questions that the designer of some textbook or of some computer statistical package assumed they would want to ask. In the end, students will use theory and their own intelligence to guide their data analysis instead of turning over the analysis to a cookbook set of procedures or to a computer program. Intelligent data analysis is our goal. Rather than applying recipes that have been learned by rote, we wish to enable students to write their own recipes as they do data analysis.

A few words are in order concerning our assumptions about the reader and the structure of the book. We assume that the reader is a student or professional researcher in the social sciences, business, education, or related fields who wants to analyze data to answer significant theoretical or practical questions in a substantive discipline. We assume the reader does not want to become a statistician but will always be more interested in the substantive discipline, with data analysis a tool rather than an end in itself.

We assume that the reader is reasonably facile with basic algebraic manipulations because almost all of our MODELs for DATA will be expressed algebraically. But we do not assume any other mathematical training such as calculus or matrix algebra. A very important assumption is that we presume the reader has access to a computer with a good multiple regression program in a statistical software package such as SAS (SAS Institute Inc., 1985; see also Freund, Littell, & Spector, 1986); SPSS-X (SPSS Inc., 1983; see also Norušis, 1985); BMDP (Dixon, 1981); MINITAB (Ryan, Joiner, & Ryan, 1985); SCSS (Nie, et al., 1980); and S (Becker & Chambers, 1984). Access to one of the many good multiple regression programs available on a personal computer is acceptable as a substitute, and even desirable as a complement.

Our assumptions about the reader and our goal of training data analysts instead of statisticians have prompted several decisions about the structure of this book.

1. We present only enough mathematical derivations to provide conceptual clarity. We will generally assume that the mathematical statisticians have done their job correctly, and so we will use many of their results without proving them ourselves. At the same time, however, we cannot abandon all mathematical details because it is extremely important that the data analyst be able to recognize when the data analysis and particularly the MODEL of the DATA are inappropriate or in need of modification. The choice of which derivations to include is therefore guided by the goal of training educated data analysts and not mathematical statisticians.

2. We let the computer do the computational work. Most statistics cookbooks present many different calculation formulas for each statistic. The different formulas facilitate hand calculation for different organizations of the raw data. We assume that the reader is interested in the science and not the calculations and will use the most efficient means to do the calculations—the computer. Ironically, the old hand-calculation formulas can be disastrous when implemented in computer programs because of problems of rounding errors and other computer idiosyncrasies. Neither the computational formulas that are best for computers nor the hand-calculation formulas are very conceptual. Hence, we avoid both computer- and hand-oriented formulas. We present instead formulas that emphasize the concepts but which may not be very useful for direct computations either by hand or by computer.

3. We try as much as possible to work from the general to the specific so that an integrated framework emerges. Many statistics books begin with details and simple statistics and then slowly build up to more general models, changing concepts and notation frequently along the way. While we begin with simple MODELs of DATA and work up, we do so within the context of a consistent overall framework, and we present the simple models using the same concepts and notation we use with the more complex models presented later. Most importantly, we use the same inferential statistics throughout. At each point, however, we provide translations between our framework and notation and the cookbook recipes that so many of us have learned in the past.

4. We do not try to cover all of statistics. There are many statistical procedures that we have left out either because they are infrequently used or because the same thing can be accomplished with a more general model that we do cover. We provide the data analyst with a limited stock of models and statistical procedures, but the models we do provide are quite general and powerful. The goal is to learn a few powerful techniques very thoroughly.

5. We tie our presentation as much as possible to the available statistical software packages. Most of those packages are themselves cookbooks, jammed full of redundant procedures. Consistent with our decision to cover a few powerful models very thoroughly, we concentrate on just a few powerful procedures from the various packages. In particular, we show how *all* the model-building and statistical techniques we present can be accomplished with a good multiple regression program. Examples of such programs that we use for illustrations include REGRESSION in SCSS and SPSS-X, PROC REG (multiple regression) and PROC GLM (general linear model) in SAS, and 1R (multiple regression) in BMDP. Many other multiple regression programs will do as well.

In general it is sufficient to learn the procedures within only one package. We assume that readers are familiar with the data input procedures for whichever package they are using; we discuss only the specifics of the particular analysis procedures in the respective packages.

6. Our framework for data analysis is consistent with what has been called the *regression* approach or the general linear model. The regression approach is often contrasted, unfortunately, with an *analysis-of-variance* approach. Historically, regression has been more often associated with surveys, quasi-experiments, and nonexperimental data, while analysis of variance has more frequently been used for randomized, laboratory experiments. These historical associations cause many people to have a false belief that there is a fundamental difference between the two approaches. We adopt the more general regression approach and show how all of analysis of variance can be accomplished within this framework. This has the important advantage of reducing the number of specialized statistical techniques that must be learned for particular data analysis problems. More importantly, we show how the regression approach provides more control in the analysis of experimental data so that we can ask specific, theoretically-motivated questions of our data—questions that are often different from the standard questions which the procedures of a traditional analysis of variance presume we want to ask.

7. We had a tough decision to make about the vocabulary to be used in this book. On the one hand, we are convinced that the traditional names for the various statistical tests perpetuate false distinctions. For that reason we would have liked to abandon them in favor of a shorter list of names from our integrated framework. However, to do so would have been irresponsible because many readers of this book will have had an introductory course using the traditional names, will have to talk to colleagues who have not read this book, and will have to read journal reports of data analysis that perpetuate the traditional names. We therefore do both: Consistent terminology and notation are used throughout the book to provide an integrated framework, but we also provide frequent translations, usually at the beginning and end of each chapter, between our terms and their traditional counterparts.

Organization of the Book

The preface or introduction in most statistics textbooks describes alternative orders in which the chapters may be studied. That is precisely what we think is wrong with most statistics textbooks. When each chapter or section is self-contained, students are often befuddled by the abrupt change of topics across chapter boundaries. To avoid these abrupt changes, we have organized the chapters in a specific sequence and used a unifying framework for data analysis throughout. Each chapter generally focuses on a single concept, but the understanding of that concept will depend on the concepts developed in the previous chapters. Thus, we do not think the chapters should be read in any order other than the one in which they are presented. This means, of course, that our book cannot be used as a cookbook. But then, we have made clear that we think the cookbook organization of statistical knowledge is misguided.

While the reader who uses our book to look up a specific test may be frustrated by the sequential organization of our book, we are convinced that this organization represents a better way to learn statistics. It substantially reduces the number of separate concepts that must be mastered and allows progressive accumulation of integrated knowledge about data analysis rather than disconnected amassing of discrete recipes.

Chapter 1 presents an overview of data analysis through the concepts DATA, MODEL, and ERROR and integrates them in the equation DATA = MODEL + ERROR. The concept of proportional reduction in error (PRE) is introduced as a tool for sorting our way through alternative MODELs for a given set of DATA. Chapter 2 considers alternative definitions of ERROR and shows the implications for MODEL for each of the alternative definitions. In the course of examining the alternative definitions of ERROR, we develop the usual descriptive statistics for location and spread. Chapter 3 develops some useful graphical techniques for displaying DATA. This chapter completes the material on traditional descriptive statistics. Chapter 4 introduces a small set of reasonable assumptions about ERROR and uses those assumptions to choose from among the alternative definitions offered in Chapter 2. The sum of squared errors (SSE) is chosen to be our standard definition of ERROR. This chapter also introduces the concept of sampling distributions of statistics. Chapter 5 uses the material of Chapter 4 to make inferences about MODELs and their parameters. The inferential test developed in this chapter is equivalent to a test usually identified as the *one-sample t-test*, but we present it in a more general form that we will be able to use in all later chapters. All the necessary concepts for statistical inference used throughout the book are contained in Chapters 2, 4, and 5, although the models that are explored in these chapters are exceedingly simple.

The remainder of the book is mostly about building MODELs that vary in their complexity and appropriateness for different kinds of DATA. Chapter 6 is about MODELs that make conditional predictions of DATA based on a single continuous concomitant variable. Such models are usually referred to as *simple regression*. Chapter 7 uses the inferential techniques developed in Chapter 5 to ask questions about the MODELs and their parameters from Chapter 6. Chapter 8 extends the concepts of Chapters 6 and 7 to MODELs that make conditional predictions of DATA based upon multiple continuous concomitant variables. Elsewhere the material in this chapter is often referred to as *multiple regression*. Chapter 9 considers the problems that a few unusual DATA observations known as *outliers* can cause for the MODELs of Chapters 6, 7, and 8. We use the concepts of Chapter 8 to develop an *outlier MODEL*, which can be used to detect outliers and to mitigate their effects on the MODEL for the remainder of the DATA. This is the one chapter of the book that may be profitably read at any point after the first eight chapters have been digested. Subsequent chapters do not depend on its content. Chapter 10 introduces the important technique of including multiplicative products of concomitant variables in MODELs. We then use that technique to develop curvilinear models and to consider the interaction between two or more predictor variables. Chapters 6 through 10 contain all the essential information for what is generally known as *regression analysis*.

Chapters 11 through 15 consider MODELs that use categorical concomitant variables to make conditional predictions of DATA. Such MODELs are often known as the *analysis of variance*. The key link between this material and the previous chapters is provided by Chapter 11, which introduces contrast codes. The use of contrast codes allows all the MODEL-building techniques of Chapters 6 through 10 and all the inferential statistical concepts of Chapters 2 through 5 to be applied *without modification* to MODELs with categorical predictor variables. Chapter 11 develops these important contrast codes for the case of single categorical predictor variables, often known as *one-way analysis of variance*. Chapter 12 shows how MODELs using products, developed in Chapter 10, can be applied to the contrast codes of Chapter 11 to produce MODELs of increasing complexity when there are multiple categorical predictor variables. The MODELs of Chapter 12 are often referred to as *analysis of variance for factorial designs*. Chapter 13 makes the easy generalization to MODELs that include both continuous and categorical predictor variables; these MODELs are sometimes known as the *analysis of covariance*.

An important assumption underlying statistical inference with all the MODELs is that each DATA observation is independent from all other observations. This assumption is unlikely to be true when more than one observation comes from each unit of analysis (e.g., when each person or group provides more than one DATA observation). Chapters 14 and 15 present an approach for building MODELs in such situations that we believe is new and which is entirely consistent with the material in previous chapters. This problem is known in psychology as *within-subjects analysis of variance* in contrast to the MODELs in Chapters 11 through 13, which apply to *between-subjects analysis of variance*. More generally, this problem is referred to as *nonindependent* or *correlated errors*. Chapter 14 presents the basics of our approach for analyzing DATA with correlated ERRORs. This approach consists of developing a separate set of contrast codes for the multiple observations from each unit of analysis, using those codes to construct new DATA variables and then using the machinery of previous chapters to analyze those new DATA variables. Chapter 15 shows how the approach of Chapter 14 can be used to develop MODELs of arbitrary complexity for sophisticated designs that arise in experimental research. Included here are MODELs for the analysis of repeated measures latin square designs and within-subject designs having covariates.

Chapter 16 considers techniques for the detection and treatment of violations of assumptions underlying the procedures for MODEL building and statistical inference presented in the previous chapters. The effect of all the remediation techniques presented is to transform DATA or otherwise restructure the problem so that all the machinery previously developed may be appropriately applied.

The book includes three appendices. Appendix A consists of data and analyses of those data that illustrate the major topics discussed in the body of the book. Thus, we take this single data set and develop increasingly complex MODELs, show the computer output generated by the estimation of those MODELs, and provide substantive interpretations of the results. This appendix is meant to serve as an extended example for the book as a whole. The reader is encouraged to input the data provided in this appendix to his or her own computer package and to replicate the analyses that we outline.

Appendix B consists of assorted problems and exercises that are tied to individual chapters of the book. These should be useful for review and illustration. Answers to selected problems are included.

Appendix C contains numerical exhibits essential for statistical inference and power analysis using PRE. The unified approach means that all statistical inference can be accomplished with only a few statistics; so the set of exhibits included here is much smaller than that usually found in most statistics books. These exhibits were all generated using the SAS statistical computer system. The SAS code for each exhibit is included in the appendix.

Acknowledgments

We began teaching the graduate statistics course in the Psychology Department at the University of Colorado during the academic year 1982–1983. It slowly became apparent to us during that year and the subsequent one that the existing textbooks in the areas of multiple regression and analysis of variance did not meet our needs. Accordingly, we began to write the present one. Since then, the many students who have taken our course have had to put up with our draft attempts at writing this book. We thank them for their patience, their help in showing us what worked and what did not, and for being such cooperative test subjects.

Five different teaching assistants have served us over the years in this course: Marcy Cooper, Craig Gillette, Cynthia Lusk, Avigail Moor, and Carey Ryan. Their assistance, both in the course and in the writing of this book, has been invaluable. They have given us feedback about points where we were unclear, points where greater detail was needed or new examples necessary, and points where we either were proceeding too quickly or too slowly. Both this book and the course would have been much poorer without their assistance.

Four individuals assisted with secretarial and adminstrative chores in the writing of this book. We thank Rae Sullivan, Doreen Victor, Mary Luhring, and Janet Grassia for their very able assistance.

We wish to thank a number of colleagues and teachers. Some of these provided comments on draft chapters. Others have been more instrumental in teaching us what we needed to know in order even to contemplate the writing of this book. We jointly and individually express our appreciation to Clyde Coombs, John Hammond, David Kenny, Lou McClelland, Carol Nickerson, Robert Rosenthal, J.E.K. Smith, and John Smith. We especially want to thank Bernadette Park for helping to teach the course while one of us was on leave and for providing feedback on all of the chapters. Finally, we thank the following reviewers: Robert Abelson, Yale University; Jeffrey Berman, Memphis State University; John Cotton, University of California at Santa Barbara; Raymond Frankmann, Michigan State University; Lawrence Jones, University of Illinois; David Kenny, University of Connecticut; Jeffrey Miller, University of California at San Diego; Robert Seibel, The Pennsylvania State University; and Rebecca Warner, University of New Hampshire.

A number of institutions have supported the work that went into this book. We gratefully acknowledge the support and assistance of the Department of Psychology and the Institute of Cognitive Science at the University of Colorado, the Center for Advanced Study in the Behavioral Sciences, and our publisher, Harcourt Brace Jovanovich. Marcus Boggs, as our editor, has been particularly supportive and cooperative.

Lastly, we thank our wives and children for giving us the support and affection that permitted us to write this book. Our wives, Liz Judd and Lou McClelland, have been our biggest supporters and constant companions during the years we have devoted to this project. Our children, Abby, Emily, and Jean, have put up with much during the course of our writing. Without the love and support of our families, this book never would have been written, and, more importantly, our lives would have been much poorer.

CONTENTS

1

Introduction to Data Analysis

This book is about data analysis. In the social sciences we often collect batches of DATA that we hope will answer questions, test hypotheses, or disprove theories. To do that we must analyze our DATA. In this chapter, we present an overview of what data analysis means. This overview is intentionally abstract with few details so that the "big picture" will emerge. Data analysis is remarkably simple when viewed from this perspective, and understanding the big picture will make it much easier to comprehend the details that will come later.

1.1
Overview of Data Analysis

The process of data analysis is represented by the following simple equation:

DATA = MODEL + ERROR

DATA represents the basic scores or observations, usually but not always numerical, which we want to analyze. The MODEL is a more compact description or representation of the DATA. Our DATA are usually bulky and of a form that is hard to communicate to someone else. The compact description provided by the MODEL is much easier to communicate,

1

say, in a journal article, and is much easier to think about when trying to understand phenomena, to build new theory, and to make predictions. To be a representation of the DATA, all the MODELs we will consider will make a specific prediction for each observation or element in DATA. MODELs range from the simple—making the same prediction for every observation in DATA—to the complex—making differential predictions conditional on other known attributes of each observation. To be less abstract, let's consider an example. Suppose our DATA observations were the automobile fatality rates for each state in the United States for 1978; these DATA are listed in Exhibit 1.1. A simple MODEL would predict the same fatality rate for each state. A more complex MODEL would adjust the prediction for each state according to that state's legal drinking age, population density, enforcement of speed limits, climate, etc. The amount by which we adjust the prediction for a particular attribute (e.g., legal drinking age) is an unknown *parameter* which must be estimated from the DATA.

EXHIBIT 1.1 ▶

Automobile fatality rates by state for 1978 (deaths per 100 million vehicle miles)

i	State	Rate	i	State	Rate
1	Alabama	4.2	26	Montana	4.0
2	Alaska	4.7	27	Nebraska	2.9
3	Arizona	5.3	28	Nevada	5.6
4	Arkansas	3.6	29	New Hampshire	2.8
5	California	3.4	30	New Jersey	2.2
6	Colorado	3.5	31	New Mexico	5.8
7	Connecticut	2.3	32	New York	3.6
8	Delaware	3.3	33	North Carolina	3.6
9	Florida	3.2	34	North Dakota	3.7
10	Georgia	3.3	35	Ohio	2.9
11	Hawaii	4.0	36	Oklahoma	3.5
12	Idaho	4.8	37	Oregon	3.9
13	Illinois	3.0	38	Pennsylvania	3.0
14	Indiana	2.9	39	Rhode Island	1.7
15	Iowa	3.0	40	South Carolina	3.8
16	Kansas	3.5	41	South Dakota	3.4
17	Kentucky	3.2	42	Tennessee	3.3
18	Louisiana	4.6	43	Texas	4.0
19	Maine	3.1	44	Utah	3.9
20	Maryland	2.5	45	Vermont	3.4
21	Massachusetts	2.7	46	Virginia	2.7
22	Michigan	3.2	47	Washington	3.5
23	Minnesota	3.3	48	West Virginia	4.0
24	Mississippi	4.8	49	Wisconsin	3.1
25	Missouri	3.5	50	Wyoming	5.4

The last part of our basic equation is ERROR. ERROR is simply the amount by which the MODEL fails to represent the DATA accurately. It is an index of the degree to which the MODEL mispredicts the DATA observations. We often refer to ERROR as the *residual*—the part that is left over after we have made our best prediction. In other words,

ERROR = DATA − MODEL

One goal of data analysis is then clear: we want to build MODEL to be a good representation of DATA by making ERROR as small as possible. In the unlikely extreme case when ERROR = 0, DATA would be perfectly represented by MODEL.

How do we reduce ERROR and improve our MODELs? One way is to improve the quality of the DATA so that the original observations contain less ERROR. This involves better research designs, better data collection procedures, more reliable instruments, etc. In this book we will not say much about such issues but will leave those problems to texts and courses in experimental design and research methods. Those problems tend to be much more discipline-specific than the general problems of data analysis and so are best left to the separate disciplines. Excellent sources covering those issues are Campbell and Stanley (1963), Cook and Campbell (1979), Judd and Kenny (1981), and Kidder and Judd (1986). Although we will often note some implications of data analysis procedures for the wise design of research, we will in general assume that the data analyst is confronted with the problem of building the best MODEL for DATA which have already been collected.

The method available to the data analyst for reducing ERROR and improving MODELs is straightforward and, in the abstract, the same across disciplines. ERROR can almost always be reduced (never increased) by making the MODEL's predictions conditional on additional information about each observation. This is equivalent to adding parameters to the MODEL and using DATA to build the best estimates of those parameters. The meaning of "best estimate" is clear: we want to set the parameters of the MODEL to whatever values will make ERROR the smallest. The estimation of parameters is sometimes referred to as "fitting" the MODEL to the DATA. Our ideal data analyst has a limited variety of basic MODELs. It is unlikely that any of these MODELs will provide a good fit "off the rack"; instead, the basic MODEL will need to be fitted or tailored to the particular size and bulges of a given DATA customer. In this chapter, we are purposely vague about how ERROR is actually measured and about how parameters are actually estimated to make ERROR as small as possible because that would get us into details to which we devote whole chapters later. But for now the process in the abstract ought to be clear: add parameters to the MODEL and estimate those parameters so that MODEL will provide a good fit to the DATA by making ERROR as small as possible.

To be a bit less abstract, let's again consider the example of automobile fatality rates by state. An extremely simple MODEL would be to predict that the fatality rate for each state is 3.7 deaths per 100 million vehicle miles traveled. This qualifies as a MODEL according to our definition, because it makes a prediction for the fatality rate in each of the 50 states. But in this MODEL there are no parameters to be estimated from the DATA to provide a good fit by making ERROR as small as possible. No matter what the DATA, our MODEL predicts 3.7. We will introduce some notation so that we will have a standard way of talking about the particulars of DATA, MODEL, and ERROR. Let Y_i represent the ith observation in the DATA; in this example Y_i is simply the fatality rate for the ith state. Then our basic equation

$$DATA = MODEL + ERROR$$

becomes for this extremely simple model

$$Y_i = 3.7 + ERROR$$

We can undoubtedly improve our MODEL and reduce ERROR by using a MODEL which is still simple but which has one parameter: predict that the fatality rate is the same in all states, but leave the predicted value as an unspecified parameter to be estimated from the DATA. For example, the average of all 50 fatality rates might provide a suitable estimate. We will let β_0 represent the unknown value that is to be estimated so that our slightly more complex, but still simple, MODEL becomes

$$Y_i = \beta_0 + ERROR$$

It is important to realize that we can never know β_0 for certain; we can only make estimates of it.

We can make our MODEL yet more complex and reduce ERROR further by adding more parameters to make *conditional predictions*. For example, our MODEL could be a basic fatality rate (β_0) for all states which is adjusted upward by a certain amount (β_1) if the legal drinking age is 18 and reduced by that same amount if the legal drinking age is 21. More formally, our basic equation now has a more complex representation, namely

$$Y_i = \beta_0 + \beta_1 + ERROR \quad \text{if the legal drinking age} = 18$$

$$Y_i = \beta_0 - \beta_1 + ERROR \quad \text{if the legal drinking age} = 21$$

The legal drinking age is the condition in this MODEL on which we base our differential or conditional prediction. The substantive hypothesis implicit in this MODEL is that a lower drinking age will mean more drunk drivers and that will mean a higher fatality rate.

We can continue making our MODEL yet more complex by adding parameters to make similar adjustments for climate, population density, etc. By so doing we will be adding still more implicit hypotheses to the MODEL.

It might appear that the best strategy for the data analyst would be to add as many parameters as possible; such is not the case. The number of observations in DATA imposes an inherent limit on the number of parameters that may be added to MODEL. At the extreme we could have separate parameters in our MODEL for each observation and then estimate the value of each such parameter to be identical to the value of its corresponding DATA observation. For example, our prediction might contain statements such as, *If the state is Kentucky, then estimate its parameter to be 3.2*, which is its fatality rate. That procedure would clearly reduce ERROR to zero and provide a perfect fit. But such a MODEL would be uninteresting because it would simply be a duplicate of DATA and would provide no new insights, no bases for testing our theories, and no ability to make predictions in slightly different circumstances. A paramount goal of science is to provide simple, parsimonious explanations for phenomena. A MODEL with a separate parameter for each observation is certainly not parsimonious. Our ideal MODEL, then, is a compact description of the DATA and has many fewer parameters than the number of observations in DATA.

We now have an obvious conflict. The goal of reducing ERROR and providing the best description of DATA causes us to add parameters to the MODEL. On the other hand, the goal of parsimony and the desire for a compact, simple MODEL cause us to remove parameters from the MODEL. The job of the data analyst is to find the proper balance between these two conflicting objectives. Thus, the ultimate goal is to find the smallest, simplest MODEL which provides an adequate description of the DATA so that ERROR is not too large ("too large" will be defined later). In still other words, the data analyst must answer the question of whether it is worthwhile to add yet more parameters to a MODEL.

Returning to the example of automobile fatality rates, we will want to ask whether the extra complexity of making predictions conditional on legal drinking age, population density, climate, etc., is worth the trouble. By so doing, we will simultaneously be asking the question of whether the hypotheses implicit in the more complex models are true. For example, if we decide that conditioning our prediction of fatality rates on each state's legal drinking age is not worthwhile, then we will have effectively rejected the hypothesis that a lower drinking age contributes to an increased automobile fatality rate. This is the essence of testing hypotheses.

Although we are still being vague about how to measure ERROR, we can be more precise about what we mean by, "Are more parameters worthwhile?" We will call the MODEL without the additional parameters the *compact model* and will refer to it as MODEL C. The alternative, *augmented model*, MODEL A, includes all the parameters, if any, of MODEL C plus some additional parameters. The additional parameters of MODEL A may reduce ERROR or leave it unchanged; there is no way the additional parameters can increase ERROR. So it must be that

$$\text{ERROR(A)} \leq \text{ERROR(C)}$$

where ERROR(A) and ERROR(C) are the amounts of ERROR when using MODELs A and C, respectively. The question of whether it is worthwhile to add the extra complexity of MODEL A now reduces to the question of whether the difference between ERROR(C) and ERROR(A) is big enough to worry about. It is difficult to decide based on the absolute magnitude of the ERRORs. We will therefore usually make relative comparisons. One way to do that is to calculate the *proportional reduction in error* (PRE), which represents the proportion of MODEL C's ERROR which is reduced or eliminated when we move to MODEL A. Formally,

$$\text{PRE} = \frac{\text{ERROR(C)} - \text{ERROR(A)}}{\text{ERROR(C)}}$$

The numerator is simply the difference between the two ERRORs—the amount of ERROR reduced—and the denominator is the amount of ERROR for the compact model with which we started. An equivalent expression is

$$\text{PRE} = 1 - \frac{\text{ERROR(A)}}{\text{ERROR(C)}}$$

If the additional parameters do no good, then ERROR(A) will equal ERROR(C), so PRE = 0. If MODEL A provides a perfect fit, then ERROR(A) = 0 and (assuming MODEL C does not also provide a perfect fit) PRE = 1. Clearly, values of PRE will be between 0 and 1. The larger the value of PRE, the more it will be worth the cost of increased complexity to add the extra parameters to the MODEL. The smaller the value of PRE, the more we will want to stick with the simpler, more parsimonious compact model.

For example, ignoring for the moment how we calculate ERROR, assume that total ERROR = 50 for the simple model which says that the fatality rate is the same for all states and that ERROR = 30 for the

MODEL with the additional parameter for legal drinking age. Then, ERROR(C) = 50, ERROR(A) = 30, and

$$PRE = 1 - \frac{30}{50} = 0.40$$

That is, increasing the complexity of the MODEL by considering the legal drinking age would reduce ERROR by 40%.

Let's review where we are. We have transformed the original problem of the conflicting goals for MODEL—parsimony and accurate representation of DATA—into a consideration of the size of PRE for comparing MODEL C and MODEL A. Unfortunately, we have still not solved the problem of the conflicting goals for MODEL, because now we must decide whether a given PRE (e.g., the 40% reduction in the previous example) is big enough to warrant the additional parameter(s). The transformation of the original problem has moved us closer to a solution, however, for now we have a PRE index that will be useful no matter how we finally decide to measure ERROR. More important, PRE has a simple, intuitive meaning which will provide a useful description of the amount of improvement provided by MODEL A over MODEL C.

Deciding whether a PRE of, say, 40% is really worthwhile involves inferential statistics. An understanding of inferential statistics must await the details of measuring ERROR, sampling distributions, and other topics which are developed in Chapters 2, 4, and 5. We can, however, now specify two considerations that will be important in inferential statistics. First, we would be much more impressed with a PRE of, say, 40% if it were obtained with the addition of only one parameter instead of with four or five parameters. Hence, our inferential statistics will need to consider the number of extra parameters added to MODEL C to create MODEL A. *PRE per parameter added* will be a useful index. Second, we noted that n, the number of observations in DATA, serves as an upper limit to the number of parameters that could be added to the MODEL. We will be more impressed with a given PRE as the difference between the number of parameters that were added and the number of parameters that could have been added becomes greater. Hence, our inferential statistics will consider how many parameters *could have been added* to MODEL C to create MODEL A but were not. In other words, we will be more impressed with a PRE of 40% if the number of observations greatly exceeds the number of parameters used in MODEL A than if the number of observations is only slightly larger than the number of parameters.

The use of PRE to compare compact and augmented models is the key to asking questions of our DATA. For each question we want to ask of DATA, we will find appropriate MODELs C and A and compare them by using PRE. For example, if we want to know whether a state's legal drinking age is useful for predicting auto fatality rates, we would compare a MODEL C which does not include a parameter for legal drinking age to a MODEL A which includes all the parameters of MODEL C plus an additional parameter for legal drinking age. If MODEL C is a simple MODEL, i.e., a single-parameter model that makes a constant prediction for all observations, then we are asking whether legal drinking age *by itself* is a useful predictor of fatality rates. If there are other parameters in MODEL C, then we are asking whether legal drinking age is a useful predictor of fatality rates *over and above* the other parameters. (We discuss this at length in Chapter 8.) As another example, if we want to ask whether several factors such as population density, climate, and speed limit enforcement are simultaneously useful in predicting fatality rates, we would use PRE to compare a MODEL C which did not have parameters for any of those factors to a MODEL A which did have those parameters in addition to those in MODEL C.

In the usual language for statistical inference, MODEL C corresponds to the *null hypothesis* and MODEL A corresponds to the alternative hypothesis. More precisely, the null hypothesis is that all the parameters included in MODEL A but not in MODEL C are zero (hence, the name "null"). If we reject MODEL C in favor of MODEL A, then equivalently we reject the null hypothesis implied by the difference between MODELs C and A. That is, we conclude that it is unreasonable to presume that all the extra parameter values in MODEL A are zero. We discuss this fully in Chapter 5.

1.2

Summary

The basic equation for data analysis is

DATA = MODEL + ERROR

The data analyst using this equation must resolve two conflicting goals: (a) to add parameters to MODEL so that it is an increasingly better representation of DATA with correspondingly smaller ERROR, and (b) to remove parameters from MODEL so that it will be a simple, parsimonious representation of the DATA. This is equivalent to asking the question of whether the additional parameters are worth it. We use PRE, the index of the proportional reduction in ERROR, to answer this question by comparing appropriately chosen MODELs C and A. In the traditional language of statistical inference, this is equivalent to comparing a null hypothesis and an alternative hypothesis. The next several chapters provide the information necessary to judge when PRE is large enough to warrant rejecting MODEL C in favor of MODEL A.

1.3

Notation

To facilitate seeing interrelationships between procedures, we use consistent notation throughout. Y_i represents the ith observation from DATA. The first observation is numbered 1 and the last is n, for a total of n observations in DATA. $\hat{Y}_i$ represents the MODEL's prediction of the ith observation. Y will always represent the variable that we are trying to predict with our MODEL. Other variables giving information about each observation on which we might base conditional predictions will be represented by X so that X_{ij} represents the value on the jth associated variable for the ith observation. For example, in the automobile fatality example the 50 fatality rates would be represented as $Y_1, Y_2, \ldots, Y_{50}$ with $n = 50$. X_{i1} could be 1 if the legal drinking age were 18, and -1 if it were 21. In this example we could use X_{i2} to represent the population density in which case the value of X_{i2} would be the population density for the ith state.

For MODEL parameters we will use $\beta_0, \beta_1, \ldots, \beta_j, \ldots, \beta_{p-1}$, for a total of p parameters. Even if we were to know the values of these parameters exactly, we would not expect the MODEL to predict the DATA exactly. Instead, we expect that some random error will cause the MODEL to predict less than perfectly. We let ε_i represent the unknown amount by which we expect MODEL to mispredict Y_i. Thus for the simple MODEL, the basic equation

DATA = MODEL + ERROR

can be expressed in terms of the true parameter β_0 and the error ε_i as

$$Y_i = \beta_0 + \varepsilon_i$$

We can never know the true β parameters exactly. Instead we will have estimates of those parameters, calculated from the DATA, which we will label $b_0, b_1, \ldots, b_j, \ldots, b_{p-1}$, respectively. We use $\hat{Y}_i$ to represent the prediction for the ith observation based on the calculated b's. We then let e_i represent the amount by which $\hat{Y}_i$ mispredicts Y_i; that is,

$$e_i = Y_i - \hat{Y}_i$$

The Greek letters β and ε represent the true but unknowable parameters, and the italic letters b and e represent estimates of those parameters calculated from DATA. For the simple MODEL, the MODEL part of the basic data analysis equation is

MODEL: $\hat{Y}_i = b_0$

and we can express that basic equation in terms of our parameter estimates as either

$$Y_i = \hat{Y}_i + e_i$$

or

$$Y_i = b_0 + e_i$$

Either of the two previous equations are estimates for the basic equation expressed in terms of the unknown parameters as

$$Y_i = \beta_0 + \varepsilon_i$$

The quantity $\beta_j X_{ij}$ tells us how much we should adjust the basic prediction for the ith observation based on the jth variable. For example, if $X_{ij} = 1$ for states with legal drinking ages of 18 and $X_{ij} = -1$ for states with legal drinking ages of 21, then β_j specifies how much to adjust, upward or downward, depending on the sign of X_{ij}, the fatality rate prediction for particular states. A more complicated MODEL involving more parameters can be expressed as

$$Y_i = \beta_0 + \beta_1 X_{i1} + \beta_2 X_{i2} + \cdots + \beta_j X_{ij} + \cdots + \beta_{p-1} X_{i,p-1}$$

$\hat{Y}_i$, the MODEL portion of the data analysis equation, is then represented in terms of the parameter estimates as

$$\text{MODEL: } \hat{Y}_i = b_0 + b_1 X_{i1} + b_2 X_{i2} + \cdots + b_j X_{ij} + \cdots + b_{p-1} X_{i,p-1}$$

The equation

$$\text{DATA} = \text{MODEL} + \text{ERROR}$$

can again be expressed in two ways:

$$Y_i = \hat{Y}_i + e_i$$

or

$$Y_i = b_0 + b_1 X_{i1} + b_2 X_{i2} + \cdots + b_j X_{ij} + \cdots + b_{p-1} X_{i,p-1} + e_i$$

Note that when β's are used on the right side of the equation that the appropriate symbol for the ERROR is always ε_i, and when b's, estimates of β's, are used on the right side of the equation that the appropriate symbol for the ERROR is always e_i. The reason is that in the first instance the ERROR ε_i is unknown, while in the second instance an estimated value e_i can actually be calculated once $\hat{Y}_i$ is calculated.

We will have to develop a few special symbols here and there, but, in general, the above notation is all that is required for all the MODELs we consider in this book.

2

Simple Models: Definitions of ERROR and Parameter Estimates

In this chapter we will consider the very simplest models—models with one or even no parameters. These simple models make the same prediction for all DATA observations; there are no differential predictions conditioned on whatever else we might know about each observation. Such a simple model may not seem very realistic or useful. However, this simple model provides a useful baseline against which we can compare more complicated models, and it will turn out to be more useful than it might appear at first. For many of the questions we will want to ask about our DATA, the appropriate MODEL C will be the simple MODEL with no parameter or one parameter; this will be compared to more complex MODEL A's. Also, the simple model provides a useful first-cut description of DATA.

2.1

Overview of the Simple Model

Formally, the simplest model is

$$Y_i = B_0 + \varepsilon_i$$

where B_0 is some specified value not based on this particular batch of DATA; ε_i is the true error or the amount by which Y_i differs from B_0. The simple model with no estimated parameters is not frequently used in the social sciences because we seldom have theories sufficiently powerful to make an explicit prediction for a parameter. Although we will sometimes want to consider a specified or hypothesized value of B_0 in order to ask an explicit question about DATA, it is much more common to consider the equation

$$Y_i = \beta_0 + \varepsilon_i$$

where β_0 is an unknown parameter which must be estimated from the DATA. In that case, ε_i is the amount by which Y_i differs from β_0 if we were ever to know β_0 exactly. We use b_0 to indicate the estimate of β_0 that we derive from the DATA. Then the predicted value for the ith observation is

$$\hat{Y}_i = b_0$$

and

$$\text{DATA} = \text{MODEL} + \text{ERROR}$$

becomes

$$Y_i = b_0 + e_i$$

where e_i is the amount by which our prediction misses the actual observation. Thus, e_i is the estimate of ε_i. The goal of tailoring the MODEL to provide the best fit to the DATA is equivalent to making the errors

$$e_i = Y_i - b_0$$

as small as possible. We have only one parameter, so this means that we want to find the estimate b_0 for that one parameter that will minimize the errors. However, we are really interested not in each e_i but in some aggregation of all the individual e_i. There are many different ways to perform this aggregation. In this chapter we will consider some of the different ways of aggregating the separate e_i into a summary measure of ERROR. Then we show how each choice of a summary measure of ERROR leads to a different method of calculating b_0 to estimate β_0 so as to provide the best fit of the DATA to the MODEL. Next we consider expressions for a "typical" error. Finally, we illustrate the use of computer programs for calculating the appropriate summary measures of ERROR and their corresponding estimates of β_0.

Measures of location or *measures of central tendency* are the traditional names for the parameter estimates of β_0 developed from the different definitions of ERROR. These names are appropriate because the parameter estimates in the simple MODEL tell us about the location of a typical observation or about the center of a batch of DATA. Specific instances include the mode, median, and mean. *Measures of variability* or *measures of spread* are the traditional names for the expressions for a typical error. These names are appropriate because expressions for typical errors tell us how variable the observations are in a batch of DATA or, equivalently, how far the DATA spread out from the center. Specific instances include median absolute deviation and standard deviation. Together, measures of central tendency and spread are known as *descriptive statistics*. However, this suggests a false distinction between these statistics and those to come later. We want to emphasize that the parameter estimates for β_0 in the simple MODEL are no more nor less descriptive than the parameter estimates we will develop for more complicated MODELs. MODELS and their parameter estimates always provide descriptions of DATA. Hence, we will generally avoid the phrase "descriptive statistics" and just refer to parameter estimates. The reader should be aware, however, that when other textbooks refer to descriptive statistics they are generally referring to the material in this chapter.

2.2

Conceptual Example

Before considering simple MODELs and measures of ERROR more formally, we consider some conceptual examples which will help build useful intuitions so that the subsequent mathematical formulas will be less abstract. Suppose that DATA consisted of the five observations 1, 3, 5, 9, 14. These observations are plotted in Exhibit 2.1. The simple MODEL must make the same prediction for all five observations. The horizontal line represents the value of that constant prediction. The

EXHIBIT 2.1 ▶

ERROR as sum of line lengths (estimate is $\hat{Y}_i = b_0 = 5$)

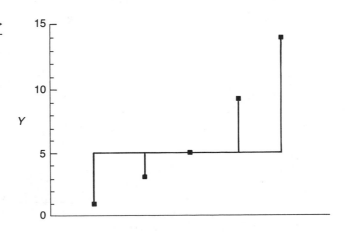

vertical lines drawn from each observation to the prediction line represent the amount by which the prediction misses the actual data value. In other words, the length of the line is e_i. One way to find the best value for $\hat{Y}_i$ and, equivalently, the best estimate b_0 for β_0 is to adjust the $\hat{Y}_i$ line up or down so that the length of the lines is a minimum. In other words, we can use trial and error to find the best estimate. For example, if we were to try 7 as our estimate, the five line lengths would be 6, 4, 2, 2, 7 with a sum of 21. For an estimate of 5, the line lengths would be 4, 2, 0, 4, 9 with a sum of 19. The estimate $b_0 = 5$ produces less total ERROR than $b_0 = 7$, so we can eliminate 7, in favor of 5, as an estimate if our goal is to minimize the total ERROR. We can continue to try other estimates until we find the best one. Exhibit 2.2 shows the sum of the line lengths for different choices of b_0 between 0 and 10. The sum of the line lengths reaches a minimum of 19 when $b_0 = 5$, so that is our best estimate of β_0. We would get more total ERROR, a larger sum of line lengths, if we used a value of b_0 that was either lower or higher than 5. Hence, $b_0 = 5$ is the optimum estimate. Note that 5 is the middle of our five observations; the middle observation in a batch of DATA which have been sorted from smallest to largest is often called the *median*.

It is interesting to ask how we would have to adjust the estimate b_0 if one of the observations were dramatically changed. For example, what if the 14 were replaced by 140 so that the five observations were 1, 3, 5, 9, 140? Before reading on, test your intuitions by guessing what the new value for b_0 will be. Exhibit 2.3 shows the sum of the line lengths for different possible values of b_0. Although all of the sums are much larger than before, the minimum of 145 still occurs when $b_0 = 5$! The middle or median observation is still the best estimate even though one of the observations has been increased by a factor of 10.

EXHIBIT 2.2 ▶

Sum of absolute error as a function of $\hat{Y}_i$

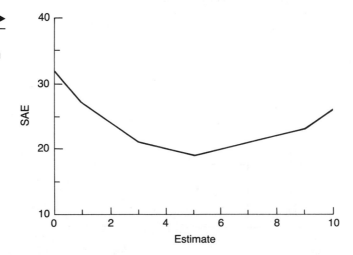

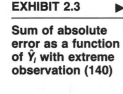

EXHIBIT 2.3 ▶

Sum of absolute error as a function of $\hat{Y}_i$ with extreme observation (140)

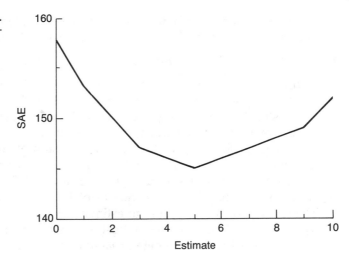

Above we used the sum of the error line lengths as an aggregate summary index of ERROR. The simple sum may not always be reasonable. For example, the simple sum implies that several small errors (e.g., four errors of length 1) are equivalent to one large error (e.g., one error of length 4). Instead, we may want to charge a higher penalty in the error index for big errors so that an error of 4 counts more than four errors of 1. One way to accomplish this is to square the line lengths before summing them. For example, $4^2 = 16$ adds a lot more to the error sum than $1^2 + 1^2 + 1^2 + 1^2 = 4$. Exhibit 2.4 depicts the original set of five observations with this new definition of error; each e_i is now represented by a square, the length of whose side is determined by the distance between the observation and the horizontal line representing the constant prediction $\hat{Y}_i$ of the simple model. The aggregate ERROR is simply the sum of those squares. Again, we can use brute force to find a value of $\hat{Y}_i$ and b_0 that will make that sum of squares as small as possible. Let's consider the possible estimates of 5 and 7, which we

EXHIBIT 2.4 ▶

ERROR as sum of squares (estimate is $\hat{Y}_i = b_0 = 5$)

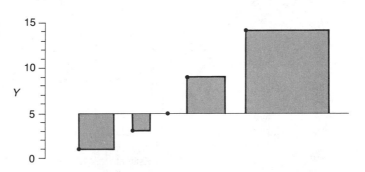

evaluated when we were using the sum of the line lengths as the ERROR measure. For $b_0 = 5$, the five areas of the squares are

$$4^2 = 16, \quad 2^2 = 4, \quad 0^2 = 0, \quad 4^2 = 16, \quad 9^2 = 81$$

and the sum of those squares is 117. For $b_0 = 7$, the five areas are 36, 16, 4, 4, 49, and the sum of squares is 109. So $b_0 = 5$, which was the best estimate when using line lengths, is no longer the best estimate when we use squares, because $b_0 = 7$ produces a smaller sum of squares or smaller ERROR. Exhibit 2.5 shows the sum of squares for different possible values of b_0 between 1 and 14. The best value for b_0 is about 6.4 with a minimum sum of squares of about 107. The estimates of 5 and 7 are not bad—sums of squares of 117 and 109, respectively—but clearly inferior to the optimum estimate of 6.4. Although not obvious, we will prove later that the best estimate when using squared errors is simply the arithmetic average or *mean* of the observations. For the five observations,

$$\frac{1 + 3 + 5 + 9 + 14}{5} = \frac{32}{5} = 6.4$$

produces b_0, the best estimate of β_0.

It is interesting to ask again what would happen to the estimate b_0 if one of the observations were dramatically changed; say, the 14 were replaced by 140. Before reading on, again check your intuition by guessing the new estimate b_0. Exhibit 2.6 shows the sum of squares for the revised set of observations. The minimum sum of squares no longer occurs when $b_0 = 6.4$; instead, the minimum now occurs when b_0 is a whopping 31.6, which is again the average of the five observations. But note that although that estimate is the best, it is not very good with a total sum of squares of about 14,723.

EXHIBIT 2.5 ▶

Sum of squared error as a function of $\hat{Y}_i$

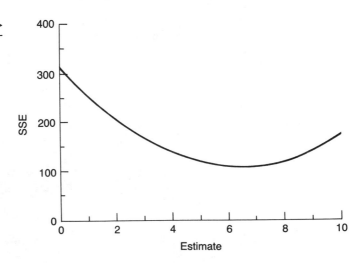

EXHIBIT 2.6 ▶

Sum of squared error as a function of $\hat{Y}_i$ with extreme observation (140)

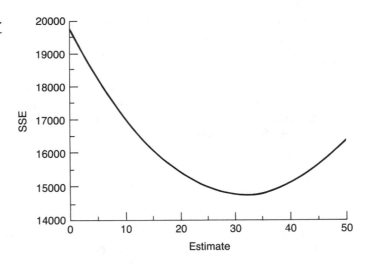

Before formalizing these examples in equations, it is useful to summarize the concepts introduced. First, the best estimate b_0 for a simple, one-parameter model is the constant prediction $\hat{Y}$ which minimizes the sum of the errors. Although we will generally have better ways to estimate the parameter than brute force, it is important to realize that the best estimate could be found by trial and error until we could no longer make ERROR any smaller. In fact, computer programs sometimes use precisely this strategy. Second, the choice of a method for summarizing or expressing the error—the lengths of the error lines or their squares in the above examples—affects the best estimate b_0. We will soon see that there are many other plausible choices for error terms. Third, if total error is the sum of the line lengths, then the median of the observations provides the best estimate b_0, where the median is simply the middle observation. Fourth, if total error is the sum of the squared line lengths, then the best estimate b_0 is the arithmetic average or mean of the observations. Fifth, the median does not change when an extreme observation is made more extreme, but the mean can change dramatically. Sixth, many times in this book we will encounter the phrase "sum of squares"; it is useful to realize that it can indeed be represented geometrically as a literal summation of squares.

2.3

Formalities for Simple Models

As always, we begin with the basic equation for data analysis,

DATA = MODEL + ERROR

For simple models, the MODEL states that all observations in DATA are essentially the same, so

$$Y_i = \beta_0 + \varepsilon_i$$

where β_0 represents the true, but unknown, parameter and ε_i represents the individual error disturbances about the unknown parameter. Then b_0 is the estimate of that parameter based on the DATA at hand. So the actual MODEL used for predicting each Y_i becomes

$$\text{MODEL: } \hat{Y}_i = b_0$$

The basic data analysis equation can then be written as

$$Y_i = \hat{Y}_i + e_i \quad \text{or} \quad Y_i = b_0 + e_i.$$

The ERROR or residual associated with each observation is then simply the difference between the DATA and the MODEL prediction, or

$$e_i = Y_i - \hat{Y}_i$$

Our problem is how to select a single value for b_0 to represent all of the DATA. Clearly, we want b_0 to be in the "center" of the data so that it will be more or less close to all of the observations. Hence, estimates of b_0 are often called *measures of central tendency*. But we need to be much more precise about defining the center and what we mean by "close." As always, the key is to make e_i as small as possible. Instead of looking at each individual e_i, we need to consider ways of aggregating the separate e_i into a summary measure of the total ERROR. Once we have done that, it should be a simple procedure to choose a b_0 that will make the summary measure of ERROR as small as possible. We now turn to a consideration of possible summary measures.

Count of Errors (CE).   One possibility is simply to count the number of times Y_i does not equal $\hat{Y}_i$. This ignores the size of the individual errors and only counts whether an error occurred. Formally,

$$\text{ERROR} = \sum_{i=1}^{n} I(e_i) = \sum_{i=1}^{n} I(Y_i - \hat{Y}_i) = \sum_{i=1}^{n} I(Y_i - b_0)$$

where $I(e_i) = 1$ if $e_i \neq 0$ and $I(e_i) = 0$ if $e_i = 0$. Functions such as $I(\ )$ are often called *indicator* functions and are simply a fancy way of representing whether or not something is to be included in an equation.

Sum of Errors (SE).   In order not to lose information about the size of the e_i, we might add all the e_i so that

$$\text{ERROR} = \sum_{i=1}^{n} e_i = \sum_{i=1}^{n} (Y_i - \hat{Y}_i) = \sum_{i=1}^{n} (Y_i - b_0)$$

But this is clearly unsatisfactory because it allows positive and negative errors to cancel one another. For example, suppose b_0 underestimated one observation by 1000 and overestimated another observation by the same amount so that $e_1 = 1000$ and $e_2 = -1000$. Adding those two errors would produce zero, incorrectly implying that there was no ERROR. We have no reason to be more interested in overestimates than underestimates, so one obvious solution is to ignore the positive and negative signs of the e_i.

Sum of Absolute Errors (SAE). One way to remove the signs is to sum the absolute values of the errors; that is,

$$\text{ERROR} = \sum_{i=1}^{n} |e_i| = \sum_{i=1}^{n} |Y_i - \hat{Y}_i| = \sum_{i=1}^{n} |Y_i - b_0|$$

The sum of absolute errors is the formal equivalent of summing the line lengths in Exhibit 2.1. As noted in the conceptual example above, it may not always be desirable to count one big error (e.g., an error of 4) the same as the equivalent amount of small errors (e.g., four errors of 1). The conceptual example therefore suggests the next measure of ERROR.

Sum of Squared Errors (SSE). Another way to remove the signs from the e_i is to square each one before summing them; that is,

$$\text{ERROR} = \sum_{i=1}^{n} e_i^2 = \sum_{i=1}^{n} (Y_i - \hat{Y}_i)^2 = \sum_{i=1}^{n} (Y_i - b_0)^2$$

The sum of squared errors is the formal equivalent of adding up the error squares in Exhibit 2.5. Besides removing the signs, the squaring has the additional effect of giving greater importance to large errors.

Weighted Sum of Squared Errors (WSSE). So far, all of the suggested ERROR measures have given equal weight to each observation. For a variety of reasons we may want to give more weight to some observations and less weight to others when calculating the aggregate error. For example, we may have reason to believe that certain observations are questionable or suspect because they were collected with less precision or less reliability than the other observations. Or we may not want to count an error of 10 the same when $\hat{Y}_i = 1000$ as when $\hat{Y}_i = 5$. In the former instance, the error of 10 amounts to only a 1% error, while in the latter it is an error of 200%. Or, finally, we might be suspicious of a couple of extreme observations just because they are "outliers" with respect to other observations. Whatever our reasons, it is easy to incorporate a weight w_i for each observation into the formal definition:

$$\text{ERROR} = \sum_{i=1}^{n} w_i e_i^2 = \sum_{i=1}^{n} w_i (Y_i - \hat{Y}_i)^2 = \sum_{i=1}^{n} w_i (Y_i - b_0)^2$$

The weights w_i might be assigned a priori based on judgments of data quality or some formal index of each observation's reliability. One possibility is to weight all observations equally, in which case $w_i = 1$ for all i. The weighted sum of squared errors becomes simply the sum of squared errors above.

To take care of the problem of 10 being a more important error when the estimate is 5 than when the estimate is 1000, we can use the size of $\hat{Y}_i$ as a weight; that is,

$$w_i = \frac{1}{\hat{Y}_i}$$

so that the aggregate measure of ERROR becomes

$$\text{ERROR} = \sum_{i=1}^{n} \frac{1}{\hat{Y}_i} e_i^2 = \sum_{i=1}^{n} \frac{(Y_i - \hat{Y}_i)^2}{\hat{Y}_i} = \sum_{i=1}^{n} \frac{(Y_i - b_0)^2}{b_0}$$

Such weights will not have much effect in the case of simple models because $\hat{Y}_i = b_0$ for all i, so we will not have the problem of some predictions being small and others being large. However, we will encounter such problems with more complex models, and we will find weights inversely proportional to $\hat{Y}_i$ to be extremely useful.

Statisticians have created some very clever ways of defining weights to solve a variety of complicated problems. We will encounter examples of those weights later in the context of specific problems. For now, just be aware that the use of weights gives us a great deal of flexibility in defining the aggregate measure of ERROR.

2.4

Estimators of β_0

As demonstrated by the conceptual examples presented earlier in this chapter, the choice of a method for aggregating the e_i influences the estimate b_0. It should not be surprising, therefore, that for each definition of aggregate ERROR presented above, there is a different way of calculating b_0 from the DATA. We could use the brute-force method for each definition of ERROR by trying different values of b_0 until we found the one that gave the minimum value for ERROR. However, it turns out that for each of the above definitions of ERROR we can define a way of calculating b_0 from the DATA so that b_0 is guaranteed to produce the minimum possible value for ERROR. While we will almost always use the calculation method, it is important to remember that the definition of the best estimate of β_0 is that value of b_0 which produces the least ERROR. We list in Exhibit 2.7 the definition of b_0 for each definition of ERROR considered so far.

EXHIBIT 2.7 ▶

Estimators for each definition of ERROR

ERROR Definition	b_0, *Estimator of β_0*
Count of Errors Sum of Absolute Errors Sum of Squared Errors Weighted Sum of Squared Errors	MODE = most frequent value of Y_i MEDIAN = middle observation of all the Y_i MEAN = average of all the Y_i WEIGHTED MEAN = weighted average of all the Y_i

2.4.1 Proof That the Mean Minimizes SSE

In this section we present a formal proof that the mean $\overline{Y}_i$ does indeed produce the smallest possible value of SSE. Although we generally avoid proofs, we think it is important to understand that the choice of the mean as an estimator is not arbitrary; instead, the choice of SSE as an aggregate measure of ERROR also dictates the choice of the mean as the best estimator. Similar proofs can be given to show that the indicated estimator minimizes the corresponding definition of ERROR in the above list.

Let us begin by assuming that $\hat{Y}$, the best estimator for reducing the sum of squared errors, is something other than $\overline{Y} = \Sigma_{i=1}^{n} Y_i/n$. (Note that here $\hat{Y}$ does not have an i subscript because we make the same prediction for all observations in the simple model.) Our strategy is to proceed with that assumption until we reach a point where we can see that it is a bad assumption. At that point we will know that the only reasonable assumption is $\hat{Y} = \overline{Y}$.

The sum of squared errors is

$$\text{SSE} = \sum_{i=1}^{n} (Y_i - \hat{Y})^2$$

Obviously, $\overline{Y} - \overline{Y} = 0$; we can add zero within the parentheses without changing the sum of squared errors. That is,

$$\text{SSE} = \sum_{i=1}^{n} (Y_i + \overline{Y} - \overline{Y} - \hat{Y})^2$$

Rearranging the terms slightly, we get

$$\text{SSE} = \sum_{i=1}^{n} [(Y_i - \overline{Y}) + (\overline{Y} - \hat{Y})]^2$$

Squaring gives

$$\text{SSE} = \sum_{i=1}^{n} [(Y_i - \overline{Y})^2 + 2(Y_i - \overline{Y})(\overline{Y} - \hat{Y}) + (\overline{Y} - \hat{Y})^2]$$

Breaking the sums apart yields

$$SSE = \sum_{i=1}^{n} (Y_i - \overline{Y})^2 + \sum_{i=1}^{n} [2(Y_i - \overline{Y})(\overline{Y} - \hat{Y})] + \sum_{i=1}^{n} (\overline{Y} - \hat{Y})^2$$

The last term contains no subscripts so the summation is equivalent to adding up the same quantity n times; hence, the summation sign can be replaced by multiplication by n. Similarly, the quantities without subscripts in the middle term can be taken outside the summation sign to give

$$SSE = \sum_{i=1}^{n} (Y_i - \overline{Y})^2 + 2(\overline{Y} - \hat{Y}) \sum_{i=1}^{n} (Y_i - \overline{Y}) + n(\overline{Y} - \hat{Y})^2$$

Now let's concentrate on the middle term. Note that

$$\sum_{i=1}^{n} (Y_i - \overline{Y}) = \sum_{i=1}^{n} Y_i - n\overline{Y}$$

$$= \sum_{i=1}^{n} Y_i - n\left(\frac{\sum_{i=1}^{n} Y_i}{n}\right)$$

$$= \sum_{i=1}^{n} Y_i - \sum_{i=1}^{n} Y_i$$

$$= 0$$

Hence, the middle term of SSE includes a multiplication by zero, which eliminates that term. We are left with

$$SSE = \sum_{i=1}^{n} (Y_i - \overline{Y})^2 + n(\overline{Y} - \hat{Y})^2$$

We want SSE to be as small as possible. We have no freedom in the first term: Y_i and $\overline{Y}$ are whatever they happen to be. We do, however, have freedom to choose $\hat{Y}$ in the second term to make SSE as small as possible. Clearly, $n(\overline{Y} - \hat{Y})^2$ is positive, so it is making SSE larger. But if we let $\hat{Y} = \overline{Y}$, then $n(\overline{Y} - \hat{Y})^2 = 0$ and we are no longer adding anything extra to SSE. For any estimate of $\hat{Y}$ other than $\overline{Y}$, we will be making SSE larger. Hence, SSE is as small as possible when $\hat{Y} = \overline{Y}$, and the minimum is

$$SSE = \sum_{i=1}^{n} (Y_i - \overline{Y})^2$$

Any other choice for $\hat{Y}$ would produce a larger SSE; thus, the mean is the best estimator for reducing SSE in the simple model.

2.4.2 Describing ERROR

If the goal is simply to describe a batch of DATA, then we can apply the simple model and use one or all of the measures of central tendency—mode, median, and mean—as descriptive statistics. When doing so, it is also useful to present a description of the typical ERROR. Reporting the total error (e.g., SAE or SSE) is not desirable because the total depends so heavily on the number of observations. For example, aggregate ERROR based on 50 observations is likely to be larger than aggregate ERROR based on 15 observations, even if the typical errors in the former case are smaller. For each measure of central tendency there is a corresponding customary index of the typical error. We consider each below.

Modal Error.   When we use the count of the errors (CE) as the aggregate index of ERROR, there can only be two values for e_i. Either $e_i = 0$ when $Y_i = \hat{Y}$ or $e_i = 1$ when $Y_i \neq \hat{Y}$. The typical error is simply the more frequent or modal error. Modal error is seldom used, but we have presented it for completeness.

Median Absolute Deviation.   When we use the sum of absolute errors (SAE) as the aggregate index of ERROR, it is customary to use the median absolute error or deviation from the prediction to represent the typical error. To find the median absolute deviation, simply sort the $|e_i|$ into ascending order and find the middle one.

Standard Deviation.   When we use the sum of squared errors (SSE) as the aggregate index of ERROR, the index is somewhat more complex. We will be making extensive use of SSE throughout this book. To avoid having to introduce more general formulas later, we present the more general formula now and then show how it applies in the case of simple models. In a general model with p parameters, those p parameters have been used to reduce ERROR. In principle, the maximum number of parameters we could have is n—one parameter for each observation—in which case ERROR would equal zero. Thus, there are $n - p$ potential parameters remaining which could be used to reduce the remaining ERROR. A useful index of ERROR is then the remaining ERROR per remaining potential parameter. This index has the name *mean squared error* and is given by

$$\text{MSE} = \frac{\text{SSE}}{n - p} = \frac{\sum_{i=1}^{n} (Y_i - \hat{Y}_i)^2}{n - p}$$

For the simple model considered in this chapter there is only one parameter β_0 to be estimated, so $p = 1$ and the estimate of $\hat{Y}_i$ is $b_0 = \overline{Y}$, the mean value. For the simple model MSE has the special name *variance* and is commonly represented by s^2; that is,

$$\text{Variance} = s^2 = \text{MSE} = \frac{\text{SSE}}{n-1} = \frac{\sum_{i=1}^{n}(Y_i - \overline{Y})^2}{n-1}$$

MSE represents the typical squared error; to express the typical error in the units in which the original DATA were recorded, it is useful to take the square root of MSE, which is often referred to, especially on computer printouts, as *ROOT MSE*. For the simple model, the square root of the variance or the MSE has the special name *standard deviation* and is given by

$$\text{Standard Deviation} = s = \sqrt{\text{MSE}} = \sqrt{\frac{\sum_{i=1}^{n}(Y_i - \overline{Y})^2}{n-1}}$$

Another index sometimes used when SSE is used as the aggregate index of error is the *coefficient of variation*. It is common for the size of the standard deviation to be proportional to the size of the mean. For example, if $\overline{Y} = 10{,}000$, we would expect the typical error or standard deviation to be much larger than when $\overline{Y} = 10$. Although this need not to be the case, it usually is true. To remove the effect of the overall magnitude of the data from the description of the error, the coefficient of variation expresses the size of the standard deviation as a proportion of the mean; that is,

$$\text{Coefficient of Variation} = \text{CV} = s/\overline{Y}$$

An Example.   We will use the automobile fatality rates by state listed in Exhibit 1.1 as an example to illustrate the simple model and the descriptors of central tendency and error. To facilitate finding the mode and the median, we have rearranged the data of Exhibit 1.1 in Exhibit 2.8 in order of increasing fatality rates per 100 million vehicle miles traveled. Our goal is to fit the simple model with just one parameter to these data. That is, the basic data analysis equation is

$$Y_i = \beta_0 + \varepsilon_i$$

and we want to fit the MODEL to the DATA by finding the estimate b_0 for β_0 which minimizes ERROR—the e_i in the equation

$$Y_i = b_0 + e_i$$

How we find the estimate b_0 depends on which definition of aggregate ERROR we adopt.

i	State	Rate	Rank	i	State	Rate	Rank
39	Rhode Island	1.7	1	47	Washington	3.5	26
30	New Jersey	2.2	2	36	Oklahoma	3.5	27
7	Connecticut	2.3	3	16	Kansas	3.5	28
20	Maryland	2.5	4	6	Colorado	3.5	29
46	Virginia	2.7	5	25	Missouri	3.5	30
21	Massachusetts	2.7	6	4	Arkansas	3.6	31
29	New Hampshire	2.8	7	32	New York	3.6	32
35	Ohio	2.9	8	33	North Carolina	3.6	33
27	Nebraska	2.9	9	34	North Dakota	3.7	34
14	Indiana	2.9	10	40	South Carolina	3.8	35
38	Pennsylvania	3.0	11	44	Utah	3.9	36
15	Iowa	3.0	12	37	Oregon	3.9	37
13	Illinois	3.0	13	26	Montana	4.0	38
19	Maine	3.1	14	48	West Virginia	4.0	39
49	Wisconsin	3.1	15	43	Texas	4.0	40
22	Michigan	3.2	16	11	Hawaii	4.0	41
9	Florida	3.2	17	1	Alabama	4.2	42
17	Kentucky	3.2	18	18	Louisiana	4.6	43
10	Georgia	3.3	19	2	Alaska	4.7	44
23	Minnesota	3.3	20	12	Idaho	4.8	45
8	Delaware	3.3	21	24	Mississippi	4.8	46
42	Tennessee	3.3	22	3	Arizona	5.3	47
41	South Dakota	3.4	23	50	Wyoming	5.4	48
45	Vermont	3.4	24	28	Nevada	5.6	49
5	California	3.4	25	31	New Mexico	5.8	50

EXHIBIT 2.8 ▲

Automobile fatality rates by state for 1978 (deaths per 100 million vehicle miles traveled, sorted by fatality rate)

If CE is adopted as the criterion, then the best estimate for β_0 is the mode. To find the mode, we simply observe which fatality rate is the most frequent. For these data, the value 3.5 is the only value that occurs five or more times, so the best estimate is $b_0 = 3.5$. In one sense, however, there is really no mode; each of these fatality rates is rounded so no two fatality rates are exactly equal. This is frequently the case with continuous variables, so the mode is usually not as useful as either the median or the mean for such data. If we do use the mode of 3.5 to predict the rounded data, then the prediction is accurate 5 times and incorrect 45 times.

If SAE is adopted as the criterion, then the best estimate for β_0 is the median. There are 50 observations, so there are two middle values— the 25th and 26th. (If there are an odd number of observations then

i	State	Rate	MEDIAN $\hat{Y}_i$	e_i	$|e_i|$	MEAN $\hat{Y}_i$	e_i	e_i^2
1	Alabama	4.2	3.45	.75	.75	3.57	.63	.39
2	Alaska	4.7	3.45	1.25	1.25	3.57	1.13	1.27
3	Arizona	5.3	3.45	1.85	1.85	3.57	1.73	2.99
4	Arkansas	3.6	3.45	.15	.15	3.57	.03	.00
5	California	3.4	3.45	−.05	.05	3.57	−.17	.03
6	Colorado	3.5	3.45	.05	.05	3.57	−.07	.01
7	Connecticut	2.3	3.45	−1.15	1.15	3.57	−1.27	1.62
8	Delaware	3.3	3.45	−.15	.15	3.57	−.27	.07
9	Florida	3.2	3.45	−.25	.25	3.57	−.37	.14
10	Georgia	3.3	3.45	−.15	.15	3.57	−.27	.07
11	Hawaii	4.0	3.45	.55	.55	3.57	.43	.18
12	Idaho	4.8	3.45	1.35	1.35	3.57	1.23	1.51
13	Illinois	3.0	3.45	−.45	.45	3.57	−.57	.33
14	Indiana	2.9	3.45	−.55	.55	3.57	−.67	.45
15	Iowa	3.0	3.45	−.45	.45	3.57	−.57	.33
16	Kansas	3.5	3.45	.05	.05	3.57	−.07	.01
17	Kentucky	3.2	3.45	−.25	.25	3.57	−.37	.14
18	Louisiana	4.6	3.45	1.15	1.15	3.57	1.03	1.06
19	Maine	3.1	3.45	−.35	.35	3.57	−.47	.22
20	Maryland	2.5	3.45	−.95	.95	3.57	−1.07	1.15
21	Massachusetts	2.7	3.45	−.75	.75	3.57	−.87	.76
22	Michigan	3.2	3.45	−.25	.25	3.57	−.37	.14
23	Minnesota	3.3	3.45	−.15	.15	3.57	−.27	.07
24	Mississippi	4.8	3.45	1.35	1.35	3.57	1.23	1.51
25	Missouri	3.5	3.45	.05	.05	3.57	−.07	0.01

EXHIBIT 2.9 ▲

Predictions and errors using the median and mean to estimate b_0 in the simple model

there will be only one middle observation.) These two values are 3.4 and 3.5, which can be averaged to produce the single estimate of the median; so in this case the best estimate is $b_0 = 3.45$. The middle columns of Exhibit 2.9 present the prediction $\hat{Y}_i$, the error $e_i = Y_i − \hat{Y}_i$, and the absolute error based on the median as the estimate b_0. In this case, total ERROR = 31.00. Any other estimate for β_0 would produce a larger value for SAE. Although it is not obvious from Exhibit 2.9, the 25th and 26th largest absolute errors are both equal to 0.45, so the median absolute deviation = 0.45.

If SSE is adopted as the criterion, then the best estimate for β_0 is the mean. The average of the 50 observations gives 3.57 as the estimate b_0. The last set of columns in Exhibit 2.9 gives the values of $\hat{Y}_i$ (or b_0 in the case of the simple model), $e_i = Y_i − \hat{Y}_i$, and e_i^2. Note that the sum of the errors equals zero exactly and, necessarily, that the sum of the

			MEDIAN			MEAN		
i	State	Rate	$\hat{Y}_i$	e_i	$|e_i|$	$\hat{Y}_i$	e_i	e_i^2
26	Montana	4.0	3.45	.55	.55	3.57	.43	.18
27	Nebraska	2.9	3.45	−.55	.55	3.57	−.67	.45
28	Nevada	5.6	3.45	2.15	2.15	3.57	2.03	4.11
29	New Hampshire	2.8	3.45	−.65	.65	3.57	−.77	.60
30	New Jersey	2.2	3.45	−1.25	1.25	3.57	−1.37	1.88
31	New Mexico	5.8	3.45	2.35	2.35	3.57	2.23	4.96
32	New York	3.6	3.45	.15	.15	3.57	.03	.00
33	North Carolina	3.6	3.45	.15	.15	3.57	.03	.00
34	North Dakota	3.7	3.45	.25	.25	3.57	.13	.02
35	Ohio	2.9	3.45	−.55	.55	3.57	−.67	.45
36	Oklahoma	3.5	3.45	.05	.05	3.57	−.07	.01
37	Oregon	3.9	3.45	.45	.45	3.57	.33	.11
38	Pennsylvania	3.0	3.45	−.45	.45	3.57	−.57	.33
39	Rhode Island	1.7	3.45	−1.75	1.75	3.57	−1.87	3.50
40	South Carolina	3.8	3.45	.35	.35	3.57	.23	.05
41	South Dakota	3.4	3.45	−.05	.05	3.57	−.17	.03
42	Tennessee	3.3	3.45	−.15	.15	3.57	−.27	.07
43	Texas	4.0	3.45	.55	.55	3.57	.43	.18
44	Utah	3.9	3.45	.45	.45	3.57	.33	.11
45	Vermont	3.4	3.45	−.05	.05	3.57	−.17	.03
46	Virginia	2.7	3.45	−.75	.75	3.57	−.87	.76
47	Washington	3.5	3.45	.05	.05	3.57	−.07	.01
48	West Virginia	4.0	3.45	.55	.55	3.57	.43	.18
49	Wisconsin	3.1	3.45	−.35	.35	3.57	−.47	.22
50	Wyoming	5.4	3.45	1.95	1.95	3.57	1.83	3.34
	SUM	178.6	172.5	6.10	31.00	178.6	.00	36.04

EXHIBIT 2.9

Continued

▲ data observations equals the sum of the predictions. This is characteristic of predictions based on minimizing the SSE. The actual SSE equals 36.04. Again, any other estimate for β_0 would produce a larger SSE. The variance or, more generally, the MSE equals

$$s^2 = \frac{\text{SSE}}{n-1} = \frac{36.04}{49} = .74$$

and the standard deviation or root mean squared error equals

$$s = \sqrt{\text{MSE}} = \sqrt{.74} = .86$$

Finally, CV is given by

$$s/\overline{Y} = \frac{.86}{3.57} = .24$$

Note that in this particular example the three estimates of β_0 (using the three definitions of error) were very similar: 3.5, 3.45, and 3.57. This is often the case for "well-behaved" data, but there is no guarantee that data will be well behaved and that the three estimates will be similar. Later we will see that a major discrepancy between the three estimates, especially between the median and the mean, should alert us to special problems in the analysis of such data. Note also in this example that the median absolute deviation and the standard deviation produce different estimates for the typical error—.45 and .86, respectively. This is not surprising given the different definitions of error used.

Computer Examples. We seldom do the explicit calculations as illustrated above. Instead we use one of the standard statistical computer packages to do the computations. Exhibit 2.10 displays the output produced by the UNIVARIATE procedure in SCSS. It calculates the mean, median, variance, standard deviation, and sum as in the above example. Note that it reports NA (not applicable) for the mode, because during the input phase SCSS was told that FATRATE was a continuous variable (as opposed to a discrete variable) for which the mode is not generally appropriate. SCSS also reports information about skewness and kurtosis which we will consider much later. SCSS, unfortunately, does not report SSE, but it is easily obtained by multiplying the variance by $n - 1$. SCSS also does not report SAE or the median absolute deviation, and neither is easily computed within SCSS.

EXHIBIT 2.10 ▶

Descriptive statistics for auto fatality rates produced by UNIVARIATE procedure in SCSS

```
FATRATE   FATALITIES PER 100M VMT

       MEAN = 3.572
   S E MEAN = .121
       MODE = NA
     MEDIAN = 3.450
   VARIANCE = .736
    STD DEV = .858
   SKEWNESS = .721
   S E SKEW = .337
   KURTOSIS = .714
   S E KURT = .662
    MINIMUM = 1.700
    MAXIMUM = 5.800
      RANGE = 4.100
        SUM = 178.600

TOTAL N = 50      VALID N = 50
```

Exhibit 2.11 displays the descriptive statistics produced by the UNI-VARIATE procedure in SAS. Like SCSS it produces the usual descriptive statistics of n, mean, median, variance, standard deviation, and sum. SAS also reports the SSE, which it labels CSS (corrected sum of squares). USS represents the uncorrected sum of squares and is the sum of squared errors that would be obtained from using the estimate $b_0 = 0$. Note also that CV is reported by SAS. Many other statistics that need not concern us now are also displayed by the UNIVARIATE procedure. SAS does not provide any information about SAE or the median absolute deviation.

EXHIBIT 2.11 ▶

Descriptive statistics for auto fatality rates produced by UNIVARIATE procedure in SAS

VARIABLE=FATRATE

MOMENTS

N	50	SUM WGTS	50
MEAN	3.572	SUM	178.6
STD DEV	0.857628	VARIANCE	0.735527
SKEWNESS	0.720735	KURTOSIS	0.714056
USS	674	CSS	36.0408
CV	24.0098	STD MEAN	0.121287
T:MEAN=Q	29.4508	PROB>|T|	0.0001
SGN RANK	637.5	PROB>|S|	0.0001
NUM /= 0	50		
W:NORMAL	0.945081	PROB<W	0.044

QUANTILES (DEF=4)

100% MAX	5.8	99%	5.8
75% Q3	4	95%	5.49
50% MED	3.45	90%	4.8
25% Q1	3	10%	2.7
0% MIN	1.7	5%	2.255
		1%	1.7

RANGE	4.1
Q3-Q1	1
MODE	3.5

EXTREMES

LOWEST ID	HIGHEST ID
1.7(Rhode_Is)	4.8(Mississi)
2.2(New_Jers)	5.3(Arizona)
2.3(Connecti)	5.4(Wyoming)
2.5(Maryland)	5.6(Nevada)
2.7(Virginia)	5.8(New_Mexi)

SAS also reports quantiles. The $X\%$ *quantile* is simply the observation such that $X\%$ of the observations are below it and $(100 - X)\%$ of the observations are above it. The median is identical to the 50% quantile. The 25% quantile is the middle value between the median and the minimum, and the 75% quantile is the middle value between the median and the maximum.

2.5

Summary

In terms of the basic data analysis equation

DATA = MODEL + ERROR

the simple MODEL with one parameter is expressed as

$$Y_i = \beta_0 + \varepsilon_i$$

Fitting the simple MODEL to the DATA consists of finding the estimator b_0 of β_0 which makes the ERRORs e_i as small as possible in the equation

$$Y_i = b_0 + e_i$$

To fit the simple MODEL to DATA, we must first define how the individual ERROR terms e_i are to be aggregated into a summary index of ERROR. Once we have chosen an aggregate index of ERROR we can find, by trial and error if necessary, the best estimate b_0 of β_0 which minimizes ERROR. Important definitions of aggregate ERROR are (a) the count of errors, (b) the sum of absolute errors, and (c) the sum of squared errors. For each of these definitions there is a different, well-defined best estimator for β_0 which can be found by calculation rather than by trial and error. These estimators are, respectively, (a) the mode—the most frequent value of Y_i, (b) the median—the middle value of all the Y_i, and (c) the mean—the arithmetic average of all the Y_i. Also, for each of these three definitions of aggregate ERROR there is an expression for representing the "typical" value for e_i. These expressions are, respectively, (a) the modal error, (b) the median absolute deviation, and (c) the standard deviation. Collectively, these best estimators and these expressions for the typical ERROR are known as *descriptive statistics* because they provide a first-cut description of a batch of DATA. We prefer to view them simply as estimators for the simple MODEL using different definitions of ERROR.

In Chapter 4 we will choose one of the three definitions of ERROR to be our standard definition. We will make this choice on the basis of reasoned principles. However, the computer examples in this chapter suggest that the estimates and aggregate indices for the sum of squared errors are more easily obtained from the standard computer statistical systems than are those for other definitions of aggregate ERROR. The reader should therefore anticipate that we will choose the sum of squared errors to be our standard definition of aggregate ERROR.

3

Simple Models: Graphing Data

As we have seen, the simplest MODEL consists of a single parameter to be estimated from some batch of DATA. How we define and interpret this single parameter depends on our definition of ERROR. If we minimize the number of errors, the best estimate of the parameter is the mode. If we minimize the sum of the absolute value of the errors, the best parameter estimate is the median. Finally, if we minimize the sum of the squared errors, the best estimate of the parameter is the mean.

In this chapter and the next two we continue to probe in more detail this simple single-parameter model. Our purpose in this chapter is to describe graphic procedures for displaying our basic equation

DATA = MODEL + ERROR

To display this basic equation, we need to discuss graphic representations of the DATA, graphic representations of the MODEL, and graphic representations of ERROR. Some displays present information about all three, as we shall see. These graphic displays can be informative regardless of the complexity of the MODEL that one develops. In this chapter we will be concerned principally with the simple single-parameter model. However, some of the graphic displays presented in this chapter will be used later for models containing many more parameters.

3.1

Displaying DATA

Let us continue to use the fatality rate data of Exhibit 1.1 to illustrate graphic display procedures. Exhibit 1.1 lists the fatality rate of each state in the alphabetical order of states. Exhibit 2.8 reorders the data so that states and their fatality rates are in ascending order, from the lowest fatality rate to the highest. Exhibit 3.1 graphically presents this same information in what is called a *frequency polygon*. The possible values of the fatality rate variable are ordered along the horizontal axis of the frequency polygon. The vertical axis displays the frequency with which each fatality rate is observed in the data.

This visual display somehow seems to present much more information about these data than does the tabular listing in Exhibit 2.8, even though the actual information in the two exhibits is the same. We are able to process more information about data more quickly when they are displayed in a graph rather than in a simple table. We immediately perceive the shape of the data distribution. We can clearly see the large hump in the frequency polygon around the fatality rate values of 3.4 to 3.6. Without calculating the mode, the median, or the mean, we obtain from this display an eyeball estimate of a "typical" fatality rate. We know that the typical rate ought to lie somewhere around the big hump in the graph.

EXHIBIT 3.1 ▶

Fatality rate frequency polygon

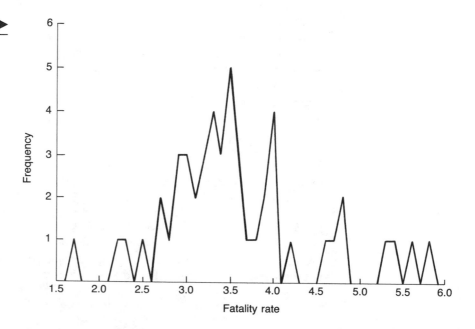

From the visual display we also perceive the relative spread of the fatality rate distribution. While most of the values seem to be bunched in the range from 2.7 to 3.9, there are a few states with considerably discrepant values. The state with the smallest fatality rate, Rhode Island, seems to be somewhat off by itself. Similarly, the four states at the upper end of the distribution, Arizona, Wyoming, Nevada, and New Mexico, seem fairly discrepant from the rest of the distribution.

We might make this frequency polygon a little more compact by collapsing some of the fatality values that currently are spread out across the horizontal axis in Exhibit 3.1. For instance, we might group together states whose fatality rates vary from 1.5 to 1.9, from 2.0 to 2.4, from 2.5 to 2.9, and so forth. The frequency polygon that results is presented in Exhibit 3.2. The shape of the distribution of data now looks quite different from the way it did before grouping. This frequency polygon is quite peaked. We can also see that the distribution is not quite symmetrical around the peak. That is, relatively more states seem to lie above the peak of the distribution than below it. Distributions that are not symmetric around their peak are called *skewed* distributions. This one is said to be positively skewed, because more cases are above the peak or central tendency than below it.

EXHIBIT 3.2 ▶

Grouped frequency polygon—fatality data

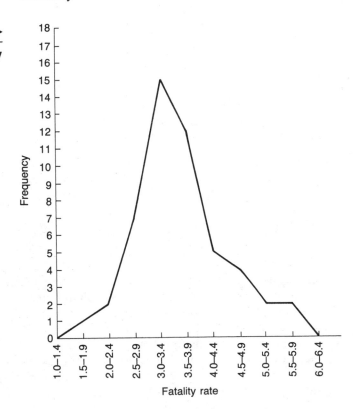

The disadvantage of this grouped frequency polygon is that a great deal of information about the actual fatality rates that was contained in Exhibit 2.8 and in the ungrouped frequency polygon has been lost. Another way of drawing this frequency polygon, suggested by Tukey in his important book, *Exploratory Data Analysis* (1977), preserves this raw data information. This graphical display is called a *stem and leaf* display and is illustrated for these data in Exhibit 3.3. In this display, the vertical column of figures to the left of the straight line is called the stem. Listed in this column are the first digits of the fatality rates. Thus the numbers in this column tell us whether a given fatality rate starts with a 1, a 2, or whatever. The digits in the rows to the right of the vertical line are called the leaves. They tell us about the number to the right of the decimal point for each state's fatality rate. For instance, in Exhibit 3.3 we see that the lowest fatality rate among the states is 1.7, reading the 1 from the stem and the .7 from the leaf to the right of the stem. The next stem digit is 2, with two leaves (i.e., .2 and .3). Notice that 2 appears in the stem column twice, because for each stem value we have put leaves ranging from .0 to .4 on one row and leaves ranging from .5 to .9 on the next row.

EXHIBIT 3.3 ▶

Fatality rate stem and leaf

1	7
2	23
2	5778999
3	000112223333444
3	555556667899
4	00002
4	6788
5	34
5	68

Not only does this stem and leaf display preserve all of the raw data that was in Exhibit 2.8, but, if we turn it on its side, it retains the shape of the grouped frequency polygon of Exhibit 3.2. This is so because the display is constructed so that each leaf occupies the same amount of space in its row as every other leaf. Thus the first row of leaves opposite the stem of 3 is 15 digits long, since there are 15 states with fatality rates between 3.0 and 3.4.

Stem and leaf displays can be produced by SAS, MINITAB, and many other statistical packages. Exhibit 3.4 presents the display for these data from the SAS output. Notice that the stem in this display is defined as the first two digits in the fatality rates, while all leaves are zero. Thus,

EXHIBIT 3.4 ▶

Stem and leaf display for auto fatality rates produced by SAS

```
                    VARIABLE=FATRATE

      STEM   LEAF                         #
        58   0                            1
        56   0                            1
        54   0                            1
        52   0                            1
        50
        48   00                           2
        46   00                           2
        44
        42   0                            1
        40   0000                         4
        38   000                          3
        36   0000                         4
        34   00000000                     8
        32   0000000                      7
        30   00000                        5
        28   0000                         4
        26   00                           2
        24   0                            1
        22   00                           2
        20
        18
        16   0                            1

      MULTIPLY STEM LEAF BY 10**−01
```

as the note at the bottom of the display indicates, in order to reconstruct the original values from this SAS generated display, the values in the display must be multiplied by 10^{-1}. The column of numbers to the right of the display gives the frequency of each value in the display.

Let us consider another data set. Exhibit 3.5 presents the 1983 season attendance figures for each of the 26 major league baseball teams, expressed in hundreds of thousands of spectators. The descriptive statistics and stem and leaf display for these data, generated by the UNIVARIATE procedure in SAS, are given in Exhibit 3.6. Notice that the last digit for these attendance figures has been lost in the SAS-produced stem and leaf. Notice also that there seems to be one attendance figure that is quite discrepant from all of the others: the Los Angeles Dodgers have a yearly attendance figure well above the attendance figure for any other team. Such an observation is known as an *outlier*. As we will see later in this chapter, outliers can have some unfortunate consequences for certain parameter estimates. Later, in Chapter 9, we discuss procedures for detecting and dealing with outliers in a systematic manner.

EXHIBIT 3.5   ▶

1983 Major league baseball attendance (in hundreds of thousands of spectators)

Team	Attendance
Atlanta	21.2
Chicago	14.8
Cincinnati	11.9
Houston	13.5
Los Angeles	35.1
Montreal	23.2
New York	11.0
Philadelphia	21.3
Pittsburgh	12.3
St. Louis	23.4
San Diego	15.4
San Francisco	12.5
Baltimore	20.4
Boston	17.8
California	25.6
Chicago	21.3
Cleveland	7.7
Detroit	18.3
Kansas City	19.6
Milwaukee	24.0
Minnesota	8.6
New York	22.6
Oakland	12.9
Seattle	8.1
Texas	13.6
Toronto	19.3

3.2

Displaying both the MODEL and ERROR

From the data displays that have been presented, it is relatively easy to calculate some of the parameter estimates of the simple single-parameter model. The mode is easily identified from the two stem and leaf displays we presented. Assuming these variables were discretely measured, the mode for the fatality rate data is 3.5 and from the baseball attendance data it is 21.3. Both of these figures are simply the most frequently occurring stem and leaf combinations. Recall that the mode is the best parameter estimate when we minimize the number of errors in the simple single-parameter model.

EXHIBIT 3.6 ▶

Descriptive statistics and stem and leaf display for baseball attendance data produced by SAS

VARIABLE=ATTEND

Moments

N	26	Sum Wgts	26
Mean	17.51538	Sum	455.4
Std Dev	6.398793	Variance	40.94455
Skewness	.5775743	Kurtosis	.6666137
USS	9000.12	CSS	1023.614
CV	36.53242	Std Mean	1.254907
T:Mean=0	13.95752	Prob>|T|	0.0001
Sgn Rank	175.5	Prob>|S|	0.0001
Num ≠ 0	26		
W:Normal	.9512193	Prob<W	0.264

Quantiles(Def=5)

100% Max	35.1	99%	35.1
75% Q3	21.3	95%	25.6
50% Med	18.05	90%	24
25% Q1	12.5	10%	8.6
0% Min	7.7	5%	8.1
		1%	7.7

Range	27.4
Q3-Q1	8.8
Mode	21.3

Extremes

Lowest	ID	Highest	ID
7.7	(Clevelan)	23.2	(Montreal)
8.1	(Seattle)	23.4	(St._Loui)
8.6	(Minnesot)	24	(Milwauke)
11	(New_York)	25.6	(Californ)
11.9	(Cincinna)	35.1	(Los_Ange)

Stem	Leaf	#
3	5	1
3		
2	6	1
2	001113334	9
1	55889	5
1	1223344	7
0	889	3

Multiply Stem.Leaf by 10**+01

The median is also easily derived from stem and leaf displays. We simply count the total number of observations in a batch of data and then count down the stem and leaf until we find the halfway point in the batch. The median is the value attached to that middle-most observation. So, for instance if there were 11 observations in some batch of data, we would line the batch up in order from lowest to highest, and then count down until we found the sixth observation. This sixth observation is the middle-most one, because there are five above it and five below it in the batch. The value attached to the sixth observation would be the median. With an even number of observations in a batch, there is no one observation that is the middle-most. So we have to average the values of the two observations that are closest to the middle of the batch to calculate the median. From Exhibit 3.6 we see that the median in the baseball attendance data (i.e., 50% quantile) is 18.05. Since there are an even number of baseball teams (26), this median value comes from averaging together the attendance figures of the two teams that are the closest to the middle of the distribution: 17.8 (Boston) and 18.3 (Detroit). In the last chapter, we saw that the median in the fatality rate data is 3.45. Recall again that the median is the best parameter estimate that results in the simple model if we minimize the sum of the absolute errors of prediction.

Unlike the other two single-parameter estimates of the central tendency of a distribution of data, the mean is not readily calculated from a graphical data display. To calculate the mean, we need to add up all the values and then divide the sum by the total number of observations. We saw in the last chapter that the mean for the auto fatality data set is 3.57. The mean baseball attendance during the 1983 baseball season is 17.5 hundreds of thousands of spectators. Both of these numbers are the best single-parameter estimate for the simple model when we minimize the sum of the squared errors of prediction in their respective data sets.

In addition to the problem of not being easily calculated from a graphic display of data, the mean suffers from one other unfortunate characteristic when compared with the median. It is relatively more affected by outliers in a distribution of data. This is a disadvantage because outliers or unusual observations frequently represent data errors or other abnormalities. For instance, when entering data into the computer, one might make a data entry error, such as misplacing a decimal point or adding one too many digits. We would like our parameter estimates to be relatively unaffected by such errors.

Although the outlying attendance figure for the Los Angeles Dodgers did not arise from a data coding error, consider what happens to our various measures of central tendency when we delete this outlier from the data set. The mode remains unchanged at 21.3. The median changes slightly, from 18.05 to 17.8. The mean changes considerably more, from 17.5 to 16.8.

Let us return to graphic displays to see how we might display simultaneously the data and the single parameter that constitutes the model. Suppose we drew a vertical axis that displayed the possible data values. We might then arrange the data points in a single continuum along that axis and indicate the parameter estimate with a horizontal line drawn through the data points. Exhibit 3.7 presents such displays for both the baseball attendance and automobile fatality data sets, estimating the single-parameter estimate, or $\hat{Y}_i$, as the median. The two models that are displayed, therefore, are

$$Y_i = 3.45 + e_i \qquad \text{for the fatality data}$$

and

$$Y_i = 18.05 + e_i \qquad \text{for the attendance data}$$

EXHIBIT 3.7 ▶

Simple model displays for fatality and baseball data

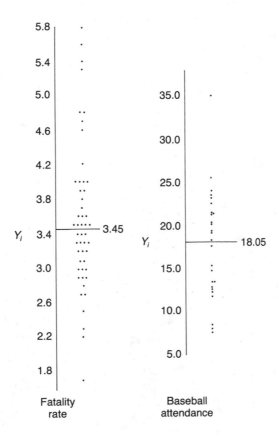

Since the horizontal lines through the data sets indicate the parameter estimates, vertical departures of individual data points from those parameter estimates represent the models' errors of prediction, e_i. Accordingly, we could redefine the vertical axes in these displays so that they represent values of e_i rather than values of Y_i. Such displays are known as *residual plots* and will be used with some frequency in later chapters. Median residual plots for both of these data sets are given in Exhibit 3.8. Note that the data points in these plots are identical to those presented in Exhibit 3.7. The only difference between the displays of these two exhibits arises from the redefinition of the vertical axes. Notice further that in the residual plots of Exhibit 3.8, we have retained the horizontal lines to indicate the median values of e_i. Given that the estimated parameters equal the medians of Y_i, the medians of the residuals are necessarily equal to zero.

The only problem with the displays contained in Exhibits 3.7 and 3.8 is that with large data sets they become relatively unwieldy and somewhat inelegant, consisting of a hodgepodge of dots on top of each

EXHIBIT 3.8 ▶

Simple model residual plots— fatality and baseball data

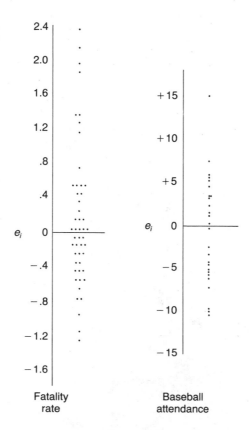

other. In order to avoid this situation and to make the display more readable, let us summarize the distribution of individual data points not by graphing all of them but by presenting the median distance of the data points from the predicted value or parameter estimate, both above and below that predicted value. We could decide to use the median absolute error both above and below the predicted value, the median, to summarize how far individual data points tend to be from the predicted value, or we could calculate separate median absolute errors for those observations above the predicted value and for those below it. Let us illustrate the two alternatives.

Using the baseball attendance data and defining the vertical axis in the display to represent values of Y_i rather than of e_i, we have constructed two displays in Exhibit 3.9. The one on the left presents a box with a line drawn through the middle of it. On the vertical axis to the left of the box are the possible data values that occur in the data set. The line in the middle of the box is drawn at the value of the median, the parameter estimate from the single-parameter model. The two lines that define the top and bottom of the box are exactly the median absolute error in distance away from the median. In other words, the value of the median in these data is 18.05. The median absolute error for this set of data,

EXHIBIT 3.9 ▶

Median box and whiskers baseball attendance

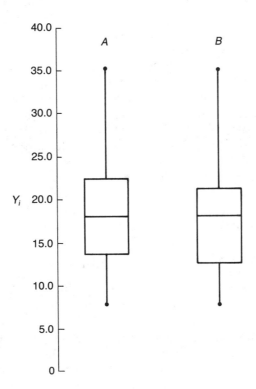

given the predicted value $\hat{Y}_i$ of 18.05, equals 4.35. (We figured out the value for this median absolute error exactly as we did in the last chapter, by writing out all of the absolute errors in the order of their magnitude and then finding the median of these absolute errors.) Hence the top line of the box in the display equals the predicted value plus the median absolute error:

$$18.05 + 4.35 = 22.4$$

The bottom line of the box in the display is the median absolute error below the predicted value, 13.7. We also have drawn two lines vertically from the top and the bottom of the box to tell us about the most extreme observation in each direction. The top line goes up to 35.1, which represents the outlying value of the Los Angeles Dodgers' attendance figure; the line from the bottom ends at the value of 7.7, which is the attendance figure of the Cleveland Indians.

So, in sum, this display tells us not only what the predicted value is for each observation, but it also tells us the median amount of error, both above and below the predicted value, and finally it tells us the amount of error in the two observations furthest above and furthest below the predicted value. The display would appear identically if we redefined the vertical axis to represent values of e_i rather than of Y_i. The horizontal line in the middle of the box would then be located at the value of zero on the vertical axis and the top and bottom of the box would be at 4.35 and −4.35.

Except for the differences between the two most extreme errors, this display assumes that the distribution of errors is symmetric around the predicted value. That is, the upper and lower lines of the box are equidistant from the predicted value. We use the median absolute error to show how far the typical observation is above the median and how far the typical observation is below the median. It may be more accurate to display any skewness in the data by separately calculating the median absolute error of observations above the median and the median absolute error of observations below the median. The display in panel B of Exhibit 3.9 does just that. For the 13 observations that lie above the median, the median absolute error equals 3.25. Hence, the upper end of the box is drawn at the value of 21.3 (18.05 + 3.25). The median absolute error for observations below the median equals 5.55; hence, the bottom of the box in panel B is at the value of 12.5 (18.05 − 5.55). Notice from this display, which preserves the most extreme values at the top and bottom of the distribution, that while the most extreme outlier is at the upper end of the distribution, observations below the median are typically further from the predicted value than observations above the median.

A bit of terminology may be helpful at this point. The displays that are presented in Exhibit 3.9 are called *median box and whiskers* displays. They too were first used by Tukey. The values that mark the bottom and top of the box in panel B of Exhibit 13.9 are the 25% quantile and the 75% quantile scores, respectively. They are also called the *hinges* of the distribution. These values are derived by simply taking the median value for observations lying below the median and the median value for observations lying above the median. Note that the average of the two median absolute errors for observations above and below the median does not always equal the median absolute error across all observations.

We could develop the same sort of displays using the mean as the single-parameter estimate and minimizing the sum of the squared errors. Then the horizontal line in the middle of the box would be drawn at the mean of the distribution, and the upper and lower limits of the box might be drawn one standard deviation above and below the mean. Such a display might be called a *mean box and whiskers* display.

Box and whiskers plots are particularly informative when the distributions of data from two different groups of observations are compared. For instance, we might want to display the results of single-parameter models applied separately to baseball teams from the American and National leagues, because we are interested in comparing the attendance figures across leagues. Exhibit 3.10 presents two median box

EXHIBIT 3.10 ▶

Box and whiskers by league

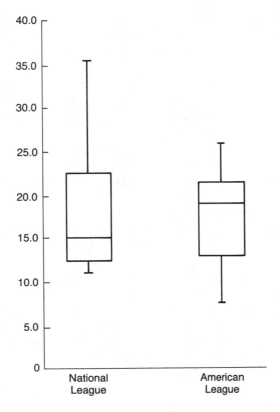

and whiskers displays, one from the American league teams and one from the National league teams. Since the boxes in these displays are not symmetric around the medians, we have obviously computed the median absolute error separately for observations above and below the median in each league.

Comparing these displays, we see that the median attendance is higher in the American league than it is in the National league. However, that simple conclusion hides a considerable amount of further information about the comparison of these two data distributions. While the American league has a higher median, it is negatively skewed, so most of the very low attendance figures are from American league teams. On the other hand, the distribution in the National league is positively skewed, with quite a few teams showing fairly high attendance figures even though the median is relatively low. So, simply to conclude that there is better typical attendance in the American league than in the National league is at least in part misleading.

Exhibit 3.10 is actually a display of a two-parameter model, even though we have not yet formally discussed such models. The two-parameter model in this display is

$$\hat{Y}_i = b_0 + b_1X_i$$

where X_i is used to identify a team's league, defining its values as +1 if a team is in the American league and −1 if a team is in the National league. Accordingly, we can redefine the horizontal axis in this display to represent the values of X_i. We will deal extensively with this sort of two-parameter model with a discrete X_i as a predictor variable in Chapter 11. The important point for the present is that the displays that we have defined can be used with much more complicated models than the simple single parameter one.

Exhibit 3.11 contains a residual plot from this two-parameter model, defining the vertical axis to represent values of e_i and the horizontal axis to represent values of X_i, and plotting the individual values of e_i rather than a summary box and whiskers plot. This plot has also been derived by using parameter estimates that result from minimizing the sum of squared errors rather than the sum of absolute errors. As we will see in Chapter 11, a two-parameter model with a discrete X_i predictor variable yields values of $\hat{Y}_i$ equal to the means of the two groups defined by the predictor variable. Thus, for the two-parameter model under present consideration, the value of $\hat{Y}_i$ for each team is the mean attendance figure for the league to which that team belongs. Accordingly, the mean value of e_i from each of the two leagues equals zero, and the two distributions of residuals from the two leagues will be centered at the same zero point on the vertical axis of the residual plot.

EXHIBIT 3.11 ▶

**Attendance resid-
ual plots within
league**

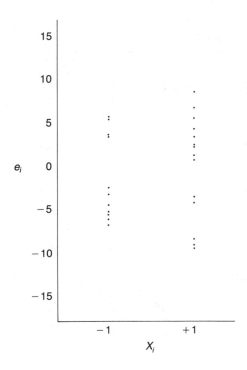

Consider displays from another two-parameter model. Suppose we thought that automobile fatalities might have something to do with bad driving conditions, induced perhaps by bad weather. To see if there was any merit to this idea, we might decide to use each state's mean minimum January temperature in a model to predict the state's automobile fatality rate. Thus, we define Y_i as fatality rate and X_i as January minimum temperature, and we estimate the parameters of the two-parameter model

$$Y_i = \beta_0 + \beta_1 X_i + \varepsilon_i$$

The values of Y_i and X_i for each state are given in Exhibit 3.12. While we have not yet discussed how the parameters of this sort of model are estimated (that will come in Chapter 6), the following parameter estimates result in values of $\hat{Y}_i$ that minimize the sum of squared errors:

$$Y_i = 3.299 + .011X_i + e_i$$

From this model we can generate values of $\hat{Y}_i$ for each state by substituting each state's minimum January temperature value in the model equation

$$\hat{Y}_i = 3.299 + .011X_i$$

Y_i	X_i	$\hat{Y}_i$	e_i	Y_i	X_i	$\hat{Y}_i$	e_i
4.2	40	3.75	.45	4.0	8	3.39	.61
4.7	18	3.50	1.20	2.9	12	3.44	−.54
5.3	38	3.73	1.57	5.6	16	3.48	2.12
3.6	29	3.63	−.03	2.8	10	3.41	−.61
3.4	47	3.83	−.43	2.2	24	3.57	−1.37
3.5	16	3.48	.02	5.8	24	3.57	2.23
2.3	22	3.55	−1.25	3.6	26	3.59	.01
3.3	24	3.57	−.27	3.6	32	3.66	−.06
3.2	45	3.81	−.61	3.7	−3	3.27	.43
3.3	33	3.67	−.37	2.9	22	3.55	−.65
4.0	65	4.04	−.04	3.5	26	3.59	−.09
4.8	21	3.54	1.26	3.9	33	3.67	.23
3.0	17	3.49	−.49	3.0	23	3.56	−.56
2.9	20	3.53	−.63	1.7	25	3.58	−1.88
3.0	11	3.42	−.42	3.8	37	3.72	.08
3.5	21	3.54	−.04	3.4	2	3.32	.08
3.2	25	3.58	−.38	3.3	29	3.63	−.33
4.6	44	3.80	.80	4.0	38	3.73	.27
3.1	12	3.44	−.34	3.9	19	3.52	.38
2.5	25	3.58	−1.08	3.4	8	3.39	.01
2.7	23	3.56	−.86	2.7	32	3.66	−.96
3.2	19	3.52	−.32	3.5	25	3.58	−.08
3.3	3	3.33	−.03	4.0	24	3.57	.43
4.8	41	3.77	1.03	3.1	10	3.41	-.31
3.5	23	3.56	−.06	5.4	15	3.47	1.93

EXHIBIT 3.12 ▲

States' fatality rate (Y_i), minimum temperature (X_i), predicted values ($\hat{Y}_i$), and residuals (e_i) resulting from the model $\hat{Y}_i =$ 3.299 + .011X_i

As always, the difference between Y_i and $\hat{Y}_i$ equals e_i. In addition to the raw data values on the fatality rate and minimum January temperature variables, Exhibit 3.12 also provides for each state the values of $\hat{Y}_i$ and e_i.

A variety of displays can be constructed to portray this model and its residuals. First, we might construct a simple scatterplot, defining values on the vertical axis as Y_i and values on the horizontal axis as X_i. Within this scatterplot we might then draw a line that represents the values of $\hat{Y}_i$ predicted for each observation by the least squares model. Such a display is given in Exhibit 3.13. The values of e_i equal the vertical distance between this model's prediction for each state, $\hat{Y}_i$, and the actual fatality rate for that state, Y_i.

We can also construct a residual plot from this model, defining the vertical axis by values of e_i and the horizontal one by values of X_i. Such a residual plot is given in Exhibit 3.14. Residual plots such as this one

EXHIBIT 3.13 ▶

Fatality rate–temperature scatterplot

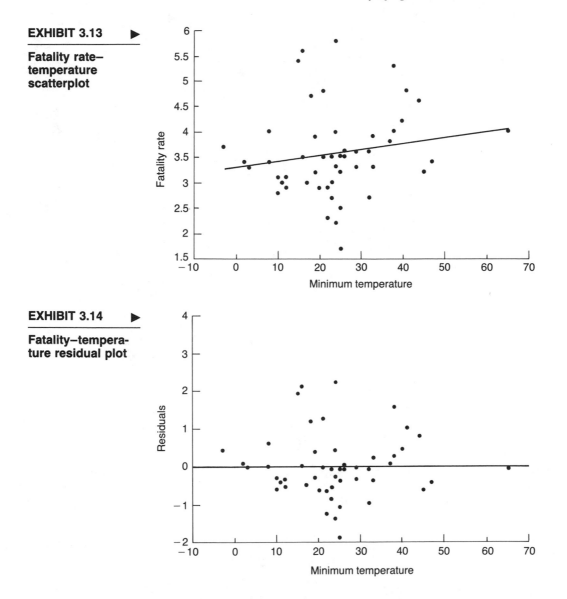

EXHIBIT 3.14 ▶

Fatality–temperature residual plot

will be used extensively later in the book. We will be concerned there about statistical inference procedures that are designed to enable us to evaluate the relative quality of a model whose parameters we have estimated. These procedures make assumptions about the distribution of residuals that result from a given model. We discuss these assumptions in Chapter 5 and elsewhere. Residual plots are useful in examining whether such assumptions are tenable, and, if they are not, in determining what corrective action (e.g., modifications to the model) need to be made. Hence, we will see a lot of residual plots.

4

Simple Models: Models of ERROR and Sampling Distributions

In Chapter 2 we considered alternative aggregate summary measures for ERROR and saw how different choices of an index led us to different estimates for the single parameter of the simple model. Now we need to make a choice of which aggregate index of ERROR we will generally use. To do so, we must state our assumptions about the behavior of the errors ε_i. We need to have a model for ERROR. In this chapter we will consider a reasonable model of ERROR that is often appropriate and show how that model of ERROR directs us to a certain aggregate index. In later chapters we show how to check the appropriateness of the chosen model for ERROR, and we will then consider what remedies to apply to our data analysis when the model for ERROR is inappropriate.

In this chapter our focus is on the error term ε_i which should be included in the full statement of our MODELs. For the simple model, the complete statement is:

MODEL: $\quad Y_i = \beta_0 + \varepsilon_i$

This model says that were it not for random perturbations represented by the ε_i all the Y_i would equal β_0 exactly. What are these random perturbations? anything which causes the observed datum Y_i to deviate from the true value β_0. For the example of automobile fatality rates some states may have had unusually bad weather, others may have had either unusually strong or unusually lax enforcement of speed laws, and still others may have disproportionately low numbers of young drivers. For the example of major league baseball attendance, some teams may have had unusually good or bad teams that year, or their cities may have had good or bad weather that summer, or there may have been rumors about the team moving to another city. Any of these or countless other factors may have caused the observed fatality rates or the observed attendance figures to deviate from the single value β_0 predicted by the simple model.

You might object that a factor such as a baseball team's performance ought to be included in the MODEL of attendance rather than in ERROR. Indeed, a team's performance and the other factors listed above as causes of ERROR may be important predictors that ought to be included in the MODEL. However, if we are using a simple model with only one parameter, then we must include all those factors in ERROR because those factors cause the observed Y_i to deviate from the single value β_0 predicted by the MODEL. Later we will consider more complex models which will allow us to move such factors from ERROR to MODEL. To the extent that moving a factor from ERROR to MODEL reduces ERROR, we will have improved our MODEL and its predictions. How to do that must await subsequent chapters; for now our problem is what assumptions we can reasonably make about the nature of ERROR.

4.1

Sampling Distributions

As was shown in Chapter 2, for each aggregate index of ERROR there is an associated estimator of β_0 in the simple model. For example, for the sum of absolute errors the median is the best estimator, and for the sum of squared errors the mean is the best estimator. Part of our strategy for selecting an aggregate index of ERROR will be to examine the performance of various estimators under some reasonable assumptions about the behavior of the ERRORs ε_i. Below we develop a metaphorical representation of the simple model which will help our intuitions about ERROR and which will provide a context for examining the relative performance of the median and the mean.

4.1.1   Metaphorical Representation of ERROR

Suppose that Nature has a bag containing a large number of tickets and on each ticket is written a particular value for ε_i. Exhibit 4.1 is a list of 100 values for ε_i which might be on the tickets. To determine the value

EXHIBIT 4.1 ▶

100 hypothetical values of ε_i in nature's bag of tickets

−1	−6	−11	−25	−1
−9	20	−24	4	−7
−13	−5	−37	−19	0
38	−17	−5	6	42
20	−17	11	22	23
−19	−9	36	−37	79
−12	16	31	−13	−19
−1	−5	39	1	26
−32	−3	−24	12	−21
−12	1	1	−2	30
21	−17	−25	10	25
−19	7	8	20	11
−9	16	39	45	−8
22	−39	−21	−17	11
−12	27	−33	25	9
6	9	62	−24	−9
−9	−8	−24	−15	17
12	−19	0	−16	5
−22	8	−41	−16	26
−52	−3	−31	−43	38

for a particular observation Y_i, Nature reaches into her bag of tickets and *randomly* draws one ticket; she then adds the number on the ticket, the value of the error ε_i, to the true value β_0. Let us assume, for example, that $\beta_0 = 65$ so that the simple model becomes

MODEL: $Y_i = 65 + \varepsilon_i$

Suppose the following 15 values were on tickets randomly drawn from a bag containing the tickets of Exhibit 4.1:

−9	38	−17	22	45
−12	−24	1	10	11
6	−24	−19	−21	−37

Then the first datum would equal $65 + (-9) = 56$ because -9 is on the first error ticket drawn. The second datum would equal $65 + 38 = 103$ and so on. The 15 observed values would be

56	103	48	87	110
53	41	66	75	76
71	41	46	44	28

Note that for the moment we are ignoring the issue of how it is determined which numbers are to be written on the tickets representing the errors. This is a very important issue, to which we will return later.

Had a different set of error tickets been drawn we would have obtained a different set of data. Statisticians often use the word *sample* to refer to a batch of data that could have been different if, in terms of our metaphor, a different set of error tickets had been drawn. Thus, the 15 data observations above represent a sample of the possible data values that could have been obtained. The mean and median for this particular sample of 15 observations are 63 and 56, respectively. Note that neither the mean nor the median exactly equal the actual value of β_0 specified in the MODEL as 65 for this example. Had a different sample been drawn, the mean and median would likely have been different. For some samples the mean and median will be closer to the true value, and for others they will be farther away. If the mean and median are to be good estimates of β_0, we would hope that on the average they would be close to β_0. For this example we can perform a simulation experiment to determine likely values for the mean and median for samples of size 15. On each simulation round we randomly select another sample of 15 error tickets, add 65 to each one, and then calculate the mean and median of the resulting sample. If we perform many, many simulation rounds, generating many, many different samples and computing the mean and median in each, then we can treat each mean or median as a datum itself. We can then construct a frequency polygon for these data. Such frequency distributions are known as *sampling distributions* because they show the distribution of a particular statistic based on many, many samples.

4.1.2   Properties of Estimators

Sampling distributions provide all the information necessary for us to evaluate the relative performance of various estimators. Below we examine the performance of the median and mean with respect to three desirable properties of an estimator: unbiased, efficient, and consistent. Each concept is illustrated and defined in terms of Exhibit 4.2, which depicts the sampling distributions for both the mean and the median based on 500 samples of size 15 from the bag of ERROR tickets in Exhibit 4.1. With only 500 samples the frequency distributions are somewhat jagged; if the number of samples were increased substantially, the curves would become much smoother but the general picture would be the same.

Unbiasedness.   Reassuringly, both distributions have peaks at 65, indicating that 65 is the most likely value for both the mean and the median. If the peak and the average value from the sampling distribution for an estimator or statistic equal the specified value for the parameter (65 in this case), then the estimator is said to be *unbiased*.

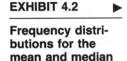

EXHIBIT 4.2 ▶

Frequency distributions for the mean and median for *n* = 15

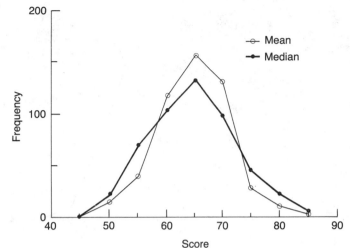

Efficiency. For these sampling distributions, there are very few instances for which the mean or the median are very far away from 65; the bulk of the observed values are between about 57 and 73. Note, however, that the mean appears to be a slightly better estimator than the median because there are somewhat fewer values of the median near 65 and there are somewhat more values of the median in the "tails" of the distribution far away from 65. For this example the mean is said to be more efficient than the median because with the same number of observations the mean provides more precision.

Consistency. It is interesting to ask what the sampling distributions would be like if the sample sizes were larger. For example, what if the mean and median were based on samples of size 50 instead of samples of size 15? Exhibit 4.3 shows the sampling distributions for the mean and the median based on 500 samples of size 50. Compared with Exhibit 4.2 it is clear that the sampling distributions based on samples of size 50 are very much narrower than those based on samples of size 15. The narrowness indicates that a greater proportion of the observed values of the mean and median were near 65 and that even fewer observed values were far away from 65. If the sampling distribution of an estimator or statistic becomes narrower as the sample size increases, then it is said to be a *consistent* estimator. Note also that again the mean is slightly more efficient than the median because its sampling distribution is a little bit narrower.

EXHIBIT 4.3 ▶

Frequency distribution for mean and median for $n = 50$

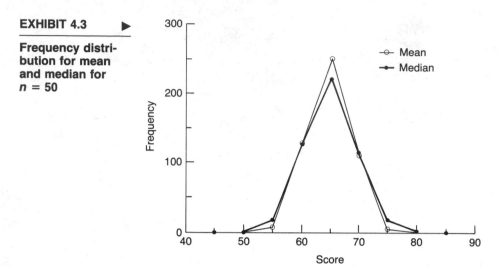

4.2

Normal Distribution of Errors

Unbiasedness, consistency, and efficiency are obviously desirable attributes for an estimator of β_0 in the simple model. Both the mean and the median and many other estimators are unbiased and consistent, so those properties offer no basis for choosing an estimator and its corresponding index of aggregate ERROR. The efficiency of estimators does differ, and in the above example the mean was slightly more efficient than the median. Hence, our example suggests that choosing the sum of squared errors as our aggregate index of ERROR and using its associated estimator (i.e., the mean) would serve us well. But that conclusion depends on the particular distribution of ERROR tickets in Exhibit 4.1. Had there been some other distribution of ERROR tickets in Nature's bag, we might have found the median to be more efficient. Thus, we must make an assumption or state our model about the contents of Nature's bag of ERROR tickets. Equivalently, we will be stating our assumption about the distribution of the ERROR tickets.

We will assume that the ERRORs have a *normal distribution*. That is, we assume that a frequency distribution for the ERROR tickets would have the general shape of the normal curve depicted in Exhibit 4.4. This is an idealized representation that would only be obtained from a bag containing an infinite number of tickets. The 100 ERROR tickets of Exhibit 4.1 were, in effect, randomly selected from a bag containing an infinite number of normally distributed ERRORs. The stem and leaf display for the 100 ERROR tickets is depicted in Exhibit 4.5; although it

EXHIBIT 4.4 ▶

Normal probability curve

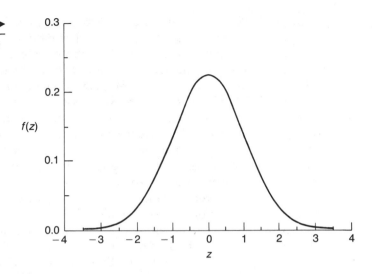

EXHIBIT 4.5 ▶

Stem and leaf display for the error tickets of exhibit 4.1 (produced by MINITAB)

```
Stem and leaf of TICKETS N = 100
Leaf Unit = 1.0

    1    −5   2
    3    −4   31
    9    −3   977321
   18    −2   554444211
   36    −1   9999977777665332221
  (19)   −0   9999988765553321110
   45     0   0111456678899
   32     1   011122667
   23     2   000122355667
   11     3   0168899
    4     4   25
    2     5
    2     6   2
    1     7   9
```

does have the general shape of the normal distribution, it is far from an exact match.

There are many other possible distributions of ERRORs that we might have assumed, but there are good reasons for assuming the normal distribution. First, there is an abundance of empirical data indicating that the distribution of ERRORs is often approximately normal. That is in fact how it acquired the name "normal" distribution. Second, as we shall see in Chapter 16, it is often possible to use various remedies to transform a nonnormal distribution of ERRORs into a nearly normal distribution. Third, and most importantly, there is a reasonable model of the ERRORs which causes us to expect them to be distributed normally. We turn now to a description of that model.

Above we mentioned a number of possible components of the ERRORs for both the fatality rate data and the baseball attendance data. It is unlikely that in any particular case only a single ERROR component is perturbing the observed value away from the parameter value specified in the simple model. For example, it might be that the attendance was altered because of unusual weather that year *and* unusual team performance *and* rumors of the team's impending move to another city. Some of the factors will push the observed value above the model value, and others will push it below the model value. The observed difference between the observed and model values, $Y_i - \hat{Y}_i$, will actually be determined by the *sum* of the individual ERROR components. The central limit theorem, a well-known theorem in mathematical statistics, shows that the distribution of a sum or the average of a number of components will approximate a normal distribution no matter what the original distribution of the individual components. Thus, if we assume that the actual ERROR is the sum of a number of individual errors, then it is reasonable to expect that the distribution of the ERRORs will approximate a normal distribution. The central limit theorem also shows that the greater the number of components in the sum or average, the better the approximation to a normal distribution.

The central limit theorem is of such importance that a demonstration of the concept is worthwhile. Suppose that the distribution of the individual error components is such that any value between $-.5$ and $+.5$ is just as likely as any other. This distribution is known as the *uniform distribution* because each possible value has the same probability. As Exhibit 4.6 illustrates, the uniform distribution is very different from a normal distribution. Suppose that each value on an ERROR ticket is the sum of 12 small individual error components randomly selected from the uniform distribution. Exhibit 4.7 shows the frequency distribution for 1000 such ERROR tickets. Clearly, even though the distribution for the individual components was not normal, the distribution for the sum closely approximates a normal distribution. Thus, if it is reasonable to assume that the observed ERROR is actually the sum of a lot of small random error components, then it is reasonable to assume that the distribution of the ERRORs is approximately normal.

4.2.1 Formal Specification of the Normal Distribution

Fortunately, there are precise mathematical statements of the normal distribution, so we do not have to depend on simulations of drawing tickets from a bag, as we used in our metaphor above. The curve for

EXHIBIT 4.6 ▶

Uniform probability curve

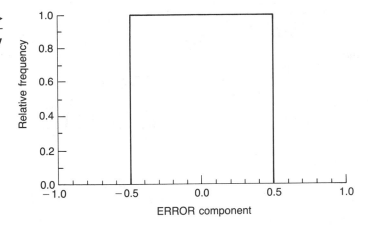

EXHIBIT 4.7 ▶

Frequency distribution for the sum of 12 uniform errors

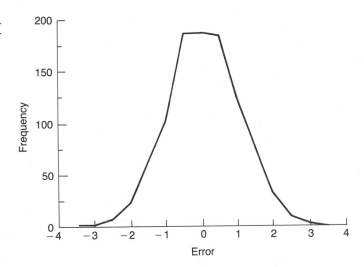

the relative frequency of the normal distribution represented in Exhibit 4.4 is given by

$$f(x) = \frac{1}{\sigma\sqrt{2\pi}} e^{-(x-\mu)^2/2\sigma^2}$$

This equation has two parameters: μ, the expected value or mean of the distribution, and σ^2, the variance of the distribution. Different values of μ simply shift the curve of Exhibit 4.4 back and forth along the horizontal axis. Exhibit 4.8 shows two normal curves which have the same variance ($\sigma^2 = 1$) but different means ($\mu_1 = 0$, $\mu_2 = 4$). The variance parameter σ^2 determines the spread of the normal curve. The larger σ^2 is, the wider the distribution. Exhibit 4.9 shows three normal curves which each have a mean of $\mu = 0$ but increasing variances of 1, 4, and 9.

EXHIBIT 4.8 ▶

Normal probability curves with same variance and different means

EXHIBIT 4.9 ▶

Normal probability curves with same mean but different variances

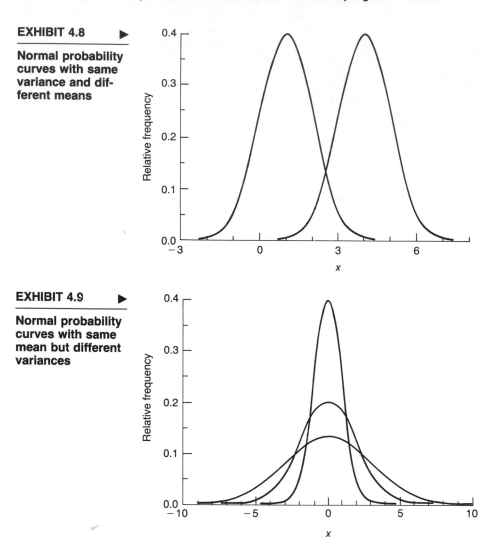

Exhibits of the normal distribution are available in many statistical books, and most computer packages provide functions for easily generating the required probabilities. All normal distributions have the same shape, so it is common to use the distribution with $\mu = 0$ and $\sigma^2 = 1$ as a standard reference distribution. Exhibit 4.10 gives the probability that a value x randomly sampled from the normal distribution will be less than the tabled values of z ranging between -3 and $+3$. For example, the probability for $z = 1.0$ equals .841, which indicates that 84.1% of the time a randomly sampled value from this distribution will be less than 1.0. Note that the probability for $z = 0$, the mean for this particular distribution, equals .5, indicating that we would expect 50% of the observations to be below zero and 50% of the observations to be above zero.

EXHIBIT 4.10 ▶

Cumulative probabilities for the normal distribution for $\mu = 0$ and $\sigma^2 = 1$

z	p(x < z)	z	p(x < z)
−3.0	.002	.0	.500
−2.9	.002	.1	.540
−2.8	.003	.2	.579
−2.7	.004	.3	.618
−2.6	.005	.4	.656
−2.5	.006	.5	.692
−2.4	.008	.6	.726
−2.3	.011	.7	.758
−2.2	.014	.8	.788
−2.1	.018	.9	.816
−2.0	.023	1.0	.841
−1.9	.028	1.1	.864
−1.8	.036	1.2	.885
−1.7	.044	1.3	.903
−1.6	.055	1.4	.919
-1.5	.067	1.5	.933
−1.4	.081	1.6	.945
−1.3	.097	1.7	.956
−1.2	.115	1.8	.964
−1.1	.136	1.9	.972
−1.0	.159	2.0	.977
−.9	.184	2.1	.982
−.8	.212	2.2	.986
−.7	.242	2.3	.989
−.6	.274	2.4	.992
−.5	.308	2.5	.994
−.4	.344	2.6	.995
−.3	.382	2.7	.996
−.2	.421	2.8	.997
−.1	.460	2.9	.998
.0	.500	3.0	.998

To find the expected proportion of observations between any two particular values, we simply subtract their associated probabilities. For example, the proportion of observations between $z = 0$ and $z = 1$ equals $.841 - .500 = .341$. Exhibit 4.11 shows the expected proportion of observations between various landmarks. We will not be using the z table of Exhibit 4.10 very much; instead we will be using similar tables for some special distributions. For most purposes it is sufficient to remember that approximately 68% of the observations from a normal distribution fall between −1 and +1, approximately 95% fall between −2 and +2, and almost all (approximately 99.6%) fall between −3 and

EXHIBIT 4.11 ▶

**Standard normal
probability curve,
$\mu = 0$, $\sigma^2 = 1$**

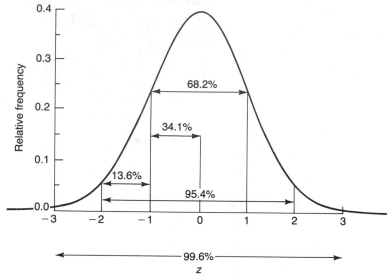

+3. The tails of the normal distribution theoretically extend to $+\infty$ and $-\infty$; however, observations more extreme than 3 are infrequent, and observations more extreme than 4 are very rare.

Normal distributions with means other than 0 and/or variances other than 1 are easily compared with the reference distribution in Exhibit 4.10. Suppose that Y is an observation from a normal distribution with mean μ and variance σ^2. Subtracting μ from Y will shift the distribution along the horizontal axis, so the mean for the constructed variable $Y - \mu$ equals 0. Although it is not obvious, it can be shown that dividing $Y - \mu$ by σ will change the spread of the distribution so that it coincides with our reference distribution. (Note that we divide by σ, not σ^2.) The division by σ rescales the original variable so that it is measured in units of the standard deviation. Thus if Y is from a normal distribution with mean μ and variance σ^2, then z, defined by

$$z = \frac{Y - \mu}{\sigma}$$

has a normal distribution with mean 0 and variance 1. Values calculated according to this formula are known as z *scores* or, because of their use with the standard reference distribution, *standard normal deviates*. The "deviates" refers to the size of the deviation from the mean measured in units of the standard deviation. For example, Graduate Record Examination (GRE) scores are scaled so that $\mu = 500$ and $\sigma = 100$. To find the proportion of students we would expect to have a GRE score less than or equal to 650, assuming that GRE scores are normally distributed, we would first compute the corresponding z score. In this case,

$$z = \frac{650 - 500}{100} = 1.5$$

That is, a GRE score of 650 is 1.5 units (of standard deviation) above the mean (of 500). The associated cumulative probability in Exhibit 4.10 for $z = 1.5$ is .933, so we would expect about 93% of students to have lower GRE scores than 650.

We also can convert from a z score back to the original scale. The Y score that corresponds to a particular z is given by

$$Y = \mu + z\sigma$$

In the same GRE example if we wanted to know what GRE score corresponded to $z = 1.8$ (i.e., a score 1.8 standard deviations above the mean), we would calculate

$$500 + 1.8(100) = 680$$

4.2.2 Sampling Distributions Revisited

Now that we have made an explicit assumption about the distribution of the errors, we can reconsider the sampling distributions for estimators such as the mean and median. Let us again return to our example of the simple model in which $\beta_0 = 65$. That is, our model is

$$Y_i = 65 + \varepsilon_i$$

We now make the explicit assumption that the ε_i are randomly sampled from a normal distribution with $\mu = 0$ and some constant but unknown variance σ^2. Adding 65 to each error value simply translates the normal distribution along the horizontal axis, so the data values Y_i will also have a normal distribution with mean $\mu = 65$ and variance σ^2. In order to be able to draw a picture of this distribution, we have assumed that $\sigma^2 = 558$. Then the distribution of the Y_i would have the theoretical curve depicted in Exhibit 4.12 as the broad curve. If we were to calculate the mean from samples of size n, the theoretical sampling distribution of such means would also have a normal distribution. The mean of the sampling distributions of means equals the mean of the original theoretical distribution, which in this case is 65. Mathematical statisticians have shown that the variance of this sampling distribution would equal

$$\frac{\sigma^2}{n}$$

EXHIBIT 4.12 ▶

Normal distribution of observations and sampling distribution of the mean for $n = 15$

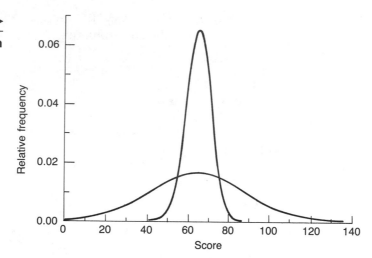

if the error tickets are drawn from a normal distribution. In our example, if the sample size were 15, then the variance of the sampling distribution for the means would equal $558/15 = 37.2$. If we were to collect many, many samples of size 15 and calculate the mean for each sample, the sampling distribution of those means would approximate the theoretical sampling distribution also depicted in Exhibit 4.12 as the peaked curve. Note that, as was the case when we simulated the sampling distribution, the spread for the mean is very much smaller than the original spread. If we were to collect larger samples, the sampling distribution for the mean would be even narrower because we would be dividing σ^2 by a larger value in order to determine its variance.

Mathematical statisticians have also shown that the variance for the sampling distribution of the median based on samples of size n is approximately equal to

$$\frac{\pi}{2} \frac{\sigma^2}{n}$$

if the error tickets are drawn from a normal distribution. This is the same as the variance for the mean except that it is multiplied by $\pi/2$ (which equals approximately 1.57), so the variance for the median must be larger. That is, the median is less efficient when error values have a normal distribution. In particular, the variance for the sampling distribution of the mean is about $2/\pi = 64\%$ smaller than the variance for the sampling distribution of the median. Another way to say this is that a sample of size 100 using the sample median has about the same efficiency as using the mean with a sample of size 64. As our earlier simulation suggested, but did not prove, the mean is clearly preferable to the median if the distribution of errors is normal. However, for some nonnormal distributions of errors, the median can actually be more efficient than the mean.

4.3
Choice of an Estimator and Index of ERROR

Now that we have made an explicit assumption about the distribution of the errors, we can choose the estimator and its corresponding definition of aggregate ERROR. We want an estimator that is unbiased, efficient, and consistent.

It can be shown mathematically that if the distribution of errors is normal, then the mean is a more efficient estimator than any other unbiased estimator. That is, the mean is more efficient than the median, the mode, and any other statistic whose sampling distribution would be centered at the parameter value specified in the simple model. The mean is also a consistent estimator. Hence, we will choose it as the best estimator. We also will adopt its corresponding definition of aggregate error which is the sum of squared errors (SSE).

There are other good reasons for selecting SSE and the mean besides the theoretical reasons above based on the assumption that the errors ε_i have a normal distribution. One very important reason is practicality. By far the greatest number of statistical procedures have been developed for SSE. Consequently there are very good computer procedures for accomplishing the statistical tests based on SSE. There are some very practical reasons for the ubiquity of statistical procedures based on SSE. It is much easier to work with squares in mathematical proofs than with absolute values. Calculating an average is also generally easier than ordering all of the data to find the middle one. More importantly, for complex models with many parameters the only way to estimate the best values for the parameters using most other aggregate indices of ERROR such as the sum of absolute errors (SAE) is brute-force or iterative search algorithms. In contrast, when using SSE, we will almost always be able to use explicit formulas for calculating the best parameter estimates. Even worse, the parameters based on SAE are not necessarily unique. That is, sometimes many different values for the parameters all produce the same minimum value of SAE. This is never a problem with SSE.

4.3.1 Other Distributions of ERRORs

It is important to remember that our choice of the mean and SSE is highly dependent on our assumption that the ERRORs are normally distributed. If the ERRORs have some other distribution, then choosing the mean and SSE might not be appropriate. Exhibit 4.13 shows another possible distribution for the ERRORs. Asymmetric distributions such as this one are *skewed* distributions. Note that in this case very large positive errors are more likely than very large negative errors. There are many situations which can produce data with a skewed distribution. For example, in any study measuring reaction times the smallest scores are obviously constrained to be above zero, but there is no constraint, other than the experimenter's patience, on how large the scores can be. This will produce a scattering of observations in the distribution's skewed tail. In general, the median is a better estimator for skewed distributions of errors. In Chapter 16 we discuss procedures for detecting and correcting skewed and other problem distributions of the ERRORs.

One of the most troubling possible error distributions is one that has the general shape of the normal distribution except that it has "thicker" tails. That is, extreme, especially very extreme, errors are more likely to occur than would be expected from the normal distribution. These extreme errors produce extreme observations which can have a very deleterious effect on the mean. As we demonstrated in Chapter 2, one wild observation can cause a dramatic change in the mean. The problem is that SSE pays a lot of attention to extreme observations in order to reduce the really big errors, so estimates get pulled a lot in the direction of the extreme observations, so much so that the mean may not be a very good estimate of central tendency when there are a few extreme observations. The median is much more resistant to effects of these wild observations or outliers, but we have to give up a lot of efficiency to get this robustness. We will stick with the mean and SSE, but we will have to remember that they are not very resistant to outliers.

EXHIBIT 4.13 ▶

Example of skewed distribution

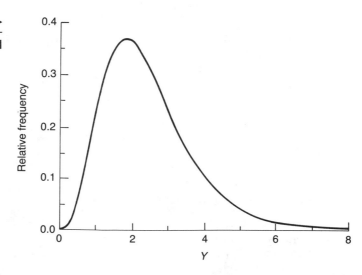

To make sure that a few extreme observations are not seriously distorting our results, we will have to check carefully for outliers each time we use statistical procedures based on SSE. A number of useful follow-up procedures have been developed precisely for this purpose, and we will examine them in Chapter 9.

4.3.2 Other Criteria for Estimators

We have adopted unbiasedness, efficiency, and consistency as reasonable criteria for an estimator. These criteria have been adopted by many statisticians. However, not all statisticians agree on the desirability of these criteria or, especially, on their relative desirability. For example, some statisticians argue that we should be willing to accept a little bit of bias in order to achieve greater efficiency. For some of the complex models we consider later there exist biased estimators which may have greater efficiency than the unbiased estimators we present. Other statisticians argue that the mean and SSE are so susceptible to outlier problems that estimators which are somewhat less efficient but more robust should be preferred. In general our approach is to stick with the mean and SSE while always checking assiduously for potential outliers which may be distorting the results.

4.3.3 Other Assumptions about Errors

In the preceding discussion of our model of errors and its metaphorical representation of Nature drawing error tickets from a bag, we have made several implicit assumptions. We need to make these assumptions explicit so that we will understand what assumptions have been made and so that we can be alert for potential violations of these assumptions. Below we consider in turn three standard assumptions: that the ε_i are independent of one another, that they are identically distributed, and that their mean is zero. These assumptions will be especially important in considering the sampling distributions for statistics developed later, particularly in Chapter 5.

Independence. The formal assumption is that each error is independent of the value of any other error. In terms of our metaphor, this means that each error ticket is selected randomly from the bag and then replaced in the bag before the next ticket is drawn. A violation of independence occurs when the value on one error ticket allows us to make a reasonable guess about the value on another error ticket. In terms of the metaphor, it would be a violation of independence if error tickets came in pairs attached to one another so that if we drew one we automatically drew the other. As a practical example, suppose our data are the automobile fatality rates for each state for each of several years. If a given state's fatality rate is above the mean or median one year, then it is likely that it will be above the mean or median in other years. Thus, when we use the simple model, all the errors for that state are likely to be positive and probably of about the same size. Thus, knowing the error for that state one year allows us to make a reasonable guess about the errors for other years. As a result, the errors would not be independent. This is an example of *time-series* data—the same units being observed or measured across a number of different time periods.

Time-series data seldom have errors which satisfy independence. As a similar example, suppose that we have two attitude scores from each subject, one score measured before the subject reads a persuasive communication and one measured after the subject reads the communication. This is known as a *within-subjects* design. Again, it is probable that someone who is below the mean or median on the first measure (the "pretest") will also be below the mean or median on the second measure (the "posttest"). Thus, if the simple model is used, the errors for each subject are likely to be either both positive or both negative, so independence is once again violated. As a final example, consider a survey which asks husbands and wives what proportion of various household tasks they each perform. For a given couple if the husband, say, claims to perform a small proportion of a particular task, then it is likely that the wife will claim to perform a large proportion of that particular task. If we tried to use a single simple model for all the data, it is likely that independence would be violated within couples. Knowing that the error for one spouse is negative (i.e., proportion claimed below the mean or median) would cause us to expect that the error for the other spouse would be positive (i.e., proportion claimed above the mean or median). Note that this dependence, unlike that in the other examples, is a *negative dependence* because the signs of the errors for each spouse are likely to be opposite.

Unlike the assumption about the normal distribution of errors which is very robust, the assumption that the errors are independent of each other is not at all robust. That is, our statistical inference will be seriously affected if the independence assumption is incorrect. Thus we must be especially alert for possible dependencies among the errors. If the independence assumption is violated, then all is not lost. We show in Chapters 14 and 15 how to analyze such data so that, after suitable transformations and rearrangements, independence is satisfied.

Identically Distributed.   Another very important assumption is that all the errors are sampled from the *same* distribution. In terms of our metaphor, this assumption would be violated if Nature had *two* bags of error tickets, one bag containing error values of a reasonable size and another bag containing error tickets with very much larger values. If Nature draws mostly from the first bag, then most of the resulting data values will be of a reasonable size. But if Nature occasionally draws an error ticket from the second bag, we will observe several "wild" data values which are very different from the other observations. Such data values are known as *outliers*. In other words, a violation of this assumption occurs if most of the errors are sampled from a normal distribution with variance σ^2 and a few errors are sampled from a normal distribution with a variance very different from σ^2. Although it would technically be a problem if the second variance were much smaller than the first one, the greater problem occurs when the second variance is very much larger than the first.

A slightly different type of violation of this assumption occurs, for example, in experiments when the manipulation itself causes the error variance to change. In general, there is a problem whenever the size of the variance depends on the mean. In this context the assumption of identical distributions is equivalent to assuming that the variances are equal, so it is sometimes called the *homogeneity of variance* assumption or sometimes *homoscedasticity*. Its violation is *heterogeneity of variance* or *heteroscedasticity*.

The identical distribution assumption is fairly robust. The variances must be very different before there are important problems for the data analysis. The most serious problems arise from outliers—a few observations which have errors sampled from a distribution with a very much greater variance. In Chapter 9 we consider procedures for detecting outliers and consider what to do about them. In Chapter 16 we develop techniques for detecting heterogeneity of variance and the use of transformations to reduce the heterogeneity to acceptable limits.

Errors Are Unbiased.   The final important assumption is that the errors are unbiased or, equivalently, that the expected value or mean of the distribution from which the errors are sampled equals zero. That is, our assumption is that on average the errors do not change the model parameters. If, instead, the errors were not random but systematic, such that errors averaged, say, below zero, then the systematic bias would appear in the MODEL rather than in the ERROR. For example, in the automobile fatality rate data suppose that reporting systems are organized such that deaths that occur in hospitals several weeks after accidents are not properly attributed as automobile fatalities. Then any estimate of the true fatality rate would necessarily be an underestimate. In effect, the systematic underreporting of error would be represented in the MODEL and not the ERROR. As data analysts we cannot do much to detect a systematic bias in the ERROR by examining the DATA. Hence, it is incumbent on the collector of the DATA to ensure that the ERRORs are indeed random with mean zero. Depending on the substantive domain, ensuring that the ERRORs are random involves aspects of experimental design, construction of survey questionnaires, interviewing procedures, instrument reliability, etc. We do not address such issues because they are highly domain-specific. However, if those issues have not been addressed in the actual collection of the data, then the use of the statistical procedures described in this book may be very misleading. As data analysts we offer no remedies for the problems of systematic error. Hence, we will always assume that errors are sampled from a distribution which has a mean of zero.

4.3.4   Estimator for σ^2

A final issue we need to consider is an estimator of σ^2. We know that the mean is an estimator for μ or β_0. It turns out that the mean squared error (MSE) is an unbiased estimator of σ^2. For the simple model, MSE has the special name *variance* and special symbol s^2. Thus,

$$\text{Variance} = s^2 = \frac{\text{SSE}}{n-1} = \frac{\sum_{i=1}^{n}(Y_i - \hat{Y}_i)^2}{n-1} = \frac{\sum_{i=1}^{n}(Y_i - \overline{Y})^2}{n-1}$$

estimates σ^2 for the simple model. For more complex models with p parameters,

$$\text{MSE} = \frac{\text{SSE}}{n-p} = \frac{\sum_{i=1}^{n}(Y_i - \hat{Y})^2}{n-p}$$

estimates σ^2. Obviously, root mean squared error, the standard deviation in the case of the simple models, estimates σ. Thus, the mean and the variance calculated from a sample of data provide estimates of the parameters μ and σ^2 which characterize a normal distribution.

5

Simple Models:
Statistical Inferences
about Parameter
Values

In Chapter 2 we considered various alternatives for how we should measure total ERROR in the equation

DATA = MODEL + ERROR

Although both the sum of the absolute errors and the sum of the squared errors seem to be reasonable alternatives, we decided in Chapter 4, for reasons of efficiency, practicality, and tradition, to define total ERROR as the sum of the squared errors. In the simplest models, where we are estimating the single parameter β_0, the choice of the sum of squared errors as the definition of ERROR implies that the best estimate is the sample mean (as was proved in Chapter 2).

In this chapter we develop procedures for asking questions or testing hypotheses about simple models. Defining and answering interesting questions is the purpose of data analysis. We first consider the logic of answering questions about DATA for the case of the simplest models because it is easy to focus on the logic when the models are simple and because the logic generalizes easily to more complex models. The specific statistical test presented in this chapter is equivalent to the "one-sample t test" usually given in traditional textbooks. We do not derive this test in terms of the t statistic; we prefer instead to construct this test using concepts and procedures that are identical to those required for the more complex models we will consider later.

The generic problem is that we have a batch of DATA for which we have calculated b_0, the mean, as an estimate of β_0. Then the question is whether β_0 is equal to some specific value. We will let B_0 equal the value specified in our question. The statement

$$\beta_0 = B_0$$

represents our *hypothesis* about the true value of β_0. Such statements are often called *null hypotheses*. The calculated value of b_0 will almost never exactly equal B_0, the hypothesized value of β_0. That is, the compact model

MODEL C: $Y_i = B_0 + \varepsilon_i$

in which no parameters are estimated will almost always produce a bigger ERROR than the augmented model

MODEL A: $Y_i = \beta_0 + \varepsilon_i$

in which β_0 is estimated by b_0, the mean of the batch of DATA. We will calculate PRE, the proportional reduction in error index developed in Chapter 1, to see how much better the predictions of MODEL A are than those of MODEL C. The original question then becomes not whether MODEL A is better than MODEL C, but whether MODEL A is *enough* better than MODEL C that we should reject the hypothesis that $\beta_0 = B_0$. Deciding what value of PRE is "enough better" is the essence of statistical inference and is the focus of this chapter.

To be less abstract, we will consider a detailed example. Suppose that the principal of an elementary school knows that the scores of her third grade students on a particular mathematics test have averaged about 65 over the past several years. One of her third grade teachers tries a new, experimental mathematics curriculum in his classroom of 15 students. The principal can think of some reasons why the new curriculum might improve the students' performance, but she also can think of other reasons why it might impair performance. At the end of the year the 15 students take the mathematics test and obtain the following scores:

72   52   93   86   96   46   55   74   129   61   57   115   79   89   68

The average score is 78.1. Exhibit 5.1 shows a stem and leaf diagram, box plot, and dot plot for these data.

EXHIBIT 5.1 ▶

Stem and leaf, box plot, and dot plot for the 15 math scores (produced by MINITAB)

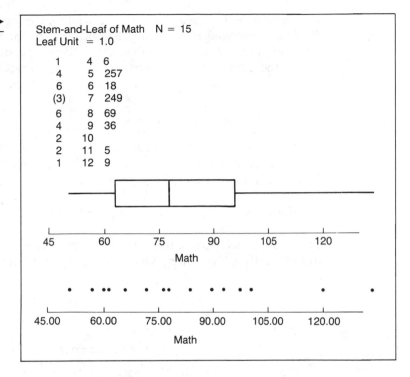

```
Stem-and-Leaf of Math   N = 15
Leaf Unit = 1.0

    1      4   6
    4      5   257
    6      6   18
   (3)     7   249
    6      8   69
    4      9   36
    2     10
    2     11   5
    1     12   9
```

The principal wants to know whether performance in this class was really different from the 65 she expected or whether the kids were "just lucky." In this example, β_0 represents the typical or expected performance on the examination of those students receiving the new curriculum. We do not know, nor can we ever know, exactly what this expected value is. The *hypothesized* value for β_0 is B_0, and in this example it equals 65, the typical performance of similar students in previous years who had not received the new curriculum. The *estimated* value for β_0 is b_0, and in this case it equals 78.1, the mean or average of the 15 students using the new curriculum, because the mean minimizes the sum of squared errors. In other words, for the compact model (which represents the hypothesis), the prediction is given by

MODEL C: $\hat{Y}_i = 65$

and for the augmented model (in which β_0 is estimated), the prediction is given by

MODEL A: $\hat{Y}_i = 78.1$

So the principal's question is whether the predictions of MODEL A are enough better to infer that MODEL C is unreasonable.

To help the principal answer her question, we want to calculate PRE. To do so, we need to calculate ERROR for each model. The necessary calculations are displayed in Exhibit 5.2. For the compact model, $\hat{Y}_{iC} = 65$, so the sum of squared errors from the compact model, SSE(C), is given as

$$\text{SSE(C)} = \sum_{i=1}^{n} (Y_i - \hat{Y}_{iC})^2 = \sum_{i=1}^{n} (Y_i - 65)^2$$

The squared error using the compact model for each student is listed in the third column of Exhibit 5.2 along with the sum of 10,403 for SSE(C). For the augmented model $\hat{Y}_{iA} = 78.1$, so

$$\text{SSE(A)} = \sum_{i=1}^{n} (Y_i - \hat{Y}_{iA})^2 = \sum_{i=1}^{n} (Y_i - 78.1)^2$$

The squared error using the augmented model for each student is listed in the fourth column along with its sum of 7,815.7 for SSE(A). Then the

EXHIBIT 5.2 ▶

Mathematics test scores and error calculations for 15 third grade students

Student Number	Score Y_i	Squared Errors	
		Compact $(Y - B_0)^2$	Augmented $(Y - b_0)^2$
1	72	49	37.6
2	52	169	683.0
3	93	784	221.0
4	86	441	61.9
5	96	961	319.2
6	46	361	1,032.6
7	55	100	535.2
8	74	81	17.1
9	129	4,096	2,587.4
10	61	16	293.6
11	57	64	446.6
12	115	2,500	1,359.2
13	79	196	.8
14	89	576	118.1
15	68	9	102.7
SUMS	1172	10,403	7,815.7
MEAN	78.1		

proportional reduction in error using MODEL A instead of MODEL C is given by

$$PRE = \frac{SSE(C) - SSE(A)}{SSE(C)} = \frac{10,403 - 7,815.7}{10,403} = .25$$

That is, MODEL A using b_0, the *estimated* value of β_0, has 25% less ERROR than MODEL C using B_0, the *hypothesized* value of β_0.

We note in passing that for both MODEL C and MODEL A two observations (students 9 and 12) are responsible for most of the total SSE. Although the presentation of formal procedures for investigating outliers must wait until Chapter 9, the large errors associated with a few observations should make us suspicious of outliers. Remember that SSE and its associated estimators such as the mean are not resistant to outliers.

5.1

Decomposition of SSE

At this point it is useful to introduce a table which summarizes our analysis so far. Let

SSR = SSE(C) − SSE(A)

be the amount of ERROR which is reduced by using MODEL A instead of MODEL C. Then it is obvious that

SSE(C) = SSR + SSE(A)

In other words, the original ERROR SSE(C) can be decomposed into two components: (a) the reduction in ERROR due to MODEL A, SSR, plus (b) the ERROR remaining from MODEL A, SSE(A). It is common to summarize the results of an analysis in a table having separate rows for SSR, SSE(A), and SSE(C). Exhibit 5.3 presents such a table for our example. Note that the SS (sum of squares) for the total line, which represents SSE(C), is indeed the sum of SSR and SSE(A); for our example, 10,403 = 2,587 + 7,816. PRE is readily obtained from the SS column using the formula

$$PRE = \frac{SSR}{SSE(C)}$$

We will use these tables that give the decomposition of the sums of squares as the basic summary for all our statistical tests. We will add several other useful columns to such tables.

EXHIBIT 5.3 ▶

**Generic ANOVA
layout**

Source	SS	PRE
Reduce, Model A	SSR	$\dfrac{\text{SSR}}{\text{SSE(C)}}$
Error for Model A	SSE(A)	
Total	SSE(C)	

SSR is easily understood and often easily calculated as the difference between SSE(C) and SSE(A). However, there is another representation for SSR which provides additional insight for the comparison of MODELs C and A. It can be shown (we essentially did it in Chapter 2 for the case of the simple model; the more general proof does not provide useful insights so we omit it) that

$$\text{SSR} = \sum_{i=1}^{n} (\hat{Y}_{iC} - \hat{Y}_{iA})^2 \tag{5.1}$$

where $\hat{Y}_{iC}$ and $\hat{Y}_{iA}$ are, respectively, the predictions for the ith observation using MODEL C and MODEL A. This formula will be useful later for calculating certain SSRs that are not automatically provided by typical computer programs. More important are the insights it provides. For a fixed SSE(C), the larger SSR is, the larger PRE is, and the larger the improvement provided by using MODEL A instead of MODEL C. This formula shows that SSR is small when MODELs C and A generate similar predictions for each observation. In the extreme case when MODELs C and A are identical (i.e., they produce the same predictions), then SSR = 0 and then PRE = 0. Conversely, SSR will be large to the extent that MODELs C and A generate different predictions. Thus, SSR is a direct measure of the difference between MODELs C and A and PRE = SSR/SSE(C) is a proportional measure of that difference.

Equation 5.1 is useful for calculating the SSR for the simple models considered in this chapter. Although we generally avoid multiple calculational formulas, we present this one because many computer programs do not conveniently provide the necessary information for computing PRE in our terms. We will illustrate the use of Equation 5.1 by computing the SSR for the math scores example. The value predicted by MODEL A is $\hat{Y}_{iA} = \overline{Y} = 78.133$, and the value predicted by MODEL C is the hypothesized value $\hat{Y}_{iC} = B_0 = 65$. So, according to Equation 5.1,

$$\text{SSR} = \sum_{i=1}^{n} (\hat{Y}_{iC} - \hat{Y}_{iA})^2 = \sum_{i=1}^{15} (65 - 78.133)^2 = \sum_{i=1}^{15} (-13.133)^2$$

EXHIBIT 5.4 ▶

ANOVA summary exhibit for math quiz example

Source	SS	PRE
Reduction (using β_0)	2,587	.25
Error (using β_0)	7,816	
Total (Error using B_0)	10,403	

That is, SSR equals the constant $-13.133^2 = 172.484$ summed 15 times. Thus, SSR $= 15(172.484) = 2587.26$, which is, within a small rounding error, the same value we obtained by calculating SSR directly as SSE(C) − SSE(A) in Exhibit 5.4. Thus, for simple models, the following formula is often handy for calculating SSR when an appropriate computer program cannot be found:

$$\text{SSR} = \sum_{i=1}^{n} (B_0 - \overline{Y})^2 = n(B_0 - \overline{Y})^2 \tag{5.2}$$

We will have many occasions to use Equation 5.2.

5.2
Sampling Distribution of PRE

It would appear obvious that a difference in parameters of $78.1 - 65 = 13.1$ and PRE = 25% are "large enough" to infer that MODEL C is unreasonable relative to MODEL A. But, unfortunately, such a conclusion is not obvious statistically, and it is important to understand why it is not obvious. To gain this understanding, we need to focus on the error term ε_i that is included in the full statement of MODEL C:

MODEL C: $Y_i = B_0 + \varepsilon_i$

As noted before, this model says that were it not for random perturbations represented by the ε_i all the Y_i would equal B_0 exactly. In Chapter 4 we made the assumption that the ε_i are all sampled randomly and independently from a normal distribution with mean 0 and variance σ^2. We also saw in Chapter 4 that the exact value for the mean calculated from a sample of size n would depend on the particular sample of errors. Sometimes the calculated mean would be above the true value B_0, and sometimes it would be below. That is, there would be a sampling distribution for the mean. If MODEL C were correct, sometimes the sample mean would be somewhat higher than 65 and other times it would be somewhat lower, but it would seldom equal 65 exactly. For example, we would most likely have obtained a different mean if the test had been given before lunch or the day before or a day later, because the pattern of random perturbations would have been different.

Similar to the sampling distribution for the mean, there is also a sampling distribution for PRE. Just as b_0, calculated from DATA, is the estimate of the unknown true parameter β_0, so too PRE, calculated from DATA, is the estimate of the unknown true proportional reduction in error η^2. For the moment, let's assume that MODEL C is correct (i.e., that $\beta_0 = B_0$) and consider what the sampling distribution for PRE would be. In other words, we are assuming that the null hypothesis is true. In these terms, $\eta^2 = 0$ is equivalent to MODEL C being correct and to MODEL A making absolutely no improvement relative to MODEL C. We saw in Chapter 4 that b_0 has a sampling distribution around β_0, so even if MODEL C is correct we would not expect our estimate b_0 to equal B_0 exactly. But we know that b_0 produces the smallest possible sum of squared errors, so SSE(A), using b_0, must always be at least a little bit smaller than SSE(C), using B_0. For example, in the math score data the mean will seldom equal 65 exactly, even if the parameter value were 65, and thus the SSE calculated using the sample mean will always be a little bit less than SSE(C) (see the proof in Chapter 2). Hence, even if the true proportional reduction in error $\eta^2 = 0$ (as it must when MODEL C is correct), the calculated PRE will always be at least a little greater than zero (never less than zero). PRE is therefore a biased estimator of η^2 because PRE will always overestimate the true value η^2. We will return to this issue of the bias in PRE later. For now, the important point is that we should not expect the calculated PRE to equal zero even when MODEL A makes no improvement on MODEL C. Thus, we cannot base our decision about the validity of MODEL C simply on whether or not PRE = 0.

If we cannot use PRE = 0 as a criterion for MODEL C being correct, then we need to consider the sampling distribution of PRE to determine whether the calculated value of PRE is a *likely* value, *assuming* MODEL C *were correct*. If the calculated value of PRE is a likely value, then we ought not to reject MODEL C and its equivalent null hypothesis that $\beta_0 = B_0$. On the other hand, if the calculated value of PRE is an unexpected value for MODEL C, then we ought to reject MODEL C in favor of MODEL A. In terms of our example, we need to consider the sampling distribution of PRE to determine for this case whether PRE = .25 is a likely value, assuming that MODEL C is correct (i.e., that $\beta_0 = 65$). If it is a likely value, then we ought not to reject MODEL C and its equivalent hypothesis that $\beta_0 = B_0 = 65$; in other words, there would be no evidence that the new mathematics curriculum produced test scores different from what was expected. If PRE = .25 is an unexpected value, then we ought to reject MODEL C and its hypothesis in favor of MODEL A and its estimate that $\beta_0 = b_0 = 78.1$; in other words, we would conclude that the new curriculum produced test scores reliably different from our expectations based on the scores from previous years.

We could develop the sampling distribution for PRE in this example using the same simulation strategy we used in the previous chapter. That is, we could put error tickets of the appropriate size into a bag and then do many simulation rounds on each of which we would randomly select 15 error tickets, add 65 to each, and calculate PRE for that sample. The only problem with this strategy is that we do not know what size error tickets to place in the bag to be sampled. In other words, we do not know the variance σ^2 of the normal distribution of errors. However, as was noted in the previous chapter, the mean squared error provides an estimate of σ^2. In particular, for MODEL A with one parameter the estimate is

$$s^2 = \frac{SSE}{n-1} = \frac{\Sigma_{i=1}^{n} (Y_i - \overline{Y})^2}{n-1} = \frac{7815.7}{14} = 558.3$$

We could therefore conduct the simulation by sampling error values from a normal distribution with mean 0 and variance 558.3. The 100 ERROR tickets in Exhibit 4.1 were sampled from such a normal distribution, so they could be used as the bag of ERROR tickets for the simulation.

As an example of a simulation round, suppose that the following 15 ERROR tickets were drawn from Exhibit 4.1:

$$
\begin{array}{rrrrr}
-9 & -37 & -17 & 22 & 45 \\
-12 & -24 & 1 & 10 & 11 \\
6 & -24 & -19 & -21 & 38
\end{array}
$$

These error terms when added to the value of $B_0 = 65$ of MODEL C yield the following 15 scores:

$$
\begin{array}{rrrrr}
56 & 28 & 48 & 87 & 110 \\
53 & 41 & 66 & 75 & 76 \\
71 & 41 & 46 & 44 & 103
\end{array}
$$

The mean of the resulting 15 scores is 63 and SSE(C), using 65 as the model prediction for all the observations, and SSE(A), using 63 as the model prediction, are easily calculated to be 8048 and 7988, respectively. Thus,

$$PRE = \frac{8048 - 7988}{8048} = .0075$$

Then a new simulation round with a new sample of ERROR values would produce a different mean and PRE. These simulation rounds could conceptually be repeated until there were enough PRE values to make a sampling distribution for PRE.

Alas, the simulation strategy outlined above for generating the sampling distribution of PRE will not work because $s^2 = 558.3$ is only an *estimate* of the true variance of the errors σ^2. Just as it is unlikely that $\overline{Y} = b_0$, the calculated mean for a sample, will equal B_0 exactly, it is unlikely that the calculated variance s^2 will equal σ^2 exactly. In other words, we are uncertain about the exact size of the ERROR tickets that should be placed in the bag.

We could conduct a more complex sampling simulation to account for our uncertainty about the size of the ERROR tickets. However, it would be tedious if we had to do a new simulation round for each data analysis. Fortunately, this is not necessary because mathematical statisticians have specified the sampling distribution for PRE based on the assumptions we made in Chapter 4 about the behavior of the ERRORs ε_i. Even though we will not actually do simulations for generating a sampling distribution, it is important to remember that the mathematical formula for that distribution is derived from the assumption that the ERROR values are randomly sampled from a distribution with mean 0 and variance σ^2 and that that sampling could be represented by drawing ERROR tickets from a bag.

Exhibit 5.5 provides a tabular description of the sampling distribution of PRE for the particular case of samples of size 15, again assuming the validity of MODEL C. That is, if MODEL C were correct (in our case, $\beta_0 = 65$), and if we compared MODEL C ($\hat{Y} = 65$) to MODEL A ($\hat{Y} = b_0 = \overline{Y}$) from samples, then Exhibit 5.5 presents the proportional frequency and cumulative proportion for each range of PRE. The proportional frequencies are plotted in Exhibit 5.6. As we would expect, the sampling distribution in Exhibit 5.6 shows that values of PRE near zero are the most likely. It also shows that values of PRE greater than .2 are infrequent.

EXHIBIT 5.6 ▶

Sampling distribution of PRE for testing the simple model with 15 observations

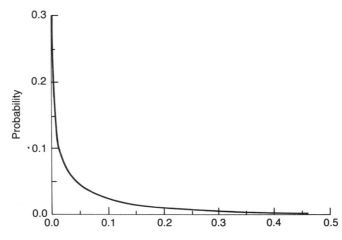

EXHIBIT 5.5 ▶

PRE range	Proportion	Cumulative Proportion
.00–.01	.287	.287
.01–.02	.111	.399
.02–.03	.080	.479
.03–.04	.064	.542
.04–.05	.053	.595
.05–.06	.045	.639
.06–.07	.038	.678
.07–.08	.034	.712
.08–.09	.030	.741
.09–.10	.026	.767
.10–.11	.023	.790
.11–.12	.021	.811
.12–.13	.019	.830
.13–.14	.017	.847
.14–.15	.015	.862
.15–.16	.014	.875
.16–.17	.012	.887
.17–.18	.011	.899
.18–.19	.010	.909
.19–.20	.009	.918
.20–.21	.008	.926
.21–.22	.007	.933
.22–.23	.007	.940
.23–.24	.006	.946
.24–.25	.005	.951
.25–.26	.005	.956
.26–.27	.004	.961
.27–.28	.004	.965
.28–.29	.004	.969
.29–.30	.003	.972
.30–.31	.003	.975
.31–.32	.003	.978
.32–.33	.002	.980
.33–.34	.002	.982
.34–.35	.002	.984
.35–.36	.002	.986
.36–.37	.002	.988
.37–.38	.001	.989
.38–.39	.001	.990
.39–.40	.001	.991
.40–.41	.001	.992
.41–.42	.001	.993
.42–.43	.001	.994
.43–.44	.001	.995
.44–.45	.001	.996
.45–.46	.001	.996
.46–.47	.001	.997

The cumulative proportions are generally more useful than the proportions for individual ranges. The cumulative proportion is simply the total proportion for the range of PRE's from zero to the value of interest. For example, to find the cumulative proportion for the range from 0 to .03, we simply add the proportions for the three component ranges: 0 to .01, .01 to .02, and .02 to .03. For this range, .287 + .111 + .080 = .479. That is, 47.9% of the simulated PRE values are less than or equal to .03. The cumulative proportions are displayed in the last column of Exhibit 5.5 and graphed in Exhibit 5.7. We can see, for example, from both the table and the graph of the cumulative proportions that PRE is less than .1 about 77% of the time.

EXHIBIT 5.7 ▶

Cumulative proportions for $n - PA = 14$

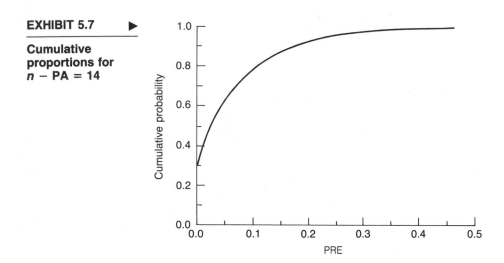

We can now ask whether a value for PRE of .25 is likely if MODEL C is correct. From the table in Exhibit 5.5 we see that slightly more than 95% of the time PRE would be less than .25. Or in other words, a PRE as large as .25 would be obtained less than 5% of the time if MODEL C were correct. We can finally answer the principal's question. It is unlikely (less than 5% chance) that we would have obtained a PRE this large had MODEL C been correct, therefore we can reasonably reject MODEL C in favor of MODEL A. This is equivalent to rejecting the hypothesis that $B_0 = 65$.

5.3

Critical Values

From the mathematical equations describing the sampling distribution for PRE, we can determine that the precise value for which we would expect 95% of the simulated values to be below if MODEL C were correct for our example data is .247. In the social sciences it is customary to consider a value of PRE surprising if it would occur by chance less than 5% of the time. Thus, .247 is the *critical value* for this example; any value of PRE > .247 causes us to reject MODEL C. Using the equations, we can calculate for any number of observations the value of PRE for which we would expect 95% of the simulated PRE values to be below if MODEL C were correct. Exhibit 5.8 gives the 95% critical value for selected numbers of observations.

5.4

*F**

Exhibits of the critical values for PRE are rare in statistics books. Much more common, for largely historical reasons, are tables of *F**, a statistic closely related to PRE. As we shall see below, *F** is a simple function of PRE, so if we know PRE, the number of observations, and the number of parameters in MODELs C and A, then we also know *F**, and vice-versa. By reexpressing PRE, *F** also provides additional insights about the proportion of error reduced. We therefore turn to the motivation for calculating *F** and then consider its sampling distribution.

The two reasons for calculating *F** are (a) to examine proportional reduction in error *per additional parameter* added to the model and (b) to compare the proportion of error that was reduced (PRE) to the proportion of error that remains (1 − PRE). In the context of the simple models which we are considering in this chapter, PRE is obtained by the addition of only one parameter. But later we will want to consider the improvement produced by models that add many parameters. To avoid having to present different formulas as the models get more complex, we will present the more general definition of *F** here. The key idea is that a given PRE, let's say .35, is much more impressive when obtained by the addition of a single parameter than when it is produced by the addition of several parameters. So we want to consider "PRE per parameter." That is, we divide PRE by the number of additional parameters used in MODEL A that are not used in MODEL C. We will let PA and PC represent the number of parameters for MODEL A and MODEL C,

EXHIBIT 5.8 ▶

Critical values (95% and 99%) for PRE and F^* for testing models which differ by one parameter

$n - PA$	95%		99%	
	PRE	F^*	PRE	F^*
1	.994	161.45	1.000	4052.2
2	.902	18.51	.980	98.50
3	.771	10.13	.919	34.12
4	.658	7.71	.841	21.20
5	.569	6.61	.765	16.26
6	.499	5.99	.696	13.74
7	.444	5.59	.636	12.25
8	.399	5.32	.585	11.26
9	.362	5.12	.540	10.56
10	.332	4.96	.501	10.04
11	.306	4.84	.467	9.65
12	.283	4.75	.437	9.33
13	.264	4.67	.411	9.07
14	.247	4.60	.388	8.86
15	.232	4.54	.367	8.68
16	.219	4.49	.348	8.53
17	.208	4.45	.331	8.40
18	.197	4.41	.315	8.28
19	.187	4.38	.301	8.18
20	.179	4.35	.288	8.10
22	.164	4.30	.265	7.94
24	.151	4.26	.246	7.82
26	.140	4.22	.229	7.72
28	.130	4.20	.214	7.64
30	.122	4.17	.201	7.56
35	.105	4.12	.175	7.42
40	.093	4.08	.155	7.31
45	.083	4.06	.138	7.23
50	.075	4.03	.125	7.17
55	.068	4.02	.115	7.12
60	.063	4.00	.106	7.08
80	.047	3.96	.080	6.96
100	.038	3.94	.065	6.90
150	.025	3.90	.043	6.81
200	.019	3.89	.033	6.76
500	.008	3.86	.013	6.69
∞		3.84		6.63

respectively. Then, the number of additional parameters is simply $PA - PC$. Hence, F^* is based on the quantity

$$\frac{PRE}{PA - PC}$$

which is simply the proportional reduction in error per parameter. For the simple models of this chapter, there are no parameters to be estimated for MODEL C and only one for MODEL A, so PC = 0, PA = 1, and PA − PC = 1.

Similarly, we need to consider the remaining proportion of the error, 1 − PRE, in terms of the number of additional parameters that *could* be added to reduce it. As noted in Chapter 1, the most parameters we can have is one for each observation Y_i. If there are n observations and we have already used PA parameters in MODEL A, then at most we could add n − PA parameters to some more complex model. So

$$\frac{1 - \text{PRE}}{n - \text{PA}}$$

gives the proportion of remaining error per parameter that *could* be added to the model. In other words, this is the average remaining error per parameter. If we added a parameter to the MODEL at random, even a parameter which was not really useful, we expect at least some reduction in error. The proportion of remaining error per parameter or the average remaining error tells us the value of PRE to expect for a worthless parameter. Obviously, if the parameter or parameters added to the MODEL are genuinely useful, then the PRE per parameter we actually obtain ought to be substantially bigger than the expected PRE per parameter for a useless, randomly selected parameter. An easy way to compare PRE per parameter obtained to the expected PRE per parameter is to compute the ratio of the two quantities; this gives the definition of F^* as

$$F^* = \frac{\text{PRE}/(\text{PA} - \text{PC})}{(1 - \text{PRE})/(n - \text{PA})} \tag{5.3}$$

We can think of the numerator of F^* as indicating the average proportional reduction in error per parameter added, and the denominator as the average proportional reduction in error that could be obtained by adding all remaining parameters. For MODEL A to be significantly better than MODEL C, we want the average error reduction for the parameters added to be much greater than the average error reduction we could get by adding the remainder of the possible parameters. Hence, if F^* is about 1, then we are doing no better than we could expect on average, so values of F^* near 1 suggest that we should stick with the simpler MODEL C. Values of F^* much larger than 1 imply that the average PRE per parameter added in MODEL A is much greater than the average which could be obtained by adding still more parameters. In that case, we would want to reject MODEL C (and its implicit hypothesis) in favor of MODEL A.

For the example of Exhibit 5.2 where PRE = .25 and $n = 15$,

$$F^* = \frac{\text{PRE}/(\text{PA} - \text{PC})}{(1 - \text{PRE})/(n - \text{PA})}$$

$$= \frac{.25/(1 - 0)}{.75/(15 - 1)} = \frac{.25}{.0536} = 4.66$$

In other words, we obtained a 25% reduction in error per parameter by using MODEL A, and the further reduction we could get by adding all the additional parameters is only 5.36% per parameter. Their ratio of 4.66 suggests that adding the one specific additional parameter β_0 which is estimated by the mean to MODEL C yields a substantially better— about 4.7 times better—PRE than we could expect by randomly adding a parameter from the remaining ones. In other words, the increased complexity of MODEL A is probably worth it. But again we need to consider the sampling distribution of F^* to determine whether a value of 4.66 is indeed "surprising."

Again, mathematical equations exist for describing F^* given the assumptions about ERROR discussed in Chapter 4. If we assume that the errors ε_i are independently, identically, normally distributed, then F^* has what is known as an F distribution.[1] The 95% critical values for F^* for testing simple models are listed in Exhibit 5.8 next to their corresponding values of PRE. F^* and PRE are redundant in the sense that one exceeds its critical value if and only if the other one exceeds its critical value. For the example, PRE = .25, which exceeds its critical value of .247, and the corresponding $F^* = 4.66$ exceeds its critical value of 4.60. Thus, either PRE or F^* causes us to reject MODEL C and its implicit hypothesis that $B_0 = 65$. Note that for most reasonable numbers of observations the 95% critical value for F^* is about 4. If we ignore the fractional part of F^*, then a useful rule of thumb which reduces the need to consult statistical tables frequently is to reject MODEL C in favor of MODEL A whenever F^* is greater than 5. If F^* is between 4 and 5, then you will probably have to look it up in the table, and if it is below 4, then there is no hope unless the number of observations is extremely large. Critical values of PRE and F^* for testing more complex MODEL A's which differ from MODEL C by more than one parameter are listed in Appendix C as a function of PA − PC, often called the "numerator degrees of freedom" for historical reasons and because that term appears in the numerator of the formula for F^* (Eq. 5.3), and n − PA, often called the "denominator degrees of freedom" because it appears in the denominator of the formula for F^*.

---

[1] We use the * on F^* to remind us that it can be calculated from DATA and that given appropriate assumptions it will have an F distribution. We can calculate F^* from any set of data. It will have an F distribution, however, only if the appropriate assumptions are met.

Source	SS	df	MS	F*	PRE	p
Reduce, Model A	SSR	PA − PC	$MSR = \dfrac{SSR}{PA - PC}$	$\dfrac{MSR}{MSE}$	$\dfrac{SSR}{SSE(C)}$	
Error for Model A	SSE(A)	$n - PA$	$MSE = \dfrac{SSE(A)}{n - PA}$			
Total	SSE(C)	$n - PC$				

EXHIBIT 5.9 ▲

Analysis of variance summary exhibit: decomposition of sums of squares

It is useful to add degrees of freedom (df) and F^* to the basic summary table we started earlier. Exhibit 5.9 presents such a table for our example. It is our policy to avoid multiple calculational formulas for the same quantity and instead to present only one conceptual formula. However, we must break that policy for F^* in this instance because F^* is traditionally calculated by an equivalent but different formula based on Exhibit 5.9. Exhibits constructed using the alternative formula for F^* are ubiquitous, so the reader has no choice but to learn this alternative in addition to the conceptual formula for F^* presented above. The alternative formula for F^* is

$$F^* = \frac{SSR/(PA - PC)}{SSE(A)/(n - PA)} = \frac{MSR}{MSE}$$

For our example, this yields

$$F^* = \frac{SSR/(PA - PC)}{SSE(A)/(n - PA)} = \frac{2587/(1 - 0)}{7816/(15 - 1)} = \frac{2587}{558} = 4.64$$

This agrees with our previous calculation except for a small rounding error. MSR represents the *mean squares reduced*, and MSE represents the *mean square error*. To facilitate this calculation, we usually add an "MS" column to the summary table. The final column, labeled "p," gives the probability of obtaining a PRE and F^* that large or larger if $\eta^2 = 0$. With the additional columns Exhibit 5.10 provides a detailed summary of our analysis of the math quiz scores.

EXHIBIT 5.10 ▶

ANOVA summary exhibit for math quiz example

Source	SS	df	MS	F*	PRE	p
Reduction (using $b_0 = 78.1$)	2,587	1	2587	4.64	.25	.05
Error (using $b_0 = 78.1$)	7,816	14	558			
Total (Error using $B_0 = 65$)	10,403	15				

5.5

Statistical Decisions

We have now defined the essence of statistical inference: if PRE and F^* exceed their respective critical values then the simpler MODEL C is rejected in favor of the more complex MODEL A. We now have a rule for resolving the inherent tension in data analysis between reducing ERROR as much as possible and keeping the MODEL of DATA as parsimonious as possible. It is important to recognize, however, that statistical inference is probabilistic and therefore not infallible. That is, if MODEL C is actually the correct model, then 5% of the time we will obtain values of PRE and F^* that exceed their 95% critical values. Our rule is to reject MODEL C if those statistics exceed their 95% critical values, so in such instances we will have made a mistake in rejecting MODEL C. There is no way to avoid making occasional mistakes of that type. By adopting a 95% critical value, we are implicitly accepting that for those data for which MODEL C is correct, we are willing to risk a 5% chance of incorrectly rejecting it. Mistakes of this type are known as *Type I* errors. The choice of 5% as an acceptable rate of Type I errors is inherently arbitrary. If we want to be more cautious, we could choose a rate of 1% or, if we are willing to risk more Type I errors, then we might choose a rate of 10%.

We also can commit a *Type II* error. A Type II error occurs when MODEL C is incorrect but the obtained values of PRE and F^* may still not exceed their critical values. Thus, a Type II error occurs when we fail to reject MODEL C when we should. That is, MODEL C is incorrect and MODEL A is reliably better, but we are unlucky in terms of the error tickets drawn and miss seeing the difference. Exhibit 5.11 summarizes the statistical decision that confronts us and defines the ways in which both the right and wrong decisions can be made. Statistical inference can be viewed as a game with Nature. Nature determines whether MODEL C is correct or incorrect. The goal of the data analyst is to "guess" which is the case. The data analyst uses the DATA to make an informed guess. Specifically, if PRE and F^* exceed their critical values, then the decision is to "reject MODEL C"; otherwise the decision is "do not reject MODEL C." If Nature has determined that MODEL C is correct, then, if we use a 95% critical value, we will decide correctly 95% of the time and incorrectly (i.e., make a Type I error) 5% of the time. The chance of making a Type I error is often labeled α and referred to as the *significance level*.

On the other hand, if Nature has determined that MODEL C is incorrect, then we will decide correctly the proportion of times that PRE

		True State of Nature	
		MODEL C Correct	MODEL C Incorrect
Statistical Decision	"Reject MODEL C"	Type I Error	Correct Decision
	"Do NOT Reject MODEL C"	Correct Decision	Type II Error

EXHIBIT 5.11 ▲

The statistical decision and the two types of errors

and F^* exceed their critical values, and we will decide incorrectly (i.e., make a Type II error) the proportion of times that PRE and F^* fall below their critical values. The chance of making a Type II error is, unfortunately, often labeled β which should not be confused with β_0, β_1, etc., which we use to represent parameters in a MODEL. The proportion of times the correct decision is made when Nature has determined that MODEL C is incorrect, $1 - \beta$, is often referred to as the *power* of a statistical test.

5.6

Estimating Statistical Power

To determine the chances of a Type II error or to determine the power, we need to know the sampling distribution for PRE and F^*, *assuming that MODEL C is incorrect*. We cannot determine such a sampling distribution in general because to say that MODEL C is incorrect is to say only that the true proportional reduction in error $\eta^2 > 0$. However, using the equations provided by mathematical statisticians, we can easily derive the sampling distributions for specific values of η^2 we might want to consider. Exhibit 5.12 displays the cumulative probability distribution for observed values of PRE for η^2 equal to 0, .05, .1, .3, .5, and .75, but only for the very particular conditions of our example: PA − PC = 1, n − PA = 14. Different distributions would be obtained for other combinations of PA − PC and n − PA. The column for $\eta^2 = 0$ corresponds exactly to the cumulative probability distribution of Exhibit 5.5. Each entry in Exhibit 5.12 is the probability that PRE calculated from DATA would be less than the value of PRE specified for that row. For example, the value of .11 in the row for PRE = .30 and the column for $\eta^2 = .50$ means that if η^2 (i.e., the true PRE) were really .5, then the chances of obtaining a PRE (calculated from DATA) of .3 or lower is 11%.

PRE	True PRE, η^2					
	0	.05	.1	.3	.5	.75
.00	.00	.00	.00	.00	.00	.00
.05	.59	.45	.33	.06	.00	.00
.10	.77	.62	.48	.12	.01	.00
.15	.86	.73	.61	.19	.02	.00
.20	.92	.82	.71	.28	.04	.00
.25	.95	.88	.79	.38	.07	.00
.30	.97	.92	.85	.48	.11	.00
.35	.98	.95	.90	.59	.18	.00
.40	.99	.97	.94	.68	.26	.00
.45	1.00	.98	.96	.77	.36	.00
.50	1.00	.99	.98	.84	.48	.01
.55	1.00	.99	.99	.90	.60	.03
.60	1.00	1.00	.99	.94	.72	.07
.65	1.00	1.00	1.00	.97	.82	.14
.70	1.00	1.00	1.00	.99	.90	.27
.75	1.00	1.00	1.00	1.00	.96	.46
.80	1.00	1.00	1.00	1.00	.98	.69
.85	1.00	1.00	1.00	1.00	1.00	.88
.90	1.00	1.00	1.00	1.00	1.00	.98
.95	1.00	1.00	1.00	1.00	1.00	1.00

We can use the cumulative probability distributions of PRE for different values of η^2 to perform "what if" analyses. For example, we can ask, "*what* would the chances of making a Type II error be *if* $\eta^2 = .3$?" To answer this question, we first must decide what chance of a Type I error we are willing to risk. If we adopt the customary value in the social sciences of $\alpha = .05$, then, as before, we select the critical value of PRE so that the calculated value of PRE has only a .05 probability of exceeding that critical value if $\eta^2 = 0$. In this case, we see from Exhibit 5.12 that the probability of obtaining a PRE < .25 equals .95 (approximately), so only 5% of the observed values of PRE should be greater than .25 if $\eta^2 = 0$. Remember that $\eta^2 = 0$ implies that MODEL C and MODEL A are identical, so our decision rule will be to reject MODEL C in favor of MODEL A only if PRE > .25. Now we can use the column for $\eta^2 = .3$ to answer our "what if" question. The entry in that column for the row for PRE = .25 reveals that the probability that the calculated PRE will be less than .25 is .38. That is, even if $\eta^2 = .3$ (i.e., there is a real difference between MODEL C and MODEL A), there is still a 38% chance that we will obtain a value of PRE below the critical value and hence will not reject MODEL C. In other words, the probability of making a Type II error is .38. Conversely, $1 - .38 = .62$ is the probability of obtaining a PRE > .25 and hence rejecting MODEL C in favor of MODEL A if $\eta^2 = .3$. In other words, the power (probability of not making a Type II error) is .62.

We can easily do the "what if" analysis for other values of η^2. For example, if $\eta^2 = .05$, which implies a small difference between MODELs C and A, then power equals $1 - .88 = .12$. That is, the chances of obtaining a PRE large enough to reject MODEL C in favor of MODEL A would be only 12% for this small difference between the two models. On the other hand, if $\eta^2 = .75$, which implies a very large difference between MODELs C and A, then power equals $1 - .00 = 1$. That is, for this large difference we would be virtually certain to obtain a PRE large enough to reject MODEL C in favor of MODEL A.

The cumulative sampling distributions are unwieldy, and only a few of the numbers are actually needed for the "what if" analyses, so a "power table" that only gives the power probabilities for specified levels of α is more useful. Exhibit 5.13 gives the power probabilities for selected values of η^2 and $n - $ PA, assuming PA $-$ PC $= 1$ and $\alpha = .05$. We can use this table to do the same "what if" analyses we did above as well as many others. For our example problem we simply use the row for $n - $ PA $= 14$. For $\eta^2 = .05$, power $= .13$, and for $\eta^2 = .3$, power $= .63$. (The small differences from the power calculations above are due to using the more precise critical value of .247 for PRE instead of .25.)

The power table allows us to ask another kind of "what if" question: "What would power be if the degrees of freedom $n - $ PA were increased?" For example, how much would power increase if the mathematics curriculum were evaluated with 31 students instead of 15? For 31 students we would use the row for $n - $ PA $= 31 - 1 = 30$. If $\eta^2 = .05$, then power $= .23$, which is better than .13 for 15 students but still not very good. If $\eta^2 = .3$, then power $= .93$, which is much higher than .63 for 15 students and gives an excellent chance of rejecting MODEL C in favor of MODEL A. Note that for $n - $ PA $= 50$ we are virtually certain of rejecting MODEL C whenever the true PRE η^2 is equal to or greater then .3.

Too many researchers fail to ask "what if" power questions before they collect their data. The consequence is too often a study which has virtually no chance of rejecting MODEL C even if the idea which motivated the study is correct. With power tables such as Exhibit 5.13 and similar tables in Appendix C, asking "what if" power questions is so easy that there is no excuse for not asking those questions before collecting data.

df	Critical Values		Prob(PRE > Critical Value)							
			True PRE, η^2							
$n - PA$	F	PRE	0	.01	.03	.05	.075	.1	.2	.3
1	161.45	.994	.05	.05	.05	.05	.05	.05	.06	.06
2	18.51	.902	.05	.05	.05	.05	.06	.06	.07	.09
3	10.13	.771	.05	.05	.06	.06	.06	.07	.10	.13
4	7.71	.658	.05	.05	.06	.07	.07	.08	.12	.17
5	6.61	.569	.05	.05	.06	.07	.08	.09	.15	.22
6	5.99	.499	.05	.06	.07	.08	.09	.11	.18	.27
7	5.59	.444	.05	.06	.07	.08	.10	.12	.21	.32
8	5.32	.399	.05	.06	.07	.09	.11	.13	.24	.37
9	5.12	.362	.05	.06	.08	.09	.12	.15	.27	.42
10	4.96	.332	.05	.06	.08	.10	.13	.16	.30	.46
11	4.84	.306	.05	.06	.08	.11	.14	.17	.33	.51
12	4.75	.283	.05	.06	.09	.11	.15	.19	.36	.55
13	4.67	.264	.05	.06	.09	.12	.16	.20	.39	.59
14	4.60	.247	.05	.06	.09	.13	.17	.21	.41	.63
15	4.54	.232	.05	.07	.10	.13	.18	.23	.44	.66
16	4.49	.219	.05	.07	.10	.14	.19	.24	.47	.69
17	4.45	.208	.05	.07	.11	.15	.20	.25	.49	.72
18	4.41	.197	.05	.07	.11	.15	.21	.27	.52	.75
19	4.38	.187	.05	.07	.11	.16	.22	.28	.54	.77
20	4.35	.179	.05	.07	.12	.16	.23	.29	.57	.80
22	4.30	.164	.05	.07	.12	.18	.25	.32	.61	.84
24	4.26	.151	.05	.08	.13	.19	.27	.35	.65	.87
26	4.23	.140	.05	.08	.14	.20	.29	.37	.69	.89
28	4.20	.130	.05	.08	.15	.22	.31	.40	.72	.92
30	4.17	.122	.05	.08	.15	.23	.33	.42	.75	.93
35	4.12	.105	.05	.09	.17	.26	.37	.48	.82	.96
40	4.08	.093	.05	.10	.19	.29	.42	.54	.87	.98
45	4.06	.083	.05	.10	.21	.33	.46	.59	.91	.99
50	4.03	.075	.05	.11	.23	.36	.51	.64	.93	*
55	4.02	.068	.05	.11	.25	.39	.55	.68	.95	*
60	4.00	.063	.05	.12	.27	.42	.58	.72	.97	*
80	3.96	.047	.05	.14	.34	.53	.71	.84	.99	*
100	3.94	.038	.05	.17	.41	.62	.81	.91	*	*
150	3.90	.025	.05	.23	.57	.80	.93	.98	*	*
200	3.89	.019	.05	.29	.70	.90	.98	*	*	*
500	3.86	.008	.05	.61	.98	*	*	*	*	*

◄ **EXHIBIT 5.13**

Power exhibit for $\alpha = .05$ and PA − PC = 1 (generated using SAS function PROBF)

Now that we know how to answer easily "what if" power questions, we need to know what values of true PRE or η^2 are appropriate for those "what if" questions. There are several ways to obtain an appropriate value for η^2 to use in the power analysis. First, with sufficient experience in a research domain, researchers know what values of PRE are important or meaningful in that domain. Those values of PRE from experience can be used directly in the power table. For example, if, based on past experience, we thought that important effects (such as the effect of a curriculum innovation) produced PREs greater than or equal to .1, then we could use the $\eta^2 = .1$ column of the power table. If we wanted to ensure that power > .7, then going down the column we find the first power > .7 requires $n − PA = 60$, which is a much greater number of students than the principal and the teacher originally included in the evaluation of the new curriculum.

In using the results of past studies to select an appropriate η^2 for the "what if" power analysis, we must remember that calculated values of PRE are biased because on average they overestimate η^2. The following simple formula can be used to remove the bias from PRE:

$$\text{Unbiased Estimate of } \eta^2 = 1 - (1 - \text{PRE})\left[\frac{n - \text{PC}}{n - \text{PA}}\right]$$

For our example in which we calculated PRE = .25, the unbiased estimate of η^2 equals

$$1 - (1 - .25)\left[\frac{15 - 0}{15 - 1}\right] = 1 - .75\left[\frac{15}{14}\right] = .20$$

Thus, although the value of PRE calculated from the DATA is .25, our best unbiased guess for the true value of η^2 is only .20. The correction for bias has more of an effect for small values of $n − PA$ than for large values. In essence, the adjustment corrects for the ability of least squares to capitalize on chance for small sample sizes. As we shall see later, many computer programs which calculate PRE also provide a corrected estimate, which is labeled an "adjusted" PRE.

A second and related method for finding appropriate values of η^2 is to use the values suggested by Cohen (1977) as "small" ($\eta^2 = .02$), "medium" ($\eta^2 = .13$), and "large" ($\eta^2 = .26$). Our power table does not have columns for these specific values of η^2, but .03, .1, and .3 could be used instead. Although these suggested values for small, medium, and large effects are inherently arbitrary, they do represent experience across a wide range of social science disciplines. If you have sufficient experience in a research domain to consider these suggested values unreasonable, then simply use those values which are reasonable based upon your experience. The goal of a power analysis conducted before the collection of data is not an exact calculation of the statistical power but an indication of whether there is much hope for detecting the effect you want to find with the sample size you have planned. If a study would not have much chance of distinguishing between MODEL C and MODEL A for a large effect ($\eta^2 = .26$ or $.3$), then there is little if any reason for conducting the study.

As an example of this approach, let's estimate the power for detecting small, medium, and large effects of the mathematics curriculum using the class of 15 students. Using the row of the power table for $n - PA = 14$ and the columns for $\eta^2 = .03, .1,$ and $.3$, we find that the respective powers are $.09, .21,$ and $.63$. In other words, we would not have much chance of detecting small and medium effects but a decent chance of detecting a large effect. If we wanted to be able to detect medium effects, then we would need to increase the number of students involved in the evaluation.

A third approach to finding an appropriate value of η^2 to use in "what if" power analyses involves guesses about the parameter values and variance. To have reasonable expectations about the parameter values and variance generally requires as much or more experience in a research domain as is necessary to know typical values of PRE. Thus, this third approach is generally less useful than the first two. We present this approach in order to be complete and because the derivation of this approach provides further useful insights about the meaning of PRE and η^2. Also, this approach requires describing in detail the data one expects to obtain, and that exercise can often be useful for identifying flawed research designs.

We begin with our familiar definition of PRE:

$$PRE = \frac{SSE(C) - SSE(A)}{SSE(C)} = \frac{SSR}{SSE(C)}$$

We have noted before that $SSE(C) = SSE(A) + SSR$ (i.e., the error for the compact model includes all the error of the augmented model plus the error that was reduced by the addition of the extra parameters in the augmented model). Hence, substituting for $SSE(C)$ yields

$$PRE = \frac{SSR}{SSE(A) + SSR} = \frac{1}{SSE(A)/SSR + 1}$$

To obtain a definition of the true proportional reduction in error η^2, we simply estimate $SSE(A)$ and SSR, using not the data but the parameter values of B_0 and β_0 that are of interest.

For example, we noted above that

$$SSR = \sum_{i=1}^{n} (\hat{Y}_{iC} - \hat{Y}_{iA})^2$$

If we thought that the effect of the mathematics curriculum would be to raise the mean score from 65 to 75, then $\hat{Y}_{iC} = B_0 = 65$ represents the null hypothesis and $\hat{Y}_{iA} = \beta_0 = 75$ represents an alternative hypothesis we want to test. For that situation we would *expect*

$$\text{SSR} = \sum_{i=1}^{15} (65 - 75)^2 = \sum_{i=1}^{15} 10^2 = \sum_{i=1}^{15} 100 = 1500$$

In other words, the SSR we expect is simply 100 added up 15 times (once for each student). We saw in Chapter 2 that $\text{SSE}/(n - \text{PA})$ was an estimate of the variance σ^2. If we use our expected value of $\beta_0 = 75$ to calculate SSE(A), then we are not using data to estimate any parameters, so PA = 0. Hence, $\text{SSE(A)}/n = \sigma^2$, so the value of SSE(A) we *expect* to obtain is

$$\text{SSE(A)} = n\sigma^2$$

Thus, if we have a reasonable guess or expectation for the variance, then we can easily calculate the value of SSE(A) we would expect. Having good intuitions about what variance to expect is usually as difficult, or more difficult, than knowing what PRE to expect. Both are based on previous experience in a research domain. Good guesses for the variance often depend on previous experience with the particular measure for Y. For our example, suppose that past data for the mathematics quiz lead us to expect that σ^2 is about 400; then, we would expect

$$\text{SSE(A)} = n\sigma^2 = (15)400 = 6000$$

We now can return to our formula for PRE to calculate the value we expect for the true proportional reduction in error η^2 (given our guesses for B_0, β_0, and σ^2).

$$\text{Expected } \eta^2 = \frac{1}{\text{SSE(A)/SSR} + 1} = \frac{1}{6000/1500 + 1} = \frac{1}{4 + 1} = .2$$

In other words, $\eta^2 = .2$ corresponds to our guesses about B_0, β_0 and σ^2. We now can use the power tables to find the power we would have for comparing MODEL C, which predicts the mean score will be 65, against MODEL A, which predicts the mean score will be 75 when the variance is about 400. Using Exhibit 5.13, we find that for 15 observations the probability of rejecting MODEL C (i.e., deciding that the new curriculum did make an improvement) is only about .41 even if we think that it will on average make an improvement of 10 points (65 to 75). This means that the principal and the teacher have less than a 50-50 chance of *deciding* that the new curriculum does make a difference even when it really does make a difference of 10 points. Using the power table, we can see that doubling the number of students in the test of the curriculum from 15 to 30 would increase the power substantially to about 0.75. In this case it would seem advisable to increase the sample size rather than test the curriculum with a sample size that offered little hope of finding that the curriculum helped. We can similarly calculate the power for other "what if" values of B_0, β_0, and σ^2 we might want to consider.

5.7

Improving Power

The relatively low power—the high probability of making a Type II error—for the apparently reasonable evaluation of the mathematics curriculum we have been considering may be startling. Unfortunately, low power is a problem that plagues data analysis far more frequently than is commonly realized. Low power creates serious difficulties. For example, consider the plight of the principal trying to evaluate the success of her teacher's innovative mathematics curriculum. She has only about a 41% chance of detecting an improvement of 10 points on the math test and 10 points represents a large improvement in this context. Even if the new curriculum is successful, she is unlikely to recognize that success using the statistical decision rule we have developed. In this particular example, the obtained value of PRE allowed her to reject the hypothesis that $B_0 = 65$; she was either lucky, or the true value of β_0 was considerably greater than the alternative value of 75 that we considered above. In general, however, we want to increase the power of the statistical inference. There are three basic strategies for improving power: reduce ERROR, increase α, and/or increase the number of observations. We consider each in turn.

5.7.1 Reducing ERROR

One way to reduce ERROR is to control as many of the possible random perturbations as possible. In the mathematics example, one might reduce ERROR and obtain more power by making sure that each child got a good night's sleep before the exam, controlling what the children ate for lunch before the exam, using a more reliable mathematics exam, etc. In other words, ERROR is reduced by obtaining DATA of better quality. In the equation

$$DATA = MODEL + ERROR$$

the MODEL will account for a higher proportion of the DATA if the DATA are of higher quality and hence have less ERROR. Less ERROR allows us to obtain a more powerful look at our DATA. Although reducing ERROR by such means may be the most effective method for improving power, the techniques for doing so are usually domain-specific and outside the scope of this book.

Another way to reduce ERROR is to improve the quality of the MODEL. Again in the equation

DATA = MODEL + ERROR

ERROR will be smaller for DATA of fixed quality if the MODEL can be improved to account for more of the DATA. How to use models more complex than the simple models we have been considering in these beginning chapters is the subject of the remainder of the book, so we cannot give too many details here. The general idea is to build models that make predictions conditional on additional information we have about the observations. In the mathematics curriculum example we might know, say, which students had which teachers the previous year. If the teacher from the previous year makes a difference in terms of the child's score on the math examination, then we can make different predictions conditional on which teacher the student had last year. Doing so we will have in essence removed what was formerly a random perturbation—the student's teacher last year—from ERROR and included it in the MODEL. Again the reduced ERROR will give us a more powerful look at our DATA. In later chapters we explicitly consider the addition of parameters to the MODEL for the purpose of improving power.

5.7.2 Increasing α

A different way to improve power is to increase α, the probability of a Type I error. The probabilities of Type I and II errors are linked in that if we choose a critical value which increases (decreases) α, then we simultaneously and unavoidably decrease (increase) the probability of a Type II error. For our example mathematics data with $n - PA = 14$, Exhibit 5.14 shows power as a function of η^2 and α. As α increases from .001 to .25 the critical values of F^* and PRE decrease. It obviously becomes easier for the values of F^* and PRE calculated from DATA to beat these critical values, so the power increases as α increases. For example, if we do a "what if" power analysis with $\eta^2 = .2$, then the power at $\alpha = .05$ is .41, but if we increase α to .1, then power increases to .55. A power of .55 is not great, but at least we would have better than a 50-50 chance of finding an effect if it existed.

Editors of scientific journals are wary of Type I errors and will seldom accept the use of $\alpha > .05$ for statistical inference. However, there are many practical data analysis problems when a higher α is justified to increase power. Characteristics of such data analyses are (a) that increasing power in any other way is infeasible, (b) that rejection of MODEL

	Critical Values		Prob(PRE > Critical Value) True PRE, η^2							
α	F	PRE	0	.01	.03	.05	.075	.1	.2	.3
.001	17.14	.550	.00	.00	.00	.00	.01	.01	.04	.10
.005	11.06	.441	.01	.01	.01	.02	.03	.04	.12	.24
.01	8.86	.388	.01	.01	.02	.04	.05	.07	.18	.34
.025	6.30	.310	.03	.03	.05	.07	.10	.14	.30	.50
.05	4.60	.247	.05	.06	.09	.13	.17	.21	.41	.63
.1	3.10	.181	.10	.12	.17	.21	.27	.33	.55	.75
.25	1.44	.093	.25	.28	.34	.40	.47	.54	.75	.89

EXHIBIT 5.14 ▲

Power exhibit for PA – PC = 1 and n – PA = 14 (generated using SAS function PROBF)

C if it is indeed false would have important practical consequences, and (c) that the costs associated with a Type I error are not great. The statistical decision problem faced by the principal is a case in point. It may be difficult for her to control any other sources of ERROR to increase power. It would certainly be important to identify a program that could increase math performance by 10 points. The consequence of a Type I error would probably be the use of the program next year in several classrooms and that would probably not involve a significant cost. Thus, the principal might well have adopted a higher α to choose the critical values for PRE and F^* for her statistical inference.

Conversely, note that reducing α also reduces power. In the mathematics example, lowering α to .01 would increase our protection against the possibility of a Type I error but would reduce power to .18, a level for which it would almost certainly not be worth conducting the study. If the costs of a Type I error are very high—for example, if the use of the new mathematics curriculum required extensive teacher retraining—then the use of restrictive values of α is appropriate. However, in this particular example, reducing α would have so reduced power that it would no longer be worthwhile to do the study—the chances of seeing anything are too low with such a low-powered "microscope."

5.7.3   Increasing *n*

Probably the most common technique for increasing the power of statistical tests is to increase the number of observations. Exhibit 5.15 is a graphical display of the 95% (α = .05) and 99% (α = .01) critical values of Exhibit 5.8 as a function of the number of observations. The value of PRE required to reject MODEL C drops dramatically as the number of observations increases. For example, had there been 50 students instead

EXHIBIT 5.15 ▶

Critical values of PRE as a function of the number of observations

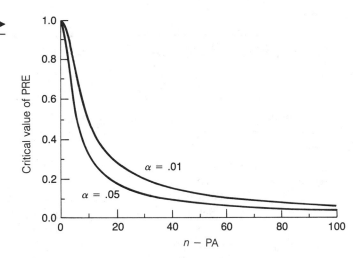

of 15 in the new mathematics program, a PRE of only about .075 would have been required ($\alpha = .05$) to reject the MODEL C that assumed $B_0 = 65$ instead of the PRE of .247 required in our example. The drop in the critical values of F^* and PRE needed to reject MODEL C corresponds to an increase in power, as we have noted several times. For example, for $\eta^2 = .2$ as a "what if" value of the true proportional reduction in error, the power for 15 observations is .41 (see Exhibit 5.13), but with 50 observations power increases to above .9.

There are two reasons for not routinely using a large number of observations. First, it may be infeasible due to cost or other data collection constraints to obtain more observations. Second, power might be so high that some statistically significant results may be misleading. By turning up the power on our metaphorical statistical microscope to extraordinary levels, we might detect flaws in MODEL C which are statistically reliable but which are trivial substantively. For example, with 120 observations any PRE greater than .032 is cause to reject MODEL C in favor of MODEL A. However, the 3.2% reduction in ERROR means that MODEL A may be a trivial improvement over MODEL C. For this reason, one should always report not just the statistical inference about whether MODEL C is or is not rejected but also the obtained values for PRE and F^* so that the reader can evaluate the magnitude by which MODEL A improves on MODEL C. All else being equal, more statistical power is always better; we just need to be careful in interpreting the results as substantively important when power is very high.

It is also important not to dismiss a small but reliable PRE just because it is small. Rejecting MODEL C in favor of MODEL A may be important theoretically even if MODEL A provides only a slight improvement. Whether a given PRE is substantively interesting will depend on prior research experience in the particular domain.

5.8

Confidence Intervals

Confidence intervals provide an alternative way for considering statistical inference. Although as we shall see later, confidence intervals are exactly equivalent to statistical inference as described above, they reorganize the information in a way which can give useful insights about the DATA.

A *confidence interval* simply consists of all those possible values of a parameter which, when used as a hypothesis for MODEL C, would not cause us to reject MODEL C. For example, the mean for the 15 mathematics scores is 78.1 and estimates the parameter β_0 in MODEL A. We have already determined that 65 is not in the confidence interval for β_0 because, when we used 65 as the prediction for MODEL C, we obtained an unlikely PRE value that would occur less than 5% of the time. Any value less than 65 would produce an even larger PRE, so none of those values is included in the confidence interval. Conceptually, we could find the boundary of the confidence interval by trying increasingly higher values for B_0 in MODEL C until we found a value for B_0 which produced a PRE that would not cause us to reject MODEL C. For example, if we tried $B_0 = 70$, the respective sums of squared errors for MODELs C and A would be 8808 and 7815.7, yielding PRE = .11, which is below the critical value for $\alpha = .05$; hence, 70 is in the confidence interval for β_0, and the boundary must be somewhere between 65 and 70. We also would need to search for the upper boundary above the estimated value $b_0 = 78.1$. We can avoid this iterative search because it can be shown that the boundaries are given by

$$b_0 \pm \sqrt{\frac{F_{1,n=1;\alpha}\text{MSE}}{n}} \tag{5.4}$$

For the simple model of the math scores, the MSE $= s^2 = $ SSE$/(n - 1) = 7815.7/14 = 558.3$. $F_{1,n-1;\alpha}$ is the critical value at level α for F with 1 degree of freedom for the numerator (i.e., the difference in the number of parameters between the two models) and $n - 1$ is the degrees of freedom for the denominator (i.e., the number of observations minus the number of parameters in MODEL A). For $\alpha = .05$, $F_{1,14;.05} = 4.60$. For these DATA, $b_0 = $ the mean $= 78.1$, so boundaries of the confidence interval are given by

$$78.1 \pm \sqrt{\frac{(4.6)558.3}{15}} \qquad \text{or} \qquad 78.1 \pm 13.08$$

Thus, the lower boundary is $78.1 - 13.08 = 65.02$, and the upper boundary is $78.1 + 13.08 = 91.18$. We are therefore 95% $(1 - \alpha)$ confident that the true value for β_0 is in the interval [65.02, 91.18]. Any B_0 not in this interval which we might try for MODEL C would, with the present DATA, produce values of PRE and F^* that would cause us to reject MODEL C. Any B_0 in this interval would produce values of PRE and F^* below the critical values, so we would not reject MODEL C.

5.9

Equivalence to the *t* Test

In this optional section we demonstrate the equivalence between the statistical test for the simple model developed in this chapter and the traditional *one-sample t test* presented in most statistics textbooks. We do so to allow readers with exposure to traditional textbooks to make the comparison between approaches.

The one-sample *t* test answers whether the mean of a set of observations equals a particular value specified by the null hypothesis. The formula for the one-sample *t* test is

$$t^*_{n-1} = \frac{\sqrt{n}(\overline{Y} - B_0)}{s}$$

where n is the number of observations, $\overline{Y}$ is the calculated mean, B_0 is the value specified by the null hypothesis, and s is the standard deviation of the set of observations. With the appropriate assumptions about Y—the same assumptions that we made about the distribution and independence of the ε_i—values of t^* can be compared to critical values of *Student's t distribution*. Tables of this distribution are available in many statistics textbooks. However, separate tables are not really needed because squaring t^* with $n - 1$ degrees of freedom yields an F^* with 1 and $n - 1$ degrees of freedom. Thus, the F tables in Appendix C may readily be used.

To show the equivalence between F^* as presented in this chapter and the usual t test, we begin with the definition of F^* for the simple model; that is,

$$F^*_{1,n-1} = \frac{\text{PRE}/1}{(1 - \text{PRE})/(n - 1)}$$

We know that PRE = SSR/SSE(C), and it is easy to show that

$$1 - \text{PRE} = 1 - \frac{\text{SSR}}{\text{SSE(C)}} = \frac{\text{SSE(C)} - \text{SSR}}{\text{SSE(C)}} = \frac{\text{SSE(A)}}{\text{SSE(C)}}$$

Substituting these values into the definition for F^* yields

$$F^*_{1,n-1} = \frac{\text{SSR}/\text{SSE(C)}}{(n - 1)^{-1}[\text{SSE(A)}/\text{SSE(C)}]} = \frac{\text{SSR}}{\text{SSE(A)}/(n - 1)}$$

But from Eq. 5.2 we know that for the simple model SSR can be replaced with $n(B_0 - \overline{Y})^2$, and from Chapter 2 we know that $SSE(A)/(n-1)$ is s^2, the variance of the set of observations. Substituting these values yields

$$F^*_{1,n-1} = \frac{n(B_0 - \overline{Y})^2}{s^2}$$

Taking the square root of this last equation gives the final result of

$$\sqrt{F^*_{1,n-1}} = t^*_{n-1} = \frac{\sqrt{n}(\overline{Y} - B_0)}{s}$$

We provide the above derivation not to present yet another calculational formula but to show that our model comparison approach to statistical inference is not different statistically from the traditional approach. The use of PREs and F^*'s for comparing models is nothing more than a repackaging of the traditional approach. This repackaging has the important consequence of making it easy to generalize to more complicated models and data analysis questions. We will use PRE and F^* just as we did in this chapter for statistical inference throughout the remainder of the book. In contrast, the traditional t test does not generalize nearly so easily. Also, even though the t test must produce exactly the same conclusion with respect to the null hypothesis, it does not automatically provide a measure of the magnitude of the result. In our model comparison approach, PRE automatically provides a useful measure of the magnitude.

5.10

An Example

In this section we illustrate the techniques of this chapter by presenting some examples based on the automobile fatality data. Suppose that the goal of a traffic safety organization had been to keep the fatality rate per 100 million vehicle miles traveled, averaged across states, under 3.9. Was the average fatality rate for 1978 reliably below 3.9? These data were presented in Exhibit 1.1, and the necessary computer outputs for answering this question are in Exhibits 2.4 and 2.5. The question is equivalent to comparing the following two models:

MODEL A: $Y_i = \beta_0 + \varepsilon_i$
MODEL C: $Y_i = 3.9 + \varepsilon_i$
            $H_0:$ $\beta_0 = 3.9$

From the computer outputs we know that the mean is $\overline{Y} = 3.572$, so the estimated MODEL A is

$$\hat{Y}_i = 3.572$$

For the statistical inference we need to calculate PRE and F^* from SSE(A) and SSE(C). Also from the outputs, we know the variance or the MSE is 0.7355. Since MSE = SSE(A)/(n − 1), we can easily obtain SSE(A) by multiplying MSE by $n - 1$; thus, SSE(A) = 0.7355(49) = 36.04. We can compute SSR using

$$\text{SSR} = n(B_0 - \overline{Y})^2 = 50(3.9 - 3.572)^2 = 5.379$$

Then it is easy to get SSE(C) from

$$\text{SSE(C)} = \text{SSE(A)} + \text{SSR} = 36.04 + 5.379 = 41.419$$

Then, the computations of PRE and F^* are easy.

$$\text{PRE} = \frac{\text{SSR}}{\text{SSE(C)}} = \frac{5.379}{41.419} = 0.13$$

and

$$F^*_{1,49} = \frac{\text{PRE}/1}{(1 - \text{PRE})/(n - 1)} = \frac{.13}{.87/49} = 7.32$$

From the appendix tables, the critical values for PRE and F, for $\alpha = .05$, are, respectively, about .075 and 4.03. The obtained values clearly exceed the critical values, so we can reject MODEL C in favor of MODEL A. Thus, the 13% reduction in error obtained by using the estimate $b_0 = 3.572$ instead of the null hypothesis value of $B_0 = 3.9$ is statistically reliable. Thus, we can conclude that the actual fatality rate was reliably lower than the goal.

From the above it is also easy to calculate the 95% confidence interval for β_0, the true average fatality rate across states. Substituting the appropriate values into Eq. 5.4 yields

$$3.572 \pm \sqrt{\frac{4.03(0.7355)}{50}} \quad \text{or} \quad 3.572 \pm 0.243$$

which gives an interval of [3.329, 3.815]. Using this interval, we can easily ask other questions. For example, had the traffic safety organization's goal been $B_0 = 3.8$, we would not conclude that the actual fatality rate was reliably less than the goal, because 3.8 is included in the 95% confidence interval.

5.11

Summary

In Chapter 1 we noted that the equation

DATA = MODEL + ERROR

implies an inherent tension in data analysis between reducing ERROR as much as possible and keeping MODEL as simple or parsimonious as possible. Whenever we consider adding an additional parameter to the MODEL so that it will fit the DATA better and thereby reduce ERROR, we must ask whether the additional complexity of the MODEL is worth it. In this chapter we have developed inferential machinery for answering whether the additional complexity is worth it.

To decide whether the benefits of adding parameters to the MODEL outweigh the disadvantages of the increased complexity, we first calculate SSE(A) and SSE(C), respectively, the sum of squared errors for the augmented model, which incorporates the additional parameters, and the compact model, which does not include those parameters. The sum of squares reduced, SSR, is simply the difference between them:

$$SSR = SSE(C) - SSE(A)$$

Then we calculate the proportional reduction in error attributable to the additional parameters, which is given by

$$PRE = \frac{SSE(C) - SSE(A)}{SSE(C)} = \frac{SSR}{SSE(C)}$$

Another related statistic is the ratio of the proportional reduction in error per parameter added to the potential proportional reduction in error per remaining unused parameter, which is given by

$$F^* = \frac{PRE/(PA - PC)}{(1 - PRE)/(n - PA)}$$

We then compare the calculated values of PRE and F^* to the distribution of values we would expect *if* MODEL C, *the compact model, were true*. If the calculated values of PRE and F^* would have been unlikely if MODEL C were true, then we reject MODEL C and conclude that the extra complexity of MODEL A is worth it. On the other hand, if the calculated values are ones that might reasonably have been obtained if MODEL C were true, then we do not reject MODEL C, and without further evidence we would not accept the additional complexity of MODEL A.

This inferential machinery is merely a guide for decision making and is not infallible. There are two kinds of errors that we can make. A

Type I error occurs when MODEL C is in fact correct but by chance we happen to get unusual values of PRE and F^* and so reject MODEL C. The probability of a Type I error is α and defines how unusual PRE and F^* have to be before we reject MODEL C. A Type II error occurs when MODEL C is in fact false or inferior to MODEL A but by chance we happen to get values of PRE and F^* that are not unusual and so fail to reject MODEL C. We generally select α, the probability of a Type I error and try to reduce the chances of a Type II error by collecting better DATA with less ERROR and by increasing the number of observations. Reducing the chances of Type II error is often referred to as increasing the statistical power of an inference.

We developed this inferential machinery in the context of asking a question for the simple model. However, exactly the same procedure will work for all the more complex models we consider in subsequent chapters. In this chapter we have learned all we need to know as data analysts about statistical inference. The remainder of our task is to learn how to build more complex and interesting models of our data.

6

Simple Regression: Estimating Models with a Single Continuous Predictor

We have used the simple single-parameter model to explicate the use of models, the notion of error, and inference procedures to be used in comparing augmented and compact models. We have focused on them in so much detail because the estimation and inference procedures that we developed within this very simple context generalize to much more complicated models. That is, regardless of the complexity of a model, estimation from here on will be done by minimizing the sum of squared errors, just as we did in the single-parameter case, and inference will be done by comparing augmented and compact models using PRE and F^*. So the detail on single-parameter models has been necessitated by our desire to present in a simple context all of the statistical tools that we will use in much more complex situations.

However, we should admit that single-parameter models are only infrequently of substantive or theoretical interest. To take the example from the last chapter, we may occasionally wish to test the hypothesis that the mean in some group equals some a priori hypothesized value. More frequently, however, such a priori values don't exist, and instead we are exploring whether the mean in one group of students (i.e., those that received the innovative mathematics curriculum) differs from the mean in another group of students (i.e., those that received the old or traditional curriculum). Or, returning to the automobile fatality data, while it is certainly possible that we would be interested in testing whether some a priori value is a good prediction for the fatality rate in a given year, and hence in testing the single-parameter model versus a compact zero-parameter model, it is much more likely that we would be interested in examining the determinants or correlates of automobile fatality rates. In other words, our interest is more likely to center on attempts to explain the fatality rate data than on tests of alternative values for the mean fatality rate.

To examine these sorts of substantive issues, we need to consider models having more than a single parameter. Initially, we will consider only two-parameter models, taking the following form:

$$Y_i = \beta_0 + \beta_1 X_i + \varepsilon_i$$

The exact definition of the terms in this two-parameter model will be spelled out in more detail below. For the time being we simply note that we are making predictions of Y_i conditional upon some other variable X_i, since the model's predictions from this two-parameter model obviously change as X_i changes, assuming that β_1 takes on some value other than zero.

Actually, there are two forms of this two-parameter model, each of which is illustrated by one of the two examples we have just discussed. In the first example, having to do with the evaluation of a third grade mathematics curriculum, we want to examine whether the test scores for students taught under the new curriculum are reliably higher than test scores of students taught under the old curriculum. This amounts to asking whether we need separate predictions from a model for the two groups of students or whether a single prediction suffices regardless of which curriculum a student receives. In other words, we want to compare a model in which predictions are made conditional on knowing whether a given student received the new or old curriculum with one where the same prediction is made for every student. For this comparison, the augmented model is a two-parameter model, defining X_i in such a way that it identifies which curriculum a student has received. We might, for instance, define X_i as follows:

$X_i = -1$ if a student received the old curriculum

$X_i = +1$ if a student received the new curriculum

If the estimated value of β_1 in the above two-parameter model is something other than zero, this two-parameter model then gives different predicted values for students taught under the different curricula. For example, if b_0, the estimated value of β_0, equals 70 and b_1, the estimated value of β_1, equals 5, then the prediction for the group with the old curriculum is

$$b_0 + b_1 X_i = 70 + 5(-1) = 70 - 5 = 65$$

and the prediction for the group with the new curriculum is

$$b_0 + b_1 X_i = 70 + 5(1) = 70 + 5 = 75$$

Notice that there are only two possible values for X_i in this example. Students are taught under one curriculum or the other, and our decision about the numerical values used to represent curriculum is arbitrary. For instance, had we defined X_i differently, giving students in the new curriculum a value of 2 on X_i and students in the old curriculum a value of 4, the two-parameter model still would generate different predictions for the two groups of students, assuming the estimated value of β_1 does not equal zero.

Now consider the second example. Suppose we wanted to explain the auto fatality data, and we suspected that population density of the states might be a reasonable candidate for an explanatory factor. In other words, we thought that fatality rates might be systematically different in states that are sparsely settled compared with states that are densely settled. So we might use the two-parameter model to make predictions for states conditional on their population densities, defining X_i as population density. Population density can take on all different values, and it would be highly unlikely that any two states would have exactly the same density and, hence, the same value on X_i. Therefore, instead of making two different predictions as in the curriculum example, our two-parameter model now is likely to make different predictions for each state, since each state is likely to have a unique value of X_i. Another difference between this two-parameter model and the one in the curriculum example is that here values on X_i are not arbitrary, whereas they were in the curriculum example. That is, a given state has an actual population density, and if we want to represent that value as X_i then we have no choice in the value we assign to X_i for each state.

The difference between these two examples lies in what is called the scale of measurement of the predictor variable, the variable upon which the predictions are conditional. In the curriculum example, new versus old curriculum is measured on a nominal scale. This means that while X_i needs to code the distinction between the two curricula, it doesn't matter which curriculum is given the higher value on X_i nor does it matter which two values are used. X_i needs to code the curriculum distinction, and it doesn't really matter how this is done. On the other hand, population density is measured on a ratio scale. That is, zero is a meaningful value and the unit of measurement is also meaningful.

The values that we use to code density as X_i are not at all arbitrary, but dictated by the desire to preserve all the information contained in the data. For this variable we want X_i to reflect not only the relative differences between states in density but also the absolute value of density for each state.

While all of the procedures for building models, estimating parameters, and comparing augmented and compact models can be used regardless of the scale of measurement of the predictor variable or variables, it is conceptually useful to treat models with nominal predictor variables separately from models whose predictors are assumed to be continuously measured on either interval or ratio scales. Initially we will deal with models that contain only predictors presumed to be measured on interval or ratio scales. In this chapter and the next we treat two-parameter models having a single, continuously measured predictor variable. Then, in Chapters 8 and 10, we consider models with multiple continuously measured predictors. In traditional statistical jargon these chapters deal with simple and multiple regression, including polynomial and interactive models. Then we turn our attention to models having predictors measured on nominal scales of measurement. Again, in traditional statistical jargon, the chapters on nominally coded predictors deal with analysis of variance. Finally, we will consider models in which some predictors are nominal variables and some are continuous variables. Such models are typically referred to as analysis of covariance models. Our approach, however, to each type of models will be uniform. Rather than describing seemingly different statistical techniques for multiple regression, analysis of variance, and analysis of covariance, we will estimate parameters just as we have done in the simple single-parameter case, and we will test hypotheses by comparing augmented and compact models. So, while our treatment of nominally coded predictors is located in different chapters from our treatment of continuously measured predictors, the same procedures will be used throughout.

6.1

Defining a Linear Two-Parameter Model

We now confine our attention to two-parameter models with a single continuous predictor variable. We will use examples from both the auto fatality data and from the baseball attendance data. Suppose in the baseball data we wanted to understand why it was that some teams had greater attendance than others. That is, suppose we wanted to speculate about what might be contributing to variation in attendance from team to team. We might think about possible factors that should lead to an increase or decrease in attendance. We might, for instance, reasonably suspect that spectators like to watch baseball games where there is a lot of action. In other words, they would prefer to watch a high-scoring slugfest than a low-scoring pitching duel. To determine whether this hypothesis makes sense, we might see whether a team's total attendance can be predicted by knowing how well they, on average, hit the ball throughout the year. The team batting average is a reasonable measure of how well each baseball team hits. Exhibit 6.1 presents each baseball team's 1983 yearly attendance figure (expressed as hundreds of thousands of spectators) and 1983 team batting average (proportion of hits per official times at bat).

EXHIBIT 6.1 ▶

Baseball data: season attendance and batting average

Team	Y_i Attend	X_i Bat. Avg.
Atlanta	21.2	.272
Chicago	14.8	.261
Cincinnati	11.9	.239
Houston	13.5	.257
Los Angeles	35.1	.250
Montreal	23.2	.264
New York	11.0	.241
Philadelphia	21.3	.249
Pittsburgh	12.3	.264
St. Louis	23.4	.270
San Diego	15.4	.250
San Francisco	12.5	.247
Baltimore	20.4	.269
Boston	17.8	.270
California	25.6	.260
Chicago	21.3	.262
Cleveland	7.7	.265
Detroit	18.3	.274
Kansas City	19.6	.271
Milwaukee	24.0	.277
Minnesota	8.6	.261
New York	22.6	.273
Oakland	12.9	.262
Seattle	8.1	.240
Texas	13.6	.255
Toronto	19.3	.277

The data that are presented in Exhibit 6.1 are graphed in Exhibit 6.2 in a scatterplot. The vertical axis represents team attendance, and the horizontal axis is team batting average. Each point in this plot represents one of the 26 baseball teams. The question that we would like to ask is whether we can use team batting average successfully in predicting team attendance. Or, expressed differently, do our predictions of team attendance improve by making those predictions conditional on knowledge of team batting average? This chapter and the next are concerned with answering this sort of question. In the present chapter, we focus on the nature of a two-parameter model and how those parameters are estimated and interpreted. In the next chapter, we discuss procedures for determining how much improvement in a model we get by adding an additional parameter.

In our two-parameter model, we wish to make different predictions about baseball attendance depending on a team's batting average. We will use a simple linear model to generate predictions of attendance that are conditional on batting average. Such a linear model is presented in the equation

$$Y_i = \beta_0 + \beta_1 X_i + \varepsilon_i$$

where Y_i is team attendance and X_i is team batting average. By referring to our generic equation

DATA = MODEL + ERROR

we see that the model in this two-parameter equation is represented by

$$\beta_0 + \beta_1 X_i$$

In terms of estimated parameter values, the predictions made by this model for each team's attendance are given by

$$\hat{Y}_i = b_0 + b_1 X_i$$

ERROR equals DATA minus MODEL, so the residuals in this two-parameter model can be expressed as follows:

$$e_i = Y_i - \hat{Y}_i$$
$$= Y_i - (b_0 + b_1 X_i)$$

Let us look at each of the parameter estimates in this model and see what each is telling us. First of all, what does b_0 represent in this model? In the single-parameter model, we saw that b_0 equaled the mean value of Y_i, assuming we define error as the sum of squared errors. Another way of saying the same thing is that in the single-parameter model, b_0 is our prediction for each team or each data point. Here, however, in this two-parameter model, we wish to take further information into account in making each team's prediction. We are making each prediction conditional on a team's batting average. b_0 is therefore not our

EXHIBIT 6.2

Scatterplot

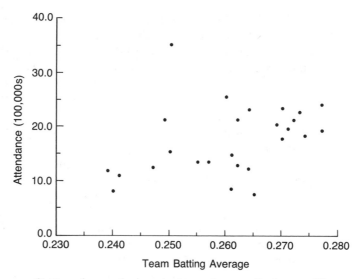

prediction for each team, since the predictions will vary as a function of team batting average:

$$\hat{Y}_i = b_0 + b_1 X_i$$

There is one time, however, based on this model, when our team attendance prediction will equal b_0. This is clearly when X_i equals zero, for then

$$\hat{Y}_i = b_0 + b_1(0) = b_0$$

This, then, provides the interpretation for the parameter estimate b_0 in this two-parameter model: According to the model, b_0 is our prediction of Y_i conditional on X_i equaling zero. As we will see for our example, this prediction may not be very useful, for the data from which we estimate this parameter may not include data points having values of X_i near zero. Nevertheless, according to the model, b_0 is the prediction of Y_i when X_i equals zero. In the terminology of simple regression, b_0 is called the *intercept*, for reasons we discuss below.

The second parameter estimate in the model, b_1, informs us about how our predictions change, according to the model, as X_i changes. Suppose we had two observations differing in their values on X_i by 1 unit, X_i for the first observation being 1 unit larger than X_i for the second. According to the model, our predictions for the two data points would differ by b_1, since

$$\hat{Y}_1 - \hat{Y}_2 = (b_0 + b_1 X_1) - (b_0 + b_1 X_2)$$
$$= b_1 X_1 - b_1 X_2$$
$$= b_1(X_1 - X_2)$$
$$= b_1$$

So, b_1 tells us by how much our predictions of Y_i change as X_i changes by one unit. Notice that in this derivation, we did not specify what the actual values of X_1 and X_2 were. We only specified that they were 1 unit apart from each other. Hence, this implies that b_1 in this two-parameter model is constant, regardless of the level of X_i. This is what was meant by the definition of this sort of two-parameter model as a linear model. As X_i changes by some set amount, our predictions of Y_i change by a constant amount, regardless of the value of X_i. In the terminology of simple regression, b_1 is known as the *slope*.

Let us look at this two-parameter model graphically. Exhibit 6.3 presents the graphical equivalent for the model. All of the predictions $\hat{Y}_i$ lie on the line defined by the model. Errors of prediction, as in the single-parameter model, are defined as vertical distances between the line and an actual observation. That is, an error or residual is the difference between Y_i and $\hat{Y}_i$. The intercept b_0 is the value of $\hat{Y}_i$ when X_i equals zero; hence it is the value on the vertical axis of the graph where the prediction function crosses or "intercepts" it. The slope b_1 is the change in $\hat{Y}_i$ for each unit increase in X_i. Hence it indicates how steeply the line goes up or down. Notice that the slope can take on any positive or negative value. If the slope is positive, it means that the model predicts higher values of Y_i as X_i increases. With a negative slope, higher values of Y_i are predicted from the model as X_i decreases.

EXHIBIT 6.3 ▶

Prediction line

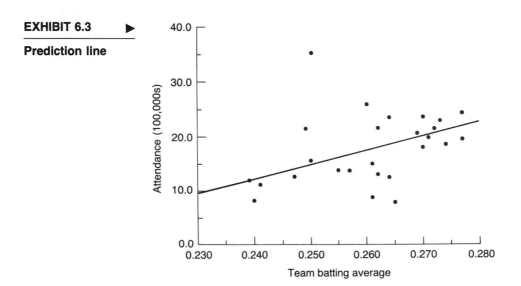

6.2

Estimating a Linear Two-Parameter Model

Given some sample of data, how do we estimate the paramaters of this sort of model? What we would like to do is generate values of b_0 and b_1 in the equation

$$\hat{Y}_i = b_0 + b_1 X_i$$

based on our sample of data, that are good estimates of the parameters β_0 and β_1. Just as we found in the single-parameter model, estimation of the parameters in this model depends on how we define aggregate error. What we want to do is find estimates of β_0 and β_1 that make as small as possible the total errors of prediction made by the model. But there are a variety of ways to define what we mean by the total errors of prediction. We could estimate β_0 and β_1 by minimizing the sum of the absolute errors:

$$\text{Minimize} \sum |Y_i - \hat{Y}_i|$$

How would we go about doing this? One way is to look at the scatterplot and attempt to draw freehand a line that seems to come as close as possible to the data points in the scatterplot. In Exhibit 6.3 we have done just this with the baseball attendance and team batting average data. For this line we would then calculate the sum of the absolute errors. Then we would proceed to slowly change both b_0 and b_1 systematically until we found values that seemed to reduce the sum of absolute errors about as far as we could go. This sort of iterative solution, while ultimately effective, is obviously not very efficient.

In Chapter 4 we showed that we generally preferred parameter estimates that minimize the sum of squared errors to those that minimize the sum of absolute errors. This preference is due to the fact that if the errors are normally distributed, least squares parameter estimates are unbiased, consistent, and more efficient than estimates that minimize the sum of absolute errors. This is true in the case of models with two parameters as well. Hence, we will derive estimated values of β_0 and β_1 by minimizing $\sum (Y_i - \hat{Y}_i)^2$. The resulting *least squares* parameter estimates are given as

$$b_1 = \frac{\sum (X_i - \overline{X})(Y_i - \overline{Y})}{\sum (X_i - \overline{X})^2}$$

$$b_0 = \overline{Y} - b_1 \overline{X}$$

The derivation of these estimates is given in Box 6.1 on page 121. They are unbiased, consistent, and relatively efficient estimates, assuming a normal error distribution.

A convenient way to reexpress the equation for b_1 is to divide both the numerator and denominator by $n - 1$:

$$b_1 = \frac{\Sigma (X_i - \overline{X})(Y_i - \overline{Y})/(n - 1)}{\Sigma (X_i - \overline{X})^2/(n - 1)}$$

$$= \frac{s_{xy}}{s_x^2}$$

In this last expression, s_{xy} is known as the *covariance* between x and y, and it is defined by the numerator of the preceding expression:

$$s_{xy} = \frac{\Sigma(X_i - \overline{X})(Y_i - \overline{Y})}{n - 1}$$

The denominator of b_1 in this expression is the variance of X_i. Since the variance of X_i is necessarily positive, the sign of b_1 will be determined by the sign of the covariance between Y_i and X_i. Let us examine for a minute what determines the sign of the covariance. Using the above formula, we see that for each observation we multiply together the X_i deviation from $\overline{X}$ and the Y_i deviation from $\overline{Y}$. If both X_i and Y_i are above their means, or if both of them lie below their means, then this product will have a positive sign. If, however, one of the two variables for a given observation lies above its mean and the other below its mean, then the product for that observation will have a negative sign. It follows from this that if high values on one variable tend to be found with relatively low values on the other variable, then the sign of the covariance will be negative and the slope will also be negative. On the other hand, if high values on the two variables tend to co-occur and if low values tend to co-occur, then the covariance and the slope will be positive.

Using the expressions for b_0 and b_1, or, more efficiently, using a regression routine in one of the various statistical software packages, we can calculate the estimated intercept and slope for our baseball example when we regress 1983 season attendance on team batting average. (Notice here that in regression terminology one regresses Y_i on X_i, not the other way around.) The resulting estimated two-parameter model for these data is

$$\hat{Y}_i = -33.77 + 197X_i$$

This prediction function is graphed as a straight line on the scatterplot we saw before in Exhibit 6.4.

EXHIBIT 6.4 ▶

Regression line

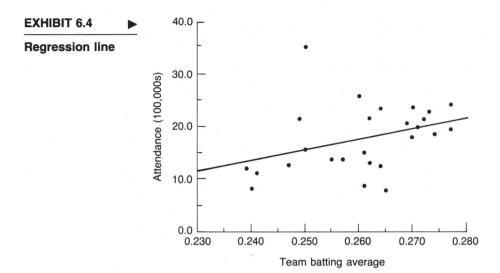

Let us interpret each of the regression coefficients, b_0 and b_1, in this equation. The first coefficient, b_0, equals -33.77. This is the value predicted by the model for a team's 1983 attendance if its season batting average were .000. While this intercept is the best unbiased estimate of this prediction based on these data, it is clearly an uninterpretable value, because no team in our sample of data had a season batting average approaching .000.

The value of the slope, 197, tells us that if we found two teams differing in season batting average by 1.000, our model predicts that season attendance for the better-batting team would be 197 hundreds of thousands of spectators higher than in the poorer-hitting team. Talking about a difference in season batting average of 1.000 is silly, since batting averages are expressed as proportions and can vary only between .000 and 1.000. It would be much more reasonable with these data to rescale this coefficient so that we are predicting .197 hundreds of thousands of spectators increase with every .001 increase in team batting average.

In Exhibit 6.5 we present for each team its Y_i, X_i, $\hat{Y}_i$, residual, and squared residual. The sum of these squared residuals, $\Sigma (Y_i - \hat{Y}_i)^2$, across all 26 teams is also given. The meaning of the least squares criterion in estimating the parameters of this model is contained in the fact that no other values of b_0 and b_1 would give us a smaller sum of squared residuals for these data.

EXHIBIT 6.5   ▶

Baseball data: simple regression
$Y_i = \beta_0 + \beta_1 X_i + \varepsilon_i$
$Y_i = -33.77$
$+ 197 X_i + \varepsilon_i$

Team	Y_i	X_i	$\hat{Y}_i$	e_i	e_i^2
Atlanta	21.2	.272	19.72	1.48	2.18
Chicago	14.8	.261	17.56	−2.76	7.62
Cincinnati	11.9	.239	13.23	−1.33	1.78
Houston	13.5	.257	16.77	−3.27	10.73
Los Angeles	35.1	.250	15.40	19.70	388.20
Montreal	23.2	.264	18.15	5.05	25.49
New York	11.0	.241	13.63	−2.63	6.90
Philadelphia	21.3	.249	15.20	6.10	37.20
Pittsburgh	12.3	.264	18.15	−5.85	34.23
St. Louis	23.4	.270	19.33	4.07	16.56
San Diego	15.4	.250	15.40	.00	.00
San Francisco	12.5	.247	14.81	−2.31	5.32
Baltimore	20.4	.269	19.13	1.27	1.60
Boston	17.8	.270	19.33	−1.53	2.34
California	25.6	.260	17.36	8.24	67.83
Chicago	21.3	.262	17.76	3.54	12.55
Cleveland	7.7	.265	18.35	−10.65	113.37
Detroit	18.3	.274	20.12	−1.82	3.30
Kansas City	19.6	.271	19.53	.07	.01
Milwaukee	24.0	.277	20.71	3.29	10.84
Minnesota	8.6	.261	17.56	−8.96	80.30
New York	22.6	.273	29.92	2.68	7.18
Oakland	12.9	.262	17.76	−4.86	23.60
Seattle	8.1	.240	13.43	−5.33	28.41
Texas	13.6	.255	16.38	−2.78	7.73
Toronto	19.3	.277	20.71	−1.41	1.98

$$\Sigma(Y_i - \hat{Y}_i)^2 = 897.25$$

We can divide the sum of squared errors by the remaining degrees of freedom for error, $n - 2$, to calculate the mean square error:

$$\text{MSE} = \frac{\Sigma (Y_i - \hat{Y}_i)^2}{n - 2} = \frac{897.25}{24} = 37.39$$

Just as b_0 and b_1 are unbiased estimates of β_0 and β_1 under the least squares criterion, so also the mean square error is an unbiased estimate of the variance of ε_i. It estimates how variable the errors of prediction are at each level of X_i. As we will discuss in the next chapter, it is assumed that the variance of these errors is constant across all values of X_i. The square root of this mean square error is known as the *standard error of prediction*.

Let us now switch to the auto fatality data and regress states' fatality rates on their population densities. If Y_i is fatality rate, measured as the number of fatalites per 100 million vehicle miles traveled, and X_i is population density, measured as hundreds of people per square mile, the resulting parameter estimates are

$$\hat{Y}_i = 3.91 - .24X_i$$

The value of b_0, 3.91, tells us that our best estimate, based on these data, of the number of auto fatalities in a state with zero population density is 3.91. Since there are no data points from states with zero density, this value does not mean very much. The value of b_1, $-.24$, means that our best prediction, in terms of minimizing the sum of squared errors of prediction, of auto fatalities goes down by .24 as a state's population density increases by 100 people per square mile. In other words, unlike the observed relationship between baseball attendance and team batting average, auto fatality rates and population density seem to be negatively related. High fatality rates tend to be found in more sparsely populated states. The sum of squared errors that results from this two-parameter model equals 22.89, and the standard error of prediction equals .69.

6.3

An Alternative Specification

It will prove useful at later points to be able to specify regression models in which the predictor variables, in this case X_i, are expressed in mean deviation form. That is, we want to examine the two-parameter model we have been considering when we use the deviation of X_i from its mean, $\overline{X}$, to predict Y_i, rather than using simply X_i. To examine what effect this has on the model, let us take the estimated model

$$\hat{Y}_i = b_0 + b_1X_i$$

and add to it both a negative and a positive $b_1\overline{X}$ (thus changing it not at all):

$$\hat{Y}_i = b_0 + b_1X_i - b_1\overline{X} + b_1\overline{X}$$
$$= b_0 + b_1(X_i - \overline{X}) + b_1\overline{X}$$
$$= (b_0 + b_1\overline{X}) + b_1(X_i - \overline{X})$$
$$= b_0^* + b_1(X_i - \overline{X})$$

where

$$b_0^* = b_0 + b_1\overline{X}$$

The implication of this is that if we were to regress Y_i on $X_i - \overline{X}$ rather than more simply on X_i, the intercept would change in value but the slope would not. Putting the predictor in mean deviation form has no effect on the slope of the prediction function, but it does affect the value of the intercept.

Conceptually this makes a great deal of sense, for what are we doing when we put the predictor into mean deviation form? All we are really doing is changing the scale of the X_i axis in the scatterplot, redefining the value of zero so that the mean value of X_i equals zero. We have not changed the observations in the scatterplot at all, we have simply shifted the origin point in the plot. In a fundamental sense, our prediction function has not changed at all, the same line, having the same slope, minimizes the squared errors of prediction. The only change derives from the change in the location of the zero point on the X_i axis. That zero point is now at the mean of X_i and, accordingly, the value of the intercept (i.e., the value of $\hat{Y}_i$ where the prediction function crosses the Y_i axis) changes.

To see how the estimated intercept changes as a function of expressing X_i in mean deviation form, let us solve for b_0^* using the derived least squares formula for b_0 given above. We have just shown that

$$b_0^* = b_0 + b_1\overline{X}$$

If we now substitute for b_0 according to our derivation that

$$b_0 = \overline{Y} - b_1\overline{X}$$

we get

$$b_0^* = (\overline{Y} - b_1\overline{X}) + b_1\overline{X} = \overline{Y}$$

Hence under a mean deviation respecification of the model, the value of the intercept equals $\overline{Y}$. If we think about how we interpret the intercept, this result is not surprising. Under this respecfication, b_0^* is the predicted value of Y_i when $X_i - \overline{X} = 0$. Clearly, $X_i - \overline{X} = 0$ only when $X_i = \overline{X}$. Hence, this intercept tells us that $\hat{Y}_i$, the predicted value of Y_i, equals $\overline{Y}$ when X_i equals $\overline{X}$. This means that the point in the scatterplot defined by $(\overline{X}, \overline{Y})$ lies on the regression line. In sum, when a model is respecified so that the predictor variable is in mean deviation form, the slope will not change. The intercept will, however, change. It will equal the mean value of Y_i.

For the baseball data, reexpressing team batting average in mean deviation form (i.e., computing a new variable for each team, $X_i - \overline{X}$) and then regressing season attendance, Y_i, on this mean-deviated team batting average, $X_i - \overline{X}$, we get the parameter estimates

$$\hat{Y}_i = 17.51 + 197(X_i - \overline{X})$$

This model naturally generates exactly the same predicted values as the model prior to respecification and thus the sum of squared errors is also the same as it was before. The slope still equals 197, just as it did under the original specification. The intercept now equals the mean season attendance for all 26 baseball teams.

For the auto fatality data, the two-parameter model used to predict states' fatality rates from their population density was

$$\hat{Y}_i = 3.91 - .24X_i$$

If we put X_i in mean deviation form, the parameter estimates are

$$\hat{Y}_i = 3.57 - .24(X_i - \overline{X})$$

The intercept under this reexpression equals the mean fatality rate from the 50 states. The slope has not changed at all nor has the sum of squared errors.

BOX 6.1

Algebraic Derivation of Least Squares Estimates of β_0 and β_1

$$SSE = \sum (Y_i - \hat{Y}_i)^2 = \sum (Y_i - b_0 - b_1X_i)^2$$

given that $\hat{Y}_i = b_0 + b_1X_i$. We now add $(\overline{Y} - \overline{Y})$ and $b_1(\overline{X} - \overline{X})$ inside the parentheses to this expression for SSE. Since both of these expressions equal zero, we have not changed the equality. Thus,

$$SSE = \sum (Y_i - \overline{Y} + \overline{Y} - b_0 - b_1X_i + b_1\overline{X} - b_1\overline{X})^2$$

Grouping terms yields the equivalent expression

$$SSE = \sum [(Y_i - \overline{Y}) + (\overline{Y} - b_0 - b_1\overline{X}) - b_1(X_i - \overline{X})]^2$$

If we square the term in brackets and distribute the summation sign, this gives the equivalent expression

$$SSE = \sum (Y_i - \overline{Y})^2 + 2(\overline{Y} - b_0 - b_1\overline{X}) \sum (Y_i - \overline{Y})$$
$$- 2b_1 \sum (Y_i - \overline{Y})(X_i - \overline{X}) + n(\overline{Y} - b_0 - b_1\overline{X})^2$$
$$- 2b_1(\overline{Y} - b_0 - b_1\overline{X}) \sum (X_i - \overline{X}) + b_1^2 \sum (X_i - \overline{X})^2$$

Since both $\sum (Y_i - \overline{Y})$ and $\sum (X_i - \overline{X})$ equal zero, this expression reduces to

$$SSE = \sum (Y_i - \overline{Y})^2 - 2b_1 \sum (Y_i - \overline{Y})(X_i - \overline{X})$$
$$+ n(\overline{Y} - b_0 - b_1\overline{X})^2 + b_1^2 \sum (X_i - \overline{X})^2$$

Since the third term in this expression, $n(\overline{Y} - b_0 - b_1\overline{X})^2$, is necessarily positive, to minimize SSE we would like to set it equal to zero. Therefore, we wish values of b_0 and b_1 such that

$$n(\overline{Y} - b_0 - b_1\overline{X}) = 0$$

Dividing both sides of this equality by n gives us

$$\overline{Y} - b_0 - b_1\overline{X} = 0$$

or, equivalently,

$$b_0 = \overline{Y} - b_1\overline{X}$$

We have now reduced our expression for SSE, assuming the desire to minimize it, to

$$SSE = \sum (Y_i - \overline{Y})^2 - 2b_1 \sum (Y_i - \overline{Y})(X_i - \overline{X}) + b_1^2 \sum (X_i - \overline{X})^2$$

$$= \sum (Y_i - \overline{Y})^2 + \sum (X_i - \overline{X})^2 \left[b_1^2 - 2b_1 \frac{\sum (Y_i - \overline{Y})(X_i - \overline{X})}{\sum (X_i - \overline{X})^2} \right]$$

Let us now add to and subtract from this expression the quantity

$$\sum (X_i - \overline{X})^2 \left[\frac{\sum (X_i - \overline{X})(Y_i - \overline{Y})}{\sum (X_i - \overline{X})^2} \right]^2$$

$$SSE = \sum (Y_i - \overline{Y})^2$$

$$+ \sum (X_i - \overline{X})^2 \left[b_1^2 - 2b_1 \frac{\sum (X_i - \overline{X})(Y_i - \overline{Y})}{\sum (X_i - \overline{X})^2} + \left(\frac{\sum (X_i - \overline{X})(Y_i - \overline{Y})}{\sum (X - \overline{X})^2} \right)^2 \right]$$

$$- \sum (X_i - \overline{X})^2 \left(\frac{\sum (X_i - \overline{X})(Y_i - \overline{Y})}{\sum (X_i - \overline{X})^2} \right)^2$$

Rearranging terms and taking the square root of the term in brackets gives us

$$SSE = \sum (Y_i - \overline{Y})^2 - \sum (X_i - \overline{X})^2 \left(\frac{\sum (X_i - \overline{X})(Y_i - \overline{Y})}{\sum (X_i - \overline{X})^2} \right)^2$$

$$+ \sum (X_i - \overline{X})^2 \left[b_1 - \frac{\sum (X_i - \overline{X})(Y_i - \overline{Y})}{\sum (X_i - \overline{X})^2} \right]^2$$

The last term in this expression for SSE is necessarily positive. Therefore, to minimize SSE, we want this last term to equal zero. This occurs if

$$b_1 = \frac{\sum (X_i - \overline{X})(Y_i - \overline{Y})}{\sum (X_i - \overline{X})^2}$$

7

Simple Regression: Statistical Inference in Models with a Single Continuous Predictor

The last chapter was devoted to estimating the coefficients of two-parameter models where predictions are made conditional on some continuous variable, X_i. This estimation was done by defining aggregate error as the sum of squared errors and deriving the least squares parameter estimates. In other words, our parameter estimates were the best possible estimates according to the agreed upon criterion of minimizing the sum of squared errors. In this chapter we explore whether those "best" possible parameter estimates are in fact any good. We want to know whether the increase in accuracy of prediction of individual data points that the two-parameter model brings us, when compared with a single-parameter model, is worth the added complexity of the model with more parameters.

The strategy we will follow to answer this question is identical to the strategy we used in Chapter 5 to determine whether a single-parameter model was preferable to a model in which no parameters were estimated. In that case, we calculated PRE, the proportional reduction in aggregate errors, as we moved from the less complicated zero-parameter model to the more complicated single-parameter model. We then looked at whether the obtained value of PRE was sufficiently surprising, assuming that the compact model is the appropriate one and the added complexity of the augmented model buys us nothing, to cause us to reject the compact model as inadequate. We did this by comparing the obtained PRE with the sampling distribution of PRE if the null hypothesis embodied in the compact model were true (i.e., $\eta^2 = 0$), or, equivalently, by comparing F^* with its sampling distribution under the null hypothesis. We will make exactly the same kind of comparison in the present case to determine whether the added complexity of predictions based on two parameters is worthwhile.

7.1

Inferences about β_1

There are actually two different single-parameter models with which we could compare the two-parameter model in which predictions of Y_i are made conditional on some predictor variable. On the one hand, we could compare this augmented model with the single-parameter model that was extensively discussed in Chapters 4 and 5 and that makes a single constant prediction, i.e., the mean, for each case. Such a comparison yields values of PRE and F^* that can be used to test whether predictions are reliably more accurate when they are made conditional on some X_i, compared to simply predicting the mean Y_i for each case. The null hypothesis in this case is that the value of β_1 in the augmented model equals zero.

A second single-parameter model which might be used as a compact model with which to compare the augmented two-parameter model is one in which β_0 is fixed at some value B_0, possibly zero, rather than being estimated from the data. In other words, we might have a single-parameter compact model of the form

$$Y_i = B_0 + \beta_1 X_i + \varepsilon_i$$

We might be interested in testing the null hypothesis that β_0 in the two-parameter model equals B_0. Later we identify occasions when such a test is likely to be of interest.

We start with the first of these two tests: whether predictions that are conditional on some predictor variable X_i are reliably improved over a constant mean prediction for each case. Thus, the simple compact model is

MODEL C: $Y_i = \beta_0 + \varepsilon_i$

which implies the same prediction for all observations. Notice that this compact model is the same model that we referred to as the augmented model in Chapter 5, where we were asking the question of whether the single-parameter model, estimating β_0, was preferable to a model with a hypothesized prediction B_0 for each case. This is the nature of statistical tests: the augmented model for one test may well become the compact model for another. The more complex model to which we want to compare MODEL C is the two-parameter model from the previous chapter. That is,

MODEL A: $Y_i = \beta_0 + \beta_1 X_i + \varepsilon_i$

MODEL A makes predictions conditional on the value of X_i. PC, the number of parameters to be estimated in MODEL C, equals 1; PA, the number of parameters to be estimated in MODEL A, equals 2.

We now must estimate the parameters in both models and calculate the respective sums of squared errors. Exhibit 7.1 presents the data and additional calculations that we will explain presently. For MODEL C the best estimate of β_0 is the mean attendance, so $b_0 = 17.5$. That is,

MODEL C: $\hat{Y}_{iC} = 17.5$

The columns grouped under the heading "MODEL C" in Exhibit 7.1 give, respectively, $\hat{Y}_{iC}$, the error e_i, and e_i^2. The sum of the e_i^2 column is the sum of squared errors, which in this case equals 1023.6. Dividing this sum of squared errors by $n - PC = 26 - 1 = 25$ yields an estimate s^2 of the variance σ^2. That is,

$$s^2 = \frac{1023.6}{25} = 40.9$$

is an estimate of the variance of the attendance data. Note that a very large portion of the squared error is due to one team, the Los Angeles Dodgers, which had an unusually large attendance. Such large errors make us concerned about the appropriateness of least square estimation. We will return to this issue later.

We can obtain the estimates of the two parameters for MODEL A either from a computer program or from the equations derived in Chapter 6. These best estimates are $b_0 = -33.8$ and $b_1 = 197$, as we calculated in Chapter 6. That is,

MODEL A: $\hat{Y}_{iA} = -33.8 + 197X_i$

The columns grouped under the heading "MODEL A" in Exhibit 7.1 give, respectively, $\hat{Y}_{iA}$, the error e_i and e_i^2. Note that unlike the attendance predictions of MODEL C which were constant, the attendance predictions of MODEL A vary because they depend on batting average

		MODEL C			MODEL A			COMPARE
Y_i	X_i	$\hat{Y}_{iC}$	e_i	e_i^2	$\hat{Y}_{iA}$	e_i	e_i^2	$(\hat{Y}_{iA} - \hat{Y}_{iC})^2$
21.2	.272	17.5	3.7	13.7	19.8	1.4	1.9	5.3
14.8	.261	17.5	−2.7	7.3	17.6	−2.8	8.1	.0
11.9	.239	17.5	−5.6	31.4	13.3	−1.4	2.0	17.6
13.5	.257	17.5	−4.0	16.0	16.9	−3.4	11.3	.4
35.1	.250	17.5	17.6	309.8	15.5	19.6	384.9	4.1
23.2	.264	17.5	5.7	32.5	18.2	5.0	24.6	.5
11.0	.241	17.5	−6.5	42.2	13.7	−2.7	7.3	14.4
21.3	.249	17.5	3.8	14.4	15.3	6.0	36.2	4.8
12.3	.264	17.5	−5.2	27.0	18.2	−5.9	35.3	.5
23.4	.270	17.5	5.9	34.8	19.4	4.0	15.8	3.7
15.4	.250	17.5	−2.1	4.4	15.5	−.1	.0	4.1
12.5	.247	17.5	−5.0	25.0	14.9	−2.4	5.7	6.8
20.4	.269	17.5	2.9	8.4	19.2	1.2	1.4	3.0
17.8	.270	17.5	.3	.1	19.4	−1.6	2.6	3.7
25.6	.260	17.5	8.1	65.6	17.4	8.1	66.4	.0
21.3	.262	17.5	3.8	14.4	17.8	3.5	11.9	.1
7.7	.265	17.5	−9.8	96.0	18.4	−10.7	115.2	.9
18.3	.274	17.5	.8	.6	20.2	−1.9	3.6	7.3
19.6	.271	17.5	2.1	4.4	19.6	.0	.0	4.4
24.0	.277	17.5	6.5	42.2	20.8	3.2	10.2	10.9
8.6	.261	17.5	−8.9	79.2	17.6	−9.0	81.8	.0
22.6	.273	17.5	5.1	26.0	20.0	2.6	6.7	6.3
12.9	.262	17.5	−4.6	21.2	17.8	−4.9	24.4	.1
8.1	.240	17.5	−9.4	88.4	13.5	−5.4	29.3	15.9
13.6	.255	17.5	−3.9	15.2	16.5	−2.9	8.2	1.1
19.3	.277	17.5	1.8	3.2	20.8	−1.5	2.2	10.9
				SSE(C) = 1023.6			SSE(A) = 897.2	126.4 = SSR

EXHIBIT 7.1 ▲

Model comparisons for baseball data

X_i. The sum of squared errors for MODEL A is 897.2, which, as it must be, is a reduction from the sum of squared errors for MODEL C. We have estimated two parameters in this model (i.e., PA = 2), and n, the number of observations, equals 26, so

$$n - PA = 26 - 2 = 24$$

are the remaining degrees of freedom or the degrees of freedom for error. Hence, the resulting mean square error, which is an unbiased estimate of the variance of ε_i in MODEL A, equals 897.25/24 = 37.39. Note that the Los Angeles Dodgers are still responsible for a large proportion of the total error.

Both MODEL C and MODEL A are graphed over the raw data in Exhibit 7.2. The horizontal line at the value of 17.5 on the vertical axis represents MODEL C. The positively sloped prediction function is MODEL A. The values of e_i that are tabled in Exhibit 7.1 represent the vertical distances of the individual data points from the two lines generated by the MODELs.

To determine whether our predictions are reliably better once we make them conditional on X_i, we want to examine the reduction in error that occurs as we add the second parameter to our model. If we determine that this reduction is sufficiently compelling or large, then we will conclude that the two-parameter model, predicting attendance by taking into account season batting average, yields reliably better conclusions than simply making the same prediction, i.e., the mean attendance, for each and every baseball team. We will thus have demonstrated that batting average is a useful predictor of attendance, or, in traditional statistical jargon, that the two variables are reliably related to each other.

To determine whether conditional predictions of Y_i based on knowledge of X_i are worth the added complexity of an additional parameter, we wish to compare aggregate squared errors of prediction from MODEL C and MODEL A. Before doing so we rewrite MODEL C as

Model C: $Y_i = \beta_0 + 0X_i + \varepsilon_i$

This makes clear that testing whether X_i is a useful predictor of Y_i is equivalent to testing the null hypothesis that β_1 equals zero.

EXHIBIT 7.2 ▶

MODEL C and MODEL A

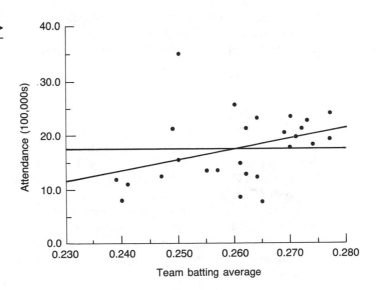

Our measure of improvement in prediction as we move from a compact to an augmented model is PRE, defined as

$$PRE = \frac{SSE(C) - SSE(A)}{SSE(C)}$$

For the two models we are comparing with these data,

$$PRE = \frac{1023.61 - 897.25}{1023.61} = .123$$

In other words, our errors of prediction are reduced by 12.3% as we move from the compact to the augmented model. Equivalently, we can say that making predictions conditional on knowledge of a team's season batting average improves our predictions of season attendance figures by 12.3% when compared with simply predicting the mean season attendance for each team.

The null hypothesis that is represented as the compact model is that team batting average is unrelated to attendance or, equivalently, that β_1 equals zero in the augmented model. The decision whether to reject this null hypothesis depends on whether this particular value of PRE, .123, is sufficiently surprising if the null hypothesis were true. To determine this, we need to compare this value of PRE with the critical value of PRE, given PA − PC = 2 − 1 = 1 and n − PA = 26 − 2 = 24 degrees of freedom. From Exhibit C.1 we find that for $\alpha = .05$ PRE needed to be greater than .151 to reject MODEL C in favor of MODEL A. Thus, the data do not indicate that team batting average is a reliable predictor of attendance.

Equivalently, we can convert the PRE statistic into F^*, which has an F distribution so long as the assumptions of normally, independently, and identically distributed errors are met. The PRE to F^* transformation is identical to the one that was used in Chapter 5:

$$F^* = \frac{PRE/(PA - PC)}{(1 - PRE)/(n - PA)} = \frac{.123/1}{(1 - .123)/24} = 3.38$$

That is, adding batting average to the model reduces error about 3.38 times more than adding a randomly chosen parameter to the model. Assuming that the assumptions about the error distribution are met, this F^* is distributed as an F statistic with 1 and 24 degrees of freedom. From Exhibit C.3 we see that the critical value of F with 1 and 24 degrees of freedom for $\alpha = .05$ equals 4.26. Hence, this value of F^* does not constitute a sufficiently surprising case to cause us to reject the null hypothesis. What this means is that we cannot conclude, based on the present data, that higher attendance is reliably found with better-hitting baseball teams. We are unable to reject the null hypothesis that the value of β_1 equals zero.

EXHIBIT 7.3 ▶

Summary table for testing batting average as a predictor of attendance

Source	SS	df	MS	F*	p	PRE
Reduction using $b_1 = 197$	126.4	1	126.4	3.38	n.s.	.12
Error (using $b_1 = 197$)	897.2	24	37.4			
Total Error (using $b_1 = 0$)	1023.6	25	40.9			

Exhibit 7.3 summarizes the results of the statistical analysis in a table of the same type as we developed in Chapter 5. The first row provides information about the reduction in error achieved by including batting average in the model (i.e., by using MODEL A instead of MODEL C). The entry in the SS column for that row is SSR = SSE(C) − SSE(A). In Exhibit 7.1 (see the column grouped under the heading "Compare") SSR is calculated directly from the equation

$$SSR = \sum (\hat{Y}_{iC} - \hat{Y}_{iA})^2$$

which was introduced in Chapter 5. The next row provides information about the error remaining even when batting average is used as a predictor (i.e., when MODEL A is used). The final row provides similar information when batting average is *not* included in the model (i.e., MODEL C is used). Calculating MS = SS/df for the first two rows provides an alternative means for calculating $F* = MSR/MSE$. MSE estimates variance of ε_i for MODEL A; this estimate is sometimes called the "mean squared error of prediction." MS_{total}, which is not traditionally included in summary tables of this type, estimates the variance of ε_i for MODEL C; this estimate is simply the variance of the original data Y_i. The same $F*$ and PRE are calculated as before. The "n.s." in the "p" column is an abbreviation for "not significant" and indicates that, if MODEL C is correct, the probability of obtaining an $F*$ as large as 3.38 is greater than .05 and hence not surprising. The conclusion, as before, is that there is insufficient evidence to reject MODEL C and its implicit null hypothesis that $\beta_1 = 0$.

7.1.1   The Pearson Correlation Coefficient

We have just examined whether predictions that are conditional on some continuous predictor variable X_i are worth the added complexity introduced by estimating a second parameter. We have done this by exactly the same procedures that were developed in Chapter 5 to infer whether a single-parameter model is preferable to one in which no parameters are estimated. As we increase the complexity of the models we consider, in this and later chapters, the inferential procedure and the formulas we use in following that procedure remain constant. We will continue to use the same formulas for PRE and F^* in comparing augmented and compact models, regardless of the complexity of those models and regardless of the differences between the two models.

In the present context, however, it is useful to explore other, equivalent formulas for PRE in order to relate the procedures we are developing to those that are found in more traditional statistics textbooks.

In the case at hand, where we wish to determine whether a continuous predictor variable X_i is useful in predicting our dependent variable, PRE is also known as the squared Pearson product moment correlation coefficient, r^2. The square root of PRE, then, in this very specific situation of comparing the simple single-parameter compact model that estimates the mean against the two-parameter augmented model that includes a continuous predictor, is known as the Pearson correlation coefficient. PRE amounts to an index of proportional reduction in errors of prediction that subsumes, in the particular case at hand, the correlation coefficient. We will also show that the inferential test we have conducted to determine whether the two-parameter augmented model is to be preferred to the single-parameter simple model amounts to a test of whether the correlation coefficient differs from zero, as that test is traditionally defined in most statistics textbooks. In other words, in the case at hand our test based on F^* subsumes the usual inferential test concerning a sample correlation coefficient.

Consider the generic formula for PRE:

$$PRE = \frac{SSE(C) - SSE(A)}{SSE(C)}$$

The formula for the sum of squared errors, regardless of the model from which those errors derive, is expressed as $\Sigma (Y_i - \hat{Y}_i)^2$. For the single-parameter compact model, the least squares estimate of β_0 equals $\overline{Y}$, and hence in this case the sum of squared errors is defined as $\Sigma (Y_i - \overline{Y})^2$. Accordingly, the formula for PRE can be rewritten as follows when only a single parameter is estimated in the compact model:

$$PRE = \frac{\Sigma (Y_i - \overline{Y})^2 - \Sigma (Y_i - \hat{Y}_i)^2}{\Sigma (Y_i - \overline{Y})^2}$$

where $\overline{Y}$ is the predicted value for each case from the compact model containing a single predictor variable. This is one of the standard formulas given in most statistics textbooks for r^2. It also is the formula for the *coefficient of determination*, or multiple R^2, in multiple regression where we have two or more predictor variables. We discuss such models in detail in the next chapter. For the time being it is sufficient to say that when we have two or more predictors in our augmented model, we can still compare it with a single-parameter compact model to ask whether the set of predictor variables is useful in predicting Y_i. The PRE statistic that results from this comparison between a compact model with a single-parameter estimate and an augmented one based on multiple predictors and hence multiple-parameter estimates is traditionally known as the coefficient of determination R^2. We generally do not recommend that models be compared when they differ by more than a single parameter. Nevertheless, PRE can still be defined in such cases, and the coefficient of determination is simply a special case of PRE, defined by specific compact and augmented models.

If PRE corresponds to r^2, then testing whether PRE = 0 is equivalent to testing whether $r^2 = 0$ and, equivalently, whether the correlation coefficient $r = 0$. Thus, when we compare PRE or its corresponding F^* to their critical values, we are testing a null hypothesis that can be expressed in the following different but equivalent ways:

1. MODEL A, which makes predictions conditional on a single continuous predictor, is not preferable to MODEL C, which makes a single constant prediction for all observations.
2. The single predictor used in the augmented model does not reliably reduce our errors in predicting Y_i.
3. In MODEL A, $\beta_1 = 0$.
4. The true value of PRE, η^2, and, equivalently, the true value of the correlation coefficient equal zero.
5. There is no correlation or linear relationship between X_i and Y_i.

7.1.2 Confidence Intervals for β_1

Recall from Chapter 5 that the confidence interval defines the range of values for the parameter for which we would fail to reject the null hypothesis. In other words, if we tested a null hypothesis that the parameter equals a value that lies within the confidence interval, we would fail to reject that null hypothesis. If the null hypothesis to be tested specifies that the parameter equals a value that lies outside of the confidence interval, we would reject that null hypothesis. In this sense, the confidence interval is entirely redundant with inference tests about the value of a parameter.

In the case of the test at hand involving inferences about β_1, the confidence interval for β_1 is defined as

$$b_1 \pm \sqrt{\frac{F_{1,n-2;\alpha}\text{MSE}}{\text{SSX}}}$$

where $F_{1,n-2;\alpha}$ is the critical value of F at level α, with degrees of freedom of PA − PC = 1 and n − PA = n − 2. MSE is the mean square error from the augmented model, again based on $n - 2$ degrees of freedom. SSX is the total sum of squares for X_i, the predictor variable, defined as $\Sigma (X_i - \overline{X})^2$.

For the baseball data that we have been examining, the critical F with 1 and 24 degrees of freedom, using $\alpha = .05$, equals 4.26. The mean square error from the augmented model (see Exhibit 7.3) equals 37.4. The sum of squares total for X_i equals .00326. We have not given this value before. It is simply the sum of squared deviations of X_i around $\overline{X} = .261$ (see Exhibit 7.1).

The confidence interval for β_1 is thus equal to

$$197 \pm \sqrt{\frac{4.26(37.4)}{.00326}} = 197 \pm 221$$

or

$$-24 \leq \beta_1 \leq 418$$

Based on the present data, we can thus say, with 95% confidence, that the true value for the slope in this two-parameter regression model, predicting season attendance from season team batting average, lies somewhere between -24 and 418. Notice that zero is a value for the slope β_1 that lies within this interval. This is consistent with the result of our earlier test where we concluded that we could not reject the null hypothesis that β_1 equals zero. The formula for the confidence interval provides some insights into the factors that influence the power—the probability of rejecting the null hypothesis when it is in fact false—and how it might be improved. The narrower the confidence interval, the more likely it is to *exclude* the value specified by the null hypothesis and therefore reject MODEL C in favor of MODEL A. Conversely, the wider the confidence interval, the more likely it is to *include* the value of the null hypothesis and therefore not provide a basis for rejecting MODEL C. What affects the size of the confidence interval? Clearly, the critical value of F affects its size. As we use a larger critical value, which is equivalent to setting α at some smaller value and thereby reducing the probability of a Type I error, the confidence interval becomes wider. In other words, as we reduce the probability of a Type I error, the confidence interval becomes wider and hence, we will in general have less power to reject a specific null hypothesis when some alternative hypothesis is true. Conversely, increasing the chances of a Type I error by decreasing the critical value of F, will produce a narrower confidence interval and hence more power.

Second, the width of the confidence interval is affected by the mean square error of Y_i from the augmented model. As the variability of errors of prediction is reduced, the confidence interval becomes narrower.

Thus, whatever we can do to reduce error such as improving the quality of the measurement of Y_i or using a better predictor variable will also increase power by narrowing the confidence interval.

Finally, SSX appears in the denominator of the confidence interval, so as it gets larger the confidence interval gets smaller. Hence, SSX, the variability of X_i around its mean, affects the width of the confidence interval. As X_i is more variable, other things being equal, the width of the confidence interval for β_1 is reduced. The most useful predictors therefore are often those that vary greatly across cases.

7.1.3 Power Analysis for Simple Regression

We can perform the same type of "what if" power analyses for simple regression, which uses one continuous predictor variable, that we performed in Chapter 5 for the simple model, which uses a single constant predictor. We perform "what if" power analyses for particular values of the true proportional reduction in error η^2 which may be of interest in exactly the same way as before. For example, for the baseball attendance data we can determine the power—the probability of concluding that team batting average is a useful predictor—when $\eta^2 = .2$, say. PA − PC = 1 as it did in Chapter 5, so we can use the same power table, Exhibit C.5 in Appendix C. Using the row for n − PA = 24 and the column for $\eta^2 = .2$, we find that power is .65, a fairly reasonable value. Hence, there is nothing new to be learned to perform "what if" power analyses here.

Now that we know how to answer easily "what if" power questions, we need to know what values of η^2 are appropriate for those "what if" questions. As before, prior experience in a research domain may provide values of PRE which can be used directly in the power table. For simple regression we might have estimates of PRE available from previous research, or we might have the correlation coefficient. In the latter case we need only square the correlation coefficient to obtain an estimate of PRE, because r^2 = PRE. As before, we would probably want to convert past empirical values of PRE, no matter how they were obtained, to unbiased estimates of η^2, using the same adjustment formula as before. That is,

$$\text{Unbiased Estimate of } \eta^2 = 1 - \frac{(1 - \text{PRE})(n - \text{PC})}{n - \text{PA}}$$

For the baseball attendance example for which PRE = .12, the unbiased estimate of η^2 equals

$$1 - \frac{(1 - .12)(26 - 1)}{26 - 2} = 1 - .88\left(\frac{25}{24}\right) = .08$$

Thus, although the value of PRE calculated from the DATA is .12, our best unbiased guess for the true value of η^2 is a rather modest .08. If we wanted to do a "what if" power analysis in preparation for doing a similar analysis of the attendance data for a different year, $\eta^2 = .08$ would be an appropriate value to use. The closest value to .08 in Exhibit C.5 of Appendix C is $\eta^2 = .075$, which we can use for a "what if" power analysis. In this case, power equals only .27. With such low power it may not be worthwhile to try to predict attendance with team batting average for another year if the magnitude of the effect (.075) is indeed so low.

If we do not have relevant prior experience for estimating η^2, we can use the values suggested in Chapter 5 for "small" ($\eta^2 = .03$), "medium" ($\eta^2 = .1$), and "large" ($\eta^2 = .3$) effects. For the baseball data the respective powers would be .13, .35, and .87. In other words, unless the effect of team batting average on attendance is large, we won't have much chance of detecting it given that our sample size is necessarily limited to 26 observations.

A third and final approach to finding an appropriate value of η^2 for "what if" power analyses for the simple regression model involves guesses about the parameter values and variance, just as in Chapter 5. Again, to have reasonable expectations about the parameter values and variance generally requires as much or more experience in a research domain as is necessary to know typical values of PRE. We present it, however, for completeness.

Although the formula for relating true values of the parameters to η^2, the true value of PRE, is easy to derive from the formula for the coefficient of determination presented earlier, we present the formula without proof:

$$\eta^2 = \beta_1^2 \frac{\sigma_x^2}{\sigma_y^2}$$

where σ_x^2 is the true variance of the predictor variable and σ_y^2 is the true variance for the dependent or criterion variable. In other words, given some alternative hypothesis that specifies what we think is the correct value for the slope β_1, and given that we want to determine the power of our test of the null hypothesis that β_1 equals zero, we can calculate the corresponding η^2 using the above expression, assuming we have estimates of σ_x^2 and σ_y^2. Then we simply use the column for the calculated value of η^2 in Exhibit C.5 to determine the power.

In the case at hand, we can use the estimated values of β_1, σ_x^2 and σ_y^2 to do an after-the-fact analysis of the power in our statistical test of whether team batting average is a useful predictor of attendance. Appropriate values would be $\beta_1 = 200$ (close to the estimate $b_1 = 197$), $\sigma_y^2 = 37$ (close to the mean square error for the augmented model; see Exhibit

7.3), and $\sigma_x^2 = .00013$ (close to $s_x^2 = \Sigma (X_i - \overline{X})^2/(n - 1) = .00326/25 = .00013$). Using these values for the true parameters, the corresponding value of η^2 is given by

$$\eta^2 = \frac{\beta_1^2 \sigma_x^2}{\sigma_y^2} = \frac{200^2(.00013)}{37} = .14$$

There is no entry in Exhibit C.5 for $\eta^2 = .14$, but we can interpolate between the power values given for $\eta^2 = .1$ and $\eta^2 = .2$ to determine that power for $\eta^2 = .14$ and $n - PA = 24$ would be approximately .47. In other words, given our estimates of σ_x^2 and σ_y^2, and given that we are going to test the null hypothesis that β_1 equals zero, setting α at .05, the chances of rejecting the null hypothesis when in fact β_1 equals 200 are roughly 50-50.

7.2

Inferences about β_0

Our discussion of inferences about the two-parameter, single-predictor model has so far been confined to comparisons with a compact model where the single parameter is β_0. But since there are two parameters in our augmented model, there are actually two different single-parameter compact models with which this augmented model could be compared. An alternative compact model with which this augmented model could be compared is one in which β_1 is estimated while β_0 is not. We could either set β_0 equal to zero in this compact model, as follows:

MODEL C: $Y_i = \beta_1 X_i + \varepsilon_i$

or we could set it equal to some a priori hypothesized value B_0:

MODEL C: $Y_i = B_0 + \beta_1 X_i + \varepsilon_i$

The choice of compact models is a crucial one, as always, since the difference between the compact and augmented models defines the null hypothesis being tested. By comparing the two-parameter augmented model with a compact one in which β_0 has been fixed at zero, we are testing the null hypothesis that the intercept equals zero. A model in which the intercept has been fixed at zero is, in regression terminology, known as regression through the origin, because the prediction function will necessarily pass through the (0,0) point in the scatterplot. A compact model in which β_0 has been fixed at some value B_0 defines a null hypothesis in which the intercept has been fixed at some known value. If B_0 equals zero, these two compact models are identical.

Inferences about β_0 are not often interesting in the social sciences because we seldom have theories strong enough to specify hypothesized values for β_0. There is one particular case in which inferences about β_0 are likely to be of interest. We saw in the last chapter that when the predictor variable is transformed so that its mean equals zero (i.e., define the predictor variable as $X_i - \overline{X}$), the intercept equals $\overline{Y}$. Hence, with a predictor variable in the model we can use a test of β_0 to test inferences about the mean Y_i value when we have transformed the predictor variable so that it represents mean deviations. Such a test of a null hypothesis concerning an a priori value of β_0 or $\overline{Y}$ with a predictor variable in the model will be more powerful than an inference test about the value of β_0 in the single-parameter model with no predictor variables, as was discussed in Chapter 5, so long as the predictor variable in the two-parameter augmented model is reliably related to Y_i. We will show this difference in power by using the fatality rate data.

In the last chapter we saw that the two-parameter model for the fatality data, predicting states' fatality rates conditional on their densities, is

$$\hat{Y}_i = 3.91 - .24X_i$$

where Y_i represents the number of fatalities per 100 million vehicle miles traveled and X_i measures states' densities as hundreds of people per square mile. The sum of squared errors from this two-parameter model equals 22.89. With 48 degrees of freedom remaining for error (number of states minus two parameters), the resulting mean square error equals .48.

A test of the null hypothesis that density is unrelated to fatality rates, or, equivalently, that β_1 in this model equals zero, is conducted by comparing this augmented model with the single-parameter compact model

MODEL C: $\hat{Y}_i = 3.57$

The estimated value of the single parameter β_0 in this compact model equals the mean fatality rate. This compact model yields a sum of squared errors of 36.04.

Comparing the augmented and compact models to determine whether X_i and Y_i are reliably related gives

$$\text{PRE} = \frac{36.04 - 22.89}{36.04} = .365$$

The resulting F^* statistic, with 1 and 48 degrees of freedom, equals

$$F^*_{1,48} = \frac{.365}{(1 - .365)/48} = 27.57$$

This obtained F^* statistic far exceeds the critical value of F with 1 and 48 degrees of freedom for α set at .05. As a result, we reject the null hypothesis that β_1 equals zero, and we therefore conclude that population density is reliably related to auto fatality rates in the 50 states. The negative slope value indicates that as population density increases, fatality rates tend to go down.

The preceding test is a second illustration of the procedures developed in the first half of this chapter. We now want to illustrate an inference test about the value of β_0. First, we want to recompute our augmented model so that X_i, population density, is transformed into mean deviation form. The mean population density, in hundreds of people per square mile, equals 1.45. We define X_i' as $X_i - 1.45$ and then regress Y_i on X_i'. The resulting model is

MODEL A: $\hat{Y}_i = 3.57 - .24X_i'$

Note once again that this transformation of X_i has not affected the value of the slope b_1, but it has changed the intercept b_0 so that it now equals the mean of Y_i. Since this model makes exactly the same predictions for each Y_i as did the earlier model prior to transforming X_i, the resulting sum of squared errors equals 22.89, just as it did earlier. Two parameters have been estimated from the data, so the remaining degrees of freedom for error equal 48.

Now suppose that in previous years the mean automobile fatality rate had been 3.80, and we wanted to determine whether the mean rate in this particular year for which we have data reliably differs from the a priori value of 3.80. To test the null hypothesis that β_0 equals 3.80, we could compare the above augmented model with the compact one

MODEL C: $Y_i = 3.80 + \beta_1 X_i' + \varepsilon_i$

It turns out that, when we have transformed X_i as we have into mean deviation form, the least squares estimate of β_1 does not change regardless of whether β_0 is estimated from the data or is fixed at some a priori value representing a null hypothesis to be tested. This is *not* the case unless we have converted X_i to X_i'. If we are interested in testing hypotheses about β_0 and we do so without transforming X_i to mean deviation form, then we are no longer testing hypotheses about $\overline{Y}$, and the least squares estimate of β_1 will change from compact to augmented models. Because of this complication and because inferences about β_0 are generally of interest only when X_i is in mean deviation form, we will confine our discussion in the remainder of this chapter to this case.

Following the above discussion, the estimated compact model is

MODEL C: $\hat{Y}_i = 3.80 - .24X_i'$

The sum of squared errors for this compact model equals 25.535. This value can be determined, as always, by computing $\hat{Y}_i$ for each case and then summing the resulting squared residuals. Equivalently, we can use the following formula (from Chapter 5), which expresses the error reduced in terms of the two alternative predictions from each model:

$$SSR = \sum (\hat{Y}_{iC} - \hat{Y}_{iA})^2$$

Substituting the specific values for $\hat{Y}_{iC}$ and $\hat{Y}_{iA}$, we obtain

$$SSR = \sum [(3.8 - .24X_1) - (3.57 - .24X_1)]^2$$
$$= \sum (3.8 - 3.57)^2 = 50(.23)^2 = 2.65$$

In general form, if we define B_0 as the value of the intercept in the compact model and b_0 as the value of the intercept in the augmented model, then the difference in the sum of squares between the compact and augmented models equals $n(B_0 - b_0)^2$. In other words, when dealing with X_i in mean deviation form and when testing a null hypothesis that the intercept, and hence the mean of Y_i, equals some value B_0, the following equality holds:

$$SSE(C) = SSE(A) + n(B_0 - b_0)^2$$

Once again, this equality holds only if X_i is in mean deviation form.

Accordingly, the sum of squares for the compact model in the example being discussed equals 22.89 + 2.65 or 25.54. The value of PRE for testing the null hypothesis is

$$PRE = \frac{2.65}{25.54} = .104$$

This in turn converts to F^* as follows:

$$F^*_{1,48} = \frac{.104}{(1 - .104)/48} = 5.55$$

This F^* has 48 degrees of freedom for error since the augmented model estimates two parameters and we have 50 observations. The critical value of F with 1 and 48 degrees of freedom, α set at .05, equals 4.04. Hence, we reject the null hypothesis that β_0 equals 3.80, and we conclude that in fact this year's fatality rates are on average lower than those of previous years.

We could have tested this same null hypothesis about the value of β_0 using our simple single-parameter model and the procedures developed in Chapter 5. As we will show, however, doing so results in a less powerful test, because X_i is reliably related to Y_i, as we have seen. To illustrate, let us test the same null hypothesis about the mean auto fatality rate in these data by using the procedures of Chapter 5. The two models to be compared, augmented and compact, are

Model A: $\hat{Y}_i = 3.57$

Model C: $\hat{Y}_i = 3.80$

The sum of squared errors for the augmented model, equal to $n - 1$ times the variance of the auto fatality data, equals 36.04. The sum of squared errors for the compact model equals 38.69. Notice that the difference between these two sums of squares equals 2.65, just as it did when we compared the sums of squares for the augmented and compact models that included X_i'. It is still the case that

$$\text{SSE(C)} = \text{SSE(A)} + n(B_0 - b_0)^2$$

where B_0 is the hypothesized value of $\overline{Y}$ given by the null hypothesis, and b_0 is the mean that is estimated from the data.

The PRE that results from comparing the augmented and compact models equals

$$\text{PRE} = \frac{2.65}{38.69} = .068$$

Since the augmented single-parameter model has 49 degrees of freedom for error, this PRE converts to an F^* with 1 and 49 degrees of freedom:

$$F^*_{1,49} = \frac{.068}{(1 - .068)/49} = 3.58$$

This F^* statistic does not exceed the critical value of F, setting α at .05; hence we fail to reject the null hypothesis that the mean fatality rate equals 3.80.

We have tested the same null hypothesis twice with exactly the same data. The null hypothesis for both tests was that the mean fatality rate was equal to the a priori value from previous years of 3.80. In the first test, we tested this null hypothesis by comparing augmented and compact models that included a predictor variable X_i'. In the second test, we did not include the predictor variable in either model. In the first test we rejected the null hypothesis, while in the second we did not. Clearly, therefore, the first test is, in this case, the more powerful of the two. Why is this?

The difference in the two F^* statistics was due to two factors. First, the degrees of freedom for error in the two tests differed. In the first test, we estimated two parameters in the augmented model, and, hence, degrees of freedom for error equaled 48. In the second test, the error degrees of freedom equaled 49 because only a single parameter was estimated in the augmented model. Since the denominator of the F^* ratio is divided by the degrees of freedom for error, this difference, considered by itself, should have resulted in a larger F^* statistic for the second test than for the first. However, this difference was more than compensated for by the other factor that affects the relative magnitude of these two F^* statistics. The value of PRE in the first test equaled .104, while in the second it equaled only .068. The larger PRE resulted in a larger F^* statistic, even though the degrees of freedom for error in the first test was smaller.

To understand why the first test yielded a larger F^* than the second, we therefore need to understand why the two values of PRE differ. In the two tests we saw that the differences in the sum of squared errors between the compact and augmented models were identical. In other words, in both cases SSR or the numerator of PRE equaled 2.65. So the difference in the two PRE values is due to the denominator of PRE, i.e., the sum of squared errors for the compact model. In the first test, when we included X_i' in the models, the sum of squared errors for both the augmented and compact models was considerably smaller than it was in the second test. This difference occurred because the presence of X_i' in the model improved our predictions of Y_i. In other words, the sums of squared errors for both the augmented and compact models in the first test were considerably smaller than they were in the second test because predictions in the first models were made conditional on X_i'. And, as we saw earlier, the predictions that are made conditional on X_i' are in this case substantially better than those made without information on X_i', since we showed that fatality rates and density are reliably related in these data.

Our conclusion, therefore, goes as follows. Tests of null hypotheses about the mean in some sample of data can be conducted as tests of β_0 both in models that include no predictors and in models that include a predictor or predictors, so long as the included predictors are in mean deviation form. The same test will be more powerful and yield higher values of PRE and F^* in the case where predictors are included in the model whenever those predictors reliably increase the quality of our predictions of Y_i, or whenever the sum of squared errors with the predictors in the model is reliably smaller than it is without them.

7.2.1 Computing Confidence Intervals and Power for β_0

In Chapter 5 we gave formulas for computing confidence intervals for β_0 and for calculating the power of a test of β_0. Both of those formulas continue to hold in the present case when we have a predictor variable in the equation, so long as that predictor variable is in mean deviation form. To repeat those formulas, the confidence interval for β_0 is

$$b_0 \pm \sqrt{\frac{F_{1,n-2;\alpha}\text{MSE}}{n}}$$

where MSE results from the two-parameter model where both β_0 and β_1 are estimated. Actually, there is a change in this formula from the one given in Chapter 5. Here F has $n-2$ degrees of freedom for error, while the earlier one had only $n-1$. The difference is due to the fact that an additional parameter has been estimated with a predictor variable in the model. With a predictor in the equation that is reliably related to Y_i, MSE from this two-parameter model will be smaller than it is without the predictor, and hence the confidence interval for β_0 will be smaller. This is equivalent to saying that tests of β_0 will be more powerful when a reliably related predictor is included in the model, as we have just shown.

The above formula for the confidence interval holds only when the predictor variable is in mean deviation form. If it is not, the expression for the confidence interval of β_0 is only slightly more complicated:

$$b_0 \pm \sqrt{\frac{F_{1,n-2;\alpha}\text{MSE}(\Sigma\ X_i^2)}{n\ \Sigma\ (X_i - \overline{X})^2}}$$

This expression reduces to the earlier one when X_i is in mean deviation form, since then $\overline{X} = 0$ and hence $\Sigma\ X_i^2 = \Sigma\ (X_i - \overline{X})^2$.

The calculation of the power of a test of β_0 with a predictor variable in the model is also the same as it was in Chapter 5, assuming that X_i is in mean deviation form. When B_0 is the value for the intercept under the null hypothesis and β_0 is the correct value of the intercept under the alternative hypothesis, the power of the test to reject the null hypothesis can be calculated by deriving η^2 according to the formula

$$\eta^2 = \frac{n(B_0 - \beta_0)^2}{n\sigma^2 + n(B_0 - \beta_0)^2}$$

and then using the exhibit in Appendix C for converting η^2 to power. The only complication is that σ^2 must be estimated. As always, it is the variance of ε_i in the augmented model. In the case where that model only involved a single parameter and no predictor variables, as in Chapter 5, the variance of ε_i is equivalently the variance of Y_i. Therefore estimates of the variance of Y_i serve as σ^2 in calculating power. However, with a reliably related predictor variable in the model, the variance of ε_i will no longer be well estimated by the variance of Y_i. A reliable predictor results in a smaller sum of squared errors, and hence the variance of ε_i will generally be overestimated if one uses the variance of Y_i to estimate σ^2. In other words, in calculating the power of a test of β_0, no relative difference in power with and without the inclusion of a predictor variable will be noticed if one uses the variance of Y_i to estimate σ^2 in calculating η^2 in the two cases. The power advantage that comes from including a reliably related predictor variable results from the fact that the variance of ε_i is reduced when we include a reliable predictor variable, as compared with when we do not.

7.3

One Final Example Using SAS Output

By way of summary and to illustrate simple regression output from the SAS statistical computing package, we will examine some simple regression models, using the third grade mathematics test scores of Chapter 5 as the dependent variable. This time around, however, we are going to act as if we also had measured each child's mathematics performance at the end of the second grade. We will refer to the third grade performance as Y_i and the second grade performance as X_i, and we will regress Y_i on X_i. The raw data are given in Exhibit 7.4. (The values of Y_i are identical to those given in Chapter 5.)

EXHIBIT 7.4 ▶

Third and second grade mathematics test scores

Third Grade (Y_i)	Second Grade (X_i)
72	88
52	76
93	89
86	89
96	94
46	74
55	67
74	78
129	90
61	70
57	77
115	94
79	76
89	82
68	74

		Analysis of Variance			
Source	DF	Sum of Squares	Mean Square	F Value	Prob > F
Model	1	5085.89871	5085.89871	24.220	.0003
Error	13	2729.83462	209.98728		
C Total	14	7815.73333			
Root MSE		14.49094	R^2	.6507	
Dep Mean		78.13333	Adj R	.6239	

		Parameter Estimates			
Variable	DF	Parameter Estimate	Standard Error	t for H_0: Parameter = 0	Prob > |t|
Intercept	1	−97.5558	35.8947	−2.718	.0176
X	1	2.1637	.4396	4.921	.0003

EXHIBIT 7.5 ▲

SAS PROC REG output: simple regression of Y_i on X_i

The output presented in Exhibit 7.5 is generated by SAS when we regress Y_i on X_i for these 15 observations. (We encourage the reader to input the data contained in Exhibit 7.4 into whatever regression package he or she has access to and duplicate the regression output provided in Exhibit 7.5.)

There are two major parts to this output. The first section, labeled Analysis of Variance, consists of a source table, similar to the source table we presented in Exhibit 7.3, that provides the sums of squares, degrees of freedom, and mean squares used for comparing the augmented two-parameter model with a compact single-parameter one in which predictions of Y_i are not conditional on X_i. The row in this section of the output that is labeled Model gives the reduction in the sum of squared errors when we move from the compact to the augmented model. The degrees of freedom for the Model row equals the difference in the number of parameters estimated for the compact and augmented models. The Error row in this source table refers to residual sum of squared errors remaining given the augmented two-parameter model. The degrees of freedom for error equal 13, i.e., $n -$ PA. The row labeled C Total tells us the sum of squared errors and the error degrees of freedom for the compact single-parameter model.

Just below these three rows in this analysis of variance section of the output, the program provides the Root MSE, which is simply the square root of the mean square from the error row of the source table. In Chapter 6 we called this term the standard error of prediction. "Dep Mean" gives us the mean of the dependent variable. R^2 equals PRE for the comparison of the augmented model with the compact single-parameter one, and Adj R^2 equals the unbiased estimate of η^2, using the formula we have used in this chapter and earlier ones.

The next section of the output provides the parameter estimates and tests of the null hypotheses that each of these parameters equals zero. The Intercept row provides the estimate of β_0 and the t^* statistic that results when the null hypothesis is tested that β_0 equals zero. As defined in Chapter 5, this t^* statistic is simply the square root of the F^* that results if we compare this augmented two-parameter model with a compact single-degree-of-freedom one in which β_0 is forced to equal zero. Thus, we must square this t^* value (i.e., -2.718) to give us the F^*, with 1 and 13 degrees of freedom, that results from a comparison of the following two models:

MODEL C: $Y_i = \beta_1 X_i + \varepsilon_i$

MODEL A: $Y_i = \beta_0 + \beta_1 X_i + \varepsilon_i$

We are not told the PRE value that results from this comparison, but we can easily get it since we know that the F^* is a function of the degrees of freedom and PRE. If F^* is known, the formula for PRE is

$$PRE = \frac{F^*/(n - PA)}{F^*/(n - PA) + 1/(PA - PC)}$$

For the values at hand, given that F^* equals $(-2.718)^2$, PRE equals .362. This test is not very informative in the present case, since the intercept value, -97.5558, equals the predicted value on the third grade mathematics test of an individual who had a score of zero on the second grade test. Since none of the second grade scores were anywhere near zero, this predicted value, although reliably different from zero, is not informative.

The second row of this section of the output provides the β_1 parameter estimate, i.e., the regression coefficient associated with X_i. This slope value is 2.1637, indicating that as second grade performance increases by 1 unit, our best estimate from these data is that third grade performance will increase by 2.1637 units. Again we are given a t^* statistic for testing whether this parameter, β_1, equals zero. Squaring this t^*, we get an F^* value of 24.22, which converts to PRE, using the above formula, of .65. These values come from the comparison of the following two models:

MODEL C: $Y_i = \beta_0 + \varepsilon_i$

MODEL A: $Y_i = \beta_0 + \beta_1 X_i + \varepsilon_i$

Note that these values of PRE and F^* are the same as those given in the first section of the output, where the source table is provided.

When we get to models with more than just a single predictor variable, the source table provided in the first section of the output will always test the full augmented model, estimating parameters for all predictor variables, against the compact model in which β_0 is the only parameter. On the other hand, tests of individual coefficients in the second half of the output will result from comparing the full augmented model with a compact model in which *only that* particular parameter has been forced to equal zero. Since in this case there is only a single predictor, these tests are equivalent. With multiple predictor variables this will no longer be the case.

The only values in this output that we have not defined are the values referred to as the standard errors in the parameter estimates part of the output. If we take a particular parameter value and divide it by its standard error, the t^* statistic results for testing whether the parameter equals zero. If we also multiply this standard error value by the critical value of the t statistic, i.e., the square root of the critical value of F, then we get another expression for a parameter's confidence interval:

Confidence Interval for Parameter β_j

$$= b_j \pm (\text{Standard Error})t_{\text{crit}}$$

Substantively, we conclude from this analysis that there is a reliable positive relationship between third grade mathematics test performance and performance one year earlier. The resulting slope value is positive and reliably different from zero. The intercept also reliably differs from zero, although it does not have any meaning in the present context since the value of zero on X_i lies far outside of the range of data values on which the analysis is based.

In Chapter 5 we were interested in these data primarily to determine whether third grade mathematics performance differed reliably on average from 65, following the introduction of the new curriculum. To answer this question, we compared the augmented model

MODEL A: $\hat{Y}_i = 78.1$

with a sum of squared errors equal to 7815.7, to the compact model

MODEL C: $\hat{Y}_i = 65$

having a sum of squared errors of 10,403. The difference between these two sums of squares, i.e., the sum of squares reduced, equaled 2587.3. The resulting PRE equaled .25 with an associated F^*, having 1 and 14 degrees of freedom, of 4.64. Let us now use SAS to answer the same question, about whether third grade performance reliably differs on average from 65, but this time we will control for second grade performance.

Analysis of Variance					
Source	df	Sum of Squares	Mean Square	F Value	Prob > F
Model	1	5085.89871	5085.89871	24.220	.0003
Error	13	2729.83462	209.98728		
C Total	14	7815.73333			
Root MSE		14.49094	R^2	.6507	
Dep Mean		78.13333	Adj R^2	.6239	

Parameter Estimates					
Variable	df	Parameter Estimate	Standard Error	t for H_0: Parameter = 0	Prob > $\|t\|$
Intercept	1	78.1333	3.7415	20.883	.0001
X_{dev}	1	2.1637	.4396	4.921	.0003

Test: Intercept = 65
      Numerator: 2587.2667 df: 1 F value: 12.3211
      Denominator: 210.0 df: 13 Prob > F: .0038

EXHIBIT 7.6 ▲

SAS PROC REG output: simple regression of Y_i on X_{dev}

Recall that the intercept will equal $\overline{Y}$ if the predictor variable is transformed so that its mean equals zero. In other words, we need to transform X_i into mean deviation form, by subtracting the mean of X_i from each of the 15 individual X_i scores. Then when we regress Y_i on this transformed X_i, the intercept will equal $\overline{Y}$ and we can proceed to test whether the mean of Y_i differs reliably from 65. We use X_{dev} to refer to the transformed X_i. The SAS output in Exhibit 7.6 results when we use the SAS PROC REG procedure to regress Y_i on X_{dev}. We use the Test option in this SAS procedure to ask for a test of whether the intercept in the model reliably differs from 65.

Notice that the analysis of variance part of this output has not changed at all as a result of using X_{dev} as the predictor rather than X_i. This is as it should be, since the estimate of β_1 does not change as a function of the transformation of X_i. We still conclude that third grade performance is reliably related to second grade performance. The parameter estimate for the intercept has changed, as we expect it to. The intercept now equals 78.13, the value of $\overline{Y}$. A test of whether this mean reliably differs from zero yields a t^* statistic of 20.883 or a value of F^*, with 1 and 13 degrees of freedom, of 436.10.

The last lines of the exhibit present the results of the Test procedure, testing whether the intercept reliably differs from 65.[1] Here we are comparing the following two models:

MODEL C: $\hat{Y}_i = 65 + 2.16X_{dev}$

MODEL A: $\hat{Y}_i = 78.13 + 2.16X_{dev}$

Although the slope coefficient for X_{dev} is not printed for MODEL C, we have stated previously that when the predictor is transformed into mean deviation form, the value of b_1 will remain constant regardless of the a priori value given to the intercept. In the last two lines of the output, we are told that the numerator of the F^* comparing these two models equals 2587.3 with 1 degree of freedom. Accordingly, SSR for this comparison equals 2587.3. It is not surprising that SSR, as we move between MODEL C and MODEL A, equals exactly the same value as it did in Chapter 5, comparing MODELs that did not include X_{dev} as a predictor. Recall that

$$SSR = \sum (\hat{Y}_{iC} - \hat{Y}_{iA})^2$$
$$= \sum [(65 + 2.16X_{dev}) - (78.13 + 2.16X_{dev})]^2$$
$$= \sum (65 - 78.13)^2$$

The denominator of the F^* equals 210.0. This naturally is equal to the mean square error from MODEL A, i.e., the sum of squared errors for MODEL A divided by the degrees of freedom. The resulting value of F^*, with 1 and 13 degrees of freedom, equals 12.32. Notice that this value of F^* is considerably larger than F^* that resulted when we earlier asked if β_0 equaled 65 without including X_{dev} as a predictor in the model. This substantial increase in power results from the fact that the sum of squares for MODEL A is considerably smaller when X_{dev} is included in the model as a predictor when compared with the MODEL A used in Chapter 5 that had no predictor variables.

---

[1]While all statistical regression packages routinely provide tests that parameter values are equal to zero, to our knowledge very few allow the researcher to test null hypotheses that parameters equal other values. The TEST procedure in SAS is clearly an exception. If using another statistical package that does not have a comparable procedure, testing a null hypothesis that the intercept takes on a specific value other than zero can be accomplished by deviating the data variable Y_i from that value. In other words, in the present example, one would subtract 65 from each observation's value of Y_i and regress the resulting scores on the predictor. Following such a transformation, a test of whether the intercept equals zero will provide results identical to those provided by the SAS TEST option.

8

Multiple Regression: Models with Multiple Continuous Predictors

In the previous chapters we considered the simple model which makes the same prediction for all the observations in DATA and the simple regression model which makes predictions conditional on one other predictor variable. In this chapter we increase complexity still further by considering models which make predictions conditional on multiple predictor variables. For example, in our discussion of the automobile fatality rate data we suggested several plausible hypotheses about variables which might be predictive of fatality rates—winter driving conditions, population density, legal drinking age, and enforcement of the 55 mph speed limit. With the simple regression model we were limited to testing one predictor variable at a time. To test our different hypotheses using the simple regression model we would have to first test the model with one predictor, say, mean annual temperature, and then test another one-variable model with, say, population density as the predictor. It is obviously inefficient to test these simple models one at a time so it would be desirable to test more than one predictor simultaneously. More importantly, there is no reason why more than one of our hypothesized explanations of differential fatality rates might not be correct. That is, it may be necessary to make our predictions conditional on more than one predictor. For example, we might need to base our predictions on *both* population density and mean annual temperature simultaneously. The solution presented in this chapter is to use *multiple regression*.

Multiple regression is very similar to simple regression. There are, however, a few important differences. We begin by briefly considering these similarities and differences with respect to the model, the new problem of redundancy among the predictors, and statistical inference. Then we will consider an extended example designed to illustrate the interpretation of the parameters in the multiple regression model.

8.1

Multiple Regression MODEL

We want to consider MODELs of the form

$$Y_i = \beta_0 + \beta_1 X_{i1} + \beta_2 X_{i2} + \cdots + \beta_{p-1} X_{i,p-1} + \varepsilon_i \tag{8.1}$$

where as before Y_i represents an observation and ε_i represents the error disturbance. X_{ij} represents the value of the ith observation on the jth predictor variable and β_j is the *partial regression coefficient* representing the weight we should give to X_{ij} in making our predictions conditional on X_{ij}. In other words, the partial regression coefficients are the proportion of each observation's X_{ij} value by which we adjust our prediction $\hat{Y}_i$.

In the multiple regression model the coefficients are called *partial* regression coefficients because, as we shall see later, the value of, say, β_1 may well depend on whether, say, the predictor X_{i2} and its parameter β_2 are included in the model. To remind us that the meaning of β_j is conditional on the other predictor variables included in the equation, we sometimes use the notation $\beta_{j.123...p-1}$. The number before the dot in the subscript represents the variable with which the β is associated, and the numbers after the dot represent the other variables which are simultaneously included in the MODEL equation. But this notation is cumbersome, so we, and certainly most computer programs, more often just use β_j with the understanding that its meaning depends on the other parameters and predictors included in the model.

We often refer to the MODEL of Eq. 8.1 as the *multiple regression* or sometimes as the *general linear* model. *Linear* means that the separate components, after first being weighted by their respective β_j, are simply added together.

The general linear model is indeed very general and constitutes an extremely important tool for data analysis. As we shall see in subsequent chapters, even the "linear" part is not much of a restriction because many apparently nonlinear models can be represented in terms of Eq.

8.1 by a suitable choice of the predictor variables. It is also clear that the models of the previous chapters are simply special cases of the multiple regression model. In fact, a great many statistical procedures can be represented in terms of Eq. 8.1 with clever construction of the X_{ij} predictor variables. The following chapters are devoted to consideration of a number of interesting and very important special cases, such as analysis of variance, and a number of special problems in the context of this model, such as violation of the assumption that the ε_i error terms are independent. In this chapter, we present the basics of the general model—basics which we will use again and again.

Redundancy. The power and generality of the multiple regression model does not come without a cost; that cost is a definite increase in complexity and the introduction of some special problems that do not arise in the case of the simple models considered previously. One such problem is redundancy among the predictors. Suppose, for example, that we were attempting to predict the weights of a sample of elementary school children with two predictor variables: height measured in inches and height measured in centimeters. Our two predictor variables are obviously completely redundant—either would do as well as the other for predicting weight, and if we had already used one as a predictor there would clearly be no benefit to adding information from the other predictor.

Redundancy among the predictor variables is seldom so extreme as measuring height in inches and centimeters. A more typical example would be predicting the weights of the elementary school children using height and age as predictors. Height and age are obviously related—knowing a child's age we can make a reasonable guess as to his or her height—but they are not completely redundant, because our guess of height from age would not be perfect. This means that height and age will share in their ability to reduce error in the predictions of weight. If we first used height as a predictor, we would be improving our predictions (and reducing our error) in some of the same ways we would have had we first used age as a predictor. Sorting out the effects of predictor variables and their relative importance is clearly going to be difficult when there is redundancy among our predictors. In general, there is redundancy when it is possible to predict, at least somewhat, one or more of the X_{ij} with some combination of the other predictor variables. In our analysis of multiple regression models we will have to be alert for redundancy and very careful about the model interpretations we make in such cases. We will consider special techniques for doing so.

Statistical Inference. Although we will have more choices of models to compare and test with multiple predictor variables, the multiple regression model poses no new problems for statistical inference. For inference we use what has now become our standard operating procedure for dealing with any statistical model. We first fit our MODEL to the DATA by estimating parameters so as to minimize ERROR. Next we calculate PRE for our augmented model (MODEL A) relative to some suitably chosen compact model (MODEL C) defined by the null hypothesis which we wish to test. Then we calculate F^*, an index of how much PRE we get per extra parameter, and compare it with a critical value obtained from its sampling distribution under the null hypothesis to determine whether we should be surprised by the size of PRE. If the obtained values of PRE and F^* are surprising, then we reject MODEL C in favor of MODEL A. On the other hand, if the obtained values of PRE and F^* are not surprising, then we do not reject MODEL C. We consider, in turn, each of these steps for the multiple regression model, but only the details of estimating parameters are really new. The statistical inference process itself is the same as before.

8.2

Estimating Parameters in Multiple Regression

As in previous models, we want to find the least square estimators of $\beta_0, \beta_1, \ldots, \beta_{p-1}$ that will minimize SSE, the sum of squared errors. That is, we want to find estimates $b_0, b_1, \ldots, b_{p-1}$ in the estimated model

$$\hat{Y}_i = b_0 + b_1 X_{i1} + \cdots + b_{p-1} X_{i,p-1}$$

so that

$$SSE = \sum_{i=1}^{n} (Y_i - \hat{Y}_i)^2$$

is as small as possible. In that way we will ensure that the MODEL fits the DATA as closely as possible so as to make ERROR (as measured by SSE) as small as possible.

If there is no redundancy among the predictors, then the same procedures we used in Chapter 6 to estimate slopes in the simple regression model will produce the appropriate estimates for the parameters in the multiple regression model. That is,

$$b_j = \frac{\sum (X_{ij} - \overline{X}_j)(Y_i - \overline{Y})}{\sum (X_{ij} - \overline{X}_j)^2}$$

This formula applies whenever there is no redundancy among the predictors. To say there is no redundancy among the predictors is equivalent to saying that the correlation between every pair of predictors equals zero. Unless the predictor variables are especially constructed to meet this condition (as in experimental designs), at least some redundancy among the predictors will always be present. In the presence of redundancy, deriving the least squares parameter estimates is considerably more complicated. We can no longer use the procedures outlined in Chapter 6 and given by the above formula for b_j to estimate those parameters.

There exist well-defined algorithms for finding the unique least square estimates when there is redundancy among the predictors. However, these algorithms are extremely tedious on hand calculators for even just a few predictors and are, on the whole, neither very conceptual nor helpful in aiding our understanding of multiple regression. We therefore will leave all the calculation of parameter estimates to the computer. All the standard computer statistical packages have multiple regression procedures which can estimate the parameters of any of the models we consider in this book. Many good multiple regression programs are also now available for personal computers.

Before turning over all of our calculations to the computer, however, it is important that we have a firm understanding of the underlying concepts. For the simple single-parameter model we found the single value b_0—a point, geometrically—that minimized SSE. For simple regression we found two values b_0 and b_1 which defined a line; b_0 is the intercept of that line, and b_1 is its slope. For a multiple regression model with two predictors the three estimates b_0, b_1, and b_2 define a plane, as depicted in Exhibit 8.1. The two predictor variables define two of the axes in the three-dimensional space (the two horizontal ones), and the data variable provides the vertical one. Error is represented geometrically as the vertical distance between each observation and the plane that represents the model.

In simple regression we conceptually moved the line around, changing its slope and its intercept, until we found the position of the line which minimized total error. Similarly, for the multiple regression model we move the plane around until we find that location which minimizes total error. (Actually we want to minimize squared error, but we have not complicated the picture in Exhibit 8.1 by adding the appropriate squares; conceptually the idea is the same.) The intersection of the plane with the Y axis defines b_0, the slope of the plane with respect to X_{i1} defines b_1 and the slope with respect to X_{i2} defines b_2. Conceptually the complicated computer algorithms simply find the location of the plane which minimizes the sum of squared errors, where an error is defined as the vertical distance from each observation to the model plane. For more than two predictors the model is equivalent to a hyperplane in spaces with four or more dimensions. Although it is impossible to draw

EXHIBIT 8.1 ▶

Fitting a plane with two predictor variables

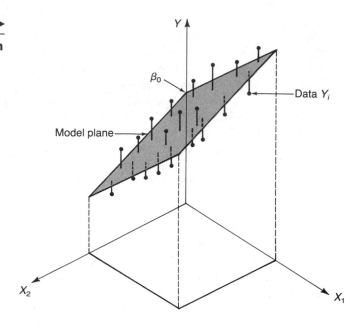

a picture of such hyperplanes, the concept is exactly the same. The best location for the hyperplane minimizes the sum of squared errors, and the hyperplane's intercept and slopes define the parameter estimates.

8.3

Statistical Inference in Multiple Regression

The general strategy for doing statistical inference or asking questions about DATA is exactly the same as before. In particular, the calculation of PRE and F^* poses no new problems. As before,

$$PRE = \frac{SSE(C) - SSE(A)}{SSE(C)} = 1 - \frac{SSE(A)}{SSE(C)}$$

and

$$F^*_{PA-PC,\,n-PA} = \frac{PRE/(PA - PC)}{(1 - PRE)/(n - PA)}$$

where MODEL A and MODEL C are suitably chosen and PA and PC represent the number of parameters, respectively, in the two models.

The only change is that the extra parameters in Eq. 8.1 give us lots of freedom in defining MODEL A and MODEL C. As we shall see, different choices allow us to ask different questions and test different hypotheses. The only difficulty then is selecting the appropriate compact and augmented models to test a specific hypothesis. Once we have the appropriate models, estimation of the parameters (using the computer statistical packages) and calculation of PRE and F* are straightforward. Each question will have its own PRE and F*.

For any set of DATA there will be many possible questions. There are several generic types of questions that occur frequently in multiple regression models. We consider each generic type separately.

8.3.1 Testing an Overall Model

Sometimes we want to ask whether our predictors as a group are any better than the simple model which uses no predictors but predicts the mean for every observation. For example, college admissions offices have the practical and interesting question of whether student information such as high school percentile rank and Scholastic Aptitude Tests (SAT), both verbal and quantitative, predict performance in college. To answer that question, we could compare a model that made predictions of first-year cumulative grade point average conditional on high school rank, SAT verbal, and SAT quantitative to a simple model that made a single unconditional prediction of grade point average using the mean. In general, we are comparing the following MODELs C and A:

MODEL C: $Y_i = \beta_0 + \varepsilon_i$

MODEL A: $Y_i = \beta_0 + \beta_1 X_{i1} + \beta_2 X_{i2} + \cdots + \beta_{p-1} X_{i,p-1} + \varepsilon_i$

To be a test of the overall model, MODEL C must be the simple model with only one parameter. The null hypothesis being tested—that MODEL C is sufficient—is equivalent to saying that it does no good to make the predictions conditional on *all* of the $p - 1$ predictor variables. Formally,

H_0: $\beta_1 = \beta_2 = \cdots = \beta_{p-1} = 0$

MODEL C has 1 parameter and MODEL A has p parameters (one for each of the $p - 1$ predictors plus one parameter for the constant β_0). The appropriate sums of squared errors are given by

$$\text{SSE(C)} = \sum (Y_i - \overline{Y})^2 \quad \text{and} \quad \text{SSE(A)} = \sum (Y_i - \hat{Y}_i)^2$$

where

$$\hat{Y}_i = b_0 + b_1 X_{i1} + b_2 X_{i2} + \cdots + b_{p-1} X_{i,p-1}$$

To remind us of precisely which variables are included in the model for which we have minimized the error, we will use the additional notation

$$\text{SSE(C)} = \text{SSE}(X_0) \quad \text{and} \quad \text{SSE(A)} = \text{SSE}(X_0, X_1, \ldots, X_{p-1})$$

where X_0 is a "variable" consisting of the value 1 for all observations; it is a placeholder to remind us that β_0 has been included in the model. $X_1, \ldots, X_{p-1}$ are the $p - 1$ predictor variables. Then

$$\text{PRE} = 1 - \frac{\text{SSE(A)}}{\text{SSE(C)}}$$

or, equivalently,

$$\text{PRE} = 1 - \frac{\text{SSE}(X_0, X_1, \ldots, X_{p-1})}{\text{SSE}(X_0)} \tag{8.2}$$

The PRE of Eq. 8.2 testing the overall model relative to the simple mean model has the special name of "coefficient of multiple determination" and is usually represented by the symbol R^2. All multiple regression computer programs which estimate the parameters will also provide R^2 directly so it is seldom necessary to calculate PRE by hand for the overall model. However, it is exceedingly important to remember that R^2 is nothing more than PRE for this special case of testing an overall model against the simple mean model. Also, for many questions we will want to ask about our models, the computer programs will *not* provide the relevant PRE, so it is important to know how to calculate it directly from SSE(A) and SSE(C).

The calculation of F^* for this case is straightforward once $\text{PRE} = R^2$ is known; that is,

$$F^* = \frac{\text{PRE}/(\text{PA} - \text{PC})}{(1 - \text{PRE})/(n - \text{PA})} = \frac{R^2/(p - 1)}{(1 - R^2)/(n - p)} \tag{8.3}$$

If we make the normal assumptions that the errors ε_i have mean zero, are normally distributed, and are independent, then we can compare F^* to the sampling distribution for the F statistic with $p - 1$ and $n - p$ degrees of freedom. Most computer programs which report R^2 will also report F^*. Many will also report the "significance of F," which is simply the probability that if the null hypothesis were true a value of F^* this big or bigger would be found. If this probability is lower than our desired level for α, the Type I error probability, then we can reject H_0 that none of the predictors are useful.

The probability tables for PRE and F^* that we developed in Chapter 5 are for the special case when the number of parameters in MODELs A and C differed by exactly one (i.e., PA − PC = 1). Eq. 8.3 allows for MODEL A having many more parameters than the simple mean model which serves as MODEL C. We therefore need new tables. The logic of developing these tables is exactly the same as for the tables developed in Chapter 5. Appendix C Exhibits C.2 and C.4 give the critical values for PRE and F^*, respectively, for $\alpha = .05$ for selected values of PA $-$ PC.

The ANOVA Exhibit. Many computer packages report the results of the regression analysis in terms of an analysis of variance (ANOVA) table like the ones we used in Chapters 5 and 7. For that reason it is useful to consider the ANOVA representation for the test of the relatively straightforward overall model. The ANOVA table will also be very useful because it will help us sort our way through more complex models, and because it often will be the only means for obtaining SSE(A) for models we might want to test but for which the computer programs do not provide the necessary PRE and F^*. The analysis, or decomposition, of the variance of our DATA rests upon the following equation relating sums of squares:

$$\sum_{i=1}^{n} (Y_i - \hat{Y}_{iC})^2 = \sum_{i=1}^{n} (\hat{Y}_{iA} - \hat{Y}_{iC})^2 + \sum_{i=1}^{n} (Y_i - \hat{Y}_{iA})^2$$

$$\sum_{i=1}^{n} (Y_i - \overline{Y})^2 = \sum_{i=1}^{n} (\hat{Y}_i - \overline{Y})^2 + \sum_{i=1}^{n} (Y_i - \hat{Y}_i)^2 \qquad (8.4)$$

$$\text{SST} \quad = \quad \text{SSR} \quad + \quad \text{SSE}$$

In our terms, SST is simply SSE(C), where C is the simple model and SSE is SSE(A) for our augmented model with $p - 1$ predictors. SSR (sum of squares due to regression) is thus the amount of the original error measured by SSE(C) which can be removed by using the $p - 1$ predictors. Equivalently it equals the difference between SSE(C) and SSE(A). Using our extended notation for SSE, we therefore have

$$\text{SSE}(X_0) = \text{SST} = \text{SSR} + \text{SSE}(X_0, X_1, \ldots, X_{p-1})$$

The difference in the predictor variables between the two models is responsible for the reduction in squared error which equals SSR. To remind us of which variables are doing the work, we will sometimes write SSR as $\text{SSR}(X_1, X_2, \ldots, X_{p-1})$, so the complete equation for decomposing the variance is

$$\text{SSE}(X_0) = \text{SST} = \text{SSR}(X_1, \ldots, X_{p-1}) + \text{SSE}(X_0, X_1, \ldots, X_{p-1})$$

Later we will generalize this equation to more complicated situations.

Exhibit 8.2 depicts the generic ANOVA table for testing the overall regression model of Eq. 8.1. The source column identifies each row of the table. The respective sums of squares (SSR, SSE, and SST) are in the SS column, and the associated degrees of freedom (either the extra parameters associated with that row or the number of remaining parameters) are in the df column. Note that the first two rows in the SS and

EXHIBIT 8.2

Generic ANOVA layout

Source	SS	df	MS	F*	PRE
Reduce, Model A	SSR	PA − PC	$MSR = \dfrac{SSR}{PA - PC}$	$\dfrac{MSR}{MSE}$	$\dfrac{SSR}{SST}$
Error for Model A	SSE	n − PA	$MSE = \dfrac{SSE}{n - PA}$		
Total	SST	n − PC			

df columns sum to produce the values in the row for Total. This simply reflects the relationship in Eq. 8.4 that SST = SSR + SSE. MS represents "mean square," which is simply the appropriate SS divided by its degrees of freedom. MSR is the mean square for regression, and MSE is the mean squared error. A little algebra (substituting the definition of PRE into the formula for F^*) reveals the following equivalent definition of F^*, which is handy when results are presented in terms of an ANOVA table.

$$F^* = \frac{PRE/(PA - PC)}{(1 - PRE)/(n - PA)} = \frac{[SSE(C) - SSE(A)]/(PA - PC)}{SSE(A)/(n - PA)}$$

In this case, SSE(C) = SST, SSE(A) = SSE, SSE(C) − SSE(A) = SST − SSE = SSR, PA − PC = $p - 1$, and $n - PA = n - p$, so

$$F^* = \frac{SSR/(p - 1)}{SSE/(n - p)} = \frac{MSR}{MSE}$$

Thus, we can compute F^* in the last column of Exhibit 8.2 as simply the ratio of the two values in the MS column. The degrees of freedom associated with that F^* are given by the values in the df column. PRE, in the last column of Exhibit 8.2, is obtained from the equation

$$PRE = R^2 = \frac{SSE(C) - SSE(A)}{SSE(C)} = \frac{SST - SSE}{SST} = \frac{SSR}{SST}$$

In other words, dividing the sum of squares for regression in the first row by the total sum of squares in the last row gives PRE or R^2 in this case.

An Example of an Overall Model Test. An example will help make all the above formulas and generic tables less abstract. For college admissions offices, a practical and interesting question is whether student information such as high school percentile rank and Scholastic Aptitude Tests (SAT), both verbal and quantitative, predict performance in college. In this example, we have the first-year cumulative grade point average

(GPA), high school rank (HSRANK), SAT verbal (SATV), and SAT math (SATM) scores for 414 students. The question we want to ask is whether we can use those variables to make conditional predictions of each student's GPA or whether we would do just as well if we simply used the group mean as an unconditional prediction of everyone's GPA. In other words, does MODEL A, which uses all the predictor variables, do better than MODEL C, which uses none of the predictors? In terms of equations we are comparing

MODEL C: $GPA_i = \beta_0 + \varepsilon_i$

MODEL A: $GPA_i = \beta_0 + \beta_1 HSRANK_i + \beta_2 SATV_i + \beta_3 SATM_i + \varepsilon_i$

For this comparison, PA = 4 and PC = 1. MODEL A and MODEL C would be the same if β_1, β_2, and β_3 all equal zero. Thus, comparing MODELs C and A is equivalent to testing the null hypothesis

H_0: $\beta_1 = \beta_2 = \beta_3 = 0$.

Exhibit 8.3 displays part of the output from the SAS multiple regression procedure (PROC REG) for a test of an overall multiple regression model in which cumulative grade point average in college for a sample of 414 students is predicted by high school percentile rank, SAT verbal, and SAT math test scores. Note that this output is very similar to the outputs for simple regression in Exhibits 7.5 and 7.6; the only difference is additional information about each individual predictor variable. It is so important to understand this output that we first review the common aspects between the multiple regression output in Exhibit 8.3 and the simple regression output in Exhibit 7.5; then we consider the additional information that is only relevant for multiple regression.

Most standard computer programs that perform multiple regression analyses (such as SAS, BMDP, SPSSX, SCSS, and MINITAB) produce an ANOVA table similar to the one displayed in Exhibit 8.3. Some of these programs perversely omit the row for TOTAL, but it is easily calculated as the sums of the DF and SUM OF SQUARES (or SS) columns. Exhibit 8.3 has the same generic structure as Exhibit 8.2. So, for example, SSR = 48.78949 and MSR = SSR/$(p - 1)$ = 48.78949/3 = 16.26316. F^* equals the ratio of the two MEAN SQUAREs, in this case 16.26316/0.421936 = 38.544.

The value of .0001 for PROB > F in Exhibit 8.3 means that if the simple, compact model were adequate and if our standard assumptions about normality and independence of the error terms are appropriate, then we would expect to find a value of F^* this large or larger 1 time out of 10,000 (1/10,000 = .0001). Thus, we would clearly reject the null hypothesis that $\beta_1 = \beta_2 = \beta_3 = 0$. Note that while there is no doubt about rejecting H_0, PRE = R-SQUARE = .2200 is not all that big. With

DEP VARIABLE: GPA   freshman grade pt average

ANALYSIS OF VARIANCE

SOURCE	DF	SUM OF SQUARES	MEAN SQUARE	F VALUE	PROB > F
MODEL	3	48.78949	16.26316	38.544	.0001
ERROR	410	172.9938	.421936		
C TOTAL	413	221.7833			

ROOT MSE	.649566	R-SQUARE	.2200
DEP MEAN	2.699203	ADJ R-SQ	.2143
C.V.	24.06511		

PARAMETER ESTIMATES

VARIABLE	DF	PARAMETER ESTIMATE	STANDARD ERROR	T FOR H0: PARAMETER = 0	PROB > |T|
INTERCEP	1	−1.739	.4237053	−4.104	.0001
HSRANK	1	.02681512	.003222922	8.320	.0001
SATV	1	.0113693	.00442991	2.566	.0106
SATM	1	.02234704	.004983883	4.484	.0001

VARIABLE	DF	PARTIAL CORR TYPE II	TOLERANCE	
INTERCEP	1	.	.	INTERCEPT
HSRANK	1	.1444511	.994517	high school percentile
SATV	1	.01581147	.8926182	SAT-Verbal score
SATM	1	.04674444	.8900306	SAT-Math score

EXHIBIT 8.3   ▲

Output from SAS PROC REG (multiple regression) for predicting GPA with high school rank and SAT scores

three predictors that should be related to college performance, we are able to reduce the error relative to guessing the mean for every observation by only 22%.

When considering more complex models or hypotheses, the important number to be able to locate in computer output such as Exhibit 8.3 is the SUM OF SQUARES for ERROR in the ANOVA table because that value is equal to SSE for whatever MODEL has been estimated. In this case, SSE = 172.9938. Once we know the SSEs for appropriate MODELs, calculating PRE and F^* will be easy.

Most computer programs also provide other useful information. SAS, as do many programs, gives ADJ R-SQ (for "adjusted R-square"), which is simply the original R^2 or PRE adjusted to give an unbiased estimate of η^2.

$$\eta^2 = \text{ADJ R-SQ} = 1 - (1 - \text{PRE})\left[\frac{n - PC}{n - PA}\right]$$

$$= 1 - (1 - .2200)\left(\frac{414 - 1}{414 - 4}\right)$$

$$= 1 - (.78)(1.0073) = 1 - .7857 = .2143$$

Also useful is the ROOT MSE, which is simply the square root of the value in the MEAN SQUARE column in the ERROR row. In this case, ROOT MSE $= \sqrt{\text{MSE}} = \sqrt{.421936} = .649566$. Remember from Chapter 2 that ROOT MSE is given by

$$\sqrt{\frac{\sum_{i=1}^{n}(Y_i - \hat{Y}_i)^2}{n - PA}}$$

and provides an estimate of σ, the standard deviation of the distribution of ε's. Thus, the ROOT MSE may be thought of as the "standard" or "typical" error when using MODEL A to predict the DATA. SAS also gives the value of DEP MEAN, which is the mean of the dependent variable. So, in this case, the mean first-year cumulative GPA is 2.699203. Note that this is b_0, the estimate of β_0, for MODEL C.

Any regression program, even those that do not provide the ANOVA table, will give the parameter estimates for MODEL A. In this case the intercept $b_0 = -1.739$, $b_1 = .0268$, $b_2 = .0113$, and $b_3 = .0223$. SAS, as do many other programs, also provides some other information about each parameter estimate that we will discuss later. We now have all the information necessary to specify the two prediction equations. Rounding, they are

MODEL C: $\widehat{\text{GPA}}_i = 2.70$

MODEL A: $\widehat{\text{GPA}}_i = -1.74 + .027\text{HSRANK}_i + .011\text{SATV}_i$

$\qquad\qquad\qquad + .022\text{SATM}_i$

The results of the hypothesis test imply that MODEL A provides statistically significantly better predictions of the DATA than does MODEL C. By basing predictions of GPA on HSRANK, SATV, and SATM, we reduce error in these DATA by 22%. Thus, it is useful to make conditional predictions of GPA by using all three predictor variables.

Problems with Overall Model Tests. On the whole, overall model tests such as this one are not particularly useful for two reasons. First, it is easy when testing a large overall model to be in the position of losing a needle in a haystack. For example, suppose we were testing a large model in which only one predictor was any good; the other predictors have all been added inadvertently and they are of no value in reducing ERROR. We would get approximately the same value of PRE for this example whether we were testing the overall model or the simple regression model in which we used only the one good predictor. However, PRE per parameter (the numerator of F^*) would be much reduced for the overall model because we would be dividing approximately the same PRE by a larger number of extra, unnecessary parameters. Simultaneously, the remaining error $(1 - \text{PRE})$ per unused potential parameter (the denominator of F^*) would be larger for the overall model with the extra useless predictors because we would be dividing approximately the same residual error by a smaller number of potential unused parameters ($n - p$ instead of $n - 2$). Both of these effects will cause F^* to be considerably smaller than it otherwise would have been without the extra useless predictors. From Exhibit C.3 in Appendix C, we see that the value of the critical value of F decreases as the numerator degrees of freedom increase, so F^* may sometimes still be significant. However, in general, we risk losing the needle—the one good predictor—in a haystack of useless predictors. The essence of the problem is that by throwing away parameters for useless predictors we lose statistical power.

A second reason for avoiding overall tests of models is that the results are often ambiguous. If the null hypothesis is rejected, then we only know that at least one of the partial regression coefficients is not equal to zero, but we don't know which predictor or predictors are useful. For example, for the GPA data we concluded that β_1, β_2, and β_3 are not *all* equal to zero, but we do not know precisely which ones are not equal to zero. There are seven different ways in which the overall null hypothesis could be false:

1. $\beta_1 \neq 0, \beta_2 \neq 0, \beta_3 \neq 0$
2. $\beta_1 \neq 0, \beta_2 \neq 0$
3. $\beta_1 \neq 0, \beta_3 \neq 0$
4. $\beta_2 \neq 0, \beta_3 \neq 0$
5. $\beta_1 \neq 0$
6. $\beta_2 \neq 0$
7. $\beta_3 \neq 0$

That is, HSRANK, SATV, and SATM *as a group* are useful predictors of GPA, but we do not know whether all are needed or what combination is best. For instance, maybe SATV and SATM are redundant, so only one SAT score needs to be included in the regression equation.

The question we ask with the test of the overall model is so diffuse that we are generally unsure what the answer means. For the reasons of power and removing ambiguity discussed above, it is almost always better to ask more specific or, in the words of Rosenthal and Rosnow (1985), more *focused* questions of our data. Focused questions will generally ask about a single predictor. That does not mean that we will ignore all the other predictors, because, as we shall soon see, we can ask about the usefulness of a particular predictor in the context of all the other predictors.

So for reasons of statistical power and specificity, we prefer null hypotheses which pertain to a single parameter, i.e., where PA and PC differ by 1. The F^* for testing such null hypotheses will always have one degree of freedom in the numerator. If the compact model representing the null hypothesis is rejected, then the answer is unambiguous—the extra parameter in MODEL A is required. Next we consider an important one-degree-of-freedom test.

8.3.2 Testing the Addition of One More Predictor

It is usually best to start with a simple MODEL for our DATA and to make it more complex by adding more parameters only when necessary. The general question we want to ask is, therefore, "If we already have $p - 1$ predictors in our model, is it worthwhile to add one more?" In this case,

$$\text{MODEL C:}\quad Y_i = \beta_0 + \beta_1 X_{i1} + \beta_2 X_{i2} + \cdots + \beta_{p-1} X_{i,p-1} + \varepsilon_i \tag{8.5}$$

$$\text{MODEL A:}\quad Y_i = \beta_0 + \beta_1 X_{i1} + \beta_2 X_{i2} + \cdots + \beta_{p-1} X_{i,p-1} + \beta_{ip} X_{ip} + \varepsilon_i$$

That is, MODEL C and MODEL A are the same except that MODEL A has been augmented by exactly one extra parameter (β_p) and predictor variable (X_p). Thus, MODEL C has p parameters, and MODEL A has $p + 1$ parameters.

By comparing MODEL A with MODEL C, we are asking whether we need the predictor X_{ip} *given* that we are already using predictors X_1, X_2, . . . , X_{p-1}. The β's in Eq. 8.5 are partial regression coefficients in that their values depend on what other β's are included in the MODEL. That is, the estimated value of, say, β_2 is likely to depend on whether or not β_1 is included in the model. Thus, we should use the more complete notation that reminds us of this dependence. In particular, the extra coefficient added to MODEL A is represented by $\beta_{p.12\ldots p-1}$. The subscript before the dot indicates the particular coefficient, and the subscripts after the dot indicate the other coefficients also included in the MODEL. Clearly, we don't need the extra predictor if its partial regression coefficient equals zero, so our null hypothesis is

$$H_0: \quad \beta_{p.12\ldots p-1} = 0$$

Note that this is merely a generalization of the test that we did for the simple regression model with one predictor. If $p = 1$, then MODEL C has $p = 1$ parameters, so it is the simple model, while MODEL A has $p + 1 = 2$ parameters, so it is the simple regression model with one predictor variable.

One strategy for model building is to start simple and add complexity only when necessary. Thus, a frequent question is whether the addition of another predictor would be worthwhile. As always, we answer the question about whether the extra parameter is worthwhile by calculating PRE and F^*. To do that, we need the sum of squared errors for each model:

$$\text{SSE(C)} = \text{SSE}(X_0, X_1, \ldots, X_{p-1}) = \sum_{i=1}^{n} (Y_i - \hat{Y}_{iC})^2$$

$$\text{SSE(A)} = \text{SSE}(X_0, X_1, \ldots, X_{p-1}, X_p) = \sum_{i=1}^{n} (Y_i - \hat{Y}_{iA})^2$$

The difference between these two SSEs is the "extra sum of squares" or ERROR that is removed by adding X_p to the model. To remind us that this sum of squares is extra, relative to the other variables already in the model, we use the notation

$$\text{SSR}(X_p \mid X_0, X_1, \ldots, X_{p-1}) = \text{SSE}(X_0, X_1, \ldots, X_{p-1})$$
$$- \text{SSE}(X_0, X_1, \ldots, X_{p-1}, X_p)$$

This SSR is read as "the sum of squares regression due to X_p *given* that $X_0, X_1, \ldots, X_{p-1}$ are already in the model." Once we know the SSEs for the two models, it is easy to calculate PRE using the usual formula. That is,

$$\text{PRE} = \frac{\text{SSE(C)} - \text{SSE(A)}}{\text{SSE(C)}} = \frac{\text{SSR}}{\text{SSE(C)}}$$

This PRE for the addition of exactly one parameter has the special name of "coefficient of partial determination" and is often represented by $r^2_{Yp.123\ldots p-1}$. The square root of this special PRE is usually called the "partial correlation coefficient" because it is the simple correlation between Y and X_p when the effects of the other $p - 1$ predictors have been removed from *both* Y and X_p.

Once we have PRE (or the coefficient of partial determination in this case), it is simple to use the standard formula for calculating F^*. That is,

$$F^* = \frac{\text{PRE}/(\text{PA} - \text{PC})}{(1 - \text{PRE})/(n - \text{PA})} = \frac{\text{PRE}}{(1 - \text{PRE})/(n - p - 1)}$$

The second equation follows because the difference in the number of parameters between the compact and augmented models in this case is 1 (hence the name "one-degree-of-freedom test"), and the total number of parameters in the augmented model is now $p + 1$. In terms of sums of squares, this F^* can be equivalently expressed as

$$F^* = \frac{\text{SSR}(X_p \mid X_0, X_1, \ldots, X_{p-1})}{\text{SSE}(X_0, X_1, \ldots, X_{p-1}, X_p)/(n - p - 1)}$$

Given F^*, we can compute a confidence interval for $\beta_{p.12\ldots p-1}$ using the same logic we used to construct a confidence interval for β_1 in the case of simple regression in Chapter 7. That is, for a specific set of data we can ask how extreme a null hypothesis could be so that F^* would still be less than the critical value of F for some α under the usual assumptions. The resulting equation is

$$b_{p.12\ldots p-1} \pm \sqrt{\frac{(F_{\text{crit}})(\text{MSE})}{\Sigma (X_{ip} - \overline{X}_p)^2(1 - R^2_p)}} \tag{8.6}$$

MSE is the mean squared error for the MODEL, and F_{crit} is the appropriate value of F obtained from Exhibit C.2 in Appendix C for degrees of freedom PA − PC = 1, n − PA, and the desired level of α. For whatever level of α is chosen, Eq. 8.6 gives the $(1 - \alpha)\%$ confidence interval. Eq. 8.6 is exactly the same formula for the confidence interval that was developed in Chapter 7 for simple regression except for the addition of the term $1 - R^2_p$ in the denominator. R^2_p is simply the R^2 or PRE obtained when all the other $p - 1$ predictors are used to predict X_p. Thus, R^2_p is a measure of the redundancy of X_p with the predictors already included in the model.

Conversely, the term $1 - R^2_p$, which has the special name of *tolerance* in some computer outputs, is a measure of X_p's uniqueness from the other predictors. Only the unique part of X_p does any good in reducing the error further; if the tolerance $1 - R^2_p$ is low, then it will be diffcult for X_p to be useful. This is reflected in the formula for the confidence interval by including it in the denominator. A low tolerance in the denominator will cause the confidence interval to be large, and a large confidence interval will be more likely to include zero. Because a low tolerance makes the confidence interval wider, some programs report the *variance inflation factor (VIF)*, which equals $1/(1 - R^2_p)$, the inverse of tolerance.

There is an exact equivalence between using F^*, compared with a critical value of F for a certain α, to test the addition of a parameter and seeing whether or not the confidence interval constructed using that same critical value of F includes zero. The confidence interval excludes zero if and only if F^* exceeds the critical F.

It is seldom necessary to calculate by hand the F^* for the addition of a parameter because most regression programs will routinely produce F^* (or sometimes the equivalent $t^* = \sqrt{F^*}$). Many programs will also give the 95% confidence interval (corresponding to $\alpha = .05$) for $\beta_{p.12\ldots p-1}$. Very few programs will directly give the corresponding PRE, which in this case is the proportional reduction in error due to adding the pth predictor. However, almost all programs will give the partial correlation coefficient, which for this model can be squared to yield PRE. The important things to remember therefore are not the calculational formulas but that the coefficient of partial determination or, equivalently, the squared partial correlation, is simply PRE for the special case of comparing a compact model with an augmented model which has one extra predictor. Similarly, the associated F^* or t^* tests whether the partial regression coefficient for X_{ip} is zero. Thus, the following are equivalent null hypotheses:

$$H_0: \quad \beta_{p.12\ldots p-1} = 0 \qquad \text{and} \qquad H_0: \quad r^2_{Yp.123\ldots p-1} = 0$$

If one is false, then the other must be false also.

We will use the GPA data analyzed previously to illustrate the use of the conceptual formulas for calculating PRE and F^* from the SSEs obtained by estimating two separate models—MODEL A, which includes the extra parameter, and MODEL C, which does not. Then, we show how those values can be obtained from the computer output for just MODEL A, so the extra step of estimating MODEL C is usually not necessary. However, it is important to understand that conceptually the process is equivalent to estimating the two MODELs separately, so we begin there.

Suppose that we want to ask whether it is useful to add SATM to the MODEL when HSRANK and SATV are already in the MODEL. This question not only has practical importance—it would be easier for the clerks in the admissions office if they only had to include HSRANK and SATV in their calculations of predicted GPA—but it also is substantively interesting to know whether quantitative skills as measured by SATM make a contribution to GPA that is independent of HSRANK and SATV. These particular data are for engineering students, so one would suppose that SATM as a measure of quantitative skills that engineers would need in their courses would be required even when HSRANK and SATV as measures of overall ability were already included in a MODEL. In other words, we want to compare these two MODELs:

MODEL C: $\quad \text{GPA}_i = \beta_0 + \beta_1\text{HSRANK}_i + \beta_2\text{SATV}_i + \varepsilon_i$

MODEL A: $\quad \text{GPA}_i = \beta_0 + \beta_1\text{HSRANK}_i + \beta_2\text{SATV}_i + \beta_3\text{SATM}_i + \varepsilon_i$

Note that PA = 4 and PC = 3, so PA − PC = 1; we therefore are asking a focused, one-degree-of-freedom question. MODEL A and MODEL C

DEP VARIABLE: GPA   freshman grade pt average

ANALYSIS OF VARIANCE

SOURCE	DF	SUM OF SQUARES	MEAN SQUARE	F VALUE	PROB > F
MODEL	2	40.30646	20.15323	45.642	.0001
ERROR	411	181.4768	.4415494		
C TOTAL	413	221.7833			

ROOT MSE		.6644918	R-SQUARE		.1817
DEP MEAN		2.699203	ADJ R-SQ		.1778
C.V.		24.61808			

PARAMETER ESTIMATES

VARIABLE	DF	PARAMETER ESTIMATE	STANDARD ERROR	T FOR H0: PARAMETER = 0	PROB > |T|
INTERCEP	1	−.71499	.365091	−1.958	.0509
HSRANK	1	.02766411	.003291284	8.405	.0001
SATV	1	.01782277	.004285853	4.159	.0001

EXHIBIT 8.4 ▲

Output from SAS PROC REG (multiple regression) for predicting GPA with high school rank and SAT (verbal only)

would be the same if β_3 equaled zero. Thus, comparing MODELs C and A is equivalent to testing the null hypothesis

H_0: $\beta_3 = 0$

MODEL A here is the same as the MODEL A we used when testing the overall model. Thus, we already have SSE and the parameter estimates for MODEL A from the SAS computer output in Exhibit 8.3; in particular, SSE(A) = 172.9938. To complete the analysis, we need only ask SAS to fit MODEL C. Exhibit 8.4 displays part of the output from the SAS multiple regression procedure (PROC REG) for the model of GPA that only includes HSRANK and SATV. Here the parameter estimates are for MODEL C. We now have all the information necessary to specify the two prediction equations. Rounded, they are

MODEL C: $\widehat{GPA}_i = -0.71 + .028 HSRANK_i + .018 SATV_i$

MODEL A: $\widehat{GPA}_i = -1.74 + .027 HSRANK_i + .011 SATV_i$

$+ .022 SATM_i$

Note that the coefficients for HSRANK and SATV are similar but not identical in the two models and that the values of b_0, the intercepts, differ substantially. The differences reflect that these are partial regression coefficients whose values depend on what other parameters and predictor variables are included in the model.

For determining whether SATM is also necessary, the important number in Exhibit 8.4 is the SUM OF SQUARES in the ERROR row of the ANOVA table because that is SSE for MODEL C. Thus, SSE(C) = 181.4768. To answer the question of whether SATM is also necessary, we compute PRE and F^* in the usual way. That is,

$$PRE = \frac{SSE(C) - SSE(A)}{SSE(C)} = \frac{181.4768 - 172.9938}{181.4768} = .0467$$

and

$$F^* = \frac{PRE/(PA - PC)}{(1 - PRE)/(n - PA)} = \frac{.0467/(4 - 3)}{(1 - .0467)/(414 - 4)} = \frac{.0467}{.002325} = 20.1$$

The obtained F^* greatly exceeds the critical value for $F_{1,410;.05} = 3.9$. We therefore can reject the null hypothesis that the partial regression coefficient for SATM is zero, and we can conclude that it is worthwhile to add SATM to the model that already includes HSRANK and SATV. In this case, the remaining error—the error left after using HSRANK and SATV in the MODEL—is reduced by 4.7%.

Although we shall see that it is usually not necessary, the strategy of doing separate regressions for MODEL C and MODEL A and then computing PRE and F^* by hand always works and is a useful strategy to remember for more complicated models. It also is what is being done conceptually even when other means are used for the calculations.

To compute a confidence interval for β_3, we need all the components of Equation 8.6. MSE = 0.421936 and $b_3 = 0.0223$ are available from the regression output in Exhibit 8.3 and F_{crit} is found in Exhibit C.3. For $\alpha = .05$, F_{crit} is about 3.87 (interpolating between the tabled values for $n - PA = 200$ and 500). We can do another regression analysis to get the other two components: $\Sigma (X_i - \overline{X})^2$, the SSE for a simple model of SATM, and R_p^2, the PRE when using HSRANK and SATV to predict SATM, the predictor to be added. Exhibit 8.5 displays the appropriate parts of the SAS output from that regression. The SSE for a simple model of SATM is the SUM OF SQUARES in the row for TOTAL, which is 19085.60628. R^2 (the PRE for comparing a simple model of SATM with a model that includes HSRANK and SATV) is .11, indicating that SATM is somewhat redundant with the other predictor variables. TOL = 1 − R_p^2 = 1 − .11 = .89 is the *tolerance* or the degree to which SATM is *not* redundant with the other predictors.[1]

---

[1]If tolerance is very low the accuracy of the numerical computations will be affected. Good computer programs will complain or issue a warning if tolerance is lower than .01 or .001. This means that the predictor variable is too redundant to be added to the model. Be wary of any regression results when one or more of the predictor variables has a very low tolerance.

EXHIBIT 8.5 ▶

Output from SAS PROC REG (multiple regression) for predicting SATM with HSRANK and SATV

DEP VARIABLE: SATM   SAT-Math score

ANALYSIS OF VARIANCE

SOURCE	DF	SUM OF SQUARES	MEAN SQUARE	F VALUE	PROB > F
MODEL	2	2098.83210	1049.41605	25.391	.0001
ERROR	411	16986.77418	41.33035080		
C TOTAL	413	19085.60628			

ROOT MSE	6.428869	R-SQUARE	.1100
DEP MEAN	64.65459	ADJ R-SQ	.1056
C.V.	9.943406		

We now have all the numbers necessary to construct the confidence interval.

$$b_{SATM.HSRANK,SATV} \pm \sqrt{\frac{(F_{crit})(MSE)}{\Sigma\,(X_{ip} - \overline{X}_p)^2(1 - R_p^2)}}$$

$$= \quad .0223 \quad \pm \quad \sqrt{\frac{(3.87)(.421936)}{(19085.60628)(.89)}}$$

$$= \quad .0223 \quad \pm \quad .0098$$

$$= (.0125, .0321)$$

Consistent with the statistical inference based on PRE and F^*, as it must be, the 95% confidence interval does not include zero.

8.3.3 The Overall Model Revisited

We noted earlier that a single test of the overall model was usually unsatisfactory because rejection of the null hypothesis does not indicate which of the many β_j's are not equal to zero. The test for adding the pth variable which we have just considered suggests a solution. The numbering of the predictor variables is arbitrary, so we can treat each predictor in turn as if it were the pth and last variable to be added. In this way we will test separately for each predictor whether its partial regression coefficient (i.e., its coefficient with all the other $p - 1$ variables in the MODEL) is different from zero. Conceptually this means that we need to do p separate regression analyses in which we first enter the other $p - 1$ predictor variables and then test whether it is worthwhile to add the pth. In practice, it is possible to compute the separate values for PRE and F^* for each of these tests from intermediate results in the overall regression analysis, so the computer programs do not need to do the p separate regressions. But we should still consider them to be separate analyses, because each of the resulting PREs and F^*'s asks a different question.

Most regression computer programs routinely present F^* (or sometimes the equivalent t^*), and many will give the square root of PRE—the partial correlation coefficient between Y and X_p—for all possible choices for the pth predictor, but almost none will give PRE directly.

As an example, again consider the SAS output for the overall test of the GPA data in Exhibit 8.3. PRE and F^* for adding SATM with HSRANK and SATV already in the equation, the test we did in two steps in the previous section, can readily be obtained from this output. Note the column labeled "T FOR H0: PARAMETER = 0." These are the values of t^* for testing that $\beta_j = 0$ *given* that all the other listed predictor variables are included in the equation. To get the appropriate F^*, we need only square t^*. For example, the value of t^* in the row for SATM is 4.484. Squaring that yields $F^* = 20.1$, which is the same value we obtained in the two-step process above for testing whether SATM should be included in the MODEL when HSRANK and SATV were already in the MODEL. The column labeled "PARTIAL CORR TYPE II" according to the *SAS User's Guide: Statistics* (SAS, 1985) is supposed to be the partial correlation coefficient. However, this is incorrect[2] because the values given are actually the coefficients of partial determination or the PRE for adding the row variable to the model given that the other variables are already in the equation. (If the correct partial correlation coefficient of .216205 had been given, simply squaring it would give the appropriate PRE.) The given value of .04674444 is the same as the value we calculated for PRE above when testing whether SATM should be added to a model which already included HSRANK and SATV. Note that the output also provides the TOLERANCE for each variable, so separate regressions to check redundancy are not needed. The TOLERANCE of .89 for SATM is also the same as obtained in Exhibit 8.5. So instead of doing three regressions to get the information necessary to compute the PRE, F^*, and confidence interval for the test of adding one more parameter, we can get all the required numbers from the computer output testing the overall model. Note, however, that the estimated parameters for

---

[2]This error in the SAS program should serve as ample warning to any user of statistical software. *Never assume that the computer program or its manual are correct!* You should always test any regression program you use by analyzing some data for which you know the correct PRE and parameter estimates.

MODEL C are not available from this output.

To ask whether the other variables should be added to the MODEL were they to be added last, we simply have to look in the appropriate rows of Exhibit 8.3. For example, if we want to ask whether HSRANK is a useful predictor of GPA given that predictions are already conditional on SATV and SATM, we are comparing these MODELs:

MODEL C: $GPA_i = \beta_0 + \beta_2 SATV_i + \beta_3 SATM_i + \varepsilon_i$

MODEL A: $GPA_i = \beta_0 + \beta_1 HSRANK_i + \beta_2 SATV_i + \beta_3 SATM_i + \varepsilon_i$

From the row for HSRANK in Exhibit 8.3, the F^* for this comparison equals $(t^*)^2 = (8.32)^2 = 69.2$ and PRE $= 0.14$. These values greatly exceed the respective critical values from the appropriate appendix tables, so we can reject the null hypothesis that $\beta_{1.23} = 0$. In other words, HSRANK reduces ERROR over and above the reductions in ERROR achieved by SATV and SATM. Note also that TOLERANCE for HSRANK $= 0.99$, indicating that HSRANK is essentially not redundant with the predictive information provided by the two SAT scores.

Similarly, we can ask whether SATV is usefully added to the model when HSRANK and SATM are already included. Then we are comparing

MODEL C: $GPA_i = \beta_0 + \beta_1 HSRANK_i + \beta_3 SATM_i + \varepsilon_i$

MODEL A: $GPA_i = \beta_0 + \beta_1 HSRANK_i + \beta_2 SATV_i + \beta_3 SATM_i + \varepsilon_i$

From the rows for SATV in Exhibit 8.3 we find that $F^* = 2.566^2 = 6.58$ and PRE $= .016$. With the large value of $n - PA = 410$, these also exceed the critical values for $\alpha = .05$, so the reduction in error due to adding SATV is statistically reliable; however, error is only reduced by 1.6%.

In asking several questions, we have the problem of doing multiple statistical tests on the same set of data. If we use a given level of α in repeated tests, our chances of making at least one Type I error increases rapidly. It is safer (but seldom done) to use α/p as the cutoff for each of the repeated tests.[3] Using the computer programs, we do not need to find the critical value of F for the α/p level; instead we need only compare the value reported for "PROB $> |T|$" in Exhibit 8.3 to α/p. In this example, $\alpha/p = .05/4 = .013$. Using this criterion, we are very close to not rejecting the null hypothesis for SATV because the probability in its row of the Exhibit 8.3 is only .0106.

---

[3]Using α/p as the criterion is known as the "Bonferroni inequality for multiple comparisons."

8.3.4 Summarizing Tests of Each Predictor and the Overall Model

Exhibit 8.6 presents the results of the various tests we have conducted so far on these data in a single analysis of variance source table. Three of the rows of this table correspond to the generic layout in Exhibit 8.2. These are the rows whose sources are labeled REGRESSION, ERROR, and TOTAL. As in that earlier source table, the TOTAL sum of squares equals the sum of squared errors for the simple single parameter model where our model predictions equal the mean value of GPA in our sample. The ERROR sum of squares equals the residual or error sum of squares from the model which includes SATV, SATM, and HSRANK as predictors. The sum of squares regression, SSR, equals the difference between these two sums of squared errors. The values of PRE and F^* given in the first row of the table labeled REGRESSION derive from a test of the overall model—comparing MODEL A, which includes all three predictors with a single parameter MODEL C. As discussed earlier, the value of PRE is equivalent to the coefficient of multiple determination or R^2.

The next three rows of the table are labeled by each of the three predictors in the model, SATV, SATM, and HSRANK. Each of these rows has values for F^* and PRE that are those given above for testing the addition of that particular predictor to a model that already includes the other two. The sum of squares for each of these rows corresponds to the difference between the sum of squared errors for a MODEL C, which does not include the particular predictor but does include the other two, and the sum of squared errors for MODEL A, which includes all three predictors. For example, for the SATV row, 2.779 equals the amount by which SSE increases if SATV were dropped from the model that includes the other two predictors. Accordingly, we can calculate that the sum of squared errors for a model that included only SATM

EXHIBIT 8.6 ▶

ANOVA summary exhibit for GPA multiple regression results

Source	SS	df	MS	F^*	PRE
REGRESSION	48.789	3	16.263	38.5	.220
SATV	2.779	1	2.779	6.6	.016
SATM	8.483	1	8.483	20.1	.047
HSRANK	29.209	1	29.209	69.2	.144
Error	172.994	410	.422		
Total	221.783	414			

and HSRANK as predictors would be 175.773 (i.e., the sum of squared errors for the model with all three predictors, 172.994, plus the sum of squares due to SATV, 2.779; $172.994 + 2.779 = 175.773$).

The three sums of squares corresponding to each of the three predictors are frequently called the sums of squares "due to" each predictor, controlling for the others. Again, they tell us by how much the sum of squared errors for the model as a whole would be increased if that particular predictor were dropped from the model. Notice that if we add up the sum of squares due to SATV, the sum of squares due to SATM, and the sum of squares due to HSRANK, we do not obtain the sum of squares explained by the model as a whole, SSR. The reason is that these three predictors are partially redundant with each other.

Notice also that the three values of F^* for the three tests of the individual predictors can be computed either by converting the associated PRE to F^* or by dividing the mean square for a particular predictor by the mean square error (MSE). Most regression programs provide the value of these F^*'s for each predictor included in a model, so the associated sums of squares due to each can be readily computed by multiplying the value of F^* by the MSE. For example, the sum of squares due to SATV, controlling for SATM and HSRANK, equals 6.6 (the value of F^* for SATV) times .422 (the value of MSE); that is, $6.6 \times .422 = 2.78$, which, within rounding, is the same value given in Exhibit 8.6. As a result, we can calculate from this table the sum of squared errors for any model which includes any two of these predictors without actually having the computer estimate the model for us. For instance, the sum of squared errors for the model with all three predictors equals 172.994. If we removed HSRANK from the model, but left in the two SAT predictors, the sum of squared errors would increase by 29.209. Accordingly, the sum of squared errors for a model that included only SATV and SATM as predictors would be 202.203.

8.3.5 Testing the Addition of a Set of Predictors

Instead of asking whether the addition of just one additional parameter is worthwhile, we sometimes want to know whether the addition of a set of predictors would be useful. For example, suppose our DATA Y_i was some measure of voting behavior for a sample of registered voters. Suppose also that we have several psychological (e.g., personality and attitude) measures for each voter as well as several sociodemographic measures (e.g., age, income, education). Depending on whether we were sociologists or psychologists, we might want to ask whether one set of variables was sufficient to predict voting behavior or whether extra information was added by the other set. By now it should be clear how we would answer such a question.

We begin by estimating the parameters and calculating SSE(C) for our compact model, which in this case is the model with just one of the two sets of predictors included. Then we estimate the parameters and calculate SSE(A) for our augmented model which includes both sets of predictors. As always, PRE = 1 − SSE(A)/SSE(C). This PRE will be due to the extra parameters added for the variables in the second set. Thus, to calculate PRE per parameter for the numerator of F^*, we will divide PRE by the number of variables in the second set, namely PA − PC. The denominator of F^* is simply 1 − PRE divided by the number of potential remaining parameters which is $n − 1$ (for the intercept) minus the number of variables in the first set minus the number of variables in the second set; that is, we divide 1 − PRE by $n − PA$.

Although few computer programs automatically test the addition of a set of predictors, it is simple to do two regressions—one for the compact model and one for the augmented model to obtain the necessary SSE(C) and SSE(A) and then do the simple calculations of PRE and F^* by hand. Again, some programs (e.g., SAS) will provide F^*, but few, if any, will provide PRE directly.

As an example, we will ask whether the two SAT scores should be added to a model which already includes high school rank. MODEL C corresponds to the model with only high school rank as a predictor and MODEL A includes all three predictors. That is,

MODEL C: $GPA_i = \beta_0 + \beta_1 HSRANK_i + \varepsilon_i$

MODEL A: $GPA_i = \beta_0 + \beta_1 HSRANK_i + \beta_2 SATV_i + \beta_3 SATM_i + \varepsilon_i$

If β_2 and β_3 are *both* zero, then MODEL A reduces to MODEL C; so the null hypothesis is

H_0: $\beta_2 = \beta_3 = 0$

Note that the augmented model has two extra parameters. The SSE for MODEL C is 189.113 (this number is not available in any of the previous tables), and the SSE for MODEL A is 172.994 (the residual or error sum of squares from Exhibits 8.3 and 8.6). So, PRE = 1 − 172.994/189.113 = .085 and $F^*_{2,410} = 19.1$, which exceeds the critical value for $\alpha = .05$. Hence, the set of SAT scores is a useful addition to the model.

Interpreting tests of the addition of a set of parameters has the same problems as interpreting tests of an overall model. If the null hypothesis is rejected, then we know that it is unreasonable to assume that all the β_j for the set equal zero; however, we don't know which one or ones do. Thus, it is probably best to ask separately whether each variable in the second set should be added to the model by using the above test for the addition of a single variable. On the other hand, sometimes we don't care which predictors in the second set are useful but just whether any are useful. Our example using psychological and sociodemographic variables to predict voting behavior is a case in point. For example, we may for theoretical reasons want to know, once we have controlled for the sociodemographic variables, whether we are able to improve our prediction of voting by using any other psychological variables; we may not care which other psychological variables are useful, just whether any are useful. Then the test for the addition of a set of variables is appropriate.

8.3.6 Testing Other Special Hypotheses

The number of special hypotheses that can be tested is virtually limitless. We cannot list here even a fraction of the questions one might want to ask within the multiple regression framework. We can, however, describe the general strategy for answering any of these questions. This strategy is simply a slight generalization and formalization of the procedure we have used above to answer questions about additional predictors or sets of predictors. There are four steps to this general strategy.

1. Formulate the question as a null hypothesis about the β_j's or as a linear combination of the β_j's.
2. Estimate the parameters and calculate SSE(C) for the compact model which incorporates the null hypothesis.
3. Estimate the parameters and calculate SSE(A) for the augmented model which removes the restrictions imposed by the null hypothesis.
4. Use SSE(C) and SSE(A) to calculate PRE and F^*.

This general strategy is straightforward and should now be very familiar, because we have used it to develop the tests for all the special questions considered above. However, there can be some tricky issues. Translating some questions into a statement about a linear combination of the β_j's sometimes requires ingenuity, and determining the effective number of parameters added in the augmented model is not always obvious. Also, getting a regression program in one of the standard computer packages to perform the required regression for the compact model is not always easy. We cannot hope to make you expert in these matters in a book of this scope. However, we can illustrate this strategy and some of the tricky issues encountered by considering a few examples.

Suppose in our example of predicting college GPA with high school percentile rank, SAT verbal, and SAT math scores, that we wanted to ask whether the two tests required separate coefficients or whether it was reasonable to use the same coefficient for both. We might have theoretical reasons (e.g., a hypothesis that both tests measure one general ability so that neither should be weighted more than the other) or practical reasons (e.g., it is easier for the admissions office if they only have to use one coefficient for both test scores) for asking this question.

Step 1.   First translate the question into a statement about the β_j's. The question is whether the same coefficient applies to both SATV and SATM. If we continue the convention above of using β_1 for HSRANK, β_2 for SATV, and β_3 for SATM, then our question is equivalent to the null hypothesis

$$H_0: \quad \beta_2 = \beta_3$$

Note that this null hypothesis does not state that β_2 or β_3 equal zero or anything else; it just states that they are equal to each other. It is customary and convenient to express null hypotheses as a linear combination of the β_j's that equals zero. In this case,

$$H_0: \quad \beta_2 - \beta_3 = 0$$

Such null hypotheses are often called *contrasts*, and we will encounter many such special hypotheses when we consider analysis of variance for experimental designs in Chapters 11 and 12.

Step 2.   For this null hypothesis let β_2 represent the common coefficient for SATV and SATM, whatever it happens to be; then the corresponding compact model is

$$\text{MODEL C:} \quad \text{GPA}_i = \beta_0 + \beta_1 \text{HSRANK} + \beta_2 \text{SATV} + \beta_2 \text{SATM} + \varepsilon_i$$

This is equivalent to

$$\text{GPA}_i = \beta_0 + \beta_1 \text{HSRANK} + \beta_2(\text{SATV} + \text{SATM}) + \varepsilon_i$$

Estimating the parameters of this and similar compact models can be tricky. Most regression programs will not estimate the coefficients of this model directly. The trick, and it is a fairly general trick, is to construct a new variable, say SATC, for SAT combined, which equals SATV + SATM. Most packages have data manipulation and transformation procedures which make it easy to create new variables. The compact model in terms of the new variables is then

$$\text{GPA}_i = \beta_0 + \beta_1 \text{HSRANK} + \beta_2 \text{SATC} + \varepsilon_i$$

We can easily use standard regression programs to fit this model to our data and obtain SSE(C). The appropriate output from SAS is displayed in Exhibit 8.7. In this case, SSE(C) = 173.8584.

Step 3.   The augmented model is the model without the restriction that $\beta_2 = \beta_3$, which is simply the usual regression model of

$$\text{MODEL A:} \quad \text{GPA}_i = \beta_0 + \beta_1 \text{HSRANK} + \beta_2 \text{SATV} + \beta_3 \text{SATM} + \varepsilon_i$$

DEP VARIABLE: GPA   freshman grade pt average
ANALYSIS OF VARIANCE

SOURCE	DF	SUM OF SQUARES	MEAN SQUARE	F VALUE	PROB > F
MODEL	2	47.92487	23.96244	56.647	.0001
ERROR	411	173.8584	.4230131		
C TOTAL	413	221.7833			

ROOT MSE	.6503946	R-SQUARE	.2161	
DEP MEAN	2.699203	ADJ R-SQ	.2123	
C.V.	24.0958			

PARAMETER ESTIMATES

VARIABLE	DF	PARAMETER ESTIMATE	STANDARD ERROR	T FOR H0: PARAMETER = 0	PROB > |T|
INTERCEP	1	−1.63039	.4173898	−3.906	.0001
HSRANK	1	.02692853	.003226058	8.347	.0001
SATC	1	.01637144	.002726269	6.005	.0001

EXHIBIT 8.7 ▲

Output from SAS PROC REG for predicting GPA with high school rank and SAT combined

Remember that β_2 means something different in this equation than in the one for the compact model because partial regression coefficients depend on what else is included in the equation. The appropriate SAS output for estimating this model is the same as in Exhibit 8.3. In this case, SSE(A) = 172.9938.

Step 4. The PRE for using the augmented instead of the compact model in this example is

$$\text{PRE} = 1 - \frac{172.9938}{173.8584} = .0050$$

To calculate F^*, we need to know the difference in the number of parameters between the two models. In this case it is clear that the compact model has three parameters and the augmented model has four parameters, so the difference is 1. In general, each statement in the null hypothesis about a linear combination of the β_j's is equivalent to one less parameter for the compact model. For example, we would express the null hypothesis that $\beta_1 = \beta_2 = \beta_3$ as two statements:

$$H_0: \quad \beta_1 - \beta_2 = 0; \quad \beta_2 - \beta_3 = 0$$

This would mean that our compact model would have two fewer parameters than the augmented model. If we actually write out the compact model, the number of parameters will generally be obvious. For the example of determining whether the coefficients for the two SAT tests are equal,

$$F^* = \frac{\text{PRE}/1}{(1 - \text{PRE})/(n - 4)} = 2.05$$

The critical value for $F_{1,410;.05}$ is about 3.84, so for these data we would *not* reject the null hypothesis that $\beta_2 = \beta_3$. In other words, using separate coefficients for SAT verbal and SAT math does not appreciably improve the predictions of GPA. Thus, the simple equation

$$\widehat{\text{GPA}}_i = -1.63 + .02693(\text{HSRANK}_i) + .01637(\text{SATC}_i)$$

does about as well in terms of accuracy of prediction as the more complicated model in which SAT verbal and SAT math are treated separately.

The same four-step strategy can answer countless other questions. For example, if we knew that the equation last year for predicting GPA was

$$\widehat{\text{GPA}}_i = -2.15 + .03(\text{HSRANK}_i) + .031(\text{SATM}_i) + .006(\text{SATV}_i)$$

we might want to ask whether the predictions using that equation were significantly worse than the predictions derived from the current data. In performing such a test, the above equation represents the compact model and it has no parameters to be estimated. We simply use it to make a prediction for each of the 414 observations and compute $\text{SSE(C)} = \Sigma (Y_i - \hat{Y}_{iC})^2$ directly; in this case $\text{SSE(C)} = 183.373$. The augmented model is

MODEL A: $\text{GPA}_i = \beta_0 + \beta_1\text{HSRANK}_i + \beta_2\text{SATM}_i + \beta_3\text{SATV}_i + \varepsilon_i$

and its parameters are easily estimated and SSE(A) calculated by any regression program (as in Exhibit 8.3); in this case $\text{SSE(A)} = 172.994$, so $\text{PRE} = 1 - 172.994/183.373 = .058$. That is, estimating four new parameters does about 5.8% better than using last year's parameters. There are four extra parameters in the augmented model, so F^* has 4 and $n - 4 = 410$ degrees of freedom; in this case $F^*_{4,410} = 6.27$, which falls beyond the critical value for $\alpha = .05$. The equivalent null hypothesis implied by this choice of augmented and compact models is

$$H_0: \quad \beta_0 = -2.15; \quad \beta_1 = .03; \quad \beta_2 = .031; \quad \beta_3 = .006$$

or, equivalently,

$$H_0: \quad \beta_0 + 2.15 = 0; \quad \beta_1 - .03 = 0; \quad \beta_2 - .031 = 0; \quad \beta_3 - .006 = 0$$

The large value for F^* indicates that the null hypothesis should be rejected. However, as with all multiple-degree-of-freedom tests, it is not clear whether all or just some of last year's parameters have changed.

As a more complex example, we might want to ask whether β_1 equals the average of β_2 and β_3. It is difficult to provide a rationale for asking whether the coefficient for HSRANK is the average of the two SAT coefficients, but we will ask the question in this context anyway just to provide an illustration. The null hypothesis is

$$H_0: \quad \beta_1 = \frac{\beta_2 + \beta_3}{2}$$

or, equivalently,

$$H_0: \quad \beta_1 - \frac{\beta_2 + \beta_3}{2} = 0$$

The augmented model is the usual

MODEL A: $GPA_i = \beta_0 + \beta_1 HSRANK + \beta_2 SATV + \beta_3 SATM + \varepsilon_i$

The compact model is not obvious. The above H_0 clearly implies $\beta_1 = (\beta_2 + \beta_3)/2$; substituting that value for β_1 into the augmented model produces the compact model

MODEL C: $GPA_i = \beta_0 + \dfrac{\beta_2 + \beta_3}{2} HSRANK + \beta_2 SATV$

$$+ \beta_3 SATM + \varepsilon_i$$

Rearranging terms yields

MODEL C: $GPA_i = \beta_0 + \beta_2(.5HSRANK + SATV)$

$$+ \beta_3(.5HSRANK + SATM) + \varepsilon_i$$

If we construct new variables

$$X'_{i2} = .5HSRANK_i + SATV_i \quad \text{and} \quad X'_{i3} = .5HSRANK_i + SATM_i$$

then our compact model becomes

MODEL C: $GPA_i = \beta_0 + \beta_2 X'_{i2} + \beta_3 X'_{i3} + \varepsilon_i$

and that model can be easily estimated with standard multiple regression programs. For these data, SSE(C) = 175.173 and SSE(A) = 172.994; thus PRE = 1 − 172.994/175.173 = .012. There is one linear constraint in the null hypothesis, and consequently a difference of 1 in the number of parameters between models; so $F^*_{1,410} = 5.16$, which does exceed the critical value of F for $\alpha = .05$. Hence, the null hypothesis that β_1 equals the average of β_2, and β_3 is rejected.

The usual questions we ask in the context of multiple regression models are not so complex as whether twice β_1 equals the sum of β_2 and β_3. However, it is important to know that should you wish to ask such complex questions in some situation, it can be done rather easily.

MODEL 1:   Last Year's Equation

GPA = −2.15 + .03HSRANK + .006SATV + .031SATM + ε_i
No Parameter Estimates
SSE = 183.373

MODEL 2:   Simple (Mean) Model

GPA = β_0 + ε_i
b_0 = 2.7
SSE = 221.783

MODEL 3:   High School Rank Only

GPA = β_0 + β_1HSRANK + ε_i
b_0 = .184; b_1 = .028
SSE = 189.113

MODEL 4:   High School Rank and SAT Verbal

GPA = β_0 + β_1HSRANK + β_2SATV + ε_i
b_0 = −.715; b_1 = .028; b_2 = .018
SSE = 181.477

MODEL 5:   High School Rank and Total SAT [SATC = SATV + SATM]
GPA = β_0 + β_1HSRANK + β_2SATC + ε_i
b_0 = −1.63; b_1 = .027; b_2 = .016
SSE = 173.859

MODEL 6:   Complex Constraint [β_1 = (β_2 + β_3)/2]

GPA = β_0 + β_2(SATV + .5 HSRANK) + β_3(SATM + .5 HSRANK) + ε_i
b_0 = −1.74; b_2 = .015; b_3 = .027; (implies b_1 = .021)
SSE = 175.173

MODEL 7:   Full Regression Model

GPA = β_0 + β_1HSRANK + β_2SATV + β_3SATM + ε_i
b_0 = −1.74; b_1 = .027; b_2 = .011; b_3 = .022
SSE = 172.994

EXHIBIT 8.8   ▲

Summary of models, parameter estimates, and SSEs for the college GPA data

Also, we will make extensive use of this technique in the analysis of variance of experimental designs where we often ask questions as complex as the one we just considered.

As a summary of the types of questions and null hypotheses that can be addressed, Exhibit 8.8 lists all the models for GPA considered in this section, their least squares parameter estimates, and their SSEs.

Is high school rank, by itself, a good predictor of GPA? (simple regression)

H_0: $\beta_1 = 0$
MODEL 2 vs. MODEL 3
PRE = .147; $F^*_{1,412} = 71.1$, $p < .001$

Is it worth adding the set of SAT scores to the model of GPA which includes high school rank? (addition of set)

H_0: $\beta_2 = \beta_3 = 0$
MODEL 3 vs. MODEL 7
PRE = .085; $F^*_{2,410} = 19.1$, $p < .01$

Should SAT verbal and SAT math be weighted equally?

H_0: $\beta_2 = \beta_3$
MODEL 5 vs. MODEL 7
PRE = .005; $F^*_{1,410} = 2.05$, *n.s.*

Compared to the mean, are high school rank, SATV, and SATM useful predictors of GPA? (overall regression)

H_0: $\beta_1 = \beta_2 = \beta_3 = 0$
MODEL 2 vs. MODEL 7
PRE = .22, $F^*_{3,410} = 38.5$, $p < .01$

Is it useful to add SAT math to a model predicting GPA which already includes high school rank and SAT verbal? (Adding pth predictor)

H_0: $\beta_3 = 0$
MODEL 4 vs. MODEL 7
PRE = .047; $F^*_{1,410} = 20.1$, $p < .01$

Does last year's model apply to the current GPA data?

H_0: $\beta_0 = -2.15$, $\beta_1 = .03$, $\beta_2 = .006$, $\beta_3 = .031$
MODEL 1 vs. MODEL 7
PRE = .058; $F^*_{4,410} = 6.3$, $p < .01$

Is the weight for high school rank equal to the average of the two SAT weights?

H_0: $\beta_1 - (\beta_2 + \beta_3)/2 = 0$
MODEL 6 vs. MODEL 7
PRE = .012; $F^*_{1,410} = 5.16$, $p < .05$

EXHIBIT 8.9

Summary of questions, null hypotheses, PREs, and F^*'s for the college GPA data

▲ Exhibit 8.9 lists many of the questions and their associated null hypotheses along with the comparison of models that answers the question or, equivalently, tests the null hypothesis. An entry such as "MODEL 1 vs. MODEL 4" means that MODEL 1 corresponds to MODEL C and MODEL 4 corresponds to MODEL A.

8.4

Computer Programs for Multiple Regression

A large variety of computer packages are available on mainframe and minicomputers for performing the calculations required for multiple regression. There is also a growing number of good statistical packages, including several of the standard mainframe packages, with excellent multiple regression programs available for personal computers. You should find a package you like and become familiar with its multiple regression procedure. In this section we consider outputs from some of the standard computer multiple regression procedures.

Exhibits 8.10 through 8.16 present computer outputs from the regression programs of standard computer packages for the GPA data. These outputs are comparable to Exhibit 8.3 which displays output from SAS (SAS, 1985; see also Freund & Littell, 1986) procedure PROC REG and which we used above for testing the various models of GPA. The illustrated packages are SAS (SAS, 1985; see also Freund, Littell, & Spector, 1986), PROC GLM (Exhibit 8.10), SPSS-X (SPSS Inc., 1987; see also Norusis, 1985) procedure REGRESSION (Exhibit 8.11), BMDP (Dixon, 1983) procedure 1R (Exhibit 8.12), MINITAB (Ryan, Joiner, Ryan, 1985) procedure REG (Exhibit 8.14), S (Becker & Chambers, 1984) procedure REG (Exhibit 8.14), BLSS (Abrahams & Rizzardi, 1987) procedure REGRESS (Exhibit 8.15), and SCSS (Nie et al., 1980) procedure REGRESSION (Exhibit 8.16).

The reader should carefully compare these various outputs. Although they all present the same basic information, they do so in various formats and use different labels. Remember that the most important piece of information to be able to find in each output is the SSE for the overall model being tested. If you can find that, then you can answer almost any question by asking the regression procedure to test different overall models, corresponding to the appropriate MODELs C and A to answer your question. The SSE for the model which uses HSRANK, SATV, and SATM to predict GPA is 172.9938 (rounded). You should try to locate that number and see how it is labeled in each of the outputs. To know what the model means you also need to be able to find the parameter estimates in each of these outputs. The estimates, rounded, are

$$b_0 = -1.74; \quad b_{\text{HSRANK}} = .0268; \quad b_{\text{SATV}} = .0114; \quad b_{\text{SATM}} = .0223$$

If you have the formulas for PRE and F^* handy, being able to find SSE and the parameter estimates for a MODEL is all the information

GENERAL LINEAR MODELS PROCEDURE

DEPENDENT VARIABLE: GPA   freshman grade pt average

SOURCE	DF	SUM OF SQUARES	MEAN SQUARE	F VALUE
MODEL	3	48.78949131	16.26316377	38.54
ERROR	410	172.99377365	.42193603	PR > F
CORRECTED TOTAL	413	221.78326496		.0001

R-SQUARE	C.V.	ROOT MSE	GPA MEAN
.219987	24.0651	.6956603	2.69920290

SOURCE	DF	TYPE I SS	F VALUE	PR > F
HSRANK	1	32.67064566	77.43	.0001
SATV	1	7.63581477	18.10	.0001
SATM	1	8.48303088	20.11	.0001

SOURCE	DF	TYPE III SS	F VALUE	PR > F
HSRANK	1	29.20831782	69.22	.0001
SATV	1	2.77922933	6.59	.0106
SATM	1	8.48303088	20.11	.0001

PARAMETER	ESTIMATE	T FOR H0: PARAMETER = 0	PR > |T|	STD ERROR OF ESTIMATE
INTERCEPT	-1.73899501	-4.10	.0001	.42370528
HSRANK	.02681512	8.32	.0001	.00322292
SATV	.01136930	2.57	.0106	.00442991
SATM	.02234704	4.48	.0001	.00498388

EXHIBIT 8.10 ▲

Sample output for the GPA data from SAS PROC GLM

```
* * * * MULTIPLE  REGRESSION * * * *

Equation Number 1     Dependent Variable..    GPA     freshman grade pt average

Beginning Block Number 1. Method: Enter    HSRANK  SATV   SATM

Variable(s) Entered on Step Number
     1..      SATM       SAT-Math score
     2..      HSRANK     percentile rank in high school class
     3..      SATV       SAT-Verbal score
```

Multiple R	.46903
R Square	.21999
Adjusted R Square	.21428
Standard Error	.64957

Analysis of Variance

	DF	Sum of Squares	Mean Square
Regression	3	48.78949	16.26316
Residual	410	172.99377	.42194

F =   38.54415   Signif F =   .0000

------------------------------------ Variables in the Equation ------------------------------------

Variable	B	SE B	95% Confdnce Intrvl B		Beta
SATM	.022347	.004984	.012550	.032144	.207304
HSRANK	.026815	.003223	.020480	.033151	.363901
SATV	.011369	.004430	.002661	.020077	.118485
(Constant)	−1.738995	.423705	−2.571901	−.906089	

------------------------------ Variables in the Equation ------------------------------

Variable	Correl	Part Cor	Partial	Tolerance	F	Sig F
SATM	.271597	.195574	.216205	.890031	20.105	.0000
HSRANK	.383808	.362902	.380067	.994517	69.225	.0000
SATV	.202691	.111943	.125744	.892618	6.587	.0106
(Constant)					16.845	.0000

End Block Number   1   All requested variables entered.

EXHIBIT 8.11 ▲

Sample output for the GPA data from SPSSX

you really need from the sometimes complicated computer outputs from multiple regression programs. However, the programs also provide a great deal of other information, and there is no reason not to take advantage of the work that has been done for you. But if things get too complicated, particularly when one is first using a particular computer

STEP NO.   3

VARIABLE ENTERED   3 SATV

MULTIPLE R   .4690
MULTIPLE R-SQUARE   .2200
ADJUSTED R-SQUARE   .2143
STD. ERROR OF EST.   .6496

ANALYSIS OF VARIANCE

	SUM OF SQUARES	DF	MEAN SQUARE	F RATIO
REGRESSION	48.789486	3	16.26316	38.54
RESIDUAL	172.99390	410	.4219363	

VARIABLES IN EQUATION FOR GPA

VARIABLE		COEFFICIENT	STD. ERROR OF COEFF	STD REG COEFF	TOLERANCE	F TO REMOVE
(Y-INTERCEPT		−1.73900)				
HSRANK	2	.02682	.0032	.364	.99452	69.22
SATV	3	.01137	.0044	.118	.89262	6.59
SATM	4	.02235	.0050	.207	.89003	20.10

STEPWISE REGRESSION COEFFICIENTS

VARIABLES STEP	0 Y-INTCPT	2 HSRANK	3 SATV	4 SATM
0	2.6992*	.0283	.0194	.0293
1	.1837*	.0283*	.0178	.0265
2	−1.4166*	.0270*	.0114	.0265*
3	−1.7390*	.0268*	.0114*	.0223*

NOTE − 1) REGRESSION COEFFICIENTS FOR VARIABLE IN THE
           EQUATION ARE INDICATED BY AN ASTERISK
        2) THE REMAINING COEFFICIENTS ARE THOSE WHICH WOULD
           BE OBTAINED IF THAT VARIABLE WERE TO ENTER IN THE
           NEXT STEP

EXHIBIT 8.12 ▲

Sample output for the GPA data from BMDP

package, our advice is to go back to basics and just use the SSEs to calculate your own PREs and F^*'s. To become familiar with these different output formats, you should try to locate R^2, the PRE for testing the overall model against the simple model, and its associated F^*, probability under the null hypothesis, and unbiased estimate of η^2. For these

EXHIBIT 8.13 ▶

Sample output for the GPA data from MINITAB

The regression equation is

gpa = −1.74 + .0268 hsrank + .0114 satv + .0223 satm

Predictor	Coef	Stdev	t-ratio
Constant	−1.7390	.4237	−4.10
hsrank	.026815	.003223	8.32
satv	.011369	.004430	2.57
satm	.022347	.004984	4.48

s = .6496   R-sq = 22.0%   R-sq(adj) = 21.4%

Analysis of Variance

SOURCE	DF	SS	MS
Regression	3	48.789	16.263
Error	410	172.994	.422
Total	413	221.783	

SOURCE	DF	SEQ SS
hsrank	1	32.671
satv	1	7.636
satm	1	8.483

EXHIBIT 8.14 ▶

Sample output for the GPA data from S procedure REGRESS

	Coef	Std Err	t Value
Intercept	−1.738995	.4237052	−4.104258
hsrank	.02681513	.003222923	8.320129
satv	.01136930	.004429910	2.566486
satm	.02234705	.004983883	4.483862

Residual Standard Error = .649566
Multiple R-Square = .2199873

N = 414   F Value = 38.54415 on 3, 410 df

data, the respective values (rounded) are $R^2 = .22$, $F^*_{3,410} = 38.54$, $p < .0001$, and estimated $\eta^2 = .21$. Note that this information is *not* provided in all the outputs in Exhibits 8.10–8.16. Also of use is the ROOT MSE or the standard error of the estimate, which for these data is .6496; remember that this estimates σ, the standard deviation of the normal distribution from which the error terms ε_i are sampled. With respect to testing other models, you should look in these outputs for the tests

Dependent variable: (gpa)
Independent variables: (hsrank,satv,satm)[1 2 3]
Observations   414   Parameters   4

Var	Coef	SE	t-Ratio	P-Value
intcp	−1.7390	.42371	−4.1043	.0000
1	.026815	.0032229	8.3201	.0000
2	.011369	.0044299	2.5665	.0106
3	.022347	.0049839	4.4839	.0000

Residual SD	.64957	Residual Variance	.42194	
Multiple R	.46903	Multiple R-squared	.21999	Centered
Multiple R	.46290	Multiple R-squared	.21428	Centered, df-adjusted
Multiple R	.97292	Multiple R-squared	.94657	Uncentered
Res Autocor	.02939	Durbin-Watson	1.93156	

Anova Exhibit

Source	df	SS	MS	F	P-Value
Fit	3	48.789	16.263	38.544 (df=3,410)	.0000
Residual	410	172.99	.42194		
Total	413	221.78			
Mean	1	3016.3			
Grand Total	414	3238.1			

EXHIBIT 8.15 ▲

Sample output for the GPA data from BLSS

of adding each predictor as the last variable. The respective rounded F^*'s for testing the addition of HSRANK, SATV, and SATM are 69.2, 6.6, and 20.1. Remember that you may have to square the corresponding values of t^* reported in some of the outputs to obtain the appropriate values for F^*.

There is great diversity among these programs in whether for the individual predictor variables they report confidence intervals, tolerance (which can be used to compute the confidence interval), and partial correlations (the square of which is the PRE for testing the addition of the last variable to the model). These values are clearly labeled in those outputs which provide them, and you should locate them in the exhibits where they do occur.

The outputs in Exhibits 8.10–8.16 are the typical amounts of information provided by these programs by default. Almost all of the programs have facilities for requesting more kinds of information. In Chapter 9 we consider the regression diagnostics provided by these programs. However, we leave most of the additional types of information provided for you to explore on your own with the aid of the appropriate manual for your preferred computer package.

```
DEPENDENT:  GPA    3 VARIABLES IN.    LAST IN:  HSRANK

MULTIPLE R =     .46903  R SQUARE =       .21999   ADJ R SQUARE =   .21428
STD ERROR =      .64957  F =            38.54415   SIGNIF F =       .00000

ANALYSIS OF VAR.      DF           SUM OF SQUARES   MEAN SQUARE
REGRESSION            3                  48.789      16.26316
RESIDUAL            410                 172.994        .42194

IN EQUATION
  VARIABLE              B       SE B         95% CONF INT B            F
  SATM              .02235   4.984-03      .01255      .03214     20.105
* SATV              .01137   4.430-03     2.661-03     .02008      6.587
  HSRANK            .02682   3.223-03      .02048      .03315     69.225
  (CONSTANT)      -1.73900    .42371     -2.57190     -.90609     16.845

IN EQUATION
  VARIABLE        SIGF   CORR   PART   PRTL   TOLER
  SATM            .000   .272   .196   .216    .890
* SATV            .011   .203   .112   .126    .893
  HSRANK          .000   .384   .363   .380    .995
  (CONSTANT)      .000

IN EQUATION
  VARIABLE        LABEL
  SATM            SAT-Math score
* SATV            SAT-Verbal score
  HSRANK          percentile rank in high school class
  (CONSTANT)
```

EXHIBIT 8.16   Sample output for the GPA data from SCSS

8.5

Interpretation of Partial Regression Coefficients

We now know how to ask and answer sophisticated questions about DATA using multiple regression. To complete our understanding of multiple regression, we need to know what the partial regression coefficients in the resulting MODELs mean. Once we decide that MODEL A does indeed significantly improve predictions relative to MODEL C, we have to understand what MODEL A tells us about DATA.

We will use a detailed examination of the data in Exhibit 8.17 to further our understanding of the meaning of coefficients. These data are the number of people unemployed (in millions) and the Federal Reserve Board Index of Industrial Production for 1950 to 1959. We will use simple

EXHIBIT 8.17 ▶

Unemployment and Federal Reserve Board Index of Industrial Production for 1950–1959. From Velleman and Welsch (1981, p. 235), by permission of American Statistical Association.

	Unemployment (millions)	Industrial Production	Year Code
1950	3.1	113	1
1951	1.9	123	2
1952	1.7	127	3
1953	1.6	138	4
1954	3.2	130	5
1955	2.7	146	6
1956	2.6	151	7
1957	2.9	152	8
1958	4.7	141	9
1959	3.8	159	10
Mean	2.8	138	5.5

regression[4] to answer several questions about these data, and in so doing will work up to a multiple regression analysis. As we do each regression, we will pay special attention to the proper interpretation of each coefficient. From this will emerge an understanding of the partial regression coefficients in a multiple regression analysis.

8.5.1 UN and IP

For the unemployment data, an obvious question to ask is whether unemployment goes down when industrial production goes up. It seems reasonable to expect that as industrial production increases more jobs will be created and that will obviously reduce unemployment. To answer this question, we can compare the following two MODELs.

MODEL C: $UN_i = \beta_0 + \varepsilon_i$

MODEL A: $UN_i = \beta_0 + \beta_1 IP_i + \varepsilon_i$

In other words, do we improve over a simple model of unemployment UN when we make predictions conditional on the industrial production IP for each year?

---

[4] The data set is small, so we urge the reader to perform each of the simple regression analyses in this section both by computer and by hand with the aid of the formulas in Chapters 6 and 7. These data may have a serial dependence problem (see Chapter 14), violating the independence of errors assumption because the errors for adjacent years may be correlated. This means that the inferential tests may be biased and should be treated with caution. However, the parameter estimates are not biased, and that is the focus of this section, so we follow the lead of Velleman & Welsch (1981) in using this interesting data set for didactic purposes.

The scattergram in Exhibit 8.18 between UN and IP suggests, to our surprise, that there is very little relationship between industrial production and unemployment. If there is any relationship, it is the counterintuitive result that unemployment *increases* as industrial production increases. The simple regression to confirm the apparent lack of relationship yields

MODEL C: $\widehat{UN}_i = 2.82$

MODEL A: $\widehat{UN}_i = -.035 + .02IP_i$

$$PRE = .098, F^*_{1,8} = .87, \text{n.s.}$$

Thus, the approximately 10% reduction in error when using IP to predict UN is not reliable. That is, we do *not* reject the null hypothesis that the β for IP is zero.

8.5.2 UN and YR

The counterintuitive result that industrial production is not related to unemployment requires that we look closer at the data. An examination of the data in Exhibit 8.17 and the scattergram in Exhibit 8.19 suggests that, as we would expect, unemployment generally increased from year to year, presumably because the potential workforce increased. It is therefore natural to ask whether YR is a reliable predictor of UN. That simple regression yields

MODEL C: $\widehat{UN}_i = 2.82$

MODEL A: $\widehat{UN}_i = 1.67 + .21YR_i$

$$PRE = .428, \quad F^*_{1,8} = 5.99, \quad p < .05$$

EXHIBIT 8.18 ▶

Scattergram for relationship between industrial production and unemployment

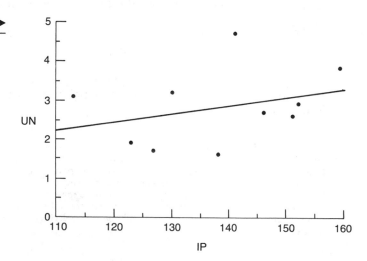

EXHIBIT 8.19 ▶

Scattergram for relationship between year and unemployment

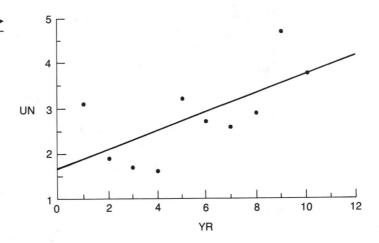

Thus, using YR to predict UN reliably reduces ERROR; for these data the proportional reduction in error is about 43%. The coefficient of .21 for YR means that for each unit increase in YR (i.e., each year) UN increases on average by approximately .21 (million) = 210,000 workers. Note in Exhibit 8.17 that sometimes the yearly increase is larger than 210,000, and sometimes it is less; in fact, for some years there is even a decrease.

8.5.3 UN Residuals

To examine these data further, let's look at the ERROR, or residuals, remaining from the yearly model of unemployment. These residuals are listed in the middle column of Exhibit 8.20. We use the awkward notation

EXHIBIT 8.20 ▶

Residuals from yearly models for unemployment and industrial production. From Velleman and Welsch (1981, p. 235), by permission of American Statistical Association.

Year	UN.0,YR	IP.0,YR
1	1.22	−5.36
2	−.19	.27
3	−.60	−.09
4	−.91	6.55
5	.48	−5.82
6	−.22	5.82
7	−.53	6.45
8	−.44	3.09
9	1.15	−12.27
10	.04	1.36
Sum	.00	.00
SSE	4.79	343.09

UN.0,YR for the residuals left when predicting UN with YR; the ".0,YR" reminds us that this is the part of UN that is left over *after* using both the intercept (β_0) and YR (β_{YR}) to predict UN. That is,

$$e_i = \text{UN.0,YR}_i = \text{UN}_i - \widehat{\text{UN}}_i$$

where $\widehat{\text{UN}}_i$ is the conditional prediction based on YR.

What exactly does UN.0,YR mean? Looking at particular values of UN.0,YR tells us when, *relative to our* MODEL, UN is unexpectedly large or small. For example, for year 1, the actual unemployment was 3.1 million but the MODEL using YR predicted unemployment of

$$\widehat{\text{UN}}_i = 1.67 + .21\text{YR} = 1.67 + .21(1) = 1.88$$

Thus, the residual is

$$e_i = \text{UN.0,YR} = \text{UN}_i - \widehat{\text{UN}}_i = 3.1 - 1.88 = 1.22$$

That is, according to the yearly model, unemployment was 1.22 million workers *higher than expected*. The other values of UN.0,YR in Exhibit 8.20 are similarly interpreted. For example, the value of -0.53 for year 7 means that in that year unemployment was, according to the yearly model, .53 million workers *lower than expected*.

Another way to think about UN.0,YR is that it is the part of the original UN data that could *not* be predicted using YR. It is simply the ERROR remaining after we have based conditional predictions on YR. Remember that the PRE for predicting UN by YR relative to the simple model was about 43%; that means that UN.0,YR represents the $1 - 43\% = 57\%$ proportion of the original data that could not be predicted by YR. If any other variable is to be useful for making conditional predictions in a multiple regression, then that variable must be able to predict UN.0,YR. That is, if another variable is to be added to the MODEL (to form a multiple regression equation), it must be useful for predicting when UN.0,YR is higher or lower than expected relative to the model using YR. If a new variable cannot reduce UN.0,YR still further, then ERROR will not have been reduced and the corresponding PRE and F^* will be small.

It now makes sense to reexamine the original question about the relationship between unemployment and industrial production. Although IP was not a useful predictor by itself of UN, maybe IP is useful for predicting when UN is higher or lower than expected relative to a model of yearly changes; that is, it may be possible to model UN.0,YR in terms of IP. Note the subtle but important distinction between these two questions. Predicting UN directly is a different problem from predicting when UN will be unusually high or low. And because they are different questions, they may well have different answers. There are a number of phrases that statisticians and social scientists use to indicate that they are talking about the second question of whether, in this case, IP is a useful predictor of UN.0,YR. We are asking whether IP is a useful predictor of UN after *controlling for* YR or after *statistically removing the effects of* YR. Or, equivalently, whether IP reduces error in predicting UN *over and above* the reduction achieved by using YR. The important distinction is that asking whether a predictor variable is useful by itself is a very different question from asking whether it is useful after controlling for one or more other variables.

8.5.4 IP and YR

We could proceed directly to test the ability of IP to predict UN.0,YR. Although doing so would give us the correct statistical inference for answering whether IP is useful for predicting UN after controlling for YR, the resulting coefficient for IP is difficult to interpret because of the redundancy problem we discussed earlier (see Section 8.1). Remember that two (potential) predictor variables in a multiple regression equation are redundant if it is possible to predict one at least somewhat from the other. In this case, IP and YR are undoubtedly partially redundant because industrial production tends to increase over years; thus, we can use YR to predict IP. We can assess that redundancy formally by comparing these two estimated MODELs:

MODEL C: $\widehat{IP}_i = 138$

MODEL A: $\widehat{IP}_i = 114 + 4.75YR$

$$PRE = .821, \quad F_{1,8}^* = 36.6, \quad p < .0001$$

Thus, there is ample evidence that industrial production does increase yearly by about 4.75 units on average. The PRE = 82% assesses the magnitude of the redundancy between IP and YR. Another way to say this is that the *tolerance* between IP and YR is only $1 - .82 = .18$.

We can define IP.0,YR just as we did UN.0,YR. In particular, IP.0,YR is the residual after using an intercept term and YR to predict IP. Therefore, IP.0,YR is the part of industrial production that could *not* be predicted by YR. If YR cannot predict IP.0,YR, it therefore follows that YR and IP.0,YR are *not* redundant. Thus, IP.0,YR is precisely the part of IP that might be useful for adding to our MODEL that already includes YR for predicting UN. The values of IP.0,YR are also listed in Exhibit 8.20. Values of IP.0,YR are interpreted similarly to UN.0,YR. For example, the value of -5.36 for year 1 means that according to the yearly model industrial production was 5.36 units lower than expected in that year and the value of 6.45 for year 7 means that according to the yearly model industrial production was 6.45 units higher than expected in that year.

8.5.5 UN and IP Revisited

Now we can ask the crucial question of whether IP.0,YR reduces the error in predicting UN.0,YR relative to a simple model for UN.0,YR. Maybe when unemployment is unexpectedly high, industrial production is unexpectedly low? Note that this is a still more sophisticated version of our original question, which simply asked whether unemployment was high when industrial production was low without reference to any expectations. UN.0,YR tells us when unemployment is unexpectedly low or high, and IP.0,YR tells us when industrial production is unexpectedly low or high. The effects of YR (in this case the typical yearly changes) have been removed from *both* UN and IP. This allows us to have a purer look at the relationship between UN and IP with the confounding effects of YR eliminated. Again, we often use the phrase "controlling for" as in "the relationship between UN and IP after controlling for YR." So an examination of the scattergram in Exhibit 8.21 between UN.0,YR and IP.0,YR will suggest an answer to our question. Indeed, it appears in Exhibit 8.21 that when unemployment is unexpectedly low, industrial production is high, and vice versa.

To confirm our conclusion from Exhibit 8.21 that UN.0,YR and IP.0,YR are related, we need our usual procedures for inferential statistics. Does a model which used IP.0,YR to make conditional predictions of UN.0,YR significantly reduce error relative to a simple model of UN.0,YR? That is simply asking whether industrial production is unexpectedly high in those years when unemployment is unexpectedly low, and vice versa. That is a question we know how to answer with a straightforward application of the simple regression procedures of Chapters 6 and 7. We simply apply those procedures to the residuals UN.0,YR and IP.0,YR.

EXHIBIT 8.21 ▶

Scattergram between the residuals UN.0,YR and IP.0,YR

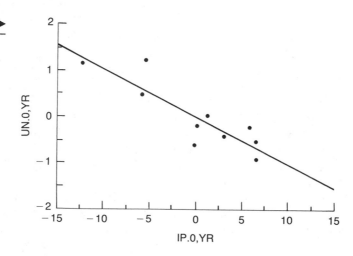

There is, unfortunately, a subtle complication, but it can easily be resolved. The complication is that we know a priori that the means of UN.0,YR and IP.0,YR are zero because the sum of the residuals must be zero for any least squares model. This in turn means that the intercept for a model predicting UN.0,YR with a predictor in mean deviation form (such as IP.0,YR) must also be zero. Thus, we have one less parameter to estimate than in the typical simple regression. In particular, to answer our question we will compare

MODEL C: $UN.0,YR = 0 + \varepsilon_i$

MODEL A: $UN.0,YR = 0 + \beta_1 \, IP.0,YR + \varepsilon_i$

For this comparison, PC = 0 and PA = 1. A second subtle complication is that UN.0,YR in one sense represents "used" DATA because it is the part of the original DATA that were left over after basing predictions on a two-parameter model (β_0 for the intercept and β_1 for YR). Thus, instead of the original $n = 10$ degrees of freedom there are only $n - 2 = 8$ degrees of freedom remaining. So the effective n for statistically comparing MODELS A and C from Eq. 8.7 is 8, instead of 10. Thus "n" − PA = 8 − 1 = 7.

Most regression programs have an option that allows estimation of the regression equation without estimating an intercept. In this case, the results are

MODEL C: $\widehat{UN.0,YR_i} = 0$

MODEL A: $\widehat{UN.0,YR_i} = -.103 IP.0,YR$

$$PRE = .76, \quad F^*_{1,7} = 22.8, \quad p < .001$$

The PRE of 76% is a substantial and statistically significant reduction in the error for predicting UN.0,YR. This confirms our visual conclusion from Exhibit 8.21 that when industrial production is unexpectedly high, unemployment tends to be unexpectedly low. In particular, MODEL A implies that for each unit increase in IP.0,YR (i.e., for each unit for which industrial production is unexpectedly high relative to a yearly model), then, on average, UN.0,YR (i.e., the amount by which unemployment is unexpectedly high or low relative to a yearly model) decreases by .103 million = 103,000 workers. This is the key coefficient for interpretation so let's state the conclusion again as it might appear in a journal article:

Over and above the yearly changes or, controlling for year, unemployment decreases, on average, by .103 million workers for each unit increase in the index of industrial production.

This conclusion contrasts sharply with the result of our first simple regression trying to predict UN. The yearly changes were masking or suppressing the relationship between IP and UN and we could only see them when YR was effectively removed from both IP and UN. Variables which mask or suppress the simple relationship between other variables are known as *suppressor* variables. The important lesson is that a variable which appears to be a poor predictor in a simple regression (in this case IP) may be a good predictor when combined with another predictor in a more complicated model. This demonstrates that asking whether two variables are related is a very different question than asking whether they are related when controlling for a third or more variable(s).

Note that relative to a simple model, using IP.0,YR reduces the error in UN.0,YR by approximately 76%. But remember that UN.0,YR was the part of UN remaining after using YR so that it represented the 57% of original data that was remaining. Thus, reducing 76% of the error in UN.0,YR is equivalent to reducing the error (relative to a simple model) in the original data by .76 × .57 = .43. The total reduction in error is the 43% obtained by using YR and the additional 43% obtained by adding IP.0,YR, or a total of 86%.

8.5.6   Multiple Regression: UN with YR and IP

By doing a series of simple regressions, some of them involving simple regressions of residuals, we have developed a more complete understanding of the relationship between industrial production and unemployment over and above their yearly changes. What would have happened if we had simply used the multiple regression procedures developed in the first half of this chapter? Exhibit 8.22 presents the output from a multiple regression analysis of the unemployment data, using both year and industrial production to predict unemployment. Look carefully at this table and note the similarities with the results we obtained above from the series of simple regressions. First, note the results for IP: the estimate of b for IP is $-.103$, the coefficient of partial determination, the PRE for comparing a MODEL of UN with IP and YR to one which only includes YR, is .76, and the resulting $F^*_{1,7}$ (obtained by squaring the t^* reported in the output) is $-4.772 = 22.8$. These are, except for rounding errors, *exactly* the same values we just obtained in Section 8.5.5 when we predicted UN.0,YR with IP.0,YR. Therefore, and this is the punch line we have been working toward, the interpretation of a parameter estimate in multiple regression is the same as the interpretation we developed in Section 8.5.5. In this case, the $b = -.103$ for IP means that when controlling for YR, or over and above the typical yearly changes, for each unit increase in IP, there is on average a decrease in unemployment of .103 million workers. Or in still other words, for each unit by which IP is unexpectedly high relative to a model involving YR, then UN is on average unexpectedly lower by 103,000 workers

DEP VARIABLE: UNEMP

ANALYSIS OF VARIANCE

SOURCE	DF	SUM OF SQUARES	MEAN SQUARE	F VALUE	PROB > F
MODEL	2	7.249764	3.624882	22.530	.0009
ERROR	7	1.126236	.1608909		
C TOTAL	9	8.376			

ROOT MSE	.4011121	R-SQUARE	.8655
DEP MEAN	2.82	ADJ R-SQ	.8271
C.V.	14.22383		

PARAMETER ESTIMATES

VARIABLE	DF	PARAMETER ESTIMATE	STANDARD ERROR	T FOR H0: PARAMETER = 0	PROB > |T|
INTERCEP	1	13.45394	2.483847	5.417	.0010
YR	1	.6594171	.104305	6.322	.0004
IP	1	−.103339	.02165515	−4.772	.0020

VARIABLE	DF	SEMI-PARTIAL CORR TYPE II	PARTIAL CORR TYPE II	TOLERANCE
INTERCEP	1	.	.	.
YR	1	.76772365	.85096168	.17925335
IP	1	.43741932	.76488056	.17925335

EXHIBIT 8.22 ▲

Output from PROC REG in SAS for unemployment data

relative to a model involving YR. PROC REG in SAS also produces "partial regression residual plots" such as the one in Exhibit 8.23. Note that although the labels are UN and IP, the plotted variables are really UN.0,YR and IP.0,YR, and this plot is identical to the scattergram in Exhibit 8.21.

Clearly, we fortunately do not need to do the laborious series of simple regressions because we can get the same information from a single multiple regression analysis. But it is important to remember that *conceptually* the algorithms of the multiple regression computer programs are merely doing that series of simple regressions for us and that the resulting coefficients have exactly the same interpretation as if we had done the series of simple regressions. To help generate interpretations of parameter estimates in multiple regressions, the following two generic statements may be useful:

When statistically controlling for the other variables in the model, or statistically holding the other variables in the model constant,

EXHIBIT 8.23 ▶

Partial regression residual plot from SAS PROC REG for UN and IP

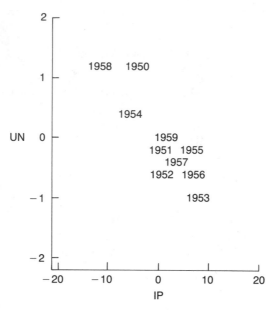

When statistically controlling for the other variables in the model, or statistically holding the other variables in the model constant, or over and above the predictions of the other variables in the model, for each unit increase in X_j, Y changes on average by amount b_j.

For each unit by which X_j is unexpectedly high relative to a model involving all the other predictor variables, then Y differs from its expectation, based on a model involving all the other predictor variables, by amount b_j.

To use these generic statements one simply has to replace the phrases "all other predictor variables," X_j, and Y with their appropriate variable names.

As an example of how to use the generic statements, let's consider the results for YR reported in the multiple regression output in Exhibit 8.22. We did not do the series of simple regressions resulting in YR being added last, after IP; but the results from the multiple regression analysis are as if we did. PRE = .85 and $F^*_{1,7} = 6.3^2 = 39.7$ indicate that the coefficient for YR of .659 is reliably different from zero. Substituting into the two generic statements yields the statements:

When statistically controlling for industrial production, or statistically holding industrial production constant, or over and above the predictions based on industrial production, for each unit increase in year (i.e., each year), unemployment increases on average by .659 million = 659,000 workers.

For each unit by which year is unexpectedly high relative to a model based on industrial production, then unemployment is unexpectedly high relative to a model based on industrial production by 659,000 workers.

The first statement makes sense. If there had not been increases in industrial production, unemployment would have increased at the rate of 659,000 workers per year instead of the actual average increase of 210,000 workers per year.[5] This time the relationship between industrial production and unemployment has been removed first or "partialed out" so that we can see the unmasked relationship between unemployment and year.

The second statement may seem a bit strange because it implies that a year can be unexpectedly high or low. But it does make sense in the context that knowing a year's level of industrial production gives us a clue to guessing the number of the particular year, and that guess might be high or low. Note that, as the statement indicates, .659 would be the value of the slope if we were to regress UN.0,IP on YR,0.IP and that the PRE would equal 85% for comparing that simple regression to a simple model that predicted 0 for the value of UN.0,IP.

8.5.7 Summary of Multiple Regression Model for Unemployment

Using both partial regression coefficients gives us a good model of unemployment for this period. Interpreting the partial regression coefficients allows us to examine the separate relationships between YEAR and UN and between IP and UN, relationships which are confounded and entangled in the original data. The model predicts that if there were no changes in industrial production, unemployment would have increased about 600,000 each year for a total increase of over 6 million during the 10-year period. That unemployment did not increase that much (it was only 3.8 million in the 10th year) is due to the fact that industrial production did not remain constant but also increased over that same period. According to the model, if there were no yearly increases in the number of workers seeking employment, each unit increase in the index of industrial production predicts a decrease in unemployment of about 100,000 workers. There was an increase of 46 index units of industrial production over this period, so had there been no changes in the number of workers there would have been a decrease in unemployment of 4.6

---

[5]The value of 210,000 workers comes from the simple regression of UN on YR in Section 8.5.2.

million workers. That unemployment did not decrease that much is in turn due to the fact that there were yearly increases in the number of workers. This is a much more complete and reasonable understanding of these data than was provided by the two simple regressions. Remember that the simple regression model predicted an increase in unemployment with an increase in industrial production because of the masking effects of the yearly changes. Only when those effects were removed could the relationship between industrial production and unemployment be seen.

8.6

Cautions about Using Multiple Regression

Multiple regression is probably the most widely used statistical procedure in the social sciences. As a consequence, it is also the most widely abused procedure. In this section we comment on some important cautions about using and interpreting multiple regression.

8.6.1   Causal Conclusions from Nonexperiments

We interpret the partial regression coefficient b_j as the amount the predicted value $\hat{Y}_i$ changes for each unit increase in the predictor variable, controlling for all other variables in the MODEL. It is important to remember that this is only a prediction based on the existing data and may not represent a causal relationship between X_j and Y. Users of multiple regression sometimes forget this fact and incorrectly presume that manipulating X_j will *cause* a change in Y. For example, it is tempting to conclude based on the relationship between industrial production and unemployment modeled above that if the government could have intervened somehow to raise industrial production in years when it otherwise would have been low, unemployment could have been substantially reduced. However, the problem with this conclusion is that unemployment probably has other causes and that intervention in the economic system might have caused other changes, which might, in turn, have negated the employment benefits of increasing industrial production artificially.

Another example may make the problem clearer. In almost any city with seasonal temperature variation it is easy to demonstrate that the number of ice cream cones sold in a month is a good predictor of the number of suicides in that month: the more cones sold the more suicides there will be. However, it would be ludicrous to suggest that by banning ice cream sales, suicides could be reduced. The problem with such a conclusion is that ice cream is not causing suicides; rather, it is probably just a proxy variable for temperature, which might be the cause. And even temperature is probably just a proxy variable for uncomfortableness or unpleasantness that might send a depressed person over the brink.

The causal error is obvious in the ice cream example. But many researchers do not realize that the dangers of presuming that manipulation of the predictor variable will cause a change in Y are no less serious whenever the regression analysis is based on observational data.

On the other hand, it is also incorrect to assume that causal conclusions can never be based on regression analyses. If the values of the predictor variables have been determined by the researcher and if those values were randomly assigned to the cases, then it is quite proper to presume that changing the predictor variable will cause a change in Y. For example, to test the sensitivity of demand for bank cards to the annual fee for the card, a bank might mail a bank card offer with one of, say, five different annual fees randomly assigned to each prospective customer. If a regression analysis revealed that the fee was a reliable predictor of the number of people who returned applications, then it would certainly be reasonable to presume that manipulation of the fee by the bank would affect the number of people seeking cards.

There are some other situations, such as what Campbell and Stanley (1963) have called quasi-experiments, in which limited causal conclusions from regression analyses of observational data are warranted. For further treatment of these issues see Cook and Campbell (1979) and Judd and Kenny (1981). In general, however, one should be extremely cautious about making causal conclusions from regression analyses of nonexperimental data.

8.6.2 Relative Importance of Predictor Variables

Many researchers are tempted to make inferences about the relative importance of predictor variables in multiple regression models. It should be obvious that it is not reasonable to compare directly the relative sizes of the b_j's because they clearly are dependent on the unit of measurement. By making the unit of measurement for a given predictor variable smaller we can make b_j arbitrarily small without changing the impact of that variable in the model. For the example of the baseball data, we can make the magnitude of the partial regression coefficient for batting average in a model predicting attendance relatively large by using the standard percentage units or relatively small by using units of thousandths.

Sometimes predictor variables will be measured on the same scale so that we can be sure to use the same units of measurement for all predictors. For example, consider trying to model attitudes toward a particular political party as a function of economic status. It might be reasonable to use both income and savings as predictor variables. We could measure both variables in dollars, so we could be assured of using the same units. But even here comparing the b_j's as a measure of importance would probably not be appropriate because the ranges of the variables would be so different. One variable might have a smaller b_j— that is, a smaller predicted change in Y for a unit increase in X_j—but still have a larger overall impact because it had a larger range.

The dependence of the overall effect of a predictor variable on its range suggests that we might normalize the partial regression coefficients by multiplying them by their ranges or, more typically, their respective standard deviations. This effectively makes the unit of measurement either the range or the standard deviation, respectively. The *standardized regression coefficients* are also traditionally normalized to include the standard deviation of Y according to the formula

$$b_j^* = b_j \left[\frac{s_{X_j}}{s_Y} \right] \tag{8.6}$$

Some books and computer programs unfortunately use β_j to refer to standardized regression coefficients; we prefer b_j^* to emphasize that they are simple transformations of the partial regression coefficients b_j.

Unfortunately, the standardized regression coefficients do not solve the problem of inferring relative importance. First, they still depend on the particular range and distribution of the predictor in the particular data set. If this distribution were to change for any reason—for example, if the researcher were to include a wider range of cases—then the standardized regression coefficients could change dramatically even if the underlying relationship between the predictor and the data remained the same. This hardly provides a good basis for inferring relative importance. Second, relative importance is also clouded by redundancy. A regression coefficient (standardized or not) might be low not because its associated predictor variable has no relationship with Y, but because that predictor variable is at least partially redundant with the other predictors. Thus, standardized regression coefficients do not really allow us, as they were intended, to make relative comparisons of predictors. As a consequence, we seldom find standardized regression coefficients to be useful; we always work with the usual partial regression coefficient b_j.

In sum, relative importance of predictor variables turns out to be a slippery concept. Any statement about relative importance must be accompanied with many caveats that it applies to this particular range of variables in this particular situation. As a result they are, in our opinion, seldom useful. Thus, although it is tempting to compare the importance of predictors in multiple regression, it is almost always best not to do so.

8.6.3 Automatic Model Building

Many regression programs have procedures for automatically building models. The most commonly used such procedure is *stepwise regression*, which, as its name implies, builds a model step by step. On each step a predictor variable may be added or deleted from the model. Usually the criterion for adding or deleting a variable is defined in terms of F^* or PRE when considering the variable as the last one in the model. On the first step the variable with the highest F^* or PRE is added (so long as it exceeds a preset minimum threshold). On subsequent steps, the variable not in the model that has the highest F^* is added to the model *or* a variable in the model whose F^* has fallen below the threshold is removed. The latter can happen because of redundancy. A predictor variable that had a high F^* when it was with few other variables in the model can have a much lower F^* on later steps after a number of variables have been added with which it is redundant. The stepwise procedure terminates when all the variables in the model have F^*'s above the threshold and all the variables not in the model have F^*'s below the threshold. Many programs for stepwise regression allow for fine-tuning of the threshold parameters. Common variations are *forward selection*—start with the simple model and add variables in the order of their usefulness until none exceeds the criterion—or *backward selection*—start with all the variables in the model and remove variables in decreasing order of usefulness until all variables remaining in the model exceed the criterion.

Stepwise regression and its variants present the alluring promise of finding the "best" model with virtually no effort by the researcher or data analyst. However, the allure is deceptive because it can be shown that for redundant predictors the stepwise procedure will not always find the best model. For example, a stepwise procedure may stop, say, with four predictor variables in the model, but when all possible four-variable regressions are computed another model will be found with a higher overall PRE. This problem can be solved with clever algorithms[6] which make it feasible to check all possible subsets of variables up to some fixed size. But then one has the problem of deciding between

---

[6]Most of the large statistical packages such as BMDP, SAS, and S have such procedures; these algorithms are infrequent in statistical packages designed for personal computers.

models of different size which do not have a MODEL C–MODEL A relationship because one model will not necessarily be a subset of the other. In such cases, the model with the highest adjusted R^2 (the unbiased estimate of η^2) is selected or the related Mallow's C_p criterion is used.

We do not recommend the use of the automatic model building procedures for three reasons. First, an unfocused search through many possible models (sometimes referred to as a "fishing expedition") increases the likelihood of capitalizing on chance and finding a model which represents only a spurious relationship. Models found by step-wise regression not infrequently fail to replicate when applied to new sets of comparable data. Second, as we saw above, the interpretation of the coefficients and the meaning of the question being asked depends on the other variables included in the model. For example, testing the relationship between industrial production and unemployment asked very different questions, depending on whether year was or was not included in the model. It seems unwise to let an automatic algorithm determine the questions we do and do not ask of our data. Someday there may indeed be artificial intelligence procedures in statistical packages, but the automatic model building procedures are not they. Third, it is our experience and strong belief that better models and a better understanding of one's data result from focused data analysis, guided by substantive theory. For an interesting illustration of the superiority of substantively guided data analysis over automatic model building, see Henderson and Velleman (1981). They state a fundamental axiom of their philosophy of data analysis with which we agree: "the data analyst knows more than the computer." Failure to use that knowledge produces inadequate data analysis.

8.7

Statistical Power in Multiple Regression

The discussion of statistical power in the context of simple regression, using a single predictor variable, generalizes quite readily to the multiple regression case, with multiple predictors, with a couple of additional caveats or qualifiers. The generalization goes as follows. If we have an estimate of the true proportional reduction in error, η^2, due to adding an additional predictor variable to others already included in a compact model, then we can employ Table C.5 in Appendix C to calculate the probability that if we included the predictor we would conclude that it reliably reduced the sum of squared errors in the model. In other words, given an estimate of η^2, we can use the same approach to calculating power that was employed in Chapter 7. If our estimate of η^2 is derived from a value of PRE from a prior study, then we need to convert that PRE value to an unbiased estimate of η^2 using the conversion formula presented earlier.

The interesting complexities in discussing power in the case of multiple predictors arise from the presence of the other predictors in the model. As we have already discussed, the denominator of the confidence interval for the coefficient for a particular predictor includes the tolerance of that predictor. As that tolerance decreases, so the confidence interval for its regression coefficient increases in width. Accordingly, as the tolerance of a predictor decreases, as it becomes more redundant with the other predictors in the model, tests of the reliability of its regression coefficient become less powerful.

Other predictors may also enhance the power of tests of a regression coefficient's reliability in multiple regression. Recall that in the numerator of the confidence interval (Eq. 8.6) is the mean square error for the augmented model. As that mean square error decreases in size, i.e., as the predictors in the augmented model do a better job of predicting Y_i, the width of the confidence interval decreases. Factors which reduce the mean square error thus increase the power of tests of the regression coefficients included in the model. Concerning the power of a test of the regression coefficient of a particular predictor, power will be increased as a function of including other predictors in the model that reliably reduce the errors of prediction in both the augmented and compact model, assuming those other predictors are not redundant with the one whose regression coefficient is being tested. When they are redundant there is a trade-off: the gain in power from reducing MSE may be compensated by a reduction in power due to redundancy. It is difficult to estimate this trade-off in power. However, the implication is that to improve power one should try to add reliable, nonredundant predictors to the model, assuming their presence makes substantive sense. The presence of predictors in the compact and augmented model that do not reliably relate to Y_i will result in less power, since the degrees of freedom for error for augmented and compact models will be reduced, thus increasing the mean square error.

9

Outliers and Data Having Undue Influence

The multiple regression techniques developed in the previous chapter for estimating and testing parameters in complex linear models give us powerful means for asking interesting questions of our DATA. We can now build and test fairly sophisticated MODELs for DATA so that ERROR is substantially reduced. However, when using these powerful techniques there is a potential problem for which we must always be alert. We observed in Chapter 2 that SSE and estimators which minimize SSE are very sensitive to extreme observations or *outliers*. The multiple regression procedures we considered in Chapter 8 are all based on the minimization of SSE. Hence, although the estimates of the regression parameters developed in Chapters 6, 7, and 8 have many desirable features, they also have the serious weakness that they are not resistant to outliers. If the least square regression estimators are routinely applied to data which contain a few wild observations, then the obtained estimates can be seriously misleading. Therefore, it is critically important to examine carefully the data for outliers whenever least square regression procedures are used. In this chapter we will examine useful ways for carefully examining DATA for outliers or for data values which have undue influence on the estimates. We begin with a general discussion of the causes of outliers and their effects on data analysis. Then we consider a detailed example to develop our intuitions about outliers and their detection. Next, we present a formal treatment of methods for detecting outliers and observations with undue influence in regression analysis. Finally, we conclude with a set of examples which illustrate the detection techniques and which demonstrate the serious consequences of failing to detect outliers.

9.1

Outliers

Outliers are extreme observations that for one reason or another do not belong with the other observations in DATA. There are many ways in which outliers can be introduced into DATA. The first cause of outliers we consider is scientifically uninteresting but quite troublesome. Data recording or, especially, data entry errors can put wild values into our DATA. The use of computers for data analysis increases the possibility of producing such outliers in our data and at the same time reduces our chances of finding them unless we carefully look for them. Consider for example the effects of entering the heights in inches and the weights in pounds for a number of individuals and for one observation reversing the numbers for the height and the weight. If we were doing our calculations with the aid of a pocket calculator, we would be likely to notice the reversal. However, when using the computer we are rather far removed from our data, so we would be unlikely to notice such a mistake unless we looked at our data with the intention of checking for outliers.

The effect of a large data entry error would be to bias the parameter estimates and to inflate SSE. It might not be obvious that our estimates had been biased. We also would be unlikely to recognize that the outlier had dramatically increased SSE, thereby making it very difficult to test other more complex models by examining changes in SSE. When a few outliers contribute a large proportion of the total ERROR, they overshadow any reductions in ERROR achieved by increasing model complexity. We obviously need statistical techniques for identifying erroneous observations so that they can be removed or corrected in DATA.

As an example of the deleterious effects of a data recording error, let's again consider the following two sets of numbers which we examined in Chapter 2.

Set 1: 1 3 5 9   14 $\overline{Y} = 6.4$ MSE $= s^2 = $ 26.8

Set 2: 1 3 5 9 140 $\overline{Y} = 31.6$ MSE $= s^2 = 3680.8$

Set 2 is identical to Set 1 except that a data entry error has added an extra digit to 14 to make it 140. As we noted before, this error has a dramatic impact on the mean, which is our estimate of β_0 for the simple model. The effects on SSE and, consequently, MSE are at least as bad.

The inflated MSE makes any hypothesis testing extremely difficult. This is easily seen by examining the 95% confidence interval for β_0 for both sets of numbers.

Set 1:   [0, 12.8]

Set 2:   [−43.7, 106.9]

The confidence interval for Set 2 is much larger than that for Set 1; in fact, the confidence interval for Set 1 is entirely included in the confidence interval for Set 2. Hence, many hypotheses about β_0 which could be easily rejected for Set 1 will not be rejected for Set 2. Hence, the effect of the data entry outlier is not only to produce a misleading parameter estimate but also to reduce the power of any statistical inferences. In other words, the outlier has so inflated SSE that it is much harder to detect any proportional reduction in ERROR produced by using β_0 instead of B_0 in a MODEL for these DATA.

Outliers are not necessarily erroneous observations. A second cause of outliers is that the cases are not a homogeneous set to which a single MODEL will apply, but rather a heterogeneous set of two or more types of cases, one of which is much more frequent. The infrequent cases of the other types will appear as outliers. For example, the set of 15 third grade students which we considered in Chapter 4 might consist of predominantly normal third grade students but might also include one or two exceptionally gifted students in mathematics who were fundamentally different from the other children. The scores for such children would appear as outliers in the data. A reexamination of Exhibit 4.2 suggests that this may indeed be the case because there are two very high scores (115 and 129) which are not very close to any of the other scores. Outliers such as these, unlike outliers which are erroneous, can be very valuable scientifically. Discovering that there are really two kinds of things in our DATA when only one was expected is almost always interesting scientifically. Looking at other characteristics of the extreme observations, especially if they are outliers, can provide clues for building more complex models. In this case we again need statistical techniques for identifying extreme or outlier observations, not necessarily so that they can be removed or corrected, but so that they can be examined with great care to extract their full informational value.

A third cause of outliers is what statisticians refer to as error distributions with "thick tails" in which extreme observations occur with greater frequency than expected for a normal distribution. Our assumption that the ERRORs have a normal distribution is fairly robust in the sense that error distributions can be rather unlike the normal distribution without appreciably altering any conclusions based upon the normality assumption. A major exception is nonnormal distributions which have thick tails. Exhibit 9.1 shows a normal distribution for the errors and a

EXHIBIT 9.1 ▶

Normal and Cauchy distributions of ERRORs (Cauchy has thicker tails)

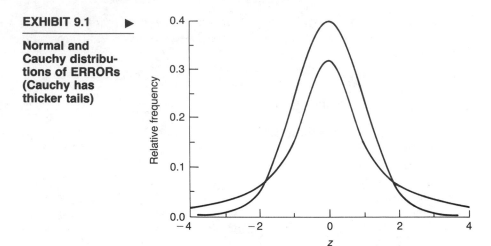

Cauchy[1] distribution for the errors. The Cauchy has the same general shape as the normal but much thicker tails. The problem is that when extreme observations are more frequent than expected for the normal distribution, SSE is greatly inflated and the sampling distribution for our test statistic F^* is no longer very accurate. In that case it is not appropriate to compare calculated values of F^* to critical values of F in the exhibits which were constructed with the assumption that the errors were normally distributed. In other words, our statistical tests may be very misleading. Also, the efficiency of our parameter estimates is greatly reduced. Ironically, sampling distributions which look very different from the normal distribution cause little or no problem as long as they do not have thick tails; the most problematical distributions have virtually the same shape as the normal distribution except for the thicker tails. Again, we need statistical techniques for identifying extreme observations that may indicate a distribution of errors with thick tails.

What one does when outliers are identified in the data is not without controversy. If the outlier is the result of a data entry error or is otherwise suspect in terms of its reliability or accuracy, then it should clearly be removed from the DATA or repaired before any further analysis. But what should be done about outliers which are not clearly erroneous? In our opinion, such observations should never be completely discarded, but neither should they be blindly included in the analysis. We will have more to say about this issue after we consider techniques for detecting outliers.

---

[1]The Cauchy distribution can be derived as the *ratio* of two random variables which are normally distributed (see, for example, Hogg & Craig, 1978, p. 142).

9.2

An Example

We now consider a detailed example to demonstrate the serious consequences of outliers and to motivate the detection techniques to be presented later. Exhibit 9.2 displays the SAT verbal scores and high school ranks for 13 students randomly selected from the data set considered in the previous chapter. The data values on the left side of the exhibit are the correct values. The values on the right side of the exhibit are identical except we have simulated an outlier (such as could be caused by a data entry error) by reversing the SAT and high school rank values for the sixth student. Below each data set are the results of simple regression analyses using high school rank to predict SAT verbal scores. Also given are the values for PRE and F^* to examine whether high school rank is a useful predictor of SAT verbal scores. Note that PRE and, consequently, F^* are slightly larger for the data set which contains the data reversal for the sixth student but that the parameter estimates are dramatically different. The intercept changes from about 6 to 97, and

EXHIBIT 9.2 ▶

SAT verbal and high school rank scores with and without data error (reversal of scores for Case 6)

Student	Original Data SAT	HSRANK	with Reversal SAT	HSRANK
1	42	90	42	90
2	48	87	48	87
3	58	85	58	85
4	45	79	45	79
5	45	90	45	90
6	48	86	86	48
7	51	83	51	83
8	56	99	56	99
9	51	81	51	81
10	58	94	58	94
11	42	86	42	86
12	55	99	55	99
13	61	99	61	99

	$b_0 = 5.95$		$b_0 = 96.55$	
	$b_1 = .50$		$b_1 = -.50$	
	PRE $= .29$		PRE $= .33$	
	$F^*_{1,11} = 4.53$		$F^*_{1,11} = 5.35$	

the slope changes sign from $+0.5$ to -0.5. The PRE and F^* are statistically significant (at $\alpha = .05$) for the data set with the data entry error, so we would conclude that as high school rank increases, SAT verbal scores decrease! This nonsensical result might cause us to check the data further, but there is nothing in the basic regression results nor a quick scan of the data in tabular form which would indicate that a serious problem exists.

How might we detect the outlier in the second data set? It is almost always easier to see outliers in graphs than in exhibits. Hence, the first step is to examine the scatterplot for SAT and HSRANK. The scatterplots along with the best-fitting line for the data sets with and without the reversal of the scores for the sixth observation are displayed in Exhibit 9.3. The y axes in both scatterplots are drawn to the same scale so that the size of an error (i.e., deviation from the least square regression line) is comparable.

The scatterplot for the original data in the top half of Exhibit 9.3 has the pattern we would expect when the model is appropriate. The data values are clustered around a straight line (which has a slope of .5 as revealed by the regression above). Note that none of the observations is unusually far from the line nor from the other observations. Thus, no outlier is apparent in the first scatterplot. In contrast, an outlier stands out clearly in the scatterplot in the bottom half of Exhibit 9.3 for the data set with the reversed observation. Again, none of the observations is particularly far from the best-fitting line (hence, the significant value of PRE $= .33$ from the above regression). However, the outlier observation in the upper left-hand corner of the second scatterplot is unusual in three different ways. First, the value of this outlying observation on the predictor variable X (HSRANK) is unusually small. If we look at the values on the predictor variable for all observations, there is only one large gap in those values and that occurs between the predictor value for this unusual observation (48) and the next lowest predictor value (79). Second, the Y value (SAT score) for the outlier is unusually large. Again, there is only one large gap between the Y values, and that is the gap between the data value for the unusual observation (86) and the next highest data value (61). Third, if the outlier case were omitted from the analysis, then the best-fitting line would have a positive slope (as in the first scatterplot) rather than a negative slope. This makes the outlier case unusual because it does not appear that omitting any other observation would have nearly as large an impact on the best slope for the regression line. These three ways in which the outlier is unusual suggests that to detect outliers we will want to ask the following three questions for each observation:

1. Is X_{i1} or, more generally, is the set of predictors $X_{i1}, X_{i2}, \ldots, X_{ip}$ unusual?

EXHIBIT 9.3 ▶

Scattergram for SAT and HSRANK with and without the reversed observation

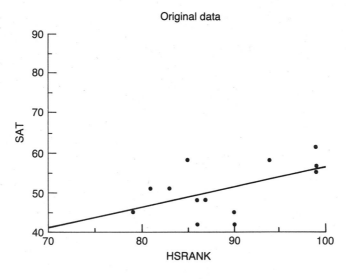

Original data

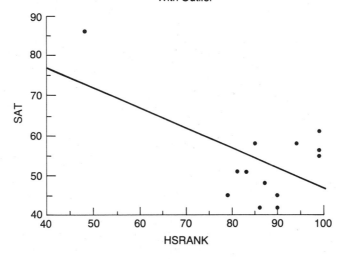

With Outlier

2. Is Y_i unusual?

3. Would omission of the observation produce a dramatic change in the parameter estimates b_0, b_1, b_2, . . . , b_p, or equivalently, in the predictions $\hat{Y}_i$ (since the values of $\hat{Y}_i$ are a direct function of the parameter estimates)?

If the answer to any of these questions is yes, then we have an outlier which requires attention. For the HSRANK and SAT data it appears as if the answer to all three questions is yes for the artificial outlier we produced by reversing the scores.

We now consider formal techniques for answering the three outlier questions. The statistical literature abounds with various mathematical indices and graphical procedures for each question. Except in the most unusual of circumstances most of these different procedures give essentially the same answer, so we will consider only a small subset of the possible techniques. We have selected those techniques which are most consistent with the general approach to data analysis presented in this book.

9.3

Are the Predictors X_{i1}, X_{i2}, ... , X_{ip} Unusual?

Of our three questions, this one is the easiest to answer. Also, its answer will provide a statistic which we will use in answering the other two questions. Hence, it is natural to begin by considering whether an observation's set of predictor values is unusual. We do so by digressing momentarily to consider a different but equivalent formula for $\hat{Y}_i$. This alternative formula for $\hat{Y}_i$ is not particularly useful for actually calculating $\hat{Y}_i$, so we will seldom use it for that purpose. Instead of calculation our interest will center upon the interpretation of the coefficients in this new expression for $\hat{Y}_i$. After the digression we will use these coefficients to answer the question about whether the set of predictors is unusual for particular observations. But first the digression.

$\hat{Y}_i$ as a Linear Function of Y_i's. Until now we have used the following expression for $\hat{Y}_i$:

$$\hat{Y}_i = b_0 + b_1X_{i1} + b_2X_{i2} + \cdots + b_pX_{ip}$$

That is, $\hat{Y}_i$ is a linear function of the X's with the b_j serving as weights in the linear combination. The b_j's are the partial regression coefficients which tell us by how much we should adjust our prediction for each unit change in the associated predictor variable X_j. While this representation for $\hat{Y}_i$ is extremely useful for calculations and has a straightforward interpretation, it does have the one disadvantage of obscuring the fact that the best prediction of $\hat{Y}_i$ is not only influenced by the predictor values X_j but also by all the other data values Y_i in the set. The other data values Y_i have their influence on $\hat{Y}_i$ through their use in the least squares estimation of the b_j's.

Alternatively, we can express $\hat{Y}_i$ as a linear function of the Y_{ij}'s (where both i and j refer to observations). Specifically,

$$\hat{Y}_i = \sum_{j=1}^{n} h_{ij}Y_j \tag{9.1}$$

where the h_{ij} depend only upon the values of the predictors X_j. We could have developed the least squares estimation procedure and the calculation of SSE(C), SSE(A), and PRE in terms of Eq. 9.1. For any given model we would obtain exactly the same $\hat{Y}_i$'s and, consequently, exactly the same sums of squared errors and PREs. We have not used Eq. 9.1 before because the translation of questions we want to ask of our DATA into appropriate MODELs C and A is less direct than for the usual equations expressing $\hat{Y}_i$ as a function of the b_j's and the X's. Although Eq. 9.1 is therefore not useful for normal analysis, its reexpression of MODEL will help us to answer the question about whether the set of predictors for a particular observation is unusual.

The important feature of Eq. 9.1 is that it separates the information from the X predictors and the information from the DATA Y_i into distinct parts. The coefficients h_{ij} depend only on the values of the predictors. If we know the values of $X_1, \ldots, X_p$ for all the observations, then we can compute h_{ij} before we know the actual DATA values Y_i. In contrast, the coefficients b_j in our usual representation are jointly determined by both the X predictors and the DATA Y_i. Thus, unlike the coefficients b_j, the h_{ij}'s give us a pure look at the effect of the X predictors. And a pure look at the effect of the X predictors is exactly what we need to answer our question about whether the set of predictors is unusual for particular observations.

There is a further interpretation of Eq. 9.1 which will help us answer our question. The equation expresses each $\hat{Y}_i$ as a linear combination of all the other Y_i's. In the equation h_{ij} thus represents the weight accorded the jth observation in the determination of the predicted value for the ith observation: the larger the value of h_{ij} then the greater the influence of the jth observation on $\hat{Y}_i$.

Calculating h_{ij}. The calculation of the h_{ij}'s is not easily accomplished by hand so their estimation is best left to matrix algorithms in computer programs. However, we will consider the calculational formulas for the h_{ij}'s for the simple model and the simple regression model in order to develop our intuitions about this alternative representation for $\hat{Y}_i$. For the simple model

$$\hat{Y}_i = b_0 = \overline{Y} = \sum_{j=1}^{n} \left(\frac{1}{n}\right) Y_j$$

or, in other words, if we let $h_{ij} = 1/n$, then

$$\hat{Y}_i = \sum_{j=1}^{n} h_{ij} Y_j$$

Thus, each Y_j is equally important in determining the prediction $\overline{Y}$ used for all the $\hat{Y}_i$'s because h_{ij} is the same for all i and j. This is just a fancy way of expressing the fact that all observations are equally weighted when computing the mean.

For the simple regression model it is easy to show (although we omit the algebra here) that

$$h_{ij} = \frac{1}{n} + \frac{(X_{i1} - \overline{X}_1)(X_{j1} - \overline{X}_1)}{SSX}$$

where

$$SSX = \sum_{i=1}^{n} (X_{i1} - \overline{X}_1)^2$$

From the formula for h_{ij} for the simple regression model it is easy to see that h_{ij} will be large whenever the values of X_{i1} and X_{j1} are far from the mean value for X_1. That is, h_{ij} will be large whenever the X_1 values for the ith and jth observations are unusual.

We will demonstrate the calculation of the h_{ij}'s and their use in the calculation of $\hat{Y}_i$ using the SAT-HSRANK data set with the outlier. The value for h_{11}, the influence of the first observation on determination of the first prediction, is given by

$$h_{11} = \frac{1}{13} + \frac{(90 - 86.15)(90 - 86.15)}{2131.7} = .084$$

In a similar fashion we calculate the following values of h_{1j} for all j: .084, .078, .075, .064, .084, .008, .071, .100, .068, .091, .077, .100, and .100. Unlike the case for the simple model, the h_{ij} in regression models are unlikely to be equal. However, they should be approximately the same size. In this case, all the values of h_{1j} are reasonably close to the average value $1/n = 1/13 = .077$ except for $h_{1,6} = .008$. The very low value of $h_{1,6}$ means that the sixth observation (which we know to be the outlier) essentially has no impact on the determination of the prediction of $\hat{Y}_1$.

We then use the values of h_{1j} to calculate the predicted value for the first SAT score by multiplying each SAT score by its respective weight above and then calculating the sum. That is,

$$\hat{Y}_1 = .084(42) + .078(48) + .075(58) + .064(45) + .084(45)$$
$$+ .008(86) + .071(51) + .100(56) + .068(51) + .091(58)$$
$$+ .077(42) + .100(55) + .100(61)$$
$$= 51.8$$

which, except for a small rounding error, agrees with the usual method for calculating $\hat{Y}_1$ which yields

$$\hat{Y}_1 = b_0 + b_1 X_{11} = 96.55 - .5(90) = 51.6$$

Thus, we can express $\hat{Y}_i$ either as a linear combination of the X's or as a linear combination of the Y's.

Levers h_{ii}. Of particular interest are the values of h_{ii} which indicate how influential the ith observation is for the determination of its own prediction. If h_{ii} is relatively large, then essentially all the other observations in DATA are being ignored during the estimation of that particular $\hat{Y}_i$. That is clearly an undesirable situation. The h_{ii} are often referred to as *levers*, and an observation with an unusually high lever is said to have *leverage* in the model estimation. As was noted above, h_{ii} is a function solely of the X_j's; h_{ii} is large only when the values of the predictors for the ith observation are unusual. This is easy to see for the case of simple regression for which

$$h_{ii} = \frac{1}{n} + \frac{(X_{i1} - \overline{X}_1)^2}{\text{SSX}}$$

The numerator in the second term is simply the squared error resulting from fitting a simple model to the X variable. The denominator is the total squared error for that simple model of X, so the ratio in the second term is simply the proportion of the variation in X which is due to the ith observation. Clearly, h_{ii} will be large only when X_{i1} is unusual, that is, when it is very far from $\overline{X}_1$. Although the formulas for h_{ii} for more complex models are much more complicated and best left to computers, the same principle applies: the larger h_{ii}, the more unusual is the set of predictors for the ith observation relative to the sets of predictors for the other observations.

The h_{ii} are referred to as the *levers* because they determine the leverage of each observation in determining its own predicted value. Several facts about the h_{ii} aid in their interpretation. It is easy to show that

$$0 \le h_{ii} \le 1$$

$$\sum_{i=1}^{n} h_{ii} = \text{PA} \quad \text{and so} \quad \overline{h}_{ii} = \frac{\text{PA}}{n}$$

An h_{ii} of zero indicates an observation with no influence on its fit to the MODEL; an h_{ii} of one means that the equivalent of one of the PA parameters has been allocated to fitting that one observation. Velleman and Welsch (1981) suggest that values of h_{ii} two or three times the average value expected ought to be considered large and in need of further attention in the data analysis. Thus, $h_{ii} > 2\,\text{PA}/n$ or $3\,\text{PA}/n$ indicate observations with unusual sets of predictors.

Huber (1981) suggests another interpretation of the h_{ii} which might aid our intuitive understanding. He says that $1/h_{ii}$ may be thought of as the "equivalent number of observations" involved in the determination of $\hat{Y}_i$. Obviously if h_{ii} is near 1, then $1/h_{ii}$ will be near 1, so essentially that one observation completely determines the prediction of $\hat{Y}_i$. If $h_{ii} = .5$, then only the equivalent of $1/.5 = 2$ observations are determining $\hat{Y}_i$. If there are many observations in our data set, then basing $\hat{Y}_i$ on the equivalent of two observations ought to make us very uncomfortable. Huber therefore suggests that any $h_{ii} > .2$ (5 equivalent observations) deserves special attention whenever n is reasonably large.

Exhibit 9.4 presents the values of the levers h_{ii} for the SAT-HSRANK data with the outlier; Exhibit 9.5 displays those values in a graph. In both the exhibit and the graph one aberrant lever is apparent; $h_{66} = .76$ while the next largest $h_{ii} = .15$. In other words, about 76% of one of the two parameters in the simple regression model is allocated to fitting the sixth observation, or, in Huber's terms, there are only the equivalent of $1/.76 = 1.3$ observations being used to determine $\hat{Y}_6$. None of the other observations has unusual leverage.

EXHIBIT 9.4 ▶

Levers h_{ii} for SAT-HSRANK data

OBS	SAT	HSRANK	LEVER
1	42	90	.08
2	48	87	.08
3	58	85	.08
4	45	79	.10
5	45	90	.08
6	86	48	.76
7	51	83	.08
8	56	99	.15
9	51	81	.09
10	58	94	.11
11	42	86	.08
12	55	99	.15
13	61	99	.15

EXHIBIT 9.5 ▶

Levers h_{ii} for SAT-HSRANK data

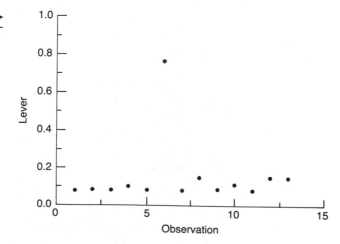

In summary, to answer the question whether the values for the set of predictors $X_1, X_2, \ldots, X_p$ for the ith observation are unusual, we need only consider the value of the lever h_{ii}. We do not have any formal rules for deciding whether a particular lever is large. Instead, we have informal guidelines which suggest the careful consideration of any observation which has a lever greater than $2\,PA/n$ or $3\,PA/n$ or, for reasonably large n, any lever greater than .2. We consider later what to do about observations which are found to have unusually high levers.

The regression programs in some computer packages (e.g., SAS) will provide the levers directly. However, most regression programs do not provide direct calculations of the levers so they must be computed from other quantities that those programs do provide. Velleman and Welsch (1981) show how to compute leverage and other regression diagnostics from other quantities typically provided by regression programs. BMDP1R, SPSSX REGRESSION, and SCSS report a statistic under the label "Mahalanobis distance," which is given by

$$MD = (n - 1)\left(h_{ii} - \frac{1}{n}\right)$$

If we can obtain MD from whatever program we are using, then simple algebra allows us to invert the above equation to obtain this equation for the lever:

$$h_{ii} = \frac{1}{n} + \frac{MD}{n - 1}$$

Obviously, h_{ii} will be large only when MD is large. Hence, it is not necessary to calculate by hand all the h_{ii} using the formula based on MD; instead, only those with the largest values of MD need be calculated.

9.4

Is Y_i Unusual?

Residuals. If we want to find those Y_i which are unusual, we must ask "unusual with respect to what?" The obvious answer is that we want to find those Y_i which are unusual with respect to the MODEL that we are considering. Obviously, the errors

$$e_i = Y_i - \hat{Y}_i$$

tell us how unusual the ith observation is with respect to the MODEL. If the absolute value of e_i is small, then the MODEL makes a good prediction for that Y_i, so it is not unusual. On the other hand, if e_i is large, then the MODEL makes a bad prediction for that Y_i, so it is unusual. The individual error e_i is often referred to as the *residual* because it is the part of the original observation Y_i that is "left over" after the prediction $\hat{Y}_i$ has been subtracted. Hence, we often refer to an examination of the individual error terms as an "analysis of the residuals."

It is generally difficult to identify outliers by examining the absolute magnitude of the e_i for two reasons. First, the importance of an error of a given magnitude is relative to the other errors and the magnitude of the prediction. For example, an error of 14 would be a very large residual if our model pertained to the automobile fatality rate per 100 million vehicle miles traveled because that error is about four times the mean of 3.54. But that same error would be inconsequential if our model pertained to the weight in kilograms of various automobiles because 14 would be a very small proportion of the mean. We therefore need some way to transform the residuals to a common scale on which we know what are large and small values. We might, for instance, standardize them by dividing each one by the root mean square error.

A second problem is that there is a paradox in using the standardized residual for identifying unusual values of Y_i. Extreme data values tend "to grab" the model so that the estimated parameters minimize e_i for those extreme values. We are asking if Y_k is unusual with respect to the MODEL, but the extreme Y_k has itself been used to determine the MODEL. If it has seriously altered or biased the parameter estimates in the model, then Y_k may not be unusual in terms of the magnitude of its residual. Instead, we ought to determine whether Y_k is unusual with respect to a model determined by all the other observations *except* Y_k.

Mathematical statisticians have developed a multitude of transformations of the residuals e_i which solve these two problems in interpreting the magnitude of particular residuals. Most regression programs in computer statistical packages can produce a large variety of these transformed residuals. Some of these transformed residuals only solve the scaling problem, others eliminate the paradox by removing the effect of the kth observation when considering the kth residual, and some do both. We choose to consider only one of these many residual indices, the *studentized deleted residual*, for three reasons. First, the studentized deleted residual both solves the scaling problem and eliminates the paradox, so there are good theoretical reasons for choosing it as an index of whether Y_k is unusual. Second, the studentized deleted residual has a natural interpretation in the context of the PRE approach used in this book. In particular, we will demonstrate that the square of the studentized deleted residual is simply the F^* for comparing appropriately chosen MODELs C and A. Third, it is very unlikely that the studentized deleted residual would fail to detect an unusual Y_k that could be detected by any of the other transformed residuals. Thus, we might as well just select one type of transformed residual, a type that is consistent with the PRE approach.

The Outlier Model and Studentized Deleted Residuals. We develop the studentized deleted residual by considering a specific MODEL for an outlier. If an observation is so extreme that it is unlike the other observations, then we should be able to reduce ERROR appreciably by adding a specific parameter to the MODEL just for that one observation. Designating a parameter for a single observation will ensure that there will be no error in our prediction for that observation. The other parameters are thereby freed to describe the remainder of the data. As a consequence, we will eliminate all error due to the outlier and the other parameters will generally provide a better fit to the remaining data so our overall measure of ERROR will inevitably be less. In effect we will be considering the outlier to be fundamentally different from the other DATA observations. We will refer to an original multiple regression model augmented by the addition of a specific parameter for the suspected outlier as an *outlier model*. To screen DATA for outliers, we will test the outlier model for each observation. That is, we will test one observation at a time to see if it is so extreme that we should allocate a specific parameter to it.

As with all other models, the question in considering the outlier model is whether the additional complexity is worth it. Adding a parameter for the suspected outlier to the MODEL will inevitably reduce ERROR, but will the reduction in ERROR justify the increased complexity of the MODEL? We can use PRE and F^* to answer this question. To be more formal, we can define the outlier model, which in this case represents our augmented model, to be

$$\text{MODEL A:}\quad Y_i = \beta_0 + \beta_1 X_{i1} + \cdots + \beta_{p-1} X_{i,p-1} + \varepsilon_i \qquad \text{for } i \neq k$$
$$= \beta_0 + \beta_1 X_{i1} + \cdots + \beta_{p-1} X_{i,p-1} + \beta_p + \varepsilon_i \qquad \text{for } i = k$$

where Y_k is the suspected outlier. In other words, there is a special parameter, β_p, just for Y_k. For all the other observations, the model is the same as the original model. We can construct a new variable X_{ip} such that

$$X_{ip} = 1 \qquad \text{for } i = k$$
$$= 0 \qquad \text{for } i \neq k$$

and then we can express the augmented model with the single equation

$$\text{MODEL A:}\quad Y_i = \beta_0 + \beta_1 X_{i1} + \cdots + \beta_{p-1} X_{i,p-1} + \beta_p X_{ip} + \varepsilon_i$$

As always, our first problem in considering a new model is to find the estimates of the model parameters which minimize SSE. We could compute the new variable X_{ip} and submit the augmented model to a standard multiple regression program. Were we to do so, we would obtain the exact parameter estimates for $b_0, \beta_1, \ldots, b_{p-1}$ as we would if we were to reanalyze the original model with the kth observation deleted. If b_p' is then freed to produce the best fit for Y_k, the error for that one observation will be zero. Hence, it must be the case that

$$b_p = Y_k - \hat{Y}_{k,[k]}$$

where the subscript $[k]$ indicates that the prediction was derived without using the kth observation. Clearly, there is no error for that one observation so $e_k = 0$. In sum, then, the error from the outlier model, MODEL A, is equal to the sum of squared errors that would result from the reanalysis of the original model with the kth observation deleted.

The compact model against which we want to compare the outlier model, which is now our MODEL A, is the original regression model for all the observations, including Y_k. To compare the two models, we need to calculate the sum of squared errors for each model and then calculate PRE and F^* as usual. For this comparison PA $-$ PC $= 1$ and $n -$ PA $= n - (p + 1)$.

As an example, let us return to the SAT and HSRANK data set which contains an outlier. If we consider the sixth observation to be the suspected outlier, then our two models are

MODEL C: SAT $= \beta_0 + \beta_1 \text{HSRANK} + \varepsilon_i$

MODEL A: SAT $= \beta_0 + \beta_1 \text{HSRANK} + \beta_2 X_{i2} + \varepsilon_i$

where $X_{i2} = 0$ except that when $i = 6$, $X_{i2} = 1$. In other words, X_{i2} simply indicates the sixth observation. PC $= 2$, PA $= 3$, so PA $-$ PC $= 1$ and $n -$ PA $= n - 3$. The regression for MODEL C is the same as the original regression displayed on the right side of Exhibit 9.2. It and the new regression for MODEL A are summarized below:

MODEL C: $\widehat{\text{SAT}} = 96.55 - .50 \text{ HSRANK}$

MODEL A: $\widehat{\text{SAT}} = 6.71 + .50 \text{ HSRANK} + 55.49 \, X_{i2}$

$$\text{PRE} = .68, \quad F^*_{1,10} = 21.4, \quad p < .01$$

Thus, devoting one parameter to the sixth observation, or equivalently, omitting the sixth observation from the DATA used to fit the MODEL, reduces the ERROR by 68%. With 11 degrees of freedom for ERROR left after estimating b_0 and b_1, we would expect the omission of any one observation would, on average, reduce error by only about $1/11 = 9\%$. The very much larger proportional reduction in ERROR obtained by omitting the sixth observation suggests that it is a very unusual observation with respect to the MODEL for the DATA. This is confirmed by the very large value of $F^*_{1,10} = 21.4$.

Note that the sign of the coefficient changed between MODEL C and MODEL A. Omitting the sixth observation thus causes a dramatic difference in the estimation of the coefficients. We return to this fact later.

It is interesting to consider what would happen if we were to test the outlier model for an observation which is not an outlier. Suppose, for example, that we tested the outlier model for the first observation in the SAT-HSRANK data set. In this case $X_{i2} = 0$ except $X_{i2} = 1$ when $i = 1$. Estimating the coefficients in the compact and augmented models yields

MODEL C: $\widehat{SAT} = 96.55 - .50\ HSRANK$

MODEL A: $\widehat{SAT} = 95.71 - .48\ HSRANK - 10.67X_{i2}$

$$PRE = .096, \quad F^*_{1,10} = 1.06, \text{ n.s.}$$

Devoting a special parameter to the first observation is clearly not worth it. The proportional reduction in error of 9.6% is little more than we would expect by chance (9%); this is confirmed by the low, nonsignificant value of F^*. Note that in contrast to omitting the sixth observation, omitting the first observation produces minimal changes in the estimates b_0 and b_1.

The above results suggest that we can use the outlier model as a means of screening our data for possible outliers. We simply test the outlier model n times, each time letting a different observation be the "odd one out." Exhibit 9.6 displays the values of PRE and F^* for testing each observation as an outlier in the SAT-HSRANK data set. The last column of Exhibit 9.6 is $t^* = \sqrt{F^*}$, which is more commonly provided by regression programs under the name *studentized deleted residual*. The only large PRE and F^* again identify the sixth observation, which we know to be an outlier.

EXHIBIT 9.6 ▶

PRE, F^*, and $t^* = \sqrt{F^*}$ for the outlier model applied to each observation

Student	SAT	SAT*	ERROR	PRE	F^*	t^*
1	42	51.8	−9.8	.10	1.1	−1.0
2	48	53.3	−5.3	.03	.3	−.5
3	58	54.3	3.7	.01	.1	.4
4	45	57.3	−12.3	.15	1.8	−1.3
5	45	51.8	−6.8	.05	.5	−.7
6	86	72.7	13.3	.68	21.4	4.6
7	51	55.3	−4.3	.02	.2	−.4
8	56	47.3	8.7	.08	.9	.9
9	51	56.3	−5.3	.03	.3	−.5
10	58	49.8	8.2	.07	.7	.9
11	42	53.8	−11.8	.14	1.6	−1.3
12	55	47.3	7.7	.06	.7	.8
13	61	47.3	13.7	.20	2.6	1.6

Although the outlier model is conceptually clear, it would not be very practical if we had to compute n separate regressions and n separate PRE and F^* values in order to screen DATA for outliers. It would be extremely tedious, although not difficult, to do the n required regressions using the computer. Fortunately, this is not necessary, for Belsley, Kuh, and Welsch (1980) have shown that F^* for testing the outlier model for the ith observation is given by

$$F^* = \frac{e_i^2(n - PA - 1)}{SSE(1 - h_{ii}) - e_i^2}$$

All of the components for computing F^* for the outlier model are therefore available either from the original regression or from the levers h_{ii}; hence, the computational cost is not great. For example, we can calculate the value of F^* for testing the sixth observation as an outlier using $e_6 = 13.33$, obtained from Exhibit 9.6, SSE $= 1085.3$, obtained from the original regression analysis or by summing the squared values in the ERROR column of Exhibit 9.6, $h_{66} = .76$, obtained from Exhibit 9.4, and $n - PA = 13 - 2$ for the original regression analysis. So,

$$F^*_{1,10} = \frac{(13.3)^2(13 - 2 - 1)}{(1085.3)(1 - .76) - (13.3)^2} = 21.2$$

which, within rounding error, is the same value reported in Exhibit 9.6.

We know of no computer programs which will report F^* for the outlier model directly, so the above formula may be useful to calculate F^* from the individual components. However, a number of programs will report the studentized deleted residual, which is simply the square root of the F^* for the outlier model for a given observation, assigning that square root the sign of that observation's residual. The name "studentized deleted residual" reflects an equivalent but very different derivation of this procedure for identifying outliers. In order, therefore, to answer the second question about whether an observation's Y value is unusual, we want to square that observation's studentized deleted residual. This then equals F^* for testing the outlier model against MODEL C, which does not include an additional parameter for that particular observation. If the resulting F^* is large, then we conclude that allocating an additional parameter for that particular observation is worthwhile. This conclusion is equivalent to saying that that particular observation's value of Y is quite unusual.

We must be careful about using the outlier model to screen DATA for outliers. We are performing the equivalent of n statistical tests on the same set of data. If we use $\alpha = .05$ to determine the critical values of PRE and F^* for rejecting the original model in favor of the outlier model, then we have a 5% chance of making a Type I error for *each* of the n model tests we perform. The probability that we do *not* make a

Type I error in n trials equals $.95^n$. For example, for the SAT-HSRANK data for which we have 13 observations, the probability that we do not make a Type I error when using $\alpha = .05$ for each test is $.95^{13} = .51$, so the probability of making at least one Type I error while screening the data with the outlier model equals $1 - .51 = .49$. That is unacceptably large. One solution is to use what is known as the *Bonferroni inequality*. According to the Bonferroni inequality, the probability of making at least one Type I error will be less than α if the critical value for each test is chosen so that $\alpha' = \alpha/n$.[2] Thus, for the SAT-HSRANK data we would use $\alpha' = .05/13 = .004$, which would imply a critical value for F of about 13 or 14. The F^* for the sixth observation still easily beats this more conservative standard and so would be declared an outlier.

In general, we do not recommend that the squared studentized deleted residual or the F^* that results from evaluating the outlier model be used as a formal statistical test unless one has external information questioning the validity or reliability of a particular observation. Rather we suggest that large values of F^* simply be used to indicate observations which require closer scrutiny. The square root of F^*, or the studentized deleted residual itself, is particularly useful for this screening purpose because we can suggest an easy rule of thumb for identifying outliers. For reasonably large n, approximately 95% of the studentized deleted residuals (which have a t distribution) will be between -2 and $+2$. Thus, studentized deleted residuals with an absolute value less than 2 are not surprising, and we will not consider them to be unusual. However, if the absolute value of the studentized deleted residual is greater than 2, then it probably deserves another look because values that large should occur less than 5% of the time (approximately). Only about 1% of the studentized deleted residuals should be less than -3 or greater than $+3$. So, if the absolute value of the studentized deleted residual is greater than 3 careful attention to that observation is required. Finally, absolute values of studentized deleted residuals greater than 4 ought to be extremely rare; if the absolute value is greater than 4, then all alarm bells ought to sound. A studentized deleted residual that large is clear indication of an unusual value of Y_k. Accepting a MODEL for which a studentized deleted residual is greater than 4 could be very misleading.

In summary, we can use a test of the outlier model or, equivalently, the studentized deleted residual to identify Y_k's which are unusual with respect to the other observations. We therefore have answered our second question.

---

[2]The Bonferroni inequality is sometimes impractical because of the difficulty in finding the critical values for α/n. The SAS programs in Appendix C which were used to generate the significance and power exhibits can be easily modified to obtain the required critical values of PRE and F^* for any desired values of α and n.

9.5

Would Omission of Y_k Dramatically Change $b_0, b_1, \ldots, b_p$?

While considering the graph of the SAT and HSRANK data and while examining the results of the outlier model applied to the sixth observation, we noted that omitting the sixth observation causes a dramatic change in the estimate of b_1: $b_1 = -.5$ when the sixth observation is included, and $b_1 = .5$ when the sixth observation is omitted. It did not appear that omitting any other observation would have an appreciable impact on the estimate b_1 and certainly would not change the sign of the estimate. This suggests that we look for outliers by considering the change in the parameter estimates resulting from the deletion of each observation from the analysis. The deletion of a "typical" observation should have little or no impact on the parameter estimates, but the deletion of an unusual observation that may have "grabbed" the estimates might result in a large change in the parameter estimates.

To be more formal we will let $b_{j,[k]}$ be the estimate of β_j when the kth observation has been omitted from the estimation. We can use SSE to measure the effect of omitting the kth observation. That is, we can compute the respective SSEs for the following two models:

$$\hat{Y}_{i,[k]} = b_{0,[k]} + b_{1,[k]}X_{i1} + \cdots + b_{p-1,[k]}X_{i,p-1}$$
$$\hat{Y}_i = b_0 + b_1X_{i1} + \cdots + b_{p-1}X_{i,p-1}$$

where $\hat{Y}_{i,[k]}$ equals the prediction for the ith observation when the kth observation has been deleted from the estimation procedure. We know that the difference in the SSE for two models can be represented as the sum of the squared differences between their predictions. That is,

$$\text{SSE}[k] - \text{SSE} = \sum (\hat{Y}_i - \hat{Y}_{i,[k]})^2$$

If we were to compute the usual PRE and F^* values for this reduction in error we would be testing the following null hypothesis:

$$\beta_0 = b_{0,[k]}, \quad \beta_1 = b_{1,[k]}, \ldots, \beta_{p-1} = b_{p-1,[k]}$$

We would then be testing a compact model with no estimated parameters against a model with p estimated parameters. Unfortunately, this would not be a legitimate use of PRE and F^* because the hypothesized values for β_j in the compact model are really estimated parameters. Although we therefore cannot compare PRE and F^* to their usual critical values, we still can compute PRE and F^* for this situation in order to provide useful indices of the degree to which omitting a particular observation would affect the parameter estimates and, equivalently, the predicted values.

To remind ourselves that the F^* calculated for this situation is not truly an F which could be compared to the usual critical values of F, we will use the notation D_k to refer to the F^* for comparing the reduction in error obtained by using all observations versus omitting the kth observation.[3] Cook (1977, 1979) has shown that

$$D_k = \frac{\Sigma_i \, (\hat{Y}_i - \hat{Y}_{i,[k]})^2}{PA(MSE)}$$

For any particular observation that was of concern for external reasons, it would be relatively simple to compute the two regressions (with and without Y_k) and then compute the sum of squared differences for the two predictions. However, this again would be tedious as a screening procedure for outliers if we had to perform n separate regressions, each time omitting a different observation. Fortunately, as was the case for the outlier model and studentized deleted residuals, this is not necessary because the following equivalent formula for D_k shows that it can be calculated from basic components available from the original regression. That is,

$$D_k = \frac{e_k^2}{PA(MSE)} \left[\frac{h_{kk}}{(1 - h_{kk})^2} \right]$$

For example, for the sixth observation the only quantity we have not determined is MSE, but this is easily obtained as $SSE/(n - PA) = 1085.3/11 = 98.66$; so,

$$D_6 = \frac{13.3^2}{2(98.66)} \left[\frac{.76}{(1 - .76)^2} \right] = 11.83$$

which, within rounding error, is the same as the value in Exhibit 9.7.

Many regression programs will report D_k for each observation as *Cook's D*, so the above calculational formula will seldom be needed. However, the calculational formula is important for two reasons. First, it shows that it is not necessary to do many regressions in order to use D_k to screen for outliers. Instead, D_k may be calculated from the residuals, PA, MSE, and the levers h_{ii}. Thus, computational expense is not an excuse for not considering the values of Cook's D. Second, and more importantly, the calculational formula demonstrates that D_k is a multiplicative function of the squared error for that observation and the lever for that observation. Thus, the most influential observations in terms of their impact upon the parameter estimates will be those which have large squared errors (an unusual Y_k value) *and* high leverage (an unusual set of predictor values). Conversely, if either Y_k is not unusual with

---

[3]The notation D is chosen because it can be shown that D_k is a generalized measure of distance.

EXHIBIT 9.7 ▶

Values of Cook's *D* for the SAT-HSRANK data set

i	SAT	Cook's D
1	42	.05
2	48	.01
3	58	.01
4	45	.09
5	45	.02
6	86	11.86
7	51	.01
8	56	.08
9	51	.02
10	58	.05
11	42	.06
12	55	.06
13	61	.21

respect to the model for the other observations (i.e., low value for the studentized deleted residual) *or* if the set of predictors for the kth observation is not unusual with respect to the sets of predictors for the other observations, then D_k will not be large. But also note that if Y_k is not quite unusual enough to attract our attention and if h_{kk} is also not quite large enough to be considered a high lever, then D_k can and often will be large enough to require attention.

There are only informal guidelines for thresholds above which values of Cook's D should require attention. A frequent recommendation is to consider values of Cook's D to be large which exceed $4/PAn$. Another suggested rule is to consider any value of D_k greater than 1 or 2 as indicating that the kth observation requires a careful look. Another suggestion is to look for gaps between the largest D_k's.

As an example of the use of D_k, the values of Cook's D for each observation in the SAT-HSRANK data set with the outlier are displayed in Exhibit 9.7. The whopping value of 11.86 for the value of Cook's D for the sixth observation clearly identifies it as a very influential observation which has seriously distorted the analysis. Whether or not that sole observation is included in the analysis dramatically influences the parameter estimates. This confirms our observation that deleting the sixth observation would dramatically change the predictions by changing the sign of b_1 but that the omission of any other observation would have very little impact on the estimate of b_1. The next largest value of Cook's D is only .21 (for the 13th observation), but it is more than twice as large as the next largest D_k so it probably deserves at least a quick look.

In summary, D_k or Cook's D assesses the global impact of each observation on the parameter estimates and, equivalently, on the predictions for all the other observations. Large values of D_k identify those observations with large impacts. We therefore can use D_k to answer our third outlier question.

9.6

Summary of Outlier Detection

There are three issues in the identication of outliers. First, are the values for the predictors X_1, X_2, . . . , X_p for this observation unusual with respect to the values of those predictors for the other observations? Values of the levers h_{ii} usefully answer this question. Second, is the value of Y_i for the observation unusual with respect to a model for other observations? PRE and F^* for the outlier model or, equivalently, the studentized deleted residual are excellent techniques, completely consistent with the PRE approach of this book, for determining whether Y_i is unusual. Third, does the observation have an undue impact on the estimation of the model parameters and, equivalently, on the determination of the predicted values for all observations? Cook's D is an excellent procedure, motivated by the PRE approach of this book, for assessing the overall impact of a particular observation on the fit of the model.

The three questions are very interrelated, and it is not unusual for an outlier to be detected by all three procedures. However, each question is slightly different, so it is possible to have any combination of answers to the three questions. Thus, all three questions need to be asked. Exhibit 9.8 illustrates the distinctness of the questions for the case of simple regression. Let's consider the effect on the regression analysis of each of the unusual points marked A, B, and C. In the comments below we assume that in a particular analysis only one of these three unusual cases is present.

The observation marked A has an unusual Y value relative to a simple regression model for these data because it lies off the line defined by the other observations, but its X value is in the middle of the other X values, so it is not unusual in that respect. We would therefore expect the studentized deleted residual to be high for observation A but would expect the lever and Cook's D to be low. The net effect of observation A on the MODEL would be to pull the intercept towards A but to leave the slope essentially unchanged. Although observation A would therefore have a minimal effect on the slope, it would adversely affect statistical inference by inflating the sum of squared errors for DATA. This

EXHIBIT 9.8   ▶

Illustration of three
different types of
outliers:
A = unusual *Y*,
B = unusual *X*,
C = unusual *Y*
and *X*

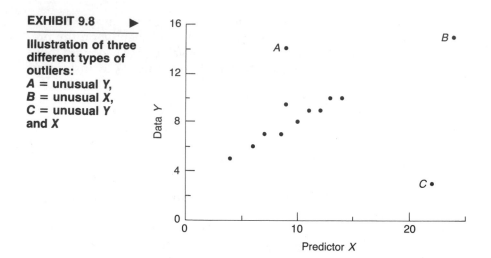

inflation, as demonstrated above, would make it harder to detect differences between any MODEL C and MODEL A, thereby increasing the probability of a Type II error—failing to reject the null hypothesis when it in fact is false.

The observation marked *B* has an unusual *X* value far beyond the *X* values of the other observations. Hence, we would expect it to have a high leverage value. However, *B* lies on the line defined by the other observations so its *Y* value is not unusual with respect to a MODEL defined by those other observations; hence, its studentized deleted residual would be low. The consistency with the other observations means that *B* would have little impact on the parameter estimates or the predicted values for the other observations; hence, Cook's *D* would be low. Although observation *B* would therefore, like *A*, have a minimal impact on the MODEL estimation, it would adversely affect statistical inference by inflating the sum of squared errors for *X*. Remember that SSX is a term in the denominator for the confidence interval for the slope (Eq. 8.6). The inflated value of SSX would therefore make the confidence interval *smaller* than it otherwise would have been. The resulting small confidence interval may be unrealistically small thereby increasing the chances of a Type I error—rejecting the null hypothesis when it should not have been rejected.

The observation marked *C* is unusual in all respects. Its *Y* value is unusual with respect to a MODEL defined by the other observations, so it would have a large studentized deleted residual. Its *X* value is also unusual, so its lever would be high. The combination of an unusual *Y* value and an unusual *X* value would mean that *C* would pull the regression line in its direction; thus, Cook's *D* would be high. An outlier such

EXHIBIT 9.9 ▶

Usual effects of outliers

Index	Parameter Estimates	Increase Error Type
Lever	OK	Type I
Student. deleted residual	OK	Type II
Cook's D	Biased	Either

as C, which is detected by all three questions, is especially disastrous for two reasons. First, it can alter statistical inference in the same ways as A or B, either inflating Type I or Type II errors—but we won't know which! Second, an outlier like C also biases the parameter estimates for fitting MODEL to DATA. Thus, with an outlier like C we can trust neither the parameter estimates in the MODEL nor any statistical inferences.

We can summarize the *usual* effects of these different types of outliers with the following rules outlined in Exhibit 9.9. The reader is cautioned that these rules summarize the usual effects and that other effects are possible. Another less formal summary is that large levers can fool us into falsely thinking that we have found something interesting, large studentized residuals are akin to shooting ourselves in the foot by causing us to miss something interesting, and for large Cook's D all bets are off.

9.7

Dealing with Outliers

Once we have identified outliers we have the problem of what remedial action, if any, we should take. The SAT-HSRANK example highlights the crux of the outlier problem. If we were simply to report the results for the regression model with no indication that there is an outlier, we would essentially be reporting a model which is determined by a single observation! It would be misleading in such situations to pretend that the model is really based on n, the reported number of observations. Somehow, however, in the social sciences the reporting of results with outliers included has come to be viewed as the "honest" thing to do and the reporting of results with outliers removed is sometimes unfortunately viewed as "cheating." Although there is no doubt that techniques for outlier identification and removal can be abused, we think it is far more honest to omit outliers from the analysis with the explicit admission in the report that there are some observations which we do not understand and to report a good model for those observations which we do understand. If that is not acceptable, then separate analyses, with and without the outliers included, ought to be reported so that the reader can make his or her own decision about the adequacy of the models. *To ignore outliers by failing to detect and report them is dishonest and misleading.*

Anscombe's Example. To provide additional motivation to check *always* for outliers, we present a famous example constructed by Anscombe (1973).[4] Exhibit 9.10 displays four sets of Y and X variables. Note that the X variable is the same for the first three data sets. Testing a simple regression model for each of these data sets is equivalent to comparing the following compact and augmented models:

MODEL C: $\quad Y_i = \beta_0 + \varepsilon_i$

MODEL A: $\quad Y_i = \beta_0 + \beta_1 X_{i1} + \varepsilon_i$

For the first data set we would obtain the following estimates:

MODEL C: $\quad \hat{Y}_i = 7.5$

MODEL A: $\quad \hat{Y}_i = 3.0 + .5X_{i1}$

$$\text{PRE} = .666, \quad F^*_{1,9} = 17.95, \quad p < .01$$

The remarkable property of the Anscombe data sets is that we obtain exactly the same parameter estimates and exactly the same PRE and F^* for the other three data sets! Even though the data are clearly different in the four sets, we obtain the same results. Obviously, the parameter estimates, PRE, and F^*, are not sufficient to distinguish among these four very different data sets.

EXHIBIT 9.10 ▶

Four hypothetical data sets from Anscombe (1973)

i	Set 1 Y_1	X_1	Set 2 Y_2	X_2	Set 3 Y_3	X_3	Set 4 Y_4	X_4
1	8.04	10	9.14	10	7.46	10	6.58	8
2	6.95	8	8.14	8	6.77	8	5.76	8
3	7.58	13	8.74	13	12.74	13	7.71	8
4	8.81	9	8.77	9	7.11	9	8.84	8
5	8.33	11	9.26	11	7.81	11	8.47	8
6	9.96	14	8.10	14	8.84	14	7.04	8
7	7.24	6	6.13	6	6.08	6	5.25	8
8	4.26	4	3.10	4	5.39	4	12.5	19
9	10.84	12	9.13	12	8.15	12	5.56	8
10	4.82	7	7.26	7	6.42	7	7.91	8
11	5.68	5	4.74	5	5.73	5	6.89	8

[4]From Anscombe (1973), by permission of American Statistical Association.

Just how different these data sets are is revealed by an examination of their scatterplots in Exhibit 9.11; the best-fitting line, which is the same for all four data sets, is also displayed in each scatterplot. The scatterplot and the fit of the best line to the data for Set 1 are as we expect them to be for the linear regression model. The points are scattered about, but reasonably close to, the regression line. The first is the only set of the four for which the statistical analysis is really appropriate. In Set 2 it is clear that there is a strong relationship between X_2 and Y_2 but that it is a *curvilinear* relationship instead of the linear relationship presumed by simple regression. The linear statistical analysis reported above understates the strength of the true relationship between the two variables because it does not consider the curvilinear part of that relationship. In the next chapter we consider techniques for adding curvilinear information to the MODEL. In Set 3 there is an obvious outlier. Except for the one outlying observation there would be a perfect linear relationship between X_3 and Y_3. The statistical analysis including this outlier yielded PRE = .666, which considerably understates the linear relationship among most of the observations in this set. In Set 4 there is also an obvious outlier. Except for the one outlying observation there would be no relationship between X_4 and Y_4 because all observations would have the same value of X_4, making it useless as a predictor of

EXHIBIT 9.11 ▶

Scattergrams and best-fitting lines for all four Anscombe data sets

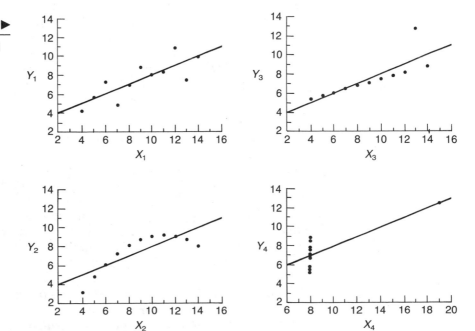

Y_4. However, the one extreme observation fools the statistical analysis into reporting a linear relationship (PRE = .666). Hence, in this case the usual analysis considerably overstates the true relationship between X_4 and Y_4.

If the usual regression analyses do not distinguish among these four very different data sets, then we cannot depend upon the parameter estimates, PRE, or F^* to alert us to situations for which the MODEL is not appropriate. Thus, any analysis which stops with those estimates and statistics is necessarily incomplete! To complete the analysis of any DATA, we must also consider graphs of the ERRORs and outlier indices. Exhibit 9.12 displays the outlier indices and Exhibit 9.13 the graph of the residuals ($e_i = Y - \hat{Y}_i$) against the predictor for each of the four data sets. For Set 1 none of the outlier indices is remarkable, and the graph of the residuals reveals a random scattering as it should.

For Set 2 none of the outlier indices is remarkable, but the graph of the residuals reveals a patterned, rather than random, scattering. Such a pattern in the residuals indicates that there is more information available in the predictor X_2 for improving the predictions of Y_2. How to extract this information is the subject of the next chapter.

For Set 3 the outlier indices indicate that the third observation is unusual because its studentized deleted residual equals 3.9. So F^* for testing whether a special parameter should be allocated to this observation in the outlier model is $F_{1,8}^* = 3.9^2 = 15.2$. If we use the conservative $\alpha = .05/11 = .005$ from the Bonferroni inequality, the critical value for $F_{1,8;.005} = 14.7$, so we should conclude that the observation does have an unusual Y value with respect to the MODEL. Converting F^* to PRE yields PRE = .992; in other words, 99.2% of the squared error is due to that single observation. The graph of the residuals also clearly indicates the outlier. Note that the lever h_{ii} for the outlier is not unusual, so the net effect on the slope is slight. The real effect of the outlier has been to reduce PRE for the simple regression model from about 1 to .666.

Finally, for Set 4 the outlier indices again indicate an unusual observation, the eighth. The extremely high value for the lever $h_{8,8} = 1$ (in fact, this is the highest possible value for a lever) indicates that the eighth observation is very unusual with respect to the other values of X_4. In effect, one of the two parameters in the regression model is allocated entirely to the eighth observation. Essentially this one observation is responsible for determining the slope. If the eighth observation were deleted there would be no slope and if its Y value were changed, the slope would change accordingly. The graph of the residuals certainly does not show a random scattering; instead, the unusual predictor value is clearly indicated.

In summary, the Anscombe's four data sets provide a dramatic warning that only estimating parameters and calculating PRE and F^* can sometimes be very misleading. On the other hand, there is comfort in

		SET 1	
i	Lever	Studentized Deleted Residual	Cook's D
1	.1	.0	.0
2	.1	.0	.0
3	.2	−1.5	.3
4	.1	.9	.0
5	.1	−.1	.0
6	.3	.0	.0
7	.2	.9	.1
8	.3	−.6	.1
9	.2	1.4	.2
10	.1	−1.2	.1
11	.2	.1	.0

		SET 3	
i	Lever	Studentized Deleted Residual	Cook's D
1	.1	−.4	.0
2	.1	−.1	.0
3	.2	3.9	.9
4	.1	−.3	.0
5	.1	−.5	.0
6	.3	−.9	.2
7	.2	.1	.0
8	.3	.3	.0
9	.2	−.6	.0
10	.1	−.1	.0
11	.2	.2	.0

		SET 2	
i	Lever	Studentized Deleted Residual	Cook's D
1	.1	.8	.0
2	.1	.8	.0
3	.2	−.5	.1
4	.1	.9	.0
5	.1	.5	.0
6	.3	−1.6	.5
7	.2	.1	.0
8	.3	−1.6	.5
9	.2	.1	.0
10	.1	.5	.0
11	.2	−.5	.1

		SET 4	
i	Lever	Studentized Deleted Residual	Cook's D
1	.1	−.3	.0
2	.1	−.8	.0
3	.1	.5	.0
4	.1	1.3	.1
5	.1	1.0	.1
6	.1	.0	.0
7	.1	−1.2	.1
8	1.0	*a	*
9	.1	−1.0	.1
10	.1	.6	.0
11	.1	−.1	.0

[a]Uses $1 - h_{ii}$ in the calculations and so is undefined because $h_{ii} = 1$ for this case.

EXHIBIT 9.12 ▲

Outlier indices for each of the four Anscombe data sets

EXHIBIT 9.13 ▶

**Residual plots for
each of the
Anscombe data
sets**

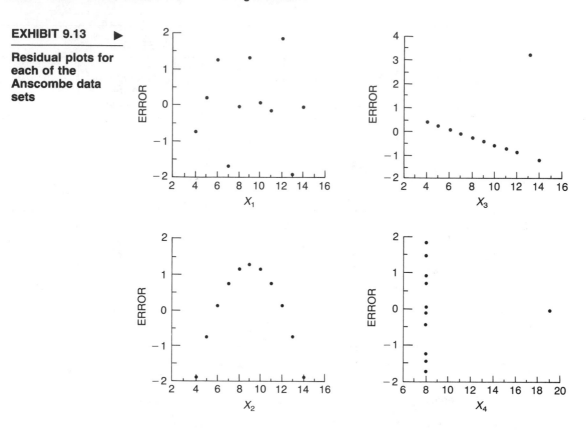

knowing that the three outlier indices—levers, studentized deleted residuals, and Cook's D—and graphs of the residuals provide ample warning about the dangers in these data sets. The moral is that one must always calculate the outlier indices and examine the residual plot.

Partial Regression Plots. We have noted the usefulness of plotting the residuals against the predictor variable for detecting outliers and unusual observations. In all of the examples presented so far, we have used simple regression with only one predictor. What do we do for multiple regression when there are two or more predictors? Ideally, we would like to examine the plot of the residuals graphed simultaneously against all the predictors. For two predictors the required three-dimensional plot is difficult, and for three or more predictors the p-dimensional plot is impossible. The best we can do is examine the partial regression plot that follows naturally from our development of multiple regression.

In Chapter 8 we developed multiple regression as a series of simple regressions. At each step, we computed the simple regression between the data residual (i.e., the error remaining after using the other predictors) and the predictor residual (i.e., the error remaining in the predictor after predicting it with the other predictors). The partial regression leverage plot is just the scatterplot for this simple regression. Exhibit 8.4, which plots UN.0,YR versus IP.0,YR, is an example of a partial regression plot. It allows us to examine the simple relationship between UN and IP with the effects of YR removed, and it makes it easier to identify unusual (with respect to the yearly changes predicted by YR) IP values, unusual UN values, and observations unusual in both respects. In this case there do not appear to be any serious outliers although year 9 (IP.0,YR = −12.27) may be exerting undue leverage that ought to be checked by examining its lever.

9.8

Summary

Outliers, whether they are data recording and data entry mistakes or truly unusual observations, can wreak havoc on both parameter estimation and statistical inference. Whether outliers ought to be omitted or included in the analysis is a matter of judgment that depends on the substantive topic, the cause of the outlier, and other issues. But failure to detect and identify outliers whether or not they are included in the analysis is scientifically irresponsible. Detection techniques are easy and closely related to our approach to model fitting and testing. Levers detect unusual predictor variables; studentized deleted residuals or, equivalently, F^* for testing the outlier model detects unusual DATA values; and Cook's D detects observations that are unusual in terms of both the predictors and DATA. Further aid in detection is provided by examining plots of residuals against predictors and, in particular, examining partial regression plots. These detection procedures should be a routine part of every regression analysis.

10

Interactions and Polynomial Regression: Models with Products of Continuous Predictors

Now that we have an appreciation for the damage that outliers can inflict on model estimation and inference, and the various procedures that might be used to detect and deal with such outliers, let us return to our general development of models which permit us to address more complicated and perhaps more interesting questions about our data. In Chapter 8 we considered in some detail models with multiple predictor variables. In this chapter we extend these models by discussing the addition of predictors that are themselves products of other predictors. Such models, as we will show, permit us to extend dramatically the range of questions which we can ask of our data. In the models of Chapter 8, our questions about individual predictor variables had the following generic form:

Is one predictor useful over and above or controlling for the set of other predictors in the model?

In this chapter we will ask a set of rather different questions about predictors. The questions considered in this chapter take the following generic form:

> Does the utility of one variable as a predictor depend on the value of other variables or even of that particular variable?

At this point, it may not be clear why this second sort of generic question is likely to be of interest. It probably is not even clear exactly what this second question means. To clarify things, we start this chapter with an extended example, using new data. We first recapitulate some of the major points of Chapter 8, in a somewhat different language, once again clarifying the sorts of questions about models that we asked there. We then show how the questions we will ask of our data with the models developed in this chapter differ from and extend the questions we asked earlier. Our hope is that this initial section will give an understanding of the second generic question mentioned above and will further the understanding of the sorts of questions addressed earlier in Chapter 8.

The models we consider in this chapter go by a variety of names elsewhere. Occasionally they are known as *moderator regression* models. Elsewhere they are known as *polynomial, interactive, nonadditive,* or *nonlinear* models. Regardless of the name we give them, the goal in this chapter is to discuss the estimation, interpretation, and tests of models that include, as predictors, products of other predictors.

Let us now turn to the data that we will rely on. These are hypothetical data, supposedly gathered from eighty individuals who are all runners. Three variables have been measured. The first variable, Time, is each runner's most recent 5-kilometer race time, measured in minutes. Next we have each runner's age. The final variable is the average number of miles per week that each runner runs when in training for a race. These data, all hypothetical, are presented in Exhibit 10.1.

Our interest in these data will focus on how age of runner and amount of training relate to race times in the 5-kilometer race. Let us start by examining how these two variables relate to race time individually, using the single-predictor models developed in Chapters 6 and 7. If we regress Time on Age, the following simple regression equation results:

$$\widehat{\text{Time}} = 15.104 + .213\text{Age}$$

The sum of squared errors for this model equals 1729.635. The sum of squared errors for a single-parameter compact model in which we predict the mean time for each case equals 2210.942. Testing the null hypothesis to determine whether Age is a reliable predictor of race time yields a value of PRE of .218, which converts to F^* with 1 and 78 degrees of freedom of 21.705. These values indicate that indeed Age is a reliable predictor of Time.

EXHIBIT 10.1 ▶

Hypothetical running data

Time	Age	Miles	Time	Age	Miles
24.91	29	10	29.68	22	10
21.82	25	20	20.36	24	30
21.54	27	40	18.07	22	40
23.03	25	50	28.78	39	10
25.35	37	20	18.80	39	30
22.84	31	40	14.87	39	50
30.16	43	10	32.19	47	20
27.00	44	20	19.46	40	30
16.42	46	40	35.32	58	10
24.87	53	20	20.83	59	30
24.95	58	40	22.69	27	20
18.32	30	30	15.69	24	40
16.66	27	50	30.89	32	10
25.08	36	20	23.11	34	30
16.53	32	40	19.17	35	50
35.29	45	10	26.09	41	20
26.41	45	30	21.81	50	40
22.48	48	50	37.75	51	10
34.38	55	10	30.30	51	20
19.00	53	30	22.95	51	40
21.86	24	10	20.14	20	20
22.11	24	30	15.23	24	40
17.45	25	40	18.53	22	50
24.58	34	20	24.96	35	30
19.97	36	40	19.21	31	50
34.34	45	10	25.07	41	20
25.22	49	30	20.99	43	40
20.52	44	50	29.94	59	10
29.98	55	20	23.08	59	30
21.62	57	40	21.52	53	50
19.35	29	20	21.38	27	30
20.45	24	40	19.52	28	50
16.07	28	50	27.00	37	10
23.06	38	20	17.61	39	30
20.94	31	40	15.19	39	50
28.77	42	10	26.03	45	20
29.86	46	30	21.51	42	40
22.96	46	50	34.53	58	10
25.62	56	20	23.68	56	30
24.98	55	40	23.50	53	50

	Mean	St. Dev.
Time	23.55	5.29
Age	39.70	11.60
Miles	29.87	13.83

This simple regression result is graphed in Exhibit 10.2. As the positive slope makes clear in the graph, our best prediction based on these data is that race times increase with age. Since this is a simple regression model and no other predictor variables have been included, we are unable to answer questions about what other variables may be related to Time, why Age may be related to Time, or what would happen to the Time-Age relationship if we controlled for some other variable, such as Miles. It may be that Age and Miles are redundant or confounded in these data, such that older runners train with fewer miles. If this were the case, then if we included Miles in the model, we would reach rather different conclusions about how Age was related to Time when Miles was controlled.

The simple relationship between Time and Miles is captured by the least squares simple regression equation

$$\widehat{\text{Time}} = 31.911 - .280\text{Miles}$$

The sum of squared errors from this model equals 1028.963. To determine whether Miles and Time are reliably related, we want to compare the sum of squared errors from this model with the sum of squared errors from the compact single-parameter model. This compact model is the same one we used to test whether Age is reliably related to Time. Its sum of squared errors equals 2210.942. The value of PRE that we get when comparing these two models equals .535, which converts to an F^* statistic with 1 and 78 degrees of freedom of 89.60. Again, this value of F^* is highly significant, and we conclude that Miles and Time are reliably related. The simple relationship is graphed in Exhibit 10.3.

EXHIBIT 10.2 ▶

Time-Age simple regression

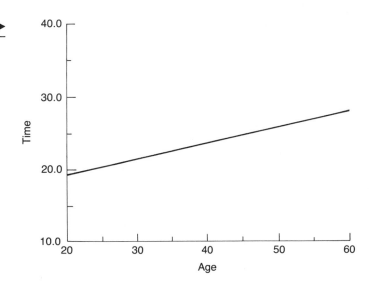

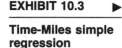

EXHIBIT 10.3   ▶

Time-Miles simple regression

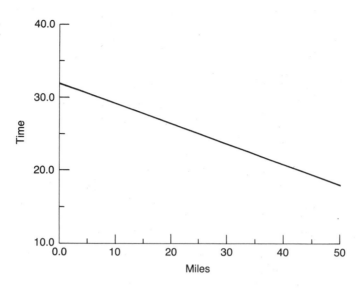

When we regress Time on both Miles and Age, the following multiple regression equation results:

$$\widehat{\text{Time}} = 24.716 - .258\text{Miles} + .165\text{Age}$$

The sum of squared errors for this three-parameter model equals 746.339, which gives a PRE of .662 when compared to the single-parameter compact model that included neither predictor. The overall F^* statistic to compare this three-parameter model with the single-parameter one equals 75.552 with 2 and 77 degrees of freedom.

We can also compare this three-parameter model with each of the simple regression models to determine whether each predictor variable reliably increases the accuracy of our predictions controlling for the other predictor variable. The value of PRE when comparing compact and augmented models without and with Age equals .275, which converts to an F^* statistic of 29.158 having 1 and 77 degrees of freedom. The value of PRE when comparing compact and augmented models without and with Miles equals .568, which converts to an F^* statistic of 101.447 with 1 and 77 degrees of freedom. Hence we conclude that each of these predictor variables reliably increases the accuracy of our predictions of Time even when the other predictor is controlled. The source table in Exhibit 10.4 summarizes the results of the inference tests we have just conducted using this multiple regression model.

It is instructive to graph this multiple regression equation much like we did in the case of the simple equations. In Exhibit 10.5, we have graphed the prediction plane that this model generates in a three-dimensional space, where the vertical axis is Time and Miles and Age are the

EXHIBIT 10.4 ▶

Source table for time multiple regression results

Source	b	SS	df	MS	F*	PRÉ
Regression		1464.60	2	732.30	75.55	.662
Miles	−.258	983.30	1	983.30	101.45	.568
Age	.165	282.62	1	282.62	29.16	.275
Error		746.34	77	9.69		
Total		2210.94	79			

EXHIBIT 10.5 ▶

Age-Miles additive model

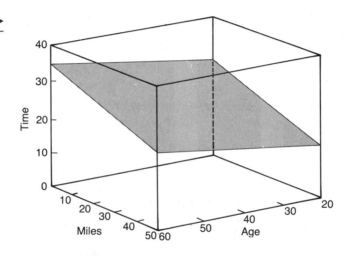

two horizontal axes. As this exhibit makes clear, a specific predicted Time value is made by the model at each pair of values for Miles and Age.

To make the presentation of this model a little simpler, we could also take slices of this prediction plane, treating for instance Age as the predictor on the horizontal axis and graphing Time-Age prediction lines at different levels of Miles. If we group terms in the multiple regression equation a little differently, we get the reexpression

$$\widehat{\text{Time}} = (24.716 - .258\text{Miles}) + .165\text{Age}$$

We can think of this reexpression as telling us about the "simple" relationship between Time and Age, allowing the intercept in the simple regression to change as Miles changes. In other words, suppose we wanted to predict race time conditional on age for someone who trained

20 miles per week. We would substitute 20 for Miles in the above reexpression and get

$$\widehat{\text{Time}} = (24.716 - .258(20)) + .165\text{Age}$$

$$= 19.556 + .165\text{Age}$$

For a runner who trained 30 miles per week, our "simple" predicted relationship between Time and Age would be

$$\widehat{\text{Time}} = (24.716 - .258(30)) + .165\text{Age}$$

$$= 16.976 + .165\text{Age}$$

In other words, if we graphed the Time-Age relationship from this multiple regression equation where we also use Miles as a predictor, we would get many different "simple" regression prediction functions between Time and Age, one for each of the possible levels of Miles. Each of these separate "simple" prediction functions would have the same slope, but their intercepts would change as Miles changes. For the two cases where Miles equals 20 and 30 that we have just presented, the two intercepts differ by 2.58, which is equal to 10 times the regression coefficient for Miles. The difference is 10 times the regression coefficient for Miles because we are looking at two "simple" relationships between Time and Age at two different values of Miles which differ by 10 units. The two intercepts thus differ by the difference in the two values of Miles times the regression coefficient for Miles.

Since Miles is in theory a continuous variable, our plot of the Time-Age relationship within levels of Miles contains an infinite number of lines, one for each of the possible levels of Miles. All of these "simple" prediction lines combine to form the prediction plane of Exhibit 10.5. We can look two-dimensionally at a few of the individual lines that contribute to this prediction plane. Thus, Exhibit 10.6 presents a few "simple" Time-Age prediction functions at representative values of Miles. These lines differ in their intercepts, which change as Miles changes, but not in their slopes. In other words, the assumption is being made in this multiple regression equation that as Miles changes the change in Time is constant regardless of one's Age. Another way of saying this is that the relationship or slope between Time and Age is assumed to be invariant across levels of Miles.

Now let's turn the equation around and graph the Time-Miles "simple" relationship at different Age levels. Reexpressing our multiple regression equation, we get

$$\widehat{\text{Time}} = (24.716 + .165\text{Age}) - .258\text{Miles}$$

For representative values of Age, we have graphed this function in Exhibit 10.7, putting Miles on the horizontal axis this time. Again, we

EXHIBIT 10.6 ▶

"Simple" Time-Age relations: additive model

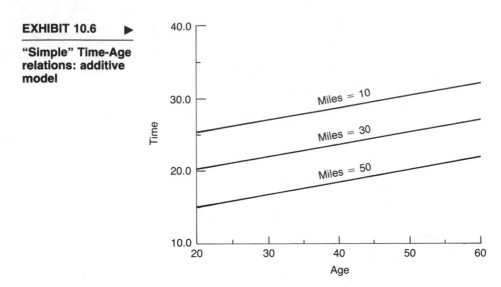

EXHIBIT 10.7 ▶

"Simple" Time-Miles relations: additive model

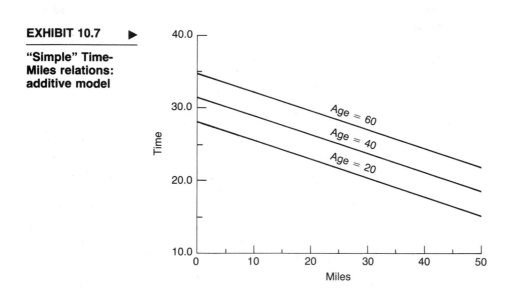

see that as Age changes the intercept for the Time-Miles relationship changes, but the slope does not. In other words, age changes are assumed to affect our predicted race times to the same extent regardless of the number of miles one runs in a week.

10.1

Interactions between Predictor Variables

The assumption that we are making in this multiple regression equation that these graphical displays make clear is known as the additive assumption. In slightly more abstract language, if we regress some variable Y_i on predictors X_1 and X_2, we are assuming that the contribution of each predictor to the best predicted values, $\hat{Y}_i$, does not depend on the value of the other predictor. The two contributions are thus additive: regardless of the level of X_1, the relationship (i.e., slope) between Y_i and X_2 does not change. Likewise, regardless of the level of X_2, the relationship between Y_i and X_1 is presumed not to change. We can simply "add" up the two predictors in deriving $\hat{Y}_i$ without worrying about the particular values of X_1 and X_2.

How reasonable is this additive assumption? The answer is that its reasonableness depends on the substantive domain under examination. For the variables at hand, it may not be a very good assumption. For instance, it seems reasonable to suggest that the age difference in race times might be greater when dealing with people who don't run very much than when dealing with people who run a lot. To put this hypothesis another way, training a lot may reduce the relationship between Age and Time, such that differences in race times associated with age may be smaller with more training. Graphically this hypothesis is portrayed in Exhibit 10.8. Notice that the slope of the prediction function

EXHIBIT 10.8 ▶

Hypothesized "simple" Time-Age relations

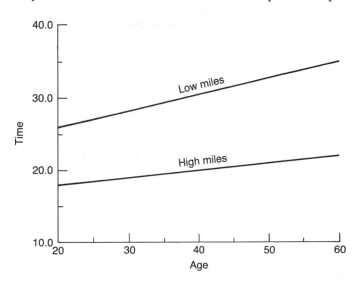

linking Age and Time is hypothesized to be steeper when Miles is relatively low than when it is relatively high. In other words, the relationship between Age and Time is hypothesized to be stronger when Miles is low than when it is high.

We are suggesting that rather than Age and Miles combining *additively* in giving us our best predictions of Time, they may *interact* in affecting time. An *interaction* between two variables, say X_1 and X_2, is said to occur whenever the effect of one of them, say X_1, on the dependent variable Y_i varies with or depends on the value of the other variable X_2. In the case at hand, we are hypothesizing that Age and Miles interact in affecting Time. This means that we suspect that the relationship between Age and Time depends on or varies with Miles.

Whether or not there is an interaction between two variables in predicting a third is an issue that is totally independent of whether or not the two predictor variables are correlated or redundant with each other. To suggest that Age and Miles may interact in predicting Time is to suggest that the "simple" relationship between Age and Time may depend on or vary with Miles. This may be true regardless of whether Age and Miles are themselves correlated or redundant predictor variables.

To test this hypothesis about the interaction between Age and Miles, we want to compare our three-parameter additive model with one in which the slope of one predictor variable is allowed to change as the other predictor variable changes. We saw earlier that the simple additive model allows the intercept of one predictor variable to change as the other predictor variable changes. However, the slope does not. The slope of Age, for instance, is invariant across changes in Miles.

To allow for changing slopes, we need to build a model that includes as a separate predictor the product of the two variables that are hypothesized to interact. To show how this allows for changing slopes, let us examine models for predicting Time from Age and Miles both additively and interactively. The additive model is given as

$$\text{Time} = \beta_0 + \beta_1\text{Age} + \beta_2\text{Miles} + \varepsilon_i$$

As we saw above, the "simple" relationship between Age and Time in this multiple regression model can be reexpressed as

$$\text{Time} = (\beta_0 + \beta_2\text{Miles}) + \beta_1\text{Age} + \varepsilon_i$$

Let us now define a new intercept for this equation, β_0', where

$$\beta_0' = \beta_0 + \beta_2\text{Miles}$$

We can now write the reexpression as

$$\text{Time} = \beta_0' + \beta_1\text{Age} + \varepsilon_i$$

As before, as Miles changes, the intercept for the "simple" relationship between Time and Age changes, but the slope does not.

Now let us look at a model that includes not only the separate predictors of Age and Miles but also a predictor that is the product of the two.

$$\text{Time} = \beta_0 + \beta_1\text{Age} + \beta_2\text{Miles} + \beta_3(\text{AgeMiles}) + \varepsilon_i$$

As we did before, let us reexpress this model to examine the Time-Age relationship and see how that relationship changes as Miles changes in value. We can group together terms on the right side of this model that do and do not include Age. This reexpression gives

$$\text{Time} = (\beta_0 + \beta_2\text{Miles}) + (\beta_1 + \beta_3\text{Miles})\text{Age} + \varepsilon_i$$

Define

$$\beta_0' = \beta_0 + \beta_2\text{Miles}$$

$$\beta_1' = \beta_1 + \beta_3\text{Miles}$$

We can write this reexpression as

$$\text{Time} = \beta_0' + \beta_1'\text{Age} + \varepsilon_i$$

As this reexpression makes clear, the "simple" relationship between Time and Age now changes as Miles changes in two ways. First, the value of the intercept changes as Miles changes, just as it did in the model before we included the product of Age and Miles. The β_2 parameter tells us by how much the intercept changes for each unit change in Miles. Second, the inclusion of the product of the two as a predictor variable results in a "simple" slope for age in the reexpression that changes as Miles changes. In other words, the value of β_1' changes as Miles changes whenever β_3, the coefficient for the product predictor, is nonzero. The parameter β_3 tells us by how much the slope of Age changes as Miles changes by 1 unit. (Note that we are still assuming in this model that the change in the intercept and in the slope of the "simple" Time-Age relationship is a function of Miles but is invariant across the values of Miles. At a later point in this chapter, we will see how this restriction can be relaxed as well.)

Notice that the interpretation of β_1 in the model that includes β_3 and the product predictor is rather different from what was the interpretation of β_1 in the additive model that did not contain the product predictor. In the additive model, the coefficient β_1 tells us by how much our predictions of Time change per unit change in Age, controlling for Miles or on average within levels of Miles. In the model that includes the product term, the "simple" slope of Age, β_1', equals $\beta_1 + \beta_3\text{Miles}$. From this expression it is clear that β_1 equals the slope of Age in only one particular case: when Miles equals zero. When Miles equals any value other than zero, the slope coefficient for Age equals β_1 plus a quantity that depends on the value of Miles, i.e., β_3Miles.

We have reexpressed the additive and interactive models so that they tell us about the "simple" relationship between Time and Age, showing that the intercept changes as Miles changes in the additive model and that both the intercept and the slope change as Miles changes in the interactive model. We can equivalently reexpress both models to tell us about the "simple" relationship between Time and Miles. Re-expressing the additive model in this way gives us

$$\text{Time} = (\beta_0 + \beta_1\text{Age}) + \beta_2\text{Miles} + \varepsilon_i$$

The interactive model can be reexpressed as

$$\text{Time} = (\beta_0 + \beta_1\text{Age}) + (\beta_2 + \beta_3\text{Age})\text{Miles} + \varepsilon_i$$

This equivalent reexpression tells us that in the additive model, if we are looking at the "simple" Time-Miles relationship, as Age changes, the intercept of that simple relationship changes, but the slope does not. However, when we look at the model that incorporates the product term, both the intercept and the slope for the "simple" Time-Miles relationship change as Age changes.

Since we can reexpress both the additive and the interactive models in two ways, once telling us about the "simple" relationship between Time and Age and once telling us about the "simple" relationship between Time and Miles, each of the parameters in these models can be interpreted in two ways, depending on which "simple" relationship we have chosen to talk about. If we are interested in the "simple" relationship between Time and Age, the parameters in the additive model are interpreted as

β_0 = intercept when Miles equals zero

β_1 = slope for Age

β_2 = change in the intercept as Miles changes

The parameters in the interactive model are interpreted as

β_0 = intercept when Miles equals zero

β_1 = slope for Age when Miles equals zero

β_2 = change in the intercept as Miles changes

β_3 = change in the slope for Age as Miles changes

If we are interested in the "simple" relationship between Time and Miles, the parameters in the additive model are interpreted as

β_0 = intercept when Age equals zero

β_1 = change in the intercept as Age changes

β_2 = slope for Miles

The parameters in the interactive model are interpreted as

β_0 = intercept when Age equals zero

β_1 = change in the intercept as Age changes

β_2 = slope for Miles when Age equals zero

β_3 = change in the slope for Miles as Age changes

We have already estimated the parameters of the additive model from our data. Let us now estimate the interactive model's parameters. To do this we need to create a new predictor variable that is the product of Age and Miles. Nearly all statistical packages permit us to define new variables that are functions of variables that already exist in a data file. Accordingly, we simply compute some new variable and define it as the product of Age times Miles. Every observation will have a value on this new variable equal to the product of that observation's value on Age and his or her value on Miles. Using any one of the regression subroutines, we regress Time on Age, Miles, and their product, yielding the following parameter estimates:

$$\widehat{\text{Time}} = 19.200 + .302\text{Age} - .076\text{Miles} - .005\text{AgeMiles}$$

The sum of squared errors for this model equals 705.104.

Let us compare this estimated model to the results that we have already given for the additive model. The estimated coefficients for that model are

$$\widehat{\text{Time}} = 24.716 + .165\text{Age} - .258\text{Miles}$$

with a sum of squared errors equal to 746.339. We can compare these two models in a variety of ways: we can compare the quality of the predictions they make to determine whether the interactive model does a reliably better job of predicting Time than does the more parsimonious additive model. We can also compare the parameter estimates in the two models.

Since the additive model contains one fewer parameter than the interactive one, i.e., β_3, we can compare the two models by computing PRE and F^*. The null hypothesis that is being tested is that β_3 equals zero, since that parameter is added to the compact additive model to form the augmented one. This null hypothesis can be 'expressed in a number of equivalent ways, however, since, as we have just seen, there are a number of ways of interpreting β_3. If β_3 is zero, it means that the "simple" slope linking Time and Age does not depend on Miles. Equivalently, it means that the "simple" slope linking Time and Miles does not depend on Age. In other words, the null hypothesis is that the magnitude of the Time-Age relationship does not depend on Miles. Equivalently it means that the magnitude of the Time-Miles relationship does not depend on Age. Much more simply and concisely, the null hypothesis is that Age and Miles do not interact in predicting Time. To test this null hypothesis, we compute PRE:

$$\text{PRE} = \frac{\text{SSE(C)} - \text{SSE(A)}}{\text{SSE(C)}}$$

$$= \frac{746.339 - 705.104}{746.339}$$

$$= .055$$

As always, PRE tells us the proportional reduction in errors of prediction moving from the compact to the augmented model. In this case, it tells us that when we allow for the interaction between Age and Miles our errors of prediction in predicting Time are reduced by 5.5%. Our augmented model has four parameters in it, while the compact model has only three. Hence the degrees of freedom for the F^* statistic to test the null hypothesis equal 1 and 76. The value of F^* is 4.445 which exceeds the critical value with 1 and 76 degrees of freedom, having set α at .05. Hence we conclude that the interactive model gives us reliably better predictions than does the more parsimonious additive model. In other words, we conclude that the relationship between Time and Age does depend on Miles or, equivalently, that the relationship between Time and Miles depends on Age.

Now let us compare the additive and interactive estimated models by interpreting the various parameter estimates in each. We have already interpreted the various parameter estimates in the additive model twice, once as we examined the "simple" Time-Age relationship within levels of Miles and once as we examined the "simple" Time-Miles relationship within levels of Age. These relationships from the additive model were graphed in Exhibits 10.6 and 10.7. Parallel interpretations will be given for the interactive model. First, looking at the "simple" Time-Age relationship within levels of Miles, we reexpress the estimated interactive model as follows:

$$\widehat{\text{Time}} = (19.200 - .076\text{Miles}) + (.302 - .005\text{Miles})\text{Age}$$

Suppose we were interested in examining the Time-Age relationship that this model implies at particular values of Miles. For instance, based on these data, we might be interested in how Age would relate to race times for people who never ran, i.e., who did zero Miles per week. This interpretation must be looked at quite cautiously since our sample includes no observations from individuals who did not run. Nevertheless, based on these data, we can substitute the value of zero for Miles in the above regression equation. Our predicted Time-Age "simple" relationship for this case is

$$\widehat{\text{Time}} = 19.200 + .302\text{Age}$$

This exercise should make clear the interpetation of b_0 and b_1 in the interactive equation when interpreted from the point of view of the "simple" Time-Age relationship. The intercept in the interactive equation gives us our best estimate of the intercept for the "simple" Time-Age relationship when Miles equals zero. The coefficient for Age in the interactive model, also known as b_1, with a value of .302, tells us the estimated "simple" slope for the Time-Age relationship when Miles equals zero. Note that this interpretation is quite different from the interpretation given for the regression coefficient for Age in the additive model. There, b_1, the regression coefficient for Age, was interpreted as the slope for the Time-Age relationship within levels of Miles, regardless of the actual value of Miles. In other words, there the "simple" slope did not change as Miles changed and hence the value of b_1 was that simple slope regardless of the value of Miles.

Now suppose we were interested in the "simple" relationship between Time and Age for runners who average 30 miles per week. The prediction function for such runners is

$$\widehat{\text{Time}} = (19.200 - .076(30)) + (.302 - .005(30))\text{Age}$$

$$= 16.92 + .152\text{Age}$$

Clearly this simple relationship between Time and Age is not what it was for the prediction function when Miles was set equal to zero. As Miles has increased both the intercept and the slope for Age have decreased. For each unit change in Miles, the intercept has decreased by .076 unit. This, then, is the interpretation for the b_2 coefficient, the coefficient for Miles in the interactive model, when reexpressing that model as the "simple" relationship between Time and Age. That is, the coefficient for Miles tells us by how much our predicted value of Time changes as Miles changes when Age equals zero.

Comparing the slopes for the "simple" Time-Age relationship when Miles equals zero and 30, we see that the slope for age has decreased by 30 times b_3. In other words, the coefficient for the Age by Miles product tells us the amount by which the "simple" slope between Age and Time changes as Miles changes one unit. Here, since the slope of Age when Miles equals zero is positive, the coefficient for the product tells us by how much the "simple" slope for Age decreases as Miles changes 1 unit. We have graphed a few representative "simple" Time-Age relationships in Exhibit 10.9 from this interactive model. These graphed regression lines have been calculated simply by substituting various values for Miles, such as the values of 0 and 30 as we have just done. Notice that in this graph as Miles changes, both the intercept and slope of these "simple" relationships change. Since we have concluded that the interactive model that allows for different slopes as Miles changes makes reliably better predictions than the additive model which maintains homogeneous slopes, our rejection of the null hypothesis that β_3 equals zero is equivalent to concluding that the slopes of these "simple" Time-Age relationships reliably change as Miles changes. In other words, these "simple" regression lines are reliably nonparallel.

Let us now turn the interpretation of the coefficients in this interactive model around, reexpressing it so that it portrays the "simple" Time-Miles relationship at different levels of age. We saw earlier that in the additive model, under this reexpression, the coefficient for Age, b_1, tells us the degree to which the intercept for the "simple" Time-Miles relationship changes as Age changes. However, in that model, the "simple" slope was invariant across levels of Age. In the interactive model that is no longer the case. Reexpressing the interactive model gives us

$$\widehat{\text{Time}} = (19.200 + .302\text{Age}) + (-.076 - .005\text{Age})\text{Miles}$$

EXHIBIT 10.9 ▶

"Simple" Time-Age relations: interactive model

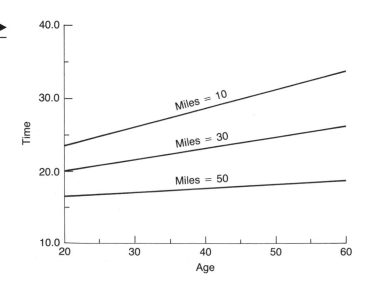

Interpreting the coefficients from this perspective, we see that b_0 in the interactive model tells us the intercept for the "simple" Time-Miles relationship when Age equals zero. As Age changes values, the intercept for this "simple" relationship changes by b_1 units. The coefficient for Miles, b_2, tells us the slope of the "simple" Time-Miles relationship when Age equals zero. The coefficient for the product term, b_3, tells us the degree to which the "simple" slope or the "simple" relationship between Time and Miles changes as Age changes. We have graphed representative "simple" Time-Miles relationships for various values of Age in Exhibit 10.10. Again, the reliable improvement in fit of the interactive model over the more parsimonious additive one tells us that the slopes we have graphed for the "simple" relationships are reliably nonparallel.

Exhibit 10.11 presents a three-dimensional graph of the prediction plane generated by this interactive model. As the graphs of the "simple" relations in Exhibits 10.9 and 10.10 make clear, if we take slices of this prediction plane parallel to one of the horizontal axes, the slope of the resulting prediction lines change. Thus, as we move up the Age horizontal axis, the slope of the plane becomes more and more negative. Compared to the prediction plan generated by the additive model, graphed in Exhibit 10.5, this prediction plane seems to twist as we move across values of one of the horizontal axes.

10.1.1 Tests of Other Parameters in the Interactive Model

We have already tested the null hypothesis that the value of β_3 equals zero when we compared the augmented interactive model with the

EXHIBIT 10.10 ▶

"Simple" Time-Miles relations: interactive model

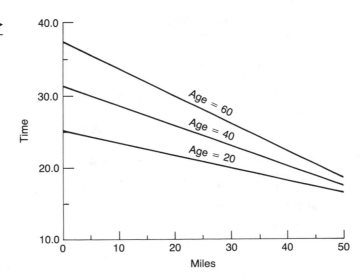

EXHIBIT 10.11 ▶

Age Miles inter-active model

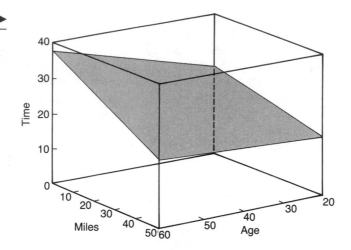

compact additive one. We could certainly conduct tests of other parameters in the interactive model as well. For instance, suppose we constructed a compact model in which β_1 was set equal to zero and compared such a model with the full interactive one. This amounts to testing the null hypothesis that β_1, the regression coefficient for Age, equals zero in the interactive model. Estimating a compact model with the regression coefficient for Age fixed at zero gives us

$$\widehat{\text{Time}} = 31.554 - .415\text{Miles} + .004(\text{Age Miles})$$

with a sum of squared errors of 870.927. Comparing this model with the augmented one in which the regression coefficient for Age is estimated, we get

$$\text{PRE} = \frac{870.927 - 705.104}{870.927} = .190$$

This PRE converts to an F^* statistic, with 1 and 76 degrees of freedom, of 17.873. This value of F^* exceeds the critical value, and hence we conclude that the regression coefficient for Age in the interactive model reliably differs from zero.

We can also test the null hypothesis that β_2, the regression coefficient for Miles in the interactive model, equals zero. Estimating a compact model with only Age and Age Miles as predictors, we get

$$\widehat{\text{Time}} = 16.861 + .355\text{Age} - .006(\text{Age Miles})$$

with a sum of squared errors of 711.704. Again, comparing this model with the augmented interactive model, we get

$$\text{PRE} = \frac{711.704 - 705.104}{711.704} = .009$$

which converts to an F^* statistic with 1 and 76 degrees of freedom of .711. We therefore cannot reject the null hypothesis that the regression coefficient for Miles in the interactive model, β_2, equals zero.

At the very start of this chapter we tested null hypotheses about the parameters β_1 and β_2 in the additive model that did not include the product term. Testing whether β_1, the regression coefficient for Age in the additive model, differed reliably from zero, we obtained a PRE value of .275 and an F^*, with 1 and 77 degrees of freedom, of 29.158. Testing whether β_2, the regression coefficient for Miles in the additive model, differed reliably from zero, we obtained a PRE value of .568 and an F^*, with 1 and 77 degrees of freedom, of 101.447. Clearly these tests of the regression coefficients for Age and Miles in the additive model do not give the same results as do the tests of the partial regression coefficients for these same predictor variables in the interactive model. For the tests of β_1, the regression coefficient for Age, the resulting PRE value in the additive model was .275, while in the interactive model it equaled .190. For the tests of β_2, the regression coefficient for Miles, the resulting PRE value in the additive model was .568, while in the interactive model it equaled only .009. Why this difference?

In a general sense, we have already discussed the reason for this difference. As shown in Chapter 8, the interpretation of a partial regression coefficient depends on what other predictors are included in a given model. Since the interactive model includes a different set of predictors than does the additive one, we would naturally expect the partial regression coefficient for a given predictor variable to differ between the two models.

In this case, a more specific and substantive answer to this question is also instructive, although in fact this more specific answer is just a restatement of the general one given in Chapter 8 and in the above paragraph. The partial regression coefficients for Age and Miles, β_1 and β_2, have quite different interpretations in the interactive model than they do in the additive one, as we have repeatedly stressed in interpreting the interactive model. Hence, testing whether they reliably differ from zero in the two models amounts to testing rather different substantive hypotheses. In the additive model, β_1 is interpreted as the slope for Age within levels of Miles or holding Miles constant. But that slope is presumed not to change in the additive model as Miles changes. Hence, we can interpret the slope as something like the average Time-Age slope within levels of Miles.

On the other hand, the regression coefficient for Age in the interactive model is the slope for Age when *and only when* Miles equals zero.

Therefore in the additive model, when we test whether β_1 equals zero, we are testing whether Time and Age are reliably related on average within levels of Miles or holding Miles constant. On the other hand, in the interactive model, we are testing whether Time and Age are reliably related *when Miles equals zero*. Similarly, when we test whether the regression coefficient for Miles, β_2, equals zero in the additive and interactive models, we are testing rather different substantive null hypotheses. In the additive case, we are testing whether the slope for Miles on average within levels of Age, or holding Age constant, differs reliably from zero. On the other hand, in the interactive model, the test of whether β_2 differs from zero amounts to testing whether Time and Miles are reliably related *when Age equals zero*.

In the interactive model both tests, of β_1 and of β_2, must necessarily be interpreted with a grain of salt, since we have no data in our sample from observations with zero values on Age or with zero values on Miles. The test of β_1 tells us that based on the present data, we might find that Age and Time are reliably related for individuals who ran no miles per week. This conclusion must be rather tentative since in fact we have no observations from runners with zero miles per week. The test of β_2 in the interactive model leads us to conclude that race times and number of training miles per week would not be reliably related if we had data on runners who were zero years old! Clearly such a conclusion lies outside the realm of what we might reasonably want to conclude from our data, since our data contain no observations even approaching zero years of age.

In Chapter 7 we saw that inferences about β_0, the intercept, are useful particularly when the predictor variables have been transformed into mean deviation form. As always, the intercept is the predicted value of Y_i when the predictor variables equal zero. When predictors are in mean deviation form, their means equal zero; hence a test of β_0 is equivalently a test about $\overline{Y}$. We can use a similar strategy in the present context, with an interactive model, to make more interpretable tests of β_1 and β_2, the regression coefficients for the variables that are components of the product term, when that product term is included in the equation.

Suppose, for instance, that we transformed both Age and Miles into mean deviation form and then we regressed Time on Miles', Age', and (Miles' Age'), where Miles' equals Miles minus its mean, and Age' equals Age minus its mean. The resulting estimated regression equation is

$$\widehat{\text{Time}} = 23.439 + .164\text{Age}' - .259\text{Miles}' - .005(\text{Age}'\ \text{Miles}')$$

Notice that the estimates for β_0, β_1, and β_2 have all changed as a result of the transformations of Age and Miles, but the estimated value of β_3 has not. If we think of this interactive model as telling us about the "simple" Time-Age' relationship at various levels of Miles', then the value of the intercept b_0 equals the intercept for the "simple" Time-Age' relationship when Miles' equals zero. Miles' equals zero when Miles equals its mean. Hence the value of b_0, 23.439, is the predicted value of Time when we are dealing with an observation with mean values on Age and Miles. The regression coefficient for Age' in this equation, .164, tells us about the "simple" slope between Time and Age' when Miles' equals zero. Miles' equals zero when Miles equals its mean. Hence, the regression coefficient for Age' in this equation represents the "simple" relationship between Time and Age at the mean value of Miles. Similarly, the regression coefficient for Miles' in this equation represents the "simple" slope between Time and Miles' when Age' equals zero or, equivalently, when dealing with observations at the mean Age. Thus the mean deviation transformations radically affect the interpretation of b_0, b_1, and b_2.

The interpretation of b_3, however, is not affected by these transformations. The coefficient b_3 still tells us by how much the "simple" Time-Age' slope changes as Miles' changes 1 unit. Equivalently it tells us by how much the "simple" Time-Miles' relationship changes as Age' changes 1 unit. Neither of these interpretations of b_3 depends on what we define as zero values of the predictors. Hence the interpretation of b_3 is invariant across mean deviation transformations of Age and Miles.

Not surprisingly, if we tested whether β_1 in this interactive model involving Age' and Miles' equals zero, we come up with different values of PRE and F^* than we did when we tested the same hypothesis in the interactive model prior to mean deviation transformations of Age and Miles. The test of β_1 prior to mean deviation transformations was a test of the "simple" Time-Age relationship when Miles equals zero. We showed that the resulting PRE was .190 and the value of F^* was 17.873. A test of β_1 in the interactive model involving transformed predictors is a test of the "simple" Time-Age relationship when Miles' equals zero, or equivalently when Miles equals its mean. The resulting value of PRE is .283, which converts to an F^*, with 1 and 76 degress of freedom, of 30.042. In other words, we reject the null hypothesis that Time and Age are not reliably related when dealing with observations at the mean of Miles.

The test of β_2 prior to the mean deviation transformation was a test of whether the "simple" Time-Miles relationship was reliable when Age equals zero. It yielded a PRE of .009 and an F^* of .711. In the transformed equation, a test of whether β_2 equals zero gives us a PRE of .583, which converts to an F^*, with 1 and 76 degrees of freedom, of 106.453. In other words, while we could not reject the null hypothesis that Time and Miles were reliably related when dealing with hypothetical cases with ages of zero, we can certainly reject the null hypothesis that Time and Miles are not reliably related when dealing with observations at the mean of Age.

Just as the value of the estimate of β_3, and its interpretation, has not changed as a result of the mean deviation transformation of Age and Miles, so the inferential test of whether β_3 equals zero has not changed either. The resulting value of PRE is .055, and the value of F^* is 4.445. In other words, regardless of whether we transform Age and Miles into mean deviation form, the test of the regression coefficient for their product is always a test of whether the "simple" slope of one variable changes as the other variable changes in value, *so long as the two variables involved in the product term, Age and Miles or Age' and Miles', are included as separate predictors in the augmented model.* The italics are to emphasize that the regression coefficient for a product of two predictor variables estimates the effect of the interaction between those variables only when the regression coefficient is a partial one, partialing out or controlling for the component variables that were multiplied together to yield that product. So long as the components are included as separate predictors in the model, a test of whether the regression coefficient for the product departs from zero will be invariant across all linear transformations of the component variables (Cohen, 1978).

The use of a mean deviation transformation for both Age and Miles in order to increase the interpretability of the regressions coefficients b_1 and b_2 can be generalized to other sorts of deviation transformations in order to test hypotheses about particular "simple" relationships in which one might be interested. Suppose, for instance, in the interactive model, allowing for different Time-Age relationships at various levels of Miles, we were interested in determining whether Time and Age were reliably related for runners who averaged 50 miles a week. Since the coefficient for Age in the interactive model, b_1, estimates the "simple" Time-Age relationship when the other predictor with which Age interacts equals zero, we could transform Miles by subtracting 50 from the value of Miles for each observation, thus resulting in a deviation transformation defined as

Miles" = Miles − 50

Now if we regressed Time on Age, Miles", and the Age by Miles" product, the regression coefficient for Age, b_1, tells us about the magnitude of the "simple" Time-Age relationship when Miles" equals zero. Since Miles" equals zero when Miles equals 50, a test of whether β_1 equals zero in this model is equivalently a test of whether the "simple" Time-Age relationship is reliable when dealing with runners who run 50 miles per week. The coefficient for Miles" in this interactive model, b_2, would have the same value it had in the original interactive regression model we presented, prior to transforming either Age or Miles. Since Age was not transformed in the equation that included Miles", the coefficient for Miles" continues to equal the Time-Miles "simple" slope when Age equals zero. Thus, when we transform one of the two component variables that is involved in the product term in an interactive regression model, by subtracting off some constant, but we do not transform the other component variable, the regression coefficient for the transformed component variable is not altered while the regression coefficient for the component variable that has not been transformed is affected by the transformation. This seemingly counterintuitive result simply follows from the interpretation of these regression coefficients as "simple" slopes. The regression coefficient for variable X_1, when some X_2 and the X_1X_2 product are included in the regression equation as predictors, tells us about the "simple" slope for X_1 when X_2 equals zero. If we undertake a transformation of X_2 that alters its zero value, the regression coefficient for X_1 will be altered accordingly, while the coefficient for X_2 will not, since we have not changed the zero value of X_1.

In general, deviation transformations of either or both component variables do not affect the regression coefficient for the product of the components, so long as both components are also included as predictors in the model. The regression coefficient for the product tells us about the change in the "simple" relationship between one component variable and the dependent variable as the other component variable changes in value. Such an interpretation makes no reference to how one has defined the values of zero of the component variables.

10.1.2   Power Considerations in Interactive Models

In Chapter 8, we presented the general formula for the confidence interval of a regression coefficient in multiple regression. That formula, reproduced from Chapter 8, is

$$b_{p.12...p-1} \pm \sqrt{\frac{F_{\text{crit}}\text{MSE}}{\Sigma\,(X_{ip} - \overline{X}_p)^2(1 - R_p^2)}}$$

where $b_{p.12...p-1}$ is the regression coefficient for the pth predictor variable. This formula is the appropriate one regardless of the nature of the predictor variable. Thus, for instance, it provides the confidence intervals for the regression coefficients of product and interactive models as well as for the coefficients of additive models.

The same considerations affect the power of tests in interactive models as in additive models. Namely, factors which tend to increase the size of the confidence interval tend to decrease the power of the test of the null hypothesis that the estimated parameter equals some a priori value. Factors which decrease the size of the confidence interval increase power. Accordingly, as the mean square error of the model decreases, as the sum of squares for the pth predictor increases, and as the tolerance of the pth predictor increases, so inferential tests of its associated parameter are more powerful.

Within the context of interactive and product models, however, there is an interesting twist to the power issue, since the product predictor variable is computed from the other predictor variables in the model and thus is somewhat dependent upon them. Consider the following two variables and their product:

X_1	X_2	X_1X_2
3	2	6
1	3	3
4	5	20
2	1	2
5	4	20

If we were to regress some data variable Y_i on these three predictors, the confidence interval for the regression coefficient for the product variable would be a function of the critical value of F, the mean square error, the sum of squares of the product variable, and its tolerance. For these data, the sum of squares of the product variable equals 328.80. Its tolerance equals .0097. (This value is obtained by regressing the product variable on its two components and subtracting the resulting R^2 from 1. Notice that this product is exceedingly redundant with its two components.) From these two values, we can compute the denominator of the formula for the confidence interval for the product variable's regression coefficient: (328.8)(.0097) or 3.189.

Now consider what happens if we transform X_1 and X_2 into mean deviation form, i.e., X_1' and X_2', subtracting off their mean values, 3 in both cases, and then computing the product of the transformed variables:

X_1'	X_2'	$X_1'X_2'$
0	−1	0
−2	0	0
1	2	2
−1	−2	2
2	1	2

Now the sum of squares for the product variable equals 4.8, and its tolerance equals .663. As a function of the transformations of X_1 and X_2, their product is considerably less variable and relatively more independent (linearly) of the two components. Allowing for rounding error, the product of these two values (i.e., the denominator of the formula for the confidence interval for the product variable's regression coefficient) again equals 3.189. This is exactly as it should be, since inferential tests of a product variable's regression coefficient are not affected by linear deviation transformations of its components, as we have seen. Thus, the power of the test of the interaction or product variable is unaffected by deviation tranformation of its components, *as long as those components are included as predictors in the model.*

What is interesting about this result, however, is that deviation transformations do affect the tolerance of the product variable or its linear redundancy with its components. In our example data, the product variable was much more linearly redundant with its components prior to the deviation transformation than afterwards. Yet, the width of the confidence interval of its regression coefficient is unaffected since the change in tolerance is exactly compensated for by the change in the sum of squares of the product variable. This is an interesting exception to the general rule given earlier that redundancy among predictors tends to reduce power. When a predictor is a product of other predictors, then various transformations can radically affect its redundancy with its components. Yet such tranformations have no effect on the power of the test of the product's regression coefficient, as long as the component variables are included as predictors in the model.

For the running data, the Age-Miles product term using the raw data has a sum of squares of 30,050,580. Its tolerance, including the components Age and Miles as predictors, is .0638. After mean deviation transformations, the Age'-Miles' product term has a sum of squares of 1,917,899 and a tolerance of .9996. Within rounding error, the product of the sum of squares of the interaction term and its tolerance does not vary as a function of the transformation. Yet, in the raw data form, the product variable is exceedingly linearly redundant with its components, while in the transformed case it is virtually independent (linearly) of its component variables.

The lesson from all of this is that while a product variable may be quite redundant, in a linear manner, with its components, and while transformations of its components may reduce that redundancy, such tranformations will have no affect on statistical inference of the product variable's regression coefficient, so long as the component variables are included in the model. Many computer packages do not allow estimation of models where redundancy among the predictors exceeds a certain limit. In the case of product models, it makes sense to simply transform the component variables to reduce the redundancy between the product variable and its components in order to overcome this restriction. Generally, mean deviation transformations will accomplish this.

10.2

A General Procedure for the Derivation of "Simple" Relationships

In this section we develop a general procedure that can be used to reexpress models in terms of the "simple" relationship between the dependent variable and some predictor variable, regardless of the complexity of the model. We will use this general procedure extensively at later points in the chapter. This general procedure necessarily involves reference to some simple notions in differential calculus. Readers who know what a derivative is will have no problems understanding what follows. For those without such knowledge, we will attempt to be as clear as we can and ask that our results be taken on faith.

The preceding discussion of an interactive model relied heavily on interpretations of "simple" relationships between the dependent variable and some predictor variable within levels of another predictor variable. In the relatively simple case we have just been considering, where the model includes two predictor variables and their product, the derivation of those "simple" relationships is a relatively straightforward matter. One simply groups together terms that do and do not contain the predictor variable whose simple relationship is to be examined. The terms that do not contain that predictor variable are then combined into the "simple" intercept, while the terms that do contain that predictor variable are then combined into the "simple" slope for that predictor. To illustrate, suppose we were dealing with the following model and were interested in reexpressing it to tell us about the "simple" relationship between Y_i and X_{i1} at various levels of X_{i2}:

$$\hat{Y}_i = b_0 + b_1 X_{i1} + b_2 X_{i2} + b_3 (X_{i1} X_{i2})$$

Two terms in this model do not include X_{i1}. These are b_0 and $b_2 X_{i2}$. These terms are added together to yield the intercept for the Y_i-X_{i1} "simple" relationship. The two terms in the model that do include X_{i1} are $b_1 X_{i1}$ and $b_3 (X_{i1} X_{i2})$. These terms are also combined, factoring out the common X_{i1}, to yield the slope for the "simple" Y_i-X_{i1} relationship. Accordingly, the resulting reexpression is

$$\hat{Y}_i = (b_0 + b_2 X_{i2}) + (b_1 + b_3 X_{i2}) X_{i1}$$

This procedure for reexpressing models in terms of the "simple" relationship between Y_i and some predictor variable does not always work when the models become more complicated. The purpose of the present section of this chapter is to provide a procedure for deriving "simple" relationships between Y_i and some predictor variable regardless of the complexity of the original model. Such a procedure is extremely important, since the interpretation of individual coefficients in these more complicated models will be greatly facilitated by focusing on "simple" relationships between the dependent variable and a particular predictor variable at particular values of the other predictor variables.

In general, a model can be seen as a linear composite function of a set of predictor variables:

$$\hat{Y}_i = F(X_{i1}, X_{i2}, \ldots, X_{ip})$$

Some of these predictor variables may in fact be products of other predictor variables. Thus in practice, we may have models such as each of the following:

$$\hat{Y}_i = b_0 + b_1 X_{i1} + b_2 X_{i2} + b_3 (X_{i1} X_{i2})$$

$$\hat{Y}_i = b_0 + b_1 X_{i1} + b_2 X_{i2} + b_3 X_{i1}^2$$

What we wish to do is reexpress these models so that they tell us about the "simple" relationship between Y_i and some particular X_{ij} at particular values of the other predictor variables. We know from calculus that the slope of some function at a given point is provided by the derivative or partial derivative. Accordingly, to reexpress a model so that it tells us about the "simple" relationship between Y_i and X_{ij}, we need to take the partial derivative of the function $F(X_{i1}, X_{i2}, \ldots, X_{ip})$ with respect to that particular X_{ij}. We indicate this partial derivative as $F'(X_{ij})$. We then take the product of this partial derivative and X_{ij}, i.e., $[F'(X_{ij})]X_{ij}$. This product is then simultaneously added to and subtracted from the original model in order to yield the "simple" Y_i-X_{ij} relationship at particular values of the other predictor variable:

$$\hat{Y}_i = F(X_{i1}, X_{i2}, \ldots, X_{ip}) - [F'(X_{ij})]X_{ij} + [F'(X_{ij})]X_{ij}$$

By doing this simultaneous addition and subtraction, we have not modified the model in any fundamental sense. We have simply reexpressed it so that it tells us about the "simple" relationship between Y_i and a particular X_{ij}. We then proceed to combine terms into the "simple" intercept and the "simple" slope. The "simple" intercept equals the first two terms in this reexpression:

$$\text{"Simple" Intercept} = \{F(X_{i1}, X_{i2}, \ldots, X_{ip}) - [F'(X_{ij})]X_{ij}\}$$

The "simple" slope equals the final term: $[F'(X_{ij})]$. Thus the "simple" relationship is given by the reexpression

$$\hat{Y}_i = \{F(X_{i1}, X_{i2}, \ldots, X_{ip}) - [F'(X_{ij})]X_{ij}\} + [F'(X_{ij})]X_{ij}$$

To illustrate, let us derive the "simple" Y_i-X_{i1} relationship from each of the following models:

(1) $\hat{Y}_i = b_0 + b_1 X_{i1} + b_2 X_{i2}$

(2) $\hat{Y}_i = b_0 + b_1 X_{i1} + b_2 X_{i2} + b_3(X_{i1} X_{i2})$

(3) $\hat{Y}_i = b_0 + b_1 X_{i1} + b_2 X_{i2} + b_3 X_{i1}^2$

To do this we need a few simple rules for calculating the derivative or partial derivative of these functions with respect to some variable. There are three rules that serve for the present functions:

1. The derivative of a sum equals the sum of the derivatives of the components of the sum.
2. The derivative of aX^m equals amX^{m-1}, where a can either be a constant or another variable with which X is multiplied.
3. The derivative of a component that does not include X equals zero.

Following these rules, for model (1) the partial derivative with respect to X_{i1} equals b_1. Accordingly, to reexpress the model in terms of the "simple" Y_i-X_{i1} relationship, we need to add and subtract $b_1 X_{i1}$ to the model:

(1) $\hat{Y}_i = b_0 + b_1 X_{i1} + b_2 X_{i2} - b_1 X_{i1} + b_1 X_{i1}$

The "simple" intercept results when we combine the first four terms in this reexpression; the "simple" slope is given by the final term in the reexpression. Thus, we have the following "simple" model

(1) $\hat{Y}_i = (b_0 + b_2 X_{i2}) + b_1 X_{i1}$

The partial derivative with respect to X_{i1} from model (2) equals $b_1 + b_3 X_{i2}$. Adding and subtracting the product of this partial derivative with X_{i1} to the model (2) gives the following result:

(2) $\hat{Y}_i = b_0 + b_1 X_{i1} + b_2 X_{i2} + b_3(X_{i1} X_{i2})$

$\qquad - (b_1 + b_3 X_{i2})X_{i1} + (b_1 + b_3 X_{i2})X_{i1}$

Combining terms, we get the following reexpression for the "simple" Y_i-X_{i1} relationship:

(2) $\hat{Y}_i = (b_0 + b_2 X_{i2}) + (b_1 + b_3 X_{i2})X_{i1}$

which is the result we have dealt with extensively earlier in the chapter. Model (3) is

(3) $\hat{Y}_i = b_0 + b_1 X_{i1} + b_2 X_{i2} + b_3 X_{i1}^2$

Its partial derivative with respect to X_{i1} equals $b_1 + 2b_3 X_{i1}$. We then add and subtract the product of this partial derivative with X_{i1} to the model:

(3) $\hat{Y}_i = b_0 + b_1 X_{i1} + b_2 X_{i2} + b_3 X_{i1}^2$

$- (b_1 + 2b_3 X_{i1})X_{i1} + (b_1 + 2b_3 X_{i1})X_{i1}$

Grouping and combining terms, we get the following "simple" reexpression

(3) $\hat{Y}_i = (b_0 + b_2 X_{i2} - b_3 X_{i1}^2) + (b_1 + 2b_3 X_{i1})X_{i1}$

This procedure for reexpressing a model to show the "simple" relationship between Y_i and one of the predictor variables will work no matter how complex the model is. As we will see, this sort of reexpression will permit us to interpret the individual parameter estimates in fairly complex models with relative ease. We turn now to the interpretation of relatively simple models that involve the product of a predictor variable with itself.

10.3

Powers of Predictor Variables

A generalization of what has been learned about interactions between two predictor variables can be used to understand models that include powers of a predictor variable. Suppose, for instance, with the data at hand, we suspect that the relationship between Time and Miles depends on the level of Miles. We suspect that when one does not train a whole lot, the relationship between training and race times might be a lot stronger than it is when one trains a great deal. In other words, adding 5 more miles per week to one's training is likely to make much more of a difference to one's race time if one's base were 10 miles per week than if one's base were 50 miles per week. Such a prediction amounts to arguments about changes in the "simple" Time-Miles relationship. This time, however, we are not saying that the magnitude of that "simple" relationship changes as Age changes. Rather we are hypothesizing that the "simple" Time-Miles relationship changes as Miles changes. In essence, we are hypothesizing an interaction of Miles with itself in predicting Time. We use the same functional form to incorporate such an interaction into our model; namely, we include the product of the two variables that are hypothesized to interact as a separate predictor in the regression model. By direct analogy with the earlier discussion of interactions, such a model might look like

$\widehat{\text{Time}} = b_0 + b_1 \text{Miles} + b_2 \text{Miles} + b_3 (\text{Miles Miles})$

These coefficients could not be estimated, since Miles appears as a predictor variable twice, resulting in a tolerance of zero. To alleviate this problem, we leave out one of the Miles predictors and are left with the following model

$$\widehat{\text{Time}} = b_0 + b_1\text{Miles} + b_2(\text{Miles}^2)$$

As we did with models involving interactions between two different component variables, we can interpret this model by reexpressing it so that it informs us about the "simple" Time-Miles relationship at different levels of Miles. Following the rule for reexpression in terms of a "simple" relationship given in the preceding section of this chapter, the derivative of the model with respect to Miles equals $b_1 + 2b_2\text{Miles}$. We now add and subtract the product of this derivative and Miles to the model:

$$\widehat{\text{Time}} = b_0 + b_1\text{Miles} + b_2(\text{Miles}^2) - (b_1 + 2b_2\text{Miles})\text{Miles}$$
$$+ (b_1 + 2b_2\text{Miles})\text{Miles}$$

Grouping and combining terms into a "simple" intercept and "simple" slope gives the reexpression

$$\widehat{\text{Time}} = (b_0 - b_2\text{Miles}^2) + (b_1 + 2b_2\text{Miles})\text{Miles}$$

This reexpression tells us about the "simple" linear relationship between Time and Miles at particular levels of Miles. Clearly, that "simple" relationship is changing as Miles changes value. When Miles equals zero, the "simple" intercept is equal to b_0 and the "simple" slope is equal to b_1. But as Miles increases in value, both the "simple" intercept and the "simple" slope change in value. The degree to which they change is a function of the level of Miles and the magnitude of the b_2 coefficient.

To better understand this reexpression, it is helpful to be a little more concrete. Accordingly, we estimate the coefficients for this model from our data:

$$\widehat{\text{Time}} = 37.477 - .753\text{Miles} + .008\text{Miles}^2$$

From this model we have derived predicted values of Time at different levels of Miles. These values of $\widehat{\text{Time}}$ have been graphed as a function of Miles in Exhibit 10.12. The shape of the resulting prediction function supports our hypothesis that race times are a nonlinear function of training. Our hypothesis was that training more and more miles had diminishing returns. More miles might make a relatively large difference at first. When one's training regimen is already fairly intense, however, an additional few miles might make relatively less of a difference in expected race times.

EXHIBIT 10.12 ▶

Time-Miles non-linear model

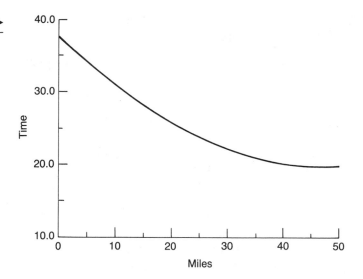

The curved prediction function in Exhibit 10.12 reflects the fact that the slope of the function relating Time and Miles is changing as Miles changes in value. At relatively low levels of Miles, the prediction function is steeper (i.e., a larger negative slope) than at higher levels of Miles. To specify what the relationship is between Time and Miles at a particular level of Miles, we can think of the slope of a line that is tangent to the curved prediction function at that particular level of Miles. The slope of such a line is equivalent to the slope of the curve at that particular level of Miles. Such a line, tangent to the curve at a particular level of Miles, has an intercept as well. These values, the intercept and slope of the line tangent to the curve at a particular value of Miles, are given by the reexpression of the model in terms of the "simple" relationship between Time and Miles at particular levels of Miles.

Given the parameter estimates provided above, the "simple" Time-Miles relationship at particular levels of Miles is given by the following reexpression of the model

$$\widehat{\text{Time}} = (37.477 - .008\text{Miles}^2) + (-.753 + 2(.008)\text{Miles})\text{Miles}$$

Using this reexpression, we could derive the "simple" relationship between Time and Miles at a few particular levels of Miles and examine how those "simple" relationships change as Miles changes value. Suppose, for instance, that we were interested in the slope of the curve for someone who does not now run. That is, we were interested in the incremental effect of running 1 mile a week given a base of zero miles per week. Substituting the value of 0 for Miles in the above reexpression of the model (in all places but the last occurrence of Miles) gives us the following "simple" relationship:

$$\widehat{\text{Time}} = (37.477 - .008(0)^2) + (-.753 + 2(.008)0)\text{Miles}$$
$$= 37.477 - .753\text{Miles}$$

This "simple" relationship makes clear the interpretation of the b_0 and b_1 terms in the model. The value of b_0, 37.477, equals the predicted value when Miles equals zero. It also equals the intercept of a line tangent to the curved prediction function depicted in Exhibit 10.12 at the point where Miles equals zero. The value of b_1 in the model equals the "simple" slope between Time and Miles when Miles equals zero. It is the slope of the line tangent to the curved prediction function when, and only when, Miles equals zero. As the expression for the "simple" Time-Miles relationship at particular levels of Miles makes clear, this "simple" slope will change as Miles changes in value. Accordingly, the coefficient for Miles in a model which includes Miles^2 as an additional predictor represents the slope for Miles only at one particular point, i.e., when Miles equals zero.

Now, suppose we were interested in examining the Time : Miles simple relationship for someone who runs 20 miles a week. That is, we were interested in the incremental effect of running an additional mile a week given a base of 20 miles a week. Substituting the value 20 for Miles in the above reexpression of the model (in all places but the last occurrence of Miles) gives us the following "simple" relationship between Time and Miles when Miles equals 20:

$$\widehat{\text{Time}} = (37.477 - .008(20)^2) + (-.753 + 2(.008)20)\text{Miles}$$
$$= 34.277 - .433\text{Miles}$$

Clearly, both the "simple" intercept and the "simple" slope have changed as a result of examining the "simple" relationship at a different value of Miles. The "simple" slope has gone from a value of $-.753$, when Miles equals zero, to a value of $-.433$ when Miles equals 20. This substantial decrease is exactly what was hypothesized: the addition of a mile more to a training regimen should have less of an effect on race times if one is already running quite a few miles than if one is running many fewer miles. A comparison of the "simple" slopes when Miles equals zero and when it equals 20 shows that the simple slope has changed by $2b_3 \times 20$. This, then, provides a compelling interpretation for the b_3 coefficient in the model. The coefficient for Miles^2 equals half the change in the slope for the "simple" Time-Miles relationship as Miles changes 1 unit. Another way of saying this is that the "simple" slope between Time and Miles changes by $2b_3$ as Miles changes 1 unit.

There is another interpretation of b_3 provided by examining the reexpression of the model in terms of the "simple" Time-Miles relationship. As Miles changes value, the intercept of the "simple" Time-Miles relationship is also changing, and the degree to which it changes is also a function of b_3. However, the changes in this intercept are not nearly as informative as are the changes in the "simple" slope that we have just interpreted. Recall that the intercept and slope of this "simple" relationship are equivalent to the intercept and slope of the line that is tangent to the curved prediction function at the point at which the "simple" relationship is evaluated. Changes in the slopes of these lines as Miles changes value are equivalent to changes in the slope of the curved prediction function as Miles changes value. Changes in the intercepts of these lines, while intimately related to changes in the slopes, are much less informative on an intuitive level. Hence, while we could interpret the b_3 coefficient by making reference to changes in the "simple" intercept as Miles changes in value, it will generally be more compelling to interpret b_3 as half the change in the "simple" slope as Miles changes by 1 unit.

Let us now summarize the interpretation of the three estimated coefficients in this model. The intercept in the model, b_0, equals the predicted value of Time for someone who runs zero miles per week. It may be equivalently interpreted as the intercept of the "simple" Time-Miles relationship when Miles equals zero. The coefficient associated with the Miles predictor variable, b_1, equals the "simple" Time-Miles slope when and only when Miles equals zero. Since, as we have seen, this "simple" slope changes in value as Miles changes in value, it tells us little about the slope of the curved prediction function at other values of Miles. Finally, the coefficient for the $Miles^2$ predictor term equals half the change in the "simple" slope as Miles changes by 1 unit.

We have seen that the coefficients of this model are consistent with our expectation that the relationship between Miles and Time should become less strong as Miles increases in value, but we have not yet tested the reliability of this curvilinear component of the prediction function. In other words, we need to test whether this model that allows changes in the "simple" Time-Miles slope as Miles changes in value does a reliably better job of predicting Time than a more simple linear model. To determine this, we compute PRE and F^*, as always, testing the null hypothesis that β_2, the parameter for the quadratic term, equals zero.

The augmented model for this test is the one we have now spent considerable time interpreting:

$$\text{Time} = \beta_0 + \beta_1\text{Miles} + b_3\text{Miles}^2 + \varepsilon_i$$

It has a sum of squared errors of 894.191. The compact model is

$$\text{Time} = \beta_0 + \beta_1\text{Miles} + \varepsilon_i$$

Earlier we gave the sum of squared errors for this model as 1028.963. A comparison of these two terms results in a PRE of .131, which converts to an F^*, with 1 and 77 degrees of freedom, of 11.605. The reliability of this F^* statistic leads us to reject the null hypothesis. In other words, we conclude that the value of β_2 in all likelihood is not equal to zero. As always, there are a variety of more substantive ways to phrase this conclusion. We might say, for instance, that this test demonstrates that the "simple" relationship between Time and Miles changes as Miles changes. We might equivalently say that Time is a nonlinear function of Miles and that the relationship is a negative decelerating one. This means that initially the slope of the prediction function is negative, and as Miles increases it become less and less negative. The relationship is now said to be a nonlinear one since we have demonstrated that a model that presumes a uniform slope at all levels of Miles does not fit the data as well as one in which the slope is allowed to change. This changing slope, graphed in Exhibit 10.12, clearly justifies the nonlinear label.

We could also test the null hypothesis that β_1, the slope for Miles, equals zero in this augmented model that includes the quadratic Miles^2 term. If we regress Time on simply Miles^2, we get the following regression equation:

$$\widehat{\text{Time}} = 28.100 - .004\text{Miles}^2$$

with a sum of squared errors equal to 1222.156. Comparing this model to the augmented model including Miles as a predictor, PRE equals .268, which converts to an F^*, with 1 and 77 degrees of freedom, of 28.242. The magnitude of this F^* statistic causes us to reject the null hypothesis that the regression coefficient for Miles, given that Miles^2 is already included in the prediction function, is equal to zero. In other words, the "simple" Time-Miles slope when Miles equals zero, and allowing that "simple" slope to change as Miles changes, is reliably different from zero. If we found a runner who trained not at all, the best prediction we could make from these data about the effects of training 1 mile per week on his or her race time would be to say that the increment in training would lead to a decrease of roughly .735 minutes in his or her race time. Of course, although this slope is reliable, we would not want to place much faith in it, for our sample includes no runners who train 0 or 1 mile per week.

Notice that this test of the regression coefficient for Miles when Miles^2 is included in the augmented and compact models is rather different from the simple test of the reliability of the regression coefficient for Miles when it is the only predictor in the augmented model. We presented such a test at the very start of this chapter, showing that when we compared the simple single-parameter model to an augmented model that included Miles as the sole predictor variable, we obtained a PRE of

.534 which converted to an F^* statistic, with 1 and 78 degrees of freedom, of 89.599. The regression coefficient for Miles when Miles^2 is not included as a predictor is a test of the slope of the Time-Miles relationship on average across all levels of Miles. In other words, it is the slope that best characterizes the Time-Miles relationship regardless of the level of Miles. On the other hand, when Miles^2 is included as an additional predictor, the test of the regression coefficient for Miles is a test of the "simple" Time-Miles slope when and only when Miles equals zero. The model presumes that the "simple" slope changes as Miles changes value, and hence a test of that slope at one particular value of Miles is not equivalent to a test of that slope at another value.

The difference between these two tests is exactly equivalent to what we found to be the case for the interactive model where we included the product between two different predictors in the models rather than the product of a single predictor with itself. In the model with an interaction between two different predictors, we showed that the regression coefficient for each of the predictor variables involved in the interaction was the "simple" effect of that variable when the other predictor variable equaled zero. Similarly, when a variable interacts with itself, the regression coefficient for that variable when the quadratic form of that variable is included in the model estimates the "simple" effect of that variable when it is equal to zero.

Concluding that the "simple" Time-Miles slope is reliably different from zero when Miles equals zero is hardly interesting, however, since, as we have said, we have no runners in our sample who average zero miles per week training. Hence, we might want to transform Miles so that the value of zero is a more meaningful value, much like we did in the case of the interaction between Miles and Age. Suppose, for instance, that we took the deviation of Miles from its mean:

$$\text{Miles}' = \text{Miles} - \overline{\text{Miles}}$$

and regressed Time on Miles' and Miles'^{2}. The resulting estimated model is

$$\widehat{\text{Time}} = 22.053 - .279\text{Miles}' + .008\text{Miles}'^2$$

The transformation of Miles has not affected the sum of squared errors for this model. It still equals 894.191. Nor has it affected the regression coefficient for the quadratic predictor. That coefficient continues to equal half the change in the "simple" Time-Miles slope as Miles changes in value by 1 unit. Accordingly, a test of the reliability of β_2, the regression coefficient for the quadratic term, is invariant across the transformation we have used. We still learn that the prediction function is reliably nonlinear, $F^*_{1,77} = 11.605$. This result parallels the conclusion reached earlier in the interactive case: linear transformations of some predictor variable will not affect a test of the regression coefficient for the quadratic function of that predictor so long as the predictor itself is included in the model.

Both the intercept and the regression coefficient for Miles', however, have been affected by the transformation. The intercept is still the predicted value of Time when Miles' equals zero, but a zero value for Miles' is equivalent to the mean of Miles. Hence, allowing for nonlinearity in the Time-Miles relationship, our predicted value of race time, when dealing with a runner who runs the average amount of miles per week for our sample, equals 22.053 minutes. The regression coefficient for Miles', $-.279$, is the "simple" slope for the Time-Miles relationship when Miles' equals zero or, equivalently, when Miles equals the sample mean. Naturally, a test of whether this parameter differs from zero would reach a rather different conclusion than the test of β_1 did in the model prior to transformation, since b_1 prior to the transformation is the "simple" slope when Miles equals zero and b_1 in the transformed case is the "simple" slope when Miles equals the sample mean.

By other transformations, taking the deviation between Miles and other representative values, we can test "simple" Time-Miles slopes at those other representative values.

10.4

More Complex Nonlinear Functional Forms

We have found evidence in our data for both an interaction between Age and Miles and a quadratic effect of Miles in predicting race times. We have examined these two nonlinear effects separately, rather than putting them both in a single model, for didactic purposes. Let us now look at a more complete model that incorporates both the Age by Miles interaction and the quadratric Miles term. The estimated model is

$$\widehat{\text{Time}} = 25.825 + .269\text{Age} - .574\text{Miles}$$
$$+ .008\text{Miles}^2 - .004(\text{Age Miles})$$

The sum of squared errors for this model equals 584.273. If we compare this model with a model that omits the Miles^2 predictor, the resulting F^*, with 1 and 75 degrees of freedom, equals 15.510. Hence, the nonlinearity in the Time-Miles relationship is still found even when we control for Age and the interaction of Age with Miles. However, when we compare this model with one which deletes only the Age Mile interaction term, the resulting F^* is not reliable. Hence, although we found that Age and Miles reliably interact in predicting Time when Miles^2 is not controlled, that effect ceases to be reliable in this more complete model.

Nevertheless, let us continue to interpret the various coefficients of this model in order to clarify the interpretation of more complex nonlinear functional forms. The curvilinear prediction plane generated by this model is graphed in three-dimensional space in Exhibit 10.13, with Age and Miles on the horizontal axes and Time on the vertical axis. Our interpretation of the coefficients of this model will make reference to this exhibit.

For the sake of interpretation, we can reexpress this equation to tell us about either the "simple" Time-Age or the "simple" Time-Miles relationship. Let us do the latter reexpression first. Accordingly, we take the partial derivative of this model with respect to Miles. This equals $-.574 + 2(.008)$Miles $- .004$Age. We now take the product of this partial derivative and Miles and add that product to and subtract it from the model:

$$\widehat{\text{Time}} = 25.825 + .269\text{Age} - .574\text{Miles} + .008\text{Miles}^2 - .004(\text{Age Miles})$$
$$- (-.574 + 2(.008)\text{Miles} - .004\text{Age})\text{Miles}$$
$$+ (-.574 + 2(.008)\text{Miles} - .004\text{Age})\text{Miles}$$

Grouping terms into the "simple" intercept and "simple" slope, as we showed earlier, we obtain the following reexpression for the "simple" Time-Miles relationship:

$$\widehat{\text{Time}} = 25.825 + .269\text{Age} - .008\text{Miles}^2$$
$$+ (-.574 + 2(.008)\text{Miles} - .004\text{Age})\text{Miles}$$

EXHIBIT 10.13 ▶

Age Miles non-linear model

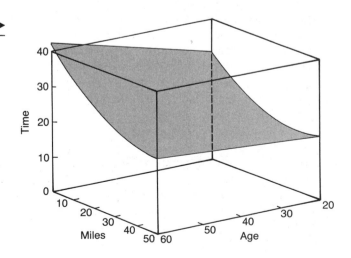

The various coefficients in this reexpression tell us about the "simple" intercept and slope of the Time-Miles relationship at particular values of Age and Miles. Graphically, they tell us about the coefficients for the Time-Miles relationship if we slice through the graph in Exhibit 10.13, parallel to the Miles axis at particular values of Age. The value of b_0 is the estimated intercept for the relationship when Age equals zero. The regression coefficient for Age, .269, tells us how that "simple" intercept changes as Age changes values. Looking at the graph in Exhibit 10.13, the Age coefficient tells us how the point of intersection of the prediction plane with the vertical axis (i.e., when Miles equals zero) changes as Age changes value. When Age equals zero, the curve intersects the vertical axis at the value of 25.825. For each unit increase in Age, the value of the intercept increases by .269.

The regression coefficient for Miles, −.574, estimates the "simple" Time-Miles slope when both Miles and Age equal zero. Notice that the interpretation for this coefficient is different from what it was in both of the earlier models, either where we included Age Miles but not $Miles^2$ or where we included $Miles^2$ but not Age Miles. Graphically, this regression coefficient equals the slope of the prediction plane at the point at which both Age and Miles equal zero. Since the graph presents the prediction plane only for Age values between 20 and 60, this point on the plane is not included in the exhibit.

The regression coefficient for $Miles^2$, .008, equals half the change in the "simple" Time-Miles slope as Miles changes by 1 unit. Notice that this interpretation does not depend on the value of Age. As Miles changes 1 unit, the "simple" slope changes by 2(.008) regardless of whether we are predicting race times for a 20-year-old or a 50-year-old individual. Its interpretation, however, does differ in one respect from the interpretation we gave to the regression coefficient for $Miles^2$ in the equation that did not include Age and Age Miles. Here we are estimating the nonlinear effect of Miles on Time within levels of Age or holding Age constant. Earlier we did not. In terms of the graph of Exhibit 10.13, if we take a vertical slice of the graph parallel to the Miles axis at any value of Age, we have a curvilinear prediction function for predicting Time from Miles at that value of Age. The amount by which the "simple" slope of that prediction function changes as Miles changes value is 2(.008). And this degree of curvilinearity in the prediction function is invariant across values of Age; i.e., it does not depend on which horizontal slice of the graph, parallel to the Miles axis, we look at. The degree of curvilinearity is constant as Age changes value. If the degree of curvilinearity of the Time-Miles "simple" relation changed as Age changed value, then there would have to be a ($Miles^2$ Age) predictor in the model.

The final coefficient in the equation, −.004, tells us the degree to which the Time-Miles "simple" slope changes as Age changes 1 unit, regardless of the value of Miles. In terms of the prediction plane of Exhibit 10.13, this value equals the change in slope of the "simple" Time-Miles prediction function as Age changes by 1 unit, i.e., moving across vertical slices of the graph from one Age value to the next, holding Miles constant.

Now let us reexpress this equation so that it tells us about the "simple" Time-Age relationship. The partial derivative with respect to Age equals .269 − .004Miles. We then multiply this partial derivative by Age and add and subtract the resulting product to the model:

$$\widehat{\text{Time}} = 25.825 + .269\text{Age} - .574\text{Miles}$$
$$+ .008\text{Miles}^2 - .004(\text{Age Miles})$$
$$- (.269 - .004\text{Miles})\text{Age} + (.269 - .004\text{Miles})\text{Age}$$

Grouping terms together, we obtain the following reexpression:

$$\widehat{\text{Time}} = (25.825 - .574\text{Miles} + .008\text{Miles}^2) + (.269 - .004\text{Miles})\text{Age}$$

To interpret this "simple" reexpression, we need to think about vertical slices of the graph in Exhibit 10.13 parallel, this time, to the Age horizontal axis. This "simple" relationship tells us about the prediction lines for these slices and how they change as Miles and Age change values. Notice first of all that these prediction lines at particular values of Miles are all linear. This is readily apparent in the exhibit: if we take any vertical slice of the graph parallel to the Age axis at some particular value of Miles, the resulting prediction function is a straight line. This is necessarily the case since the "simple" slope in the reexpressed model does not include any terms including Age.

Both the "simple" intercept and the "simple" slope change as a function of Miles, however. The "simple" Time-Age intercept changes both linearly and nonlinearly as a function of Miles. The "simple" slope for that relationship, however, changes only linearly with Miles.

Although the data that we have been using throughout this chapter are not consistent with any more complex nonlinear functional forms than those already explored, we could extend this model to a more complex one, should our theories suggest that more complex forms are plausible. There is nothing inherently more difficult about interpreting more complex nonlinear models, so long as the basic principles that we have explained are kept in mind. These might be succinctly summarized as follows:

It is generally easiest to interpret a complex nonlinear prediction function by reexpressing it as a "simple" relationship between the dependent variable and a single predictor variable. Doing so makes clear that the regression coefficient for a predictor that is a component of a higher-order product should be interpreted as the effect of that predictor variable when the other components with which it is multiplied to form those higher-order products equal zero. Accordingly, linear transformations of predictors in the model will affect the regression coefficients for other predictors whenever the two sets of predictors are components of higher-order product terms. The coefficient of the highest-order product term (or terms) included in a model will be invariant across linear transformations of its component variables, so long as those components are also included in the model, as they should be. The components of a higher-order product term include all lower-order products as well as the component variables themselves. Thus, for instance, the component terms for the X^2Z^2 product include X^2Z, XZ^2, XZ, X^2, and Z^2, as well as X and Z. If this X^2Z^2 product term is included in a model along with all these components, then the regression coefficient for any given component equals the effect of that component when the other component with which it must be multiplied to equal the highest-order product term equals zero. Thus, the regression coefficient for the X^2Z term in the model that includes X^2Z^2, equals the effect of that triple interaction when and only when Z equals zero.

Before plunging headlong into a more complex final model to illustrate these principles, we should say that while more complex models are certainly tractable if theoretical speculation suggests that they are reasonable, there is always a danger in adding complexity simply for the sake of complexity without sufficient theoretical justification. The danger of exploring more complex models than our theories call for is the danger of "profiting" from chance searches. We may eventually find a complex augmented model that compares favorably with a less complex compact one, but in the absence of a strong theoretical motivation we stand the risk of simply making a Type I statistical error. Now for the illustration.

Consider the following model:

$$\hat{Y}_i = b_0 + b_1 X_i + b_2 Z_i + b_3 X_i^2 + b_4(X_i Z_i) + b_5(X_i^2 Z_i)$$

Let us now interpret these parameters estimates. If we examine the "simple" Y_i-X_i relationship, we take the partial derivative with respect to X_i and derive the appropriate reexpression of the model using the procedures described earlier. The resulting "simple" reexpression is

$$\hat{Y}_i = (b_0 + b_2 Z_i - b_3 X_i^2 - b_5 X_i^2 Z_i) + (b_1 + 2b_3 X_i + b_4 Z_i + 2b_5 X_i Z_i)X_i$$

Within the context of this reexpression, we will interpret the various coefficients of the model. The intercept, b_0, is the predicted value of Y_i

when both X_i and Z_i equal zero. The coefficient for the Z_i term, b_2, represents the change in the "simple" intercept of the Y_i-X_i relationship as Z_i changes by 1 unit. Accordingly, it tells us the degree to which the Y_i-X_i simple relationship changes as Z_i changes 1 unit, assuming X_i equals zero. The coefficient for the X_i term, b_1, equals the "simple" slope of the Y_i-X_i relationship when both X_i and Z_i equal zero. The coefficient for the X_i^2 term, b_3, equals half the change in the "simple" Y_i-X_i slope associated with a unit change in X_i when and only when Z_i equals zero. The coefficient for the X_iZ_i term, b_4, equals the change in the "simple" Y_i-X_i slope associated with a unit change in Z_i when and only when X_i equals zero. Finally, the coefficient for the highest-order product in the model, b_5, equals half the change in the "simple" Y_i-X_i slope as the X_iZ_i interaction changes by 1 unit. A variety of parallel interpretations exist for this final term: it equals half the change in the effect of the X_iZ_i interaction as X_i changes by 1 unit. Equivalently, it tells us by how much the nonlinear effect of X_i varies as Z_i varies. Note that the only coefficient that we were able to interpret without making reference to a zero value of some term included in the model was this last, highest-order one. This is because all other terms included in the model are components of this highest-order term.

In Exhibit 10.14, we have graphed the prediction plane generated by the following coefficients, using the form of the model just discussed:

$$\hat{Y}_i = 6.0 + .4X_i - .5Z_i + .06X_i^2 - .06(X_iZ_i) + .015(X_i^2Z_i)$$

Let us interpret these coefficients in terms of the "simple" relationship between Y_i and X_i:

$$\hat{Y}_i = 6.0 - .5Z_i - .06X_i^2 - .015X_i^2Z_i$$
$$+ (.4 + 2(.06)X_i - .06Z_i + 2(.015)X_iZ_i)X_i$$

EXHIBIT 10.14 ▶

An illustrative more complex model

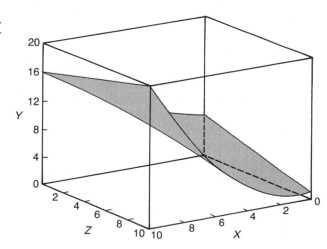

This amounts to examining the prediction function relating Y_i and X_i at particular values of Z_i or taking vertical slices of the graph in Exhibit 10.14 parallel to the X_i axis. Some of the coefficients in the model tell us about the shape of the prediction line when we take a vertical slice of the graph at the point where Z_i is equal to zero. The prediction line for this slice has an intercept of 6.0. The slope of this prediction line at the point at which X_i equals zero is .4. As X_i increases 1 unit, again looking only at the prediction line for the slice where Z_i equals zero, the slope of the prediction line increases by 2(.06). Now, if we take other vertical slices of the graph, still parallel to the X_i axis, but now at values of Z_i that are greater than 1, the prediction lines in those slices change. Specifically, as Z_i increases by 1 unit, the slope of the prediction line where X_i equals zero decreases by .06. The degree to which the prediction line is nonlinear also increases as Z_i increases. We have just said that when Z_i equals zero, the slope increases by 2(.06) for every unit increase in X_i. This increase is larger when dealing with prediction lines from slices where Z_i is greater than zero. When Z_i equals 1, the increase in the "simple" Y_i-X_i slope as X_i increases is equal to 2(.06) + 2(.015). When dealing with the slice where Z_i equals 10, the increase in the "simple" Y_i-X_i slope as X_i increases in value by 1 unit equals 2(.06) + 2(10)(.015).

We could make parallel interpretations of this function and the graph of Exhibit 10.14 by expressing it as the "simple" Y_i-Z_i relation and referring to prediction lines from vertical slices of the graph parallel to the Z_i axis.

The point in all of this is simply to demonstrate that this sort of interpretation, although somewhat cumbersome, is feasible. There may be rare occasions when models as complex as this one are theoretically quite plausible. Knowing how to interpret the resulting coefficients and their associated inferential tests is then important. However, such occasions are likely to be rare and the researcher who explores complex nonlinear functions without strong a priori motivation runs the risk of discovering "theoretical conclusions" that fail to replicate.

11

One-Way ANOVA: Models with a Single Categorical Predictor

Up to this point we have relied on regression models where the predictor variables have been treated as continuous variables. Our purpose in this chapter and the following two is to examine our basic approach to data analysis when predictors are categorical variables. In the language of traditional statistics books, earlier chapters concerned multiple regression. The present chapter concerns one-way analysis of variance models or, equivalently, models with a single categorical predictor. In the next chapter we consider models having multiple categorical predictors, or higher-order analysis of variance models. Chapter 13 is devoted to models in which some predictors are categorical and some are continuous. Such models have been traditionally labeled analysis of covariance models. Throughout we will continue to use our basic approach of simply comparing augmented and compact models.

11.1

The Case of a Categorical Predictor with Two Levels

Returning to our baseball data, suppose we were interested in determining whether a team's league is a reliable predictor of the team's seasonal batting average. While we might assume that team batting average is a continuous variable, which league a team is in, i.e., American or National, clearly is not. Our predictor is thus a categorical variable, having two categories or values. These categories cannot be meaningfully rank-ordered, so that, in the language of scale construction, we are dealing with a nominally coded predictor. Exhibit 11.1 contains the data to be used: each team's batting average and its league.

EXHIBIT 11.1 ▶

1983 team batting averages (× 1000)

	B.A.	League
Atlanta	272	National
Chicago	261	National
Cincinnati	239	National
Houston	257	National
Los Angeles	250	National
Montreal	264	National
New York	241	National
Philadelphia	249	National
Pittsburgh	264	National
St. Louis	270	National
San Diego	250	National
San Francisco	247	National
Baltimore	269	American
Boston	270	American
California	260	American
Chicago	262	American
Cleveland	265	American
Detroit	274	American
Kansas City	271	American
Milwaukee	277	American
Minnesota	261	American
New York	273	American
Oakland	262	American
Seattle	240	American
Texas	255	American
Toronto	277	American

11.1.1 Contrast Codes for a Categorical Predictor

If we are to tell the computer to construct a least squares prediction function, predicting team batting average from league, we need some way of coding or numerically representing the information about a team's league. Since league is measured on a nominal scale, it would seem that any numerical representation of the league information would do, so long as we used that arbitrary numerical representation consistently. By consistent use, we mean that if a given value on the variable that represents league numerically is assigned to one league, then any team in that league has that same value on the variable, and no team in the other league has that value.

To illustrate, suppose we created a variable X_i to represent league numerically, arbitrarily assigning the value of -1 to teams in the National League and $+1$ to teams in the American League. Since every team is in one league or the other, all teams have values of either -1 or $+1$ on variable X_i. Notice that our purpose in creating this variable is simply to differentiate numerically between the two leagues. Since league is a nominal variable, no rank order or interval information need be preserved in our coding scheme. We could just as easily have given the value of -1 to the American League teams and $+1$ to the National League teams. Similarly, we could have given the value of 203 to teams from the National League and the value of -20.5 to teams from the American League. The point is that the values that represent the nominal variable are arbitrarily defined, but they must be consistently used.

Throughout all of the rest of the book we will use a convention for coding nominal predictors known as *contrast codes*. Contrast codes are simply one of the possible arbitrary coding schemes for numerically representing categorical predictors. Two conditions define contrast codes and differentiate them from other coding schemes. For right now, we will only define one of these two conditions. The other is only relevant when the nominal variable has more than two categories and will be given later. Let us define a value on a contrast-coded categorical variable X_i as λ_k, where the subscript k refers to the level of the categorical variable being coded. Across levels of k, or across all categories of the variable, a contrast code is one where

$$\sum_k \lambda_k = 0$$

Notice that we are summing here across levels or categories rather than across individuals or observations. The coding scheme that we defined above to represent league, defining the values of X_i as -1 if a team was in the National League and as $+1$ if a team was in the American League, meets this condition for a contrast code. Namely, there are two categories that are being coded, National League and American League. The value of -1 has been assigned to the first category, and the value of $+1$ to the second. These values are the λ_k's. If we sum them across the two categories, we add together -1 and $+1$, giving us a total of zero. Notice that if we had summed the λ's across individual observations or teams, we would not have arrived at a total of zero, since there are 12 National League teams and 14 American League teams. Hence, summing across teams, the sum of the λ's would equal $+2$. Only if there are an equal number of observations in each of the categories would the sum of the λ's across individual observations equal the sum of the λ's across categories.

There are an infinite number of other possible values for X_i that also meet this condition for contrast codes. For instance, values of -3 and $+3$ for the American and National leagues also meet this condition. Our arbitrarily chosen values of 203 and -20.5 do not, however. Although we will rely exclusively on contrast codes whenever we encounter categorical predictors, at a later point in this chapter we will explore how codes other than contrast codes affect the parameters and interpretation of the model. For the time being, let us examine the least squares prediction function, predicting team batting average from league, using the contrast-coded variable X_i, coding National league as -1 and American League as $+1$.

11.1.2 Estimation and Inference with a Single Contrast-Coded Predictor

Defining batting average as Y_i and using our contrast-coded variable X_i as the predictor, we wish to estimate the parameters of the following augmented model:

MODEL A: $Y_i = \beta_0 + \beta_1 X_i + \varepsilon_i$

This is a simple regression model to which we devoted attention in Chapters 6 and 7. Assuming that β_1 equals some value other than zero, this model allows batting average values Y_i to be conditional or to vary with which league a team comes from. To see if league is in fact related to batting average, we will compare this augmented model to a compact single-parameter model in which a single predicted value is generated for all teams regardless of which league they are from. This compact model is our simplest model, discussed in Chapters 4 and 5:

MODEL C: $Y_i = \beta_0 + \varepsilon_i$

The least squares estimates of these models are

MODEL A: $\hat{Y}_i = 260.38 + 5.05X_i$

MODEL C: $\hat{Y}_i = 260.78$

The augmented model as well as the raw data on which it is based is graphed in Exhibit 11.2. The sums of squared errors for the augmented and compact models equal 2608.095 and 3266.615, respectively. The calculations for these two sums of squares are summarized in Exhibit 11.3 where we derive from each model the predicted value for each team and then calculate for each team the two squared residuals.

Accordingly, the value of PRE for predicting team batting average from league is

$$PRE = \frac{SSE(C) - SSE(A)}{SSE(C)}$$

$$= \frac{3266.61 - 2608.10}{3266.61} = .202$$

To determine whether this proportional reduction in error is reliable, we want to convert PRE to the F^* statistic. In this case, since two parameters are estimated in the augmented model and one in the compact model, the degrees of the freedom for F^* equal 1 and 24 (PA − PC and N − PA, respectively). The resulting F^* is

$$F^*_{PA-PC,N-PA} = \frac{PRE/(PA - PC)}{(1 - PRE)/(N - PA)}$$

$$F^*_{1,24} = \frac{.202/1}{(1 - .202)/24} = 6.06$$

The critical value of F, with 1 and 24 degrees of freedom, at $\alpha = .05$ is 4.26. Hence, we conclude that there is a significant reduction in our errors of prediction when those predictions are made conditional on information about a team's league.

EXHIBIT 11.2 ▶

$\hat{Y}_i = 260.38 + 5.05X$

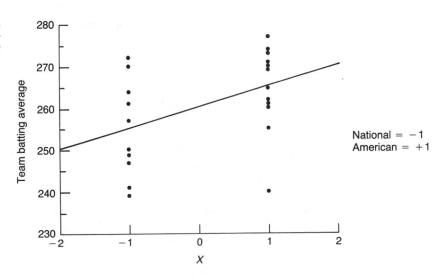

EXHIBIT 11.3 ▶

Calculating error for augmented and compact models

Team	Y_i	Augmented $\hat{Y}_i$	e_i^2	Compact $\hat{Y}_i$	e_i^2
Atlanta	272	255.33	277.89	260.78	125.89
Chicago	261	255.33	32.15	260.78	.05
Cincinnati	239	255.33	266.67	260.78	474.37
Houston	257	255.33	2.79	260.78	14.29
Los Angeles	250	255.33	28.41	260.78	116.21
Montreal	264	255.33	75.17	260.78	10.37
New York	241	255.33	205.35	260.78	391.25
Philadelphia	249	255.33	40.07	260.78	138.77
Pittsburgh	264	255.33	75.17	260.78	10.37
St. Louis	270	255.33	215.21	260.78	85.01
San Diego	250	255.33	28.41	260.78	116.21
San Francisco	247	255.33	69.39	260.78	189.89
Baltimore	269	265.43	12.74	260.78	67.57
Boston	270	265.43	20.88	260.78	85.01
California	260	265.43	29.48	260.78	.61
Chicago	262	265.43	11.76	260.78	1.49
Cleveland	265	265.43	.18	260.78	17.81
Detroit	274	265.43	73.44	260.78	174.77
Kansas City	271	265.43	31.02	260.78	104.45
Milwaukee	277	265.43	133.86	260.78	263.09
Minnesota	261	265.43	19.62	260.78	.05
New York	273	265.43	57.30	260.78	149.33
Oakland	262	265.43	11.76	260.78	1.49
Seattle	240	265.43	646.68	260.78	431.81
Texas	255	265.43	108.78	260.78	33.41
Toronto	277	265.43	133.86	260.78	263.09
SSE			2608.10		3266.62

So far, once we have coded our categorical predictor, there is nothing different about this simple regression model from those simple models using continuous predictors that were discussed in Chapters 6 and 7. The estimation of the model parameters and the calculations of PRE and F^* proceed just as before. Since all of the assumptions underlying the use of F^* involve assumptions about the distribution of Y_i, or really of ε_i, and since the categorical nature of X_i has no effect on the distribution of ε_i, none of the assumptions underlying this analysis have been violated by the presence of the categorical predictor.

What has changed somewhat, however, is the interpretation of the estimated parameters of the model and the statistical inference results. It is not the case that the old interpretations are incorrect, for the value of intercept in the augmented model, 260.38, is still the predicted value of Y_i when X_i equals zero. The coefficient for X_i is still a slope—the amount by which the predicted value of Y_i changes for each unit increase in X_i. And PRE and F^* still tell us about the reduction in errors of prediction. Rather, when we have categorical predictors, new interpretations of these statistics become possible.

To understand these new interpretations, it is helpful to consider the predicted values that the augmented model makes. These are contained in Exhibit 11.3. If we are dealing with a National League team, the predicted value from the augmented model equals

$$\hat{Y}_i = 260.38 + 5.05(-1) = 255.33$$

For the American League, the predicted value from the augmented model equals

$$\hat{Y}_i = 260.38 + 5.05(+1) = 265.43$$

These predicted values turn out to equal exactly the category means of Y_i, i.e., the mean team batting averages for the two leagues. The estimated value of the slope in the augmented model, 5.05, is in this case equal to half the difference between the means of the two leagues:

American $\overline{Y}$ − National $\overline{Y}$ = 265.43 − 255.33

$$= [260.38 + 5.05(+1)] - [260.38 + 5.05(-1)]$$

$$= [260.38 + 5.05] - [260.38 - 5.05]$$

$$= 5.05 + 5.05$$

or

$$\frac{(\text{American } \overline{Y} - \text{National } \overline{Y})}{2} = 5.05$$

In general the least squares parameter estimate or regression coefficient for a contrast-coded predictor is given by

$$b = \frac{\sum_k \lambda_k \overline{Y}_k}{\sum_k \lambda_k^2}$$

In the example at hand, this expression is evaluated as

$$\frac{(-1)255.33 + (1)265.43}{(-1)^2 + 1^2} = \frac{10.10}{2} = 5.05$$

The estimated value of the intercept, 260.38, equals, as always, the predicted value of Y_i when X_i equals zero. Since X_i equal to zero occurs halfway between the two values of $+1$ and -1 that code the two leagues, the estimated value of the intercept is necessarily equal to the average of the two league averages. This result is made clear by the graph in

Exhibit 11.2. It can also be shown algebraically as follows:

Since American $\overline{Y} = 260.38 + 5.05$,

$$260.38 = \text{American } \overline{Y} - 5.05$$

and since National $\overline{Y} = 260.38 - 5.05$,

$$260.38 = \text{National } \overline{Y} + 5.05$$

Adding these two equalities gives

$$260.38 + 260.38 = \text{American } \overline{Y} + \text{National } \overline{Y}$$

or

$$260.38 = \frac{(\text{American } \overline{Y} + \text{National } \overline{Y})}{2}$$

Notice that since the two leagues have different numbers of teams in them, the intercept in the augmented model, which we have just shown to be equal to the mean of the two league means, does not equal the overall mean batting average of all 26 teams. The intercept from the compact model equals the overall or grand mean of the 26 teams, 260.78. The intercept in the augmented model is equal to what is sometimes called the *unweighted grand mean*, averaging together the means of the two leagues without taking into account the fact that those two averages are based on different numbers of teams. If there were an equal number of teams in the two leagues, then the unweighted grand mean and the grand mean would equal each other, and in that case the intercept in the augmented model would be identical to the intercept in the compact model.

Since the slope in the augmented model equals half the difference between the two predicted values, and since those predicted values equal the means of the two leagues, then a test of whether that slope differs from zero is equivalent to testing whether the difference between the means of the two leagues equals zero. Therefore the inferential test of whether the augmented model gives us better predictions than the compact model is a test of whether the means of the two leagues reliably differ from each other. In other words, since the predicted value in the compact model for all teams equals the grand mean, and since the predicted values in the augmented model equal the league averages, testing whether the augmented models gives us better predictions than the compact model is equivalently a test of whether the two league means reliably differ from each other. We can thus state the null hypothesis that is being tested by F^* in two different but equivalent ways:

$$H_0: \quad \beta_1 = 0$$

$$H_0: \quad \text{American } \mu = \text{National } \mu$$

In this latter expression μ refers to the true but unknown values of the category or league means.

11.1.3 Reexpressions for F^*

As we saw in Chapter 7, the test statistic F^* can be expressed as a function of sums of squares instead of as a function of PRE. We know that

$$\text{PRE} = \frac{\text{SSE(C)} - \text{SSE(A)}}{\text{SSE(A)}} = 1 - \frac{\text{SSE(A)}}{\text{SSE(C)}}$$

Therefore

$$1 - \text{PRE} = \frac{\text{SSE(A)}}{\text{SSE(C)}}$$

Since

$$F^* = \frac{\text{PRE}/(\text{PA} - \text{PC})}{(1 - \text{PRE})/(N - \text{PA})}$$

Therefore

$$F^* = \frac{[(\text{SSE(C)} - \text{SSE(A)})/\text{SSE(C)}]/(\text{PA} - \text{PC})}{[(\text{SSE(A)}/\text{SSE(C)}]/(N - \text{PA})}$$

or

$$F^* = \frac{[\text{SSE(C)} - \text{SSE(A)}]/(\text{PA} - \text{PC})}{\text{SSE(A)}/(N - \text{PA})}$$

The difference between the sum of squared errors for the compact and augmented model is equal to the additional sum of squares due to regression in the augmented model as compared with the compact model. For the case where the augmented model has only a single predictor (and therefore two parameters) and the compact model has no predictors (and therefore a single parameter), this difference equals the entire sum of squares due to regression in the augmented model. In other words, for this case

$$\text{SSE(C)} - \text{SSE(A)} = \text{SSR} = \sum_i (\hat{Y}_i - \overline{Y})^2$$

since $\hat{Y}_i$ in the augmented model in our example from the two baseball leagues equals the means of the two leagues, $\overline{Y}_k$, this difference in the sum of squared errors also equals

$$\sum_i (\overline{Y}_k - \overline{Y})^2$$

In this expression we are summing across all cases. However, since $\overline{Y}$ is constant across all cases and since $\overline{Y}_k$ is constant across all cases within leagues, we can reexpress this sum of squares as

$$\sum_i = (\hat{Y}_i - \overline{Y})^2 = \sum_i (\overline{Y}_k - \overline{Y})^2 = \sum_k n_k(\overline{Y}_k - \overline{Y})^2$$

where n_k is the number of cases or teams in each league. In the example we have been using

$$\sum_k n_k(\overline{Y}_k - \overline{Y})^2 = 12(255.33 - 260.78)^2 + 14(265.43 - 260.78)^2$$

$$= 658.52$$

Similarly, the sum of squared errors for the augmented model can be expressed as

$$\text{SSE(A)} = \sum_i (Y_i - \hat{Y}_i)^2 = \sum_i (Y_i - \overline{Y}_k)^2$$

where we are summing across all observations.

Following all of this, F^* can be equivalently written in this case as

$$F^* = \frac{\sum_i (\hat{Y}_i - \overline{Y})^2/(\text{PA} - \text{PC})}{\sum_i (Y_i - \hat{Y}_i)^2/(N - \text{PA})} = \frac{\sum_k n_k(\overline{Y}_k - \overline{Y})^2/(\text{PA} - \text{PC})}{\sum_i (Y_i - \overline{Y}_k)^2/(N - \text{PA})}$$

In Chapter 7 we presented an alternative format for calculating and displaying this F^* statistic. That format was an analysis of variance source table, and it is reproduced as Exhibit 11.4. As we have just shown, we can substitute for $\hat{Y}_i$ in the expressions for the sum of squares regression and sum of squares error, since in the present case $\hat{Y}_i = \overline{Y}_k$. Thus we can rewrite this source table as shown in Exhibit 11.5. The bottom half of this exhibit contains the actual values from the example we have been considering. Notice that we have relabeled the first two rows in this source table. The sum of squares regression is now called the sum of squares *between groups* and the sum of squares error is now called the sum of squares *within groups*. The degrees of freedom column in the table of Exhibit 11.5 has also been changed so that the degrees of freedom between groups equals the number of groups minus 1 ($m - 1$), and the degrees of freedom within equals the total number of observations minus the number of groups ($N - m$). This source table is the source table that is given in most statistics textbooks for calculating an F^* statistic from a

EXHIBIT 11.4 ▶

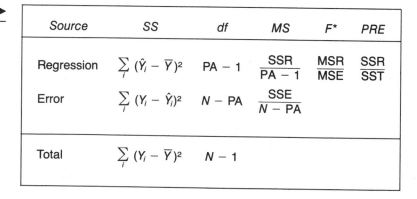

Source	SS	df	MS	F*	PRE
Regression	$\sum_i (\hat{Y}_i - \overline{Y})^2$	PA − 1	$\dfrac{\text{SSR}}{\text{PA} - 1}$	$\dfrac{\text{MSR}}{\text{MSE}}$	$\dfrac{\text{SSR}}{\text{SST}}$
Error	$\sum_i (Y_i - \hat{Y}_i)^2$	N − PA	$\dfrac{\text{SSE}}{N - \text{PA}}$		
Total	$\sum_i (Y_i - \overline{Y})^2$	N − 1			

EXHIBIT 11.5 ▶

Source	SS	df	MS	F*	PRE
Between	$\sum\limits_{k} n_k(\overline{Y}_k - \hat{Y})^2$	$m - 1$	$\dfrac{SSB}{m - 1}$	$\dfrac{MSB}{MSW}$	$\dfrac{SSB}{SST}$
Within	$\sum\limits_{i} (Y_i - \overline{Y}_k)^2$	$N - m$	$\dfrac{SSW}{N - m}$	$\dfrac{SSB}{SST}$
Total	$\sum\limits_{i} (Y_i - \overline{Y})^2$	$N - 1$			

Source	SS	df	MS	F*	PRE
Between	658.520	1	658.520	6.06	.202
Within	2608.095	24	108.671		
Total	3266.615	25			

one-way analysis of variance. We have just shown that the F^* we have derived from PRE resulting from the comparison of a single-parameter compact model with a two-parameter augmented model involving a contrast-coded predictor variable is algebraically equivalent to the F^* from what is traditionally called a one-way analysis of variance. With only two groups whose means are compared in an analysis of variance, the square root of the F^* statistic is the frequently encountered t^* statistic that is usually used to test the difference between the means of two groups.

The null hypothesis that is traditionally tested via a one-way analysis of variance is that the two group means, in this case the league means, are equal to each other. We have shown that this null hypothesis is equivalent to a null hypothesis that the value of β_1 equals zero, where β_1 is the parameter associated with a contrast-coded predictor variable that identifies which group an observation is from.

In this one-way analysis of variance source table the sum of squares error or the sum of squares within groups is, within our terminology, the sum of squared errors from the augmented model. As we have shown, the sum of squares regression or the sum of squares between groups equals the difference in the sum of squared errors between the augmented and compact model, where the augmented model estimates a parameter for a single contrast-coded predictor variable. One of the advantages of contrast codes is that this sum of squares regression or sum of squares explained by a single contrast-coded predictor can be calculated from knowledge of the group means, the number of observations in each group, and the contrast weights:

SS explained by a contrast predictor

$$= \frac{(\Sigma_k \lambda_k \overline{Y}_k)^2}{\Sigma_k (\lambda_k^2/n_k)}$$

In our example, the sum of squares explained by our single contrast-coded predictor equals

$$\frac{(-1(255.33) + 1(265.43))^2}{(-1)^2/12 + 1^2/14} = 658.52$$

This alternative expression for the sum of squares regression is useful when all one has available are the group means in a published report and one wishes to calculate tests of various differences between group means.

11.1.4 Alternative Coding Schemes for Categorical Predictors

We have a distinct preference for contrast-coded predictors for representing categorical variables. Although we will use such contrast-coded predictors exclusively in the remainder of this book, a slight excursion to discuss other sorts of coding schemes is appropriate, since these other schemes are frequently encountered and the intelligent data analyst ought to be able to interpret the resulting parameter estimates.

The most frequently used alternative to contrast codes are called *dummy codes*. For a categorical variable having two levels, such as a baseball league, a dummy-coded predictor variable is one in which one category is arbitrarily given the value of 0 and the other category is given the value of 1. Thus, for instance, using dummy codes rather than contrast codes, we might define a new X_i, assigning the value of 0 to teams from the National League and 1 to teams from the American League. If we then regressed team batting average Y_i on this new X_i, we get the following parameter estimates:

MODEL A:　$\hat{Y}_i = 255.33 + 10.1X_i$

This prediction function is graphed in Exhibit 11.6 along with the raw data on which it is based. Compare this graph with the one in Exhibit 11.2 for the contrast-coded predictor. Notice that the only difference between the two graphs concerns the definition of the X axis or abscissa.

EXHIBIT 11.6 ▶

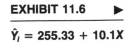

$\hat{Y}_i = 255.33 + 10.1X$

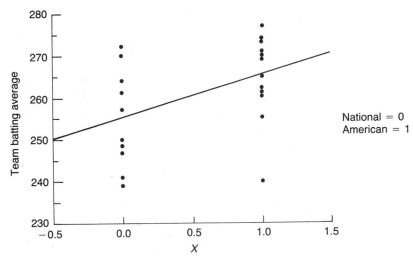

The data have not changed as a function of our change in codes nor have the predicted values. Those predicted values are still the league averages, $\overline{Y}_k$. If we are dealing with a team from the National League, the predicted value equals

$$\hat{Y}_i = 255.33 + 10.1(0) = 255.33$$

If we are dealing with a team from the American Leaque, the predicted value equals

$$\hat{Y}_i = 255.33 + 10.1(1) = 265.43$$

While superficially this prediction function looks rather different from the one that was estimated using the contrast-coded predictor variable, in a deeper sense it is exactly the same prediction function since it produces exactly the same predicted values. All that has changed is the definition of values on the abscissa.

The parameter estimates in this model are easily interpreted. The value of b_0, 255.33, equals the mean of Y_i for teams in the National League, since that is the predicted value when X_i equals zero. As we move from the National to American Leagues, the value of X_i changes by a single unit rather than by two units, as it did in the case of the contrast-coded predictor. Therefore the value of the slope, b_1, is twice as large as it was in the case of the contrast-coded predictor. It necessarily equals the difference in predicted values for the two categories of the predictor variable and therefore the difference in the values of $\overline{Y}_k$.

Since neither the data nor the predicted values have changed by our use of a dummy-coded predictor, the errors of prediction are necessarily the same. Hence the values of PRE, F^*, SSE(C), SSE(A), and SSR have not changed as a result of the redefinition of X_i. In other words, inferences about β_1 in an augmented model that includes the dummy-coded predictor arrive at the exact same conclusion as an inferential test about β_1 when a contrast-coded predictor is used. In both cases, we are testing a null hypothesis that the predicted values conditional on information about league are no better than predicting the overall mean of Y_i for each team. Since these predicted values are the league means, $\overline{Y}_k$, we are testing the null hypothesis that the two league means do not differ. The null hypothesis and results of the inferential test do not depend on how we have chosen to code our categorical predictor.

11.2

Categorical Predictors with More Than Two Levels

Suppose a developmental psychologist is interested in the effects of feedback about performance on subsequent motivation to do a task. She hypothesizes that subsequent motivation will decline if children are told that they earlier failed at the task. To test this hypothesis, she randomly assigns subjects to three conditions. In one condition, subjects are told that they failed on the task. A second condition is given no feedback. And in a third condition, subjects are told they succeeded. The experimenter then monitors the number of tasks the subject subsequently completes, after the differential feedback has been given. Twenty-four subjects are run in total, eight in each of the three conditions. The hypothetical raw data are given in Exhibit 11.7.

EXHIBIT 11.7 ▶

Hypothetical experimental data (Values represent number of tasks each subject completes)

	Conditions		
	Failure	No Feedback	Success
	2	4	4
	2	3	6
	2	4	5
	3	5	4
	4	5	6
	4	2	4
	3	4	3
	4	3	3
$\overline{Y}_k$	3.000	3.75	4.375

11.2.1 Contrast Codes for Multilevel Categorical Predictors

In order to examine the effects of feedback on the number of tasks subsequently completed, we need to derive a coding scheme to represent the three levels of the categorical feedback variable. We might think that a single variable that codes all three conditions might be appropriate, giving observations from the Success condition a higher value on the variable than observations from the No Feedback condition who in turn receive a higher value than observations from the Failure condition. We could then see if such a coded variable would be predictive of Y_i. The problem with using a single variable to code the three levels of this categorical variable is that by such a coding scheme we are assuming that the categories can be ordered in an a priori manner and that the relationship between how we order the categories and Y_i is a linear one. While we may have an a priori reason for expecting that Y_i should be lower in the Failure condition than in the other two, we do not have an a priori reason for assigning particular values to the other two conditions on the coded predictor. In other words, a single-predictor variable that codes the three conditions in a particular order does not make much sense given that we are dealing with a nominally measured categorical variable whose levels cannot be ordered in an a priori manner.

To code a categorical variable with m levels or groups (i.e., k varies between 1 and m), we need to employ $m - 1$ contrast codes. In essence, this allows us to create a set of variables that allow for all possible orders of the m groups. It is now time to introduce the second defining condition for contrast codes. The first condition, you will recall, was that for any contrast-coded variable the sum of the λ's across the levels of the categorical variable being coded must equal zero: $\Sigma_k \lambda_k = 0$. When we use more than a single contrast code to code a categorical variable having more than two levels, the second condition that must be met is that across levels of the categorical variable all pairs of contrast codes must be orthogonal to each other. Suppose we are dealing with a categorical predictor with m levels; we thus have $m - 1$ contrast codes. As long as the first defining codition of contrast codes is met, the condition of orthogonality across levels of the categorical variable will be met whenever the sum, across k or across the levels of the categorical variable, of the product of λ's from pairs of contrast codes equals zero. In our example, we have three levels of the categorical variable. We will therefore use two contrast codes to code it. Each value of λ now has two subscripts, the first one designating which contrast code we are talking about (j), and the second one designating the level of the categorical variable (k). The condition of independence is met when

$$\sum_k \lambda_{1k}\lambda_{2k} = 0$$

To make this second defining condition of contrast codes more comprehensible, let us illustrate codes that do and do not meet this condition for the example at hand. In Exhibit 11.8, two sets of codes, with two codes in each set, are given for coding the three levels of the categorical predictor variable: Failure, No Feedback, and Success.

EXHIBIT 11.8 ▶

Sets of codes for a three-level categorical predictor

	Failure	No Feedback	Success
Set I			
λ_{1k}	-2	1	1
λ_{2k}	0	-1	1
Set II			
λ_{1k}	-1	0	1
λ_{2k}	0	-1	1

Each of the four codes meets the first defining condition for a contrast code, in that the sum of the λ's for any given code, computed across the three levels of the categorical variable, equals zero. The second defining condition, however, is only met by the codes in set I. If we multiply the value of λ_{1k} by the value of λ_{2k} at each of the levels of the categorical predictor variable and then we add up the resulting three products, we get a sum of 0 from set I (i.e., $0 + (-1) + 1 = 0$), while for the codes in set II we get a sum of 1 (i.e., $0 + 0 + 1 = 1$). Accordingly, only the codes in Set I can legitimately be called contrast codes.

This second defining condition means that a given code cannot be defined as a contrast code in isolation. We could not, for instance, look at the code for λ_{1k} in set I and identify it as a contrast code, unless we looked at the other code or codes with which it is used in combination to code the categorical predictor variable. For instance, if we changed the values of λ_{2k} in set I to be -1, -1, and 2 for Failure, No Feedback, and Success, respectively, then the codes in set I would no longer be contrast codes, even though we had not changed the values of λ for the first code. This set of codes would no longer be contrast codes since the sum of the product of the λ's across the category levels would no longer equal zero.

If our categorical predictor variable had four levels, we would need three contrast codes to code it completely. The second defining condition for contrast codes would be met in such a case if the sum of the products of the λ_{jk}'s for all possible pairs of codes equaled zero. Suppose, for instance, that we had a categorical variable with four levels, as in Exhibit 11.9. We there define three contrast codes with values of λ_{1k}, λ_{2k}, and λ_{3k}.

EXHIBIT 11.9 ▶

Codes for a four-level categorical predictor

	Level 1	Level 2	Level 3	Level 4
λ_{1k}	−3	1	1	1
λ_{2k}	0	−2	1	1
λ_{3k}	0	0	−1	1

We then have three pairs of codes for each of which the sum of the product of the λ_{jk}'s must equal zero. For codes 1 and 2, the sum of the product of the λ_{jk}'s equals $(-3)0 + 1(-2) + 1(1) + 1(1) = 0$. For codes 1 and 3, the sum of the product of the λ_{jk}'s equals $(-3)0 + 1(0) + 1(-1) + 1(1) = 0$. And for codes 2 and 3, the sum of the product of the λ_{jk}'s equals $0(0) + 0(-2) + 1(-1) + 1(1) = 0$.

With a categorical predictor having three levels, then, we need two contrast codes and a single sum of products of λ's must equal zero. With a categorical predictor having four levels, we need three contrast codes. Those three codes result in three possible pairs of codes, and hence three sums of products of λ's must equal zero. In general, with a categorical variable having m levels, we need $m - 1$ contrast codes to code it. From these $m - 1$ contrast codes, there are $(m - 1)(m - 2)/2$ pairs of codes. This many sums of products of λ's must equal zero to meet the second defining condition of contrast codes.

For any given categorical predictor, there are an infinite number of sets of contrast codes that could be used. The choice of which codes should be used should be guided by some a priori theoretical or substantive notions about how the groups defined by the categorical predictor variable ought to differ on the dependent variable. For instance, in the illustration at hand, we expected subjects in the Failure condition to have lower scores than subjects in the other two conditions. Since, as we saw in the case of a categorical predictor with only two levels, the regression coefficient for a contrast code tells us about the relative mean difference between observations having different values on the contrast code, it makes sense to derive a code that will allow us to examine this a priori prediction about mean differences on the dependent variable. In other words, given that we want to see whether the observations in the Failure condition have lower scores than observations in the other two conditions, the first contrast code we gave in set I of Exhibit 11.8 is one that we may well choose to examine.

As was the case for contrast codes with a two-level categorical predictor, the regression coefficient for a contrast code equals

$$\frac{\Sigma_k \, \lambda_k \overline{Y}_k}{\Sigma_k \, \lambda_k^2}$$

even when there are many more than two levels of the categorical variable. Using the first contrast code defined in set I of Exhibit 11.8, where the code equals -2 for observations in the Failure condition and 1 for observations in both of the other conditions, the value of the regression coefficient for this contrast code, when we regress the dependent variable on it, will equal

$$b_1 = \frac{-2\overline{Y}_f + 1\overline{Y}_n + 1\overline{Y}_s}{2^2 + 1^2 + 1^2}$$

where $\overline{Y}_f$, $\overline{Y}_n$, and $\overline{Y}_s$ equal the condition means on the dependent variable for Failure, No Feedback, and Success conditions, respectively. If we divide both numerator and denominator of this expression by 2, we get the following equivalent value for the regression coefficient for this contrast code, rearranging terms in the numerator to aid interpretation:

$$\frac{(\overline{Y}_n + \overline{Y}_s)/2 - \overline{Y}_f}{3}$$

This regression coefficient will clearly equal zero if and only if the mean value of the performance dependent variable in the Failure condition equals the average of the two means in the No Feedback and Success conditions. In other words, the regression coefficient for this contrast code estimates one third of the difference between the mean in the Failure condition and the average of the other two condition means.

Once this contrast code has been defined according to our a priori interest in the difference between observations in the Failure and those in the other two conditions, the second contrast code is mandated as the second one of set I in order to meet the second defining condition of contrast codes.[1] As indicated in Exhibit 11.8, the values of λ for that contrast code were 0, -1, and 1 for Failure, No Feedback, and Success conditions, respectively. These codes indicate that the regression coefficient for this code will tell us about the relative magnitude for the mean difference between observations in the No Feedback and Success conditions.

Had we been interested in some other a priori hypothesis, we might have used some other set of contrast codes. For instance, we might have hypothesized that the mean performance level in the No Feedback condition would differ from the mean levels in the other two conditions.

---

[1]With $m - 1$ contrast coded variables, once the values of λ have been defined for the first $m - 2$ variables the values for the last one are constrained. An approach that sometimes is useful for generating codes that meet the defining condition once other theoretically motivated codes have been defined is to assign different λ values to groups or levels of the categorical variable that have not been discriminated between on the basis of earlier contrast codes.

Had this been our hypothesis, then we most probably would have defined a contrast code with values of λ of 1, -2, and 1 for the Failure, No Feedback, and Success conditions, respectively. Such a contrast code would have necessitated a second code of -1, 0, and 1 for the three conditions in order to meet the second defining condition for contrast codes.

When there exists no strong a priori hypothesis to motivate the choice of contrast codes, a simple algorithm will generate codes that meet the necessary conditions.[2] If there are m levels of the categorical predictor, one defines the first of $m - 1$ contrast codes by assigning the value of $m - 1$ to the first level and the value of -1 to each of the remaining $m - 1$ levels. For the second contrast code, the first level is given the value of 0, the second level is given the value of $m - 2$, and all remaining levels are given the value of -1. For the third contrast code, the first two levels of the categorical predictor are assigned values of 0, the third level is given the value of $m - 3$, and the remaining levels are given the value of -1. One proceeds in this manner to define all $m - 1$ contrast codes, with the last one having values of 0 for all levels of the predictor variable except for the last two. These last two levels have values of 1 and -1. The resulting code values are laid out in Exhibit 11.10.

EXHIBIT 11.10 ▶

Helmert contrast codes

Code Values	Category						
	1	2	3	...	$m - 2$	$m - 1$	m
λ_{1k}	$m - 1$	-1	-1	...	-1	-1	-1
λ_{2k}	0	$m - 2$	-1	...	-1	-1	-1
λ_{3k}	0	0	$m - 3$	...	-1	-1	-1
$\vdots$	$\vdots$	$\vdots$	$\vdots$		$\vdots$	$\vdots$	$\vdots$
λ_{m-2k}	0	0	0	...	2	-1	-1
λ_{m-1k}	0	0	0	...	0	1	-1

One other convention for contrast codes is worth knowing. Imagine that the categories of a categorical predictor variable could be ranked ordered in some way, so that groups at the bottom of the rank order were presumed to possess less of some attribute than groups at the top.

---

[2]Codes derived using this algorithm are known as *Helmert contrasts*.

Then we might want to code this ordering into a set of contrast-coded predictors. With a two-level variable this rank ordering is easily given with −1 and 1 code values. With a three-level variable, the rank ordering might be given with the values −1, 0, and +1. The second contrást code values for this three-level predictor must then be −1, 2, and −1. Notice that the first set of contrast codes codes a linear ordering of the categories, while the second set codes a curvilinear or quadratic ordering of the categories, with the middle category assigned a value higher than the other two. With a four-level categorical predictor, the linear ordering of the categories might be coded with a set of linearly ordered code values, the second contrast code values might preserve the quadratic trend in the order, and the third set of codes might order the categories in a cubic manner (i.e., low, high, low, high).

Sets of contrast codes that code the linear, quadratic, cubic, and so forth, trends in a categorical predictor that can be rank ordered have come to be known as *orthogonal polynomials*. Exhibit 11.11 presents codes for orthogonal polynomials for categorical predictors having up to five categories.

11.2.2 Estimation with a Multilevel Predictor Variable

In Exhibit 11.12, we present the DATA variable, Y_i, from Exhibit 11.7, and the values of the contrast-coded predictors, X_{i1} and X_{i2}, that define category or group.

EXHIBIT 11.11 ▶

Orthogonal polynomial contrast codes

Trend	Category				
	1	*2*			
Linear	−1	1			
	1	*2*	*3*		
Linear	−1	0	1		
Quadratic	−1	2	−1		
	1	*2*	*3*	*4*	
Linear	−3	−1	1	3	
Quadratic	1	−1	−1	1	
Cubic	−1	3	−3	1	
	1	*2*	*3*	*4*	*5*
Linear	−2	−1	0	1	2
Quadratic	2	−1	−2	−1	2
Cubic	−1	2	0	−2	1
Quartic	1	−4	6	−4	1

EXHIBIT 11.12 ▶

DATA and contrast-coded predictor variables

	DATA (Y_i)	X_{i1}	X_{i2}
	2	−2	0
	2	−2	0
	2	−2	0
Failure	3	−2	0
	4	−2	0
	4	−2	0
	3	−2	0
	4	−2	0
	4	1	−1
	3	1	−1
	4	1	−1
No Feedback	5	1	−1
	5	1	−1
	2	1	−1
	4	1	−1
	3	1	−1
	4	1	1
	6	1	1
	5	1	1
Success	4	1	1
	6	1	1
	4	1	1
	3	1	1
	3	1	1

The following parameter estimates result when we regress Y_i on X_{i1} and X_{i2}:

MODEL A: $\hat{Y}_i = 3.7083 + .3542X_{i1} + .3125X_{i2}$

As defined above, X_{i1} and X_{i2} represent the three-level categorical predictor variable. The sum of squared errors for this three parameter model equals 23.375. This aggregate error term was derived by computing for each of the 24 observations in the data set the model's predicted value and then squaring the residuals. The predicted values are simply derived by substituting the appropriate values of λ_{jk} for the two contrast codes at each level of the categorical predictor. Thus, for the eight observations in the Failure condition,

$\hat{Y}_i = 3.7083 + .3542(-2) + .3125(0) = 3.000$

The two values in parentheses in this expression, −2 and 0, are the values of λ_{jk} for this condition on the two contrast codes, X_{i1} and X_{i2}.

The predicted value for the eight observations in the No Feedback condition is given as

$$\hat{Y}_i = 3.7083 + .3542(1) + .3125(-1) = 3.750$$

The predicted value for each of the eight Success observations is

$$\hat{Y}_i = 3.7083 + .3542(1) + .3125(1) = 4.375$$

Notice that these predicted values are the mean values of Y_i for each of the three conditions, $\overline{Y}_k$. This will always be the case when predicting values of some Y_i from a single categorical predictor variable as long as we have included as predictors all $m - 1$ contrast-coded variables needed to represent the m levels of the categorical predictor. In other words, just as we saw in the case of a categorical predictor with only two levels, all values of $\hat{Y}_i$ equal the cell or condition means, $\overline{Y}_k$. Thus the sum of squared errors for this model can be written in either of two ways:

$$\text{SSE(A)} = \sum_i (Y_i - \hat{Y}_i)^2 = \sum_i (Y_i - \overline{Y}_k)^2$$

Before comparing this model with compact ones containing fewer parameter estimates, let us interpret each of the three regression coefficients. As we have already said, the regression coefficients for each of the two contrast codes are equivalent to

$$\frac{\sum_k \lambda_k \overline{Y}_k}{\sum_k \lambda_k^2}$$

Accordingly, the regression coefficient for X_{i1} equals

$$\frac{-2(3.000) + 1(3.750) + 1(4.375)}{6} = .3542$$

This expression is equivalent to

$$\frac{(3.750 + 4.375)/2 - 3.000}{3}$$

Accordingly, the regression coefficent for the X_{i1} contrast code equals one third the difference between the average of the No Feedback and Success means and the Failure mean.

This result should come as no surprise once we recall the interpretation for any regression coefficient, regardless of whether it is attached to a contrast-coded predictor or a continuous one. The regression coefficient for a given X_i estimates the change in the value of $\hat{Y}_i$ for each unit change in X_i, holding other predictors constant. In the case of the contrast code X_{i1}, we are dealing with changes in the predicted values, in this case the condition means, as we change the values of the contrast codes. Since the X_{i1} contrast code has assigned the same value of λ_k to both the No Feedback and Success conditions, but a different value to the Failure condition, as we change values of X_{i1}, we are discriminating between the predicted value for the Failure condition, on the one hand, and the values for the No Feedback and Success conditions on the other. Since Failure observations are coded as -2 on X_{i1}, while observations in the other two conditions are coded 1, we move 3 units on X_{i1} as we go from the predicted value for the Failure observations to those for the No Feedback and Success observations. Accordingly, the value of the regression coefficient for X_{i1} equals one third of the difference between the average of the predicted values for the No Feedback and Success conditions and the predicted value for the Failure condition.

Algebraically this follows from the three expressions we have given for the values of $\hat{Y}_i$ contingent on the two contrast codes:

$$\overline{Y}_f = b_0 + b_1(-2) + b_2(0)$$

$$\overline{Y}_n = b_0 + b_1(1) + b_2(-1)$$

$$\overline{Y}_s = b_0 + b_1(1) + b_2(1)$$

In order to show the relationship between the value of b_1 and the cell means, let us add together the second and third of the above equalities and divide the sum by 2. This gives us

$$\frac{\overline{Y}_n + \overline{Y}_s}{2} = \frac{2b_0}{2} + \frac{2b_1}{2} + 0b_2 = b_0 + b_1$$

Now let us subtract the first equality, that for $\overline{Y}_f$, from this result

$$\frac{\overline{Y}_n + \overline{Y}_s}{2} - \overline{Y}_f = (b_0 + b_1) - (b_0 - 2b_1 + 0b_2) = 3b_1$$

Thus, this algebraic manipulation arrives at the same interpretation for b_1, the regression coefficient for the first contrast code.

The value of the regression coefficient for the second contrast code, X_{i2}, is also derived from the expression $\Sigma_k \lambda_k \overline{Y}_k / \Sigma_k \lambda_k^2$. Substituting in the appropriate values of λ_k from this contrast code gives us

$$\frac{0(3.000) + (-1)(3.750) + 1(4.375)}{2} = \frac{4.375 - 3.750}{2} = .3125$$

In other words, this regression coefficient is equal to half the difference between the means of the Success and the No Feedback conditions. Again, this result should come as no surprise. The contrast code captures the difference between these two conditions, a difference that is not coded by X_{i1}. Compare the expressions given above for the predicted values for the No Feedback and Success conditions

$$\overline{Y}_n = b_0 + b_1(1) + b_2(-1)$$

$$\overline{Y}_s = b_0 + b_1(1) + b_2(1)$$

If we subtract the first of these equalities from the second, we have

$$\overline{Y}_s - \overline{Y}_n = (b_0 - b_0) + (b_1 - b_1) + (b_2 + b_2)$$
$$= 2b_2$$

Accordingly, the regression coefficient for X_{i2} equals half the difference in the means between the Success and No Feedback conditions.

The value of the intercept, 3.7083, equals the predicted value when all contrast codes equal zero. Since the sum of the λ_k's for any contrast, computed across levels or across k, equals zero, the average value of λ_k, again averaging across levels, equals zero. Hence, the predicted value when X_{i1} and X_{i2} equal zero equals the average of the predicted values for the three conditions. Again, this result can be easily shown algebraically. Let us add the three equalities that give the predicted values for the Failure, No Feedback, and Success conditions:

$$\overline{Y}_f + \overline{Y}_n + \overline{Y}_s = 3b_0 + 0b_1 + 0b_2$$

Thus, the intercept equals the unweighted grand mean or the mean of the condition means when all $m - 1$ contrast codes from a categorical predictor having m levels are included as predictor variables. We saw the exact same result earlier when dealing with a categorical predictor having only two levels. There, the intercept in the augmented model that included the single contrast equaled the unweighted grand mean. Note that in the present case, because we have an equal number of observations in each of the three conditions, the unweighted grand mean is identical to the mean of all of the observations. With an unequal numbers of observations in the various conditions, however, that will not be the case. In general, the intercept will equal the mean of the category means or the unweighted grand mean rather than the mean of all of the observations, assuming all $m - 1$ contrast codes are included in the model.

11.2.3 Inference with a Multilevel Predictor Variable

We start by comparing the augmented three-parameter model that includes the two contrast codes:

MODEL A: $Y_i = \beta_0 + \beta_1 X_{i1} + \beta_2 X_{i2} + \varepsilon_i$

with a compact single-parameter one in which we have the same predicted value for all observations:

MODEL C: $Y_i = \beta_0 + \varepsilon_i$

The estimated compact model is

MODEL C: $\hat{Y}_i = 3.7083$

The resulting sum of squared errors from this model equals 30.958.

The comparison we are making between the augmented three-parameter model with both contrast codes included as predictors and the compact single-parameter model allows a test of the null hypothesis that both β_1 and β_2 in the augmented model equal zero. Equivalently, since X_{i1} and X_{i2} code information about which condition an observation is in, the null hypothesis is that information about condition does not improve our predictions of Y_i. Since, as we have seen, the augmented model predicts the category or condition mean for each observation, while the compact model predicts the overall grand mean for each observation, if the augmented model yields reliably better predictions, it must be because those predicted values, i.e., the category means, $\overline{Y}_k$, are not all equal to the grand mean. Therefore an equivalent expression for the null hypothesis that is tested in this comparison is that there are no differences among the category means.

Equivalent expressions for the null hypothesis tested by comparing the augmented model with the compact single-parameter model include the following:

H_0: $\beta_1 = \beta_2 = 0$

$\mu_f = \mu_n = \mu_s$

where μ_f, μ_n, and μ_s are the unknown true value means for the Failure, No Feedback, and Success conditions.

With the values of SSE(A) and SSE(C) that we have already given, the following PRE statistic results from the comparison of the augmented and compact models:

$$\text{PRE} = \frac{30.958 - 23.375}{30.958} = .245$$

This PRE converts to an F^* statistic with 2 and 21 degrees of freedom of 3.406. Since this value does not exceed the critical value of the F statistic at $\alpha = .05$, we cannot reject the null hypothesis. Accordingly we cannot conclude that there are differences among the condition means.

As we have seen before, inferential tests with more than a single degree of freedom in the numerator are not as informative as single-degree-of-freedom tests. There are two reasons for this. First, when we reject the null hypothesis involved in a "multiple degrees of freedom in the numerator" test, we know there are some nonzero β's, but we don't know which ones are nonzero. Second, such "multiple degrees of freedom in the numerator" tests are frequently less powerful than single degree of freedom tests that examine individual parts of the omnibus null hypothesis. Tests of individual regression coefficients are usually much more useful.

Before examining the single-degree-of-freedom tests, let us reexpress the test we have just conducted in traditional analysis of variance terms. The sum of squared errors from the compact model equals what is traditionally called the sum of squares total around the grand mean of Y_i. The sum of squared errors for the augmented model equals the sum of squares residual or the sum of squares within group or category. The difference between these two equals the sum of squares reduced or regression or, in traditional analysis of variance terminology, the sum of squares between groups. Because of the equivalence in our augmented model between $\hat{Y}_i$ and the group or category means, $\overline{Y}_k$, the sums of squares within and between groups can be expressed as

$$\text{Sum of Squares within} = \sum (Y_i - \overline{Y}_k)^2$$
$$\text{Sum of Squares between} = \sum_k n_k(\overline{Y}_k - \overline{Y})^2$$

The source table for this analysis of variance thus looks as follows:

Source	SS	df	MS	F*	PRE
Between	7.583	2	3.792	3.406	.245
Within	23.375	21	1.113		
Total	30.958	23			

Two different single-degree-of-freedom tests can be conducted to determine whether β_1, the regression coefficient for the first contrast code, equals zero and to determine whether β_2 equals zero. Since, as we have seen, the estimates of β_1 and β_2 equal specific comparisons between the condition means, $\overline{Y}_k$, the two null hypotheses that are tested can each be expressed in two ways:

Test 1: H_0: $\beta_1 = 0$ or

$$\frac{\mu_s + \mu_n}{2} - \mu_f = 0$$

Test 2: H_0: $\beta_2 = 0$ or

$$\mu_s - \mu_n = 0$$

In words, the test of whether β_1 equals zero is equivalently a test of whether the mean level of Y_i under Failure equals the average of the mean levels under Success and No Feedback. The test of whether β_2 equals zero is equivalently a test of whether the mean level of Y_i under Success equals the mean level under No Feedback.

For each of these tests, the augmented model remains the same, with three estimated parameters. The compact models, however, include only two parameters. The compact model for testing whether β_1 equals zero includes X_{i2} as a predictor but not the first contrast-coded predictor. The compact model for testing whether β_2 equals zero includes X_{i1} as a predictor but not the second contrast-coded predictor. The resulting compact models and their sums of squared errors are

Test of H_0: $\beta_1 = 0$

MODEL C: $\hat{Y}_i = 3.7083 + .3125X_{i2}$

SSE(C) = 29.396

Test of H_0: $\beta_2 = 0$

MODEL C: $\hat{Y}_i = 3.7083 + .3542X_{i1}$

SSE(C) = 24.938

Notice that the value of the intercept and the regression coefficients for X_{i1} and X_{i2} do not change in these compact models when compared to the augmented model. This results from the fact that contrast codes have been used, thus making the values of λ orthogonal across levels of the categorical predictor (ensured by the second defining condition of contrast codes), and by the fact that we have an equal number of subjects in all three groups or categories. As a result, X_{i1} and X_{i2} are completely nonredundant predictors across all observations as well as across levels of the categorical predictor.

A test of the first null hypothesis, that β_1 equals zero, yields the following statistics:

$$PRE = \frac{29.396 - 23.375}{29.396} = .205$$

$F^*_{1,21} = 5.41$

This F^* statistic exceeds the critical value of F with α set at .05. Hence we conclude that β_1 reliably differs from zero. Equivalently, we conclude that the mean value of Y_i in the Failure condition is reliably different from the average of the mean values in the Success and No Feedback conditions. Since the sample mean in the Failure condition is less than the average of the other two sample means, we conclude that the debilitating effects of Failure feedback that we have observed in these data are reliable. That is, Failure feedback seems to decrease subsequent performance relative to Success and No Feedback.

Notice the difference in power between this test and the earlier two-degree-of-freedom test where the null hypothesis was that both β_1 and β_2 equaled zero. Under that two-degree-of-freedom test, we concluded that we could not be confident that there were any differences between the condition means. Now, however, with a more focused single-degree-of-freedom test, we realize that there is a reliable predicted difference between the mean in the Failure condition and the other two means. Had we left things with our omnibus test without testing the specific comparison we had hypothesized, we would have missed this supporting evidence altogether.

Testing the second null hypothesis, that β_2 equals zero, we come up with the following statistics:

$$\text{PRE} = \frac{24.938 - 23.375}{24.938} = .063$$

$$F^*_{1,21} = 1.40$$

Since this F^* statistic does not exceed the critical value of F, we conclude that β_2 does not reliably differ from 0. Accordingly, we cannot conclude that mean performance under Success is reliably different from mean performance under No Feedback.

Let us once again fit these two tests within the context of a more traditional analysis of variance. Notice that the decrease in the sum of squared errors as we move from the compact to the augmented model (i.e., the numerator of PRE) in the first test equals 6.021. We might think of this as the increase in the sum of squares explained by the inclusion of X_{i1} in the augmented model over and above X_{i2}. In other words, if we take a model which only includes X_{i2} and add to it X_{i1}, the additional sum of squares explained is 6.021.

For the second test, the decrease in the sum of squared errors as we move from the compact to the augmented model equals 1.562. We may equivalently refer to this as the increase in the sum of squares explained as we add X_{i2} to a model that already contains X_{i1}.

Adding up these two increases in sums of squares explained, we get

$$6.021 + 1.562 = 7.583$$

which is equal to the sum of squares reduced or sum of squares between groups in the two-degree-of-freedom test that we presented earlier. In other words, the total decrease in the sum of squared errors as we move from the original compact single-parameter model to one that contains both contrast codes and in which three parameters are estimated equals the sum of two decreases in sum of squared errors as we add one contrast code to a compact model that already contains the other. Another way to say this is that the total sums of squares explained by the two contrasts together equals the sum of the two sums of squares explained by each contrast individually. This result follows from the fact that *across observations* the two contrast codes are entirely nonredundant. We know this to be the case since we have met the second defining characteristic of contrast codes and since we have an equal number of observations in each level of our categorical predictor.

If our codes were not independent of each other, or if, more generally, two predictor variables in a model are partially redundant, then it will not be the case that the sum of squares explained by them both will equal the sum of the two sums of squares explained by them each individually. With contrast-coded predictors and with equal cell sizes, however, this simplifying state of affairs results.

Earlier in the chapter when we were considering categorical predictors with only two levels, we gave a formula for computing the sum of squares explained by a contrast-coded predictor when it was the only predictor in a model.

$$\text{SS Explained by a Contrast Predictor} = \frac{(\sum_k \lambda_k \overline{Y}_k)^2}{\sum_k (\lambda_k^2 / n_k)}$$

This formula continues to be appropriate in cases with multiple contrast codes, so long as these contrast codes are the only predictors used in a model. For the two contrast codes in our example,

SS Explained by X_{i1}

$$= \frac{[(-2)3.000 + (1)3.750 + (1)4.375]^2}{(-2)^2/8 + 1^2/8 + 1^2/8}$$

$$= 6.021$$

SS Explained by X_{i2}

$$= \frac{[(0)3.000 + (-1)3.750 + (1)4.375]^2}{0^2/8 + (-1)^2/8 + 1^2/8}$$

$$= 1.562$$

Each of these sums of squares and each of the single-degree-of-freedom tests that we conducted can be incorporated into the analysis of variance source table that we already gave for the two-degree-of-freedom test. This source table is presented in Exhibit 11.13.

The first F^* statistic is used to test the null hypothesis that both β_1 and β_2 in the augmented model equal zero. Equivalently the null hypothesis is that all of the condition means are equivalent. The second F^* statistic tests the null hypothesis that β_1 equals zero in the augmented model that includes both contrast codes. Equivalently, it tests the null

EXHIBIT 11.13   ▶

Summary source table

Source	b	SS	df	MS	F*	PRE
Between		7.583	2	3.792	3.406	.245
X_{i1}	.3542	6.021	1	6.021	5.409	.205
X_{i2}	.3125	1.562	1	1.562	1.403	.063
Within		23.375	21	1.113		
Total		30.958	23			

hypothesis that the mean of the Failure condition equals the average of the means in the No Feedback and Success conditions. The third F^* statistic tests the null hypothesis that β_2 in the model that includes both contrast codes equals zero. Equivalently, it tests the null hypothesis that the mean in the No Feedback condition equals the mean in the Success condition.

Each of the F^* statistics in this source table can be arrived at both by our usual way (i.e., calculating PRE for augmented and compact models and converting it to F^*) or by dividing each mean square in the source table by the mean square error or mean square within. This mean square within equals the sum of squared errors in the augmented model with both contrast codes included, divided by the degrees of freedom for error in that model.

11.2.4   A Quick Look at Alternative Contrast Codes

Earlier we stated that there were many, many possible sets of contrast codes that could be used to code a categorical predictor. Let us examine the same data that we have been focusing on using a different set of codes. Suppose we now define our contrast codes as follows:

	Failure	No Feedback	Success
λ_{1k}	−1	0	1
λ_{2k}	−1	2	−1

We redefine X_{i1} and X_{i2} as contrast-coded predictors, assigning each individual the indicated values to represent category membership. We then regress Y_i on X_{i1} and X_{i2} with the estimated parameters

$$\hat{Y}_i = 3.7083 + .6875X_{i1} + .0208X_{i2}$$

While the parameter estimates for the two contrast-coded predictors in this model are quite different from those that we estimated using the earlier set of contrast codes, in a deeper sense this model is equivalent to the model we developed under the old set of codes. Substituting for values of X_{i1} and X_{i2}, we see that the group or condition means continue to be the predictions made by the model for all observations. For the eight observations in the Failure condition, we get

$$\hat{Y}_i = 3.7083 + .6875(-1) + .0208(-1) = 3.000$$

For the eight observations in the No Feedback condition, we get

$$\hat{Y}_i = 3.7083 + .6875(0) + .0208(2) = 3.750$$

And for the eight observations in the Success condition, we get

$$\hat{Y}_i = 3.7083 + .6875(1) + .0208(-1) = 4.375$$

Since the model makes the same predictions for all observations as the model with the previous set of contrast codes, so the sum of squared errors is identical to what it was before, i.e., 23.375.

The regression coefficients for X_{i1} and X_{i2} have changed since the new contrast codes are making different comparisons among condition means from the comparisons made by the old set of codes. The contrast-coded predictor X_{i1} is now comparing the means in the Success and Failure conditions. The value of its regression coefficient equals half the difference between these two group means. The second contrast-coded predictor, X_{i2}, compares the mean in the No Feedback condition with the average of the means of the other two conditions. Its regression coefficient equals one third of the difference between the mean in the No Feedback condition and the average of the other two means. These values for the regression coefficients are easily derived using the formula we gave earlier for the regression coefficient for a contrast code. They also follow immediately once we realize the comparisons made by the contrasts and the number of units that separate observations in the various conditions on X_{i1} and X_{i2}. The intercept has not changed in value as a result of the new set of codes. It still equals the unweighted grand mean, as it will whenever a full set of contrast codes is used.

Since the change in codes has not changed the predicted values nor the sum of squared errors for this model, a test of the null hypothesis that both β_1 and β_2 equal zero produces the same values of PRE and F^* as it did under the old set of codes. The compact single-parameter model is

MODEL C: $\quad \hat{Y}_i = 3.7083$

with a sum of squared errors of 30.958. PRE continues to equal .245, which converts to an F^*, with 2 and 21 degrees of freedom, of 3.406. Thus, a test of the omnibus null hypothesis that all of the condition means equal one another reaches the same conclusion regardless of our choice of contrast codes.

Single-degree-of-freedom tests of whether β_1 or β_2 equals zero, however, reach rather different conclusions than they did before, for, as we have seen, these regression coefficients now estimate different comparisons between the condition means from those estimated with the earlier set of contrast codes. A test of whether β_1 equals zero is now equivalent to whether the means in the Failure and Success conditions are equal to each other. The compact model for this test is

$$\text{MODEL C:} \quad \hat{Y}_i = 3.7083 + .0208X_{i2}$$

with a sum of squared errors of 30.938. The resulting PRE equals

$$\frac{30.938 - 23.375}{30.938} = .244$$

This converts to an F^* statistic, with 1 and 21 degrees of freedom, of 6.973. Since this F^* exceeds the critical value, our test of this particular contrast code tells us that the means in the Failure and Success conditions are reliably different from each other. Note that the sum of squares explained by the X_{i1} predictor equals 7.562, the numerator of PRE. This value also results when we use the formula we gave earlier for the sum of squares explained by a given contrast:

$$\text{SS Explained by a Contrast Predictor} = \frac{(\Sigma_k \lambda_k \overline{Y}_k)^2}{\Sigma_k (\lambda_k^2 / n_k)}$$

SS Explained by X_{i1}

$$= \frac{[(-1)3.000 + (0)3.750 + (1)4.375]^2}{(-1)^2/8) + 0^2/8 + 1^2/8}$$

$$= 7.562$$

The test of whether β_2 equals zero is equivalently a test of whether the No Feedback mean is reliably different from the average of the Failure and Success means. The compact model for this test is

$$\text{MODEL C:} \quad \hat{Y}_i = 3.7083 + .6875X_{i1}$$

with a sum of squared errors equal to 23.396. The resulting PRE equals .001, which converts to an F^*, again with 1 and 21 degrees of freedom, of 0.019. Clearly the difference between the No Feedback mean and the average of the means in the other two conditions is not reliable. The sum of squares explained by this contrast equals .021. Since these are orthogonal contrasts and since we have an equal number of observations in each condition, the sum of squares explained by each of the two

EXHIBIT 11.14 ▶

Summary source table

Source	b	SS	df	MS	F*	PRE
Between		7.583	2	3.792	3.406	.245
X_{i1}	.6875	7.562	1	7.562	6.793	.244
X_{i2}	.0208	.021	1	.021	.019	.001
Within		23.375	21	1.113		
Total		30.958	23			

contrasts add up to give us the total sum of squares explained in the augmented model that includes both X_{i1} and X_{i2}.

The results of these tests can be equivalently summarized in the analysis of variance source table of Exhibit 11.14. Note that the only changes in this source table compared to the one using the earlier set of contrast codes occur in the two lines of the table testing the specific contrast codes, X_{i1} and X_{i2}.

11.3

Contrast Codes With Unequal Cell Sizes

We now need to discuss the additional complications that unequal numbers of observations in the various conditions introduce. Although these complications are not major, as we shall see, they are introduced by the fact that the contrast coded variables are no longer independent of each other. While it is still true, by the definition of contrast codes, that $\Sigma_k \lambda_{1k}\lambda_{2k} = 0$, it is no longer the case, with unequal numbers of observations in the various conditions, that the contrast-coded predictors are independent across observations. In other words, unequal numbers of observations in the various conditions results in some redundancy between the contrast-coded predictor variables. The major complication that this introduces is that the sum of squares explained by each contrast-coded predictor, within a set that codes a given categorical predictor, no longer adds up with the other contrast sums of squares to equal the total sum of squares explained by the full set of contrast codes. Due to their redundancy, the explanatory power of the contrast-coded predictors overlap with each other, as explained in Chapter 8 where the problem of redundancy among predictors was discussed at some length.

To illustrate the slight complications that are introduced, let us consider what the analysis of our performance data would look like if we added an observation to the Failure condition. What if we had data with the following group means and sizes:

	Failure	No Feedback	Success
$\overline{Y}_k$	3.000	3.750	4.375
n_k	9	8	8

Let us adopt the set of contrast codes that have been just discussed; namely X_{i1} and X_{i2} are defined by the following λ_{jk} values:

	Failure	No Feedback	Success
λ_{1k}	−1	0	1
λ_{2k}	−1	2	−1

We regress Y_i on both X_{i1} and X_{i2} and obtain the following estimated model

MODEL A: $\hat{Y}_i = 3.7083 + .6875X_{i1} + .0208X_{i2}$

Notice that these parameter estimates are exactly the same as they were before we added an observation to the Failure condition. This is because none of the condition means have changed as a function of adding the observation. Thus, and this is an important point, the parameter estimates are not influenced by the number of observations in each condition or category. They simply tell us about the differences in the category means, regardless of whether the number of observations varies across categories.

The sum of squared errors for this model equals 23.375. We can compare it with three different compact models to test each of the null hypotheses considered in earlier sections. First, let us use the single-parameter model as the compact model, thereby testing the null hypothesis that both β_1 and β_2 equal zero, and equivalently, that there are no differences among the condition means. Our compact model is

MODEL C: $\hat{Y}_i = 3.680$

with a sum of squared errors of 31.420. (Notice that while we have constructed this example so that the condition means were not affected by the addition of the observation to the Failure condition, the overall grand mean of all 25 observations has changed.) Comparing these two models, we get a value of PRE equal to .256, which converts to an F^* statistic, with 2 and 22 degrees of freedom of 3.786. The sum of squares reduced or the sum of squares explained by the addition of X_{i1} and X_{i2} to the model equals 8.045.

Since the contrast codes continue to make the same comparisons between condition means that they did earlier, tests of the null hypotheses that β_1 equals zero and that β_2 equals zero continue to be interpretable as tests of comparisons among the condition means. In other words, the null hypothesis that β_1 equals zero continues to be equivalent to the null hypothesis that the means of the Failure and Success conditions are equal. The null hypothesis that β_2 equals zero continues to be equivalent to the null hypothesis that the mean in the No Feedback condition equals the average of the means in the Failure and Success conditions.

To test the null hypothesis that β_1 equals zero, we compute the following compact model:

$$\text{MODEL C:} \quad \hat{Y}_i = 3.681 + .0343X_{i2}$$

with a sum of squared errors of 31.382. When we had equal numbers of observations in each condition, the parameter estimates did not change from compact to augmented models. That is no longer true, since the contrast-coded predictors, X_{i1} and X_{i2}, are no longer independent across observations. Comparing this model with the augmented one, we get a PRE of .255, which converts to an F^* statistic, with 1 and 22 degrees of freedom, of 7.536.

To test the null hypothesis that β_2 equals zero, we compute the following compact model:

$$\text{MODEL C:} \quad \hat{Y}_i = 3.708 + .689X_{i1}$$

with a sum of squared errors of 23.396. Comparing this model with the augmented one, we get a PRE of .001, which converts to an F^* statistic, with 1 and 22 degrees of freedom, of 0.020.

These three tests, the omnibus test of both β_1 and β_2, and the two single-degree-of-freedom tests, are equivalently summarized by the analysis of variance source table presented in Exhibit 11.15.

While the additional observations did not affect the sum of squared errors in the augmented model nor the parameter estimates in that model, it did affect the other entries in this source table. Since the contrast-coded predictors are no longer independent across observations, their sums of squares explained no longer sum to the total sum of squares

EXHIBIT 11.15 ▶

Unequal n_k analysis of variance summary table

Source	b	SS	df	MS	F*	PRE
Between		8.045	2	4.022	3.786	.256
X_{i1}	.6875	8.007	1	8.007	7.536	.255
X_{i2}	.0208	.021	1	.021	.020	.001
Within		23.375	22	1.062		
Total		31.420	24			

explained in the augmented model. In other words, 8.007 plus 0.021 is not equal to 8.045.

The fundamental lesson to be learned from this is that unequal cell sizes do not affect the basic computations that are conducted nor how the regression coefficients attached to contrast codes are interpreted. In addition, the tests of null hypotheses that parameters equal zero continue to be tests of specific comparisons among condition means, *so long as the full set of contrast codes are included in the augmented model (i.e., m − 1 contrast codes are included with a categorical predictor having m levels).* The only slight complication is that the contrast codes are now somewhat redundant with each other across observations, even though they continue to be independent across levels of the categorical predictor variable. This means that their sums of squares explained will not add up to the total sum of squares explained in the full augmented model that includes all contrast codes.

Note that in the two compact models where one of the two contrast-coded predictors was included but not both, the parameter estimates no longer equaled the coded differences among the category means. In general, to test differences among category means, the augmented model must include all $m − 1$ contrast-coded predictor variables. With unequal numbers of observations in the various categories, test of the regression coefficients for contrast-coded predictors will not amount to comparisons among category means unless the full set of contrast-coded predictors is included in the augmented model.

As is always the case, redundancy among predictor variables reduces statistical power. Thus, given the choice, one should favor equal numbers of observations in the various categories to unequal numbers. One does not always have that choice, however, when dealing, for instance, with intact groups rather than with ones that are experimentally formed. The important point to remember is that the redundancy introduced by unequal numbers of observations creates no special problems of interpretation. Parameter estimates in the augmented model continue to inform us about differences in condition means, even though our tests might not be as powerful as they would be given an equal number of observations equally split among the category levels.

11.4

Confidence Intervals for β_j

The formula that we gave in Chapter 8 for the confidence interval for a regression coefficient continues to be applicable in the situation where predictor variables are contrast codes. The confidence interval for the regression for any given regression coefficient is given as

$$b_j \pm \sqrt{\frac{F_{crit}\text{MSE}}{\Sigma_i\,(X_{ij} - \overline{X}_j)^2(1 - R_j^2)}}$$

In this case X_{ij} is a contrast-coded predictor. Given equal numbers of observations in each of the categories coded by a contrast code, the two quantities in the denominator of the confidence interval formula can be expressed more simply. With equal cell n, the tolerance of a contrast-coded predictor $(1 - R_j^2)$ equals 1.0 since it will be uncorrelated with all other contrast-coded predictors. Also with equal cell n, $\overline{X}_j$ will equal zero. Accordingly, in this case the formula for the confidence interval reduces to

$$b_j \pm \sqrt{\frac{F_{crit}\text{MSE}}{\Sigma_i\,(X_{ij})^2}}$$

Since the value of b_j informs us about the magnitude of differences among the contrasted category means, $\overline{Y}_k$, this confidence interval also tells us about the confidence interval for the coded difference between those category means.

11.5

Nonorthogonal Contrasts

Researchers often find that they cannot represent all the questions they want to ask of their data in terms of one set of orthogonal contrast codes. This necessarily implies that some of the questions the researcher wants to ask are partially redundant. The partial redundancy means that knowing the answer to one question gives us some information about the answer to the other question. For example, the researcher conducting the Success/Failure feedback study introduced at the beginning of this chapter might want to ask (a) Does the performance of the Failure group differ from the performance of the other two groups combined? and (b) Does the performance of the Failure group differ from the performance of the Success group? Representing these questions as contrast codes makes it easy to determine that they are *nonorthogonal* or partially redundant.

	F	N	S
Failure vs. Other	+2	−1	−1
Failure vs. Success	−1	0	+1

Checking the orthogonality for these two codes reveals that they are nonorthogonal because

$$(2)(-1) + (-1)(0) + (1)(1) = 3$$

instead of zero. The nonorthogonality implies redundancy between the two corresponding contrast-coded predictors and that implies that if we know the answer to one of the two questions we can make a reasonable guess about the answer to the other question. This is never possible with orthogonal codes. In this case, if the data analysis revealed that the performance of the Failure group differed significantly from the average performance of the other two groups combined, then it is likely, although not guaranteed, that the Failure group will also differ significantly from the Success group.

Nonorthogonality does not mean the questions to be asked are uninteresting, nor does it mean that they should not be asked. It simply means that some care is required and that we should not fool ourselves by thinking we are asking independent questions when our contrast codes are partially redundant. There are a plethora of statistical procedures for testing multiple, nonorthogonal contrasts. The ANOVA procedure in SAS currently provides 13 different methods for making multiple, nonorthogonal comparisons of group means. These methods differ primarily in how they control the Type I and Type II error rates and how they adjust the trade-off between them. For certain types of contrasts, some methods are slightly more powerful than others, but the differences between methods are subtle.

These subtleties often confuse novice data analysts. These comparison methods are also much abused. For example, some researchers use many different methods and then report the one that gives the best results. Our experience is that two of these methods, which are consistent with our integrated approach, are sufficient for almost all data analyses.

Both of our recommended methods begin with the same first steps. First, for whatever contrasts are of interest, calculate the corresponding estimate b_j and its associated SSR, using either the equations presented earlier in the chapter or a regression program. Second, use the Within MSerror from an analysis which used a complete set of codes to calculate

$F*$. This step is reasonable because if we were to do an analysis of a complete set of orthogonal codes containing our code of interest, then we would obtain the same SSE(A) or Within MSerror. For example, suppose we did want to answer the two questions posed above. The first question, comparing the failure group to the other two groups, was answered with the test of the coefficient for the contrast-coded predictor X_{i1} in the ANOVA table on p. 310. The large values of PRE = .205 and $F* = 5.409$ caused us to reject the null hypothesis of no differences; the performance of the failure group was reliably lower than that of the other two groups combined. But to answer the second question, comparing the failure and success groups, we must calculate b_j and its associated SSR. For this code,

$$b_j = \frac{-1(3) + 0(3.75) + 1(4.375)}{(-1)^2 + 0^2 + 1^2} = \frac{1.375}{2} = .6875$$

$$SSR = \frac{[-1(3) + 0(3.75) + 1(4.375)]^2}{1/8 + 0/8 + 1/8} = \frac{1.375^2}{0.25} = \frac{1.89}{0.25} = 7.56$$

From the previous analysis we know that when using a full set of contrast codes that Within MSerror = 1.113 so we can calculate

$$F^*_{1,21} = \frac{SSR}{MSerror} = \frac{7.56}{1.113} = 6.79$$

If we have $F*$ and PRE, then we must be comparing a MODEL C and a MODEL A, but it might not be obvious what those models are. MODEL A is simply a model with a complete set of orthogonal contrast codes containing our code of interest and MODEL C has the same codes *except* for the code of interest. We know that SSE(C) = SSE(A) + SSR. In this case, SSE(A) = SSerror = 23.375, and we just calculated SSR = 7.56 so SSE(C) = 23.375 + 7.56 = 30.935. So,

$$PRE = \frac{7.56}{30.935} = .244$$

To avoid having to calculate the statistics by hand, one can therefore use a standard regression program to do the calculations. Simply generate a complete set of codes including the contrast of interest and obtain the above statistics from the regression analysis output. (Note that in this case we already did this when we considered this code as part of an alternative set of contrast codes in Section 11.2.4.)

So far our analysis for the nonorthogonal contrast is no different from our analysis of any other contrast. Now we must compare $F*$ and PRE with their respective critical values to determine whether we should conclude that the difference coded by our predictor is reliable. The problem is that although each test has a Type I probability of α, the probability that we have made at least one Type I error when conducting multiple statistical tests on the same set of data is considerably larger than α. For example, if we conduct four statistical tests each with a .05 probability of a Type I error, then the probability that we will make at least one Type I error in the four tests is equal to

$$1 - (1 - .05)^4 = 1 - .95^4 = 1 - .81 = .19$$

Thus, if there were no real differences between our groups, there would be a .19 probability that we would incorrectly reject MODEL C—make a Type I error—for at least one of the four statistical tests. That risk is unacceptably large so we must use different or adjusted critical values to reduce the overall risk of making Type I errors when evaluating multiple, nonorthogonal contrasts for the same set of data. The appropriate critical values depend on whether the nonorthogonal contrast is a *planned comparison* or a *post hoc comparison*.

Planned Comparisons. Planned comparisons are those that the researcher had theoretical or substantive reasons for examining *before* conducting the experiment. In other words, the researcher should specify all the planned comparisons of interest before collecting or examining the data. Ideally, as many of these planned contrasts as possible will be included in the set of orthogonal contrast codes for the ANOVA. However, we will consider those that cannot be included in an orthogonal set by calculating the appropriate test statistics as above. There are some statistics textbooks that say it is legitimate to compare F^* and PRE to the usual critical values determined by the degrees of freedom. However, it is safer to protect against the overall Type I error rate by using α/k instead of α, where k is the number of statistical tests performed on the same data.[1] In calculating k don't forget to count all the contrast codes included in the original ANOVA. For our nonorthogonal contrast code comparing the performance of the failure and success groups we would use $k = 3$, the two orthogonal contrast codes of the original analysis plus the extra nonorthogonal contrast code. Thus, *if this code represents a planned comparison*, we can compare the calculated values of F^* and PRE to the critical values for $.05/3 = .017$. The obvious difficulty is that there is no column in Exhibits C.1 and C.3 of Appendix C for $\alpha = .017$. We could be conservative and use the next lowest value of .01 for which there is a column. However, if we use a regression program

---

[1]The use of α/k instead of α is based on the *Bonferroni inequality* and so some manuals for statistical programs refer to this as the Bonferroni method of multiple comparisons. Sometimes this is also referred to as the Dunn method.

to do the calculations, it will almost certainly provide the probability associated with F^*, which can be compared to .017. In this case, the program would report a probability for our calculated $F^* = 6.79$ of .0165. That is less than .017, so we would reject the null hypothesis of no difference between the Failure and Success groups. Also, some computer packages (e.g., MINITAB and SAS) provide facilities for obtaining the critical value of F for any specified α and degrees of freedom. The appropriate critical values for $\alpha = .017$ are $F = 6.77$ and PRE $= .244$. The values calculated above exceed these values, so we would conclude that there were reliable performance differences between the Failure and Success groups. Any *planned comparison* may be evaluated in this manner.

Post Hoc Comparisons. Post hoc comparisons are those that do not occur to us until *after* we have examined the data. It is often the case that when looking at the means after the experiment certain comparisons that we did not anticipate appear to be interesting. It is natural to want to test those interesting, unanticipated contrasts. However, it is impractical to use the above procedure for planned comparisons because when looking at the data we are implicitly doing many, many comparisons— all those that do not strike us as interesting—that ought to be included in k, the total number of comparisons made. Instead of trying to count all those implicit comparisons, standard practice is to compare F^* to the following critical value developed by Scheffé (1959):

$$(m - 1)F_{m-1,n-\text{PA};\alpha}$$

There are two important features of using the Scheffé adjusted critical value. First, the overall probability of making at least one Type I error will remain at α no matter how many contrasts are evaluated using the adjusted critical value. Thus, the researcher can do as much snooping and exploring with contrasts as desired without undue risk of making Type I errors. Second, there will be at least one contrast whose F^* exceeds the Scheffé adjusted critical value if and only if the omnibus test is statistically significant. Thus, if the omnibus test is not significant, then there is no point in evaluating any other contrasts. In the present example, the omnibus test is not significant, so we need not bother to test the additional orthogonal contrast comparing the Failure and Success groups. However, to confirm this and to illustrate the procedure, the Scheffé adjusted critical value for this example is equal to

$$(3 - 1)F_{3-1,24-3;.05} = 2F_{2,21;.05} = 2(3.47) = 6.94$$

The computed value of $F^* = 6.79$ does not exceed 6.94 so we would not conclude that there was a reliable difference between the post hoc comparison of the performance of the Failure and Success groups.

Note in this example that we reached different conclusions about the reliability of the difference between the Failure and Success groups depending on whether we considered the contrast as a planned comparison or as a post hoc comparison. Given that exactly the same data are involved, some people find this disquieting. However, a moment's reflection reveals that this is as it should be. If theoretical or other substantive issues focuses our attention on a few specific contrasts, then we do not need to be as cautious as when we implicitly do a multitude of implicit comparisons by allowing the data to focus our attention. This is just another illustration of the importance of using theory to guide data analysis. We do not mean to imply, however, that data snooping is wrong. To the contrary, one ought to extract everything one can from the data, but one needs to be appropriately cautious while snooping by using the Scheffé adjusted critical values. Once it is clear whether a nonorthogonal contrast is planned or post hoc, the procedures in this section should allow any contrast to be evaluated.

12

Factorial ANOVA: Models with Multiple Categorical Predictors and Product Terms

In this chapter we expand our consideration of models with one categorical predictor variable to models with two or more categorical predictor variables. Our reasons for wanting to include more than one categorical variable as a predictor in our MODEL are the same as those which motivated us to move from simple regression models with one predictor to multiple regression models with two or more predictors in Chapter 8. Models in which predictions are conditional on two or more categorical variables may be required by our DATA and, more importantly, by the underlying process which generates the DATA. Just as in multiple regression, controlling for one categorical variable by including it in the MODEL often allows us to have a better look at the effects of other categorical variables. Also, as in multiple regression, we are often interested in modeling the joint effect of two or more categorical variables. With categorical variables we will be especially interested in whether the effect of a given categorical variable depends on the levels of the other categorical variables; that is, we are interested in whether or not there is an interaction between the categorical variables analogous to the interactions of continuous variables in multiple regression considered in Chapter 10.

The generalization of models with one categorical predictor (one-way ANOVA of the previous chapter) to models with two categorical predictors (two-way ANOVA) and to models with more than two categorical predictors (q-way factorial ANOVA, where q is the number of categorical predictor variables) is easy. As we shall demonstrate, classical analysis of variance with two or more categorical predictors is nothing more than a simple one-way ANOVA with a specific, clever set of contrast codes. In other words, the only new thing to learn is how to generate the appropriate set of contrast codes; fitting the model and testing hypotheses are *exactly* the same as for one-way ANOVA in Chapter 11.

12.1

Factorial ANOVA as One-Way ANOVA

We begin by considering the hypothetical data set presented in Exhibit 12.1. In this hypothetical experiment, two types of clinically depressed patients, with and without Enzyme E in their blood, are randomly assigned to one of three drug treatment conditions—Drug A, Drug B, and Placebo in which an inert drug is administered. After a month of drug therapy each patient completes a mood questionnaire which is scored so that higher scores mean less depression.

The experimental design represented in Exhibit 12.1 is known as a *factorial* design because every level of one categorical variable is combined with every level of the other categorical variable. There are three levels of the Drug variable and two levels of the Enzyme variable, so there are a total of $3 \times 2 = 6$ different combinations, each defining a group or cell in the design. This is sometimes referred to as a *3 × 2 design*.

EXHIBIT 12.1 ▶

Hypothetical data (mood scores) after drug therapy for depressed patients with and without enzyme E

	Enzyme E				
	With			*Without*	
Drug A	31 31 34			17 15 19	
Drug B	25 25 28			23 18 16	
Placebo	17 18 16			9 10 8	

Although it is natural to display these data in a table with three rows and two columns as in Exhibit 12.1, we can also display the data as a one-way layout in terms of the six groups or cells as in Exhibit 12.2. Once the data are displayed in the one-way layout, it is clear that we can use any of the sets of contrast codes developed in the previous chapter to analyze these data. To illustrate this, we will first do an analysis with contrast codes which are statistically correct but which do not ask questions that are normally interesting. In this first set of contrast codes we form the first contrast λ_1 by comparing Group 1 (Drug A administered to patients with Enzyme E) with all the other groups; the corresponding contrast-coded predictor is Z_1.[1] The contrast λ_2 compares Group 2 against all the remaining groups except Group 1 and so on. These contrast codes are also displayed in Exhibit 12.2. We can verify

EXHIBIT 12.2 ▶

Hypothetical data of Exhibit 12.1 arrayed as a one-way design

Group Label	1 AwE	2 BwE	3 PwE	4 AwoE	5 BwoE	6 PwoE
	31	25	17	17	23	9
	31	25	18	15	18	10
	34	28	16	19	16	8
Mean	32	26	17	17	19	9

Contrast Codes		1	2	Group 3	4	5	6
λ_1 1 vs. 2, 3, 4, 5, 6	Z_1	5	−1	−1	−1	−1	−1
λ_2 2 vs. 3, 4, 5, 6	Z_2	0	4	−1	−1	−1	−1
λ_3 3 vs. 4, 5, 6	Z_3	0	0	3	−1	−1	−1
λ_4 4 vs. 5, 6	Z_4	0	0	0	2	−1	−1
λ_5 5 vs. 6	Z_5	0	0	0	0	1	−1

[1]We use Z's here instead of the customary X's because subsequently we will do an analysis of these same data using a different set of contrast codes. The Z's are the contrast-coded predictor variables for the first analysis and the X's will be the contrast-coded predictor variables for the second analysis.

that these codes are orthogonal by checking that the sum of each set of cross products is zero. For example,

$$\sum_{k=1}^{m} \lambda_{1k}\lambda_{2k} = 5(0) - 1(4) - 1(-1) - 1(-1) - 1(-1) - 1(-1)$$

$$= 0 - 4 + 1 + 1 + 1 + 1$$

$$= 0$$

We can regress Y_i, the mood scores, on the predictor variables Z_1, Z_2, . . . , Z_5 using a standard regression program or, equivalently, we could use the one-way ANOVA formulas from Chapter 11. Exhibit 12.3 shows the actual data matrix we would use to regress Y (mood scores) on Z_1 to Z_5. Note that the mean for each contrast-coded predictor is zero because there are equal numbers of observations in each group.

EXHIBIT 12.3 ▶

Data matrix for analyzing mood scores using multiple regression and one-way codes

Group		Data	Predictors				
Drug	Enzyme	Y	Z_1	Z_2	Z_3	Z_4	Z_5
A	E	31	5	0	0	0	0
A	E	31	5	0	0	0	0
A	E	34	5	0	0	0	0
B	E	25	−1	4	0	0	0
B	E	25	−1	4	0	0	0
B	E	28	−1	4	0	0	0
P	E	17	−1	−1	3	0	0
P	E	18	−1	−1	3	0	0
P	E	16	−1	−1	3	0	0
A	no E	17	−1	−1	−1	2	0
A	no E	15	−1	−1	−1	2	0
A	no E	19	−1	−1	−1	2	0
B	no E	23	−1	−1	−1	−1	1
B	no E	18	−1	−1	−1	−1	1
B	no E	16	−1	−1	−1	−1	1
P	no E	9	−1	−1	−1	−1	−1
P	no E	10	−1	−1	−1	−1	−1
P	no E	8	−1	−1	−1	−1	−1
Mean		20	0	0	0	0	0

The analysis of the mood scores using the contrast-coded predictors Z_1, Z_2, Z_3, Z_4, and Z_5 is presented in Exhibit 12.4. The analysis is exactly the same as the one-way analyses in the previous chapter. That is, the mood scores are modeled in terms of the five Z predictors in a multiple regression. The augmented model using all five predictors reduces the error of the compact model using the mean by $960/1010 = .9505$. We calculate F^* in the usual way. In this case,

$$F^*_{5,12} = \frac{.9505/5}{(1 - .9505)/12} = 46.1$$

This omnibus tests implies, as it did in one-way analysis of variance, that the means for the six groups are significantly different, so they cannot be adequately represented by the overall mean. That is, we reject

MODEL C: $Y_i = \beta_0 + \varepsilon_i$

in favor of

MODEL A: $Y_i = \beta_0 + \beta_1 Z_{i1} + \beta_2 Z_{i2} + \beta_3 Z_{i3} + \beta_4 Z_{i4} + \beta_5 Z_{i5} + \varepsilon_i$

because the large value of PRE (.95) is statistically surprising ($F^*_{5,12} = 46.1$, $p < .0001$). Note that the Z's will be independent of each other

EXHIBIT 12.4 ▶

Analysis of the hypothetical mood scores by the model: $Y_i = \beta_0 + \beta_1 Z_{i1} + \beta_2 Z_{i2} + \beta_3 Z_{i3} + \beta_4 Z_{i4} + \beta_5 Z_{i5} + \varepsilon_i$

Source	b_j	SS	df	MS	F^*	p	PRE
Between Groups		960.0	5	192.0	46.1	.0001	.95
Z_1	2.4	518.4	1	518.4	124.4	.0001	.91
Z_2	2.1	264.6	1	264.6	63.5	.0001	.84
Z_3	.5	9.0	1	9.0	2.2	.17	.15
Z_4	1.0	18.0	1	18.0	4.3	.06	.26
Z_5	5.0	150.0	1	150.0	36.0	.0001	.75
Within Groups		50.0	12	4.2			
Total		1010.0	17				

because there are equal numbers of observations in each group. Hence, the sums of squares in Exhibit 12.4 for the individual contrast-coded predictors sum to the overall sum of squares for the complete model.

But which groups are different from each other? The test of the Z_1 contrast indicates that the estimate $b_1 = 2.4$ is significantly different from zero and it reduces 91% of the error remaining after all the other codes are in the equation. Remember that this test is obtained by comparing an augmented model which includes all the Z's to a compact model which includes all the Z's except Z_1. In this case, we can reject the null hypothesis that $\beta_1 = 0$. Z_1 codes the comparison between Group 1 (Drug A administered to patients with Enzyme E) and the average of all the other groups; thus, we can conclude that Group 1 was significantly different from the average of all other cells in the study.

We interpret the value of the coefficient the same as we always have. Specifically, the coefficient $b_1 = 2.4$ means that for a unit increase in Z_1, the predicted mood score increases, on average, by 2.4. To verify this, reexamine Exhibit 12.2 to see that the value of Z_1 for all the other groups is -1 and for Group 1, $Z_1 = 5$. Thus, there is a change of six units on Z_1 between the two comparison groups. We therefore would predict the mean for Group 1 to be $6 \times 2.4 = 14.4$ higher than the average in all the other groups. This is indeed the case: the mean for Group 1 is 32 and the mean for all the other groups combined is $(26 + 17 + 17 + 19 + 9)/5 = 17.6$; and $32 - 17.6 = 14.4$. But why is Group 1 better, on average, than all the other groups? Is it because of Drug A? Or is it because patients with Enzyme E score higher regardless of which drug they receive? Or is it because Drug A is especially effective for patients with Enzyme E? The contrast Z_1 cannot tell us. It just indicates that there is a difference.

The contrast Z_2 can be interpreted similarly to Z_1. That the estimate $b_2 = 2.1$ is significantly different from zero indicates that Group 2 (Drug B administered to patients with Enzyme E) is different from the average of all the subsequent groups (i.e., excluding Group 1). The difference in means equals $5 \times 2.1 = 10.5$. But again we do not know whether the higher average mood scores of Group 2 are due to Drug B or Enzyme E or their combination.

The other contrast that is significantly different from zero (using $\alpha = .05$) is Z_5; this contrast compares Groups 5 and 6 or the difference between Drug B and the placebo for those patients without Enzyme E. We know in this case that the higher average score for Group 5 ($2 \times 5 = 10$) is due to Drug B relative to the placebo because all patients in this comparison do not have Enzyme E. But is Drug B also better than the placebo for those patients who do have Enzyme E? None of the Z contrasts helps us answer that question.

12.2

A Better Set of Codes

It is now clear that even though the one-way analysis of variance using the Z contrast-coded predictors is statistically correct it has failed to answer important questions we want to ask of the data. One solution would be to use the multiple comparison procedures developed in Chapter 11 to address some of the unanswered questions. However, a much more efficient way is to begin with a set of contrast codes which do ask many of the questions we would naturally want to consider. Given the two-way layout of the data (as in Exhibit 12.1), there are several codings which are more natural than the Z codes just used. "Two-way" analysis of variance turns out to be nothing more than one-way ANOVA using one of these natural codings.

To develop a more natural coding, we begin by considering each of the two categorical variables separately. The strategy is to develop contrast codes identical to the ones that we would use if each categorical variable were considered alone in its own one-way analysis of variance. That is, our first step is to code each categorical variable as if the other one did not exist. For the drug variable an interesting question is whether the drugs, on average, do better than the placebo. The contrast code λ_1, which produced the contrast-coded predictor X_1, in Exhibit 12.5 performs precisely that comparison. The $(1, 1, -2)$ pattern is repeated for each level of the other categorical variable. The contrast code λ_2, associated with predictor X_2, then asks whether there is any difference between Drugs A and B. We can verify that λ_1 and λ_2 are orthogonal by checking whether the sum of their cross products equals zero. That is,

$$\sum_{k=1}^{m} \lambda_{1k}\lambda_{2k} = 1(1) + 1(-1) - 2(0) + 1(1) + 1(-1) - 2(0)$$

$$= 1 - 1 + 0 + 1 - 1 + 0$$

$$= 0$$

The orthogonality combined with the equal numbers of observations in each cell ensures that the coded predictors X_1 and X_2 are uncorrelated. With three levels of the drug categorical variable, we can only have two orthogonal codes so λ_1 and λ_2 are sufficient for the one-way analysis of that variable.

There are only two levels of the Enzyme categorical variable, so we need only one code. Hence, λ_3 codes the contrast between having and not having Enzyme E and provides the complete one-way analysis of variance for that variable.

EXHIBIT 12.5 ▶

Hypothetical data
of Exhibit 12.1
coded for two-way
ANOVA

Group Label	1 AwE	2 BwE	3 PwE	4 AwoE	5 BwoE	6 PwoE
	31	25	17	17	23	9
	31	25	18	15	18	10
	34	28	16	19	16	8
Mean	32	26	17	17	19	9

Contrast Codes		Group 1	2	3	4	5	6
λ_1 Drugs vs. Placebo	X_1	1	1	−2	1	1	−2
λ_2 Drug A vs. Drug B	X_2	1	−1	0	1	−1	0
λ_3 Enzyme E vs. not E	X_3	1	1	1	−1	−1	−1
λ_4 Interaction: $\lambda_1 \times \lambda_3$	X_4	1	1	−2	−1	−1	2
λ_5 Interaction: $\lambda_2 \times \lambda_3$	X_5	1	−1	0	−1	1	0

So far we have only three codes, λ_1, λ_2, and λ_3, for the two separate one-way analyses of the categorical variables, but five are required for the complete analysis because there are six groups. To generate the other two necessary codes, we simply multiply the contrast codes between the two categorical variables; that is, $\lambda_4 = \lambda_1 \times \lambda_3$ and $\lambda_5 = \lambda_2 \times \lambda_3$. These are the same kind of product terms we considered in Chapter 10. In the context of two-way analysis of variance these product terms ask especially interesting questions. λ_4, the product of λ_1 and λ_3, asks whether the difference coded by λ_1 (Drugs versus Placebo) depends on the level of λ_3 (whether or not the patient has Enzyme E). Similarly, λ_5, the product of λ_2 and λ_3, asks whether the comparison coded by λ_2 (Drug A versus Drug B) depends on the level of λ_3. The order of multiplication is arbitrary, so either statement could be turned around. That is, λ_4 asks whether the comparison coded by λ_3 (Enzyme E versus no Enzyme E) depends on the level of λ_1 (whether or not a drug was administered). These product codes are often called *interactions*. We will consider the interpretation of interactions in greater detail later.

Note that we do not form a code by multiplying $\lambda_1 \times \lambda_2$ because that would give us another code for just the drug categorical variable which could not be orthogonal to the other two codes for that variable. The two codes formed from products, λ_4 and λ_5, are orthogonal to each other and to the other codes. This gives a total of five orthogonal contrast codes which is precisely the number we need for the analysis of six groups.

Exhibit 12.6 shows the actual data matrix we can submit to a multiple regression program to analyze the mood scores in terms of the X variables. That is, we can regress Y_i on X_1 to X_5. Note again that the mean for each predictor is zero because we are using contrast codes and there are an equal number of observations for each group.

Exhibit 12.7 presents the results of the regression analysis using the X contrast-coded predictors. Note that the sum of squares for the augmented model including all the predictors, and the F^* and PRE for the omnibus test of the complete model are exactly the same as when the

EXHIBIT 12.6 ▶

Data matrix for analyzing mood scores using multiple regression and two-way codes

Group Drug	Enzyme	Data Y	X_1	X_2	X_3	X_4	X_5
A	E	31	1	1	1	1	1
A	E	31	1	1	1	1	1
A	E	34	1	1	1	1	1
B	E	25	1	−1	1	1	−1
B	E	25	1	−1	1	1	−1
B	E	28	1	−1	1	1	−1
P	E	17	−2	0	1	−2	0
P	E	18	−2	0	1	−2	0
P	E	16	−2	0	1	−2	0
A	no E	17	1	1	−1	−1	−1
A	no E	15	1	1	−1	−1	−1
A	no E	19	1	1	−1	−1	−1
B	no E	23	1	−1	−1	−1	1
B	no E	18	1	−1	−1	−1	1
B	no E	16	1	−1	−1	−1	1
P	no E	9	−2	0	−1	2	0
P	no E	10	−2	0	−1	2	0
P	no E	8	−2	0	−1	2	0
Mean		20	0	0	0	0	0

EXHIBIT 12.7 ▶

Analysis of the hypothetical mood scores by the model: $Y_i = \beta_0 + \beta_1 X_{i1} + \beta_2 X_{i2} + \beta_3 X_{i3} + \beta_4 X_{i4} + \beta_5 X_{i5} + \varepsilon_i$

Source	b_j	SS	df	MS	F^*	p	PRE
Between Groups		960	5	192.0	46.1	.0001	.95
Drug		453	2	226.5	53.9	.0001	.90
X_1	3.5	441	1	441	105.8	.0001	.90
X_2	1.0	12	1	12	2.9	.11	.19
Enzyme		450	1	450	108.0	.0001	.90
X_3	5.0	450	1	450	108.0	.0001	.90
Drug × Enzyme		57	2	28.5	6.8	.01	.53
X_4	.5	9	1	9	2.2	.16	.15
X_5	2.0	48	1	48	11.5	.005	.49
Within Groups		50	12	4.2			
Total		1010	17				

Z predictors were used. This must be the case because in each analysis we used a complete set of codes so that, as in one-way ANOVA, $\hat{Y}$ is the mean of each group. If both sets of predictors produce the same $\hat{Y}$, then the total error reduced must be the same. The only difference in the two analyses is how that total error reduction is divided into separate components. The X predictors ask different questions from the Z predictors, so the individual error reduction associated with each X predictor is different from that of the Z predictors, but the total error reduction must be the same.

There are nine PRE's and F^*'s reported in Exhibit 12.7. Each one corresponds to a comparison between a particular MODEL C and a MODEL A. To understand the meaning of each test, it is important to be precise about those models for each test. The omnibus test is reported in the row labeled "Between Groups" and represents the comparison between the following two MODELs:

MODEL A: $Y_i = \beta_0 + \beta_1 X_{i1} + \beta_2 X_{i2} + \beta_3 X_{i3} + \beta_4 X_{i4} + \beta_5 X_{i5} + \varepsilon_i$

MODEL C: $Y_i = \beta_0 + \varepsilon_i$

The null hypothesis being tested is obviously

$$\beta_1 = \beta_2 = \beta_3 = \beta_4 = \beta_5 = 0$$

and that hypothesis is rejected by the large values of PRE and F^*.

The rows for each of the X_j compare a MODEL A using all the contrast-coded predictors to a MODEL C which includes all the predictors except X_j. For example, the PRE and F^* in the row labeled X_1 compare

MODEL A: $Y_i = \beta_0 + \beta_1 X_{i1} + \beta_2 X_{i2} + \beta_3 X_{i3} + \beta_4 X_{i4} + \beta_5 X_{i5} + \varepsilon_i$

MODEL C: $Y_i = \beta_0 + \beta_2 X_{i2} + \beta_3 X_{i3} + \beta_4 X_{i4} + \beta_5 X_{i5} + \varepsilon_i$

and test the null hypothesis

$$\beta_1 = 0$$

We generated X_1 and X_2 as one-way codes for the drug categorical variable for the data matrix in Exhibit 12.1. The row labeled "Drug" in Exhibit 12.7 reports the results from testing a model including all the contrast codes to one which omits *both* the drug codes X_1 and X_2. That is, we are comparing

MODEL A: $Y_i = \beta_0 + \beta_1 X_{i1} + \beta_2 X_{i2} + \beta_3 X_{i3} + \beta_4 X_{i4} + \beta_5 X_{i5} + \varepsilon_i$

MODEL C: $Y_i = \beta_0 + \beta_3 X_{i3} + \beta_4 X_{i4} + \beta_5 X_{i5} + \varepsilon_i$

which implies the null hypothesis

$$\beta_1 = \beta_2 = 0$$

In other words, we are asking the question of whether the predictions would suffer if we were to ignore the drug categorical variable. The large PRE and F^* indicate that we cannot ignore which drug a patient received. In the traditional language of analysis of variance, this is known as the test of the *main effect* of the drug categorical variable. In this case, we would conclude that overall there is a statistically significant main effect for the drug categorical variable. Note that because X_1 and X_2 are uncorrelated, their sums of squares add to produce the sum of squares attributable to both of them. We prefer the single-degree-of-freedom tests of the focused comparisons X_1 and X_2 to this global test of the drug effect because rejection of the hypothesis $\beta_1 = \beta_2 = 0$ is ambiguous. We don't know which part of this multiple-degree-of-freedom hypothesis is at fault. Maybe the global hypothesis is rejected because $\beta_1 \neq 0$ or because $\beta_2 \neq 0$ or because both β_1 and β_2 are not equal to zero. We present the omnibus test for the drug variable in Exhibit 12.7 not as a recommended practice but only to show what hypothesis is being tested in the traditional approach to analysis of variance. Unfortunately, in the traditional approach usually *only* the omnibus tests in Exhibit 12.7 are presented in a source table.

We can similarly assess the main effect for the enzyme variable. In this case there is only one code for the enzyme variable so that test is the same as the test of the null hypothesis that $\beta_3 = 0$. Finally, we can group together the two codes X_4 and X_5 which we constructed from products of other codes. Each of these two products involved one code for the drug categorical variable and one code for the enzyme categorical variable, so in the traditional language of analysis of variance they would be known together as the "Drug × Enzyme Interaction." Testing the Drug × Enzyme interaction is equivalent to comparing

MODEL A: $Y_i = \beta_0 + \beta_1 X_{i1} + \beta_2 X_{i2} + \beta_3 X_{i3} + \beta_4 X_{i4} + \beta_5 X_{i5} + \varepsilon_i$

MODEL C: $Y_i = \beta_0 + \beta_1 X_{i1} + \beta_2 X_{i2} + \beta_3 X_{i3} + \varepsilon_i$

which is equivalent to the null hypothesis

$\beta_4 = \beta_5 = 0$

A traditional analysis of variance source table similar to the one in Exhibit 12.7 would contain rows only for "Drug," "Enzyme," "Drug × Enzyme," "Within Groups," and "Total." Such a source table, because it aggregates individual contrasts into more global effects, omits information that is available in the individual contrasts. In other words, the traditional analysis of variance source table fails to analyze the variance as much as is possible using the focused comparisons of contrast codes.

The analysis in Exhibit 12.7 can be produced with any standard regression program or, equivalently, by using the equations from Chapter 11 which express the parameter estimates and their corresponding sums of squares as a function of the contrast codes and the cell means. As an illustration, let's use the formulas to calculate b_1 and its associated SSR. The coefficient which estimates β_1 is given by

$$b_1 = \frac{\sum_k \lambda_{1k} \overline{Y}_k}{\sum_k \lambda_{1k}^2}$$

$$= \frac{1(32) + 1(26) - 2(17) + 1(17) + 1(19) - 2(9)}{1^2 + 1^2 + (-2)^2 + 1^2 + 1^2 + (-2)^2}$$

$$= \frac{42}{12} = 3.5$$

Then the sum of squared error reduced by including X_1 and using the estimate $b_1 = 3.5$ is given by

$$SSR_{b_1} = \frac{(\sum_k \lambda_{1k} \overline{Y}_k)^2}{\sum_k \lambda_{1k}^2 / n_k}$$

$$= \frac{[1(32) + 1(26) - 2(17) + 1(17) + 1(19) - 2(9)]^2}{1^2/3 + 1^2/3 + (-2)^2/3 + 1^2/3 + 1^2/3 + (-2)^2/3}$$

$$= \frac{42^2}{12/3} = 441$$

Thus, in terms of parameter estimates and statistical tests there is absolutely nothing new that needs to be learned to do two-way ANOVA—it is *exactly* the same as one-way ANOVA.

12.3

Interpretation of Coefficients

There is one new difficulty introduced by the generalization to two-way and higher analysis of variance, but it is an interpretation problem and not a difficulty involving statistical procedures. The difficulty is the interpretation of the coefficients for the predictor variables that code the interactions—the products between one-way codes. What does it mean, for example, to reject the null hypothesis that $\beta_5 = 0$? Newcomers to analysis of variance whether using our approach or more traditional approaches often have initial difficulty understanding the concept of an interaction. We therefore devote considerable attention in the following to the interpretation of interactions. We do so by considering three different approaches to interpreting the coefficients in a model involving two-way codes such as those in Exhibit 12.5. Those three approaches are (a) reexpression of the codes in terms of the cell means as was done in Chapter 11; (b) interpretation of product predictors as changes in slopes as was done in Chapter 10; and (c) consideration of the parameter estimates as the adjustments required for conditional predictions. Each approach to interpretation is considered in turn. In each approach we also consider the interpretation of the coefficients for predictors not involving products because interactions are best understood in comparison.

12.3.1 Interpretation in Terms of Cell Means

The interpretation of the parameter estimates associated with the X predictors proceeds in the same manner as for the Z predictors and indeed in the same manner as for any set of predictors in the one-way analyses of Chapter 11. However, unlike the Z predictors, the X contrast-coded predictors correspond to meaningful, natural questions. The large value of $F_{1,12}^* = 105.8$ for X_1 rejects the null hypothesis that $\beta_1 = 0$. To see exactly what the rejection of this null hypothesis means, we express β_1 in terms of the contrast code using the equation from Chapter 11 which expresses the parameter estimate as a function of the codes and the cell means. That is, an equivalent statement of the null hypothesis $\beta_1 = 0$ is

$$\beta_1 = \frac{\mu_{AE} + \mu_{BE} - 2\mu_{PE} + \mu_{A\slashed{E}} + \mu_{B\slashed{E}} - 2\mu_{P\slashed{E}}}{12} = 0$$

where μ_{AE} represents the true but unknown mean for the group that had Enzyme E and received Drug A, etc. Multiplying by 12 and moving the terms for the placebo conditions to the right side of the equation yields the following equivalent statement of the hypothesis:

$$\mu_{AE} + \mu_{A\bar{E}} + \mu_{BE} + \mu_{B\bar{E}} = 2(\mu_{PE} + \mu_{P\bar{E}})$$

Dividing each side of this equation by 2 gives

$$\frac{\mu_{AE} + \mu_{A\bar{E}}}{2} + \frac{\mu_{BE} + \mu_{B\bar{E}}}{2} = 2\left(\frac{\mu_{PE} + \mu_{P\bar{E}}}{2}\right)$$

If we let $\mu_A = (\mu_{AE} + \mu_{A\bar{E}})/2$, the mean of the Drug A conditions averaged across both levels of the enzyme variable, $\mu_B = (\mu_{BE} + \mu_{B\bar{E}})/2$, and $\mu_P = (\mu_{PE} + \mu_{P\bar{E}})/2$, then the null hypothesis reduces to

$$\mu_A + \mu_B = 2\mu_P$$

Dividing each side of this equation by 2 then gives the final, useful statement of the null hypothesis as

$$\frac{\mu_A + \mu_B}{2} = \mu_P$$

That is, concluding that $\beta_1 \neq 0$ is equivalent to concluding that the average of the two drug conditions is not equal to the average for the placebo groups. Thus, unlike the ambiguous conclusions using the Z contrast codes, rejection of the null hypothesis for β_1 clearly implies that the mood scores for the two drug groups, on average, differed from the mood scores of the placebo group. With experience it is usually easy to go directly from the contrast codes to a statement of the null hypothesis without doing the formal derivation as above. For example, the $(1, -1, 0)$ code for X_2 compares the Drug A groups with the Drug B groups so the null hypothesis $\beta_2 = 0$ is equivalent to the null hypothesis

$$\mu_A - \mu_B = 0 \quad \text{or} \quad \mu_A = \mu_B$$

The direction and magnitude of a difference revealed by rejecting the null hypothesis is given by the estimate of β_j. For X_1, this estimate is $b_1 = 3.5$. As with all regression coefficients, this means that our model prediction $\hat{Y}$ increases, on average, 3.5 units for each unit increase in X_1. The change on X_1 from the placebo groups ($X_1 = -2$) to the drug groups ($X_1 = 1$) is a change of 3 units, so the predicted difference between the placebo and drug groups is $3 \times 3.5 = 10.5$. Indeed, the average of the four drug groups, $(32 + 26 + 17 + 19)/4 = 23.5$, exceeds by 10.5 the average of the two placebo groups, $(17 + 9)/2 = 13$.

We cannot conclude that the estimate for β_2 is reliably different from zero, so we will not interpret the coefficient $b_2 = 1.0$. The coefficient $b_3 = 5$ is reliably different from zero. X_3 codes the difference between the two enzyme groups, so we can conclude that on average there is a significant difference between mood scores as a function of whether or not the patient has Enzyme E. That is, we can reject the null hypothesis that

$$\mu_E = \mu_{\not E}$$

To be specific about the amount of the difference in mood scores between those with and without Enzyme E, we need to interpret the meaning of the estimate $b_3 = 5$ as before. There is a 2-unit difference on X_3 between not having Enzyme E ($X_3 = -1$) and having Enzyme E ($X_3 = 1$); thus, the predicted average difference between the two groups is $2 \times 5 = 10$. Indeed, the average of the three Enzyme E groups, $(32 + 26 + 17)/3 = 25$, exceeds by 10 the average of the three groups without Enzyme E, $(17 + 19 + 9)/3 = 15$.

The estimate of the coefficient for X_4, the product of X_1 and X_3, is not significantly different from zero so we will not interpret it. The coefficient for the other interaction contrast-coded predictor X_5, the product of X_2 and X_3, is reliably different from zero, so we will examine it closely. We will begin by considering formally the null hypothesis that is rejected. Using the contrast code for X_5, we can see that the null hypothesis $\beta_5 = 0$ is equivalent to the statement

$$\mu_{AE} - \mu_{BE} - \mu_{A\not E} + \mu_{B\not E} = 0$$

or, by grouping the A terms on the left and the B terms on the right,

$$\mu_{AE} - \mu_{A\not E} = \mu_{BE} - \mu_{B\not E}$$

The left side of the last statement is simply the difference between those with and without Enzyme E for the Drug A conditions only. The right side is the same comparison between those with and without Enzyme E but for the Drug B conditions only. Thus, this null hypothesis for an interaction is a statement that two *differences* are equal. That $b_3 = 5$ told us that *on average* the score difference between those with and without Enzyme E was 10. The above equation shows that b_5 tells us whether that difference between those with and without Enzyme E is the same *within* each drug condition or whether that difference depends on which drug was administered. Thus, concluding that $\beta_5 \neq 0$ is equivalent to concluding that the difference between those with and without Enzyme E who received Drug A is not the same as the difference between those with and without Enzyme E who received Drug B. In other words, the observed difference between those with and without Enzyme E of $32 - 17 = 15$ for those receiving Drug A is reliably different from the difference of $26 - 19 = 7$ for those receiving Drug B. In still other words, the degree to which scores for those with Enzyme E tend to be higher than scores for those without Enzyme E is not constant, but instead depends on the level of the other variable, which in this case is type of drug.

Another rearrangement of terms of the previous equation yields an equivalent expression which interprets the interaction in terms of the other variable. That expression is

$$\mu_{AE} - \mu_{BE} = \mu_{A\bar{E}} - \mu_{B\bar{E}}$$

This time we have grouped the terms with Enzyme E on the left and those without Enzyme E on the right. The left side of the last equation is simply the difference between the Drug A and Drug B groups for those patients with Enzyme E, and the right side is the same comparison but for those patients without Enzyme E. Again, this null hypothesis is simply a statement that two differences are equal. Thus, concluding that $\beta_5 \neq 0$ is equivalent to concluding that the difference between the two drug groups for those with Enzyme E is not the same as the difference between the two drug groups for those without Enzyme E. In other words, the observed difference of $32 - 26 = 6$ between the two drug groups for those with Enzyme E is reliably different from the difference of $17 - 19 = -2$ between the two drug groups for those without Enzyme E. In still other words, the superiority of Drug A over Drug B is not constant, but instead depends on the level of the other variable, which in this case is the presence of Enzyme E.

We therefore have two equivalent interpretations for the interaction which is implied by rejecting the hypothesis that $\beta_5 = 0$. Indeed, for any interaction there will be multiple ways to express it. It will often help to understand the interaction to consider all the possible interpretations, but it is important to realize that they are all equivalent statements of the same relationship.

12.3.2 Interpretation in Terms of Slope Changes

It is also useful to examine this interaction using the same procedures we developed in Chapter 10 for ordinary multiple regression involving product terms. We begin with the estimated equation for MODEL A:

$$\hat{Y} = 20 + 3.5X_1 + X_2 + 5X_3 + .5X_4 + 2X_5$$

Then we substitute the product definitions—$X_4 = X_1X_3$ and $X_5 = X_2X_3$— to get

$$\hat{Y} = 20 + 3.5X_1 + X_2 + 5X_3 + .5X_1X_3 + 2X_2X_3$$

Next we regroup the terms to express the "simple" linear relationship between $\hat{Y}$ and one of the three predictors X_1, X_2, or X_3. We will begin with X_3; regrouping terms yields

$$\hat{Y} = (20 + 3.5X_1 + X_2) + (5 + .5X_1 + 2X_2)X_3$$

which expresses the "simple" linear relationship between $\hat{Y}$ and X_3. The first term in parentheses represents the intercept (given specific values of X_1 and X_2), and the second term in parentheses represents the slope (i.e., as always, the predicted change in $\hat{Y}$ given a unit change in X_3). Remember that X_3 codes whether or not the patient has Enzyme E, so this linear relationship reflects the effect of Enzyme E on the predicted scores. That is, the larger the slope the greater the effect of whether or not the patient has Enzyme E on the predicted values.

To understand the equation expressing $\hat{Y}$ as a linear function of X_3, let's begin by examining Exhibit 12.8, which displays the relationship between $\hat{Y}$ and X_3 when $X_1 = 0$ and $X_2 = 0$. X_1 and X_2 are contrast-coded predictors with an equal number of observations in each cell, so average values of X_1 and X_2 are zero; hence, the graph in Exhibit 12.8 may be thought of as the average relationship between $\hat{Y}$ and X_3. For $X_1 = 0$ and $X_2 = 0$, the relationship between $\hat{Y}$ and X_3 reduces to

$$\hat{Y} = 20 + 5X_3$$

The intercept of 20 is, as always, the predicted value when $X_3 = 0$. X_3 is never zero (it is either $+1$ or -1), but its average value is zero, so we can interpret the intercept as the average value across levels of X_3. Indeed, 20 is the grand mean for these data. The slope for X_3 is 5, which means that for every unit change in X_3 the predicted value $\hat{Y}$ changes by 5. Hence, the change from $X_3 = -1$ to $X_3 = +1$ (from no Enzyme E to Enzyme E) predicts a change in $\hat{Y}$ of $(1 - (-1))5 = 10$. This, as it must be, is the same interpretation we obtained for b_3 in terms of cell means.

EXHIBIT 12.8 ▶

Simple relationship between $\hat{Y}$ and X_3 when $X_1 = 0$ and $X_2 = 0$

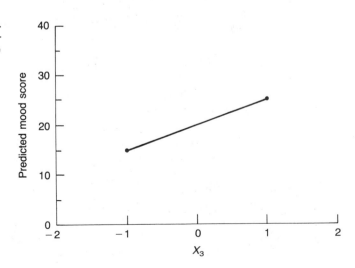

What happens to the simple relationship between $\hat{Y}$ and X_3 if we don't look at the average relationship, but instead allow X_1 and X_2 to be different from zero? The intercept term is

$$20 + 3.5X_1 + X_2$$

so if $X_1 = 1$ (Drug A or B) then the intercept will increase by 3.5 units and if $X_1 = -2$ (Placebo) then the intercept will decrease by 7 units. These represent the changes in $\hat{Y}$ due to X_1 when X_3 equals zero (which it does equal on average). On average, then, $\hat{Y}$ for the four drug groups ought to be $3.5 + 7 = 10.5$ units higher than $\hat{Y}$ for the two placebo groups. This again is the same interpretation we obtained in terms of cell means. Similarly, for $X_2 = 1$, 0, and -1, the intercept increases, stays the same, or decreases. These changes in $\hat{Y}$ (for $X_3 = 0$, on average) are similarly interpreted.

Now that we have seen what happens to the "simple" intercept for the Y-X_3 relationship as X_1 and X_2 change, let's turn to the "simple" slope and see what happens when X_1 and X_2 are not equal to zero. The slope term is

$$5 + 0.5X_1 + 2X_2$$

so the slope relating $\hat{Y}$ and X_3 *changes* as a function of both X_1 and X_2. If $X_2 = 1$ (Drug A), then the predicted slope increases by $2 \times 1 = 2$ units. If $X_2 = -1$(Drug B), then the predicted slope decreases by $2 \times 1 = 2$ units. In other words, changes in X_3 are more important when $X_2 = +1$ than when $X_2 = -1$. Translating the last statement into the categories those variables code, we have the conclusion that whether or not Enzyme E is present (coded by X_3) makes more of a difference when Drug A is administered than when Drug B is administered (coded by X_2). This is the essence of any ANOVA interaction. If there is an interaction, *the effect of one categorical variable depends on the level of another variable*.

Similarly, different values of X_1 also yield different slopes. If $X_1 = 1$, then the slope increases slightly by .5 unit, and if $X_1 = -2$, then it decreases by 1 unit. However, the coefficient b_4 which represents this interaction ($X_4 = X_1 \times X_2$) is not significantly different from zero. Hence, there is no reliable evidence from these data that whether or not Enzyme E is present (coded by X_3) makes more or less of a difference when drugs are administered than when a placebo is used (coded by X_1). That is, there is no reliable evidence that this particular interaction exists.

The changes in the intercept and the changes in the slope for X_3 due to X_1 and X_2 can be seen in Exhibit 12.9. Clearly, the different values of X_1 yield noticeably different intercepts, but the changes in the slope for X_3 due to X_1 are marginal. Although it may not appear to be the case, the slopes for the bottom set of lines for $X_1 = -2$ are slightly flatter

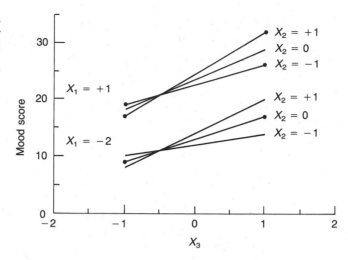

EXHIBIT 12.9 ▶

Simple relationship between $\hat{Y}$ and X_3 for different values of X_1 and X_2 (dots represent cell means)

than those for the top set of lines for $X_1 = +1$. In contrast, the intercept changes due to X_2 are noticeable but smaller than those due to X_1, but the slope changes due to X_2 are obvious. Indeed, the lines actually cross within the range of values used in this study. That is, mood scores are higher for Drug A ($X_2 = 1$) than for Drug B ($X_2 = -1$) when Enzyme E is present ($X_3 = 1$), but when Enzyme E is absent ($X_3 = -1$) the reverse is true—mood scores for Drug B are higher than those for Drug A. These differences in slope are the essence of an interaction.

Similar to the above interpretation of the augmented model in terms of the simple linear relationship between $\hat{Y}$ and X_3, we could also do the interpretation in terms of $\hat{Y}$ and X_2. Although the interpretation of the interaction between X_2 and X_3 must necessarily be equivalent, the alternative interpretation in terms of the relationship between $\hat{Y}$ and X_2 may produce different insights. We do not provide that interpretation here, but it is recommended as an exercise for the reader. Finally, we could do the interpretation in terms of the simple linear relationship between $\hat{Y}$ and X_1. However, that is not likely to be useful for these data because the only interaction involving X_1 is $X_4 = X_1 \times X_3$, and the coefficient for that interaction was not reliably different from zero.

12.3.3 Interpretation in Terms of Conditional Predictions

For yet another interpretation of the parameter estimates in the augmented model we can return to the basic ideas of data analysis outlined in Chapter 1. Those ideas are that MODELs provide predictions of DATA and that increasingly complex MODELs make conditional predictions based on other information available about each observation. The simplest MODEL makes an unconditional prediction for all the DATA. For the mood scores in our hypothetical example, that unconditional prediction is the grand mean, which equals 20. The full regression equation

$$\hat{Y} = 20 + 3.5X_1 + X_2 + 5X_3 + .5X_4 + 2X_5$$

then shows how that unconditional prediction ought to be adjusted based on the information provided by the variables X_1 to X_5. The actual adjustment is determined by $b_j X_j$. For example, if $X_1 = 1$, then the unconditional prediction is adjusted upward by $3.5 \times 1 = 3.5$ units, and if $X_1 = -2$ then the prediction is adjusted by $3.5 \times (-2) = -7$ units.

Exhibit 12.10 displays all the relevant information for determining all the conditional predictions. As was the case for one-way ANOVA in Chapter 11, the predicted values are the cell means. Thus, we need only consider the adjustments in predicted values necessary for each cell rather than for each observation. For the mood score data each adjustment is represented by six numbers, one for each cell. The contrast codes are displayed at the top of Exhibit 12.10; each code is presented as three rows and two columns corresponding to the three row, two column array in which the data were originally presented in Exhibit 12.1. Thus, the first row in each array corresponds to Drug A, the second row to Drug B, the third row to Placebo, the first column to Enzyme E, and the second column to without Enzyme E. We have also included for completeness the constant code X_0 even though it is not a contrast code. X_0 corresponds to b_0 and the unconditional prediction. Below the codes are displayed the least squares estimates of the corresponding parameters b_j. The actual adjustments are obtained by multiplying the codes by the parameter estimates; these values for $b_j X_j$ are displayed below the parameter estimates along with the cell means.

$\hat{Y}$, the predicted value for a given cell, is obtained by adding the corresponding entries in the six $b_j X_j$ arrays. For example, the predicted value for the first cell (Drug A, Enzyme E) is given by

$$32 = 20 + 3.5 + 1 + 5 + .5 + 2$$

The 20 is the unconditional or base prediction. The other numbers on the right side are the adjustments to this base prediction conditional on other information about observations in that cell. In this case, the prediction is increased 3.5 units because we know a drug was administered ($b_1 X_1$), increased by 1 unit because the drug was A instead of B ($b_2 X_2$), increased by 5 units because we know patients in that group had Enzyme E, increased .5 units because patients in that cell had Enzyme E *and* received a drug ($b_4 X_4 = b_4 X_1 X_3$), and finally increased by 2 units because patients in that cell had Enzyme E *and* received Drug A instead of Drug B ($b_5 X_5 = b_5 X_2 X_3$). Each of the other predicted values (i.e., cell means)

EXHIBIT 12.10 ▶

Decomposition of mood score means by contrast-coded predictors

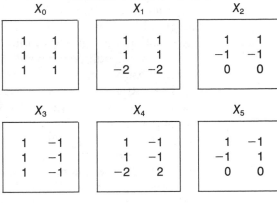

Contrast-Coded Predictors

X_0	X_1	X_2
1 1	1 1	1 1
1 1	1 1	-1 -1
1 1	-2 -2	0 0

X_3	X_4	X_5
1 -1	1 -1	1 -1
1 -1	1 -1	-1 1
1 -1	-2 2	0 0

Estimated Coefficients

$$b_0 = 20 \qquad b_1 = 3.5 \qquad b_2 = 1$$
$$b_3 = 5 \qquad b_4 = .5 \qquad b_5 = 2$$

Cell Means
$\hat{Y} = \bar{Y}$

Codes Multiplied by Appropriate Coefficient
$b_0X_0 \qquad\qquad b_1X_1 \qquad\qquad b_2X_2$

32 17	20 20	3.5 3.5	1 1
26 19	= 20 20	+ 3.5 3.5	+ -1 -1
17 9	20 20	-7 -7	0 0

$b_3X_3 \qquad\qquad b_4X_4 \qquad\qquad b_5X_5$

5 -5	.5 -.5	2 -2
+ 5 -5	+ .5 -.5	+ -2 2
5 -5	-1 1	0 0

Sum of Squares

$$960 \quad = \quad 0 \quad + \quad 441 \quad + \quad 12$$
$$+ \quad 450 \quad + \quad 9 \quad + \quad 48$$

can be interpreted similarly. Of course, not all the adjustments will be increases. For example, the predicted value for the last cell (Placebo, without Enzyme E) is given by

$$9 = 20 - 7 + 0 - 5 + 1 + 0$$

The representation of the cell means in Exhibit 12.10 in terms of the separate adjustments for each contrast is often referred to as a decomposition because the overall effect is decomposed or analyzed into the separate effects attributable to each contrast.

The pattern of the $b_j X_j$ arrays in Exhibit 12.10 indicates the type of adjustment each one makes to the prediction. The constant value for the grand mean $b_0 X_0$ shows that it is indeed an unconditional prediction because that value is added into every prediction. The patterns for $b_1 X_1$ and $b_2 X_2$ are conditional but still fairly simple. We need only know which row an observation is in to know which adjustment to make for X_1 or X_2. The pattern for $b_3 X_3$ is similar but pertains to the columns. That is, we need only know which column an observation is in to know which adjustment to make. The patterns for the $b_4 X_4$ and $b_5 X_5$ arrays are more complex. Remember that X_4 and X_5 represent interactions. For these two codes, knowing which row an observation is in does not allow us to know which adjustment to make; similarly, knowing which column an observation is in does not allow us to know which adjustment to make. Instead, we need information about both the row *and* the column to know which adjustment to make. For example, consider $b_5 X_5$. In making the prediction for a patient who received Drug A, we would not know whether to increase the prediction by 2 or to decrease it by 2; the proper adjustment depends not only on the row but also on the column. In this case, we would increase the prediction by 2 if the patient received Drug A *and* the patient had Enzyme E. Such conjunctive statements are the hallmark of interactions in the analysis of variance. To know what adjustment to the prediction to make for an interaction with two categorical variables, we need to know both the row and the column in which the observation appeared.

Examining the pattern of the appropriate adjustment array will generally lead to an interpretation of an interaction. For example, consider the array for $b_5 X_5$ (remember that $X_5 = X_2 X_3$). We know from interpreting $b_3 X_3$ that there was a difference in average mood scores associated with Enzyme E—those with Enzyme E had higher scores. The effect of the adjustment array for $b_5 X_5$ is to *increase* that difference for those receiving Drug A and to *decrease* that difference for those receiving Drug B; there is no adjustment for those receiving the placebo. Of course, this interaction can also be interpreted from the perspective of the other variable. That is, the effect of the adjustment array for $b_5 X_5$ is to increase the superiority of Drug A over Drug B for those who have Enzyme E and to decrease that superiority for those without Enzyme E. The array for $b_4 X_4$ has a similar interpretation, but we do not present it because for these data we could not reject the null hypothesis that $\beta_4 = 0$.

Note that the importance of an adjustment is directly related to the variability of the adjustments within the array. If all the adjustments for a contrast are near zero, the mean adjustment for any contrast, then obviously that contrast is not very important. In fact, it can be shown that SSR (sum of squares explainable by a contrast-coded predictor) is equal to the sum of the squared values in the adjustment arrays weighted by the number of observations. For example, for b_1X_1 the sum of squares is given by

$$3(3.5^2 + 3.5^2 + 3.5^2 + 3.5^2 + 7^2 + 7^2) = 3(12.25 + 12.25 + 12.25 + 12.25 + 49 + 49)$$

$$= 3(147) = 441$$

where the 3 is obtained from the number of observations per cell and the other numbers are directly from the adjustment array. Note that this value for the SSR for X_1 is exactly the same as obtained earlier in Exhibit 12.7. The SSR for the other adjustment arrays can be calculated similarly. These values of SSR are provided at the bottom of Exhibit 12.10. There is no SSR for b_0X_0 because the grand mean of 20 does not vary.

The top portion of Exhibit 12.11 shows the adjustment arrays aggregated into drug, enzyme, and drug × enzyme interaction adjustments. The drug adjustments in this case are simply the sum of the two adjustment arrays which were coding for drug differences. That is, the aggregate drug adjustment equals $b_1X_1 + b_2X_2$. There is only one code for enzyme so the enzyme adjustment equals b_3X_3. Finally, the total adjustment for interactions equals $b_4X_4 + b_5X_5$. This is the usual decomposition provided in traditional approaches to the analysis of variance. It obviously contains less information because the decomposition is not as detailed. Again, the magnitude of an effect is directly related to the magnitude of the adjustments in the corresponding array. In this case,

EXHIBIT 12.11 ▼

Decomposition of mood score means by aggregated adjustment arrays

							Conditional Adjustments					
Cell Means $\hat{Y}_{ik} = \overline{Y}_k$			Grand Mean b_0X_0			Drug $b_1X_1 + b_2X_2$			Enzyme b_3X_3		Interaction $b_4X_4 + b_5X_5$	
32	17	=	20	20	+	4.5	4.5	+	5	−5	+	2.5	−2.5
26	19		20	20		2.5	2.5		5	−5		−1.5	1.5
17	9		20	20		−7	−7		5	−5		−1	1

Sum of Squares

960	=	0	+	453	+	450	+	57

Cell Means $\hat{Y}_{ik} = \overline{Y}_k$			Grand Mean b_0X_0			Conditional Adjustments $b_1X_1 + b_2X_2 + b_3X_3 + b_4X_4 + b_5X_5$	
32	17	=	20	20	+	12	−3
26	19		20	20		6	−1
17	9		20	20		−3	−11

Sum of Squares

960	=	0	+	960

the drug × enzyme interaction adjustments are not nearly as large as the drug and enzyme adjustments. This is reflected in their SSRs, which are provided below the adjustment arrays in the exhibit. The adjustment arrays correspond to the "Drug," "Enzyme," and "Drug × Enzyme Interaction" rows in Exhibit 12.7. The PRE and F^*'s for those rows test the null hypotheses, respectively, that the drug adjustments are zero, the enzyme adjustments are zero, and the interaction adjustments are zero. All of those null hypotheses are rejected, but it is clear from an examination of the adjustment arrays that the drug and enzyme effects are much larger than the interaction effects. That difference in magnitude of effect is also assessed directly by the respective PREs of .90, .90, and .53.

The bottom portion of Exhibit 12.11 shows the highest level of aggregation—all the adjustments have been combined into one array. The adjustment array here is simply the sum of the three adjustment arrays in the top portion of the exhibit. The values in this aggregate adjustment array are also simply the amounts by which the respective cell means differ from the grand mean. For example, the adjustment for the Drug A, Enzyme E group is 12, which equals 32 − 20, the cell mean minus the grand mean. The omnibus model test in Exhibit 12.7 tests whether these adjustments equal zero which is equivalent to testing whether all the cell means are equal. Again, the variability of these adjustments is directly related to the sum of squares reduction for the complete model. This SSR is the same as the SSR between groups as discussed in Chapter 11 and can also be simply calculated from the means by

$$\text{SS(Between Groups)} = \sum_{k=1}^{m} n_k(\overline{Y}_k - \overline{Y})^2$$

12.3.4 Interpretation Summary

Although all three interpretation strategies yield essentially the same interpretation, each is useful for providing a slightly different perspective. For interpreting a given analysis of variance, you should use as many of the strategies as necessary until a clear interpretation emerges. Below we suggest a summary interpretation for this analysis, which might be included in a journal article.

On average, both drug treatments produced higher mood scores than the placebo condition (means 23.5 versus 13, PRE = .90, $F^*_{1,12} = 105.8$, $p < .0001$). There is no statistically significant difference in the average mood scores produced by Drug A versus Drug B (means 24.5 versus 22.5, PRE = .19, $F^*_{1,12} = 2.9$, $p = .11$). Averaged across all three drug conditions, patients who had Enzyme E in their blood had higher mood scores than those who did not (means 25 versus 15, PRE = .90, $F^*_{1,12}$ = 108, p < .0001). However, there was a significant interaction between type of drug administered (A versus B) and whether or not Enzyme E was present such that Drug A, relative to Drug B, produced an increase in mood scores for those with Enzyme E but produced a decrease in mood scores for those without Enzyme E (differential adjustment = 2 − (−2) = 4, PRE = .49, $F^*_{1,12}$ = 11.5, p < .005).

A useful adjunct to the above journal summary are graphs of the cell means (i.e., the predicted values) as a function of the drug and enzyme variables. Exhibit 12.12 and Exhibit 12.13 present the two different views of these data. In the first of these two exhibits, the differences between the lines for the drug treatments represent the "Drug" differences. In particular, the relatively large difference between the two lines for Drug A and Drug B and the line for the Placebo corresponds to the large value for b_1 and the small difference between the Drug A and Drug B lines corresponds to the small value for b_2. That the three lines for the drug treatment groups are not parallel—the differences between lines are not constant—indicates the interaction between drug and enzyme variables. In particular, the crossing of the Drug A and Drug B lines corresponds to the statistically significant value of b_5 ($X_5 = X_2X_3$ which asks whether the difference between the Drug A and Drug B lines is constant or dependent on the presence of Enzyme E). The relatively large difference between the two enzyme lines in Exhibit 12.13 similarly corresponds to the large value of b_3 and the nonparallelism corresponds to the statistically significant value of b_5. Each of these graphs depicts the interaction, but from different perspectives just as we were able to examine the interaction from different perspectives in each of the interpretation strategies presented above.

EXHIBIT 12.12 ▶

Cell means for mood scores by enzyme and drug

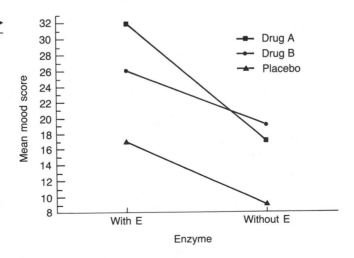

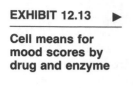

EXHIBIT 12.13 ▶

Cell means for mood scores by drug and enzyme

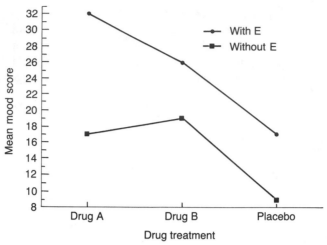

12.4

Higher-Order ANOVA

Our strategy for dealing with two-way analysis of variance is to generate an appropriate set of contrast codes and then do the statistical analysis exactly as we did for one-way ANOVA. We can use that same strategy when we have three or more categorical variables. Once we have an appropriate set of contrast codes for an experimental design with more than two categorical variables, the statistical analysis proceeds just as before. We therefore only need to learn a procedure for generating the appropriate codes. That procedure is a generalization of the procedure we used for two-way. For a factorial design of q categorical variables, the appropriate contrast codes are constructed according to the following rules:

1. For each of the q categorical variables, develop a set of one-way contrast codes.

2. For each *pair* of categorical variables, construct additional contrast codes by multiplying all possible pairs of contrast codes, one from each categorical variable.

3. For each *triple* of categorical variables, construct additional contrast codes by multiplying all possible triads of contrast codes, one from each categorical variable.

4. Continue this procedure for each *quadruple, quintuple,* etc., until products are formed using codes from all q categorical variables simultaneously.

If $k_1, k_2, \ldots, k_l, \ldots, k_q$ are the respective number of categories for each of the q categorical variables, then the above algorithm for generating contrast codes will produce the complete set of

$$\prod_{l=1}^{q} k_l - 1$$

orthogonal codes.

As an example, let's generate an appropriate set of contrast codes for a $4 \times 3 \times 2$ design. There would be a total of $(4)(3)(2) = 24$ different groups or cells in this design, so we will need $24 - 1 = 23$ contrast codes for a complete analysis. To simplify notation, we will refer to the four levels of the first categorical variables as A_1, A_2, A_3, and A_4; the three levels of the second categorical variable as B_1, B_2, and B_3; and the two levels of the third categorical variable as C_1 and C_2. The top portion of Exhibit 12.14 lists the 24 groups defined by the factorial combination of these three categorical variables.

The first step is to form an appropriate set of one-way contrast codes for each categorical variable separately. For the first variable let's assume that there is interest is asking whether the first two levels differ from the last two levels. An appropriate contrast code to ask that question is [1, 1, −1, −1]. There are four levels for Variable A, so we need two additional contrast codes. A useful strategy for generating orthogonal codes is to construct new codes that distinguish between levels that were grouped together in a previous code by having the same value. Thus, two other appropriate codes are [1, −1, 0, 0] and [0, 0, 1, −1]. So the total set of codes for the first variable would be

A_1	A_2	A_3	A_4
1	1	−1	−1
1	−1	0	0
0	0	1	−1

These codes are represented in Exhibit 12.14 as λ_1, λ_2, and λ_3, respectively. For Variable B, let's assume we want to know whether there are linear and quadratic trends. Appropriate codes are therefore

B_1	B_2	B_3
−1	0	1
−1	2	−1

These codes are represented in Exhibit 12.14 as λ_4 and λ_5, respectively. For Variable C with two levels the appropriate code must be

C_1	C_2
1	−1

Table (Exhibit 12.14) — Contrast codes for a 4 × 3 × 2 design. Columns are the 24 groups defined by factors A (1–4), B (1–3), C (1–2); rows are the contrasts λ_1–λ_{23}; the final column is the Sum.

	A	1	1	1	1	1	1	2	2	2	2	2	2	3	3	3	3	3	3	4	4	4	4	4	4	Sum
	B	1	1	2	2	3	3	1	1	2	2	3	3	1	1	2	2	3	3	1	1	2	2	3	3	
	C	1	2	1	2	1	2	1	2	1	2	1	2	1	2	1	2	1	2	1	2	1	2	1	2	
λ_{1}		1	1	1	1	1	1	-1	-1	-1	-1	-1	-1	0	0	0	0	0	0	0	0	0	0	0	0	0
λ_{2}		0	0	0	0	0	0	0	0	0	0	0	0	1	1	1	1	1	1	-1	-1	-1	-1	-1	-1	0
λ_{3}		1	1	1	1	1	1	1	1	1	1	1	1	-1	-1	-1	-1	-1	-1	-1	-1	-1	-1	-1	-1	0
λ_{4}		1	1	-1	-1	0	0	1	1	-1	-1	0	0	1	1	-1	-1	0	0	1	1	-1	-1	0	0	0
λ_{5}		1	1	1	1	-2	-2	1	1	1	1	-2	-2	1	1	1	1	-2	-2	1	1	1	1	-2	-2	0
λ_{6}		1	-1	1	-1	1	-1	1	-1	1	-1	1	-1	1	-1	1	-1	1	-1	1	-1	1	-1	1	-1	0
λ_{7}		1	1	-1	-1	0	0	-1	-1	1	1	0	0	0	0	0	0	0	0	0	0	0	0	0	0	0
λ_{8}		1	1	1	1	-2	-2	-1	-1	-1	-1	2	2	0	0	0	0	0	0	0	0	0	0	0	0	0
λ_{9}		0	0	0	0	0	0	0	0	0	0	0	0	1	1	-1	-1	0	0	-1	-1	1	1	0	0	0
λ_{10}		0	0	0	0	0	0	0	0	0	0	0	0	1	1	1	1	-2	-2	-1	-1	-1	-1	2	2	0
λ_{11}		1	1	-1	-1	0	0	1	1	-1	-1	0	0	-1	-1	1	1	0	0	-1	-1	1	1	0	0	0
λ_{12}		1	1	1	1	-2	-2	1	1	1	1	-2	-2	-1	-1	-1	-1	2	2	-1	-1	-1	-1	2	2	0
λ_{13}		1	-1	1	-1	1	-1	-1	1	-1	1	-1	1	0	0	0	0	0	0	0	0	0	0	0	0	0
λ_{14}		0	0	0	0	0	0	0	0	0	0	0	0	1	-1	1	-1	1	-1	-1	1	-1	1	-1	1	0
λ_{15}		1	-1	1	-1	1	-1	1	-1	1	-1	1	-1	-1	1	-1	1	-1	1	-1	1	-1	1	-1	1	0
λ_{16}		1	-1	-1	1	0	0	1	-1	-1	1	0	0	1	-1	-1	1	0	0	1	-1	-1	1	0	0	0
λ_{17}		1	-1	1	-1	-2	2	1	-1	1	-1	-2	2	1	-1	1	-1	-2	2	1	-1	1	-1	-2	2	0
λ_{18}		1	-1	-1	1	0	0	-1	1	1	-1	0	0	0	0	0	0	0	0	0	0	0	0	0	0	0
λ_{19}		1	-1	1	-1	-2	2	-1	1	-1	1	2	-2	0	0	0	0	0	0	0	0	0	0	0	0	0
λ_{20}		0	0	0	0	0	0	0	0	0	0	0	0	1	-1	-1	1	0	0	-1	1	1	-1	0	0	0
λ_{21}		0	0	0	0	0	0	0	0	0	0	0	0	1	-1	1	-1	-2	2	-1	1	-1	1	2	-2	0
λ_{22}		1	-1	-1	1	0	0	1	-1	-1	1	0	0	-1	1	1	-1	0	0	-1	1	1	-1	0	0	0
λ_{23}		1	-1	1	-1	-2	2	1	-1	1	-1	-2	2	-1	1	-1	1	2	-2	-1	1	-1	1	2	-2	0

EXHIBIT 12.14 ▲

Contrast codes for a 4 × 3 × 2 design

The second step is to generate products of contrast codes for each pair of categorical variables. For the pair (A, B) there are three codes for the first variable and two for the second, so all possible products will generate $(3)(2) = 6$ codes. Those six products are

$$\lambda_7 = \lambda_1\lambda_4$$

$$\lambda_8 = \lambda_1\lambda_5$$

$$\lambda_9 = \lambda_2\lambda_4$$

$$\lambda_{10} = \lambda_2\lambda_5$$

$$\lambda_{11} = \lambda_3\lambda_4$$

$$\lambda_{12} = \lambda_3\lambda_5$$

The codes λ_7 through λ_{12} represent the two-way interactions between variables A and B. Next we generate all products for the pair (A, C). The product codes are

$$\lambda_{13} = \lambda_1\lambda_6$$

$$\lambda_{14} = \lambda_2\lambda_6$$

$$\lambda_{15} = \lambda_3\lambda_6$$

The codes λ_{13} through λ_{15} represent the two-way interactions between variables A and C. Finally, we generate all products for the pair (B, C). The resulting codes are

$$\lambda_{16} = \lambda_4\lambda_6$$

$$\lambda_{17} = \lambda_5\lambda_6$$

The codes λ_{16} and λ_{17} represent the two-way interactions between variables B and C and the codes λ_7 through λ_{17} are all the two-way interactions.

The final step is to generate all products for the three-way interactions (A, B, C). There are three codes for A, two for B, and one for C, so there will be a total of $(3)(2)(1) = 6$ triple products.

$$\lambda_{18} = \lambda_1\lambda_4\lambda_6$$

$$\lambda_{19} = \lambda_1\lambda_5\lambda_6$$

$$\lambda_{20} = \lambda_2\lambda_4\lambda_6$$

$$\lambda_{21} = \lambda_2\lambda_5\lambda_6$$

$$\lambda_{22} = \lambda_3\lambda_4\lambda_6$$

$$\lambda_{23} = \lambda_3\lambda_5\lambda_6$$

Source	df
Between Groups	23
A	3
λ_1	1
λ_2	1
λ_3	1
B	2
λ_4	1
λ_5	1
C	1
λ_6	1
$A \times B$	6
λ_7	1
λ_8	1
λ_9	1
λ_{10}	1
λ_{11}	1
λ_{12}	1
$A \times C$	3
λ_{13}	1
λ_{14}	1
λ_{15}	1
$B \times C$	2
λ_{16}	1
λ_{17}	1

EXHIBIT 12.15 ▲

Schematic source table for 4 × 3 × 2 design

Codes λ_{18} through λ_{23} represent all the three-way interactions. Interpretation of these codes is much the same as the interpretation of two-way codes. For example, let's consider the question asked by λ_{18}. We note that $\lambda_7 = \lambda_1\lambda_4$, so

$$\lambda_{18} = \lambda_1\lambda_4\lambda_6 = \lambda_7\lambda_6$$

Thus, λ_{18} asks whether the answer to the question asked by λ_7 depends on the level of λ_6 or, in other words, does the two-way interaction between variables A and B that is coded by λ_7 depend on the level of Variable C? Just as there were two alternative ways of considering each two-way interaction, there are three alternative ways of considering each three-way interaction. Continuing this example, we note that $\lambda_{13} = \lambda_1\lambda_6$, so

$$\lambda_{18} = \lambda_1\lambda_4\lambda_6 = \lambda_{13}\lambda_4$$

So, equivalently, λ_{18} asks whether the answer to the question asked by λ_{13} depends on the level of λ_4 or, in other words, does the two-way interaction between variables A and C that is coded by λ_{13} depend on the level of Variable B? Finally, noting that $\lambda_{16} = \lambda_4\lambda_6$, we get

$$\lambda_{18} = \lambda_1\lambda_4\lambda_6 = \lambda_1\lambda_{16}$$

Thus, λ_{18} also asks whether the two-way interaction between B and C that is coded by λ_{16} depends on the level of Variable C.

Exhibit 12.15 presents a schematic source table for the $4 \times 3 \times 2$ design; only the source and degrees of freedom are indicated. Each λ row in the source table represents a contrast code and would have its own SSR, F^*, and PRE; these would test a MODEL with all 23 contrast codes against one which left out the indicated code. The F^* for the top row labeled "Between Groups" tests an omnibus MODEL containing all 23 contrast-coded predictors against a simple MODEL with only one parameter. Next, the table groups the one-way contrast codes into omnibus tests of the main effects of Variables A, B, and C, respectively. Next in the table are the two-way contrasts which are also grouped into omnibus tests of the two-way interaction between the categorical variables of AB, AC, and BC, respectively. Finally, the three-way codes are grouped into an omnibus test of the three-way interaction ABC.

The global tests, as for one-way ANOVA, are not generally as useful as the focussed questions represented by the one-degree-of-freedom contrasts. However, the testing of interactions is one instance in which global tests are sometimes useful. The proliferation of interaction contrasts in factorial designs makes testing and interpreting individual contrasts unwieldy. Interpretations of three-way and higher interactions are often so theoretically ad hoc that some data analysts recommended examining only those interactions for which theoretical predictions exist a priori. If the higher-order interactions are not expected and not to be

$A \times B \times C$	6
λ_{18}	1
λ_{19}	1
λ_{20}	1
λ_{21}	1
λ_{22}	1
λ_{23}	1
Within Groups	$N - 24$
Total	$N - 1$

EXHIBIT 12.15 ▲

continued

examined, then it might be better to eliminate them from the analysis and only use those contrasts that will be considered. This effectively includes those eliminated interaction contrast codes in the "Error" term. Rather than eliminating the higher-order interactions outright, a more conservative strategy that is frequently recommended is to do a global test of the higher-order interaction and then pool those contrasts in the Error term only if the null hypothesis is not rejected for the global test. This strategy protects against missing something very unusual in the data while greatly simplifying the data analysis and its presentation. An extra benefit is that the statistical power of the other contrasts will be increased if the F^* for the higher-order interactions is less than 1, because then more will be gained by adding degrees of freedom to the Within-Group (Error) term than will be lost by adding extra SS in that term.

In eliminating interaction terms one must remember the rule from Chapter 10 that products represent interactions only if all the components of the product are included in the MODEL. That means, for example, that if the three-way interactions are retained, then none of the main effect contrasts can be eliminated. Less obviously, it also means that none of the two-way interactions could be eliminated because any three-way interaction can be represented as the product of any of the two-way interactions and one of the main effects (as was demonstrated above for λ_{18}). Thus, if an interaction of a given order is retained, then all the main effects and interactions of lower order must also be included in the MODEL. However, if the three-way interactions were eliminated, then one might also consider whether some of the two-way interactions could be eliminated with a global test.

12.5

Other Details in Factorial ANOVA

In all other details factorial ANOVA with two or more categorical variables is exactly the same as one-way ANOVA with one categorical variable. Specifically, the techniques for asking other questions and for dealing with unequal numbers of observations in each group are the same as those presented in Chapter 11. Below, we briefly consider each of these issues.

12.5.1 Asking Other Questions

It often is not possible to generate a set of orthogonal contrast codes addressing all the theoretical questions that one might want to ask of a given set of data. This is often true for interactions that are of theoretical interest. The choice of the one-way codes for each categorical variable determines the products that are the interaction codes, and the resulting interaction codes may not be the ones of theoretical interest. It is therefore sometimes difficult to ask simultaneously the relevant main effect and interaction questions. For example, in a 2×2 design, there is no choice for the one-way codes for each categorical variable, so there is also no choice for the interaction code which must be the product of the two one-way codes. Thus, the necessary coding is

	A_1B_1	A_1B_2	A_2B_1	A_2B_2
λ_1	1	1	-1	-1
λ_2	1	-1	1	-1
λ_3	1	-1	-1	1

The interaction code λ_3 asks whether the average of the A_1B_1 and A_2B_2 groups equals the average of the other two groups. However, the theoretical question of interest might be whether the mean of one group, say A_2B_2, differs from the average of the other three groups. For example, this question is often of interest when one of the groups is a control condition. If so, the code of interest is $[-1, -1, -1, 3]$. Its SSR can be computed with the usual formula and then compared as a planned comparison (as in Chapter 11) to the mean within group error (MSE) resulting from the analysis of variance using λ_1 through λ_3.

Other questions may also present themselves after the initial analysis. We can use the same post hoc comparison procedures we used in Chapter 11 because statistically q-way ANCVA is the same as one-way ANOVA. For example, in the mood score data whether Drug A was better than Drug B depended on whether the patient had Enzyme E or not. Looking at the means, it appears that Drug A, instead of Drug B, should be given to depressed patients who have Enzyme E. But before making such a recommendation we ought to check it with a post hoc comparison. Comparisons such as this between categories (Drug A versus Drug B) of one variable within a single level (Enzyme E) of another variable are known as *simple effects*. Let's do the calculation for this comparison as an example. The λ coefficient for the Drug A, Enzyme E group will be $+1$ and for the Drug B, Enzyme E group will be -1; so

$$\text{SSR} = \frac{(\Sigma_k \lambda_k \overline{Y}_k)^2}{\Sigma_k \lambda_{1k}^2 / n_k} = \frac{(32 - 26)^2}{1/3 + 1/3} = 54$$

The MSError (from Exhibit 12.4 or 12.7) is 4.2, so

$$F^* = \frac{\text{SSR}}{\text{MSE}} = \frac{54}{4.2} = 12.86$$

and the comparison of a MODEL with a complete set of orthogonal contrast codes, including this one, to a MODEL which omitted just this code yields

$$\text{PRE} = \frac{\text{SSR}}{\text{SSR} + \text{SSE(A)}} = \frac{54}{54 + 50} = .52$$

If this were not a planned comparison, then it would be advisable to compare F^* with the Scheffé adjusted critical value of

$$(m - 1)F_{m-1, n-\text{PA};\alpha} = 5F_{5,12;.05} = 5(3.11) = 15.55$$

$F^* = 12.86$ is below the adjusted critical value, so we would not be able to conclude for a post hoc comparison that Drug A was reliably better than Drug B for those patients who have Enzyme E.

12.5.2 Unequal Number of Observations

It is always best, in order to maximize power, to plan factorial designs with equal numbers of observations in each group. However, equal numbers of observations are not always possible. For example, data for one or two observations might be unavoidably lost due to technical problems such as instrument failure or the number of observations in each group might not be easily controllable such as in survey research. There is an unfortunate folklore in the social sciences that unequal numbers of observations are disastrous for factorial designs. This folklore is undoubtedly due to the fact that many old ANOVA computer programs required equal group sizes. However, the problem of unequal numbers of observations is exactly the same as with one-way ANOVA and hence is no more serious.

The problem is that even with orthogonal contrast codes unequal numbers of observations induce correlations among the contrast-coded predictors. Thus, the predictors used in the analysis will be somewhat redundant with each other, and that means that the answers to the questions posed by each contrast will not be independent of each other. If only a few observations are missing from a few cells, the effect of the redundancy is likely to be of little consequence. If the cell sizes are very different, then the redundancy effects can be very large. In any case, the best strategy is to use a standard regression program to compute the *tolerance*, as defined in Chapter 8, for each predictor variable. Those predictors with low tolerances would be asking a question closely related to other questions already asked.

The question asked by a particular contrast does not depend on whether or not there are equal numbers of observations in each group so long as (1) *a complete set of contrasts is used in the analysis and* (2) *there are no groups which have no observations.* For example, if one or two observations had been missing from the mood score data example we used in the beginning of this chapter, the test of whether or not $\beta_j = 0$ could be expressed in terms of the same differences between group means as before. The problem of analyzing designs with missing groups is that some effects will be perfectly confounded with each other so that some effects may not be testable at all.

Note the importance of using a complete set of contrast codes when there are unequal numbers of observations in each group. If not, for example if some higher-order interactions are omitted as suggested in the previous section, then the predicted values from the MODEL will no longer be the group means. In that case, the contrast codes would ask questions different from those intended. Thus, the best strategy is always to use a complete set of contrast codes when group n's are unequal.

One nuisance introduced by unequal numbers of observations is that the SSRs for the individual contrast-coded predictors do not sum to give the SSR for groups of predictors. For example, in the two-way ANOVA of the mood score data summarized in Exhibit 12.7, if there were one or two missing observations there would be no guarantee that the SSRs for X_1 and X_2 would sum to the total effect for the Drug variable. To determine that SSR, you would need to compare directly a MODEL A that used all the predictors to a MODEL C that omitted *both* X_1 and X_2.

12.6

Power in Factorial ANOVA

There are two issues to consider with respect to power in two-way and, in general, in q-way ANOVA. First, how is the power affected for questions we ask about a given variable when additional categorical variables are added to the analysis? Second, how do we estimate the statistical power for particular questions we want to ask? We consider each question in turn.

As an example let's again consider the mood score data of Exhibit 12.1. If we were mainly interested in the questions about the effects of the drugs, we could have performed a one-way analysis of variance on these data, completely ignoring the Enzyme E variable. If we ignored the enzyme categories, we would have three groups—Drug A, Drug B, and Placebo—each with six observations. The respective means would be $(32 + 17)/2 = 24.5$, $(26 + 19)/2 = 22.5$, and $(17 + 9)/2 = 13$. The two contrast codes would be $(1, 1, -2)$ and $(1, -1, 0)$. Applying the usual formulas from Chapter 11, we obtain $\beta_1 = 3.5$ with SSR $= 441$ and $\beta_2 = 1$ with SSR $= 12$, exactly the same values as before. However, PRE and F^* would change if we were to ignore the categorical variable for

Enzyme E, because then testing the null hypothesis $\beta_1 = 0$ would be comparing

MODEL A: $Y_i = \beta_0 + \beta_1 X_1 + \beta_2 X_2 + \varepsilon_i$

MODEL C: $Y_i = \beta_0 + \beta_2 X_2$

This is a different question from the question asked when testing $\beta_1 = 0$ in the complete two-way analysis. There is no reason therefore to expect the statistical power for the two questions to be the same.

To see the likely changes in power due to ignoring the other categorical variable, let's consider Exhibit 12.16, which presents the complete source table for the one-way analysis of variance ignoring the enzyme variable. The parameter estimates, the sums of squares, the degrees of freedom, and the mean squares are exactly as they were in Exhibit 12.7. However, the error sum of squares and the error degrees of freedom have increased substantially. The reason is that the sums of squares that were reduced by X_3, X_4, and X_5 in the two-way analysis are now included in the error because those predictors are not used in this analysis. Given the same SSRs for X_1 and X_2 and increased SSE, then the F^*'s and PREs must be considerably less than they were before. For example, in the complete two-way analysis of Exhibit 12.7, for X_1 $F^*_{1,12} = 105.8$ and PRE = .90, but in the one-way analysis only considering the drug treatment variable, $F^*_{1,15} = 11.9$ and PRE = .44. The differences between the means for Drug A, Drug B, and Placebo have not changed, so clearly the two-way analysis provided considerably more statistical power for testing $\beta_1 = 0$ and $\beta_2 = 0$. This increase in power is generally the case in multiway analysis of variance. Using one or more other categorical variables to reduce SSE allows a more powerful test of hypotheses concerning another categorical variable. The only situation for which there

EXHIBIT 12.16 ▶

One-way analysis of variance of mood scores ignoring the enzyme variable

Source	b_j	SS	df	MS	F^*	p	PRE
Between Groups (Drug)		453	2	226.5	6.1	.012	.45
X_1	3.5	441	1	441	11.9	.004	.44
X_2	1.0	12	1	12	.3	.58	.02
Within Groups		557	15	37.1			
Total		1010	17				

would be a decrease in statistical power would be if the F^*'s for the codes of the additional variables and the codes for the interactions were less than 1.0. If $F^* < 1.0$ for a contrast, then the proportional reduction in error associated with that contrast is less than we would expect for a randomly chosen parameter. Hence, including that contrast-coded predictor would not be worth the loss of a degree of freedom due to the extra parameter, so power goes down.

The second power issue concerns estimating statistical power for analysis of variance or finding the sample size which will ensure an adequate power level. The power table in Appendix C requires us to have an estimate of η^2. Just as was the case in Chapter 5, there are several ways to obtain this estimate. First, with sufficient experience in a research domain, researchers often know what values of PRE are important or meaningful in that domain. Those values of PRE from experience can be used directly in the power table of Appendix C. For example, if based on past experience we thought that important effects had PREs greater than or equal to .1, and if we used a 3×3 design (for a total of nine groups) with six observations per group, then we would enter Exhibit C.5 in Appendix C in the row for $n - \text{PA} = (9 \times 6) - 9 = 45$ and the column for $\eta^2 = .1$ to find that the power—the probability of rejecting the null hypothesis—for each one-degree-of-freedom contrast is at least .59. If we wanted to ensure a power of at least .9 for detecting an η^2 of .1, then $n - \text{PA} = n - 9$ would need to be about 100, so n would need to be about $100 + 9 = 109$; dividing 109/9 yields the answer of about 12 observations per group to ensure power greater than .9.

In using the results of past studies, remember that calculated values of PRE are biased overestimates of η^2. To remove the bias, use the same formula we used in Chapter 5. That is,

$$\text{Estimate of } \eta^2 = 1 - (1 - \text{PRE})\left[\frac{n - \text{PC}}{n - \text{PA}}\right]$$

For the one-degree-of-freedom tests of focused contrasts which we recommend, the compact and augmented models differ by one parameter so $\text{PA} = \text{PC} + 1$. Thus, the above adjustment reduces to

$$\text{Estimate of } \eta^2 = 1 - (1 - \text{PRE})\left[\frac{n - \text{PA} + 1}{n - \text{PA}}\right]$$

As an example, the PRE calculated for X_5 in Exhibit 12.7 was .49, so the estimated η^2 for that interaction contrast is

$$1 - (1 - .49)\left[\frac{18 - 6 + 1}{18 - 6}\right] = 1 - (.51)\left[\frac{13}{12}\right] = .45$$

For n large relative to PA, the adjustment will be negligible. The adjustment essentially corrects for the ability of least squares to capitalize on chance for small sample sizes. However, small sample sizes are not unusual in analysis of variance designs, so this adjustment is sometimes important.

A second and related method for finding appropriate values of η^2 is to use the suggested values from Chapter 5 for "small" ($\eta^2 = .03$), "medium" ($\eta^2 = .1$), and "large" ($\eta^2 = .30$) effects. As an example of this approach, let's estimate the power for the two-way analysis of variance for the mood score data. With six parameters (β_0 through β_5) and six groups with three observations each, $n - PA = (6 \times 3) - 6 = 12$. Using the column for $\eta^2 = .3$ and the row for $n - PA = 12$ in Exhibit C.5 of Appendix C we see that the probability of rejecting a hypothesis that $\beta_j = 0$ is about .55 for a "large" effect.

A third approach, also introduced in Chapter 5, is to use expectations about the means and the within-cell variance to estimate η^2. To have reasonable expectations about the means and variance generally requires as much or more experience in a research domain as is necessary to know typical values of η^2. Thus, this third approach is often less useful than the first. We present this approach anyway in order to be complete and because the derivation of this approach provides useful insights about the meaning of PRE and η^2 in the analysis of variance. Also, this approach requires describing in detail the data one expects to obtain and that exercise can often be useful in identifying flawed research designs.

We begin with our usual definition of PRE:

$$ PRE = \frac{SSE(C) - SSE(A)}{SSE(C)} = \frac{SSR}{SSE(C)} $$

We have noted before that $SSE(C) = SSE(A) + SSR$ (i.e., the error for the compact model includes all the error of the augmented model plus the error that was reduced by the addition of the extra parameters in the augmented model). Hence,

$$ PRE = \frac{SSR}{SSE(A) + SSR} = \frac{1}{SSE(A)/SSR + 1} $$

To obtain a definition of η^2, we simply calculate $SSE(A)$ and SSR using the true parameter values (β_0, β_1, etc., σ^2) instead of the estimated parameters (b_0, b_1, etc., s^2). We can use the true parameter values for the individual group means, the μ_k's, to obtain

$$ SSR \text{ for a Contrast} = \frac{[\sum \lambda_k \mu_k]^2}{\sum \lambda_k^2/n_k} $$

For a complete model, $SSE(A)$ depends only on σ^2, the within-cell variance. Specifically,

$$ SSE(A) = \left(\sum_k n_k \right) \sigma^2 = N\sigma^2 $$

where N is the grand total of observations. We multiply by N instead of by $N - PA$ because we have not estimated any parameters from data in the calculation of SSE(A). Substituting these values for SSR and SSE(A) calculated from the presumed true parameters into the formula for PRE yields this formula for η^2:

$$\eta^2 = \left(\frac{N\sigma^2(\Sigma\ \lambda_k^2/n_k)}{[\Sigma\ \lambda_k\mu_k]^2} + 1\right)^{-1}$$

If n_k, the number of observations in each group, is equal for all k and if m is the number of groups in the factorial design so that $N = mn_k$, then the formula for η^2 reduces to

$$\eta^2 = \left(\frac{m\sigma^2\ \Sigma\ \lambda_k^2}{[\Sigma\ \lambda_k\mu_k]^2} + 1\right)^{1}$$

which does not depend on either the total number of observations or the number of observations in each group. Therefore, to find a value for η^2 to use in our power calculations, we need only specify the values for σ^2 and for the μ_k's which we expect to obtain in our experiment. The λ_k's specify the contrast code for which we want to estimate the power.

As an example of the direct approach for calculating η^2, suppose we are conducting a study of the effects of competition and cooperation on classroom learning, and we wish to assess whether competition and cooperation are differentially effective depending on the ability of the student. On the basis of standardized tests we divide students into two groups of high and low ability and randomly assign half of each group to the competition condition and the other half to the cooperation condition. Suppose further that we expected the means of Exhibit 12.17 on our performance task, and we were interested in the contrast code defined in Exhibit 12.17, which tests the interaction between condition and student ability. If we also expected a within-cell variance of about 10, then our expectations about the size of the effect represented by the means of Exhibit 12.17 would correspond to the following η^2:

$$\eta^2 = \left(\frac{(4)(10)(4)}{[5 - 10 - 15 + 12]^2} + 1\right)^{-1} = .286$$

EXHIBIT 12.17 ▶

Expected means and interaction contrast code for a hypothetical experiment

	Expected Means		Interaction Contrast Code	
Ability	Comp	Coop	Comp	Coop
Low	5	10	1	−1
Hi	15	12	−1	1

Given that the estimates of σ^2 and the μ_k's are necessarily approximate, we can use $\eta^2 = .3$ as an approximation to .286 to find the approximate power for this study using Exhibit C.5 in Appendix C. If we wanted to ensure power equal to about .90, then $N - PA$ would need to equal about 28, so N would be about 32. Dividing these 32 observations evenly across the four groups yields a requirement of about eight observations for each group. If we knew that a maximum of only six observations per group were feasible, then $N = 24$ and $N - PA = 20$, so the power to detect an effect as large as the one represented by the above means would be about .8.

12.7

Summary

In a factorial design, there are two or more categorical predictor variables, and all levels of each categorical variable are combined with all levels of other categorical variables. We analyze data from a two-way or higher-order factorial design by applying the one-way analysis of variance techniques from Chapter 11 to an appropriate set of contrast codes. This set of codes is generated by developing separate sets of one-way contrast codes for each categorical variable and then forming appropriate products among these codes to represent the interaction between categorical variables. Interpretation of the interaction contrasts can be difficult but can be accomplished using the techniques of Chapter 10 for interpreting products or by using several other techniques introduced in this chapter.

13

ANCOVA: Models with Continuous and Categorical Predictors

The material covered in this chapter represents an integration of the materials covered in Chapters 8 and 12. In Chapter 8 we considered models with continuous predictors. Chapter 12 was concerned with models with categorical predictors. We will now consider models that include both sorts of predictors. Such models are more traditionally covered under the heading of analysis of covariance. We feel that this is a confusing label for these models and prefer to think of them simply as models involving both categorical and continuous predictor variables.

In Chapter 10, we saw that a simple extension of models with continuous predictors included products of those predictors, or interactions between them, as predictors as well. Similarly, in the last chapter we considered as predictors interactions among categorical predictor variables. By extension, we will also consider in this chapter models that include not only categorical and continuous predictors but also interactions between the two sorts of predictor variables.

Interest in these sorts of models originally developed within the tradition of methods for the analysis of experimental and quasi-experimental research designs. In this tradition, researchers were primarily interested in the effects of experimental factors, or the categorical predictor variables, and wished to estimate those effects while controlling for some continuously measured concomitant variable, called a *covariate*.

As is detailed below, this control might be desired because of the increase in power that such control might produce or because the concomitant variable was redundant with the categorical ones. Models involving both categorical and continuous predictor variables have, however, a wide range of application outside of experimental research designs. For instance, in sociology or political science, one might be interested in the effects of both a categorical variable (e.g., sex) and a continuous one (e.g., personal income) on some dependent variable, and might wish to estimate each of these effects controlling for the other. In other words, the focus in these models need not be on the effects of the categorical variables and what happens to those effects when a continuous predictor variable is controlled. We might be just as interested in the effects of the continuous predictor variable and how those effects change when we control for a categorical one.

Given the historical tradition of these models within the context of experimental design, we start the chapter by illustrating the use of models with both categorical and continuous predictors within the context of an experimental design, where the primary interest is in the effects of the categorical variables. We use this context in order to illustrate reasons why we might want to control for a continuously measured concomitant variable. In later sections of the chapter, we illustrate the use of these models in a context where the researcher's interest is primarily in the effects of the continuous predictor when a categorical one is controlled.

13.1

Controlling for a Continuous Variable in a Factorial Design

13.1.1 The Case of an Orthogonal Continuous Variable

Suppose we were evaluating a curriculum innovation in a secondary school. Students were randomly assigned to either the new or the old curriculum. In addition, each curriculum was taught by two different teachers, and students were assigned to one of the two teachers on a random basis. Thus, the experimental design is a two-factor crossed design, with two levels of both the curriculum and teacher factors. Ten students have been randomly assigned to each of the resulting four conditions. The dependent variable is the student's score on a standardized achievement test given at the end of the curriculum. In addition, we have a pretest measure from each student, indicating his or her achievement in the domain in question prior to exposure to either the new or old curriculum. The hypothetical raw data are given in Exhibit

13.1. The variable Z_i represents each student's pretest achievement score. The X_{i1} variable is a contrast-coded variable that codes curriculum (-1 if old; 1 if new); X_{i2} is a contrast-coded variable that codes teacher (-1 if teacher A; 1 if teacher B); and Y_i represents each student's posttest achievement score.

The cell means for both Z_i and Y_i are given in Exhibit 13.2. Notice that the data have been constructed so that all four pretest means equal 50. Since students have been randomly assigned to the four treatment conditions after they took the pretest, we would expect their mean pretest scores to be very similar, although the chances are that they would not all be identical as we have here constructed them to be for didactic purposes.

EXHIBIT 13.1 ▶

Hypothetical experimental data

Y_i	X_{i1}	X_{i2}	Z_i	Y_i	X_{i1}	X_{i2}	Z_i
58	1	−1	50	57	1	−1	49
63	1	−1	49	61	1	−1	52
65	1	−1	53	57	1	−1	50
56	1	−1	47	67	1	−1	51
60	1	−1	53	56	1	−1	46
50	−1	−1	49	62	−1	−1	54
58	−1	−1	51	55	−1	−1	48
52	−1	−1	50	63	−1	−1	52
55	−1	−1	47	50	−1	−1	46
57	−1	−1	52	58	−1	−1	51
61	1	1	47	59	1	1	49
71	1	1	53	65	1	1	54
68	1	1	52	60	1	1	46
58	1	1	48	65	1	1	51
68	1	1	51	65	1	1	49
47	−1	1	46	62	−1	1	51
56	−1	1	51	51	−1	1	49
63	−1	1	53	54	−1	1	51
53	−1	1	48	58	−1	1	50
52	−1	1	47	54	−1	1	54

EXHIBIT 13.2 ▶

Pretest and posttest means by condition

Condition	Pretest	Posttest
Old Curr., Teacher A	50	56
Old Curr., Teacher B	50	55
New Curr., Teacher A	50	60
New Curr., Teacher B	50	64

The reason for constructing these data with equal pretest means is that as a result the pretest is not correlated with condition. To see this, suppose we regressed the pretest Z_i on X_{i1}, X_{i2}, and their interaction. With all three contrast codes as predictors, the predicted values of Z_i would equal the four cell means. Each of these cell means also equals the grand mean. Hence, a model with all three contrast codes as predictors generates no better predictions than a simple model in which we predict the grand mean for each case. As a result, condition is entirely unrelated to pretest.

Let us conduct a straightforward two-way analysis of variance on the posttest data, ignoring the pretest variable for the moment. We regress Y_i on X_{i1}, X_{i2}, and X_{i3}, where X_{i3} is the interaction contrast code, formed by multiplying X_{i1} and X_{i2} together. The resulting model is

$$\hat{Y}_i = 58.75 + 3.25X_{i1} + .75X_{i2} + 1.25X_{i3} \qquad \text{SSE} = 710$$

The value of the regression coefficient for X_{i1}, 3.25, equals half the difference between the average of the two mean values of Y_i under the new curriculum and the average of the two mean values of Y_i under the old curriculum. The regression coefficient for X_{i2}, .75, equals half the difference between the average under teacher B and the average under teacher A. The regression coefficient for the interaction, 1.25, equals half the difference between the average of the old curriculum, teacher A and the new curriculum, teacher B conditions and the average of the old curriculum, teacher B and the new curriculum, teacher A conditions. Conceptually it tells us the extent to which the curriculum difference for teacher B is different from the curriculum difference for teacher A.

We can calculate the sum of squares due to each contrast code by computing a series of compact models that omit each contrast code in turn. Alternatively, we can use the contrast sum of squares formula we have used before:

$$\frac{(\Sigma_k \lambda_k \overline{Y}_k)^2}{\Sigma_k (\lambda_k^2/n_k)}$$

Accordingly, the sum of squares explained by X_{i1} equals 422.5, that explained by X_{i2} equals 22.5, and that explained by X_{i3} equals 62.5. Since we have 10 observations in each of the four conditions, these sums of squares add up to the between condition sum of squares. The analysis of variance source table of Exhibit 13.3 results from these calculations.

In this analysis, we have made no use of the pretest Z_i. We might decide to add it as a predictor to the model for a number of different reasons. For instance, we might be interested in asking how curriculum and teacher affect posttest performance when we control for the pretest or when we look within levels of the pretest. In other words, we might be interested in these effects over and above differences in performance

EXHIBIT 13.3 ▶

Two-way analysis of variance source table

Source	b	SS	df	MS	F*	PRE
Between or Model		507.5	3	169.17	8.58	.42
Curriculum	3.25	422.5	1	422.50	21.42	.37
Teacher	.75	22.5	1	22.50	1.14	.03
Curr. X Teacher	1.25	62.5	1	62.50	3.17	.08
Error		710.0	36	19.72		
Total		1217.5	39			

that existed at the time of the pretest. A seemingly different reason for including it as a predictor in the model is that we might expect it to be highly correlated with the posttest, since presumably it is only an earlier version of the posttest, measuring the same domain of achievement. If this is so, then, as we shall see, it might make our tests of curriculum and teacher effects considerably more powerful.

In these data the pretest scores are highly related to the posttest scores. The sum of squared errors from a simple regression model in which Y_i is regressed on Z_i equals 855.57. From the source table of Exhibit 13.3 we see that the sum of squares of Y_i for the simplest single-parameter model equals 1217.5. Accordingly, a comparison between the two-parameter simple-regression model using Z_i to predict Y_i and a one-parameter model yields a PRE of .297 and $F^*_{(1,38)} = 16.05$. Thus, the relationship between the pretest and the posttest is substantial and highly reliable.

As we have seen, the pretest Z_i is uncorrelated with condition, since all of the pretest conditions means are identical. Accordingly, the sum of squares explained by Z_i should not overlap with the sums of squares explainable by the three condition contrast codes. Since the sum of squares explained by these three contrast codes equals 507.5, the sum of squares explained by Z_i equals 361.93, and Z_i is orthogonal to the three contrast-coded predictors, then the sum of squares explained by the pretest, Z_i, *plus* the three contrast codes ought to equal 507.5 + 361.93 or 869.43. Accordingly, the sum of squared errors for a model in which Y_i is regressed on Z_i, X_{i1}, X_{i2}, and X_{i3} should equal 1217.5 − 869.43 or 348.07.

In the analysis of variance source table of Exhibit 13.3, the denominator for each of the F^* statistics testing the reliability of the condition differences equals the mean square error within or the mean square error from the final augmented model that includes all predictor variables. If we include the pretest Z_i as an additional predictor, this mean square error ought to be reduced substantially due to the fact that the sum of squares potentially explainable by Z_i has been controlled for or removed from the sum of squared errors. Thus, by including Z_i as an additional predictor in the model, we would expect our tests of condition differences in Y_i to be more powerful, yielding larger F^* values.

The resulting augmented model is

$$\hat{Y}_i = -4.52 + 1.27Z_i + 3.25X_{i1} + .75X_{i2} + 1.25X_{i3} \qquad \text{SSE} = 348.07$$

Notice that the coefficients in this model for the three contrast-coded predictors have not changed. Since Z_i is uncorrelated with all of these predictors, its inclusion has no effect on the value of these coefficients nor on their interpretation. The coefficient for X_{i1} continues to tell us about the magnitude of the difference in Y_i due to curriculum. The coefficient for X_{i2} continues to tell us about the magnitude of the teacher difference. And the coefficient for X_{i3} continues to estimate the magnitude of the curriculum by teacher interaction.

We could test the reliability of the coefficient for Z_i by comparing this augmented model to the model presented earlier that included only the contrast-coded predictors. The value of PRE that results from this comparison is

$$\frac{710.00 - 348.07}{710.00} = .510$$

with an associated F^* statistic of

$$F^*_{(1,35)} = \frac{.510/1}{(1 - .510)/35} = 36.39$$

Accordingly, we can conclude that independent of condition, or on average within condition, one's pretest score reliably relates to one's posttest score.

We can test the reliability of the condition differences by testing the regression coefficients in this model for each of the three contrast-coded predictors. Let us start with the omnibus test of whether there are any differences in the condition means of Y_i. To do this test, we want to compare the augmented model that includes Z_i and the three contrast-coded predictors with a compact one that includes only Z_i. We have already said that the sum of squared errors from this compact simple regression model equals 855.57. Accordingly the value of PRE for the omnibus test equals

$$\frac{855.57 - 348.07}{855.57} = .593$$

And the omnibus F^* statistic, having 3 and 35 degrees of freedom, equals

$$F^*_{(3,35)} = \frac{.593/3}{(1 - .593)/35} = 17.09$$

An equivalent expression for this F^* statistic is given in terms of the sums of squares:

$$F^*_{(3,35)} = \frac{507.50/3}{348.07/35} = 17.09$$

where 507.50 is the reduction in the sum of squared errors as we move from the compact to the augmented model, and 348.07 is the sum of squared errors of the augmented model. Notice that this F^* statistic is nearly twice as large as the F^* statistic for the omnibus test based on the augmented model that did not include the pretest as a predictor. The reason for this difference is that the sum of squared errors from the augmented model is now considerably less than it was without the pretest included. It is also true that the degrees of freedom for error have been reduced by 1 as a result of the additional parameter for the pretest estimated in the augmented model. In combination, however, the substantially smaller sum of squared errors and the slightly smaller degrees of freedom for error result in a considerably smaller mean square error. In other words, the denominator of the F^* ratio for the omnibus test of condition differences when the pretest is included equals 348.07/35 or 9.94. In the model that did not include the pretest, the denominator of the F^* ratio for the omnibus test of condition differences equaled 710.0/36 or 19.72. The net result of including the pretest as a predictor, then, has been to reduce the mean square error and increase the power of tests of the condition effects. Such an increase in power will happen whenever there is a reliable relationship between the continuously measured predictor variable, in this case the pretest, and the dependent variable in the augmented model that includes the categorical predictor variables. The full source table for the model that includes the pretest and all three contrast codes is given in Exhibit 13.4. Let us compare this source table with the analysis of variance source table of Exhibit 13.3.

EXHIBIT 13.4 ▶

Analysis of covariance source table

Source	b	SS	df	MS	F*	PRE
Model		869.43	4	217.36	21.87	.71
Pretest	1.27	361.93	1	361.93	36.39	.51
Between Conditions		507.50	3	169.17	17.09	.59
Curriculum	3.25	422.50	1	422.50	42.48	.55
Teacher	.75	22.50	1	22.50	2.26	.06
Curr. X Teacher	1.25	62.50	1	62.50	6.28	.15
Error		348.07	35	9.94		
Total		1217.50	39			

First, notice that the test of the overall model, comparing this model that includes four predictor variables, with the single parameter model that includes no predictors, yields substantially higher values of both PRE and F^* than the test of the overall model that did not include the pretest. These larger values are entirely attributable to the fact that the pretest is highly related to the dependent variable. Accordingly, the sum of squares attributable to the model, 869.43, has dramatically increased from the analysis of variance table, while the error sum of squares has dramatically decreased. The decrease in the sum of squared errors for the model, and equivalently the increase in the sum of squares explained by the model, is exactly equal to the sum of squares associated with the pretest, i.e., 361.93.

Second, notice that the rows for the three contrast-coded variables, representing curriculum, teacher, and their interaction, have the same sums of squares, degrees of freedom, and mean squares as they did in the analysis of variance source table. Because the pretest is unrelated to curriculum, teacher, and their interaction, neither the regression coefficients for these contrast-coded predictor variables nor their sums of squares are affected by the inclusion of the pretest in the model. The inclusion of the pretest, however, does have a major effect on the row in the source table referring to error in the model, as just described. As a result, all of the F^* statistics used to test the teacher effect, curriculum effect, and the interaction effect on the posttest dependent variable are substantially larger than they were in the analysis of variance source table of Exhibit 13.3. Whereas the curriculum by teacher interaction was not significant in the analysis of variance source table, it now is. The positive coefficient associated with this interaction contrast code tells us that the new-old curriculum difference, while reliable on average across teachers, is reliably larger for teacher B than it is for teacher A.

This analysis has illustrated one of the major reasons for including a continuously measured predictor variable (equivalently called a co-variate) in randomized experimental research designs. If that predictor variable is measured prior to randomization of subjects to conditions, on average it will be unrelated to the contrast-coded variables that code experimental condition. The purpose of including such a variable is to increase the power of the analysis that tests for condition differences in the dependent variable. If the covariate is in fact unrelated to condition, then neither the regression coefficients for the various contrast-coded predictors that code condition differences nor their sums of squares will be affected by its inclusion in the model. The null hypothesis associated with the test of a given contrast-coded predictor will also not change. Regardless of the inclusion of the covariate, we will still be testing for differences among the condition means on the dependent variable, as coded by the λ_k's. Tests for condition differences will be more powerful as a result of including a covariate whenever the test of whether the covariate's regression coefficient in the full augmented model differs from zero yields a reliable F^* statistic. When the covariate is unrelated to the dependent variable, then the decrease in sum of squared errors resulting from the inclusion of the covariate will not offset the decrease of the degrees of freedom for error in the model. The ideal covariate, therefore, in this situation, is one that is as highly associated as possible with the dependent variable controlling for the categorical variables or within levels of the categorical variables.

Even with random assignment of subjects to condition after measuring the covariate, it will almost never be the case that the covariate will be completely orthogonal to the condition contrast codes. In other words, it will be a very rare event for all of the pretest or covariate means in the various experimental conditions to be identical. Our example, then, is obviously a constructed one, designed simply to illustrate what happens in the pure case, when the covariate is completely independent of condition. In any given study, there will in all probability be some nonsignificant relationships between the covariate and the contrast codes that represent condition. Nevertheless, the inclusion of a covariate will increase the statistical power of tests of condition differences, given a covariate that is reliably related to the dependent variable within levels of the categorical variables.

As we said in the introduction to this chapter, within the context of experimental designs, the usual interest in including a continuously measured predictor variable with a set of categorical ones is to examine what happens to tests of condition differences when we control for the continuously measured covariate. As we have seen, with a covariate measured prior to random assignment of subjects to condition, the result will generally be an increase in statistical power for tests of condition differences. There is no necessary reason, however, for confining our interpretations of the model that includes both kinds of predictors to this typical interest. In other words, there is nothing to prevent us from turning the interpretation of this model around—concentrating not on the tests of mean differences while controlling for the covariate, but on a test of the pretest-posttest relationship while controlling for condition differences on the posttest. If we simply regress the posttest on the pretest, the pretest's regression coefficient equals 1.27. The sum of squared errors for this simple regression model equals 855.57. A test of the simple pretest-posttest relationship yields a PRE of .297 and an $F^*_{(1,38)}$ of 16.05. When we examine the pretest-posttest relationship controlling for the categorical variables, as given in the ANCOVA source table of Exhibit 13.4, the pretest's coefficient is still 1.27, but a test of whether it is reliably related to the posttest within condition levels yields a PRE of .51 and an F^* of 36.39 with 1 and 35 degrees of freedom. Thus, we might equivalently look at this analysis as a way of increasing the power of tests of the pretest-posttest relationship by controlling for experimental condition.

13.1.2   Analysis of Posttest-Pretest Difference Scores

In giving a rationale for the analysis that includes pretest as a predictor, we suggested that it might make sense to examine the effects of curriculum and teacher on the posttest controlling for pretest differences or holding constant pretest performance. It might seem that an equivalent way of doing this analysis would be to examine condition differences in improvement from the pretest to the posttest. To do such an analysis, we might logically compute a new dependent variable equal to $Y_i - Z_i$. This *difference score* tells us about each individual's improvement in achievement during the course of the study. We would then be interested in condition differences in the mean $Y_i - Z_i$ difference scores. Since all Z_i condition means are identical, the mean differences among conditions on the $Y_i - Z_i$ difference scores will be equivalent to the mean differences among conditions on Y_i.

To examine condition effects on this improvement difference score, let us regress it on the three contrast-coded predictors that define condition. The following estimated parameters result:

$$\widehat{(Y_i - Z_i)} = 8.75 + 3.25X_{i1} + .75X_{i2} + 1.25X_{i3} \qquad \text{SSE} = 364.00$$

The intercept in this model equals the unweighted grand mean difference score or, equivalently, the difference between the unweighted grand mean of Y_i and the unweighted grand mean of Z_i. Somewhat surprisingly, perhaps, the regression coefficients for the three contrast codes have not changed as a result of changing the dependent variable to the $Y_i - Z_i$ difference score. Both in this difference score analysis and in the analysis where the posttest was the dependent variable and the pretest was included as a predictor, the regression coefficients continue to equal what they did in the simple analysis of variance with Y_i as the dependent variable and no pretest. This invariance is once again due to the fact that the pretest is uncorrelated with condition.

To illustrate algebraically why these regression coefficients have not changed, let us examine the algebraic expression for the regression coefficients in this difference score analysis. It equals

$$\frac{\Sigma_k \lambda_k (\overline{Y}_k - \overline{Z}_k)}{\Sigma_k \lambda_k^2}$$

which can be expressed equivalently as

$$\frac{\Sigma_k \lambda_k \overline{Y}_k - \Sigma_k \lambda_k \overline{Z}_k}{\Sigma_k \lambda_k^2}$$

Since all $\bar{Z}_k$ are identical, the expression $\Sigma_k \lambda_k \bar{Z}_k$ equals zero and this expression for the regression coefficient reduces to what it is if simply Y_i is the dependent variable in the model. In sum, these regression coefficients equal the coded differences in the mean $Y_i - Z_i$ difference scores, which, given equal $\bar{Z}_k$, are equivalent to the coded differences in $\bar{Y}_k$.

This difference score analysis gives us the difference score analysis of variance source table of Exhibit 13.5. Notice that just as the regression coefficients for the contrast codes in this difference score analysis equal what they were in the analysis that included pretest as a predictor variable, so too the sums of squares for these contrast-coded predictors equal what they have been all along. Once again, this equivalence is due to the fact that Z_i is uncorrelated with condition. Consider the algebraic expression for the sum of squares for a contrast-coded predictor in this difference score analysis:

$$\frac{(\Sigma_k \lambda_k (\bar{Y}_k - \bar{Z}_k))^2}{\Sigma_k \lambda_k^2 / n_k}$$

This expression is equivalent to

$$\frac{(\Sigma_k \lambda_k \bar{Y}_k - \Sigma_k \lambda_k \bar{Z}_k)^2}{\Sigma_k \lambda_k / n_k}$$

Since, given invariant values of $\bar{Z}_k$, $\Sigma_k \lambda_k \bar{Z}_k$ equals zero, this expression for the sum of squares reduces to what it was in the original analysis of variance model where the dependent variable was simply Y_i.

This analysis, however, differs from both the earlier analysis of variance and the analysis that included the pretest as a predictor in the sum of squares for error and the sum of squares total. The total sum of squares is now equal to the sum of squares in the $Y_i - Z_i$ difference score, which in this case is less than the total sum of squares in Y_i. Since this total sum of squares has been reduced and since the sums of squares explained by the three contrast-coded predictors are unchanged, so the error sum of squares in this analysis must be less than the sum of squared errors in the earlier analysis of variance with Y_i as the dependent variable.

EXHIBIT 13.5 ▶

Difference score analysis of variance source table

Source	b	SS	df	MS	F*	PRE
Between or Model		507.5	3	169.17	16.73	.58
Curriculum	3.25	422.5	1	422.50	41.79	.54
Teacher	.75	22.5	1	22.50	2.22	.06
Curr. X Teacher	1.25	62.5	1	62.50	6.18	.15
Error		364.0	36	10.11		
Total		871.5	39			

As a result, the F^* statistics for the omnibus test of any condition differences and for the three single-degree-of-freedom tests are all larger than they were in the original analysis of variance source table of Exhibit 13.3.

Notice, however, that the sum of squared errors in this difference score source table is larger than the sum of squared errors was in the analysis that included the pretest as a predictor variable (ANCOVA source table of Exhibit 13.4). As a result, the F^* statistics testing condition differences in this difference score analysis are all slightly smaller than they were in the source table of Exhibit 13.4. In sum, while this difference score analysis is more powerful in this case than the simple analysis of variance on Y_i, it is not as powerful as the analysis of covariance in which the dependent variable was Y_i and Z_i was included as a predictor variable.

To understand why this is so, let us examine the difference score model:

$$Y_i - Z_i = \beta_0 + \beta_1 X_{i1} + \beta_2 X_{i2} + \beta_3 X_{i3} + \varepsilon_i$$

We can reexpress this model by adding Z_i to both sides of the equation:

$$Y_i = \beta_0 + Z_i + \beta_1 X_{i1} + \beta_2 X_{i2} + \beta_3 X_{i3} + \varepsilon_i$$

This difference score model now looks very similar to the analysis of covariance model in which the pretest was used as a predictor variable. There is, however, one major difference. Instead of associating a parameter with the pretest variable, and estimating that parameter as we did in the analysis of covariance model, we have set the parameter value equal to 1.0. By doing the difference score analysis, we have in effect assumed that the parameter value for the pretest equals 1.0, rather than letting it be a free parameter and deriving its least squares estimate.

By definition, the least squares estimates are those that minimize the sum of squared errors. Accordingly, the sum of squared errors in a model where the coefficient for the covariate is fixed at 1.0 cannot be less than the sum of squared errors in the analysis of covariance model, since in that model the coefficient for the covariate is the least squares estimate. Hence, the difference score analysis can never be a more powerful analysis than the analysis of covariance. More typically, it will be substantially less powerful and may, in fact, be even less powerful than the simple analysis of variance model.

Once we realize that this difference score model is identical to the analysis of covariance model, except that we have fixed the coefficient for the covariate at 1.0 instead of estimating it, we can rewrite the difference score analysis source table as we have in Exhibit 13.6. In this revised table the sums of squares total refers to the total sum of squares of Y_i rather than the total sum of squares in the $Y_i - Z_i$ difference score.

EXHIBIT 13.6 ▶

Revised difference score analysis of variance source table

Source	b	SS	df	MS	F*	PRE
Model		853.5	3	284.50	28.14	.70
Pretest (Z_i)	1.00	346.0	0			
Between Conditions		507.5	3	169.17	16.73	.58
Curriculum	3.75	422.5	1	422.50	41.79	.54
Teacher	.75	22.5	1	22.50	2.22	.06
Curr. X Teacher	1.25	62.5	1	62.50	6.18	.15
Error		364.0	36	10.11		
Total		1217.5	39			

Notice in this source table that the degrees of freedom for the pretest, Z_i, equals zero since in this model its coefficient has been set at 1.0 rather than estimated. The sum of squares associated with Z_i equals the difference between the sum of squares total for Y_i and the sum of squares total for the $Y_i - Z_i$ difference score.

In these data the difference score analysis is nearly as powerful as the analysis of covariance. This near equivalence results from the fact that the estimated parameter for the covariate in the analysis of covariance model, 1.27, is rather close to the value of 1.0 at which it is fixed in the difference score analysis. We could test whether the analysis of covariance model results in reliably smaller errors of prediction than the difference score model. This is equivalent to testing whether the parameter associated with the covariate in the augmented analysis of covariance model reliably differs from 1.0. For this test, the analysis of covariance model, in which the covariate's parameter is estimated, is the augmented one:

MODEL A: $Y_i = \beta_0 + \beta_1 Z_i + \beta_2 X_{i1} + \beta_3 X_{i2} + \beta_4 X_{i3} + \varepsilon_i$

The compact model is the difference score model in which the pretest's parameter value is fixed at 1.0:

MODEL C: $Y_i = \beta_0 + Z_i + \beta_1 X_{i1} + \beta_2 X_{i2} + \beta_3 X_{i3} + \varepsilon_i$

Comparing the sums of squared errors for these two models, we get

$$\text{PRE} = \frac{364.00 - 348.07}{364.00} = .044$$

which converts to an F^* with 1 and 35 degrees of freedom of 1.61. Hence, in these data, we cannot conclude that the parameter for the covariate is reliably different from 1.00. This conclusion means that the analysis of covariance model for these data is not reliably more powerful than the difference score analysis.

13.1.3 The Case of a Nonorthogonal Continuous Variable

So far we have been illustrating one of the two major reasons for including a continuously measured concomitant variable in an analysis of condition differences from a factorial design. By including a covariate that is measured prior to randomization of subjects to condition (and is therefore relatively unrelated to condition), we will increase the power of the tests of condition differences, as long as the covariate is reliably related to the dependent variable within condition. There arise other cases where we are interested in controlling for some continuously measured concomitant variable precisely because it is related to condition and we wish to estimate the condition differences freed from the contaminating influence of this concomitant variable. In other words, we might like to control for a covariate precisely because there are differences between conditions on the covariate and we wish to control statistically for those differences as we look for condition differences on the dependent variable.

Suppose, for instance, in our example that students had not been randomly assigned to the four cells defined by teacher and curriculum factors. If the decision about which students got which teacher-curriculum condition was not based on a random decision rule, but was instead based on some unknown assignment rule (e.g., keeping last year's classes intact), then we might expect differences among the various conditions on the pretest, long before the students had actually been exposed to their assigned teacher or their assigned curriculum. We would then quite reasonably want to control statistically for these pretest differences in looking at condition differences on the posttest. In other words, we might then like to control for the pretest in our analysis so that we could look at differences among conditions on the posttest freed of the preexisting differences on the pretest. This second function of analysis of covariance is called the adjustment function, because, as we will show, we will be examining condition differences in Y_i, first adjusting for condition differences on the pretest or covariate Z_i. This function of analysis of covariance is particularly common in what have come to be known as quasi-experimental research designs where assignment to condition has not been on a purely random basis (Cook & Campbell, 1979; Judd & Kenny, 1981). In such designs, we might expect condition differences on some pretest, and we might like to remove those differences statistically when testing for condition differences on the dependent variable.

A strong warning is in order at this point, however. While we can include a covariate in our model and thus statistically control for some confounding concomitant variable, this strategy is *not* a general solution to the problem of causal inference in quasi-experimental research designs. There are a variety of reasons why statistically controlling for preexisting differences between conditions will seldom be an adequate strategy for estimating condition effects on the dependent variable. The analysis of covariance in this situation is a useful tool, but it is not a general panacea. One's ability to reach causal conclusions about the effects of various independent variables depends not on the statistical analyses one undertakes. Rather, research design considerations are paramount in the quest for internal validity. Attempts to adjust for pre-existing differences between treatment conditions will typically adjust insufficiently, and resulting conclusions about the condition effects are likely to be erroneous. For a further consideration of these design issues, see Cook and Campbell (1979) or Judd and Kenny (1981). Our purpose in the following discussion is to illustrate this adjustment function of analysis of covariance, not to recommend it as a general analytic procedure in quasi-experimental designs.

With this strong warning in mind, we present the data of Exhibit 13.7, where we have modified the data we used earlier so that there will now be small differences among the conditions on the pretest. All variables are defined as previously, with the four conditions defined by teacher A versus teacher B and new curriculum versus old curriculum.

EXHIBIT 13.7 ▶

Modified pretest-posttest data

Y_i	X_{i1}	X_{i2}	Z_i	Y_i	X_{i1}	X_{i2}	Z_i
58	1	−1	51	57	1	−1	50
63	1	−1	50	61	1	−1	53
65	1	−1	54	57	1	−1	51
56	1	−1	48	67	1	−1	52
60	1	−1	54	56	1	−1	47
50	−1	−1	48	62	−1	−1	53
58	−1	−1	50	55	−1	−1	47
52	−1	−1	49	63	−1	−1	51
55	−1	−1	46	50	−1	−1	45
57	−1	−1	51	58	−1	−1	50
61	1	1	50	59	1	1	52
71	1	1	56	65	1	1	57
68	1	1	55	60	1	1	49
58	1	1	51	65	1	1	54
68	1	1	54	65	1	1	52
47	−1	1	44	62	−1	1	49
56	−1	1	49	51	−1	1	47
63	−1	1	51	54	−1	1	49
53	−1	1	46	58	−1	1	48
52	−1	1	45	54	−1	1	52

Variable X_{i1} continues to code curriculum (-1 if old; 1 if new), and variable X_{i2} continues to code teacher (-1 if teacher A; 1 if teacher B). Exhibit 13.8 gives the condition means for both Z_i and Y_i for these modified data.

There is now a definite relationship in these data between condition and Z_i, the pretest, since the condition means are no longer equal to each other. If we regressed Z_i on the three contrast codes, X_{i1}, X_{i2}, and X_{i3}, we get the following model:

$$\hat{Z}_i = 50.25 + 1.75X_{i1} + .25X_{i2} + .75X_{i3} \qquad \text{SSE} = 225.94$$

To show the relationship between condition and Z_i, we use as the compact model the single-parameter model making a constant prediction of Z_i for all cases:

$$\hat{Z}_i = 50.25 \qquad \text{SSE} = 373.50$$

A comparison of these two sums of squares tests the null hypothesis of no differences among the pretest means. It yields PRE $= .40$ and $F^*_{(3,36)} = 7.84$. Hence, we have now modified the data so that the pretest is reliably related to condition. We now wish to look at the effect of condition on the posttest Y_i controlling for Z_i, in order to assess condition effects on Y_i over and above any differences that existed at the time of the pretest and were measured by it.

Since we have not changed any values of Y_i, the analysis of variance model that assessed condition differences in Y_i not controlling for the pretest yields exactly the same estimated parameters, source table (Exhibit 13.3), and interpretations as it did previously. In other words, this analysis concludes that the regression coefficient for the curriculum contrast code equals 3.25 and that it is quite reliable. This time, however, since we are acting as if subjects were no longer randomly assigned to conditions, we are concerned that the magnitude of this difference between mean posttest scores in the new and old curricula may be due to previously existing differences in achievement. To the extent that these differences are reflected in the pretest scores, it may make sense to include the pretest as a predictor in the model and to estimate the treatment differences controlling for the pretest.

EXHIBIT 13.8 ▶

Modified pretest and posttest means by condition

Condition	Pretest	Posttest
Old Curr., Teacher A	49	56
Old Curr., Teacher B	48	55
New Curr., Teacher A	51	60
New Curr., Teacher B	53	64

The resulting model for these modified data is

$$\hat{Y}_i = -4.84 + 1.26Z_i + 1.04X_{i1} + .43X_{i2} + .30X_{i3} \qquad SSE = 348.07$$

Obviously, the regression coefficients for the contrast-coded predictors have been dramatically affected by the inclusion of the pretest variable Z_i. No longer does the coefficient for X_{i1} equal half the difference between the average Y_i under the new and old curricula. Similarly, the coefficients for X_{i2} and X_{i3} can no longer be interpreted as they were previously in terms of differences among various $\overline{Y}_k$. In other words, with the inclusion of a covariate that is correlated with the contrast-coded predictors, the regression coefficients for the contrast-coded predictors are no longer equal to

$$\frac{\sum_k \lambda_k \overline{Y}_k}{\sum_k \lambda_k^2}$$

Obviously a test of whether the parameters for these contrast-coded predictors equal zero is no longer a simple test of a comparison among the Y_i means in the various conditions.

With the inclusion of a covariate the regression coefficient for a contrast-coded predictor variable is equal to

$$\frac{\sum_k \lambda_k \overline{Y}_k}{\sum_k \lambda_k^2} - b_z\left(\frac{\sum_k \lambda_k \overline{Z}_k}{\sum_k \lambda_k^2}\right)$$

where b_z is the regression coefficient associated with the covariate Z_i in the augmented model that includes both the covariate and the set of contrast-coded predictor variables.

To illustrate this expression, let us calculate the value of the regression coefficient for X_{i1} in the model that includes Z_i. Notice that the first half of this expression equals the regression coefficient for X_{i1} in the model that did not include the covariate, i.e., 3.25. The second half of the expression equals the difference coded by the contrast weights among the *covariate or pretest* condition means, weighted by the regression coefficient for the pretest. Numerically, for the coefficient for X_{i1}, the second half of this expression equals

$$1.26\left(\frac{53 + 51 - 48 - 49}{4}\right) = 1.26(1.75) = 2.21$$

In sum, then, according to this expression the regression coefficient for the X_{i1} predictor equals

$$3.25 - 1.26(1.75) = 1.04$$

This new expression for the regression coefficient for a contrast-coded predictor in the presence of a covariate is readily interpreted. It is equal to the magnitude of the difference among $\overline{Y}_k$ coded by the contrast weights, adjusting for or subtracting off the magnitude of the same difference among the covariate condition means $\overline{Z}_k$. The degree to which the coded comparison among the $\overline{Y}_k$ is adjusted by the same comparison among the $\overline{Z}_k$ depends on the magnitude of the covariate's regression coefficient. In sum, the regression coefficients for contrast-coded predictors in the presence of a covariate tell us about the difference among the $\overline{Y}_k$ coded by the contrast weights, adjusting that difference for the parallel difference that exists in the covariate condition means $\overline{Z}_k$. The degree to which this adjustment is performed depends on the magnitude of the within-condition relationship between the covariate and the dependent variable, i.e., the partial regression coefficient for the covariate.

In the case of the regression coefficient for X_{i1}, we know that half the difference between the mean Y_i score under the new and old curricula equals 3.25, i.e., the regression coefficient for X_{i1} not controlling for the pretest. The regression coefficient for X_{i1} controlling for the pretest equals 1.04. This equals half the difference in Y_i associated with the difference in curriculum over and above any pretest differences associated with curriculum.

Another way to think about the coefficient for a contrast-coded predictor in the presence of a covariate is that it tells us about the magnitude of differences among adjusted values of $\overline{Y}_k$, adjusting the condition means to get rid of differences associated with differences in the covariate condition means. More precisely, if we compute for each condition the adjusted mean

$$\overline{Y}'_k = \overline{Y}_k - b_z(\overline{Z}_k - \overline{Z})$$

where $\overline{Z}$ is the unweighted grand mean of the covariate, then we can use these adjusted means to derive the regression coefficient for a contrast-coded predictor, using the old expression for the coefficient. In other words, the regression coefficient for a contrast-coded predictor in a model that includes a covariate equals

$$\frac{\Sigma_k \lambda_k \overline{Y}'_k}{\Sigma_k \lambda_k^2}$$

where $\overline{Y}'_k$ is defined as the adjusted cell mean according to the equation immediately above.

To illustrate, in Exhibit 13.9 the values of $\overline{Y}'_k$ are given for the four teacher by curriculum conditions. These were derived using the expression given above. For example, the value of the adjusted mean for the old curriculum, teacher A condition is given by

$$\overline{Y}'_k = 56 - 1.26(49 - 50.25) = 57.58$$

where 56 is the value of $\overline{Y}_k$ for this condition, 1.26 is the regression coefficient for the pretest in the model that includes both the pretest

EXHIBIT 13.9 ▶

Posttest condition means adjusted for the pretest ($\overline{Y}'_k$)

Condition	$\overline{Y}'_k$
Old Curr., Teacher A	57.58
Old Curr., Teacher B	57.85
New Curr., Teacher A	59.05
New Curr., Teacher B	60.52

and the condition contrast codes, 49 equals the value of $\overline{Z}_k$ for this condition, and 50.25 equals the unweighted grand mean of the pretest.

We now can use these adjusted $\overline{Y}'_k$ values to compute the regression coefficient for the contrast-coded predictors. For instance, the coefficient for X_{i1} in the model that includes the covariate equals

$$\frac{(-1)57.58 + (-1)57.85 + 59.05 + 60.52}{4} = 1.04$$

Conceptually, then, the coefficients for contrast codes in the presence of a covariate tell us about the magnitude of the coded difference among adjusted condition means, adjusting those dependent variable means by the extent to which the covariate means depart from the unweighted covariate grand mean. If all covariate condition means are equivalent, then there will obviously be no adjustment, since each value of $\overline{Z}_k$ will equal $\overline{Z}$. Thus, with identical covariate condition means, there is no adjustment to the dependent variable condition means. As a result, with a covariate that is uncorrelated with condition, the contrast-code coefficients do not change as we include a covariate. With a correlated covariate included, however, the contrast-code coefficients make comparisons among condition means that are adjusted for parallel differences among the covariate condition means.

EXHIBIT 13.10 ▶

Analysis of covariance source table

Source	b	SS	df	MS	F*	PRE
Model		869.43	4	217.36	21.87	.71
Pretest	1.26	361.93	1	361.93	36.39	.51
Between Conditions		34.30	3	11.43	1.15	.09
Curriculum	1.04	27.81	1	27.81	2.80	.07
Teacher	.43	7.44	1	7.44	.75	.02
Curr. X Teacher	.30	3.29	1	3.29	.33	.01
Error		348.07	35	9.94		
Total		1217.50	39			

The source table for the analysis of covariance model with these modified data is given in Exhibit 13.10. Notice that the sums of squares and, as a result, F^* statistics for the omnibus test of condition differences and the individual contrast tests are all considerably smaller than they were in the analysis of variance source table. This is so because they are testing different null hypotheses than they were in the analysis of variance model. In the analysis of variance model, the omnibus test was testing whether there were any differences among the condition means $\overline{Y}_k$. The tests of the contrasts were testing specific comparisons among the condition means. With the inclusion of the pretest in the model, the omnibus test is now testing for the presence of differences among the adjusted condition means. Similarly, the contrast tests are now testing specific comparisons among the adjusted condition means. In other words, the tests are now examining condition differences in Y_i having adjusted for condition differences that existed on the pretest.[1]

Since the pretest is no longer orthogonal to the various contrast codes that code condition, the sums of squares in this source table are not additive as they were in the earlier analysis of variance table. Therefore, some of them must be derived through the estimation of various compact models. To get the sum of squares for the omnibus condition test, we must estimate a model with only the pretest used as a predictor, since this omnibus sum of squares is no longer equal to the sum of the three sums of squares explained by the three contrast codes. Even though the three contrast codes are still orthogonal and even though there are still an equal number of observations in each condition, the three contrast codes differ in how redundant or correlated they are with the covariate. Thus the sum of their three individual sums of squares is not equal to the difference in the sum of squares explained if they are all omitted from the model.

As we have seen, an analysis that includes a covariate that is correlated with condition tells us about condition differences in the dependent variable first adjusting for or getting rid of differences among conditions on the covariate. This is not a general solution, however, to problems of internal validity in research designs where random assignment of observations to conditions has not been used (Cook & Campbell, 1979; Judd & Kenny, 1981). While differences among conditions on a covariate may capture some of the preexisting differences that exist because of the absence of random assignment, a single covariate or set

---

[1]Should we wish to use the procedures discussed in Chapter 11 in order to make further comparisons among condition means controlling for a covariate, then we should make those comparisons among the adjusted means rather than the unadjusted ones, using the mean square error from the ANCOVA source table as the error term.

of covariates cannot be expected to capture all of the potential differences that exist among conditions. Hence, using analysis of covariance to adjust for differences among conditions is only an incomplete solution to the interpretational problems posed by the lack of a random assignment rule.

As a final comment before proceeding to consider interactions between covariates and contrast codes, we should mention that models incorporating two or more covariates are simple extensions of models with single covariates that have been discussed at some length. Multiple covariates can be used in the context of randomized experimental designs to increase the power of tests of condition differences. They can also be used if the purpose of their inclusion is to adjust for differences that exist on a variety of different pretest measures. The analyses only increase in complexity as more covariates are included. Conceptually, the extension is a relatively trivial one.

13.1.4 Models with Continuous by Categorical Interactions

The analysis that we have just conducted, examining condition differences in the posttest while controlling for the pretest, rests on an untested assumption. The assumption is that the relationship between the pretest and the posttest is invariant across conditions. Alternatively, the assumption is that the relationships between the categorical condition variables and the posttest are invariant across levels of the pretest. This assumption is critical if we are to interpret the analysis as we have done in the preceding section. To see why this is so, recall that an analysis of covariance can be somewhat simplistically thought of as an analysis of variance on adjusted Y_i scores, adjusting each observation's Y_i by the weighted covariate. Thus, we saw that the regression coefficients for contrast-coded predictors are equal to the coded differences among conditions on adjusted mean scores, adjusting each $\overline{Y}_k$ by subtracting $b_z(\overline{Z}_k - \overline{Z})$. The weight used in this adjustment, b_z, is the regression coefficient for the covariate in the model that includes the condition defining contrast-coded predictors. In other words, this adjustment weight equals the average within-condition regression coefficient of Y_i regressed on Z_i. If the relationship between the dependent variable Y_i and the covariate Z_i differs substantially in magnitude across the various conditions of the study, then we should not be assuming a single adjustment weight b_z, but should be allowing for different adjustment weights for the various conditions. Accordingly, in controlling for a covariate, it is reasonable to test whether the relationship between Y_i and Z_i is invariant or homogeneous across conditions.

To suggest that the relationship between the pretest and the posttest depends on condition is to suggest that condition and the pretest interact in affecting the posttest. Therefore, to test the homogeneity of the relationship between Y_i and Z_i across conditions, we need to test whether the interactions between Z_i, on the one hand, and the condition defining contrast-coded predictors, on the other, are reliable. To examine these interactions, we follow the by now standard procedure of computing the product of the two variables whose interaction we wish to test and then entering those product variables as separate predictor variables into a model that includes the variables that are components of the products. We then would test whether the augmented model that includes the product terms generates reliably better predictions when compared to a compact model that omits all of the pretest by contrast-code interactions.

Let us illustrate this using the data contained in Exhibit 13.7. Since we have three contrast codes that define condition in these data, X_{i1}, X_{i2}, and X_{i3}, there will be three interaction or product terms to examine the condition by pretest interaction: $X_{i1}Z_i$, $X_{i2}Z_i$, and $X_{i3}Z_i$. The contrast-coded variable X_{i1} represents the comparison between the new and old curricula; hence the interaction between it and the pretest examines whether the relationship between Y_i and Z_i depends on curriculum. The contrast-coded variable X_{i2} codes the comparison between teacher A and teacher B. Hence, including its interaction with the pretest as a predictor in the model amounts to examining whether the relationship between Y_i and Z_i depends on teacher A versus teacher B. Finally, the contrast-coded variable X_{i3} codes the interaction between curriculum and teacher. Hence its interaction with Z_i is equivalent to the curriculum by teacher by pretest interaction. Including it in the model examines whether the relationship between posttest and the pretest depends on or varies with the curriculum by teacher interaction.

The model that includes all three of these pretest by condition interactions is estimated as

$$\hat{Y}_i = -4.40 + 1.26Z_i + 6.11X_{i1} - 1.32X_{i2} - 3.93X_{i3}$$
$$- .10X_{i1}Z_i + .03X_{i2}Z_i + .08X_{i3}Z_i \quad \text{SSE} = 344.23$$

Since we wish to examine whether there exist any differences among conditions in the relationship between Y_i and Z_i, and since we have no specific predictions about any of these three interactions, we can conduct an omnibus three-degrees-of-freedom test to examine whether this model produces a reliably smaller sum of squared errors when compared with a compact model that includes no condition by pretest interaction terms. That compact model was given earlier as

$$\hat{Y}_i = -4.84 + 1.26Z_i + 1.04X_{i1} + .43X_{i2} + .30X_{i3} \quad \text{SSE} = 348.07$$

By comparing these two models, we see that the sum of squares explainable by the pretest by condition interactions equals $348.071 - 344.226$ or 3.845. The resulting PRE as we add the interaction terms is

$$\text{PRE} = \frac{348.071 - 344.226}{348.071} = .011$$

and $F^*_{(3,32)} = 0.119$. Since this F^* statistic is far from significant, we cannot reject the omnibus null hypothesis that these pretest by condition interaction terms do not add reliably to our predictive power. In other words, there is no evidence in these data that the relationship between Y_i and Z_i varies among the four conditions created by crossing curricula with teachers. As a result, we should be perfectly happy to conclude our analysis of these data with the more parsimonious model, not including the three condition by pretest interactions, and reporting the source table of Exhibit 13.10.

Had the addition of these three condition by pretest interaction terms resulted in a reliable improvement in the model, then we would have wanted to interpret the model that includes the interactions and add those interactions to the reported source table. Even though we have concluded that the condition by pretest interactions are not reliable in these data, let us examine how we would interpret them and report them in the source table if the interactions were in fact reliable. We have already seen that the sum of squares explained by the three condition by pretest interaction terms as a set equals 3.845, resulting in an F^* statistic, with 3 and 32 degrees of freedom, of .119. The sum of squared errors from this full model that includes the interaction terms equals 344.226 with 32 degrees of freedom for error. Hence, this omnibus F^* can be equivalently expressed as

$$F^*_{(3,32)} = \frac{3.845/3}{344.226/32} = \frac{1.282}{10.757} = .119$$

where 10.757 is the mean squared error from this model.

To calculate the sum of squares explained by each of the individual pretest by condition interaction terms, we could delete each one in turn from this model and calculate the increase in the sum of squared errors. Each of these sums of squares explained by a particular pretest by condition interaction term could then be converted to an F^* statistic to test the reliability of that particular interaction term by computing the resulting PRE and converting it to F^* or, equivalently, by dividing the sum of squares due to each individual pretest by condition interaction term by the mean square error for the full or augmented model.

Following this strategy, we would compute with a portion of the source table devoted to the pretest by condition interaction terms presented in Exhibit 13.11. Each of the regression coefficients for these

Source	b	SS	df	MS	F*	PRE
Pretest X Cond		3.845	3	1.282	.119	.01
$X_{i1}Z_i$	−.10	2.324	1	2.324	.216	.01
$X_{i2}Z_i$	.03	.247	1	.247	.023	.00
$X_{i3}Z_i$	.08	1.571	1	1.571	.146	.00
Error		344.226	32	10.757		

interaction terms should also be interpreted, although in practice we probably would not do so in the present analysis since none of them was predicted and none was significant. Nevertheless, for the sake of illustration, let us proceed with the interpretations. Each one can be interpreted in two ways, either by focusing on the Y_i-Z_i relationship and describing how it changes as condition changes, or by focusing on the Y_i-condition relationships and describing how they change as Z_i changes in value. Let us first give the interpretation in terms of the Y_i-Z_i relationship. Since the coefficient for Z_i in the model is positive and since the coefficient for $X_{i1}Z_i$ interaction is negative, this tells us that the Y_i-Z_i relationship becomes somewhat less positive as X_{i1} increases in value. Since X_{i1} is the contrast code that codes curriculum, and since the high value on it is found with the new curriculum, the interaction tells us that the relationship between the pretest and the posttest is slightly (although not reliably) less strong in the new curriculum than in the old one.

Now, let us interpret the same interaction by focusing on the Y_i-X_{i1} relationship and seeing how it changes as Z_i changes in value. Since the coefficient for the X_{i1} contrast code in the model that did not include the interactions was positive, and since the interaction coefficient for the $X_{i1}Z_i$ term is negative, this tells us that the difference in Y_i due to X_{i1} decreases as Z_i becomes larger. Since the X_{i1} contrast code codes the difference between the new curriculum minus the old curriculum, the fact that the coefficient for the $X_{i1}Z_i$ interaction is negative tells us that this curriculum difference becomes smaller when dealing with observations having higher scores on the pretest.

The coefficient for the $X_{i2}Z_i$ interaction is positive in sign. This tells us that the relationship between Y_i and Z_i becomes very slightly more positive as X_{i2} becomes more positive. That is, the relationship between the posttest and the pretest is slightly more positive for students taught by teacher B than those taught by teacher A. Interpreting this interaction the other way, we would recall that the coefficient for the X_{i2} contrast-coded variable was positive in the model that did not include the pretest interaction terms, meaning that teacher B produced higher Y_i scores than did teacher A. The positive sign for the $X_{i2}Z_i$ coefficient means that the teacher difference is even larger as Z_i increases: students who score well on the pretest are more affected by the teacher B versus teacher A difference.

Finally, if we were to interpret the triple interaction between X_{i3} and Z_i, we would go back to the coefficient for the X_{i3} term in the model that did not include the condition by pretest interactions. We noted there that the direction of the coefficient for the X_{i3} term indicated that the difference due to new versus old curriculum was more pronounced for teacher B than it was for teacher A. The positive sign of the coefficient for the $X_{i3}Z_i$ interaction means that this curriculum by teacher interaction is even more pronounced for individuals with relatively high values on Z_i. In other words, had this interaction been reliable, we would have concluded that the difference due to curriculum was more pronounced when taught by teacher B than when taught by teacher A, and that this teacher difference in the magnitude of the curriculum effect in turn was more pronounced for those with high pretest scores than for those with relatively low pretest scores.

Notice that in making these interpretations we did not refer to the regression coefficients for the X_{i1}, X_{i2}, or X_{i3} terms in the model that included the pretest by condition interactions. In other words, when interpreting the $X_{i1}Z_i$ interaction coefficient in terms of how the relationship between Y_i and X_{i1} changes as Z_i changes in value, we reverted to the coefficient for the X_{i1} contrast-coded variable in the model that did not include the pretest by condition interactions, and argued that that difference due to X_{i1} changed as Z_i changed. We did not attempt to interpret the value of the regression coefficient for X_{i1} in the model that includes the pretest by condition interaction terms. That coefficient equals 6.11, which is certainly a different value from the coefficient for X_{i1} in the model that did not include the pretest by condition interaction terms, i.e., 1.04.

Should we wish to interpret the regression coefficient for the X_{i1} predictor in the model that includes the pretest by condition interaction terms, then we need to recall a very important lesson that was treated extensively in Chapter 10: *When an interaction product term is included in a model, the regression coefficient for a component of that interaction tells us about the effect of that component when the other component with which it is multiplied to form the interaction equals zero.* For the case at hand, the value of 6.11 attached to the X_{i1} predictor in the model that includes the $X_{i1}Z_i$ interaction represents the effect of X_{i1} when Z_i equals zero.

To make this clear, let us reexpress the model that includes the pretest by condition interaction terms. That model was given above as

$$\hat{Y}_i = -4.40 + 1.26Z_i + 6.11X_{i1} - 1.32X_{i2} - 3.93X_{i3}$$
$$- 0.10X_{i1}Z_i + 0.03X_{i2}Z_i + 0.08X_{i3}Z_i$$

By regrouping terms, this model can be equivalently expressed as

$$\hat{Y}_i = (-4.40 + 1.26Z_i) + (6.11 - 0.10Z_i)X_{i1}$$
$$+ (-1.32 + 0.03Z_i)X_{i2} + (-3.93 + 0.08Z_i)X_{i3}$$

Accordingly, we see that 6.11 is the "simple" X_{i1} or curriculum effect when Z_i equals zero. The coefficient for X_{i2}, -1.32, is the "simple" effect of teacher when Z_i equals zero. And the coefficient for X_{i3}, -3.93, is the curriculum by teacher interaction effect when Z_i equals zero. These coefficients do not tell us about the effect of curriculum, teacher, and curriculum by teacher on average across levels of Z_i. Such "average" effects are given by the coefficients of X_{i1}, X_{i2}, and X_{i3} in the model that did not include the pretest by condition interactions.

Accordingly, if we are interested in testing the curriculum effect, for instance, on average across levels of the pretest, we should do so by comparing compact and augmented models that do not include the three condition by pretest interaction terms, just as we did earlier in the chapter. If we delete X_{i1} from the equation that includes the $X_{i1}Z_i$ interaction, and then compare augmented and compact models, we are no longer testing the average effect of curriculum. We then would be testing the effect of curriculum when and only when Z_i equals zero.

One final point before leaving these data. Since the coefficient for X_{i1}, for instance, in the model that includes the $X_{i1}Z_i$ interaction term tells us about the "simple" effect of curriculum when Z_i equals zero, we may, upon occasion, wish to interpret these coefficients and report their associated sums of squares and F^* statistics. Should we, for instance, wish to know the curriculum "simple" effect when dealing with students who scored at a given level on the pretest, say 40, we could recode Z_i by subtracting from everyone's pretest score that level:

$$Z_i' = Z_i - 40$$

Our transformed Z_i, Z_i', would then equal zero when Z_i equaled 40. The coefficient of X_i, then, in a model which included Z_i' and the $X_{i1}Z_i'$ interaction, would tell us about the "simple" curriculum difference when Z_i' equaled zero or when dealing with a pretest score of 40. This procedure is exactly the same as the one discussed in Chapter 10 when considering continuous by continuous interaction terms.

13.2

Models with Continuous and Categorical Predictors Outside of Experimental Contexts

As we stated at the beginning of this chapter, models with both categorical and continuous predictor variables have been frequently used within the context of factorial experimental designs, where the theoretical questions of interest center on the effects of the categorical variables and how those effects change when one or more continuous predictor variables, called covariates, are controlled. The data we have used to illustrate the models of this chapter have been developed within this context. That is, the primary focus of the discussion so far in this chapter has been on the ways in which we might want to control for some continuously measured pretest variable in order to examine the effects of various categorical factors of interest. But that is certainly not the only context in which models with both continuous and categorical predictors are of interest. We now turn to an example where the primary theoretical questions of interest concern the relationship between a continuous predictor variable and the dependent variable. We are interested in both what happens to this relationship as some categorical variable is controlled and how this relationship changes from one level of the categorical variable to another.

13.2.1 Controlling for a Categorical Predictor Variable

Suppose we had survey data from 400 individuals. Each of these individuals answered three questions of interest for the following example. First, they indicated on a scale of 1 to 10 whether or not they supported a woman's right to choose abortion (1 = oppose individual right to abortion; 10 = favor individual right to abortion). Second, they indicated on a scale of 1 to 10 how conservative or liberal they considered themselves to be in general (1 = very conservative; 10 = very liberal). Finally, each individual indicated their religious preference, coded as Protestant, Catholic, or Jewish. Since we are dealing with purely hypothetical data, let us suppose that the sample as a whole is rather religious, with everyone indicating one of these three responses. Of the 400 individuals, 200 indicate that they are Protestants, 140 indicate their preference for the Catholic faith, and 60 indicate their preference as Jewish. Some univariate statistics for the two attitude questions are given in Exhibit 13.12.

Right to Abortion (ABORT)	
Mean	5.883
Median	6.000
Std Dev	2.824
Skewness	.182

Conservative/Liberal (LIB)	
Mean	4.798
Median	5.000
Std Dev	2.027
Skewness	−.018

Theoretically, let us imagine that we are interested in the following question: To what extent are beliefs about the abortion issue reflective of one's ideological predisposition on other political and social issues? In terms of the measured variables, we are interested in examining the relationship between the two attitude items. Accordingly, using data from the entire sample, we regress ABORT on LIB. The following model results

$$\widehat{ABORT} = 3.60 + .48 \text{ LIB} \qquad SSE = 2811.40$$

The sum of squares total of ABORT is 3182.50. Accordingly, to test the reliability of the ABORT-LIB relationship, we get a value of PRE of .117 and an associated F^*, with 1 and 398 degrees of freedom, of 52.53. We conclude that there is a highly reliable relationship between the responses to the two attitude items. Respondents who indicate that they are relatively liberal in general are more likely to favor a woman's right to abortion.

We suspect that our three religious groups differ in their sentiments regarding abortion. It is also possible that they differ in how generally liberal or conservative they report themselves to be. To examine whether religious preference is related to one or both of the attitude items, we code religion using two contrast codes, defined in Exhibit 13.13. We then regress both ABORT and LIB on these two contrast codes. The resulting ABORT model is

$$\widehat{ABORT} = 5.97 - .84 \ X_1 + .13 X_2 \qquad SSE = 2637.46$$

EXHIBIT 13.13 ▶

Contrast codes to code religious preference

$$
\begin{aligned}
X_1 &= -1 && \text{if Protestant} \\
&= 2 && \text{if Catholic} \\
&= -1 && \text{if Jewish} \\
X_2 &= -1 && \text{if Protestant} \\
&= 0 && \text{if Catholic} \\
&= 1 && \text{if Jewish}
\end{aligned}
$$

A comparison of this model with the simple single-parameter model yields a PRE of .17 and an $F^*_{(2, 397)}$ of 41.02. Accordingly, we conclude that the three religious groups do differ in their abortion sentiments. To locate these differences, we examine the reliability of the regression coefficients for the X_1 and X_2 contrast codes. A test of the X_1 contrast yields an $F^*_{(1, 397)}$ of 75.43. A test of the X_2 contrast yields an $F^*_{(1, 397)}$ of .44. Accordingly, we conclude that the Catholic respondents differ in their abortion attitudes from the other two religious groups, while the Protestant and Jewish respondents are not reliably different on average. From this regression equation, we can derive predicted values (group means) for each of the three religious groups. These are given in Exhibit 13.14.

To determine whether the three religious groups differ in their general political sentiments, we regress LIB on X_1 and X_2:

$$\widehat{\text{LIB}} = 5.18 - .21X_1 + 1.06X_2 \qquad \text{SSE} = 1432.28$$

The total sum of squares of LIB equals 1639.55. Accordingly, the test of whether there are any differences among the three religious groups in their responses to this item yields a PRE of .126 and an $F^*_{(2, 397)}$ of 28.72. Again, tests of the individual contrast codes show both regression coefficients to be reliably different from zero: For X_1 contrast, $F^*_{(1, 397)} = 8.60$; For X_2 contrast, $F^*_{(1, 397)} = 57.38$. The derived group means are also given in Exhibit 13.14.

These tests tell us that the Catholics see themselves as more conservative than the average of the other two groups and that Jewish respondents are reliably more liberal than Protestant ones. Inspection

EXHIBIT 13.14 ▶

Religious group means on ABORT and LIB

	ABORT Group Means	LIB Group Means
Protestant	6.68	4.33
Catholic	4.30	4.76
Jewish	6.93	6.45

of the three means suggests that Jewish respondents are quite a bit more liberal in general than respondents from the other two religious groups.

These analyses have shown that religious preference is reliably related to both abortion attitudes and one's general ideological preference across issues. Accordingly, we might wonder whether these religious differences account for the relationship between ABORT and LIB that we reported earlier. In other words, since the three religious groups differ in both their attitudes toward abortion and their general political views, it might be that the relationship we observed between abortion attitudes and general political views is entirely due to the religious differences that we have documented. To determine whether this is the case, we need to control for religious preferences in examining the ABORT-LIB relationship.

Accordingly, we regress ABORT on LIB and the two religious preference contrast codes, obtaining the following parameter estimates:

$$\widehat{ABORT} = 3.28 + .52LIB - .73X_1 - .42X_2 \quad SSE = 2251.68$$

Comparing this model to the one in which only X_1 and X_2 were predictors permits a test of the reliability of LIB while controlling for religious preferences. This test yields a PRE of .146 and an $F^*_{(1, 396)}$ of 67.85. Accordingly, we can conclude that there remains a reliable ABORT-LIB relationship even when we control for religious preferences. An alternative way of saying this is that on average within the three religious groups, general political views are predictive of abortion attitudes. If anything, the ABORT-LIB relationship is stronger when controlling for religion than when religion is not controlled. The simple regression coefficient for LIB is .48. When X_1 and X_2 are included in the model, the regression coefficient for LIB increases to .52.

One useful way of interpreting this model is to substitute values for X_1 and X_2 in order to examine the simple predictions made by the model for each of the three religious groups. If we plug in the contrast code values for Protestant respondents, we get

$$\widehat{ABORT} = 3.28 + .52LIB - .73(-1) - .42(-1)$$

Grouping terms together, the resulting simple model for Protestants is

$$\widehat{ABORT} = 4.43 + .52LIB$$

For Catholic respondents, the following substitutions are made:

$$\widehat{ABORT} = 3.28 + .52LIB - .73(2) - .42(0)$$

resulting in a simple prediction function of

$$\widehat{ABORT} = 1.82 + .52LIB$$

Finally, for Jewish respondents, the following substitutions are made:

$$\widehat{ABORT} = 3.28 + .52LIB - .73(-1) - .42(1)$$

resulting in a simple prediction function of

$$\widehat{ABORT} = 3.59 + .52LIB$$

These three simple relationships are graphed in Exhibit 13.15. As this exhibit makes clear, this model presumes that the ABORT-LIB relationship is invariant across religious groups. The slopes of the three simple prediction functions are identical. This common slope represents the value of the LIB regression coefficient that minimizes the sum of squared errors given the restriction of equal slopes within each religious group. It is the best-fitting ABORT-LIB slope within groups, given this restriction. While the three simple prediction functions do not differ in their slopes, they do have different intercepts. Since the three slopes are identical, these intercept differences are preserved at each level of LIB.

We have been concerned with interpreting the ABORT-LIB relationship within the three religious groups. We might alternatively focus on the differences among the religious groups in their abortion attitudes, once LIB is controlled, much like the focus in the earlier part of this chapter. We have already seen that when we examine mean differences among the three groups, the Catholic respondents reliably differ from the other two groups, while Protestants and Jews do not have reliably different abortion attitudes. Since the slope of LIB is constant across religious groups, the intercept differences among the three religious groups are preserved at all levels of LIB. Accordingly, these intercept differences, graphed in Exhibit 13.15, tell us about the differences among religious groups in abortion attitudes when we hold constant their general political views (LIB). A test of whether the regression coefficient for X_1 reliably differs from zero, in the model that includes LIB as a predictor, yields an $F^*_{(1, 396)}$ of 65.43. Thus, this reliable coefficient continues to tell us that Catholic attitudes toward abortion differ from the attitudes of Jewish and Protestant respondents, even when we control for general political sentiments. The coefficient for X_2 also differs reliably from zero in the model that includes LIB, $F^*_{(1, 396)} = 5.08$. Thus, when general political sentiments are held constant, Jewish and Protestant respondents reliably differ in their abortion attitudes. Interestingly, while the mean abortion attitude of Jewish respondents was slightly higher than the mean of Protestant respondents, when we control for LIB differences, Protestant respondents have higher predicted ABORT responses than do Jewish ones. On average, as we have seen, Protestant respondents give lower self-ratings on the LIB question than do Jewish respondents.

When we eliminate this difference or adjust for it in examining differences among groups in abortion attitudes, we conclude that the Protestant respondents are actually somewhat more tolerant toward freedom of choosing abortion than are the Jewish respondents, given the same general political orientation (i.e., holding constant LIB).

13.2.2 Estimating Slope Differences within Levels of a Categorical Variable

So far we have seen that the relationship between abortion attitudes and general political orientation is reliable both when ignoring religious preference and when we control for religious preference. In addition, we have seen that in these hypothetical data, Catholic respondents have different abortion attitudes on average than the other two groups, and this difference continues to exist when general political orientation is controlled. Protestant and Jewish respondents do not have different abortion attitudes on average, but when general political orientation is controlled, Protestant respondents have somewhat more liberal abortion attitudes.

As we noted in presenting the model that is graphed in Exhibit 13.15, the preceding analysis was based on the assumption that the ABORT-LIB relationship was invariant across religious groups. That is, we assumed that there was a single within-group slope for that relationship, resulting in the parallel simple prediction functions graphed in the exhibit. This may or may not have been a reasonable assumption.

EXHIBIT 13.15 ▶

ABORT-LIB simple relations: additive model

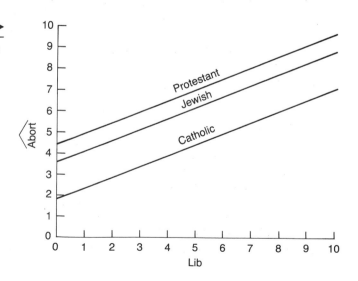

One way to examine whether it is reasonable might be to regress ABORT on LIB for each of the three religious groups and then examine the three resulting regression coefficients. (We propose to do this here for didactic purposes. It will become clear that we do not recommend this as a general analytic strategy.) Let us divide the sample into three different subsamples, based on religious preference, and estimate a simple regression model within each subsample. For Protestant respondents the resulting parameter estimates are

$$\widehat{\text{ABORT}} = 3.50 + .73\text{LIB} \qquad \text{SSE} = 1246.61$$

The test of whether this simple relationship is reliable yields a PRE of .235 and an $F^*_{(1, 198)}$ of 60.74. For Catholic respondents the resulting parameter estimates are

$$\widehat{\text{ABORT}} = 3.42 + .19\text{LIB} \qquad \text{SSE} = 732.12$$

The test of the simple relationship yields a PRE of .023 and an $F^*_{(1, 138)}$ of 3.31. Finally, for Jewish respondents the resulting parameter estimates are

$$\widehat{\text{ABORT}} = 2.93 + .61\text{LIB} \qquad \text{SSE} = 179.47$$

The test of the simple relationship yields a PRE of .306 and an $F^*_{(1,58)}$ of 25.61.

These three subsample simple regression models are graphed in Exhibit 13.16. It looks as if the assumption of a common slope for the ABORT-LIB relationship within each of the three religious groups might be unwarranted. For both the Protestant and Jewish respondents, the

EXHIBIT 13.16 ▶

ABORT-LIB simple relations: interactive model

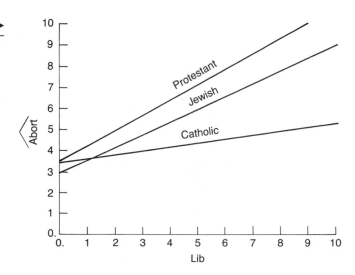

relationship between the two variables is quite reliable: General political orientation predicts with moderate strength one's attitude toward abortion. With Catholics, on the other hand, the relationship between the two variables is weak and unreliable. One is tempted to conclude that the previous analysis, assuming invariant slopes, was perhaps inappropriate and that its conclusions were premature. The differences among the three groups in the ABORT-LIB relationship do not appear to be simply differences in intercepts.

Although it is tempting to conclude from these subsample analyses that the ABORT-LIB relationship varies among the three religious groups, no test of those differences is in fact provided by these subsample models. For each religious group we simply have a test of whether the ABORT-LIB relationship is reliably different from zero. In the Jewish and the Protestant samples, it is; in the Catholic sample it is not. Nowhere do we have a test of whether the subsample slopes differ from each other. Nowhere do we have a test of whether the ABORT-LIB relationship depends on religious preference.

Conceptually, when we suggest that the relationship between ABORT and LIB may depend on religious preference, we are suggesting that the interaction between LIB and religious preference may be reliable. As always, we examine interactions by computing one or more product variables and including them in the model along with their components. Since religious preference is coded with two contrast codes, we need to include two religious preference by LIB product variables: X_1LIB and X_2LIB. The model that includes these product predictors is estimated from the full sample of 400 as follows

$$\widehat{\text{ABORT}} = 3.28 + .51\text{LIB} + .07X_1 - .28X_2$$
$$- .16X_1\text{LIB} - .06X_2\text{LIB} \qquad \text{SSE} = 2158.20$$

To test whether these product terms reliably reduce errors of prediction, we compare this augmented model with a compact one that does not include the product terms, given earlier. The sum of squared errors from the model that included only LIB, X_1, and X_2 is 2251.68. The comparison of these two models yields a PRE of .042 and an $F^*_{(2, 394)}$ of 8.53. Since this value exceeds the critical value of F, we conclude that these product terms reliably increase the accuracy of the model's predictions. Tests of the regression coefficients for the individual product terms show that the first is reliably different from zero, $F^*_{(1, 394)} = 12.75$, while the second is not, $F^*_{(1, 394)} = 0.38$.

To interpret the parameter estimates of this model, let us derive from it the simple ABORT-LIB prediction function for each of the three religious groups, just as we did in the case of the model that did not include the product terms. For Protestant respondents, we want to substitute -1 for X_1 and -1 for X_2 wherever we find them in the model

$$\widehat{ABORT} = 3.28 + .51LIB + .07(-1) - .28(-1)$$
$$- .16(-1)LIB - .06(-1)LIB$$

This becomes:

$$\widehat{ABORT} = 3.28 + .51LIB - .07 + .28 + .16LIB + .06LIB$$
$$= (3.28 - .07 + .28) + (.51 + .16 + .06)LIB$$
$$= 3.49 + .73\ LIB$$

To derive the simple prediction function for Catholics, we substitute the values of 2 and 0 for X_1 and X_2:

$$\widehat{ABORT} = 3.28 + .51LIB + .07(2) - .28(0)$$
$$- .16(2)LIB - .06(0)LIB$$

This becomes

$$\widehat{ABORT} = 3.28 + .51LIB + .14 - .32LIB$$
$$= (3.28 + .14) + (.51 - .32)LIB$$
$$= 3.42 + .19LIB$$

To derive the simple prediction function for the Jewish respondents, we substitute the values of -1 and 1 for X_1 and X_2:

$$\widehat{ABORT} = 3.28 + .51LIB + .07(-1)$$
$$- .28(1) - .16(-1)LIB - .06(1)LIB$$

This becomes

$$\widehat{ABORT} = 3.28 + .51LIB - .07 - .28 + .16LIB - .06LIB$$
$$= (3.28 - .07 - .28) + (.51 + .16 - .06)LIB$$
$$= 2.93 + .61LIB$$

If we go back and compare these simple prediction functions that have been derived from the full-sample interactive model with the simple ABORT-LIB models that we estimated earlier from each of the three religious subsamples, we notice that they are identical, within rounding error. In other words, if we derive simple prediction functions from this interactive model for each of the three religious groups, the results agree exactly with the simple regression results that emerged when we regressed ABORT on LIB for each subsample separately. Since this inter-active model therefore makes exactly the same predictions as the separate subsample simple regression models, it is not surprising that the sum of squared errors from this full-sample interactive model equals the sum of the three sums of squared errors from the three subsample analyses:

$$
\begin{array}{cccc}
Interactive\ SSE & Prot\ SSE & Cath\ SSE & Jew\ SSE \\
2158.20 & = 1246.61\ + & 732.12\ + & 179.47
\end{array}
$$

This interactive model thus subsumes the three subsample analyses reported earlier and graphed in Exhibit 13.16. That exhibit is identically a graph of the three simple prediction functions that we have derived from the full-sample interactive model.

Let us now interpret the various parameter estimates in the full interactive model. The model's intercept, 3.28, equals the predicted value of ABORT when all predictors equal zero. Since the unweighted grand means of both X_1 and X_2 equal zero, the model's intercept, 3.28, equals the unweighted mean of the three subsample intercepts. In other words, it is the average of the three intercepts from the three simple prediction functions. Similarly, the regression coefficient for LIB in the full interactive model equals the unweighted mean of the three LIB simple slopes from the three subsample prediction functions. It tells us what the ABORT-LIB slope is for the average of the three religious subsamples. The regression coefficients for X_1 and X_2 tell us by how much the simple intercepts change as we move from one religious group or subsample to the next. Thus, the coefficient for X_1, .07, equals one third of the difference between the simple intercept of the Catholic respondents and the average of the simple intercepts from the Protestant and Jewish subsamples. The coefficient for X_2, −.28, equals half the difference between the simple intercepts of the Jewish and Protestant subsamples. Notice that these coefficients tell us about differences in predicted ABORT values between the religious subsamples only when LIB equals zero. Unlike the earlier model that did not include the interactions, the simple slopes are no longer identical, i.e., the prediction functions graphed in Exhibit 13.16 are no longer parallel. Whereas in the earlier model, not including the interactions, the differences in the intercepts were preserved between religious groups at all levels of LIB, that is no longer the case. These coefficients tell us about between subsample differences *when and only when* LIB equals zero. We return to this point below.

The coefficients associated with the two product terms, X_1LIB and X_2LIB, tell us about the differences among the simple ABORT-LIB slopes for the three religious subsamples. Thus, the X_1LIB coefficient, −.16, equals one third of the difference between the simple slope for the Catholic respondents and the average of the simple slopes from the

Protestant and Jewish respondents. A test of whether this coefficient differs from zero amounts to a test of whether the simple ABORT-LIB relationship differs in the Catholic subsample when compared with the other two subsamples. As reported earlier, this coefficient does in fact differ reliably from zero. Hence, this analysis permits the conclusion that general political orientations are less strongly predictive of abortion attitudes among Catholic respondents than among Protestant and Jewish respondents. Not only are the Catholic respondents on average less liberal toward abortion (as indicated by the test of the X_1 coefficient in the model that did not include the product terms), but also there is a weaker relationship between general political attitudes and abortion attitudes among this religious subsample.

The coefficient for the X_2LIB product variable, $-.06$, equals half the difference between the simple slopes for the Jewish and Protestant subsamples. Since it does not reliably differ from zero, we cannot conclude that there is any difference between these two groups of respondents in how strongly related general political orientations are to abortion attitudes.

The general point about interpreting these product term regression coefficients, where the product is between a categorical variable and a continuous one, is that they tell us about differences in the simple slopes for the continuous predictor variable between groups defined on the basis of the categorical variable. Since the full interactive model subsumes the separate subsample analyses, and since, in addition, differences in intercepts and slopes from those separate subsample analyses are explicitly testable within the context of the full interactive model, we strongly believe that this is the most appropriate analysis for determining whether discrete groups of respondents or subjects differ in how strongly related two or more variables are to each other. Separate subsample analyses do not allow between group tests of differences in the magnitude of relationships. One needs to test the appropriate interactions within a full-sample interactive model.

One final point is worth making about this full interactive model. Since this model allows the simple slopes of the ABORT-LIB relationship to vary with religious group, it provides no overall test of whether the religious groups differ in predicted abortion attitudes on average or across levels of general political orientation. To know whether the religious groups differ in their abortion attitudes, you must specify the level of LIB that you are referring to, since the predicted values of ABORT for the religious subsamples differ by different amounts depending on the value of LIB. The coefficients for the X_1 and X_2 terms in the interactive model tell us about the predicted differences among the religious groups only when LIB equals zero, which is certainly an uninformative comparison, since the scale of measurement of LIB varies between 1 and 10.

These regression coefficients would be more informative if LIB were rescaled in mean deviation form, as recommended in earlier chapters. Thus, we define

LIB' = LIB − 4.80

where 4.80 is the mean value of LIB across all 400 respondents. The mean of LIB' is accordingly equal to zero. We now compute new product terms, X_1LIB' and X_2LIB', and regress ABORT on LIB', X_1, X_2, X_1LIB', and X_2LIB'. The resulting parameter estimates are

$$\widehat{ABORT} = 5.75 + .51LIB' - .72X_1 - .56X_2$$
$$- .16X_1LIB' - .06X_2LIB'$$

As we saw in Chapter 10, linear transformations applied to one component variable in an interactive model affect the coefficient of the other component variable involved in the interaction. Accordingly, in this model employing LIB' instead of LIB, the regression coefficients associated with LIB' and the two product predictors have not changed as a result of the transformation. They still tell us about the unweighted average slope and the differences among the religious groups in slopes. The coefficients associated with X_1 and X_2 have dramatically changed, however. Their interpretation is as follows: the X_1 coefficient, −.72, equals one third of the difference between the predicted ABORT value for Catholic respondents and the average of the predicted values for Protestant and Jewish respondents, when LIB' equals zero. Since LIB' equals zero at the mean value of LIB, −.72 estimates the difference between Catholic respondents and the other two religious groups at the mean value of LIB. This coefficient is reliably different from zero, $F_{(1, 394)}^* = 53.60$. Similarly, the coefficient for X_2, −.56, now equals half the difference between the predicted ABORT value for Jewish and Protestant respondents when LIB' equals zero or at the mean value of LIB. It too is reliably different from zero, $F_{(1, 394)}^* = 6.46$.

We can illustrate these values from the graphed prediction functions of Exhibit 13.16. Prior to tranforming LIB into mean deviation form, the coefficients of X_1 and X_2 told us about between group differences in predicted values at that point on the graph where LIB equals zero. Thus, the X_1 coefficient, .07, equals one third of the difference between the predicted ABORT values between Catholic respondents and the average of the other two groups only at the zero point on the horizontal axis of the graph. The coefficient for X_2, .28, equals half the difference between the predicted values for Jewish and Protestant respondents at that point. Once we have tranformed LIB into mean deviation form, we are simply making comparisons among the three predicted ABORT values at a different point on the horizontal axis. Specifically, we are making comparisons among the three predicted values when LIB' equals zero or when LIB equals 4.80. At that point on the horizontal axis, one third of the difference between the Catholic predicted value and the average of the other two predicted values equals $-.72$ (i.e., the coefficient for X_1 in the model involving LIB'). Also, at that point, i.e., LIB equals 4.8, one half the difference between the Jewish and Protestant respondents' predicted values equals $-.56$ (i.e., the coefficient for X_2 in the model involving LIB').

Should we wish to make other comparisons among the religious groups in their predicted ABORT values at particular levels of LIB, then we need to apply appropriate transformations to LIB and recompute the two product terms so that the transformed LIB equals zero at the levels at which comparisons are desired. What we would then be doing is making comparisons among the three religious groups in their predicted ABORT values at different points along the horizontal axis of the graph in Exhibit 13.16. The procedure is identical to that discussed in Chapter 10.

13.3
Conclusion

In many ways, this chapter marks the final point in the process of developing more complex MODELs for our DATA in order to ask more complex, and perhaps more interesting, questions of those DATA. Throughout the development of these more complex models we have kept the same basic machinery to determine whether the increase in complexity is worthwhile as more parameters are added to the model. This machinery depends on comparisons of augmented and compact models in a manner that by now ought to be totally routine. While this machinery has remained constant across the chapters, our models have, however, developed from the simplest one involving a single parameter (Chapters 4 and 5) to ones making predictions conditional on a single continuous variable (Chapters 6 and 7) to ones involving multiple continuous predictors, including product terms (Chapters 8 and 10), to models with categorical variables including products of those categorical variables (Chapters 11 and 12), and finally to models involving continuous and categorical predictor variables and their products (this chapter). This is as far as we wish to extend the complexity of the models we have considered. We believe that nearly every interesting substantive question that social science researchers might like to ask of their data can be answered by using the range of models that have been explored. This is not to say that the limits of model complexity have been reached. Rather, this is to suggest that the models we have considered are those that are most likely to be of use to the data analyst. Further, when other more complicated models seem appropriate, we hope that the reader by now is equipped to adapt the model comparison approach we have used to these other more complicated situations.

So what remains to be done? The remaining three chapters of the book are devoted to problems that are frequently encountered in data that violate various assumptions underlying the model comparison approach we have developed to data analysis. In Chapters 14 and 15 we consider how our models and data analysis need to be modified when dealing with data where we cannot assume independence of errors. Researchers routinely encounter dependencies in their data when dealing with multiple measures taken from the same person, group, or other aggregate unit. Such dependencies violate the assumptions underlying inferential statistics, and our models need to be appropriately modified to overcome the resulting problems. We will see that doing this is not particularly difficult. One simply transforms the data in order to remove the dependencies and then proceeds using the full array of models developed in the chapters already covered. In Chapter 16 we consider problems in data due to nonnormal distributions and heterogeneous variances. Again, our approach will be to solve these problems with appropriate transformations of the data so that the full range of models we have developed can be subsequently applied to the transformed data.

14

Repeated Measures ANOVA: Models with Nonindependent ERRORs

The regression model that has been used in all of the preceding chapters is

$$Y_i = \beta_0 + \beta_1 X_{i1} + \beta_2 X_{i2} + \cdots + \beta_p X_{ip} + \varepsilon_i$$

In this model, we have made no assumptions about the distributions of the predictor variables, the X_j's. They can be continuously measured or they can be contrast-coded predictors used to represent nominally measured variables. We have, however, made assumptions all along about the residuals, ε_i, in this model, and therefore, implicitly about Y_i. Specifically, we have assumed three things about ε_i throughout the preceding chapters:

1. They are normally distributed.
2. They have constant variance.
3. They are independent of each other.

In this and subsequent chapters we consider necessary modifications to the regression model when these assumptions are violated. Specifically, in this chapter we consider violations of the third assumption, that concerning the independence of ε_i, or, more colloquially, the independence of observations. Subsequent chapters consider violations of the normality and constant variance assumptions.

Independence of observations is formally defined using conditional probabilities (Kenny & Judd, 1986). Two observations are nonindependent if the conditional probability of one of them having a particular value, given knowledge of the other one, is different from the unconditional probability. All this means is that if two observations are nonindependent, then knowing the value of one of them gives us information about the value of the other, allowing us to make a reasonable guess about the other's value. To illustrate, suppose we collected data from married couples, asking each spouse to rate, on a scale of 1 to 7, how satisfied he or she is with their marriage. Presumably, there would be some agreement between spouses on the quality of their marriage. The resulting data might look as follows:

Couple	Male Spouse	Female Spouse
1	1	1
2	4	3
3	6	7
4	5	6

The relative agreement between spouses in these data results in nonindependent observations. Observations within couples on average are more similar than observations between couples. Or, in terms of conditional probabilities, if we know that the score of one spouse is below the mean, then that gives us information about whether the score of the other spouse is above or below the mean. Since couples partially agree about the quality of their marriage in these data, if one spouse's score is below the mean, the other's is likely to be as well. Similarly, if one spouse's score is above the mean, the other's is likely to be as well. Observations that are linked, in the sense that they come from the same couple, are more similar on average than observations that are not linked, i.e., that come from different couples. This illustrates what we call *positive nonindependence:* greater similarity between linked observations than between nonlinked observations.

Negative nonindependence occurs when linked observations are more dissimilar on average than nonlinked observations. Consider hypothetical ratings from these same four couples about the percentage of housework each does:

Couple	Male Spouse	Female Spouse
1	30%	80%
2	40%	75%
3	70%	40%
4	20%	100%

If there were perfect agreement between spouses in these data, the sum of each couple's percentage estimates should be 100%. That is, as one spouse estimates that he or she does a higher percentage of housework, the other estimates a lower percentage. While there is not perfect agreement in these data, there is considerable nonindependence of observations within couples. If one spouse's estimated percentage is below the mean, the other's is quite likely to be above it. Observations that come from the same couple are on average more dissimilar than are observations from different couples. They are negatively nonindependent.

Nonindependence in data is likely to be found in two classic situations: grouped data and sequential data. The couples data that we have just used to define nonindependence illustrates nonindependence due to grouped data. Observations are grouped together in the sense that pairs of them come from the same couples. Another common grouping of observations occurs when each individual provides multiple observations: each person is measured more than once or provides more than a single response. It is then likely that observations taken from the same individual will be more or less similar on average than observations taken from different individuals. Thus, the observations are nonindependent because they are grouped within individuals. A further example of grouped data is typically encountered in social psychological research on small group interaction. If different individuals within interacting groups are measured, it is exceedingly likely that nonindependence will be a problem.

Like grouped data, sequential data are also commonly encountered. Whenever lots of data are collected over time from one or more individuals, nonindependence due to sequence is likely to be encountered: observations that are close together in the sequence or in time are quite likely to be more or less similar on average than observations that are further away in time. As a simple illustration, suppose we measured the number of pages read by a college student every day for 50 days.

Because of exams, varying academic pressure, and other factors, we would expect cycles in the data: groups of days right before exams would be heavy reading periods; groups of days right after exams might show fewer pages read. In other words, there is likely to be more similarity in the number of pages read on adjacent days, on average, than on days that are nonadjacent. Thus, the observations would be nonindependent due to time sequence.

Since nonindependence is likely to be present in both grouped and sequential data, the usual regression model that we have employed needs to be modified in some way to deal with the fact that one of its underlying assumptions has been violated. For both kinds of data, the corrective strategy consists of removing the nonindependence from the data through some sort of transformation of those data. How this is done, however, typically depends on the origin of the nonindependence. Problems of nonindependence in sequential data are typically handled with somewhat different transformations from those employed in grouped data. This chapter concentrates on nonindependence problems in grouped data. Included here are data in which a few observations are gathered from each of a set of subjects over time. When many observations are gathered from the same subject over time, then other procedures, known as *time-series analysis*, are recommended for dealing with nonindependence due to sequence. Excellent discussions of time-series procedures are available in Gottman (1981) and McCleary (1980).

Let us return to our married couple example to make one further distinction relevant to our discussion of nonindependence due to grouped data. Suppose in our example we are interested in knowing whether male spouses give reliably different ratings of marital satisfaction than do female spouses. If we worried not at all about the violation of the independence assumption in these data, we would construct a contrast code to represent sex of spouse, and regress our dependent variable, i.e., each individual's rating, on this contrast-coded predictor. In this case, the groups which give rise to the nonindependence problem are said to be *crossed* with the treatment or experimental variable of interest. That is, each couple or group provides one and only one rating under each level of the treatment variable: from within each couple there is one observation coded -1 on the contrast code and one observation coded $+1$.

Now suppose that the treatment variable we are interested in was not sex of spouse, but rather some characteristic of couples. Say, for instance, that we have two sets of couples, some of whom are newly married and others who have been married more than 10 years, and we wanted to know whether the two sets of couples give reliably different ratings of marital satisfaction. Again, if we did not worry about the nonindependence in the data, we might code duration of marriage as short or long using a contrast code, and then regress ratings, one for each individual, on the resulting contrast-coded predictor. This time, however, the groups or couples which give rise to nonindependence are *nested* under the levels of the treatment or experimental variable of interest. That is, each couple or group provides two ratings of marital satisfaction, both of which receive the same code on the predictor variable. If one member of the couple is coded as -1, meaning that he or she comes from a relatively recent marriage, the other necessarily has the same code on the predictor variable.

In general, if groups of observations are nested under some factor of interest, then observations from within a group are gathered under the same level of the factor. If groups of observations are crossed with the factor, then the observations within a group are gathered under different levels of the factor.

To clarify this distinction further, consider a second example. Suppose a researcher was interested in exploring differences in short-term memory as a function of stress levels. He intends to manipulate stress levels by testing subjects' memories in the presence of loud white noise, and in a control condition without any noise. He further decides that he will measure each subject's memory twice. These two observations from any given subject can either be crossed with the experimental treatment variable of interest, i.e., the presence or absence of white noise, or nested under it. In the case where the treatment is crossed with subjects, each subject's memory would be measured once with the white noise present and once with it not present. The treatment variable in this case varies *within subjects*. In the case where the two observations from each subject are nested under the treatment, each subject's memory would be measured twice, but now it would be measured both times either with the noise present or with it not present. In this case the treatment variable varies only *between subjects*.

For didactic purposes we will start by treating these two different cases separately. That is, we will first consider how nonindependence problems are overcome when groups are nested under the treatment variable or factor whose effect is to be estimated. We will then consider solutions to nonindependence when groups are crossed with a factor of interest. Remember that "groups" refers simply to a collection of observations that are linked in some way because they come from the same individual, couple, social group, or other entity. We suspect that such observations are nonindependent because of their group links, and we have to alter our analysis procedure to deal with the problems this poses. It will become apparent that we have a general approach to solving nonindependence problems that can be used in either the nested or the crossed case. That general approach amounts to combining the data from each group into one or more summary dependent variables, which are then analyzed separately. Since only one summary measure from each group is included in each separate analysis, the observations in each analysis are independent of each other. This approach is appropriate in both nested and crossed designs. It is also applicable in designs that are known as *mixed designs*, where groups are nested under some factors of interest and crossed with others.

14.1

Nonindependence in Nested Designs

All of the data that we used in the last three chapters to explore models with categorical predictor variables were from designs in which subjects were nested under levels of the categorical treatment variable of interest. That is, each subject was measured under only one treatment level. However, in those designs, each subject was observed only a single time, so nonindependence was assumed not to be a problem. Now we are simply going to extend those designs to situations where there is more than a single observation from each subject. All of those observations, however, continue to be taken from the subject under the same level of the treatment or independent variable. More generally, we are discussing designs in which observations are linked or grouped, but each group of observations is gathered only under a single level of the treatment variable. Groups of observations need not be defined by coming from the same subject. They might instead come from the same social group or the same family. While our examples employ multiple linked observations from each subject, observations may be nonindependent because they are linked in many other ways as well.

Consider the data of Exhibit 14.1. To examine whether performance is affected by being observed by others (a "social facilitation effect"), subjects are asked to complete a number of math puzzles in a fixed amount of time. Each subject has been assigned either to a condition where the experimenter observes her while working on the puzzles or a condition where she works alone. The dependent variable is the number of puzzles correctly solved in the allotted time. Each subject does two different sets of puzzles, thus providing two different observations. Each observation is labeled Y_{hi}, where the subscript i refers to subject and the subscript h refers to order of observation within subject. In this case h has a maximum value of 2 since there are two observations from each subject. In general, h varies between 1 and s. With n subjects, i varies between 1 and n. The total number of observations thus equals ns. In the above data, $n = 6$, $s = 2$, and there are 12 observations altogether.

EXHIBIT 14.1 ▶

Social facilitation data: nested design

	Experimenter Present			Experimenter Absent		
Subject	1	2	3	4	5	6
Y_{1i}	8	9	5	3	5	3
Y_{2i}	7	9	6	3	4	4
$\bar{Y}_k$	7.33			3.67		

While we have two observations from each subject, each subject is observed under only one treatment condition. Subjects 1, 2, and 3 are observed twice each with the experimenter present, and subjects 4, 5, and 6 are observed twice with the experimenter absent. Thus, the independent variable, whether the experimenter is present or absent, varies between subjects. What we want to know is whether this independent variable reliably affects how many math puzzles subjects were able to solve in the allotted time. In other words, we want to know whether the mean number of puzzles solved with the experimenter present, 7.33, reliably differs from the mean number solved with the experimenter absent, 3.67.

Since some subjects are likely more adept at math puzzles than others, these observations are likely to show positive nonindependence due to subjects. That is, values of the dependent variable are likely to be more similar on average within subjects than they are between them. For the sake of illustration, let us analyze these data ignoring the probable violation of the independence assumption, using the analysis of variance procedures that we have discussed in earlier chapters. We will then compare the results of this *inappropriate* analysis to an analysis that more properly adjusts for or eliminates the nonindependence in these data.

To examine the effect of the categorical independent variable, we code it using a contrast-coded predictor, X_{hi}, coded 1 if the experimenter is present and -1 if the experimenter is absent. The resulting regression equation, regressing Y_{hi} on X_{hi} is

$$\hat{Y}_{hi} = 5.5 + 1.83X_{hi} \qquad SSE = 16.67$$

The intercept equals the mean of the two treatment means and the regression coefficient for X_{hi} equals half the difference between the two treatment means, $\bar{Y}_k$. To examine whether the experimenter's presence makes a difference, we would compare this augmented model with the compact single-parameter one

$$\hat{Y}_{hi} = 5.5 \qquad SSE = 57.00$$

This comparison generates the source table of Exhibit 14.2.

EXHIBIT 14.2 ▶

Source table for nested data ignoring nonindependence

Source	b	SS	df	MS	F*	PRE
Model		40.33	1	40.33	24.20	.71
X_{hi}	1.83	40.33	1	40.33	24.20	
Error		16.67	10	1.67		
Total		57.00	11			

In order to illustrate the likely nonindependence that is a source of bias in this analysis, we give in Exhibit 14.3 each of the 12 residuals, e_{hi}, from this model. Notice that residuals within subjects tend to have similar signs. If one observation from a subject is above the predicted value for that treatment condition, then the other observation from that subject tends to be as well. Similarly, if one residual is negative, then the other residual from that same subject is likely to be negative as well. Hence, nonindependence of observations, as defined earlier, would seem to be a problem for this analysis.

How do we handle this assumption violation? The general strategy is to do something to the data so that we are no longer dealing with nonindependent observations. In other words, we need to transform the data in some way so that the nonindependence is removed. Suppose, for instance, instead of analyzing two scores from each subject, we only analyzed a single score, in essence throwing out an arbitary half of our data. Then, clearly, the resulting six scores that were used to estimate the effect of the independent variable would all be independent of each other, since each one comes from a different subject. But somehow it seems inappropriate arbitrarily to throw out half of our data. Besides, we wouldn't know which of the two scores from each subject to throw out and which to keep. An alternative, of course, is to keep both scores but to combine them or to average them for a given subject. Then we would have for each subject a single composite score that combines the information from the two dependent observations. We could then analyze this composite score to estimate the effect of the independent variable.

EXHIBIT 14.3 ▶

Residuals from inappropriate analysis of nested data

Subject	Experimenter Present			Experimenter Absent		
	1	2	3	4	5	6
e_{hi}	.67	1.67	−1.33	−.67	1.33	−.67
	−.33	1.67	−.33	−.67	.33	.33

To do this, let us define δ_h as a weight to be applied to the hth observation within each subject. For each subject, we will then add up the weighted observations and divide by the square root of the sum of the squared weights:

$$W_i = \frac{\sum_h \delta_h Y_{hi}}{\sqrt{\sum_h \delta_h^2}}$$

In the present case, where we want a single score for each subject that is the composite or something like the average of the subject's two scores, we will set the value of δ_h equal to 1 for all observations and define W_{0i} as[1]

$$W_{0i} = \frac{Y_{1i} + Y_{2i}}{\sqrt{1^2 + 1^2}}$$

Notice that in fact W_{0i} is not a simple average. Rather than dividing the sum of each subject's two scores by 2, in computing W_{0i} we are dividing by the square root of 2. There are two reasons for doing this. First, we will at a later point deal with values of δ_h that are defined much like contrast codes are defined, so that within subjects they add up to 0. Since we wish to compute W_i by dividing by some function of the number of within subject observations, we need to eliminate possible negative values of δ_h prior to adding them up. The second reason for dividing by $\sqrt{\sum_h \delta_h^2}$ rather than by $\sum_h \delta_h$ is to preserve the sums of squares explained by the treatment variable at its appropriate value, as we show below.

To illustrate the computation of W_{0i}, let us compute it for the first hypothetical subject in these data:

$$W_{0i} = \frac{1 \times 8 + 1 \times 7}{\sqrt{1^2 + 1^2}} = \frac{15}{\sqrt{2}} = 10.61$$

Similar computations for the other five subjects in our design give the values of W_{0i} presented in Exhibit 14.4. We have now combined the two observations from each subject into a single composite one and can proceed to examine whether the presence or absence of the experimenter makes any difference to this composite W_{0i} score. We can use our regular procedures to answer this question, since we have eliminated the non-independence problem in these data by combining the two noninde-pendent observations from each subject into a single composite one. Regressing W_{0i} on X_i, we get the following model:

$$\hat{W}_{0i} = 7.78 + 2.59X_i \qquad \text{SSE} = 14.67$$

---

[1]We have added the subscript 0 to W_i to indicate a particular W_i where all values of δ_h are equal to 1. At a later point in this chapter we will deal with other W_i's having values of δ_h other than 1. However, W_{0i} will always be defined as W_i where all values of δ_h equal 1.

EXHIBIT 14.4   ▶

Values of W_{0i}:
nested design

	Experimenter Present			Experimenter Absent		
Subject	1	2	3	4	5	6
W_{0i}	10.61	12.73	7.78	4.24	6.36	4.95

Since each subject only contributes a single value of W_{0i} to this analysis, we have omitted the subscript h from X_i. There are now 6 observations contributing to this analysis rather than the 12 there were in the earlier analysis that ignored the potential nonindependence problem.

The coefficients in this model can be interpreted just as all coefficients for contrast-coded predictor variables. The only complication is that they tell us about values of W_{0i} rather than about values of Y_{hi}. In other words, the value of b_0 in this model, 7.78, equals the unweighted grand mean of the values of $\overline{W}_{0k}$, where $\overline{W}_{0k}$ equals the mean value of W_{0i} for all subjects in the kth treatment level. The value of b_1 in this model, 2.59, equals half the difference between $\overline{W}_{01}$ (mean W_{0i} with experimenter present) and $\overline{W}_{02}$ (mean with experimenter absent). Using the formula for the regression coefficient for a contrast-coded predictor that we put forward in Chapter 11, the value of b_1 equals

$$\frac{\Sigma_k\,\lambda_k\overline{W}_{0k}}{\Sigma_k\,\lambda_k^2}$$

Since Y_{hi} is measured in a meaningful metric (i.e., number of math puzzles solved), while W_{0i} is not, it is usually helpful to convert these parameter estimates back into the same metric as Y_{hi}. To do this, we simply divide each one by the denominator used in calculating W_{0i}. In other words, if we divide the value of b_0 in this expression by $\sqrt{2}$ (i.e., $\sqrt{\Sigma_h\,\delta_h^2}$), we get 5.50, which is equal to the unweighted grand mean of the two $\overline{Y}_k$ values. If we divide the value of b_1 by $\sqrt{2}$, we get 1.83, which equals half the difference between the mean Y_{hi} with the experimenter present and with the experimenter absent.

Comparing this augmented model with a compact single-parameter one provides a test of whether X_i is a reliable predictor of W_{0i}. This is equivalent to a test of whether the two values of $\overline{Y}_k$ reliably differ from each other. The resulting source table is presented in Exhibit 14.5. Notice that the value of the regression coefficient for X_i that we have included in this table is given in the metric of Y_{hi} rather than in the less meaningful metric of W_{0i}. We will do this throughout this chapter when we report regression coefficients in source tables. Notice also that, compared with the incorrect analysis that failed to remove the nonindependence in the

EXHIBIT 14.5 ▶

Preliminary nested source table

Source	b	SS	df	MS	F*	PRE
X_i	1.83	40.33	1	40.33	11.0	.73
Error		14.67	4	3.67		
Total		55.00	5			

data (source table of Exhibit 14.2), the error sum of squares and degrees of freedom have been substantially affected by correcting the problem, while the sum of squares and degrees of freedom due to the treatment variable have not been affected.[2]

In essence, what we have done here is remove from the analysis, and from the sum of squares and degrees of freedom for error, the within-subject variability. We are now only examining variability between subjects rather than variability that is partly between and partly within subjects. In other words, the original Y_{hi} scores varied within individuals as well as between them. By collapsing observations within individuals into a single W_{0i} score, we have eliminated any variability within individuals from this analysis. All that is left is variability between subjects.

Recognizing that we have in fact divided up the total variation in the Y_{hi} scores into within- and between-subject variation and then analyzed the effect of treatment, which varies between subjects, examining only the between-subject variability, we could now write out the full source table, integrating both between and within sources of variation in Y_{hi}. This source table is presented in Exhibit 14.6. Notice that there is in these data relatively little variability within subjects. The sum of squares within subjects equals 2.00, which is the difference between the total sum of squares in the original Y_{hi} scores (i.e., 57.00) and the total sum of squares in the W_{0i} scores that ignored within-subject variability (i.e., 55.00).

We can derive this value for the within-subject sum of squares by going back to the original Y_{hi} values and actually calculating the sum of the squared deviations of each individual Y_{hi} score from the mean of the subject from which a particular observation was taken, $\bar{Y}_i$. Thus, each of the scores from the first subject deviate from the first subject's mean by .5. Squaring this value, we get .25 as the squared deviation of each Y_{hi} from $\bar{Y}_i$ for the first subject. If we continue to do this for each of the

---

[2]The constancy of this sum of squares for treatment is due in part to having put $\sqrt{\Sigma_h \, \delta_h^2}$ in the denominator of W_{0i} rather than more simply $\Sigma_h \, \delta_h^2$. Had we simply constructed W_{0i} as the simple average, the sums of squares would not have worked out this nicely.

EXHIBIT 14.6 ▶

Full nested source table

Source	b	SS	df	MS	F*	PRE
X_i	1.83	40.33	1	40.33	11.00	.73
Error Between S		14.67	4	3.67		
Total Between S		55.00	5	11.00		
Total Within S		2.00	6	.33		
Total		57.00	11			

12 observations, adding up the 12 squared deviations of each observation from the individual subject means, we arrive at a sum of squares of 2.00. We don't have to actually calculate the sum of squares within subjects in this manner, since we can get it by subtracting the total sum of squares in W_{0i} from the total sum of squares in Y_{hi}. Nevertheless, it is useful to know that the within-subject sum of squares calculated in this way is in fact actually equal to the sum of the squared deviations of all observations from their subject means.

Comparing this analysis to the earlier incorrect analysis that failed to remove the within-subject variability, the sum of squares for error has been reduced slightly, by the magnitude of the within-subject variability, i.e., 2.00. The degrees of freedom for error, however, have been reduced substantially, from 10 to 4, since 6 of the original degrees of freedom in Y_{hi} were within subjects rather than between. Since the error sums of squares has been reduced proportionally less than the error degrees of freedom, our correct analysis that removes the nonindependence from the data results in a substantially smaller value of $F*$ for testing the treatment effect. With positive nonindependence (i.e., linked observations more similar on average than nonlinked observations) and an independent variable that varies between subjects (i.e., subjects are nested under its levels) it will nearly always be the case that if one conducts an analysis that inappropriately ignores the nonindependence in the data, the resulting value of $F*$ will be too large, resulting therefore in too many Type I errors. Should the nonindependence be negative, with relatively less similarity of observations within subjects than between, then the $F*$ that results from the analysis that inappropriately ignores the nonindependence will nearly always be too small, resulting therefore in too many Type II errors.

This source table provides us with an index of the degree to which the observations are in fact nonindependent. As we said before, if observations show positive nonindependence, they are more similar within groups (or subjects in this case) than they are between groups. The following statistic, known as the *intraclass correlation*, provides an index of the degree to which observations show nonindependence due to group:

$$\frac{MS_b - MS_w}{MS_b + MS_w(s - 1)}$$

where MS_b and MS_w are the mean squares between and within the groups or individuals and s is the total number of observations from each group or subject. This intraclass correlation varies between $+1$ and $-1/(s - 1)$. A positive value means that scores within groups are on average more similar than scores between groups. A negative value means greater dissimilarity on average within groups. For the present data, the intraclass correlation equals[3]

$$\frac{3.67 - .33}{3.67 + .33(1)} = .83$$

Thus these data show evidence of a great deal of nonindependence. The implication of this, as we have seen, is that the test of treatment differences is substantially biased if we fail to correct for the violation of the nonindependence assumption.[4]

We have illustrated this analysis with a very simple example. The same general strategy holds, however, with a between-subject treatment, regardless of the number of its levels and regardless of the number of within-subject observations. In other words, had we had more than two observations within each subject, we would simply have computed a value of W_{0i} for each subject, adding up all s observations from each subject and then dividing the sum by the square root of the number of within-subject observations. Had we had more than two treatment levels under which subjects were nested, we would have regressed the resulting values of W_{0i} on more than a single contrast-coded predictor variable.

---

[3]The values of MS_b and MS_w that are used in computing the intraclass correlation are the mean squares between subjects and within subjects after having removed any sums of squares due to the independent variables of interest. Thus, in this case, the value of MS_b equals 3.67 (the between-subject error sum of squares of Exhibit 14.6) rather than the total between-subject mean square.

[4]A test for whether the intraclass correlation differs from zero is provided by the ratio of the mean square between to the mean square within. This ratio can be treated as an F^* statistic (see Kenny & Judd, 1986). However, whenever observations can be thought to be linked, they should be treated as nonindependent observations even if the resulting intraclass correlation does not reliably differ from zero.

Consider, for instance, the data of Exhibit 14.7. Here we have three treatments of interest (m, the number of levels of the treatment variable equals 3), with two subjects measured in each one. Data are gathered from each subject three times (so $s = 3$ as well). To analyze these data, we need to create two contrast codes that code the three levels of our categorical predictor variable X_{i1} and X_{i2}. Then, to remove the within-subject variability from the data, we need to create a single W_{0i} score for each individual by adding up each individual's three scores and then dividing the sum by $\sqrt{3}$. We then would proceed with the analysis by regressing the W_{0i} values on the two contrast-coded predictors that code treatment level. The resulting regression coefficients would tell us about differences among $\overline{W}_{0k}$, just as any analysis of variance tells us about differences among the cell means on the dependent variable. To convert these coefficients back into the metric of Y_{hi} so that they tell us about differences in the Y_{hik} cell means, we would need to divide each coefficient by $\sqrt{\sum_h \delta_h^2}$, which in this case equals the square root of three. Notice that while there are a total of 18 observations in these data, the error degrees of freedom used to test the reliability of the treatment effect would only be three, since there are six values of W_{0i} in the regression and three parameters are estimated. The remaining 12 degrees of freedom are all within subjects.

We turn now to a consideration of appropriate analyses when subjects or groups of observations are crossed with treatment variables of interest or when those treatment variables vary within subjects rather than between them.

14.2

Nonindependence in Crossed Designs

Suppose that each subject's performance on the math puzzles had been observed once with the experimenter present and once with him absent. Then the independent variable of interest would vary within subjects

EXHIBIT 14.7 ▶

Nested data with $s = 3$ and $m = 3$

	Treatment A		Treatment B		Treatment C	
Subject	1	2	3	4	5	6
Y_{hi}	4	5	6	3	8	6
	3	5	7	5	9	8
	4	3	7	6	9	9

rather than between them. Equivalently, we would say that subjects are crossed with the treatment variable rather than nested under its levels. Consider the data of Exhibit 14.8. We have 16 observations, Y_{hi}, taken from eight different subjects in two different treatment conditions. The subscript i refers to subject and varies from 1 to 8; the subscript h continues to refer to which observation within subject we are looking at. Now, however, it also refers to levels of the independent or treatment variable of interest, since that variable varies within subjects. In these data, h varies between 1 and 2.[5]

Observations from within subjects are likely to display nonindependence. Again, for purely didactic purposes, we will initially ignore this probable nonindependence and erroneously conduct the sort of analysis of variance that was described in Chapter 11 for independent data.

Treatment is contrast coded as the predictor X_i, coded -1 if the experimenter is absent, $+1$ if present. The dependent variable, Y_i, is then regressed on X_i, with the following result:

$$\hat{Y}_i = 6.75 + .375X_i \qquad \text{SSE} = 20.75$$

As always with a simple analysis of variance using a contrast-coded predictor, the intercept equals the mean of the two treatment means, and the regression coefficient for the contrast-coded predictor equals half their difference.

EXHIBIT 14.8 ▶

Social facilitation data: crossed design

Subject	Experimenter Absent	Experimenter Present
1	7	8
2	5	5
3	6	6
4	7	9
5	8	8
6	7	7
7	5	6
8	6	8
$\overline{Y}_h$	6.375	7.125

[5]In the nested example, h referred to whether an observation within a subject was the first one or the second one. Now it refers to the levels of the within-subject independent variable. If some subjects were exposed to the two levels of the independent variable in one order and some in the other order, then we would need two within-subject subscripts to refer both to order and level of the independent variable. Such a design is a within-subject latin square design and is considered in Chapter 15.

A comparison of this model with a compact single-parameter one gives the source table of Exhibit 14.9. We conclude from this erroneous analysis that the treatment effect is not reliable since the obtained F^* does not exceed the critical value of F at α equal to .05.

The residuals from this analysis for all of the observations are presented in Exhibit 14.10. Notice the pattern in these residuals. With two exceptions, if subjects have a negative residual in one treatment, they do in the other as well. Similarly, positive residuals are found in the same subjects across treatments. Since the mean of the residuals is zero, if one residual from a subject is below the mean, the other is exceedingly likely to be as well. Positive nonindependence due to subjects is thus illustrated by these residuals.

To eliminate this nonindependence problem, we need to do an analysis on a single summary score from each subject, just as we did in the case where subjects were nested under treatment. Here, subjects are crossed with treatment, so rather than using a single summary score that is something like the average or sum of the within-subject observations, as we did in the nested case, we want to compute something like a within-subject difference score, using what amount to within-subject contrast weights. In other words, if we want to ask whether the

EXHIBIT 14.9 ▶

Source table for crossed data ignoring nonindependence

Source	b	SS	df	MS	F*	PRE
X_i	.375	2.25	1	2.25	1.52	.10
Error		20.75	14	1.48		
Total		23.00	15			

EXHIBIT 14.10 ▶

Residuals from inappropriate analysis of crossed data

Subject	Experimenter Absent	Experimenter Present
1	.625	.875
2	−1.375	−2.125
3	−.375	−1.125
4	.625	1.875
5	1.625	.875
6	.625	−.125
7	−1.375	−1.125
8	−.375	.875

difference between the two treatment means is reliable, we might do this by computing for each subject a composite score that is essentially a difference score between the subject's performances in the two treatments, and then ask whether this within-subject difference score on average differs from zero.

Let us use the same formula given earlier for combining the different observations from within a subject:

$$W_i = \frac{\sum_h \delta_h Y_{hi}}{\sqrt{\sum_h \delta_h^2}}$$

but this time we will set the values of δ_h equal to $+1$ if the observation is taken with the experimenter present and to -1 if the observation is taken with the experimenter absent. These are the same contrast values used to construct the contrast-coded predictor in the analysis just described that ignored the nonindependence in these data. But now, the comparison is within each subject and our composite score reflects the difference within each subject. To indicate that this within-subject composite score is a contrast or difference composite, we will refer to it as W_{1i}, rather than the W_{0i} that was used in the nested example where the composite score was like an average of all within-subject observations, with all values of δ_h set to 1.

Setting the values of δ_h equal to -1 if experimenter absent and $+1$ if experimenter present, the computation of W_{1i} for each subject is accomplished as follows:

$$W_{1i} = \frac{(-1)Y_{1i} + (1)Y_{2i}}{\sqrt{-1^2 + 1^2}}$$

where Y_{1i} is the ith subject's score when the experimenter is absent and Y_{2i} is the observation when the experimenter is present.

In Exhibit 14.11 we have calculated W_{1i} for each subject. In the column labeled $\sum_h \delta_h Y_{hi}$, we have calculated the numerator of W_{1i}. This numerator amounts to the simple difference between Y_{2i} and Y_{1i} for each subject. Since the denominator of W_{1i} is a constant for all subjects, W_{1i} will be perfectly correlated with the simple within-subject difference scores. It can also equal zero only when the simple difference score equals zero.

If the treatment difference is reliable, then it makes sense that the average of these W_{1i} scores across subjects should be reliably different from zero, since the average of each subject's difference score equals the difference between the treatment averages. In other words, the mean value of W_{1i} equals $(\overline{Y}_2 - \overline{Y}_1)/\sqrt{2}$, and hence $(\overline{Y}_2 - \overline{Y}_1)$ will equal zero only when the mean value of W_{1i} equals zero.

EXHIBIT 14.11 ▶

**Values of W_{1i}:
crossed design**

Subject	Y_{1i}	Y_{2i}	$\sum_h \delta_h Y_{hi}$	W_{1i}
1	7	8	1	.707
2	5	5	0	.0
3	6	6	0	.0
4	7	9	2	1.414
5	8	8	0	.0
6	7	7	0	.0
7	5	6	1	.707
8	6	8	2	1.414
Mean	6.375	7.125	.75	.530

We will use the simplest model of Chapters 4 and 5 to test whether the mean of the W_{1i} scores differs from zero. Our compact model is

MODEL C: $W_{1i} = 0 + \varepsilon_i$

The augmented model is

MODEL A: $W_{1i} = \beta_0 + \varepsilon_i$

A comparison of these two models is a test of whether the mean W_{1i} score differs reliably from zero. Equivalently, this provides a test of whether $\overline{Y}_h$ with the experimenter present differs from $\overline{Y}_h$ with the experimenter absent.

Compact and augmented models are estimated as

MODEL C: $\hat{W}_{1i} = 0$ SSE = 5.00

MODEL A: $\hat{W}_{1i} = 0.53$ SSE = 2.75

Since we have a total of eight W_{1i} values, the error degrees of freedom equal eight and seven for the compact and augmented models, respectively. Comparing these two models gives PRE and F^* values of

$$\text{PRE} = \frac{5.00 - 2.75}{5.00} = .45$$

$$F^* = \frac{.45}{(1 - .45)/7} = 5.73$$

The sum of squares reduced as we move from the compact to the augmented model equals 2.25. This value can be derived quite simply as

$$\sum_i (\hat{W}_{1iA} - \hat{W}_{1iC})^2$$

where $\hat{W}_{1iA}$ and $\hat{W}_{1iC}$ are the predicted values from the augmented and compact models. Since each of these models makes the same prediction for all eight subjects, the sum of squares reduced can be equivalently expressed as

$$n(\hat{W}_{1iA} - \hat{W}_{1iC})^2$$

Since $\hat{W}_{1iA}$ equals $\overline{W}_1$ and $\hat{W}_{1iC}$ equals zero, this reduces to

$$n(\overline{W}_1)^2 = 8(.53)^2 = 2.25$$

Before presenting all of this in a source table, let us once again interpret the value of the estimated parameter in the augmented model. As we saw in the nested design, if we take the estimated parameters and divide them by the denominator of W_i, i.e., $\sqrt{\Sigma_h\ \delta_h^2}$, we get a parameter estimate in the same metric as Y_{hi} rather than in the W_i metric. In this case, the denominator of W_{1i} equals $\sqrt{2}$. If we divide the single-parameter estimate in the augmented model, .530, which is also $\overline{W}_1$, by $\sqrt{2}$, we get .375. This value is the same as the value of b_1 in the model where the nonindependence in the data was ignored. Namely, it equals half the difference between the mean Y_{hi} when the experimenter is present and the mean Y_{hi} when the experimenter is absent.

The source table that summarizes our test is presented in Exhibit 14.12. Notice that the sum of squares for the treatment difference in this source table is identical to what it was before in the source table of Exhibit 14.9 that resulted when we ignored the nonindependence in the data.[6]

As in the nested design, what has happened as we eliminated the nonindependence from the data is that sum of squared errors and the degrees of freedom for error have been dramatically affected. Instead of having a sum of squared errors of 20.75, as we had in the inappropriate analysis of Exhibit 14.9, we now have a sum of squared errors of 2.75. The degrees of freedom for error have been reduced from 14 to 7. Rather than counting each value of Y_{hi} as an observation, we now have only eight observations, one from each subject, hence the degrees of freedom

EXHIBIT 14.12 ▶

Preliminary crossed source table

Source	b	SS	df	MS	F*	PRE
Treatment	.375	2.25	1	2.25	5.73	.45
Error		2.75	7	.39		
Total		5.00	8			

[6]This equivalence is ensured by the fact that the denominator of W_i equals $\sqrt{\Sigma_h\ \delta_h^2}$. Had we just computed a simple difference score for each subject, i.e., the numerator of W_{1i}, the sum of squares would not have been equivalent although the resulting PRE and F* values would have been correct.

Conceptually, the sum of squared errors in this source table represents the interaction of treatment with subjects. If all of the between treatment differences were the same across subjects, then there would be no variation in the values of W_{1i} around their mean, and hence the augmented model that predicts the mean value of W_{1i} for each case would fit the data without error. This amounts to saying that the treatment effect would not vary from subject to subject. The sum of squared errors from the augmented model derives from the fact that the magnitude of the difference between the treatment conditions varies from subject to subject. Hence, the error term in this source table can be thought of as the sum of squares associated with the treatment by subject interaction.

There is still considerable variation in the Y_{hi} scores that is not represented in this source table. In the source table of Exhibit 14.9 where nonindependence was ignored, we saw that the total sum of squares of Y_{hi} equals 23.00. The difference between this value and the total sum of squares for the W_{1i} in the source table we have just presented, 5.00, equals the total sum of squares between subjects. In other words, we have once again divided up the sum of squares of Y_{hi} into two portions: one between subjects and one within subjects. Since the treatment variable in this crossed example varies within subjects rather than between them, we have looked only at the within-subject variation in the data to estimate and test the treatment effect. We have entirely omitted the between-subject variation from this analysis. In the earlier section of this chapter, we considered the case where subjects were nested under the treatment variable or, equivalently, the treatment variable varied between subjects. There, we conducted our analysis only examining between-subject variation in the data. Here, we have conducted our analysis only examining the within-subject variation in the data, since the treatment variable varies within subjects. What we now need to do, as we did in the earlier section, is to report both the between- and within-subject variation in the values of Y_{hi} in a single source table.

To calculate the between-subject sum of squares in these data, let us use the same procedure we did earlier when considering a treatment variable that varied between subjects. There, to capture only the between subject variation, we computed values of W_{0i} for each subject, assigning δ_h weights of 1 to all observations within subjects. Let us do the same thing here. The resulting W_{0i} values are given in Exhibit 14.13. The total sum of squares of these W_{0i} values equals 18, the difference between the total sum of squares of Y_{hi} and the total within-subject sum of squares. This sum of squares total for W_{0i} equals the total between-subject sum of squares, just as it did in the earlier design where subjects were nested under treatment conditions.

EXHIBIT 14.13 ▶

Calculation of W_{0i}

Subject	Y_{1i}	Y_{2i}	$\sum_h \delta_h Y_{hi}$	W_{0i}
1	7	8	15	10.61
2	5	5	10	7.07
3	6	6	12	8.49
4	7	9	16	11.31
5	8	8	16	11.31
6	7	7	14	9.90
7	5	6	11	7.78
8	6	8	14	9.90
Mean	6.375	7.125	13.50	9.55

We are now in a position to write out the full source table for these data, incorporating variation both within and between subjects, and including the sum of squares due to treatment as a component of the within-subject variation. This source table is presented in Exhibit 14.14.

Let us review the general procedure we used in both this design and the earlier one and that we will use subsequently. First, to capture the between-subject variation in the data, we compute values of W_{0i} for all subjects, setting all values of δ_h equal to 1. This amounts to adding up all values of Y_{hi} for each subject and then dividing that sum by the square root of the total number of observations within a subject. The total sum of squares of this W_{0i} variable is the sum of squares between subjects. Associated with it are degrees of freedom between subjects,

EXHIBIT 14.14 ▶

Full crossed source table

Source	b	SS	df	MS	F*	PRE
Total Between S		18.00	7	2.57		
Total Within S		5.00	8	.63		
Treatment	.375	2.25	1	2.25	5.73	.45
Treatment by Subjects (Error within)		2.75	7	.39		
Total		23.00	15			

equal to the number of subjects minus 1. If the treatment variable of interest is between subjects, then this W_{0i} is regressed on a treatment variable contrast-code predictor to test the reliability of the treatment difference.

To obtain the within-subject sum of squares, values of W_{1i} are computed, forming a composite of each subject's two scores by taking the difference between them. This in essence amounts to using within-subject contrast codes to form W_{1i}. Assuming that there are only two observations from each subject, as in the examples we have considered so far, the total within-subject sum of squares is equal to the sum of squared deviations of this W_{1i} around zero. If the treatment variable of interest is within subjects, then this total within-subject sum of squares can be partitioned into two components, a treatment sum of squares and a sum of squares due to the treatment by subject interaction. (Recall that the sum of squared errors of W_{1i} around its mean amounts to variation between subjects in the treatment difference. Hence it amounts to the treatment by subject interaction.) The former sum of squares has associated with it a single degree of freedom, while the latter has associated with it degrees of freedom equal to the number of subjects minus 1. The ratio of the mean squares for these two within-subject terms constitutes an F^* ratio that can be used to test the reliability of the treatment effect. This test is equivalent to testing whether the mean W_{1i} value is reliably different from zero. If it is, then the within-subject treatment difference can be considered reliable, since the W_{1i} variable assesses the within-subject treatment difference.

In the example we have just been considering, scores within subjects are on average more similar than scores between subjects, as shown by the positive value of the intraclass correlation in these data:

$$\text{Intraclass } r = \frac{2.57 - .39}{2.57 + .39(1)} = .74$$

We saw that when the nonindependence assumption violation was ignored in these data, the resulting value of F^* was too small: It underestimated what the F^* for testing the treatment difference ought to be. As a result too many Type II errors will be made. With negative nonindependence, meaning greater dissimilarity on average within subjects or groups than between, and a treatment variable that is crossed with subjects, ignoring nonindependence in data will generally cause the resulting F^* value to be too large, resulting in too many Type I errors. In sum, the direction of the bias in F^* introduced by ignoring nonindependence in one's data is a joint function of the direction of that nonindependence and of whether the treatment variable to be tested varies within or between subjects. The table in Exhibit 14.15 summarizes these conclusions.

	Nonindependence	
	Positive	Negative
Groups *nested* under treatment	*F** too large	*F** too small
Groups *crossed* with treatment	*F** too small	*F** too large

14.3

Multiple Within-Subject Factors

In the example discussed in the preceding section, there was only a single within-subject factor having only two levels. The procedures we have discussed for handling nonindependence in this case generalize quite readily to more complex cases where subjects are crossed with multiple within-subject factors, each having two or more levels. Consider the following example. Each of four subjects is measured in each of four conditions, defined by crossing two factors, Letter and Color, that each have two levels. In other words, each subject is measured once in each of the unique treatment combinations defined by the 2 × 2 design portrayed in Exhibit 14.16. The hypothetical data are displayed there as well.

EXHIBIT 14.16 ▶

Data from a 2 × 2 within-subjects design

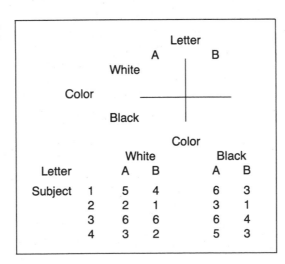

Letter	Color			
	White		Black	
	A	B	A	B
Subject 1	5	4	6	3
2	2	1	3	1
3	6	6	6	4
4	3	2	5	3

The analysis proceeds as follows: First, we need to realize that total variation in these Y_{hi} scores can be broken up into two components: between subjects and within subjects. To examine the between-subject variation in these data, we compute W_{0i} for each individual, setting all values of δ_h at 1. Since all treatment variables of interest are within subjects rather than between, we will not be regressing this W_{0i} score on any treatment contrast codes. Rather, we will simply calculate its total sum of squares and report it in the source table as the sum of squares between subjects.

Proceeding with this part of the analysis, the values of W_{0i} for each subject are given in Exhibit 14.17. To illustrate the calculations, for subject 1, W_{0i} equals

$$\frac{(1)5 + (1)4 + (1)6 + (1)3}{\sqrt{4}} = 9$$

The total sum of squares of these W_{0i} equals 31.5, with associated degrees of freedom equal to three, i.e., the number of subjects minus 1. Since all treatment variables of interest are within subjects, this sum of squares will not get divided up further. Rather it will simply be reported as the between-subjects sum of squares in the resulting source table.

Turning to the within-subject variation, the two within-subject factors can be used to generate three sets of contrast codes, one to represent the Color factor, one to represent Letter, and one to represent the interaction between Color and Letter. These contrast-code values will be used as δ_h values in computing three different W_i scores for each subject. Assuming that the first set of δ_h codes the Color difference, then the values of δ_h used to compute W_{1i} might be -1 if White and $+1$ if Black. This W_{1i} will then represent the difference between the Black and White observations for each subject. The second set of δ_h values, used in computing W_{2i}, will code the Letter difference. Finally the interaction between Color and Letter will be coded into the W_{3i} composite variable. The values of δ_h used in computing these three within-subject difference scores are given in Exhibit 14.18. The resulting values of W_{1i}, W_{2i}, and

EXHIBIT 14.17 ▶

W_{0i} values for 2 × 2 within-subjects design

	W_{0i}
Subject 1	9.0
Subject 2	3.5
Subject 3	11.0
Subject 4	6.5

EXHIBIT 14.18 ▶

Within-subject contrast codes (δ_h) for 2 × 2 within-subject design

		Color			
		White		Black	
	Letter	A	B	A	B
W_{1i}	(Color Contrast)	−1	−1	+1	+1
W_{2i}	(Letter Contrast)	+1	−1	+1	−1
W_{3i}	(Interaction Contrast)	−1	+1	+1	−1

W_{3i} tell us about the within-subject differences due to Color, Letter, and their interaction. What we want to know is whether the values of $\overline{Y}_h$ differ reliably as a function of Color, Letter, and their interaction. Since the mean of the within-subject difference for each of these factors is equal to the difference between the means, we can simply test whether W_{1i}, W_{2i}, and W_{3i} have means that reliably differ from zero. We will do this by comparing three augmented and compact models, one each for W_{1i}, W_{2i}, and W_{3i}. The augmented model in each case will be the simple single-parameter model, making the constant prediction of the mean:

MODELs A: $W_{1i} = \beta_0 + \varepsilon_i$

$W_{2i} = \beta_0 + \varepsilon_i$

$W_{3i} = \beta_0 + \varepsilon_i$

The compact model will make the constant prediction that the mean equals zero:

MODELs C: $W_{1i} = 0 + \varepsilon_i$

$W_{2i} = 0 + \varepsilon_i$

$W_{3i} = 0 + \varepsilon_i$

The comparison of these models will in each case allow a test of whether the within-subject difference coded by the W_i in question reliably differs from zero.

To be more concrete, Exhibit 14.19 presents the values of W_{1i}, W_{2i}, and W_{3i} for each subject. These were derived using the values of δ_h given in Exhibit 14.18. To test whether the Color difference is reliable, we compare the following two models:

Model C: $\hat{W}_{1i} = 0$ SSE = 3.50

Model A: $\hat{W}_{1i} = .25$ SSE = 3.25

The sum of squares reduced, as we move between these two models, equals $n(\overline{W}_1)^2 = 4(.25)^2 = .25$.

EXHIBIT 14.19

Values of W_{1i}, W_{2i}, W_{3i} for 2 × 2 within-subjects design

		W_{1i} Color	W_{2i} Letter	W_{3i} Interaction
Subject:	1	0	2	1
	2	.5	1.5	.5
	3	−1	1	1
	4	1.5	1.5	.5
Mean		.25	1.5	.75

To test whether the Letter difference is reliable, we compare the models

Model C: $\hat{W}_{2i} = 0$ SSE = 9.50

Model A: $\hat{W}_{2i} = 1.5$ SSE = .50

The sum of squares reduced, as we move between these two models, equals $n(\overline{W}_2)^2 = 4(1.5)^2 = 9.00$.

Finally, to test the Color by Letter interaction, we compare the models

Model C: $\hat{W}_{3i} = 0$ SSE = 2.50

Model A: $\hat{W}_{3i} = .75$ SSE = .25

The sum of squares reduced in this case equals $n(\overline{W}_3)^2 = 4(.75)^2 = 2.25$.

We have broken up the total within-subject variation in these data into three components: that associated with the Color contrast, that associated with the Letter contrast, and that associated with the Color by Letter interaction contrast. Each of these within-subject contrasts has associated with it a W_i difference score for each subject. For each one, we then examined whether its mean departs from zero. The resulting part of the source table that examines only the within-subject variation in these data is presented in Exhibit 14.20.

The values of b given in this table are the values of b_0 from the three augmented models, i.e., the values of $\overline{W}_1$, $\overline{W}_2$, and $\overline{W}_3$, transformed back into the metric of Y_{hi} by dividing each one by $\sqrt{\sum_h \delta_h^2}$. For each W_i in the present analysis, $\sqrt{\sum_h \delta_h^2}$ equals 2. Accordingly, we have divided each $\overline{W}$ by 2 to get the values of b included in the above source table. Equivalently, in each of the augmented models, we have divided b_0 by 2. The resulting values estimate the within-subject differences associated with the comparison that each set of within-subject contrast weights codes. For instance, the first set of contrast weights codes the within-subject distinction of Color, assigning δ_h values of -1 if White and $+1$

EXHIBIT 14.20 ▶

Within-subject portion of source table for color by letter data set

Source	b	SS	df	MS	F*	PRE
Color	.125	.25	1	.25	.23	.08
Color × Ss		3.25	3	1.08		
Letter	.75	9.00	1	9.00	53.89	.95
Letter × Ss		.50	3	.17		
Color × Letter	.375	2.25	1	2.25	27.01	.90
Color × Letter × Ss		.25	3	.08		
Total Within Ss		15.50	12			

if Black. The value of b given for this color effect in the above source table, .125, equals one half the difference between the mean of the Y_{hi} observations under the black color condition (3.875) and the mean of those under white (3.625). It also equals $\overline{W}_1/2$.

The other thing to note about this partial source table is that we have used the terms Color × Ss, Letter × Ss, and Color × Letter × Ss to refer to the three error sums of squares. The sums of squares reported in these rows of the source table are in fact the sums of squared errors from the three augmented models for W_{1i}, W_{2i}, and W_{3i}. As explained previously, since each of these W_i's represents a within-subject difference associated with a certain treatment, variation in these W_i's around their means amounts to variations between subjects in the magnitude of the associated treatment effect. Conceptually, variations between subjects in the magnitude of a treatment effect can be thought of as an interaction between that treatment and subjects. We use this label since it is most commonly used in other treatments of within-subject analysis of variance.

It is perhaps useful at this point to insert a computational note. The values in the above source table are extremely easily derived from most statistical software packages. Once one has computed the appropriate W_i value for each subject, examining the univariate statistics for that W_i across subjects provides all the necessary information for the source table. The sum of squares associated with or due to a within-subject factor is simply equal to the number of subjects times the squared mean value of the W_i that codes that particular within-subject contrast. Thus, in the case of the Color factor, the mean value of W_i that codes the within-subject Color contrast is .25. Squaring this we get .0625, which, when multiplied by the number of subjects, i.e., 4, gives a sum of squares due to the Color factor of .25. Similarly, the sum of squares due to the Letter factor, 9.00, equals the squared mean value of the W_i that codes the Letter contrast, 1.5^2, times the number of subjects.

The sum of squares associated with a factor's error term is simply the sum of squared errors from the augmented single-parameter model. This amounts to the sum of squared deviations of W_i around the mean value of W_i, which is equal to $n - 1$ times the variance of W_i. Thus, for instance, in the case of the Color factor, the variance of W_i that codes the Color contrast equals 1.083. If we multiply this by the number of subjects minus 1 (i.e., 3) we get 3.25, which is the sum of squares for the Color error term, referred to in the source table as the Color by subjects sum of squares. The degrees of freedom for this error term are simply equal to the number of subjects minus 1. As a result the mean square for the error term equals the variance of W_i.

We can now add on the between-subject sum of squares to this source table, resulting in the full source table for these data. This source table is given in Exhibit 14.21. The last line in this table represents the total sum of squares in all Y_{hi} scores. It equals the sum of the total sums of squares between and within subjects.

14.3.1 A Somewhat Technical Note

A few comments about our approach to the analysis of within-subject factors seem appropriate at this point, particularly for readers who are familiar with more traditional discussions of repeated measures analysis of variance procedures as set forth in books on experimental design.

EXHIBIT 14.21 ▶

Full source table for color by letter data set

Source	b	SS	df	MS	F*	PRE
Between Ss		31.50	3	10.50		
Color	.125	.25	1	.25	.23	.08
Color × Ss		3.25	3	1.08		
Letter	.75	9.00	1	9.00	53.89	.95
Letter × Ss		.50	3	.17		
Color × Letter	.375	2.25	1	2.25	27.01	.90
Color × Letter × Ss		.25	3	.08		
Total Within Ss		15.50	12			
Total		47.00	15			

Readers without that background may find some of these comments elucidating as well.

First, it should be noted that each within-subject comparison, coded by a specific W_i, has its own unique error term. This error term amounts to the interaction between that specific within-subject treatment comparison and subjects. This is quite unlike the case where the factors or independent variables of interest are all between subjects. In this latter case, a common error term is used for testing all of the single-degree-of-freedom between-subject comparisons. In the within-subject case, each single-degree-of-freedom comparison has its own unique error term.

In the Letter by Color example we have just considered, each single-degree-of-freedom within-subject comparison represented a comparison between the two levels of a categorical treatment variable or an interaction comparison between two categorical treatment variables. Thus, each categorical treatment variable had only two levels and its effects could be examined with a single within-subject comparison, i.e., a single W_i. If a within-subject categorical treatment variable has more than two levels, then more than one single-degree-of-freedom within-subject comparison could be formed. Accordingly, a within-subject factor having three levels will generate two W_i comparisons, a factor having four levels will generate three W_i within-subject comparisons, and so forth. Each of these within-subject comparisons will be tested by examining whether the mean of the W_i scores differs reliably from zero, just as we did in the Letter by Color example. Accordingly, each single-degree-of-freedom comparison within subjects will continue to have its own unique error term even when those single-degree-of-freedom comparisons all derive from a single categorical within-subject treatment variable having more than two levels.

In most treatments of repeated measures analysis of variance, the error terms for within-subject treatment comparisons are pooled or averaged together when those comparisons derive from a single categorical treatment variable of interest. On the other hand, pooling of within-subject error terms is generally not done in the case of within-subject comparisons from different categorical treatment variables. (A discussion of procedures for pooling terms in the within-subject portions of a source table is included near the end of this chapter.) We see little reason to pool unique error terms in either case. Since each single-degree-of-freedom comparison has its own unique error term, i.e., the interaction of that comparison with subjects, we see little reason to combine them or pool them either when they come from multiple categorical treatment variables or from a single one. The common practice of pooling derives from the common tendency to examine the effects of a categorical treatment variable with a single multiple-degree-of-freedom test rather than examining more focused single-degree-of-freedom comparisons. Our strategy of including separate error terms for each within-subject single-degree-of-freedom comparison is consistent with our general preference for focused single-degree-of-freedom tests.

A benefit of our preference for single-degree-of-freedom comparisons and our reluctance to pool their associated unique error terms is that the usually difficult assumption of homogeneity of covariance of observations within subjects, or, as it is also called, the *compound symmetry* assumption, is no longer necessary.

14.4

Nonindependence in Mixed Designs

Experimental designs in which subjects are nested under one or more factors and simultaneously crossed with one or more other factors are used with some frequency in psychological research. Suppose 16 subjects were involved in a memory study. They were all read two lists of integers. After each list, they were asked to recite from short-term memory as many of the integers they had been read as possible. Each subject then has two scores, the number of integers remembered from the first list and the number remembered from the second list. This factor thus varies within subjects (or, equivalently, subjects are crossed with it). It is labeled First versus Second lists. In addition, half of the subjects were read the integers and asked to recall them while dribbling a basketball. The other half were not so preoccupied. This factor, whether or not subjects were dribbling a basketball, is thus between subjects (or, equivalently, subjects are nested under its levels). It will be referred to as the Active versus Passive factor.

The hypothetical data are given in Exhibit 14.22. There are three questions of interest in these data. First, we might like to know whether dribbling a basketball interfered with short-term memory. Thus, we would like to know whether the average number of integers remembered by subjects in the Active condition was less than the average number remembered by subjects in the Passive condition. We will answer this question about the effect of the between-subject factor just as we did earlier, by computing W_{0i}, setting all values of δ_h equal to 1. We will then regress this W_{0i} on a contrast-coded predictor that codes whether subjects were in the Active or Passive conditions, X_i.

The second question of interest is whether subjects performed better on the Second list than they did on the First. Here we want to know about the effect of the within-subject factor. We will answer this question as we did earlier, by defining contrast codes as values for δ_h: $+1$ if Second

EXHIBIT 14.22 ▶

Hypothetical memory data: mixed design

		Passive				Active	
		First	Second			First	Second
Subject	1	7	8	Subject	9	6	6
	2	5	6		10	5	6
	3	6	9		11	4	4
	4	7	6		12	3	5
	5	8	8		13	4	5
	6	7	7		14	5	5
	7	5	6		15	3	3
	8	6	8		16	3	5

list and -1 if First list. These values for δ_h will be used to compute W_{1i}, coding the within-subject difference in the number of integers remembered. We will then ask whether the mean W_{1i} differs from zero. This will provide an answer to the question about whether the mean number of integers remembered from the Second list is different from the mean remembered from the First list.

The third question we have not met before. The two factors, First versus Second list and Active versus Passive conditions, are themselves crossed. It thus is possible and even desirable to ask about their interaction: does the Active versus Passive difference depend on whether we are looking at the First list or at the Second? An equivalent way of asking this question about the interaction of the between- and within-subject factors is to ask if the difference between the Second and First lists depends on whether subjects were Active or Passive. Intuitively, this second way of asking about the interaction seems to make more sense. If we think of the Second versus First list difference in memory as indicative of how able subjects are to improve in short-term memory performance, then the question about the interaction is a question about whether memory improvement depends on whether subjects are Active or Passive.

How do we go about answering this third question about the interaction between a within-subject factor and a between-subject factor? We want to know if the difference associated with the within-subject factor, Second versus First list, depends on or varies with the between-subject factor, Active versus Passive. Since W_{1i} estimates for each subject the within-subject difference between First and Second lists, it seems appropriate to ask whether this within-subject difference score depends in turn on the contrast-coded predictor that codes Active versus Passive, i.e., X_i.

Let us proceed with the analysis that we have just outlined. First, we focus on the analysis of the between-subject factor, Active versus Passive. For each subject, we compute W_{0i}, setting all values of δ_h equal to 1. This amounts to adding up each subject's two observations and dividing this sum by $\sqrt{2}$. The resulting values of W_{0i} are given in Exhibit 14.23. We code Active versus Passive condition using a contrast code X_i, defined as +1 if Passive and −1 if Active. We regress W_{0i} on this condition contrast code, yielding the estimated model:

$$\hat{W}_{0i} = 8.00 + 1.63X_i \qquad SSE = 24.94$$

We wish to ask whether these W_{0i} scores depend on Active versus Passive condition. Hence, we want to compare this augmented model with a compact one in which the coefficient for X_i is forced to equal zero:

$$\hat{W}_{0i} = 8.00 \qquad SSE = 67.72$$

This comparison gives rise to the between-subject portion of the source table presented in Exhibit 14.24. The value for the coefficient b in this table is equal to the value of the regression coefficient in the augmented model, i.e., 1.63, divided by $\sqrt{\Sigma_h \delta_h^2}$ or $\sqrt{2}$. It is thus expressed in the Y_{hi} metric and equals half the difference between the mean number of

EXHIBIT 14.23 ▶

Values of W_{0i} for mixed design data

		Passive			Active
Subject	1	10.61	Subject	9	8.49
	2	7.78		10	7.78
	3	10.61		11	5.66
	4	9.19		12	5.66
	5	11.31		13	6.36
	6	9.89		14	7.07
	7	7.78		15	4.24
	8	9.89		16	5.66
Mean		9.63			6.37

EXHIBIT 14.24 ▶

Between-subject portion of source table for mixed design data

Source	b	SS	df	MS	F*	PRE
Active vs. Passive	−1.15	42.78	1	42.78	24.02	.63
Error		24.94	14	1.78		
Total Between Ss		67.72	15			

integers remembered in the Passive condition and the mean number remembered in the Active condition.

We now turn to the within-subjects analysis. We first define values of δ_h for calculating W_{1i} to code the within-subject difference between Second and First lists. We will set δ_h equal to -1 if the observation is from the First list and $+1$ if it is from the second. Using these within-subject contrast values, each subject's score of W_{1i} is calculated and shown in Exhibit 14.25. We want to know two things about these W_{1i} scores. First, to test whether there is a reliable difference between Second and First lists, we want to test whether the mean W_{1i} computed across all 16 subjects differs from zero. Since W_{1i} is a composite score for each subject based on the Second versus First list difference for each subject, asking whether its mean equals zero is equivalent to asking whether the mean difference between Second and First lists equals zero.

Second, to test whether the list difference, Second versus First, depends on whether subjects were Active or Passive, we want to examine whether W_{1i} scores differ as a function of X_i, the contrast-coded predictor representing the Active versus Passive between-subject factor. This will provide a test of the interaction between the within-subject factor, Second versus First list, and the between-subject factor, Active versus Passive.

To answer both of these questions, we regress W_{1i} on X_i. As always, this is a straightforward, between-subject regression, regressing a single measure from each subject, in this case W_{1i}, on a between-subject contrast code. Since we have coded Active versus Passive condition using a contrast-coded predictor X_i the intercept in this regression equation equals the overall mean of W_{1i} for all 16 subjects, and the regression coefficient for X_i equals half the difference between the W_{1i} means for the subjects in the two different conditions. The resulting model is

$$\hat{W}_{1i} = .57 + .04X_i \qquad \text{SSE} = 8.19$$

EXHIBIT 14.25 ▶

Values of W_{1i} for mixed design data

		Passive			Active
Subject	1	.71	Subject	9	0
	2	.71		10	.71
	3	2.12		11	0
	4	−.71		12	1.41
	5	0		13	.71
	6	0		14	0
	7	.71		15	0
	8	1.41		16	1.41
Mean		.62			.53

To test whether the overall mean of W_{1i} differs from zero, we want to compare this augmented model with a compact one in which β_0 is set at zero:

$$\hat{W}_{1i} = 0 + .04X_i \qquad \text{SSE} = 13.47$$

This comparison provides a test of whether the mean number of integers recalled from the Second list differs from the mean number recalled from the First list. The sum of squares reduced as we move between these two models equals 5.28. As before, this sum of squares due to the within-subject factor is equal to

$$n(\overline{W}_1^2) = 16(.57^2)$$

To test whether the Second versus First list difference depends on the between-subject Active versus Passive factor, we want to compare the augmented two-parameter model with a compact one in which β_1 is forced to equal zero:

$$\hat{W}_{1i} = .57 \qquad \text{SSE} = 8.22$$

The sum of squares reduced between this compact model and the augmented one equals .03. This is the sum of squares explained by the interaction between the within-subject factor, Second versus First list, and the between-subject factor, Active versus Passive.

Notice that the sum of squares for the augmented two-parameter model for W_{1i} is used as the error sum of squares for testing both of these effects, i.e., both the main effect of the within-subject factor and its interaction with the between-subject factor. It has an associated 14 degrees of freedom (i.e., $N - PA$). Let us think conceptually for a minute about this error sum of squares. Since W_{1i} captures the within-subject difference due to Second versus First list, and since the predicted values of W_{1i} are equivalent to the mean Second versus First list differences for subjects in the Passive and Active conditions, variability of individual W_{1i} scores around those predicted values amounts to variability between subjects within conditions in the magnitude of the Second versus First list difference. Hence, we can think of this error sum of squares as the sum of squares associated with the interaction between the within-subject factor and subjects within levels of the between-subject factor.

This within-subject portion of the analysis of these data gives rise to the partial source table of Exhibit 14.26. The values of b given in this table have once again been converted back into the metric of Y_{hi}.

We can now merge the two partial source tables into an overall analysis of variance table for this mixed design. This is given in Exhibit 14.27. Notice that the two total sums of squares, one entirely within subjects and the other entirely between subjects, add up, as do the degrees of freedom within and between subjects. The total sum of

EXHIBIT 14.26 ▶

Within-subject portion of source table for mixed design table

Source	b	SS	df	MS	F*	PRE
List (2nd vs. 1st)	.41	5.28	1	5.28	9.03	.39
List by Active vs. Passive	.03	.03	1	.03	.05	.00
List by Ss within Active vs. Passive		8.19	14	.58		
Total within Ss		13.50	16			

EXHIBIT 14.27 ▶

Full source table for mixed design data

Source	b	SS	df	MS	F*	PRE
Between Subjects						
Active vs. Passive	−1.15	42.78	1	42.78	24.02	.63
Error Between Ss		24.94	14	1.78		
Total Between Ss		67.72	15			
Within Subjects						
List (2nd vs. 1st)	.41	5.28	1	5.28	9.03	.39
List by Active vs. Passive	.03	.03	1	.03	.05	.00
List by Ss within Active vs. Passive		8.19	14	.58		
Total within Ss		13.50	16			
Total		81.22	31			

squares reported in the table, 81.22, equals the total sum of squares of Y_{hi} around the grand mean of all 32 Y_{hi} observations, with naturally enough, 31 degrees of freedom.

We can briefly summarize the results of this hypothetical study by noting that the between-subject effect of Active versus Passive is highly reliable: subjects who attempt to recall lists of integers while dribbling a basketball do reliably less well than those who were not so occupied. Second, there is a reliable, although smaller, effect for First versus Second list, with subjects showing better short-term memory for integers on the second trial than on the first. Finally, there is no indication in these data that subjects' activity (i.e., whether or not they were dribbling a basketball) affected their improvement from the First list to the Second.

14.4.1 A More Complicated Mixed Design

The strategy for analyzing mixed designs that we have just illustrated generalizes quite readily to much more complicated designs. Before considering such a design, let us review and summarize that strategy.

When there are multiple observations (Y_{hi}) that are likely to be linked or nonindependent because they come from the same subject or are grouped in some other way, one needs to combine those observations, analyzing composite scores in order to meet the assumption that residuals in MODELs are independent of each other. With s linked observations from each subject or group, one forms a total of s composite W_i scores and these composite W_i scores are used as dependent variables in a series of between-subject regression models. The first of these W_i scores, W_{0i}, is defined by setting all values of δ_h equal to 1, adding up the s scores from each subject or group and then dividing by the square root of the number of scores, $\sqrt{s}$. This W_{0i} composite score captures all of the between-subject variation in the Y_{hi} scores. One then regresses this W_{0i} composite score on the contrast-coded predictors (or continuous predictors as well; see Chapter 15) that code any between-subject factors of interest. In this way one tests the main effects and interactions of these between-subject factors, just as they were tested in Chapter 11. If there are no between-subject factors, then the total variation in W_{0i} is simply reported as the between-subject sum of squares in Y_{hi}.

The remaining $s - 1$ composite scores are computed by using within-subject contrast codes as values of δ_h in order to code the within-subject factors of interest. Thus, each remaining W_i (from the set $W_{1i}, W_{2i}, \ldots, W_{(s-1)i}$) codes a specific within-subject comparison or difference between observations, capturing the main effects and interactions of the within-subject factors of interest. Each of these W_i composite scores represents a single-degree-of-freedom within-subject comparison. One then regresses these W_i scores on the contrast-coded predictors that code any between-subject factors of interest. In each of these regression models, a test of whether the intercept differs reliably from zero amounts to a test of the within-subject comparison or contrast coded by that particular W_i. (If there are no between-subject factors, then one uses the simple single-parameter model of Chapters 4 and 5 to test whether the mean of each W_i differs from zero.) Tests of the regression coefficients for the between-subject contrast-coded predictors in each of these models amount to tests of interactions between the within-subject contrast coded by that particular W_i and the between-subject contrasts.

Having given the strategy in its general form, let us now apply it to some hypothetical data from a relatively complicated mixed design. Consider the data in Exhibit 14.28. The data were collected by varying four different experimental factors, labeled Height, Color, Letter, and Number. Color and Letter each have three levels; Height and Number each have two levels. Subjects are nested under Height and Color, while being crossed with Letter and Number. In sum then, each subject is observed under one of six conditions defined by crossing the two between-subject variables of Height and Color. Each subject provides six different observations, being observed once in the six conditions defined by crossing the two within-subject variables of Letter and Number. Three subjects are observed in each cell defined by the between-subject factors.

The data are analyzed by first examining the effects of the between-subject factors, Color and Height. This is done by computing a W_{0i} for each subject defining all δ_h values as 1. In other words, we sum each subject's six scores and divide that sum by $\sqrt{6}$. Variation in this W_{0i} represents variation that is totally between subjects. To estimate and test the reliability of the between-subject factors and their interaction, we regress this W_{0i} on a set of contrast-coded predictors that define the between-subject factors. The between-subject contrast-coded predictors are labeled X_1 to X_5. Their contrast-code values, λ_{jk}, are given in the top half of Exhibit 14.29. As is shown there, X_1 and X_2 define specific comparisons among the three levels of the Color factor, X_3 codes Height,

EXHIBIT 14.28 ▼

Data for more complicated mixed design

Color								Height						
		High Letter							Low Letter					
		A		B		C			A		B		C	
	Number	1	2	1	2	1	2	Number	1	2	1	2	1	2
Red	Subject 1	5	6	4	5	7	8	Subject 4	7	7	5	6	8	7
	Subject 2	3	5	2	3	4	4	Subject 5	6	8	7	7	9	9
	Subject 3	6	5	4	4	6	7	Subject 6	3	4	4	5	6	3
Black	Subject 7	2	4	3	3	1	2	Subject 10	8	9	9	9	7	8
	Subject 8	3	2	2	3	1	1	Subject 11	6	5	8	7	8	9
	Subject 9	2	3	4	5	1	2	Subject 12	7	6	6	9	8	7
Green	Subject 13	9	7	6	8	7	7	Subject 16	3	1	1	2	1	1
	Subject 14	5	5	9	8	6	8	Subject 17	2	3	4	4	1	3
	Subject 15	7	9	5	8	6	8	Subject 18	3	2	5	4	2	4

Between-Subject Codes

	Red Hi	Red Lo	Black Hi	Black Lo	Green Hi	Green Lo
λ_1 (X_1)	2	2	−1	−1	−1	−1
λ_2 (X_2)	0	0	−1	−1	+1	+1
λ_3 (X_3)	−1	+1	−1	+1	−1	+1
λ_4 (X_4)	−2	+2	+1	−1	+1	−1
λ_5 (X_5)	0	0	+1	−1	−1	+1

Within-Subject Codes

	A1	A2	B1	B2	C1	C2
δ_0 (W_{0i})	+1	+1	+1	+1	+1	+1
δ_1 (W_{1i})	−2	−2	+1	+1	+1	+1
δ_2 (W_{2i})	0	0	+1	+1	−1	−1
δ_3 (W_{3i})	+1	−1	+1	−1	+1	−1
δ_4 (W_{4i})	−2	2	+1	−1	+1	−1
δ_5 (W_{5i})	0	0	+1	−1	−1	+1

EXHIBIT 14.29 ▲

Contrast-code values for mixed design

and X_4 and X_5 each code parts of the Color by Height interaction. The following model results:

$$\hat{W}_{0i} = 12.54 + .50X_1 - .20X_2 + .75X_3$$
$$+ .41X_4 - 5.92X_5 \quad \text{SSE} = 76.22$$

To test whether each between-subject contrast-coded predictor reliably affects W_{0i}, and equivalently Y_{hi}, we simply test whether each of the regression coefficients for X_1 through X_5 in this model reliably differs from zero. The top portion of the source table in Exhibit 14.30, labeled "Between Ss," summarizes the results of this analysis, giving the sum of squares associated with each between-subject contrast and the associated F^* statistic. Also included there are the regression coefficients for each of the contrasts from the model given above, having transformed each one back into the original Y_{hi} metric by dividing each coefficient by $\sqrt{6}$.

Next we turn to the within-subject variation in these data, in order to analyze both the effects of the within-subject factors, Letter and Number, and the effects of the interactions between within-subject factors and between-subject factors. To do this, we first need to create a set of within-subject contrast codes to define the within-subject factors. These within-subject contrast codes are labeled δ_1 through δ_5 in the bottom

Source	b	SS	df	MS	F*	PRE
Between SS						
X_1	.20	8.96	1	8.96	1.41	.11
X_2	−.07	.50	1	.50	.02	.01
X_3	.30	10.08	1	10.08	1.59	.12
X_4	.12	6.00	1	6.00	.95	.07
X_5	−2.43	420.50	1	420.50	66.20	.85
Error between		76.22	12	6.35		
Total between		522.27	17			
Within SS						
W_1	.09	1.67	1	1.67	.78	.06
W_1X_1	−.02	.11	1	.11	.05	.00
W_1X_2	−.02	.06	1	.06	.03	.00
W_1X_3	.12	3.37	1	3.37	1.58	.12
W_1X_4	−.01	.02	1	.02	.01	.00
W_1X_5	−.10	1.56	1	1.56	.73	.06
W_1 by Subjects		25.61	12	2.13		
W_2	.01	.01	1	.01	.01	.00
W_2X_1	−.47	31.17	1	31.17	31.61	.72
W_2X_2	−.06	.19	1	.19	.19	.02
W_2X_3	.01	.01	1	.01	.01	.00
W_2X_4	.12	2.01	1	2.01	2.03	.00
W_2X_5	.35	6.02	1	6.02	6.10	.34
W_2 by Subjects		11.83	12	.99		
W_3	−.23	5.79	1	5.79	7.10	.37
W_3X_1	.02	.07	1	.07	.09	.01
W_3X_2	−.03	.06	1	.06	.07	.01
W_3X_3	.14	2.08	1	2.08	2.56	.18
W_3X_4	.00	.00	1	.00	.00	.00
W_3X_5	.03	.06	1	.06	.07	.01
W_3 by Subjects		9.78	12	.81		
W_4	−.06	.78	1	.78	1.27	.10
W_4X_1	.09	3.17	1	3.17	5.15	.30
W_4X_2	−.08	.84	1	.84	1.36	.10
W_4X_3	.01	.04	1	.04	.07	.00
W_4X_4	.05	1.02	1	1.02	1.65	.12
W_4X_5	.03	.17	1	.17	.28	.02
W_4 by Subjects		7.39	12	.62		
W_5	−.04	.12	1	.12	.11	.01
W_5X_1	−.10	1.56	1	1.56	1.35	.10
W_5X_2	.10	.52	1	.52	.45	.04
W_5X_3	−.04	.12	1	.12	.11	.01
W_5X_4	−.10	1.56	1	1.56	1.35	.10
W_5X_5	.10	.52	1	.52	.45	.04
W_5 by Subjects		13.83	12	1.15		
Total Within Ss		133.16	90			
Total		655.43	107			

EXHIBIT 14.30 ▲

ANOVA source table for mixed design

half of Exhibit 14.30. The row of codes labelled δ_0 provides the values used in computing W_{0i}. The δ_1 values are used to compute the composite score W_{1i}, W_{2i} is formed by using the δ_2 contrast values, and so forth. As these δ_h values indicate, W_{1i} and W_{2i} capture the within-subject main effect due to the Letter factor, W_{3i} represents the Number main effect, and W_{4i} and W_{5i} capture the Letter by Number interaction.

We then estimate five different regression models, one for each of W_{1i} through W_{5i}, regressing each one in turn on the between-subject contrast-coded predictors, X_1 through X_5. The test of whether the intercept differs from zero in each of these five models is a test of whether the within-subject difference coded by the particular W_i is reliable. The sum of squares associated with this test can be found either by computing the sum of squares reduced when the full augmented model is compared with a model in which the intercept is forced to be zero or by simply squaring the intercept and multiplying it by the total number of subjects. The tests of the regression coefficients associated with X_1 through X_5 in each of these equations provide tests of the interactions between the within-subject difference coded by the particular W_i and the between-subject contrasts. The residual or error sum of squares from each of these five regression equations constitutes the error sum of squares used for testing the effect of the within-subject contrast whose W_i is being examined in the equation and for testing the interactions between that within-subject contrast and each of the between-subject contrasts. It can also be thought of as the interaction between the within-subject contrast used to code the particular W_i and subjects within levels of the between-subject factors.

In total then, there is a single error sum of squares for the between-subjects analysis and five error terms for the within-subjects analysis, one corresponding to each of the within-subject contrast codes used in computing W_{1i} through W_{5i}. Each of these error terms has 12 degrees of freedom, since they each result from a regression equation in which some composite W_i score is regressed on the five between-subject contrast-coded predictors, X_1 to X_5.

The resulting source table for the full Color by Height by Letter by Number mixed factorial design is presented in Exhibit 14.30. Notice that the total degrees of freedom between subjects equals $18 - 1$, and the total degrees of freedom within subjects equals 90. Thus the total degrees of freedom, both between and within subjects, equals 107, which equals the total number of Y_{hi} observations minus 1. Again, the regression coefficients given in this table are in the original Y_{hi} metric rather than in the metric of each W_i.

In Exhibit 14.31 we give the SAS Proc Reg input for analyzing these data. In this input W0 through W5 are the compositive variables W_{0i}

EXHIBIT 14.31 ▶

SAS Proc Reg input for analysis of complex mixed design

```
DATA ALL;
INPUT A1   A2   B1   B2   C1   C2   COLOR HEIGHT;
W0 =  (A1+A2+B1+B2+C1+C2)/6**.5;
W1 =  (−2*A1−2*A2+B1+B2+C1+C2)/12**.5;
W2 =  (B1+B2−C1−C2)/4**.5;
W3 =  (A1−A2+B1−B2+C1−C2)/6**.5;
W4 =  (−2*A1+2*A2+B1−B2+C1−C2)/12**.5;
W5 =  (B1−B2−C1+C2)/4**.5;
IF COLOR=1 THEN X1=2;
  ELSE X1=−1;
IF COLOR=1 THEN X2=0;
  IF COLOR=2 THEN X2=−1;
  IF COLOR=3 THEN X2=1;
IF HEIGHT=1 THEN X3=−1;
  ELSE X3=1;
X4=X1*X3;
X5=X2*X3;
CARDS;
5   6   4   5   7   8   1   1
3   5   2   3   4   4   1   1
6   5   4   4   6   7   1   1
7   7   5   6   8   7   1   2
6   8   7   7   9   9   1   2
3   4   4   5   6   3   1   2
2   4   3   3   1   2   2   1
3   2   2   3   1   1   2   1
2   3   4   5   1   2   2   1
8   9   9   9   7   8   2   2
6   5   8   7   8   9   2   2
7   6   6   9   8   7   2   2
9   7   6   8   7   7   3   1
5   5   9   8   6   8   3   1
7   9   5   8   6   8   3   1
3   1   1   2   1   1   3   2
2   3   4   4   1   3   3   2
3   2   5   4   2   4   3   2
; ; ; ;
PROC REG;
   MODEL W0 = X1 X2 X3 X4 X5;
   MODEL W1 = X1 X2 X3 X4 X5;
   MODEL W2 = X1 X2 X3 X4 X5;
   MODEL W3 = X1 X2 X3 X4 X5;
   MODEL W4 = X1 X2 X3 X4 X5;
   MODEL W5 = X1 X2 X3 X4 X5;
RUN;
```

through W_{5i}. The between-subject contrast-coded predictors are coded as specified in Exhibit 14.29. Note that in the raw data that are input, the last two variables for each subject indicate their level of Color and Height, the between-subject factors. In these raw data, the levels of Color are coded as 1, 2, and 3, and the levels of Height are coded as 1 and 2. The Proc Reg procedure simply asks for six regression models, regressing W0 through W5 on X1 through X5.

Exhibit 14.32 presents the SAS output of these data. This output contains for each W_i the parameter estimates and associated inferential tests as well as the sums of squared errors. Note that the t^* statistics associated with the parameter tests convert to the F^* statistics reported in the source table of Exhibit 14.30 by simply squaring them. The output from this Proc Reg procedure contains all the information necessary to generate the source table of Exhibit 14.30. To demonstrate this, examine the output for the model where W2 is the dependent variable. The error sum of squares for this model equals 11.83 which is the value reported in the source table of Exhibit 14.30 for the W2 by subjects error term.

DEP VARIABLE: W0   ANALYSIS OF VARIANCE

SOURCE	DF	SUM OF SQUARES	MEAN SQUARE	F VALUE	PROB>F
MODEL	5	446.04630	89.20925926	14.045	.0001
ERROR	12	76.22222222	6.35185185		
C TOTAL	17	522.26852			

ROOT MSE	2.520288	R-SQUARE	.8541
DEP MEAN	12.54229	ADJ R-SQ	.7932
C.V.	20.09431		

PARAMETER ESTIMATES

VARIABLE	DF	PARAMETER ESTIMATE	STANDARD ERROR	T FOR H0: PARAMETER=0	PROB > |T|
INTERCEP	1	12.54229470	.59403759	21.114	.0001
X1	1	.49897013	.42004801	1.188	.2579
X2	1	−.20412415	.72754449	−.281	.7838
X3	1	.74845520	.59403759	1.260	.2316
X4	1	.40824829	.42004801	.972	.3503
X5	1	−5.91960021	.72754449	−8.136	.0001

EXHIBIT 14.32 ▲

SAS ouput for complex mixed design data

DEP VARIABLE: W1   ANALYSIS OF VARIANCE

SOURCE	DF	SUM OF SQUARES	MEAN SQUARE	F VALUE	PROB>F
MODEL	5	5.13425926	1.02685185	.481	.7839
ERROR	12	25.61111111	2.13425926		
C TOTAL	17	30.74537037			

ROOT MSE	1.46091	R-SQUARE	.1670	
DEP MEAN	.3047126	ADJ R-SQ	−.1801	
C.V.	479.4387			

PARAMETER ESTIMATES

VARIABLE	DF	PARAMETER ESTIMATE	STANDARD ERROR	T FOR H0: PARAMETER=0	PROB > |T|
INTERCEP	1	.30471264	.34433989	.885	.3936
X1	1	−.05613128	.24348507	−.231	.8216
X2	1	−.07216878	.42172851	−.171	.8670
X3	1	.43301270	.34433989	1.258	.2325
X4	1	−.02405626	.24348507	−.099	.9229
X5	1	−.36084392	.42172851	−.856	.4090

DEP VARIABLE: W2   ANALYSIS OF VARIANCE

SOURCE	DF	SUM OF SQUARES	MEAN SQUARE	F VALUE	PROB>F
MODEL	5	39.40277778	7.88055556	7.992	.0016
ERROR	12	11.83333333	.98611111		
C TOTAL	17	51.23611111			

ROOT MSE	.9930313	R-SQUARE	.7690	
DEP MEAN	.02777778	ADJ R-SQ	.6728	
C.V.	3574.913			

PARAMETER ESTIMATES

VARIABLE	DF	PARAMETER ESTIMATE	STANDARD ERROR	T FOR H0: PARAMETER=0	PROB > |T|
INTERCEP	1	.02777778	.23405972	.119	.9075
X1	1	−.93055556	.16550521	−5.623	.0001
X2	1	−.12500000	.28666344	−.436	.6705
X3	1	.02777778	.23405972	.119	.9075
X4	1	.23611111	.16550521	1.427	.1792
X5	1	.70833333	.28666344	2.471	.0294

EXHIBIT 14.32 ▲

continued

DEP VARIABLE: W3　　　　ANALYSIS OF VARIANCE

SOURCE	DF	SUM OF SQUARES	MEAN SQUARE	F VALUE	PROB>F
MODEL	5	2.26851852	.45370370	.557	.7311
ERROR	12	9.77777778	.81481481		
C TOTAL	17	12.04629630			

ROOT MSE	.9026709	R-SQUARE	.1883	
DEP MEAN	−.567012	ADJ R-SQ	−.1499	
C.V.	−159.198			

PARAMETER ESTIMATES

VARIABLE	DF	PARAMETER ESTIMATE	STANDARD ERROR	T FOR H0: PARAMETER=0	PROB > |T|
INTERCEP	1	−.56701151	.21276158	−2.665	.0206
X1	1	.04536092	.15044516	.302	.7682
X2	1	−.06804138	.26057865	−.261	.7984
X3	1	.34020691	.21276158	1.599	.1358
X4	1	−1.85037E-17	.15044516	−.000	1.0000
X5	1	.06804138	.26057865	.261	.7984

DEP VARIABLE: W4　　　　ANALYSIS OF VARIANCE

SOURCE	DF	SUM OF SQUARES	MEAN SQUARE	F VALUE	PROB>F
MODEL	5	5.24537037	1.04907407	1.704	.2082
ERROR	12	7.38888889	.61574074		
C TOTAL	17	12.63425926			

ROOT MSE	.7846915	R-SQUARE	.4152	
DEP MEAN	−.208488	ADJ R-SQ	.1715	
C.V.	−376.373			

PARAMETER ESTIMATES

VARIABLE	DF	PARAMETER ESTIMATE	STANDARD ERROR	T FOR H0: PARAMETER=0	PROB > |T|
INTERCEP	1	−.20848760	.18495356	−1.127	.2817
X1	1	.29669389	.13078192	2.269	.0425
X2	1	−.26461887	.22652092	−1.168	.2654
X3	1	.04811252	.18495356	.260	.7992
X4	1	.16839383	.13078192	1.288	.2222
X5	1	.12028131	.22652092	.531	.6051

EXHIBIT 14.32 ▲

continued

DEP VARIABLE: W5   ANALYSIS OF VARIANCE

SOURCE	DF	SUM OF SQUARES	MEAN SQUARE	F VALUE	PROB>F
MODEL	5	4.29166667	.85833333	.745	.6051
ERROR	12	13.83333333	1.15277778		
C TOTAL	17	18.12500000			

ROOT MSE	1.073675	R-SQUARE	.2368
DEP MEAN	−.0833333	ADJ R-SQ	−.0812
C.V.	−1288.41		

PARAMETER ESTIMATES

VARIABLE	DF	PARAMETER ESTIMATE	STANDARD ERROR	T FOR H0: PARAMETER=0	PROB > |T|
INTERCEP	1	−.08333333	.25306760	−.329	.7476
X1	1	−.20833333	.17894582	−1.164	.2670
X2	1	.20833333	.30994324	.672	.5142
X3	1	−.08333333	.25306760	−.329	.7476
X4	1	−.20833333	.17894582	−1.164	.2670
X5	1	.20833333	.30994324	.672	.5142

EXHIBIT 14.32 ▲

continued

The parameter estimate for the intercept equals .027. If we divide this value by $\sqrt{\Sigma_h \delta_h^2}$ or $\sqrt{4}$, we get the value of b in the source table for W2, .01. The t^* statistic associated with this coefficient equals .119 on the SAS output. Squaring this t^*, we get a value of .01, which is the F^* value reported for the W2 comparison in the source table. The sum of squares associated with this term in the source table is obtained by multiplying its value of F^* (.01) with the mean square error from the model, .99.

For another example of how we go from the SAS output to the source table of Exhibit 14.30, take the model for W4. The sum of squared errors for this model is 7.39 with 12 degrees of freedom. These are the values reported in the source table for the W4 by subjects error term. The coefficient for the X2 predictor in the SAS model equals −.265. If we divide this coefficient by $\sqrt{\Sigma_h \delta_h^2}$ or by $\sqrt{12}$, we get −.08, which is the b value reported in the source table for the W4 by X2 interaction. The t^* statistic in the SAS output for this coefficient equals −1.168, which if squared equals the F^* of 1.36 reported in the source table. The sum of squares due to this interaction, reported in the source table, is obtained by multplying this F^* with the mean square error for the model, .62.

Once one learns the general rules for analyzing mixed model designs, as set forth in the beginning of this section of the chapter, then computerized analysis of such data sets using regression programs is simple and efficient. We hope that this example illustrates this.

14.5

Pooling Effects in Within-Subject Designs

In the analysis of the relatively complicated mixed model design that we have just completed, two of the four factors had three levels and were thus each coded using two different contrast codes. One of these factors was between subjects, i.e., Color, and was coded using the between-subject contrast-coded predictors X_1 and X_2. The other one of the factors with three levels was within subjects, i.e., Letter, and from it we generated two within-subject sets of contrast-code values, used in computing W_{1i} and W_{2i}. Nowhere in the source table presented in Exhibit 14.30 did we give, however, omnibus tests of the Color or Letter main effects or omnibus tests of the interactions of these factors with the other factors in the design. In other words, all F^*'s presented in the exhibit had only a single degree of freedom in the numerator. We did not provide the two degree-of-freedom test of the Color main effect or the two degree-of-freedom test of the Letter main effect, or the various tests of factor interactions involving more than a single degree of freedom.

Although we have given a number of reasons why we prefer tests involving single-degree-of-freedom contrasts to omnibus tests involving more degrees of freedom, in order to be complete we need to indicate how one would go about generating a source table for a mixed design that includes such omnibus tests. Doing so for the between-subject factor, Color, and its interaction with the other between-subject factor, Height, is rather straightforward. Since there is only a single between-subject error term in the source table, we can combine sums of squares in this portion of the source table and test the resulting mean squares by comparing them with this between-subject error term. This is exactly the procedure we followed in Chapters 11 and 12 for generating omnibus multiple-degree-of-freedom tests in designs where observations could be assumed to be independent.

The combined sum of squares due to the two Color contrasts equals $8.96 + .50$ or 9.46. Two different between-subject contrasts code the Color by Height interaction. Combining the sums of squares for these two contrasts gives us an omnibus interaction sum of squares of 426.50. Each of these combined sums of squares, one for the Color main effect and one for the Color by Height interaction, is associated with two degrees of freedom. Their respective mean squares can be compared with the between-subject mean square error to generate the desired omnibus F^* statistics. The resulting revision of the between-subjects portion of the source table, incorporating these omnibus tests, is given in Exhibit 14.33.

EXHIBIT 14.33 ▶

Between-subject portion of source table involving pooled effects

Source	b	SS	df	MS	F*	PRE
Color		9.46	2	4.73	.74	.11
X_1	.20	8.96	1	8.96	1.41	.11
X_2	−.07	.50	1	.50	.02	.01
Height (X_3)	.30	10.08	1	10.08	1.59	.12
Height by Color		426.50	2	213.25	33.58	.85
X_4	.12	6.00	1	6.00	.95	.07
X_5	−2.43	420.50	1	420.50	66.20	.85
Error		76.22	12	6.35		
Total		522.27	17			

Deriving the omnibus tests for the within-subject factor that has more than two levels, Letter, and its various interactions is a little more difficult since each single-degree-of-freedom within-subject contrast has its own unique error term. To combine single degrees of freedom within subjects in order to conduct omnibus tests, we may then need to also combine within-subject error sums of squares.

Two W_i scores represent the within-subject Letter factor, i.e., W_{1i} and W_{2i}. We can pool or combine their two sums of squares to come up with a sum of squares due to Letter, having two degrees of freedom. From Exhibit 14.30, the sum of squares associated with W_{1i} equals 1.67 and the sum of squares associated with W_{2i} equals .01. Combining these terms gives us a sum of squares associated with the Letter factor of 1.68, with two degrees of freedom. The Letter mean square thus equals .84.

To derive a value of $F*$ for the omnibus test of whether there are differences due to Letter, we need to pool the two error sums of squares from the W_{1i} and W_{2i} models. The sum of squared errors from the W_{1i} equation (i.e., W_{1i} by subjects within condition) equals 25.61 with 12 degrees of freedom. The sum of squared errors from the W_{2i} equation (i.e., W_{2i} by subjects within condition) equals 11.83 with 12 degrees of freedom. Pooling or combining these two into a single Letter by subjects within condition error term gives us a pooled sum of squares of 37.44 with 24 degrees of freedom. Dividing this error sum of squares by its degrees of freedom gives a Letter by Subject within condition mean square of 1.56.

We might also want to provide an omnibus test of the interactions between the Letter factor and the two between subject factors, Color and Height. Since Color has three levels, the Color by Letter interaction consists of four separate single-degree-of-freedom terms: $W_{1i}X_1$, $W_{1i}X_2$, $W_{2i}X_1$, and $W_{2i}X_2$. Combining their sums of squares gives us a sum of squares due to the Letter by Color interaction of 31.53 with four degrees of freedom. The Letter by Height interaction consists of two terms, $W_{1i}X_3$ and $W_{2i}X_3$, which provide a pooled sum of squares of 3.38 with two degrees of freedom. Finally, there are four terms that represent the Letter by Color by Height interaction: $W_{1i}X_4$, $W_{1i}X_5$, $W_{2i}X_4$, and $W_{2i}X_5$. Their pooled sums of squares equals 9.61 with four degrees of freedom. Each of these pooled interaction terms can be tested by comparing their mean squares with the pooled error mean square or Letter by Subject within condition mean square that we have already derived.

The portion of the source table that includes only these pooled terms providing omnibus tests of the Letter factor and its interactions with the between subject factors is presented in Exhibit 14.34. Notice in this partial source table that we have not included values of PRE for the various tests. Since the various tests that are reported in this table use a pooled error term, pooled from two different models, these tests cannot be expressed as a proportional reduction in error from a single augmented to a single compact model.

We can also pool the various terms that involve the within-subject factor Number and its interactions with the between-subject factors. Since Number has only two levels, it is coded with a single term, W_{3i}, and has associated with it only a single error term: W_{3i} by subjects within condition (i.e., the error sum of squares from the W_{3i} model). From the W_{3i} portion of the source table in Exhibit 14.30, we can pool the two terms that represent the Number by Color interaction, $W_{3i}X_1$ and $W_{3i}X_2$. We can also pool the two terms that represent the Number by Color by Height interaction, $W_{3i}X_4$ and $W_{3i}X_5$.

Finally, we can pool various terms from the final two sections of the source table in Exhibit 14.30, involving the W_{4i} and W_{5i} within-subject terms. These two terms represent the Letter by Number interaction. Their pooled sum of squares equals .90. We can also pool the four terms that represent the Letter by Number by Color interaction, $W_{4i}X_1$, $W_{4i}X_2$,

EXHIBIT 14.34 ▶

Portion of source table involving pooled effects due to letter and its interactions with color and height

Source	SS	df	MS	F*
Letter	1.68	2	.84	.54
Letter by Color	31.53	4	7.88	5.05
Letter by Height	3.38	2	1.69	1.08
Letter by Color by Height	9.61	4	2.40	1.54
Letter by Ss within Color and Height	37.44	24	1.56	

$W_{5i}X_1$, and $W_{5i}X_2$, the two terms that represent the Letter by Number by Height interaction, $W_{4i}X_3$ and $W_{5i}X_3$, and the four terms that represent the Letter by Number by Color by Height interaction, $W_{4i}X_4$, $W_{4i}X_5$, $W_{5i}X_4$, and $W_{5i}X_5$. Finally, the error term for testing all of these pooled terms comes from pooling the W_{4i} by subjects within condition and the W_{5i} by subjects within condition error terms (i.e., the error sums of squares from the W_{4i} and W_{5i} models). From all of this, we come up with the portion of the source table that involves only the omnibus within-subject tests presented in Exhibit 14.35.

Most statistical textbooks and computer packages that are routinely used for mixed model analyses of variance do not use the single-degree-of-freedom contrast approach that we have developed. Rather, most programs simply produce the omnibus or pooled tests that are reported in the source tables of Exhibits 14.33 and 14.35. There are two primary problems with such source tables. First, as we have argued all along, omnibus tests that involve more than a single degree of freedom are

EXHIBIT 14.35 ▶

Within-subject portion of source table involving pooled effects

Source	SS	df	MS	F*
Letter	1.68	2	.84	.54
Letter by Color	31.51	4	7.88	5.05
Letter by Height	3.38	2	1.69	1.08
Letter by Color by Height	9.61	4	2.40	1.54
Letter by Ss within Color and Height	37.44	24	1.56	
Number	5.79	1	5.79	7.10
Number by Color	.13	2	.06	.07
Number by Height	2.08	1	2.08	2.56
Number by Color by Height	.06	2	.03	.04
Number by Ss within Color and Height	9.78	12	.81	
Letter by Number	.90	2	.45	.51
Letter by Number by Color	6.09	4	1.52	1.73
Letter by Number by Height	.16	2	.08	.09
Letter by Number by Color by Height	3.27	4	.82	.93
Letter by Number by Ss within Color and Height	21.22	24	.88	

difficult to interpret since, if we reject the null hypothesis, we know that there are mean differences, but we don't know where those differences lie. Single-degree-of-freedom tests, by contrast, provide much more focused tests and conclusions.

The second disadvantage to routinely pooling effects in mixed models analysis of variance is that error terms must be pooled. For instance, in coming up with the error mean square for the pooled test of the Letter factor, we pooled the W_{1i} by subjects within condition and the W_{2i} by subjects within condition error terms. If the error sums of squares that are pooled are very different from each other, then pooling them will result in biased F^* statistics. In other words, this pooling strategy assumes that the various error terms that are to be pooled are homogeneous. Since these error terms amount to interactions of subjects with within-subject contrasts or differences, this assumption amounts to the assumption that the variability in these within-subject differences are homogeneous across the contrasts whose error terms are pooled. This is frequently a very difficult assumption to make. As a general rule, we do not recommend pooling within-subject error terms except in cases where the two mean squares are very close in value.

14.6

Considerations Due to Unequal *N* in Mixed Models

The final issue deserving a brief treatment in this chapter concerns how unequal numbers of observations are handled in the context of models involving within-subject factors. There are two ways in which we might have unequal numbers of observations. First, we may simply have unequal numbers of subjects or groups nested under levels of the between-subject factors. For instance, in a mixed design, we might have 8 subjects under one level of a between-subject factor and 10 subjects under another level. But an equal number of observations are obtained from all subjects, so that every subject provides complete data on the within-subject factors. In this case, the issues in handling the problems posed by unequal numbers of observations are the same as those discussed in Chapter 12 and earlier. Specifically, as long as one fully codes the between-subject factors and includes all between-subject contrast-coded predictors in the analyses of the W_i scores, tests of the between-subject factors and their interactions with the within-subject factors will be readily interpretable as partial tests of those effects. The sums of squares will no longer sum to the total sum of squares explained. Nevertheless tests of all coefficients proceed as before.

The more difficult situation arises when there exist missing observations within a subject. For instance, one or two subjects may not have provided data for all levels of the within-subject factor or factors. This situation is problematic, for one cannot simply compute the W_i composite scores for these subjects in this case. Two alternatives are possible. First, if the number of subjects with missing observations is quite small, one might simply omit them from the analysis, with an accompanying loss of power. This is not recommended in most cases, however, since bias may result as well as loss of power. Second, there exist a variety of procedures that can be used to estimate the value of missing observations. These procedures lie outside of the scope of this book. Unfortunately, they are not without their problems either. (See discussions in Seber, 1984, and Steel & Torrie, 1980.)

14.7

Conclusion

The approach we have developed for the analysis of nonindependent observations relies on the realization that we can combine the nonindependent observations in meaningful ways so that we can continue to ask the full range of questions of interest and yet do so preserving the assumption that residuals in the models examined are independent of each other. This is accomplished by combining observations within subjects into both a summary score and a set of difference scores. The summary combined score W_{0i} can then be used to examine the influence of the between-subject independent variables of interest. The difference scores W_{1i}, W_{2i}, . . . , $W_{(s-1)i}$ can be used to examine the effects of the within-subject factors and their interactions with the between-subject factors. Through the use of these combinatorial rules, the analysis of complex data sets involving nonindependent observations can be handled quite readily within the model comparison context we have developed in this book. As our final complex example and associated SAS analysis demonstrate, this procedure is relatively efficient and straightforward, once the few rules are learned.

There is one topic in handling nonindependent observations that we have only hinted at in this chapter. That topic concerns complications that arise when independent variables of interest are measured continuously rather than categorically. In the next chapter we consider this issue, among others. In essence, this consideration amounts to a generalization of the procedures of Chapter 13 to the case of nonindependent observations.

15

Further Models with Nonindependent ERRORs

The procedures developed in the last chapter permit one to analyze data arising in most situations where nonindependence due to groups or subjects is a problem. One simply analyzes as many W_i scores as the number of observations from each subject. The first of these W_i scores, W_{0i}, is computed by setting all values of δ_h equal to 1, with the result that the between-subject variance is examined. This W_{0i} score is then regressed on any between-subject contrast-coded predictors to test main effects and interactions involving only the between-subject variables. The remaining W_i scores are computed by taking within-subject differences, using values of δ_h that correspond to within-subject contrast codes. These W_i scores are also regressed on any between-subject contrast-coded predictors. Tests of the intercepts in these equations are equivalent to tests of the within-subject contrasts used to code the W_i's. Tests of the regression coefficients for the between-subject contrasts in these regression equations amount to tests of particular interactions between the within-subject and between-subject contrasts.

Within the context of this general analytic strategy for dealing with nonindependent observations, we now want to explore two further complications in designs involving nonindependent data. The first complication arises from designs known as *repeated measurement latin square designs*. These designs permit the researcher to examine the effects of some within-subject treatment variable while simultaneously controlling for the order in which the treatment levels are received by each subject.

This control, however, is achieved at a cost, as we will see. Second, we explore how continuously measured predictors or covariates may be incorporated into the analysis of designs with nonindependent data, in order to increase the power of such designs and in order to examine their effects in the context of repeated measures designs.

15.1

Repeated Measures Latin Square Designs

15.1.1 A 2 × 2 Latin Square

Consider a design in which two different drugs are administered on subsequent days to each of two individuals who suffer from chronic pain. The data of Exhibit 15.1 reflect each subject's pain judgment following the administration of each drug. Thus, we have a single factor with which subjects are crossed. To analyze these data, using the techniques of the last chapter, we compute two W_i scores, W_{0i} and W_{1i}. W_{0i} captures the between-subject variation in the data, setting all values of δ_h equal to 1. The sum of squares of this W_{0i} equals the sum of squares between subjects. W_{1i} is based upon the within-subject contrast that compares Drug A with Drug B, with δ_h values of -1 if Drug A and $+1$ if Drug B. A test of that contrast is given by a test of whether the mean value of W_{1i} differs from zero. This analysis results in the source table of Exhibit 15.2. Obviously, we have very little power with this design, since the Drug by Subjects error term for testing the Drug main effect has only a single degree of freedom associated with it.

There is a further problem with this analysis, however, in addition to its relative lack of power. If we assume that both subjects were administered Drug A on day 1 and Drug B on day 2, then any difference in pain ratings associated with Drug is also associated with the day on which the drug was administered. In these data, there was a nonreliable tendency for pain ratings to be higher under Drug B than under Drug

EXHIBIT 15.1 ▶

Hypothetical drug data

	Drug A	Drug B
Subject 1	4	6
Subject 2	4	5

EXHIBIT 15.2 ▶

Source table from analysis of drug data

Source	b	SS	df	MS	F*	PRE
Between Ss		.25	1	.25		
Within Ss						
Drug	.75	2.25	1	2.25	9.00	.90
Drug by Ss		.25	1	.25		
Total Within		2.50	2	2.50		

A. We might attribute this difference to Drug. On the other hand, it might be the case that regardless of which drug had been taken on the second day of the study, pain ratings on that second day would have been higher simply as a result of subjects having thought about their reactions to the pain for two successive days. In other words, any Drug effect found with this design might alternatively be due to the order in which the drugs are administered.

In order to overcome this confounding, we need to manipulate the order in which the drugs are administered. For instance, the first subject might be given Drug A first followed by Drug B, while the second subject receives the two drugs in the reverse sequence. Such a research design involves the use of what is called a 2 × 2 latin square, depicted schematically in Exhibit 15.3. As this exhibit makes clear, there are two ways in which the latin square can be equivalently presented. In the top half of the exhibit, the columns of the table indicate the day or order in which a given drug was taken. The letters in the cells of the 2 × 2 table refer to which drug was taken on which day. The equivalent design is given in the bottom half of the exhibit, with the column referring to drug and the numbers in the cells referring to day or order in which the indicated drug was taken.

EXHIBIT 15.3 ▶

2 × 2 latin square

	Order 1	2
Subject 1	A	B
Subject 2	B	A

	Drug A	B
Subject 1	1	2
Subject 2	2	1

What we would now like to do, using this latin square design, is conduct an analysis in which we analyze for or control for the effect of Order in assessing the Drug effect. Let us act as if the data we have already discussed were collected using this latin square design, and let us analyze these data to examine the effect of Order as well as the effect of Drug. The source table reported above continues to tell us about the Drug effect. Now, let us rearrange the data in the design to analyze for the Order effect. Assuming that subject 2 received Drug B first and Drug A second, the data can be rearranged as in Exhibit 15.4, so that the columns represent Order of administration. The only difference between this presentation of the data and that given in Exhibit 15.1 is that the two pain ratings provided by the second subject have been reversed, since columns in the table now refer to the day on which the drug was administered rather than to the drug that was administered.

We can now analyze these data for the effect of Order, using two W_i scores. W_{0i} captures the between-subject variation in these data and is identical to W_{0i} used before. Since only the data from within a subject have been reversed, on average each subject's scores have not been altered and, accordingly, the between-subjects portion of the resulting analysis is identical to what was given before. The W_{1i} score is derived by coding the within-subject Order contrast. The scores of both subjects for W_{1i} are as follows:

$$\text{Subject 1:} \quad W_1 = \frac{1(4) - 1(6)}{\sqrt{2}} = -1.414$$

$$\text{Subject 2:} \quad W_1 = \frac{1(5) - 1(4)}{\sqrt{2}} = .707$$

To test for the Order effect, we want to test whether the mean of these W_{1i} scores differs from zero. This analysis results in the source table of Exhibit 15.5. It is instructive to compare this source table with the one of Exhibit 15.2 that resulted from the analysis in which Drug was cast as the within-subject variable of interest. The only difference in the two source tables is that the order of the two rows in the within-subject portions of the tables has been reversed. That is, in the Drug analysis of Exhibit 15.2, the sum of squares due to Drug is equivalent

EXHIBIT 15.4 ▶

Drug data rearranged by order

	Order	
	1	2
Subject 1	4	6
Subject 2	5	4

EXHIBIT 15.5 ▶

Source table for analysis of order effect in drug data

Source	b	SS	df	MS	F*	PRE
Between Ss		.25	1	.25		
Within Ss						
Order	−.25	.25	1	.25	.11	.10
Order by Ss		2.25	1	2.25		
Total Within		2.50	2	2.50		

to the sum of squares due to the Order by Subjects interaction in the analysis of Exhibit 15.5 where Order is the within-subject variable of interest. Vice versa, the sum of squares due to Order in the Exhibit 15.5 analysis is identical with the sum of squares due to the interaction of Drug with subjects in the analysis where the within-subject factor is Drug. In other words, the effect of Order in this design is perfectly confounded with the Drug by Subject interaction and, reciprocally, the effect of Drug is perfectly confounded with the Order by Subjects interaction.

The source tables from the two analyses, one using Drug as the within-subject factor of interest and one using Order as the within-subject factor of interest, could be combined into the relabeled source table of Exhibit 15.6. Doing this, however, makes clear the fact that we really have no way to test for the effect of Drug in this design, since no appropriate error term exists once a model is specified in which both Order and Drug are within-subjects factors. In other words, if we assume in the earlier analysis that focused on Drug (i.e., Exhibit 15.2) that the Drug by Subjects interaction really is due to the effect of Order, then there is no residual Drug by Subjects interaction against which to test the Drug main effect. If we control for both Drug and Order, then all of the within-subject degrees of freedom are used up, the residual sum of squares within subjects equals zero, and no test of the Drug effect is possible.

EXHIBIT 15.6 ▶

Source table of drug data with drug and order as factors

Source	b	SS	df	MS	F*	PRE
Between Ss		.25	1	.25		
Within Ss						
Order	−.25	.25	1	.25		
Drug	.75	2.25	1	2.25		
Total Within		2.50	2	2.50		

This analysis does, however, suggest that if we used more subjects in each of the rows of the latin square design, assigning subjects at random to one sequence or the other (i.e., does Drug A come first or Drug B?), then there would be residual degrees of freedom due to the Drug by Subjects interaction, even after we removed the effect of Order from the analysis. This residual Drug by Subjects interaction might then be used to test for the effect of Drug.

15.1.2 A Replicated 2 × 2 Latin Square

Suppose, for instance, that we collected the data of Exhibit 15.7, with four subjects receiving Drug A first and B second, and four subjects receiving the drugs in the opposite sequence. In essence, what has happened is that four subjects, rather than only a single one, fill each of the rows of the 2 × 2 latin square defined previously. All subjects in the A-B sequence received Drug A on the first day or in the first order, and Drug B second. All subjects in the second sequence received Drug B first. Accordingly, these data could be reorganized so that the columns of the table refer to order or day on which a drug is administered rather than the drug that is administered. To do this, we simply rearrange the ratings from subjects in the B-A sequence, as shown in Exhibit 15.8.

To analyze these data, let us first ignore Order as a within-subject factor, and simply examine the effect of Drug, treating the data as organized in Exhibit 15.7. Since we have four subjects in each of the two possible sequences, we can code which Sequence a subject received as a between-subject contrast-coded predictor and analyze its effects and

EXHIBIT 15.7 ▶

Drug data: replicated 2 × 2 latin square

	Drug A	B
A-B Sequence		
Subj. 1	2	3
Subj. 2	4	4
Subj. 3	5	7
Subj. 4	4	5
B-A Sequence		
Subj. 5	2	3
Subj. 6	4	4
Subj. 7	3	4
Subj. 8	5	6

EXHIBIT 15.8

Drug data displayed by order: replicated 2 × 2 latin square

	Order 1	Order 2
A-B Sequence		
Subj. 1	2	3
Subj. 2	4	4
Subj. 3	5	7
Subj. 4	4	5
B-A Sequence		
Subj. 5	3	2
Subj. 6	4	4
Subj. 7	4	3
Subj. 8	6	5

its interaction with Drug. We derive W_{0i} as previously by setting all values of δ_h equal to 1. We derive W_{1i} to code the within-subject drug effect, setting the value of δ_h equal to $+1$ if Drug B and -1 if Drug A. Both of these W_i scores are then regressed on the between-subject contrast-coded predictor that represents Sequence. In the W_{0i} equation, the test of the regression coefficient for the Sequence contrast-coded predictor represents the test of the Sequence main effect. In the W_{1i} equation, the test of the intercept represents the test of the Drug main effect and the test of the coefficient for Sequence represents the test of the Sequence by Drug interaction. This analysis gives the source table presented in Exhibit 15.9.

EXHIBIT 15.9

Source table for 2 × 2 replicated latin square: order ignored

Source	b	SS	df	MS	F*	PRE
Between Subjects						
Sequence	−.19	.56	1	.56	.15	.03
Ss within Seq.		21.88	6	3.65		
Total Between		22.44	7			
Within Subjects						
Drug	.44	3.06	1	3.06	13.37	.68
Drug × Seq.	.06	.06	1	.06	.27	.01
Drug × Ss within Seq.		1.38	6	.23		
Total Within		4.50	8			

Now, let us repeat the analysis of these data, examining the effect of Order rather than that of Drug, treating the data as arranged in Exhibit 15.8. The between-subjects portion of the analysis is identical to that just completed, since each subject's value on W_{0i} does not change as a function of rearranging the data. Values on W_{1i} do change, however, since the within-subject contrast values δ_h now code the difference due to Order rather than the difference due to Drug. From this analysis of the data in Exhibit 15.8, the source table of Exhibit 15.10 results.

The major difference between this source table and that presented for these data in Exhibit 15.9 is that the rows of the within-subject portion of the table have been renamed and two of them have been put in a different order. When we treated Drug as the within-subject factor, the Drug row of the source table is identical to the Order × Sequence row of the source table when treating Order as the within-subject factor. In a corresponding manner, the row labeled as Order in the Order analysis is labeled Drug by Sequence in the Drug analysis. In other words, the sum of squares due to Drug is perfectly confounded in this analysis with the sum of squares due to the Order by Sequence interaction. Similarly, the sum of squares associated with Order in this design is perfectly confounded with the sum of squares associated with the Drug by Sequence interaction. The residual sum of squares within subjects can be attributed either to the interaction between Drug and Subjects within Sequence or to the interaction between Order and Subjects within Sequence. These two potentially discriminable sources of variance in the data are confounded in the design.

If we make the assumption that there is neither a Drug by Sequence interaction nor an Order by Sequence interaction, then we can combine the two source tables of Exhibits 15.9 and 15.10 into one table that presents both the Drug and Order effects, as in Exhibit 15.11. Notice

EXHIBIT 15.10 ▶

Source table for 2 × 2 replicated latin square: drug ignored

Source	b	SS	df	MS	F*	PRE
Between Subjects						
Sequence	−.19	.56	1	.56	.15	.03
Ss within Seq.		21.88	6	3.65		
Total Between		22.44	7			
Within Subjects						
Order	.06	.06	1	.06	.27	.01
Order × Seq.	.44	3.06	1	3.06	13.37	.68
Order × Ss within Seq.		1.38	6	.23		
Total Within		4.50	8			

EXHIBIT 15.11 ▶

Source table for 2 × 2 replicated latin square

Source	b	SS	df	MS	F*	PRE
Between Subjects						
Sequence	−.19	.56	1	.56	.15	.03
Ss within Seq.		21.88	6	3.65		
Total Between		22.44	7			
Within Subjects						
Drug	.44	3.06	1	3.06	13.37	.68
Order	.06	.06	1	.06	.27	.01
Residual within Ss		1.38	6	.23		
Total Within		4.50	8			

that the within-subject error or residual mean square that is used to test both the Drug and Order effects has been relabeled since it could be called either the Order by Subjects within Sequence interaction or the Drug by Subjects within Sequence interaction.

This simple 2 × 2 latin square design and its analysis illustrates how latin square designs are useful as well as potentially problematic to interpret. The utility of the design comes from its ability to control a concomitant variable, such as Order, while estimating the effect of some treatment variable of interest. This control, however, is gained at some expense, since, as we have seen in the example, the Drug main effect can be tested only if one assumes that there is no Order by Sequence interaction. However, if the original design had been used in which the sequence of drug administration was not varied, as it is in the latin square design, then the Drug effect can be interpreted as just that only if one is willing to assume no Order effect. While there may be occasions where Order by Sequence interactions are plausible, they seem much less likely than Order main effects. Accordingly, a latin square design in which Order, or some other concomitant variable, can be controlled, seems preferable to designs in which the concomitant variable is not controlled at all.

15.1.3 A 3 × 3 Latin Square without Replications

Suppose there were three drugs to be tested. Once again these are to be administered on subsequent days, and a 3 × 3 latin square design is used to control the confounding effect of order of administration. A latin square that might be used is given in Exhibit 15.12. Again, the columns of the design refer to the Order or day on which a given subject receives a given drug. The letters in the body of the table refer to the drug received

EXHIBIT 15.12 ▶

A 3 × 3 latin square (columns indicating order)

	Order		
	1	2	3
Subject 1	A	B	C
Subject 2	B	C	A
Subject 3	C	A	B

by a given subject on a given day. As can be seen, every letter appears once and only once in every column and in every row of the latin square. This is the defining characteristic of a latin square. As a result, across the rows of the square, Order and Drug are unconfounded. Note, however, in this latin square that there are sequences of letters that do not occur. For instance, none of the three subjects receives the drugs in the sequence A-C-B or B-A-C or C-B-A. Thus, while Order and Drug are not confounded in this design, not every drug follows every other drug and combination of drugs. All possible sequences are not part of the design.[1]

This latin square can be rearranged so that the columns refer to drugs and the cell entries refer to order, as in Exhibit 15.13. Let us present some data that might have been collected using this design and proceed to illustrate the analysis. Exhibit 15.14 presents some hypothetical pain rating data, first organized with columns defined by Drug and then organized with columns defined by Order. We will analyze these data twice, once treating Drug as the within-subject factor and once treating Order as the within-subject factor.

EXHIBIT 15.13 ▶

A 3 × 3 latin square (columns indicating drug)

	Drug		
	A	B	C
Subject 1	1	2	3
Subject 2	3	1	2
Subject 3	2	3	1

---

[1]Because not all sequences are included in this latin square (unlike the 2 × 2 latin square), there are a number of different 3 × 3 latin squares that could be used, maintaining the restriction that every drug occurs once and only once in each row and each column of the square. As the size of the latin square grows, the number of possible squares increases geometrically. For a discussion of how to choose a square and the use of randomization procedures in that choice, see Fisher and Yates (1953).

EXHIBIT 15.14 ▶

Hypothetical data for 3 × 3 latin square

| | | *Drug* | |
	A	B	C
Subject 1	3	4	5
Subject 2	6	6	7
Subject 3	3	2	5

| | | *Order* | |
	1	2	3
Subject 1	3	4	5
Subject 2	6	7	6
Subject 3	5	3	2

Treating Drug as the within-subject factor of interest (thus dealing with the data as arranged in the top half of Exhibit 15.14), we need to create three W_i scores. W_{0i} uses unit values of δ_h to capture the between-subjects sum of squares and W_{1i} and W_{2i} capture the two within-subject Drug contrasts. We define the values of δ_h for W_{1i} to compare Drug A with Drug C; we define the values of δ_h for W_{2i} to compare Drug B with the average of Drugs A and C. The sum of squares for W_{0i} gives us the between-subject sum of squares; to test each of the two within-subject contrasts, we test whether the means of W_{1i} and W_{2i} differ reliably from zero. This analysis results in the source table found in Exhibit 15.15. Using the procedures discussed at the end of the last chapter, we have pooled the two single-degree-of-freedom Drug effects at the bottom of this source table to provide a two-degrees-of-freedom test of whether there are any reliable drug differences.

EXHIBIT 15.15 ▶

Source table for 3 × 3 latin square: order ignored

Source	b	SS	df	MS	F*	PRE
Between Subjects		14.89	2	7.44		
Within Subjects						
Drug A vs. C	.83	4.17	1	4.17	25.00	.93
A vs. C × Ss		.33	2	.17		
Drug B vs. A + C	.28	1.39	1	1.39	1.92	.49
B vs. A + C × Ss		1.44	2	.72		
Pooled Drug		5.56	2	2.78	6.26	
Pooled Drug × Ss		1.78	4	.44		
Total Within		7.33	6	1.22		

We now analyze these same data with Order treated as the within-subject factor of interest (thus as they are arranged in the bottom half of Exhibit 15.14). In this analysis W_{0i} scores are identical to what they were before. We need to recompute W_{1i} and W_{2i}, however, so they capture Order contrasts. Coding the within-subject contrasts to compare Order 3 with Order 1 (W_{1i}) and Order 2 with the average of Orders 1 and 3 (W_{2i}), the source table of Exhibit 15.16 results from the Order analysis of these data.

Comparing this source table with the one in Exhibit 15.15 where Drug was treated as the within-subject variable, we see that the sum of squares between and the total within sum of squares are identical. However, the within-subject sum of squares has been divided up rather differently in the two analyses. Since, as we have seen, each drug appears in every row and every column of the latin square design, defining the columns as Order, the two within-subject variables of Drug and Order are orthogonal. As a result, the sum of squares due to Drug and the sum of squares due to Order are completely independent of each other. Accordingly, just as in the earlier 2×2 latin square analysis, the Order sum of squares must be found within the sum of squares due to Drug by subjects and the Drug sum of squares must be found within the sum of squares due to Order by subjects.

Accordingly, if we make the assumption that the sum of squares associated with Drug really is due to Drug rather than to part of the Order by Subjects interaction, and if we make a similar assumption about the sum of squares associated with Order, then we can combine the two pooled within-subject source tables to list the sum of squares due to Drug, the sum of squares due to Order, and the sum of squares residual

EXHIBIT 15.16 ▶

Source table for 3 × 3 latin square: drug ignored

Source	b	SS	df	MS	F*	PRE
Between Subjects		14.89	2	7.44		
Within Subjects						
Order 1 vs. 3	.17	.17	1	.17	.05	.03
1 vs. 3 × Ss		6.33	2	3.17		
Order 2 vs. 1 + 3	.06	.06	1	.06	.14	.07
2 vs. 1 + 3 × Ss		.78	2	.40		
Pooled Order		.22	2	.11	.06	
Pooled Order × Ss		7.11	4	1.78		
Total Within		7.33	6	1.22		

within subjects. This combined source table is presented in Exhibit 15.17. In the present data the order effect is extremely small. Had it been larger, as it may well be, then this pooled analysis that pulls the pooled Order effect out of the pooled Drug by subject interaction sum of squares will be more powerful than the analysis in which Order is simply ignored.

Notice, however, that we have not attempted to pull the sum of squares potentially associated with Order out of the single-degree-of-freedom tests of specific Drug comparisons. Each of these single-degree-of-freedom Drug tests has its own unique error sum of squares, i.e., the sum of squares due to the interaction between subjects and the specific Drug contrast being tested. Unfortunately, the degrees of freedom associated with Order do not map onto the two separate components of the Drug by subjects interaction used to test the two single-degree-of-freedom Drug contrasts. In other words, while the Order sum of squares is confounded with the Drug by subjects interaction in this design, it is confounded with both the A versus C Drug contrast by subjects and the B versus A + C Drug contrast by subjects interactions in a way that does not permit us to remove it from these individual error terms. This would be true no matter how we coded the Drug and Order single-degree-of-freedom contrasts.

The lesson then is that a latin square design is useful for unconfounding Order or some other concomitant variable from the treatment variable of interest. However, with latin squares larger than a simple 2 × 2, one can remove the sum of squares due to Order or the confounding factor from the error term used to test the treatment variable of interest only if one is content with pooled tests involving multiple degrees of freedom of the treatment variable. While the design ensures that Order will not be confounded with the treatment single-degree-of-freedom comparisons, the sum of squares due to Order cannot be removed from the individual within-subject error terms used to test those single-degree-of-freedom treatment comparisons.

EXHIBIT 15.17 ▶

Source table for 3 × 3 latin square

Source	b	SS	df	MS	F*
Between Subjects		14.89	2	7.44	
Within Subjects					
Pooled Drug		5.56	2	2.78	3.57
Pooled Order		.22	2	.11	.14
Residual within Ss		1.55	2	.78	
Total Within		7.33	6	1.22	

15.1.4 A Replicated 3 × 3 Latin Square

In the example used in the previous section, we had only a single subject in each row or sequence of the latin square design. That is, only one subject was exposed to the drugs in the sequence A-B-C. Similarly, only one subject received the sequence B-C-A and only one received the sequence C-A-B. Accordingly, Sequence could not be treated as a between-subject factor since it was entirely redundant with subjects. To gain statistical power and to unconfound Sequence with subjects, we might collect data from multiple subjects in each of the three sequences, thus using a replicated 3 × 3 latin square design. Data from such a design are presented in Exhibit 15.18. In this exhibit, the columns represent Drugs and the order of delivery of those drugs is indicated by the letters following the Sequence numbers. Thus, for instance, subject 7 received the drugs in the sequence C-A-B. And this subject's ratings were sequentially given as first a 6 (for Drug C), then a 3 (for Drug A), and finally a 3 (for Drug B). Obviously we could rearrange these data so that the columns represented Order rather than Drug, as we did in earlier examples.

Since Sequence is now a between-subject variable that is not perfectly redundant with subjects, as it was in the 3 × 3 design that did not have replications, we can examine its effects in the between-subjects portion of the analysis. Accordingly, we derive two between-subjects contrasts to code the three levels of Sequence. The contrast-coded predictor S1 compares sequences 1 and 2 and the contrast-coded predictor S2 compares the average of sequences 1 and 2 with sequence 3. Three W_i scores

EXHIBIT 15.18 ▶

Hypothetical pain rating data: 3 × 3 replicated latin square

	Drug A	B	C
Sequence 1 (A-B-C)			
Subject 1	3	4	5
Subject 2	4	6	6
Subject 3	7	8	9
Sequence 2 (B-C-A)			
Subject 4	3	6	6
Subject 5	4	5	8
Subject 6	3	6	9
Sequence 3 (C-A-B)			
Subject 7	3	3	6
Subject 8	3	5	7
Subject 9	3	4	8

are computed for each subject in the analysis that treats Drug as the within-subject factor. As always, W_{0i} represents the between-subject portion of the variability. W_{1i} codes the within-subject comparison between Drug A and Drug C. W_{2i} codes the within-subject comparison between Drug B and the average of Drugs A and C. Each of these W_i's are regressed on the two between-subject contrast-coded predictors, S1 and S2, to generate the source table given in Exhibit 15.19.

Let us now proceed to analyze these same data treating Order as the within-subject factor and ignoring Drug. To do this, we simply rearrange the data for subjects in Sequences 2 and 3 so that the ratings are in the order they were recorded, rather than corresponding to the drugs they were given in response to. We then proceed to compute three W_i's just as we did in the preceding analysis. W_{0i} captures the between-subject variability. W_{1i} compares order 1 and order 3. W_{2i} compares order 2 with

EXHIBIT 15.19 ▶

Source table for 3 × 3 replicated latin square: order ignored

Source	b	SS	df	MS	F*	PRE
Between Subjects						
S1	.11	.22	1	.22	.05	.01
S2	.33	6.00	1	6.00	1.27	.17
Pooled Sequence		6.22	2	3.11	.66	.18
Ss within Seq.		28.44	6	4.74		
Total Between Ss		34.66	8			
Within Subjects						
Drug A vs. C	1.72	53.39	1	53.39	96.10	.94
A vs. C × S1	.58	4.08	1	4.08	7.35	.55
A vs. C × S2	.14	.69	1	.69	1.25	.17
A vs. C × Ss within Seq.		3.33	6	.56		
Drug B vs. A + C	.06	.17	1	.17	.28	.05
B vs. A + C × S1	.03	.03	1	.03	.05	.01
B vs. A + C × S2	.14	2.08	1	2.08	3.52	.37
B vs. A + C × Ss within Seq.		3.56	6	.59		
Pooled Drug		53.56	2	26.78	46.64	
Pooled Drug × Seq.		6.88	4	1.72	3.00	
Pooled Drug × Ss within Seq.		6.89	12	.57		
Total Within Ss		67.33	18			

the average of orders 1 and 3. These three W_i's are then regressed on the two Sequence contrast-coded predictors, S1 and S2, to generate the source table of Exhibit 15.20.

Note that the between-subjects portions of these two source tables are identical. Note also that the total within-subjects sums of squares are identical and that the pooled within-subject error terms, whether we call it the pooled Order by Subjects within sequence term or the pooled Drug by subjects within sequence term, are also identical in the two tables. As in the case of the 3×3 latin square without replications, across the three different sequences, every drug appears in each order, and across orders, every drug appears in each sequence. Hence, it must be the case that the pooled sum of squares due to Drug is part of the

EXHIBIT 15.20 ▶

Source table for 3 × 3 replicated latin square: drug ignored

Source	b	SS	df	MS	F*	PRE
Between Subjects						
S1	.11	.22	1	.22	.05	.01
S2	.33	6.00	1	6.00	1.27	.17
Pooled Sequence		6.22	2	3.11	.66	.18
Ss within Seq.		28.44	6	4.74		
Total Between Ss		34.66	8			
Within Subjects						
Order 1 vs. 3	.55	5.56	1	5.56	14.29	.70
1 vs. 3 × S1	1.08	14.06	1	14.06	16.05	.86
1 vs. 3 × S2	.47	8.02	1	8.02	20.56	.78
1 vs. 3 × Ss within Seq.		2.33	6	.39		
Order 2 vs. 1 + 3	.11	.67	1	.67	.88	.13
2 vs. 1 + 3 × S1	.47	8.03	1	8.03	10.57	.64
2 vs. 1 + 3 × S2	−.47	24.10	1	24.10	31.71	.84
2 vs. 1 + 3 × Ss within Seq.		4.56	6	.76		
Pooled Order		6.23	2	3.11	5.46	.47
Pooled Order × Seq.		54.21	4	13.55	23.78	.89
Pooled Order × Ss within Seq.		6.89	12	.57		
Total Within Ss		67.33	18			

pooled Order by Sequence sum of squares in the Order analysis. Reciprocally, the pooled sum of squares due to Order is part of the pooled Drug by Sequence sum of squares in the Drug analysis.

It then becomes possible to reexpress the pooled portions of the within-subjects sections of these two source tables, to identify both the sums of squares due to Drug and due to Order, assuming in fact that the Drug effect is just that and not an effect of Order by Sequence, and assuming that the Order effect is just that and not an effect of Drug by Sequence. Such a reexpressed source table is given in Exhibit 15.21.

A few comments are in order about this final pooled source table. First, while we have pulled the Order effect out of the Drug by Sequence interaction and reciprocally while we have pulled the Drug effect out of the Order by Sequence interaction, there remains variation in the data, with two associated degrees of freedom, that is either residual Order by Sequence variation or Drug by Sequence variation. In the 3×3 latin square that did not include replications, analyzed in the preceding section of this chapter, this residual interaction with Sequence (or with subjects in that design, since subjects and Sequence were perfectly confounded) was used as the error term to test the pooled Order and pooled Drug effects. Now, however, in addition to this residual Sequence interaction sum of squares, we also have a sum of squares that can be equivalently identified as the Drug by subjects within Sequence interaction or the Order by subjects within Sequence interaction. It is this latter

EXHIBIT 15.21 ▶

Source table for 3 × 3 replicated latin square

Source	SS	df	MS	F*	PRE
Between Subjects					
Pooled Sequence	6.22	2	3.11	.66	.18
Ss within Seq.	28.44	6	4.74		
Total Between Ss	34.66	8			
Within Subjects					
Pooled Drug	53.56	2	26.78	46.64	.89
Pooled Order	6.23	2	3.11	5.46	.47
Pooled Residual Drug × Seq. or Order × Seq.	.65	2	.33		
Pooled Drug or Order × Ss within Seq.	6.89	12	.57		
Total Within Ss	67.33	18			

term that we have used as the error term in the final pooled source table given in Exhibit 15.21. Some discussions of latin square designs recommend pooling the last two terms in this source table into a common error term to test the pooled treatment effect. In principle, there is nothing wrong with this strategy.

The other important comment to make is that once again it is not possible within this replicated 3 × 3 latin square design to pull the Order effect out of the individual single-degree-of-freedom Drug by Sequence interaction terms that are reported in the Drug analysis of Exhibit 15.19. However, with replications, these individual Drug by Sequence interaction terms are not used as the error terms in testing the single-degree-of-freedom Drug contrasts, as was the case in the design that contained no replications (where the Drug by Sequence terms were equivalently Drug by Subjects terms). Hence, we see no advantage in latin square designs with replications to control statistically for Order in testing the treatment effect, or what is here identified as the Drug effect, either when testing its pooled effect or its individual single-degree-of-freedom contrasts. This is because the Order effect is part of the Drug by Sequence interaction and, unlike the situation where there are no replications within Sequence, this interaction is not used as the error term in testing Drug effects. Obviously, however, the use of a latin square design may be important regardless of whether or not we choose to identify the sums of squares due to Order in the analysis. Regardless of whether we identify it statistically, in a latin square design Order is unconfounded with the treatment variable of interest. If all subjects receive the levels of the treatment variable in the same order then obviously this is not the case. A viable alternative is to randomize order for each subject rather than using the preset sequences defined by a latin square. Since we see nothing to be gained in the latin square analysis that includes replications from statistically identifying the Order sum of squares, we see no reason for preferring the use of such a design over one in which order of treatment is determined randomly for each subject and subsequently ignored in the analysis.

The principles of analysis that we have illustrated extend readily to larger latin square designs. In essence with such designs, one can conduct two parallel analyses, the first analyzing for the effects of the treatment variable, using single-degree-of-freedom contrasts and then pooling the appropriate sums of squares, and the second analyzing for the effects of Order. One can then combine the two resulting source tables into a single pooled source table as we have done in the last two examples. Discussions of higher-order latin square designs and procedures for identifying higher-order squares are contained in Cochran & Cox (1957) and Edwards (1960).

15.2

Continuously Measured Predictors in Repeated Measures Designs

In Chapter 13 we explored how continuous predictors could be incorporated into models that also involve categorical independent variables. Substantively, we might be interested in such models for either of two reasons. First, we might be interested in examining the relationship between the continuous predictor and the dependent variable when controlling for the categorical one. Alternatively, we might be interested in what happens to the effect of the categorical predictor when controlling for the continuously measured one. Within the experimental design literature, these sorts of models have been known as analysis of covariance models with interest focused on the second of these two substantive questions.

What we wish to do in the remaining part of this chapter is explore how continuous predictor variables might be incorporated into models with multiple dependent observations from each subject or group. In other words, we wish to extend the analysis of nonindependent observations, as set forth in Chapter 14, to incorporate continuously measured predictor variables. Again, there may be two different reasons for doing this. First, we might be interested in how those continuous predictor variables relate to the multiple within-subject dependent scores, either controlling for some set of categorical predictors that are measured between subjects or not. Second, we might be interested in examining what happens to the effects of categorical predictor variables when we control for continuously measured ones with nonindependent observations. In this latter case, the analyses we outline amount to what has been called the analysis of covariance in repeated measures designs, where the continuously measured predictor variable is known as the covariate. It is within this latter context that we illustrate in this chapter how continuously measured predictors might be examined within mixed model designs. We will upon occasion, however, remind the reader that one might be primarily interested in the relationship between the continuously measured predictor variable and the dependent variable when confronted with nonindependent observations.

In Chapter 13 we discussed two different reasons why continuously measured predictors, or covariates, might be incorporated into models along with categorical predictor variables. First, in experimental designs, one might include a covariate in a model in order to increase the power of the statistical tests of the experimental factors. Accordingly, the ideal covariate in this case is one that is as highly correlated as possible with the dependent variable of interest but that shows little or no relationship with the experimental factors whose effects are to be examined. The second reason for including a covariate is because that covariate is partially redundant with the other predictor variables of interest and one wishes to examine the effects of those categorical predictor variables freed from the contaminating effects of the covariate. In other words, one may want to examine the effects of the predictors over and above or controlling for the partially redundant covariate.

These same two reasons exist for wanting to control for some continuously measured covariate within the context of repeated measures designs. Accordingly, we wish to generalize the procedures of Chapter 13 to the situation where one or more experimental factors are crossed with subjects, rather than subjects being nested under them all. The procedures for doing this are remarkably straightforward within the general approach we have developed for analyzing repeated measures designs. One simply computes W_i scores as usual and then regresses them not only upon the between subject factors of interest but also on the covariates and linear transformations of those covariates.

To understand this sort of analysis two different sorts of covariates in repeated measures designs need to be considered. Let us assume that we have a mixed experimental design with experimental units or subjects nested under one factor and crossed with a second. To be more concrete, let us suppose that individuals are assigned to one of two groups in an experimental session. These two groups then either compete against or cooperate with each other in some experimental task. Following this interaction each group member rates how much they like members of their own group (their ingroup) and how much they like members of the other group in the session (their outgroup). These ratings are then averaged across all members in a session, so that for each session we have a mean ingroup rating and a mean outgroup rating. Experimental session is thus the unit of analysis in this design. Four sessions are randomly assigned to the cooperative task, and four to the competitive task. Cooperation versus competition is the experimental factor under which sessions are nested. Sessions are crossed with the ingroup versus outgroup liking factor, since from each session we have a mean ingroup liking and a mean outgroup liking. The data of Exhibit 15.22 might result from such a study.

We could conduct a mixed model repeated measures analysis of variance on these data, using the procedures developed in the last chapter, in order to examine the effects of cooperation versus competition, ingroup versus outgroup, and their interaction on liking. Suppose further, however, that the eight experimental sessions lasted different amounts of time, so that individuals in some sessions had more prolonged interaction with each other than individuals in another session.

In this case, we have measured the covariate only once for each session. In other words, since sessions only have a single time measure, time varies between sessions and may differ as a function of cooperation and competition, but it does not vary within sessions. We can then ask what the effect of cooperation versus competition is on liking controlling for the amount of time spent interacting in a session, and we can ask how time of interaction relates to average liking of ingroup and outgroup members, but it makes little sense to inquire about differences between ingroup and outgroup liking controlling for time of interaction, since time of interaction does not vary with the ingroup versus outgroup distinction.

In other cases, the covariate may vary within subjects, or session in this case, as well as between them. Suppose, for instance in our example, that the experimenter had monitored each group and recorded not only the total length of interaction in the session but also the amount of time in each session devoted to interaction between groups and interaction within groups on average. Thus, for each session we might have recorded an average length of interaction with other ingroup members and an average length of interaction with outgroup members. Such data are given in Exhibit 15.24. These data have been created such that the sum of the times of interaction for the ingroup and outgroup for each session equals that session's total time of interaction given in the previous data table of Exhibit 15.23. Just as in that table, therefore, the total time of interaction in each session varies between sessions and may well vary with the between-session factor of competition versus cooperation. Now, in addition, the time covariate varies within a session, between the ingroup and outgroup. Accordingly, it may make sense to control for time of interaction in examining the effect of the ingroup

EXHIBIT 15.24 ▶

Hypothetical group liking and group interaction time data

	Ingroup Time	Ingroup Liking	Outgroup Time	Outgroup Liking
Cooperation				
Session 1	19	7.5	16	7.0
Session 2	14	6.5	14	6.5
Session 3	14	7.0	13	6.5
Session 4	12	5.5	13	6.0
Competition				
Session 5	14	6.5	12	4.3
Session 6	20	7.0	13	5.3
Session 7	18	6.8	12	4.8
Session 8	22	7.3	16	3.5

EXHIBIT 15.22 ▶

Hypothetical group liking data

	Mean Liking	
	Ingroup	Outgroup
Cooperation		
Session 1	7.5	7.0
Session 2	6.5	6.5
Session 3	7.0	6.5
Session 4	5.5	6.0
Competition		
Session 5	6.5	4.3
Session 6	7.0	5.3
Session 7	6.8	4.8
Session 8	7.3	3.5

We might suspect that the duration of interaction might affect the degree of liking one expresses for other subjects in the session, and hence, we might like both to examine the effect of duration of interaction on liking and to control for it when examining the effects of the experimental factors. We have reproduced the data in Exhibit 15.23, this time including for each session the amount of time (in minutes) of interaction.

EXHIBIT 15.23 ▶

Hypohetical group liking and time of interaction data

	Time	Mean Liking	
		Ingroup	Outgroup
Cooperation			
Session 1	35	7.5	7.0
Session 2	28	6.5	6.5
Session 3	27	7.0	6.5
Session 4	25	5.5	6.0
Competition			
Session 5	26	6.5	4.3
Session 6	33	7.0	5.3
Session 7	30	6.8	4.8
Session 8	38	7.3	3.5

versus outgroup factor and its interaction with cooperation-competition. We might also be interested in examining not only how time of interaction relates to average group liking but also in how the difference in the time of interaction between the ingroup and the outgroup relates to the ingroup-outgroup difference in liking.

We will refer to these two cases by talking about whether the covariate only varies between subjects, or sessions, or whether it also varies within subjects, or sessions. As we will show, the analysis of the former case is in fact subsumed under the more comprehensive analysis of a covariate that varies within as well as between subjects.

15.2.1 Covariate Only between Subjects

Let us start by analyzing the liking data from this design ignoring the covariate. As always with two observations from each session we compute two W_i scores, one to capture the between-session variability in the data (W_{0i}) and one to capture the within-session variability (W_{1i}). Both of these W_i scores are regressed on a contrast-coded predictor variable that represents the between-session factor of cooperation versus competition (X_1). The coefficient for this contrast-coded predictor in the W_{0i} regression informs us about the main effect of the between-session factor. In the W_{1i} regression, the intercept informs us about the ingroup-outgroup difference in liking and the coefficient for the contrast-coded predictor informs us about the interaction between ingroup-outgroup and cooperation-competition. This analysis gives rise to the source table presented in Exhibit 15.25.

EXHIBIT 15.25 ▶

Mixed model ANOVA source table for group liking data

Source	b	SS	df	MS	F*	PRE
Between Sessions						
Coop-Comp	−.44	3.06	1	3.06	5.88	.49
Session within Coop-Comp		3.13	6	.52		
Total Between		6.19	7			
Within Sessions						
Ingroup-Outgroup	.64	6.50	1	6.50	23.40	.80
In-Out × Coop-Comp	.57	5.29	1	5.29	19.03	.76
In-Out × Session within Coop-Comp		1.67	6	.28		
Total Within		13.46	8			

From this analysis we conclude that the difference in mean liking as a function of cooperation versus competition is not reliable. (The critical value of F with one and six degrees of freedom, $\alpha = .05$, is 5.99.) There is, however, a reliable difference in liking between ingroups and outgroups and this difference is larger under competition than it is under cooperation.

Inspection of the data given in Exhibit 15.23 for total time of interaction in each session suggests that sessions which competed interacted for longer periods of time on average than did sessions which cooperated. The mean time of interaction under competition is 31.75 minutes; under cooperation it is 28.75 minutes. If, as we suspect, higher liking ratings are associated with more prolonged interaction, then the difference between cooperation and competition in liking may emerge as a reliable one once we control for the difference between the two conditions in total time of interaction. In other words, the liking ratings under competition might have been even lower than those under cooperation if sessions in the two conditions had on average interacted for the same amount of time. Accordingly, we may want to examine the cooperation-competition effect while controlling for or statistically holding constant time of interaction.

To do this, we simply include Time of interaction as a predictor variable in the W_{0i} regression equation along with the contrast-coded predictor representing cooperation-competition. If the cooperation-competition contrast is now reliable, this tells us that on average, collapsing across ingroup and outgroup ratings, higher liking results under cooperation than under competition once differences between sessions in the length of interaction are controlled. For right now, it makes little sense to include Time as a predictor in the W_{1i} regression, since total Time of interaction varies only between sessions and not within, while W_{1i} captures only the within-session variability in the liking data. At a later point in this discussion we will see how we would interpret a model that includes total Time of interaction as a predictor of W_{1i}. For right now, however, it makes little sense to ask whether there is a difference in ingroup versus outgroup liking when total time of interaction is statistically controlled, since total time of interaction does not vary across the ingroup-outgroup distinction.

The W_{0i} model that includes Time and the cooperation-competition contrast-coded predictor ($X_1 = 1$ if competition; $= -1$ if cooperation) is as follows:

$$\hat{W}_{0i} = 6.32 + 0.08\text{Time}_i - 0.73X_{i1} \qquad \text{SSE} = 2.33$$

The revised source table including the between-subject covariate, Time, is given in Exhibit 15.26. Note that, as always, the coefficients we report in the source table have been transformed back into the Y_{hi} metric by dividing them by, in this case, $\sqrt{2}$.

EXHIBIT 15.26 ▶

Mixed model source table for group liking data including total time of interaction as between-session covariate

Source	b	SS	df	MS	F*	PRE
Between Sessions						
Coop-Comp	−.52	3.81	1	3.81	8.17	.62
Time	.05	.80	1	.80	1.71	.25
Residual Between		2.33	5	.47		
Total Between		6.19	7			
Within Sessions						
Ingroup-Outgroup	.64	6.50	1	6.50	23.40	.80
In-Out × Coop-Comp	.57	5.29	1	5.29	19.03	.76
In-Out × Session within Coop-Comp		1.67	6	.28		
Total Within		13.46	8			

Comparing this source table with that presented from the analysis of variance in Exhibit 15.25, three comments on the between-sessions portion of the table are worth making. First, as we suspected, the cooperation-competition main effect is now reliable, whereas it was not when differences in time of interaction were not controlled. Second, the sums of squares in the between-session portion of the table no longer add up to give us the total sum of squares between sessions, since the Time covariate and the condition contrast code are not orthogonal. Third, although the relationship between total time of interaction and liking, within cooperation-competition conditions, is positive, as we suspected it would be, it is not reliable.

This analysis, including a between-subjects or sessions covariate in the between-subjects or sessions portion of the analysis, is certainly a straightforward extension of the procedures developed in Chapters 13 and 14. One simply includes the covariate in the W_{0i} equation and interprets the resulting coefficients for the between-subject or between-session contrast codes appropriately. We can further complicate things by asking about various interactions with the covariate in addition to asking more simply, as we have done, about conditional effects of the between-subject or between-session factors once a covariate is included.

The first such interaction that seems reasonable to test involves the homogeneity of regression assumption that was discussed in the treatment of analysis of covariance in Chapter 13. We have assumed that the relationship between the covariate Time and W_{0i} does not depend on whether a session is cooperative or competitive. Phrased the other way, we have assumed that the relationship between Time and liking does not depend on whether the interaction was cooperative or competitive. To test whether this assumption is appropriate, we would include the Time by X_1 product term in the W_{0i} model. Doing so results in the following augmented regression model:

$$\hat{W}_{0i} = 6.06 + 0.09\text{Time}_i + 1.84X_{i1} - .09(\text{Time})X_{i1} \qquad \text{SSE} = 1.37$$

Comparing this model with the one that did not include the Time by X_1 interaction gives a value of F^*, with one and four degrees of freedom, of 2.81. Since this value does not exceed the critical value, we conclude that the relationship between whether a session was cooperative or competitive and the average liking of ingroup and outgroup members does not depend on how long a session lasted. Equivalently, we conclude that the relationship between average liking of session members, collapsing across the ingroup-outgroup distinction, and time of interaction in the session does not depend on whether the groups in a session cooperated or competed with one another. Had the interaction been reliable, then our conclusions about the main effect of cooperation versus competition would have had to be tempered by identification of the levels of Time at which the cooperation-competition differences emerge.

So far, this covariate analysis seems a straightforward extension of the material in Chapter 13. We simply are including a between-subject or between-session covariate in the between-subject or between-session portion of the analysis and analyzing its conditional effects and interaction just as we did earlier. Now, however, we can extend the analysis to inquire about the interaction between the between-session covariate and the within-session factor of ingroup versus outgroup. In the source table of Exhibit 15.26, we reported the somewhat surprising result that total time of interaction and liking were not reliably related to each other within levels of cooperation versus competition. In other words, the coefficient for Time was not reliably different from zero in the W_{0i} equation when looking within condition or when X_1 was controlled. It may be, however, that the relationship between Time and liking depends on whether one is looking at ingroup liking or outgroup liking. This is equivalent to saying that total time of interaction may not make a difference to the average liking of ingroup and outgroup members, but it may make a difference to the *difference* between liking of ingroup and outgroup members. Thus, to examine whether there is an interaction between the between-session covariate Time and the within-session factor of ingroup versus outgroup, we might like to include Time as a predictor variable in the W_{1i} regression equation. The W_{1i} model that includes only X_1 as a predictor and that was the basis of the within-sessions portions of the source tables given in Exhibits 15.25 and 15.26 is

$$\hat{W}_{1i} = 0.90 + 0.81X_{i1} \qquad \text{SSE} = 1.67$$

Including Time as a predictor gives us the following equation:

$$\hat{W}_{1i} = -1.32 + .70X_{i1} + .07\text{Time}_i \qquad SSE = 0.95$$

A comparison of these two models yields a value of F^*, with one and five degrees of freedom, of 3.79, which does not exceed the critical value of F. Accordingly, there is no evidence in these data that the total time of interaction in the session is any more or less predictive of ingroup than it is of outgroup liking, controlling for whether the sessions were cooperative or competitive ones. Another way of saying the same thing is to say that there is no evidence that total time of interaction relates to the difference between ingroup and outgroup liking, within levels of cooperation versus competition.

Had the coefficient for Time in the W_{1i} equation been reliable, assuming a positive coefficient, this would tell us that W_{1i} becomes more positive as time of interaction increases. Since we have coded W_{1i} so that it represents the ingroup liking minus outgroup liking, the positive coefficient would mean that as Time of interaction increases the liking of ingroup members relative to outgroup members increases.

One point of caution is appropriate here. Recall that the intercept in the W_{1i} equation is used to test the main effect of the within-subject or session factor. In this case, in the model that includes the contrast-coded X_1 as the only predictor of W_{1i}, the intercept tells us about the ingroup versus outgroup difference in liking. This interpretation of the intercept assumes that all predictor variables included in the equation have mean values of zero, since what we really want to know is whether the mean of W_{1i} differs from zero and the intercept in the W_{1i} equation will equal the mean of W_{1i} only if all predictors have means of zero. When we include a covariate such as Time in the model, however, the intercept no longer equals the mean value of W_{1i}, since the mean value of Time is not zero. Accordingly, in the model that includes Time, the test of the intercept is no longer a test of the main effect for ingroup versus outgroup in liking. Rather, it tells us about the ingroup-outgroup difference in liking, assuming zero time of interaction! Had we transformed Time, putting it in mean deviation form, the intercept could then still be interpreted as the average difference between ingroups and outgroups in liking.

We have now tested two different covariate interactions. One involved the interaction of the covariate with the between-session factor of cooperation versus competition. The other involved the interaction of the covariate with the within-session factor of ingroup versus outgroup. It is logically possible to test also the triple interaction between Time, cooperation-competition, and ingroup-outgroup by including the X_1Time product in the W_{1i} model. We see no reason to do so in the present case, since a clear interpretation for such an interaction is not apparent. However, should such covariate by within-subject factor by between-subject factor interactions be expected, they certainly can be tested using the present approach.

15.2.2   Covariate within and between Subjects

We now want to treat the case where for each subject or session in the analysis we measure the covariate as many times as we measure the dependent variable. We have given the data we will use here in Exhibit 15.24.

The dependent measure is liking for the ingroup and liking for the outgroup and our covariate is also measured twice for each session, once for time of interaction with the ingroup and once for time of interaction with the outgroup. What we want to know is whether liking differs as a function of cooperation-competition when time of interaction is controlled (i.e., the same question we asked in the last section of this chapter when the covariate varied only between subjects), whether ingroup liking differs from outgroup liking when the *difference* in the time of interaction between the two is controlled, and whether the ingroup-outgroup difference in liking depends on cooperation versus competition when the *difference* in the time of interaction between ingroups and outgroups is controlled.

Let us think for a minute about what it means to examine whether there exists an ingroup-outgroup difference in liking when we control for any difference between the ingroup and outgroup in time of interaction. If it is the case, as we have speculated, that higher liking ensues from more prolonged interaction, and if there is on average more prolonged interaction with ingroup members than with outgroup members, then the ingroup-outgroup difference in liking we have documented in these data could be entirely due to a difference in the time of interaction with the two groups. What we now want to know is whether there remains an ingroup-outgroup difference in liking if we act as if there were no difference in time of interaction with the two groups. In other words, we want to know if there persists a difference in liking over and above or getting rid of the difference in liking that is associated with the difference in time of interaction.

Phrasing our questions in this way makes clear the analytic strategy we will follow. We will code the covariate in a manner parallel to how we code the dependent variable in this analysis and then we will include those covariate codes in the appropriate regression models. As always, we use two W_i's to code the dependent variable. W_{0i} amounts to the average or sum of the two mean liking ratings for each session, adding up the two scores, and dividing by $\sqrt{2}$. W_{1i} amounts to the ingroup-outgroup difference in mean liking for each session, subtracting the outgroup value from the ingroup value, and dividing the difference by

$\sqrt{2}$. We will derive similar transformations for the covariate. Thus, we will define T_{0i} analogously to W_{0i}, adding up for each session the two Time values and dividing by $\sqrt{2}$. We will also define T_{1i} analogously to W_{1i}, taking the difference between the time of interaction with the ingroup and the time of interaction with the outgroup for each session and dividing that difference by $\sqrt{2}$. The resulting values are given in Exhibit 15.27.

Now, we will proceed with our analysis as we have done all along, regressing W_{0i} on X_1 and W_{1i} on X_1, but this time in each of these regressions we will include the appropriately transformed covariate. Thus, in the W_{0i} equation, where we are asking whether cooperation versus competition makes a difference to liking on average across ingroups and outgroups, we will now ask whether it does so controlling for T_{0i} or controlling for the average or total time of interaction across ingroups and outgroups. In the W_{1i} regression we will include as a predictor T_{1i}. We will then be asking questions about the ingroup versus outgroup difference in liking (i.e., whether that difference is reliably different from zero and whether that difference depends on cooperation versus competition) when controlling for or holding constant the ingroup versus outgroup difference in time of interaction.

Remember that our test of the ingroup-outgroup difference in liking is a test of the intercept in the W_{1i} model, testing whether the intercept differs from zero. We said above that the question we now want to ask of these data is whether there remains an ingroup-outgroup difference in liking when we control for the ingroup-outgroup difference in time of interaction or act as if there were no ingroup-outgroup difference in time of interaction. Testing the intercept when T_{1i} is included in the

EXHIBIT 15.27 ▶

Time and liking composite scores

	T_{0i}	W_{0i}	T_{1i}	W_{1i}
Cooperation				
Session 1	24.75	10.25	2.12	.35
Session 2	19.80	9.19	0	0
Session 3	19.09	9.55	.71	.35
Session 4	17.68	8.13	−.71	−.35
Competition				
Session 5	18.38	7.64	1.41	1.56
Session 6	23.33	8.70	4.95	1.20
Session 7	21.21	8.20	4.24	1.41
Session 8	26.87	7.64	4.24	2.69

model will provide a test of whether there is an ingroup-outgroup difference in liking when $T_{1i} = 0$, i.e., when the ingroup-outgroup difference in time of interaction equals zero. Thus, and this is important, we want to include T_{1i} as a predictor in the model *without* putting it into mean deviation form, allowing for the fact that on average there is a difference in time of interaction between the two groups, and then asking whether the difference in liking persists (i.e., is the intercept different from zero) when we act as if the difference in time of interaction were equal to zero.

The regression equation for W_{0i} not including the covariate is

$$\hat{W}_{0i} = 8.66 - .62X_{i1} \qquad \text{SSE} = 3.13$$

Recall that X_1 is coded so that cooperative sessions have a value of -1 and competitive ones have a $+1$ value. This is the same equation that was used previously to generate the between-sessions portion for the analysis of variance source table for these data (Exhibit 15.25). When we include the transformed covariate T_{0i}, the following regression results emerge:

$$\hat{W}_{0i} = 6.32 - .73 \, X_{i1} + .11 \, T_{0i} \qquad \text{SSE} = 2.33$$

The regression equation for W_{1i} not including the covariate is

$$\hat{W}_{1i} = .90 + .81X_{i1} \qquad \text{SSE} = 1.67$$

Again, this is the same equation that was used to generate the within-sessions portion of the source tables of Exhibits 15.25 and 15.26. When we include the covariate difference score in this analysis, T_{1i}, the following equation results:

$$\hat{W}_{1i} = .69 + .66X_{i1} + .10T_{1i} \qquad \text{SSE} = 1.55$$

To test whether the difference in average liking between cooperative and competitive sessions is reliable when we control for the amount of time spent interacting, we want to test whether the regression coefficient for X_1 is reliably different from zero in the W_{0i} equation. To test whether there is a reliable difference between ingroup and outgroup liking when controlling for the difference in the time of interaction with the two groups (i.e., asking whether there is a liking difference over and above any difference attributable to a difference in time of interaction), we want to test the intercept in the W_{1i} equation. Finally, to determine whether the difference in liking between ingroups and outgroups depends on cooperation versus competition, again controlling for the difference in interaction time, we want to test whether the X_1 coefficient differs from zero in the W_{1i} equation. These tests give rise to the analysis of covariance source table of Exhibit 15.28.

EXHIBIT 15.28 ▶

Mixed model source table for group liking data including time of interaction as between- and within-session covariate

Source	b	SS	df	MS	F*	PRE
Between Sessions						
Coop-Comp	−.52	3.81	1	3.81	8.17	.62
T_{0i}	.08	.80	1	.80	1.71	.25
Residual Between		2.33	5	.47		
Total Between		6.19	7			
Within Sessions						
Ingroup-Outgroup	.50	.95	1	.95	3.05	.38
In-Out × Coop-Comp	.47	1.27	1	1.27	4.08	.45
T_{1i}	.07	.11	1	.11	.36	.07
Residual within Sessions		1.55	5	.31		
Total Within		13.46	8			

It is informative to compare this analysis of covariance source table, with a covariate that varies within as well as between sessions, with both the earlier analysis of variance table for these data (Exhibit 15.25) and the analysis of covariance table in which the total time of interaction was the only covariate (Exhibit 15.26), varying only between sessions. Examining the between-sessions portion of this table, we see that the results are identical with the analysis of covariance table of Exhibit 15.26 where total time of interaction was included as the between-sessions covariate. This is necessarily the case since the sum of the time of inter- action with the ingroup and the time of interaction with the outgroup in these data is equal to the total time of interaction used as the covariate earlier. The only slight difference between using that sum, referred to as Time in Exhibit 15.26, and the present T_{0i} as the covariate is that T_{0i} equals the sum of the two divided by $\sqrt{2}$. As a result, the coefficient for T_{0i} reported in the current source table (Exhibit 15.28) differs from the coefficient for Time reported in the earlier analysis of covariance table (Exhibit 15.26) by a factor of $1/\sqrt{2}$. The sum of squares associated with T_{0i}, however, is identical to the sum of squares for Time reported earlier.

It is because of the equivalence of this between-sessions portion of the analysis of covariance source table with the earlier source table, in which the covariate varied only between sessions, that the earlier anal- ysis of covariance is really subsumed by the analysis we are presently conducting. In other words, using a covariate that varies only between subjects is equivalent to using the sum of the values of the covariate in the between-subjects or between-sessions part of the analysis when the covariate varies within as well as between subjects or between sessions. As in the earlier section, our conclusion is here that the difference between liking under cooperation and under competition, collapsing across the ingroup-outgroup difference, becomes a reliable difference once we control for or hold constant the total amount of time spent interacting with both ingroup and outgroup members. Surprisingly, however, average time of interaction (collapsing across ingroup and outgroup) does not reliably relate to average liking (again collapsing across ingroup and outgroup) within levels of cooperation-competition.

When we compare the within-sessions portions of the source table with the within-sessions portions of Exhibits 15.25 and 15.26, where no covariate was included, the differences in the ingroup-outgroup effect and the ingroup-outgroup by condition interaction are marked. Earlier, both of these effects were large and quite reliable, with greater liking on average for the ingroup than the outgroup, especially under competition. Now, however, both effects have been reduced in magnitude considerably (as indicated by the reported coefficients in the table) and neither one yields a value of F^* that exceeds the critical value of F at α less than .05. The difference in results when we include T_{1i} in the W_{1i} equation is produced because of the difference in time of interaction between ingroups and outgroups, with more extensive interaction with the ingroup than the outgroup, and because of the fact that this difference in time of interaction is especially pronounced for competitive sessions. The analysis here is essentially asking questions about how much of an ingroup-outgroup difference in liking there is when we act as if the ingroup-outgroup difference in time of interaction equals zero. Since the T_{1i} covariate represents the ingroup-outgroup difference in time of interaction, when we ask whether the intercept in the W_1 equation differs from zero when T_{1i} is included as a predictor, we are asking whether the ingroup-outgroup difference in liking equals zero when the ingroup-outgroup difference in time of interaction equals zero. Similarly, to determine whether the ingroup-outgroup difference in liking varies with cooperation versus competition when the T_{1i} covariate is included as a predictor, we are asking whether X_1 is reliably related to W_{1i} when we control for differences in time of interaction between the ingroup and the outgroup. Since the difference in time of interaction between the two groups is much larger, on average, under competition than it is under cooperation, we are asking whether condition explains variation in the ingroup-outgroup difference in liking when we control for the fact that the ingroup-outgroup difference in time of interaction is larger for competitive than for cooperative sessions.

Notice that the sum of squares for the individual predictors in the within-sessions portions of the source table no longer come close to adding up to the total within-sessions sum of squares once we included the covariate. This is because T_{1i} is quite redundant with X_1, as we have already said.

These results illustrate how the analysis of a within-subjects or within-sessions factor can look rather different when we control for some other variable that varies within subjects and on which there is a large difference within subjects. In other words, our analysis of the difference in liking due to the within-sessions ingroup-outgroup factor looks rather different when we statistically remove the large ingroup-outgroup difference in time of interaction. A within-subjects or within-sessions covariate can also be useful, however, even when the average difference on the covariate as a function of the within-subjects factor exactly equals zero. If the covariate difference is highly related to the dependent variable difference, i.e., if T_{1i} is highly related to W_{1i}, even when the average value of T_{1i} equals zero, then an analysis that includes the covariate will be a more powerful analysis than one that does not. In other words, when dealing with a covariate that varies within subjects, we have the same two basic rationales for including a covariate as when the covariate varies between subjects, along the lines discussed in Chapter 13. Namely, if the difference in the covariate associated with a within-subject factor exactly equals zero, then including the covariate difference will affect power, but it will not change the estimated effect of the within-subject factor on the dependent variable. However, when the mean difference on the covariate associated with the within-subject factor does not equal zero, then the estimate of the effect of the within-subject factor on the dependent variable will vary as a function of whether the covariate difference score is included in the model or not.

In the last section of this chapter, where the covariate was measured only once for each session and thus did not vary within sessions, we discussed various covariate interactions that might be of interest within the context of this mixed design. More specifically, we examined whether Time and X_1 interacted in the W_{0i} equation in order to determine whether time of interaction related differently to average liking, collapsing across ingroups and outgroups, under cooperation than under competition. We also examined whether the effect of Time of interaction on liking depended on the within-sessions factor of ingroup or outgroup. We did this by including Time as a predictor in the W_{1i} equation. Finally, we discussed how one could examine the triple interaction between Time of interaction, cooperation versus competition, and ingroup versus outgroup by including the Time by X_1 product in the W_{1i} equation. All of these interactions could be equivalently examined in the present design, with a covariate that varies within sessions as well as between, by using

T_{0i} rather than Time as a component of the various interactions. Thus, for instance, to test the homogeneity of regression assumption in the between-sessions portion of the analysis, we would include the T_{0i} by X_1 product term in the W_{0i} equation. To examine whether time of interaction relates to liking differently for ingroups versus outgroups, we would include T_{0i} in the W_{1i} equation. Finally, to test whether the triple interaction involving time of interaction, condition, and the ingroup-outgroup difference, we would include the T_{0i} by X_1 product in the W_{1i} equation. These specifications would produce identical results to those reported earlier where we simply used Time as the between-sessions covariate.

What we want to do now is discuss various interactions involving the ingroup versus outgroup difference in time of interaction, T_{1i}. The first such interaction to be examined concerns the same homogeneity of regression assumption that has come up whenever we have considered analysis of covariance. Namely, in the W_{1i} equation, we have so far assumed that the relationship between T_{1i} and W_{1i} is the same under cooperation as it is under competition. It may be that the ingroup-outgroup difference in time of interaction relates to the ingroup-outgroup difference in liking differently under cooperation than it does under competition. To test this, we simply compute the T_{1i} by X_1 product and include it as a predictor in the W_{1i} equation. The resulting model for the present data is

$$\hat{W}_{1i} = .82 + .86X_{i1} + .13T_{1i} - .12(X_{i1}T_{1i}) \qquad \text{SSE} = 1.41$$

A comparison of this model to the one that did not include the X_1 by T_{1i} product, given earlier, shows that the interaction is not reliable. Hence, we can conclude that the relationship between the difference in time of interaction and the difference in liking across ingroups and outgroups does not reliably differ as a function of cooperation versus competition.

A further question we might be interested in is whether average liking for others in one's session, averaging across ingroup and outgroup members, depends on the difference in time of interaction with ingroup and outgroup members. It is hard to imagine a theoretical rationale for such an interaction, yet it is certainly testable by including T_{1i} as a predictor in the W_{0i} equation, along with X_1 and T_{0i}. If the coefficient for T_{1i} in this equation were reliable, then we would conclude that liking for others in one's session, regardless of whether they were members of the ingroup or the outgroup, depends on the difference in time of interaction between the ingroup and the outgroup.

Finally, it is conceivable that we would be interested in knowing whether the difference in time of interaction between ingroup and outgroup members relates differently to average liking of all individuals in one's session, collapsing across the ingroup-outgroup distinction, under cooperation than it does under competition. Such an interaction could be tested by including the T_{1i} by X_1 product in the W_{0i} equation.

We discuss all of these interactions not because we mean to suggest that they ought to be examined in every design involving a within-subject or within-session covariate. In fact, our recommendation is that interactions between a covariate and experimental factors generally be examined only when there exists a theoretical reason for doing so. There will be occasions, however, when one is interested in interactions involving a within-subject covariate and between-subject or within-subject experimental factors. The point of this discussion is simply to show how such interactions can be tested and interpreted in a straightforward manner if in fact they are of theoretical interest.

15.2.3   Covariates in Designs Involving Multiple Within-Subject Factors

We have discussed the use of a covariate within the context of a relatively simple mixed design, with one two-level factor between subjects and one two-level factor within them. A few comments are in order about the generalization of what we have said to more complicated mixed designs.

First, imagine a situation in which a within-subject factor has more than two levels and in which the covariate is measured as many times as the dependent variable is measured. For instance, a within-subject factor may have four levels, and the covariate might then be measured four different times. In such a design, there would be four W_i's that would be regressed on any between-subject contrast-coded predictors. To include the covariate in the analysis, we would code it in a manner parallel to that used to code the dependent variable, thus creating four different T_i scores for each subject. In each W_i equation we would then include the T_i that codes the same within-subject covariate comparison as that coded for the dependent variable. Thus, for instance, if W_{1i} codes the difference between the first and the average of the second, third, and fourth levels of the within-subject factor, then the parallel comparison on the covariate, T_{1i}, would be included in the W_{1i} regression. We would then be asking whether the difference in the dependent variable between the first and other levels of the within-subject factor is reliable once we force the parallel difference on the covariate to equal zero.

With multiple within-subject factors and the covariate measured at all combinations of levels of those factors, the situation is hardly different. Just as specific W_i's might code the main effects and interactions of the within-subject factors, so parallel comparisons involving the covariate would be coded and included in the appropriate models.

Most treatments of analysis of covariance in repeated measures designs make the assumption that the coefficients for the covariate comparisons, T_i's, included in the various W_i equations, are homogeneous across equations or across the within-subject comparisons that are made. We see no necessary reason to make such an assumption. In other words, in each W_i equation, it seems reasonable to estimate the coefficient for the parallel T_i comparison in a way to minimize the sum of squared errors in that equation rather than forcing equivalent coefficients across models.

A somewhat more complicated situation arises when we have multiple within-subject factors and a covariate that is measured under all levels of only some of those factors. Imagine, for instance, that we have a 2×3 design within subjects, with two levels of factor A crossed with three levels of factor B. Thus, for each subject we measure the dependent variable six times. Suppose, however, that a covariate is measured only once under each level of factor A. Thus, the covariate varies between levels of factor A but is constant across the levels of factor B. We would then code the covariate in a manner parallel to the W_i codes that compare levels of factor A, including the covariate comparisons only in those regression models that capture factor A comparisons on the dependent variable.

In these more complicated within-subject designs, it is also possible to test various covariate interactions in much the same manner as we have in the simple 2×2 mixed design discussed in the last two sections of the chapter. With multiple within-subject factors and a covariate that varies with them all, the number of testable covariate interactions can be very large. Again, we strongly recommend that such interactions be examined only when prior theoretical motivation for them exists.

15.3

Conclusion

In this chapter we have focused on some further issues and designs where independence of ERRORs cannot be assumed. The first section dealt with latin square designs that involve repeated measures. The second focused on the use of covariates in repeated measures designs. More generally, the second section dealt with the use of continuously measured predictor variables in designs with multiple observations for each subject.

This concludes our discussion of how to deal with data in which the assumption of independent ERRORs is violated. Although we certainly have not dealt with every design or situation in which this is likely to be the case, we hope to have illustrated a general approach to the problem, whereby observations are combined into one or more composite scores. One then uses these composite scores, one from each subject or independent unit, as dependent variables in a series of models, thereby preserving the independence assumption within models. By the appropriate construction of these composite scores, the full range of questions of interest can normally be answered.

We turn now to violations of the normality and common variance assumptions. We will see that the general approach we have outlined here will be our approach there as well. One operates on the data or transforms it in such a way that the assumption violation is removed. One then proceeds to use the full set of models developed in earlier chapters on the transformed data.

16

Other Problems with DATA: Transformation Remedies

In the previous two chapters we encountered and solved a common problem with data values and the error terms in models—the problem of nonindependence. Nonindependence is unfortunately not the only problem which afflicts the Y's and the errors ε's. In this chapter we will consider a variety of other problems with the Y's and the ε's, problems which can make it difficult to build and test successful models for the data. In order to compare values of PRE and F^* with their critical values in the appropriate tables of Appendix C, we have assumed throughout, in addition to independence, that the ε's are sampled from a normal distribution with a common variance. Violations of these two assumptions are known, respectively, as nonnormality of errors and heteroscedasticity. In this chapter we consider diagnosis and remediation of those two problems as well as the related problem of unequal intervals on the measurement scale for Y. Although these problems are conceptually distinct from one another, we group them together because the solution to one problem generally, but not always, provides the solution to all the other problems.

On the one hand, the problems considered in this chapter are often not as serious as the nonindependence problem examined in the previous two chapters. It is often said that the linear model analysis is "robust" with respect to these issues. That is, while positive and negative nonindependence can seriously alter the chances of falsely rejecting a null hypothesis (Type I errors), simulation studies have shown that nonnormality and heteroscedasticity must be very extreme before the Type I error probabilities are appreciably altered. On the other hand, nonnormality and heteroscedasticity can cause certain difficulties for the data analysis. Two particular difficulties are loss of efficiency and increased model complexity.

Efficiency is the relative variance of an estimator. As was discussed in Chapter 4, estimators which minimize SSE are the most efficient estimators possible if the distribution of errors is normal with homogeneous variances. With nonnormality and heteroscedasticity, other estimators (such as the median) can be more efficient. The loss in efficiency usually produces inflated values of both SSE(C) and SSE(A) while leaving $SSR = SSE(C) - SSE(A)$ relatively unchanged. This means that PRE and F^* values will be artificially reduced, thereby increasing the chances that a reliable effect will be undetected (Type II error). Therefore, to improve the efficiency of parameter estimates and to reduce the chances of making Type II errors, it behooves us to detect and to remedy problems of nonnormality and heteroscedasticity.

Nonnormality, heteroscedasticity, and unequal intervals on the scale of measurement for Y can also lead to unnecessarily complex models. To accommodate the distortions introduced by these problems it is often necessary to add product terms, both polynomials and interactions, to a MODEL for DATA. Fixing problems of nonnormality, heteroscedasticity, and, in particular, unequal intervals usually produces a simpler, more parsimonious MODEL and that is the ultimate goal of data analysis. Thus, to achieve simpler MODELs it is generally to our advantage to detect and to remedy the data problems considered in this chapter.

The solution to problems of nonnormality, heteroscedasticity, and unequal measurement scale intervals is the same, at an abstract level, as the solution we offered in the previous two chapters for nonindependence. The solution there was to calculate new data values from the original data values in a clever way so that the nonindependence was eliminated. With independence then being a reasonable assumption we were able to apply the regression modeling techniques with which we are now very familiar. Our solution for the data problems in this chapter is also to calculate new data values from the original data values in a way which will eliminate the problems. The new data values are often referred to as *transformations* or *reexpressions* of the original data. With the problems eliminated or at least substantially reduced, we can then apply our familiar regression modeling techniques to the transformed or reexpressed data. Thus, in this chapter we need only consider procedures for detecting problems of nonnormality, heteroscedasticity, and unequal intervals and for identifying the appropriate transformation to remedy the detected problem. Once the data are appropriately transformed then all the data analysis techniques considered in the previous chapters can be applied without modification. Before turning to the detection procedures, we first consider some concerns often expressed about transforming or reexpressing data.

16.1
Concerns about Reexpressing Data

Transformations and reexpressions of data are sometimes controversial. Although most statisticians accept transformations as a reasonable and necessary part of data analysis and although all the major statistical computer packages provide many facilities for accomplishing such transformations, many social scientists are suspicious about the appropriateness of transformations and reexpressions of data. Most of the suspicions can be attributed to three general issues. We consider each in turn.

The first issue is a belief in the sanctity of data. Holders of this belief argue that we must accept the data as they come to us and that reexpressing data is dishonest. This argument presumes, however, that data and the predictors to be used in the model are always measured on the correct scale of measurement. To the contrary, as Mosteller and Tukey (1977, p. 89) have noted, "Numbers are primarily recorded in a form that reflects habit or convenience rather than suitability for analysis."

There are abundant examples from both the physical and social sciences that demonstrate that the form of the original data or the customary measure of a variable are often inappropriate for building a model. As an example, consider the psychophysical problem of modeling judgments of perceived brightness of a constant light as a function of distance from the light. Our data Y would be a set of brightness judgments and our predictor X would be the distance at which each judgment was made. Eschewing transformations, our only possible model would be

$$Y_i = \beta_0 + \beta_1 X_{i1} + \varepsilon_i$$

However, we know from both physics and psychophysics that this model is inappropriate. First, from physics we know that the physical intensity of the light falling upon a judge's retina changes as a function of the square root of the distance between the light and the judge. For example, doubling the distance between the judge and the light reduces the physical intensity to a fourth of what it was. Thus, $X' = \sqrt{1/X}$ would be proportional to the physical intensity of the light falling on the judge's retina and would almost surely produce a better model than X. Furthermore, we know from Weber and Fechner and the early psychophysicists that perceived or subjective intensity is not directly proportional to physical intensity; rather, subjective brightness is proportional to the logarithm of the physical intensity of the stimulus. Thus, $X'' = \log(X') = \log(\sqrt{1/X})$ would be an even better predictor in the model. Thus, we would expect the best model to have this form

$$Y_i = \beta_0 + \beta_1 \log\left(\sqrt{\frac{1}{X_{i1}}}\right) + \varepsilon_i$$

or equivalently

$$Y_i = \beta_0 + \beta_1 X''_{i1} + \varepsilon_i$$

We can obtain another version of this model by taking the antilog of both Y and X''. That is, let $Y' = e^Y$ and we get the model

$$Y'_i = \beta_0 + \beta_1 X'_{i1} + \varepsilon_i$$

Thus, transforming both Y and X produces a more appropriate model. Not only is it an appropriate model, but also it is a simple, parsimonious model in terms of the transformed variables.

The point of this example is that the way in which Y and X are originally measured does not necessarily provide the appropriate forms for those variables. In this psychophysical example, reexpressing both Y and X produces a more appropriate model. In analyzing any type of data we need to consider the possibility that the data and our predictor variables may need to be reexpressed in order to find an appropriate model. We should note in the context of this psychophysical example that subsequent to Weber and Fechner, Stevens (1951, 1961) argued that the logarithm was not the most appropriate transformation. He contended that power transformations (i.e., $X' = X^p$, $p \neq 0$) were better. These power transformations and the log transformation form the bulk of the reexpression techniques we will put into our toolbox for data analysis.

A second issue is a concern that transformations might be used to force data into the mold of the linear model even when that mold might not be appropriate. We use the linear model as a conceptual, organizing framework. By adding the use of transformations, we can include in this framework a large number of other statistical techniques, techniques whose consistency with the linear model are not generally recognized. For example, when the normal distribution assumptions are seriously violated, many researchers would advocate the use of special nonparametric statistical tests which do not make distributional assumptions. The disadvantages, in our opinion, of these nonparametric tests is that they require the researcher to learn another large set of procedures and they often require special computer programs not always available. However, as Conover and Iman (1981) have shown, the widely used nonparametric tests are identical in terms of hypotheses tested and the conclusions about those hypotheses with the PRE and F^* approach applied to data which have been suitably transformed. The suitable transformation for reexpressing Y to obtain the equivalent nonparametric test is simply the rank transformation which replaces each Y_i with its rank within the set of observations. This approach to nonparametric statistics is developed more fully later in the chapter. The point here is that transformations should not be viewed as a sledgehammer for forcing data into the linear model mold but rather many transformations should be seen as tools for including apparently disparate statistical techniques within a common conceptual framework. That is, although transformations and reexpressions are applied to the data Y_i, their real effect is often to adapt the linear model to the data rather than the other way around.

The third issue is a concern that altering the data in any way, especially when we use the data themselves to choose the appropriate transformation post hoc, substantially increases the chances that we will mislead ourselves. This is a valid concern but the danger of misleading ourselves by transformations is no greater than the danger of fooling ourselves when using regression for empirical model building. The preventive measures are the same. Use replication and cross-validation to test transformations derived from an examination of the data and whenever possible have a priori, theory-based reasons for the transformations to be applied. As we shall see later in this chapter, there are a number of common types of data for which we can prescribe an appropriate transformation even before the data are collected. Finally, it must also be remembered that not transforming data that need to be transformed will always be misleading.

16.2

Problems with Data

The goal of reexpressing data is to convert the data analysis into a form for which the modeling techniques we have used throughout this book are appropriate. This means that there is very little to learn that is new in terms of statistical procedures. The only new data analytic skills are (a) the ability to recognize various problems in the data and (b) the ability to find the appropriate transformation that will reexpress the data in a form that will remove the problem. We begin with a consideration of the specific problems, followed by an examination of a relatively small number of transformations among which we can almost always find an appropriate reexpression for our data.

16.2.1 Nonnormality

One of the statistical assumptions justifying the comparison of the statistic F^* to the F distribution is that the error terms have a normal distribution. If the assumption is correct, then a frequency distribution of the true error terms ε_i, if they were known, or their estimates $e_i = Y_i - \hat{Y}_i$, the residuals, would have the frequency distribution of the normal curve as depicted in Exhibit 16.1. Most computer packages have procedures for producing frequency distributions. The graph in Exhibit 16.1 was produced by PROC CHART in SAS. It is a good habit to examine the frequency distribution of residuals.

It turns out that statistical inference based upon F^* is very robust with respect to the normality assumption, especially in comparison to the lack of robustness for the independence assumption. Simulation studies have demonstrated that the shape of the distribution of the errors can often be very nonnormal without appreciably affecting the data analysis. Some examples of nonnormally shaped error distributions that do not cause problems were considered in Chapter 9. However, a few special cases, even some distributions with very "normal-looking" shapes such as the Cauchy distribution, also considered in Chapter 9, can cause significant and sometimes devastating data analytic problems. A general characterization of these problem error distributions is that they have "thicker" tails than the normal distribution. That is, there are

EXHIBIT 16.1 ▶

Frequency distribution of normally distributed residuals (SAS PROC CHART)

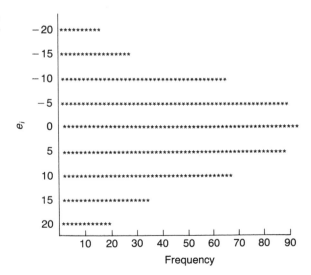

more extreme observations in the tails of the distribution than would be expected for the normal distribution. Extreme errors in the tails of the distribution can produce outliers and we have already considered in Chapter 9 how outliers can distort the least-squares model fit and subsequent statistical tests. Outlier detection and removal can remedy many of the most serious nonnormality problems. However, for distributions with very thick tails there will be many extreme observations that will not be detected as outliers. Thus, we need techniques for detecting and fixing thick-tailed error distributions.

In summary, thin-tailed error distributions cause so little problem that in such cases we can safely continue with the regular analysis without any remedial action. Thick-tailed error distributions, on the other hand, signal a serious data analysis problem that ought to be resolved before the analysis continues.

There are a number of formal statistical procedures for testing the hypothesis of normal distributions. However, these tests have serious disadvantages and problems of their own. Many are tedious and cumbersome even with computers and many of them are adversely affected by the very problem of nonnormality which they are designed to detect. Furthermore, many of these tests do not distinguish between thick- and thin-tailed distributions but simply test whether the distribution is normal. We therefore eschew these complex formal tests in favor of simple graphical examinations of the residuals. These graphical "tests" are generally effective in identifying nonnormality of a magnitude that would cause problems in the analysis. Their only disadvantage is that there are no formal critical values for deciding when a problem exists, so some experience with these graphs in one's particular research domain is usually necessary before appropriate judgments can be made.

The first graphical technique is simply a frequency distribution of the errors e_i which result from fitting the augmented MODEL to the DATA. The frequency distribution is especially effective for identifying *skewed* distributions which have thicker, longer tails on only one side of the distribution. Exhibit 16.2 is an example of a positively skewed distribution with the longer tail above the mean (if the longer tail is below the mean the distribution is negatively skewed). Skewed distributions of errors are common when the range of data values is truncated on one end so that there is either a floor or ceiling for the possible Y_i's. For example, counts, times, etc. are never negative so their range is bounded by zero below, but they are not bounded above. As a consequence, their distributions tend to look like the skewed distribution in Exhibit 16.2.

Although the frequency distribution of the errors usually easily identifies a thick tail caused by skewness, such distributions are less successful in detecting thick tails in symmetric distributions of errors. The "normal quantile-quantile" plot is a useful graphical technique for detecting tail problems for both skewed and symmetric distributions. We

EXHIBIT 16.2 ▶

**Positively skewed
distribution (SAS
PROC CHART)**

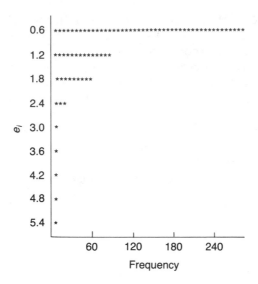

almost always have the computer produce the quantile-quantile plot, but to understand it we need to know conceptually how the computer programs generate it. First, order the residuals from smallest to largest. The ith-ordered residual will have $(i - .5)/n$ proportion[1] of the data below it. For example, the 11th-smallest residual in a group of 90 residuals would exceed $(11 - .5)/90 = .12$ or 12% of the residuals. From tables of the cumulative normal distribution we can determine the z score which exceeds a given proportion of the data. For example the z scores which exceed 25%, 50%, and 67% of the observations are $-.675$, 0, and .44, respectively. We then can plot the actual z score for that residual or, equivalently, the residual itself, against the z score that would be expected for that percentage assuming a normal distribution. For our example of the 11th residual in a group of 90 observations, the appropriate z score corresponding to 12% is -1.175. We then would plot the actual z score or the residual itself on the ordinate or y axis and -1.175 on the abscissa or x axis. Most statistical packages provide procedures for producing the normal quantile-quantile plots,[2] so they seldom need to be done by hand.

If the distribution is approximately normal, then all the points in the quantile-quantile plot should fall along a straight line on the diagonal.

---

[1]The adjustment of .5 in the formula effectively counts the residual as half above and half below itself.

[2]But be careful: some programs reverse the axes. For example, in SPSSX (Version 2), the REGRESSION procedure produces quantile plots with axes as we describe, but the MANOVA procedure reverses the axes. If the axes are reversed, then the interpretation of the plots is exactly opposite to what we describe in this section.

That is, for a normal distribution a residual which exceeds a certain proportion of the observations will have the appropriate z score. This is illustrated in the upper left quantile plot in Exhibit 16.3. Conversely, nonnormality of the errors is indicated by a systematic deviation of the points from that straight line. First, let's consider a positively skewed distribution that has more observations in the right tail than it ought to have relative to a normal distribution. An error in this tail that exceeded, say, 95% of the other residuals ought to have a z score of approximately 1.64; however, the error in the positive tail will be further from the mean than predicted by a normal distribution so its actual z score will be larger. Thus, when plotting actual against predicted z scores, a positive skew will appear as a steeply sloped curve for the high values, as is illustrated in the upper right corner of Exhibit 16.3. Conversely, if there is a negative skew, then the curve will be steeply sloped for the low values.

If the distribution has thick tails on both sides, then the curve in the quantile plot will be steeply sloped at both ends, as in the lower left corner of Exhibit 16.3. Note that the residuals in this illustration of thick tails come from a Cauchy distribution. Although it was difficult to distinguish between a normal distribution and a Cauchy distribution in a frequency distribution, the difference is clear when comparing the two left-hand quantile plots in the exhibit. Finally, a thin-tailed distribution of errors (as when the data are truncated on both ends for some reason) will have a flat slope at the ends, as in the lower right corner of Exhibit 16.3, because the tail observations are not as far from the mean as a normal distribution would predict.

In summary, the normal quantile plots indicate potential trouble— either skewness or thick tails at both ends—whenever the slope of the curve in the plot is steep at either end. However, there are no formal rules for how much steepness at the ends can be tolerated before remedial action is required. The proper interpretation of normal quantile plots requires experience examining such plots in particular research domains.

As an example of detecting nonnormality, Exhibit 16.4 displays stem and leaf and box plots for the population density for each of the 50 states based on the 1970 census. These densities were used in the analysis of the automobile fatality rate data considered earlier. The distribution is clearly not normal, with a large positive skew. The mean of the 50 population densities is 144.7. We could use this estimate of the mean as a simple model for these data. The residuals would then be given by $e_i = Y_i - 144.7$. The normal quantile-quantile plot in Exhibit 16.5 clearly indicates the deviations from the normal distribution, especially the extra observations in the tail which appear above the normal line at the high end. This plot strongly suggests that the simple mean model would be inappropriate for these data. Later in this chapter we consider possible remedies.

EXHIBIT 16.3 ▶

Sample normal quantile plots

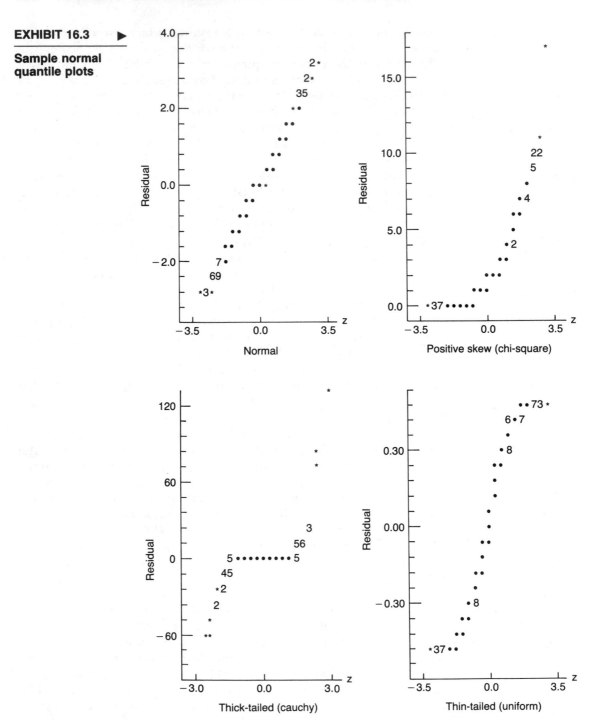

EXHIBIT 16.4 ▶

Stem and leaf and box plots of state population density

```
Stem Leaf                              #   Box Plot
9   5                                  1      *
9   1                                  1      *
8
8
7
7   3                                  1      *
6
6   2                                  1      *
5
5
4
4   0                                  1
3   8                                  1      0
3
2   668                               3     ┌─┐
2   0                                 1     │ │
1   56                                2     │ │
1   102233                            6     │ │
0   55555777888889                   14  ┌──┤ │
0   000111111222233444               18  └──┴─┘
    └─┴──┴──┴──┴──┘
       Multiply STEM LEAF by 10**+02
```

EXHIBIT 16.5 ▶

Normal quantile-quantile plot of state population densities

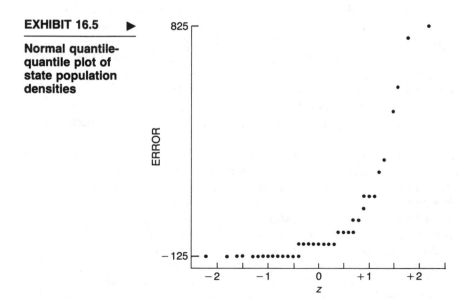

16.2.2 Heteroscedasticity

Another important assumption underlying statistical inference using least squares fits and F^* is homogeneity of variance: the assumption that all the errors (ε_i) in a given model have the same variance. This assumption is violated if the variances or spread of the errors varies systematically with the predicted values. The violation of this assumption is often referred to as *heteroscedasticity*. As with nonnormality, the least squares analysis and the PRE and F^* inferences are fairly robust with respect to this assumption. However, there is increasing concern that this may not be as robust an assumption as once thought (Wilcox, 1987).

Estimates for the partial regression coefficients will still be unbiased even in the presence of heteroscedasticity. However, those estimates will themselves have larger variances and so will be more unstable. In general, this reduces the statistical power of the inferential tests and makes it more difficult to reject the null hypothesis that $\beta_j = 0$. Also, as will be demonstrated in an example later, heteroscedasticity can also make it appear as if interactions are required in the MODEL when in fact they are not. An important caution is that for some single-degree-of-freedom contrasts in the analysis of variance, the statistical inference is not robust with respect to the homogeneity of variance assumption. In particular, heteroscedasticity is a problem for contrast codes in which the absolute values of the λ's differ (Keppel, 1982). Another important caution is that heteroscedasticity can be a more serious problem when there are very unequal numbers of observations in each group (Glass, Peckham, & Sanders, 1972; Bradley, 1978). Heteroscedasticity, therefore, can be a serious problem for which detection and treatment are very important.

Again paralleling the case for nonnormality, there are formal tests for heteroscedasticity, especially for analysis of variance designs. However, many of these formal tests, such as Bartlett's, are even more vulnerable to nonnormality than the original least squares analysis. Also, such tests do not easily generalize to regression analysis. Such formal tests are therefore not recommended.

The underlying issue in heteroscedasticity is whether the residuals are systematically related to the predictions. This is most easily ascertained by examining a plot of the residuals against the predicted values. For homoscedasticity, such a plot will appear as a random scatter of points as in Exhibit 16.6. Exhibit 16.7 depicts one of the more common forms of heteroscedasticity in which the spread of the errors systematically increases with the size of the predictions to give the plot a characteristic funnel-shaped appearance. Other patterns of heteroscedasticity are of course possible. For example, the funnel might be pointed the other way or two funnels might be joined in the middle.

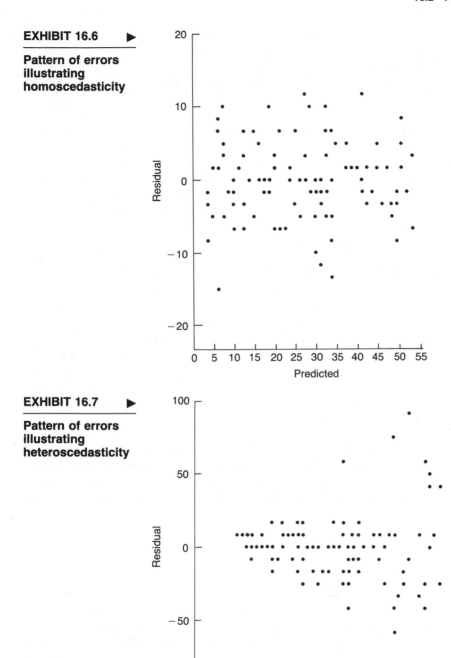

EXHIBIT 16.6 ▶

Pattern of errors illustrating homoscedasticity

EXHIBIT 16.7 ▶

Pattern of errors illustrating heteroscedasticity

Anything other than a random scatter of points as in Exhibit 16.6 is an indication of heteroscedasticity. Most regression programs in the standard statistical computer packages have facilities for easily producing the residual-by-prediction plot. An examination of that plot ought to be a routine part of any data analysis.

The residual-by-prediction plot suggests an informal test for heteroscedasticity. If we want to know whether the spread of the errors is related to the size of the prediction then we are not interested in the sign of the error. Instead, we want to know whether the size of the squared errors varies as a function of the size of the predictions. This can be determined by using the predictions $\hat{Y}_i$ to construct a model of the squared residuals e_i^2. That is, we take the e_i^2's as our data and the $\hat{Y}_i$'s as our predictors in a standard regression analysis. The funnel pattern, for example, could be modeled by

$$e_i^2 = \beta_0 + \beta_1 \hat{Y}_i + \varepsilon_i$$

The PRE for this model would be a rough index of the amount of heteroscedasticity. Anscombe (1961) and Draper and Smith (1981) have proposed similar indices of heteroscedasticity. The sign of the estimated b_1 would indicate which direction the funnel pointed in the residual-by-prediction plot. Positive values would indicate the spread of the residuals increasing with the predictions and negative values would indicate the opposite. For more complicated patterns of heteroscedasticity, powers of $\hat{Y}_i$ could be added as predictors in the model. The procedure would be the same as in Chapter 10.

We must emphasize that although modeling the squared errors may provide a useful description and index of the heteroscedasticity, a visual examination of the residual-by-prediction plot will usually suffice to identify heteroscedasticity. Later in this chapter we consider remedies designed to achieve homoscedasticity. Fortunately, the remedies for nonnormality often cure heteroscedasticity as well.

16.2.3 Unequal Intervals

The least squares procedure for fitting a MODEL to DATA attempts to minimize ERROR by making each $\hat{Y}_i$ as close as possible to the corresponding Y_i. Each residual, $e_i = Y_i - \hat{Y}_i$, of a given size is treated the same in the summation of squared errors. The implicit assumption is that an error of a given size, say 3, means the same thing no matter what the value of Y_i and $\hat{Y}_i$. There are many situations for which this is not a reasonable assumption. For example, consider a study in which the respondent's task is to judge the prices of a variety of consumer goods. Suppose that one respondent guesses $9 for an item which is really $10, and $99 for an item which is really $100. In each case the guess is off by $1. However, we have a sense that coming within $1 of an expensive item demonstrates more accuracy than coming within $1 on an inexpensive item. Even an error of $5 for the expensive item seems subjectively smaller than an error of $1 on the inexpensive item. (If the example using $100 for the expensive item is not convincing, try $1000 or $10,000.) A least squares analysis, however, would treat equally each numerically equivalent error and would count the $5 for the expensive item as being much larger than the $1 error for the inexpensive item ($5 \times 5 = 25$ versus $1 \times 1 = 1$). As was noted long ago by Bernoulli (1738/1954), it seems more compelling to treat *proportional errors* as equal in the analysis. That is, the $1 error for the $10 item is an error of 10%; an equivalent error for the $100 item would be a $10 error or a guess of $90 or $110. The $5 error for the $100 item would be an error of only 5% and would therefore be smaller than the 10% $1 error for the inexpensive item.

The problem is that the subjective size of the intervals is unequal. In this case, the size of the intervals gets smaller as the price of the item being estimated gets higher. Each unit between 90 and 100 subjectively may count about one tenth of the unit between 9 and 10. The sum of squared error equation being minimized does not know that the size of the intervals is changing and that we want to count some errors differently from others. To do so, we will either have to change our definition of ERROR, or we will have to reexpress the DATA on a new scale which does have equal intervals.

There is no general statistical procedure or graph for detecting unequal intervals in the DATA. However, unequal intervals will often produce nonnormal error distributions with thick tails and heteroscedasticity. For example, if the guesses in the range ($9, $11) for the inexpensive item are really equivalent to guesses in the range ($90, $110) for the expensive item, then the variance or spread of the guesses around the expensive item will be numerically greater. In other words, heteroscedasticity ought to be apparent as the funnel-shape in the residual-by-prediction plot. There are some sophisticated techniques for constructing and validating measurement scales with equal intervals (e.g., Anderson, 1981; Krantz, Luce, Suppes, & Tversky, 1971), but they are beyond the scope of this book.

Probably the best technique for detecting unequal intervals is for the data analyst to ask the following question: should numerically equivalent errors be treated equivalently? There are many situations for which the answer is yes. However, there are many common types of DATA for which the answer is no. We cannot give any precise rules but we can describe the general characteristics which make unequal intervals a likely problem.

The first warning characteristic is for the range of the DATA to be constrained on one or both ends. For example, in the price guessing study above, prices are constrained to be above zero, but they are not really limited on the high end. As an example of constraint on the other end, consider DATA which are speed measures (items completed per unit time) such as running paces. The current world record for the mile is equivalent to a speed of about 15.86 miles per hour. For a mile run it is obviously very difficult for anyone to go much faster than that. However, it is easy to go slower. Even though speeds must be greater than zero, they are not really constrained at that end because one can always go slower. Note that in this case the intervals for the high numbers are smaller than those for the smaller numbers because an improvement of .1 mph for a fast speed (breaking the world mile record by more than a second) is more impressive than an improvement of, say, .2 on a speed of 7.5 mph (i.e., a recreational runner improving his or her mile time from 8 minutes/mile to 7.47 minutes/mile).

Common types of DATA used in the social sciences which are constrained at one end include counts, timings (e.g., reaction times in psychology), and speeds or rates. There are also frequent situations in which the DATA are constrained at both ends. Common examples include the use of probabilities or proportions as DATA which are constrained to be in the range [0, 1] or [0, 100]. Sometimes correlations, constrained to be in the range [−1, +1], are used as DATA. Whenever the DATA are constrained at one or both ends, we should consider the possibility of unequal intervals.

The second warning characteristic for unequal intervals is a large range in the data. If the ratio of the largest to the smallest observation is 10 to 1 (one order of magnitude), then a problem of unequal intervals may exist. If the ratio is greater than 100 to 1 (two orders of magnitude), then a problem almost certainly exists. In the price guessing study above the ratio was about 10 to 1. If $1000 items had been included, the ratio would have been 100 to 1. There can be no argument that a $5 error in pricing a $1000 item is smaller than a $5 error in pricing a $10 item.

If either of these two warning characteristics is present, it is wise to consider the possibility of unequal intervals. The prescribed remedy for unequal intervals depends upon the precise way in which the intervals are unequal. These remedies will be considered below because they are in general the same remedies that are prescribed for nonnormality and heteroscedasticity.

16.2.4   Other Symptoms

To use a medical analogy, nonnormality, heteroscedasticity, and unequal intervals are all diseases, potentially very serious diseases, which can afflict DATA and, especially, an analysis of DATA. Diagnostic signs for these diseases can be found in a normal quantile-quantile plot as in Exhibit 16.5 and in a residual-by-predicted plot as in Exhibit 16.7. These diseases can also produce other symptoms such as outliers; procedures for detecting outliers are described in Chapter 9 and therefore are not presented here. However, those procedures should always be included in a complete diagnostic evaluation of the appropriateness of any MODEL.

DATA which require complex interactions or high-order polynomial components in their MODELs may or may not have problems. The complex interactions may be real or they may be an artifact introduced in the MODEL in an attempt to fit "funny," ill-behaved DATA whose ERRORs violate our standard assumptions. That complex interactions might be diagnostic of problems should not be taken as encouragement to test complex interactions without good theoretical or substantive reasons. Rather, if there are good reasons to look for these interactions and they are found, then the data analyst ought to ensure that they are not caused simply by DATA which violate the assumptions we have made throughout.

Thus, although outliers and interactions have many other causes besides nonnormality, heteroscedasticity, and unequal intervals, their presence in an analysis requires that the data analyst ought to check carefully for nonnormality, heteroscedasticity, and unequal intervals. Frequently, treating those diseases also eliminates or reduces outliers and complex interactions.

16.2.5 An Example

A detailed example will help illustrate the procedures for detecting the various potential problems with DATA and will demonstrate that those problems are often related. Consider the hypothetical data in Exhibit 16.8 from a problem-solving experiment. The design is a 2 × 3 factorial. Subjects were either given previous training on a task whose solution would transfer to the present task or on a task whose solution would not transfer. The task difficulty was also varied by altering the text describing the task so that identifying the precise problem to be solved was either easy, moderate, or difficult. Eighteen subjects were randomly assigned to the six conditions so that there were three subjects per condition. The data were the times required to solve the problem.

The required data analysis is a straightforward two-way ANOVA. A set of reasonable contrast codes is listed in the bottom half of Exhibit 16.8. A standard regression analysis of these times, using the specified contrast codes, produces the statistical results in Exhibit 16.9. The estimated b's for the codes X_1, X_2, and X_4 are statistically significant, indicating, respectively, a reliable difference due to the transfer task, a reliable difference depending on whether problem identification was easy or not, and a reliable interaction involving those two codes.

EXHIBIT 16.8 ▶

Hypothetical data from a 2 × 3 problem-solving experiment (data are times to problem solution)

Problem Identification	Transfer Task					
	No			Yes		
Difficult	40.2	35.2	68.5	10.0	7.7	13.1
Moderate	33.6	31.4	53.5	15.7	8.1	6.2
Easy	12.5	14.3	10.9	4.4	5.0	3.8

Transfer Task Problem Ident. Group	N D 1	N M 2	N E 3	Y D 4	Y M 5	Y E 6	Contrast Comparison
X_1	1	1	1	−1	−1	−1	No vs. Yes
X_2	1	1	−2	1	1	−2	(D, M) vs. E
X_3	1	−1	0	1	−1	0	D vs. M
X_4	1	1	−2	−1	−1	2	X_1X_2
X_5	1	−1	0	−1	1	0	X_1X_3

EXHIBIT 16.9 ▶

Regression analysis of a model for the data of Exhibit 16.8

Source	b_j	SS	df	MS	F*	p	PRE
MODEL		4956.2	5	991.2	11.7	.0003	.83
X_1	12.56	2840.1	1	2840.1	33.6	.001	.74
X_2	6.15	1361.6	1	1361.6	16.1	.002	.57
X_3	2.18	57.2	1	57.2	.7	.43	.05
X_4	4.24	646.9	1	646.9	7.7	.017	.39
X_5	2.05	50.4	1	50.4	.6	.46	.05
Error		1013.1	12	84.4			
Total		5969.2					

Before taking the above results too seriously, however, we need to check the adequacy of the model and assumptions for the errors. There is one very large studentized deleted residual: for the observation 68.5, the value is 4.3. The Cook's D for that observation is .62, and the next two largest values are .29; all the other values are less than .1. It is not necessary to check the levers because the levers in a balanced factorial design are all equal. The 68.5 observation therefore clearly stands out as an outlier which is probably distorting the model fit and the statistical inference related to that model.

Exhibit 16.10 displays the normal quantile-quantile plot of the residuals. The residuals appear to deviate substantially from the normal line in the high end of the data range which indicates a thicker than normal positive tail; in other words, a skewed distribution. There is good evidence, therefore, that the distribution of the residuals does not have a normal distribution.

Examining the residual-by-prediction plot in Exhibit 16.11 provides a check for heteroscedasticity. A classic funnel shape is readily apparent in Exhibit 16.11, indicating that the size of the residuals steadily increases with the size of the predictions. As a verification of this observation, the PRE for using $\hat{Y}_i$ to predict squared error is .51 and the coefficient is 4.5. The PRE for using $\hat{Y}_i$ to predict the absolute error is .72 with a coefficient of .28. The assumption of equal variances is violated for these data. Heteroscedasticity prevails.

EXHIBIT 16.10 ▶

Box plot of residuals and normal quantile plot (produced by MINITAB) for the analysis of Exhibit 16.9

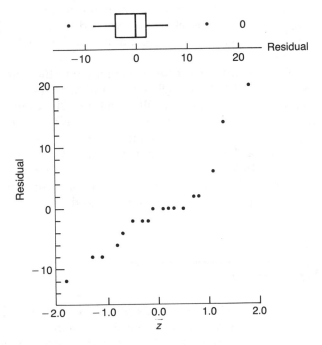

EXHIBIT 16.11 ▶

Residual plot for the problem-solving data

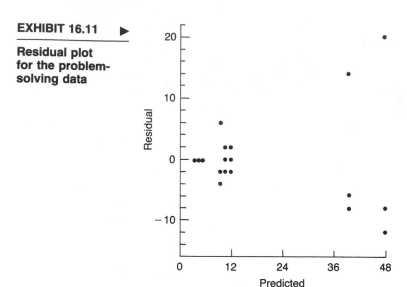

Finally, we can consider whether it is reasonable to assume equal intervals for the time scale on which the data were measured. The data are constrained at one end and the ratio of the largest to smallest observation is about 18. These are both warning indicators for unequal intervals. It does not seem that we would want to treat an error of 5 for predictions around 10 seconds the same as an error of 5 for predictions around 40 seconds, but we might need to know more about the underlying theoretical model before we had an informed opinion. On the whole, however, there is good reason to doubt the equal interval assumption.

There is little in a casual examination of the data in Exhibit 16.8 and its analysis in Exhibit 16.9 that would alert the data analyst to fundamental problems in the resulting model. The examination of the residuals, however, shows that these data have all the problems we have considered: outliers, significant interactions, nonnormality, thick tails, heteroscedasticity, and unequal intervals. As a consequence, the analysis in Exhibit 16.9 ought not to be trusted. We now turn to a consideration of remedies for data and residuals with such serious afflictions. We will then return to apply those remedies to these example data.

16.3

Remedies

The basic remedies for the distributional problems described above are transformations which reexpress data to remove the distributional problems. These reexpressions will generally solve our problems. There are three broad classes of transformations: rank transformations which lead to equivalents of nonparametric statistics; power transformations which "straighten out" relationships between variables; and theory-based transformations which correct problems with particular kinds of data. Each class of transformation is considered in turn.

16.3.1 Rank Transformations

The rank transformation is simply defined as

$$W_i = \text{Rank}(Y_i)$$

where $\text{Rank}(Y_i)$ is the ordinal position of the ith observation[3] relative to all the other observations. Effectively, all the exact information about the data values, especially the magnitude of the differences between data values, is discarded, leaving only information about relative ordering. Thus, the rank transformation is desirable for those situations in which one does not have confidence in the numerical values of the data, but only in their ordering. Sometimes the data collection procedure in effect applies the rank transformation for us. For example, we might ask a survey respondent to rank a number of attitude items in the order which he or she agreed with them.

After applying the rank transform to obtain W_i's, we can then use, without modification, the regression modeling techniques that we have developed throughout the book. If we have categorical predictors we use contrast-coded variables in the model just as we did for the analysis of variance. If we have continuous predictors, we can use those variables directly in the models. However, it is common also to apply the rank transform to the continuous predictors so that ranks will be used to predict ranks. In general, we just have to remember that in building a model for W_i we are building a model for the rank of Y_i.

The rank transformation cures many of the possible ills afflicting data which we have considered in this chapter. Outliers are controlled because the distances between extreme observations are reduced. Similarly, although the rank transformation does not produce normally distributed errors, it generally does eliminate problems of thick tails. The rank transformation does not ensure homogeneity of variance, but it usually is effective in preventing the very large differences in variance which could distort an analysis.

An example will illustrate how the rank transformation solves certain data problems. We will also use this same example to demonstrate the

---

[3]If observations are tied, then each tied observation receives the average of the ranks those observations would have received if they were not tied but in the same order relative to the remainder of the data. For example, the data 2.3, 4.5, 4.5, 6.1, 7.3, 7.3, 7.3, 9.8 would be ranked 1, 2.5, 2.5, 4, 6, 6, 6, 8.

relationship between a regression analysis of W and a traditional non-parametric statistical test. Exhibit 16.12 presents the number of steps required to solve a complex problem for 15 subjects from a hypothetical study of problem solving. Those subjects in the control condition did not work on any prior problems while those in the two transfer conditions did work on prior problems. It was expected that subjects would attempt to apply the strategies developed in solving the prior problems to the new problem. There were two transfer conditions: a positive condition in which the strategies learned were expected to facilitate solution of the new problem and a negative condition in which the strategies learned were expected to interfere with finding the new solution. The question of interest is whether the number of problem-solving steps differs between the positive and negative transfer conditions. For completeness we will also ask whether the transfer conditions as a group differ from the control condition. The appropriate contrast codes are also given in Exhibit 16.12.

Even before fitting a complex model to these data, we can see from an examination of the raw data and the simple descriptive statistics that these data are ill-behaved. As is often the case with problem-solving tasks, a few subjects had inordinate difficulty in finding the solution. One subject in the control condition required 97 steps, and one in the negative transfer condition took 105 steps. Both these values are roughly

EXHIBIT 16.12 ▶

Number of steps to solution from hypothetical problem-solving experiment (W column gives ranks)

	Control		Transfer Positive		Transfer Negative	
	Y_{i1}	W_{i1}	Y_{i2}	W_{i2}	Y_{i3}	W_{i3}
	30	7	16	2	55	13
	38	10	20	4	36	9
	97	14	27	6	40	11
	26	5	14	1	43	12
	19	3	32	8	105	15
Mean	42.0	7.8	21.8	4.2	55.8	12.0
Std Dev	31.5	4.3	7.6	2.9	28.4	2.2
λ_1	0		1		−1	
λ_2	−2		1		1	

twice the next highest data value and therefore suggest outliers or a thick-tailed distribution. Also, the variances within each condition are very different. The variance for the control condition ($s^2 = 31.5^2 = 992$) is about 17 times larger than the variance for the positive transfer condition ($s^2 = 7.6^2 = 57.8$), a clear indication of heteroscedasticity. We might also suspect the measurement scale because it is necessarily constrained at the bottom and because a difference of five steps is probably more important between 15 and 20 than between 50 and 55.

Exhibit 16.13 presents a summary of the analysis of variance of the original problem-solving data. The test for the difference between the positive and negative transfer conditions is almost reliable at the .05 level, but the test of the omnibus model is clearly not significant. An examination of outliers reveals, as expected, large values of studentized deleted residuals (or, equivalently, large values of F^* for the outlier model of Chapter 9) and Cook's D for the observations with original values of 97 and 105. Their studentized deleted residuals are, respectively, 3.38 and 2.75, compared to the next largest studentized deleted residual of 1.03. Their Cook's D values are, respectively, .41 and .51, compared to the next largest value of .09. These outliers also appear in the normal-normal quantile plot (not shown) and a residual plot (also not shown) reveals the heteroscedasticity. Thus, both a priori considerations and the residual analysis raise questions about the adequacy of the analysis of variance model fit to these data.

Exhibit 16.14 presents a corresponding analysis of variance of W_i, the data values after the rank transformation has been applied. The PRE of .54 and F^* of 14.3 for testing the difference between the positive and negative transfer conditions are now much larger and very reliable compared to the analysis of variance of the raw data. The outlier problem is now controlled but not entirely eliminated. The observation $Y_i = 105$ now has a studentized deleted residual of 1.05 and a Cook's D of

EXHIBIT 16.13 ▶

Analysis of variance for data from the hypothetical problem-solving experiment

Source	b_j	SS	df	MS	F^*	p	PRE
Model		2,934.1	2	1,467.1	2.37	.14	.28
X_1	−17.0	2,890.0	1	2,890.0	4.67	.052	.28
X_2	1.1	34.1	1	34.1	.06	.82	.005
Error		7,425.6	12	618.8			
Total		10,349.7	14				

EXHIBIT 16.14 ▶

Analysis of variance for the ranks W_i from the hypothetical problem-solving experiment

Source	b_i	SS	df	MS	F^*	p	PRE
Model		152.4	2	76.2	7.17	.009	.54
X_1	−17.0	152.1	1	152.1	14.30	.0001	.54
X_2	−.1	.3	1	.3	.03	.87	.00
Error		127.6	12	10.6			
Total		280.0	14				

.09. However, the observation $Y_i = 97$ still has the largest values of those statistics (2.58 and .38, respectively); yet the discrepancy from those of the other observations is reduced. Heteroscedasticity is also controlled because the ratio of the largest to smallest group variance (see Exhibit 16.12) is now less than four. On the whole, the analysis of W_i, the ranks of the original data, is much more satisfactory then an analysis of Y_i, the original data.

A traditional statistical method for dealing with ill-behaved data or data that were ranks originally is to use *nonparametric* statistics. We have not laid the basis for discussing the statistical models underlying nonparametric statistics and we will not do so because that basis is not easily expressed in a PRE framework. Instead, we will illustrate that applying the PRE framework to rank transformed data often produces a test as least as good as and sometimes better than the corresponding nonparametric test. For the analysis of our hypothetical problem-solving data, the appropriate nonparametric technique is the Kruskal-Wallis test. The test statistic H, corresponding to F^*, is given by

$$H = \frac{12}{N(N+1)} \sum_{k=1}^{m} n_k \overline{W_k^2} - 3(N+1)$$

where N is the total number of observations, $\overline{W}_k$ is the mean rank for group k, m is the number of groups, and n_k is the number of observations in the kth group. For the present data

$$H = \frac{12}{15(16)}[5 \cdot 7.8^2 + 5 \cdot 4.2^2 + 5 \cdot 12^2] - 3(16) = 7.62$$

For large N, H has *approximately* a chi-squared distribution with degrees of freedom $= m - 1$ where m is the number of groups. Appropriate chi-squared tables in most statistics textbooks[4] can be consulted

---

[4]We do not provide a chi-squared table in Appendix C because this would be our only use of that table. Below we provide an equivalent alternative test that uses our regular PRE and F tables.

to evaluate H. In this case, if there were no differences between groups, the approximate probability of obtaining a value of H equal to or greater than the obtained value of 7.62 is .022. Using the .05 level, we would reject the null hypothesis of no differences between groups just as we did for the linear model analysis of the ranks. Note that the Kruskal-Wallis test corresponds to the omnibus test in the linear model analysis. Although there are procedures for doing all post hoc comparisons between pairs of groups (e.g., Ryan's procedure), there is no technique for evaluating general contrasts (such as comparing the control group against both transfer groups).

The formula for calculating H in the Kruskal-Wallis test may make it appear that this nonparametric test is fundamentally different from the linear model tests we have considered so far. However, Conover and Iman (1981) have shown that there is actually a very close relationship between the Kruskal-Wallis test and the linear model analysis of the ranks. Specifically, F^* for the linear model analysis can be calculated from the following formula.

$$F^*_{m-1,N-m} = \frac{H/(m-1)}{(N-1-H)/(N-m)}$$

For the present data,

$$F^*_{2,12} = \frac{7.62/2}{(15-1-7.62)/12} = 7.17$$

which is the same value, within rounding error, of F^* for the omnibus test we obtained in Exhibit 16.14.

The formula relating F^* and H is not so important because of its calculational use but rather because of its conceptual implications. The formula shows that F^* and H are monotonically related: for any data set which had a higher F^* than our hypothetical data, H would also be higher. Thus, with very large values of N, F^* and H will have exactly the same probabilities under the null hypothesis. For small values of N, comparing H to the chi-squared distribution and comparing F^* to the F distribution yield two approximations of the same probability. Simulation studies have shown that in many situations comparing F^* with the F distribution gives a more accurate approximation than comparing H with the chi-squared distribution, but that in general there are not strong reasons for preferring either one. We therefore use other criteria—consistency with the linear model framework, ease of finding appropriate computer software, minimizing the number of statistical procedures to be learned, and ability to evaluate general contrast codes—to opt for PRE and F^* of rank transformed data over standard nonparametric statistics.

Although we have chosen PRE and F^* tests of rank-transformed data, it should be recognized that many nonparametric tests are essentially equivalent to such linear model tests. For readers familiar with some of the traditional nonparametric statistics we give a brief guide to the corresponding linear model tests.

1. Wilcoxon Rank Sum or Mann-Whitney U. The equivalent linear model test is the analysis of variance of ranks for two independent groups.

2. Kruskal-Wallis Test. As illustrated above, the equivalent linear model test is the one-way analysis of variance for three or more groups.

3. Wilcoxon Signed Ranks (for two levels of a within variable). Compute difference scores for each unit of analysis. Then rank the absolute value of the differences, but attach the original sign to each ranked difference. Finally, use PRE and F^* to test whether the mean of the signed ranks is different from zero. A similar test may be obtained by first ranking all the Y_i and then applying the techniques of Chapter 14 directly to those ranks. This latter test is most consistent with the approach presented in this book and may be better than the Wilcoxon Signed Ranks test in many ways (Iman and Conover, 1980).

4. Friedman Test (for more than two levels of a within variable). Rank order the observations within each unit of analysis. For example, if there were four levels of a within variable, the scores for each unit of analysis would be replaced with 1, 2, 3, and 4. An equivalent test is then obtained by applying the modeling procedures of Chapter 14 to these transformed data (but note that W_0 will necessarily be the same for all units so there will be no variation between units). Again, a different and probably more powerful test is obtained by ranking all the data together and then applying the analysis methods of Chapter 14 (in which case there will be a between-units component).

5. Spearman ρ. Rank X and Y separately and then regress Y on X. Spearman $\rho = \sqrt{\text{PRE}}$.

In summary, applying unaltered all the linear model techniques developed in previous chapters to rank-transformed data produces tests which are essentially equivalent to or better than corresponding nonparametric tests. Using the linear model approach on rank-transformed data also eliminates the need to learn the cookbook of nonparametric procedures and a multitude of computer programs. The rank transform is therefore an effective means for dealing with many types of ill-behaved data.

16.3.2 Power Transformations

The family of power transformations provides a very useful and important remedy for the types of problems considered in this chapter. Power transformations are of the form

$$W_i = Y_i^p \qquad p \neq 0$$

That is, the transformed value W_i is simply the original value Y_i raised to some power, hence, the name *power transformation*. Exhibit 16.15 graphs the power transformation for a number of different values of p. For purposes of this graph, the curves have also been linearly rescaled so that they pass through the same point for easier comparison. We cannot use $p = 0$ as a transformation because $Y^0 = 1$ for all Y, effectively eliminating the data! It turns out that the log transformation

$$W_i = \log Y_i$$

fills the niche in Exhibit 16.15 where the zero power would fit. Hence, we usually include the log transformation as the 0th power in the family of power transformations.

Power (and log) transformations have the effect of stretching and contracting the scale on which Y is measured. The amount of stretching or contracting depends on the portion of the scale. For example, the log transformation increasingly contracts the size of intervals as we move to higher and higher data values. That is, note that for larger values of Y in Exhibit 16.15 that the corresponding W for the log function (power "0" in the exhibit) does not increase much. Conversely, for small values of Y, the corresponding W for the log function changes dramatically for even a small change in Y. Values of $p < 1$ have the same general effect as the log function, varying only in degree.

The square transformation, on the other hand, stretches the size of intervals as we move to higher and higher data values. For larger values of Y, small changes in Y correspond to dramatic changes in W for the

EXHIBIT 16.15 ▶

Ladder of power transformations: $W = Y^p$ (based on Mosteller & Tukey, 1977, p. 80)

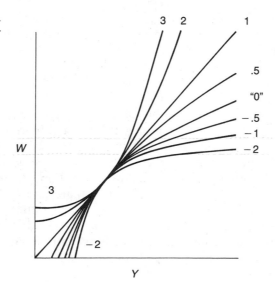

square function; and the opposite is true for small values of Y. Values of $p > 1$ have the same general effect as the square function, varying only in degree.

In general, flat portions of curves in Exhibit 16.15 indicate contraction of intervals while steep portions indicate stretching of intervals. Appropriate stretching and contracting can have many beneficial effects: repairing problems of unequal intervals, moving outliers closer to the range of the other data values, establishing normality of error terms, and eliminating heteroscedasticity. However, an inappropriate power transformation will make all those problems worse.

How, then, should we choose an appropriate value of p in the transformation $W_i = Y_i^p$? Formal statistical procedures exist for selecting a "best" transformation. Box and Cox (1964), for example, provide a statistical procedure for finding the value of p that simultaneously reduces heteroscedasticity and nonnormality. Their method is not particularly difficult but it relies on statistical principles we have not developed so we do not present it here. Instead, we will rely on direct and graphical procedures.

The direct approach is simply to try a range of values of p in the power transformation, examine the residuals from each regression analysis, and then choose that value of p producing residuals most consistent with the assumptions. In practice, p does not need to be determined exactly so trying p values of 3, 2, 1, .5, 0, $-.5$, -1, -2, and -3 will almost always be more than sufficient. The availability of high-speed computing makes it reasonable to try these nine values of p. If the improvement from using a power transformation is not appreciable then it will be preferable to report an analysis of the untransformed data ($p = 1$). However, if a power transformation produces a marked improvement in homoscedasticity and normality, then the data analyst ought to be very wary about reporting an analysis of the untransformed data. Analyzing the transformed data will usually be more appropriate and will generally result in a simpler MODEL.

A brute-force trial of all p values can usually be avoided by examining the normal quantile-quantile plot or the frequency distribution of the errors. If the problem is a long, positive tail then a value of $p < 1$ will pull in the long tail, thereby reducing heteroscedasticity, nonnormality, and reducing outliers. On the other hand, a long, negative tail can be pulled in using $p > 1$ in a power transformation. An extreme tail indicates that extreme values of p (near 3 or -3) are required while a moderate tail indicates values of p nearer 1 are appropriate.

The residual-by-prediction plot can also be diagnostic for the appropriate transformation. If there is a funnel pattern with the funnel opening to the right, then $p < 1$ ought to be tried. Conversely, for funnels opening to the left, $p > 1$ is required.

Thinking about whether intervals are likely to be of equal size can also suggest an appropriate transformation. In both the price estimation and solution time examples considered previously, we concluded that proportional rather than absolute errors ought to be equated because the size of the interval changed with Y. If the functional intervals on the untransformed scale are decreasing as Y increases, then a power transformation with $p < 1$ ought to be employed. In particular, $p = 0$ (the *log* transformation) will reduce the size of larger intervals by equating proportional errors. To illustrate how the log transformation accomplishes this, let's consider an example in the price estimation study. The size of the interval between 100 and 90 is 10, and the difference between 10 and 9 is 1. However, both differences are equal proportionately because $10/100 = 1/10 = 10\%$. If we take logarithms before computing the differences, then the size of the intervals is equal. That is,

$$\log 100 - \log 90 = 4.6052 - 4.4998 = .1054$$

and

$$\log 10 - \log 9 = 2.3026 - 2.1972 = .1054$$

In other words, differences that were proportionately equal on the untransformed scale are arithmetically equal on the log transformed scale. For data constrained on the lower end such as times, counts, and money, either the log ($p = 0$) or the square root ($p = .5$) transformations are usually required to fix problems of unequal intervals.

As an illustration of the impact of a power transformation on data analysis, let's return to the problem-solving example we considered in Section 16.2.5. The long, positive tail identified in Exhibit 16.10, the funnel pattern opening to the right in Exhibit 16.11, and our thought about the equality of intervals in that context all suggest that we try a power transformation with $p < 1$. Let's try $p = 0$ or the log[5] transformation. The transformed data ($W_i = \log Y_i$) are displayed in Exhibit 16.16.

The analysis of the transformed data is displayed in Exhibit 16.17. This analysis should be compared with the corresponding analysis of the untransformed data in Exhibit 16.9. The resulting model is a better description of the DATA because the omnibus F^* and PRE have increased from 11.7 and .83, respectively, to 26.9 and .92. Furthermore, the resulting model is simpler because there is no longer a reliable interaction (the F^* and PRE for the interaction contrast code $X_4 = X_1 \times X_3$ have decreased from 7.7 and .39, respectively, to 2.0 and .14). Only the main effects for

---

[5]We use the natural logarithm or $\log_e$, but $\log_{10}$ may be used instead. The resulting PREs and F^*s will be the same in either case.

EXHIBIT 16.16 ▶

The data of Exhibit
16.8 after a log
transformation

Problem Identification	Transfer Task					
	No			Yes		
Difficult	3.69	3.56	4.23	2.30	2.04	2.57
Moderate	3.51	3.45	3.98	2.75	2.09	1.82
Easy	2.53	2.66	2.39	1.48	1.61	1.34

EXHIBIT 16.17 ▶

Regression analy-
sis of a model for
the log-trans-
formed data of
Exhibit 16.16

Source	b_j	SS	df	MS	F*	p	PRE
MODEL		12.22	5	2.44	26.9	.0003	.92
X_1	.67	7.98	1	7.98	87.8	.0001	.88
X_2	.33	4.01	1	4.01	44.1	.0001	.79
X_3	.07	.05	1	.05	.6	.47	.04
X_4	.07	.18	1	.18	2.0	.19	.14
X_5	.02	.01	1	.01	.1	.78	.01
Error		1.09	12	.09			
Total		13.32					

the transfer task (X_1) and the comparison of the difficult and moderate problems versus the easy problems (X_2) are now statistically reliable. For both those main effects, the F* and PRE are now larger. Thus, the log transformation has resulted in a more parsimonious MODEL that better describes the DATA.

It is still necessary to examine the residuals to determine whether the errors resulting after the log transformation are better behaved in terms of heteroscedasticity and normality. The plot of e_i by $\hat{Y}_i$ in Exhibit 16.18 shows a random scattering of points consistent with homogeneity of variance. The normal quantile-quantile plot in Exhibit 16.19 shows that the errors have a normal distribution because the points lie approximately on a diagonal line with no indication of a strong deviation in the tails (compare Exhibit 16.10). The outlier situation has also improved.

EXHIBIT 16.18 ▶

Residual plot for the transformed problem-solving data of Exhibit 16.16

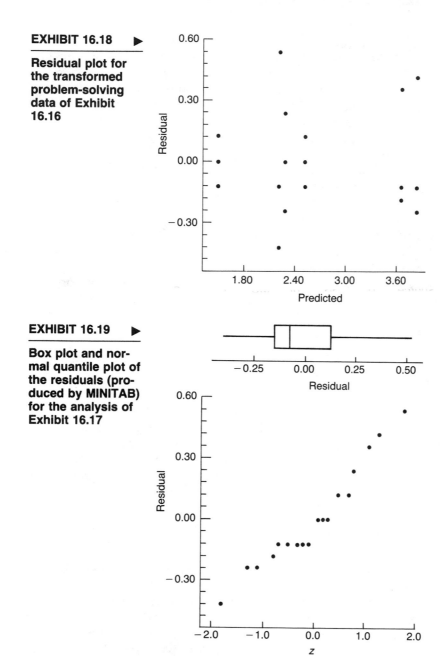

EXHIBIT 16.19 ▶

Box plot and normal quantile plot of the residuals (produced by MINITAB) for the analysis of Exhibit 16.17

The largest studentized deleted residual is now 2.6, and it is not for the largest observation 68.5 but for the observation 15.7, which is unusually large for its cell. The largest Cook's $D = .39$, which is smaller than before but still somewhat large considering only two other values of Cook's D were above .2.

In summary, the analysis of the log-transformed data produced a better analysis on all counts. The homogeneity of variance and normality assumptions are much more reasonable for the transformed data in this case. The outlier problems are substantially reduced for the transformed data. The log transformation is consistent with our speculations about the relative size of intervals in timing data that are necessarily constrained at one end. And, finally, the resulting model of the transformed data is more parsimonious and provides a better description of the data. In contrast, the analysis of the untransformed data is misleading because it suggests that an interaction exists and the presence of outliers reduces the magnitude of F^* and PRE for the other effects. Thus, when an analysis of the residuals indicates problems with the assumptions about the errors ε_i, it is wise to consider power transformations for the data.

When reporting the results for transformed data, we customarily note that the statistical inference was done on transformed data, but report group means (or indeed any predicted values) in the original metric of the DATA. Thus, the means or predicted values from the transformed analysis must be inverted. For the natural log function,

$$Y_i = e^{W_i}$$

provides the proper inversion to the original metric. For example, from Exhibit 16.17, $\overline{W} = 3.33$ for the no transfer group and $\overline{W} = 2.00$ for the transfer group. The test of the coefficient for X_1 in Exhibit 16.17 indicates that the difference between those two means is reliable. Using the inversion formula, we can convert these means to the original metric of seconds. Thus, the predicted mean in seconds for the no-transfer group would be $e^{3.33} = 28$, and for the transfer group $e^2 = 7.4$. We could conclude that the difference (in seconds) between these two groups was reliably different from zero.

16.3.3 Known DATA Problems and Their Remedies

Certain types of DATA are known to be ill-behaved in terms of heteroscedasticity and nonnormality and appropriate transformations have been developed. When analyzing data of these types, it is always wise for us to compare an analysis of the untransformed data with an analysis of the appropriately transformed data. This subsection describes those frequently encountered data types and their corresponding transformations. If an analysis is done on transformed data, it is often desirable to report the resulting predicted values on the untransformed scale. Thus, for each transformation we also provide the appropriate inverse transformation for returning predicted values to the original scale.

Counts. Data that are counts, especially counts of relatively rare events, are usually generated from a "Poisson process." The errors from models of such data are often heteroscedastic and nonnormal because the size of the error depends on the size of the count. Examples of such data in the social sciences are counts of errors in cognitive or peceptual tasks, counts of accidents, counts of people switching political parties, and counts of first admissions for a particular psychiatric problem. The appropriate transformation that eliminates the heteroscedasticity inherent in such data is the square root transformation; that is, for counts it will be appropriate to do an analysis of

$$W_i = \sqrt{Y_i} = Y_i^{1/2}$$

The inverse transformation is simply

$$Y_i = W_i^2$$

Proportions or Counted Fractions. Proportions, percentages, and population rates (e.g., an accident rate of 782 per 100,000 residents) are very common types of data in the social sciences. The data Y_i are computed as the ratio between two counts: r, the count of instances meeting some condition and n, the count of the total possible instances that might have met the condition. Thus,

$$Y_i = \frac{r_i}{n_i}$$

Examples include the proportion of items correct on a test, the proportion of women in a university department, and the population rate for skin cancer. That there were problems with counts suggests that there will also be problems with counted fractions that involve two counts. There are in fact three problems with counted fractions. First, computing the proportion amounts to adjusting the count r_i by the count n_i. Just as we saw in Chapter 13 that computing difference or change scores did not necessarily provide the best adjustment, so too dividing by n_i does not necessarily provide the best adjustment. In many cases it may be better to use r_i as the data and to include n_i as a predictor in the model of r_i. Second, the variance of the errors for proportions depends on the size of the proportion. Proportions around .5 have the largest variance, while those nearer 0 and 1 have smaller variances. For models of proportions it is not unusual to observe a diamond pattern in the plot of e_i against $\hat{Y}_i$; that is, the spread of the errors is narrow near predicted values of 0 or 1 and broad near predicted values of .5. Third, the size of the intervals on the proportion scale are not equal. Most people consider a change from 2% to 8%, a quadrupling, to be functionally much larger than the equivalent arithmetic change from, say, 47% to 53%. For these reasons it is generally useful to use a transformation that stretches *both* tails of the distribution. Two such transformations that are easy to compute are the *arcsine* and *logit* transformations. The arcsine transformation is given by

$$W_i = \sin^{-1} \sqrt{Y_i}$$

The inverse transformation for the arcsine transformation is

$$Y_i = (\sin W_i)^2$$

If r and n are small, a somewhat better arcsine transformation is given by

$$W_i = \sin^{-1} \sqrt{\frac{r_i + 3/8}{n_i + 3/4}}$$

The logit transformation is given by

$$W_i = \log \frac{Y_i}{1 - Y_i}$$

The inverse of the logit transformation is

$$Y_i = \frac{e^{W_i}}{e^{W_i} + 1} = \frac{1}{1 + e^{-W_i}}$$

For proportions the odds are given by $Y/(1 - Y)$, so the logit transformation is also known as log odds. The two transformations differ in the extent to which they stretch the tails. The logit does a little bit more stretching than the arcsine transformation. If all the values of Y_i are between about .2 and .8, then these transformations will have little effect because they operate primarily on the tails. In that case, an analysis of untransformed and transformed proportions will produce essentially the same results.

Correlations. Sometimes data will consist of correlations computed for each unit of observation. For example, in a study of stereotypes each subject might rate a number of individuals on two scales; the dependent variable might be each subject's correlation[6] between ratings on the two scales. The distributional problems of correlations are similar to those for counted fractions. The variance of the errors depends on the correlation. There is much more variability for correlations around 0 than there is for correlations near -1 or $+1$. There is also a problem with

---

[6]Remember that the correlation coefficient equals the square root of PRE for predicting the rating of one variable from the rating of the other variable.

unequal intervals. Most people consider the difference between a correlation of .95 and .85 to be functionally much greater than the equivalent arithmetic difference between, say, $-.05$ and $+.05$. Again, both tails need to be stretched. The appropriate transformation, usually known as *Fisher's* Z is given by

$$W_i = \frac{1}{2} \log \left[\frac{1 + Y_i}{1 - Y_i} \right]$$

and the inverse of this transformation is

$$Y_i = \frac{e^{2W_i} - 1}{e^{2W_i} + 1}$$

A very common use of this transformation is when one wants to compute the average or build the simple model for a set of correlations. The correlations should first be transformed to W's, those values should be averaged, and then the resulting average should be transformed back by using the inverse.

16.4

Summary

If DATA are well behaved in that the ERRORs from a MODEL are independent, identically distributed, from a common normal distribution with mean 0 and variance σ^2, then the least squares model-fitting procedures used in this book in conjunction with the inferential statistics PRE and F^* provide excellent data analysis tools. However, if those assumptions are not true, then those same tools can sometimes produce very misleading, distorted results. Our general solution is to diagnose the problems in the ERRORs and then apply appropriate transformations to DATA so that the ERRORs from MODELs of the transformed DATA satisfy those assumptions. Thus, once the transformation is applied, all of the procedures from earlier chapters may be used unaltered. Chapters 14 and 15 concern the diagnosis and correction of nonindependence. This chapter pertains mostly to diagnosis and remedy of other problems with ERRORs, especially heteroscedasticity (ERRORs from distributions with different variances) and nonnormality (particularly thick-tailed distributions). We recommend graphical detection procedures such as the normal quantile plot and the residual-by-prediction plot because these are generally sufficient to detect problems large enough to cause serious problems for the data analysis. Once a diagnosis is made, one can usually find an appropriate transformation that works by stretching or shrinking the tails of the distribution of ERRORs.

16.5

A Final Word on the Model Comparison Approach to Data Analysis

With this chapter we complete the coverage of the basic techniques that we think every data analyst ought to have in his or her bag of tricks. We hope these chapters have made clear our firm belief that good data analysis in the social sciences is not primarily a matter of statistics but rather depends on the ability to formulate and answer good substantive questions about one's DATA. After you have formulated an appropriate question, you can then use the procedures of this book to translate that question into an appropriate pair of models—a compact MODEL C and an augmented MODEL A. The resulting PRE and F^* provide both a description of the magnitude of the difference between the models—the ability of MODEL A to make better conditional predictions of the DATA than MODEL C—and a statistical answer to the substantive question that motivated the analysis.

The model comparison approach frees the data analyst from having to decide whether a particular analysis requires "regression analysis" or "analysis of variance." Instead, the data analyst performing model comparisons need only focus on which combination of continuous and categorical predictor variables provides the best MODEL for the DATA, without worrying about what the analysis procedure was traditionally called. Using the model comparison approach also frees the data analyst from the tyranny of the computer programmers. By formulating questions in terms of models, you can use a common multiple regression program to answer the questions you want to address instead of the questions the computer programmer assumed you wanted to know.

APPENDIX A

Illustration of All Model Types

In this appendix we present a complete analysis of a real data set for two reasons. First, we want to provide an example of a complete analysis and how such an analysis uses models from throughout the book. Second, we want to illustrate on a common data set all the model types considered in the book. However, instead of organizing this appendix by model types, we organize it by questions we want to ask of the data. It is always good substantive questions and not model types that guide a quality data analysis. Along the way, we do point to the relevant chapter so that the interested reader can consult the appropriate chapter for more detailed information about the particular model type.

Each fall many entering college freshmen complete a questionnaire in the Cooperative Research Program conducted jointly by the American Council on Education and the Higher Education Research Institute at the University of California, Los Angeles. The data for our analysis come from 170 entering freshmen at a large public university. The questionnaire asks about educational background, abilities, interests, goals, and demographics.

A.1

The Question

An important question in survey research is whether people respond accurately and truthfully to survey questions. People may be inaccurate simply because they do not remember or because they purposely misrepresent the facts to make themselves look better. In either case, the obtained survey results would not be an accurate characterization of the population surveyed if the resondents' self-reports are inaccurate. In this survey students reported their verbal and quantitative scores 'from the Scholastic Aptitude Test (SAT). The Educational Testing Service (ETS) reports each student's official score on the SAT to the university, and the university places it in the student's official record. A natural question, and the one that drives our analysis in this appendix, is whether self-reported SAT scores match the official scores. If they do not match, then the question becomes what factors predispose students to be accurate or inaccurate in reporting their SAT scores.

It is important to note that a number of factors besides student error, willful or not, could cause a mismatch between stated and recorded SAT scores. For example, some students take the SAT more than once and all their scores may not be reported to the university.[1] Another example, the university receives most scores on computer tape and most of these scores are added electronically to student records. Sometimes, however, these scores are added manually, which raises the possibility of numerical typing errors by the university.

Another caution to note is that this analysis is only for those respondents who answered affirmatively to the following question, which was the last question in a long survey:

> The Higher Education Institute at UCLA actively encourages the colleges that participate in this survey to conduct local studies of their students. If these studies involve collecting follow-up data, it is necessary for the institution to know the students' ID numbers so that follow-up data can be linked with the data from this survey. If your college asks for a tape copy of the data and signs an agreement to use it only for research purposes, do we have your permission to include your ID number in such a tape?

We need to consider possible sources of bias associated with responses to this question. It is possible that students who had misrepresented some of their answers, including their response to the SAT question,

---

[1]The university does have a policy of recording only the highest score for students who take the SAT more than once.

might be less likely to respond affirmatively to the above question. This is potentially a serious problem because of the 275 students who reported their SAT scores, only 179 (65%) explicitly gave permission for their other university records to be used in follow-up studies while 24 (9%) explicitly denied permission and 72 (26%) did not respond to the question. The permission question was at the bottom of the last page of a long questionnaire, did not have a question number unlike the other questions, and had the highest nonresponse rate. Thus, many students may have simply missed this item.

Another possibile source of bias, although it seems less plausible, is that after giving permission students rechecked the accuracy of their previous answers. In any case, we need to consider the possibility that the differences between self-reported and official SAT scores are smaller for those students who gave permission than for those who did not. Note, however, that the direction of the bias is toward finding no differences. If we do find differences, we can be reasonably confident that the true differences are at least that large.

In summary, our question is whether students reported their SAT scores accurately and, if not, what other factors or characteristics are associated with either over- or under-reporting of SAT scores. If we find a difference, we can be confident that the true difference is at least that large. If we find no difference, then we can make no conclusion because of the issues discussed above which would bias the results towards no difference.

A.2

The DATA

We were able to find the recorded SAT scores in the university's records for 170 of the 179 students who gave explicit permission for their records to be used. The responses from these students constitute the data for our illustrative analysis. The Educational Testing Service reports SAT scores to students as a three-digit number, but the last digit is always 0 and so is superfluous. ETS reports SAT scores to universities as two-digit numbers between 20 and 80 without the superfluous zero. So, in our data set we have divided the self-reported SAT scores by 10 to place them on the same scale of 20 to 80. In addition to the students' self-stated and recorded SAT scores we have included in the data set some other variables from the survey that might be related to any differences, should they exist. Exhibit A.1 describes the variable names for the survey questions included in the analysis. Exhibits A.2–A.8 present the actual data. We urge the reader to use these data with his or her favorite computer statistical package to conduct the analyses described in this appendix.

SATV Self-reported SAT verbal score

SATM Self-reported SAT quantitative score

RSATV Recorded SAT verbal score from university records

RSATM Recorded SAT quantitative score from university records

SEX Coded as "M" for male and "F" for female

HSGPA Self-reported average high school grades

HSENGL Years of English in high school

HSMATH Years of mathematics in high school

ACDABIL Self-rating of academic ability

ACHIEVE Self-rating of drive to achieve

WRITING Self-rating of writing ability

A.3

Power Analysis

We begin with a power analysis, as every good data analysis ought to begin, to determine if we have a reasonable chance of detecting differences in self-stated and officially recorded SAT scores. Ideally, we would perform the power analysis before collecting the data so that we could make changes in the study design and the number of observations if the statistical power were inappropriate. But even when the data have already been collected by someone else, we ought to do a power analysis to determine whether the considerable work of a quality data analysis is likely to be fruitful.

Let's begin by asking what are our chances of rejecting the null hypothesis for what Cohen, as we discussed in Chapter 5, describes as a medium effect for the social sciences, about $\eta^2 = .1$. For the focused, single-degree-of-freedom tests which we favor, PA − PC = 1. The other degrees of freedom are $n -$ PA = 170 − PA, which depends on the number of parameters in the augmented model. For the simple model, PA = 1, so there would be 170 − 1 = 169 degrees of freedom. Consulting Exhibit C.5 in Appendix C, we find that the approximate power for detecting a medium effect using $\alpha = .05$ is greater than .98. Even in the context of a complicated MODEL A that had 20 parameters (so, $n -$ PA = 170 − 20 = 150), power for detecting a medium effect would still be .98. This is certainly an acceptable level of statistical power.

OBS	SATV	SATM	RSATV	RSATM	SEX	HSGPA	HSENGL	HSMATH	ACDABIL	ACHIEVE	WRITING
1	63	65	63	65	M	7	6	5	4	3	4
2	54	68	58	66	M	3	6	6	4	4	3
3	48	58	48	58	M	4	6	6	4	3	2
4	43	67	43	67	M	5	6	7	4	4	2
5	53	67	53	67	M	5	6	5	4	4	3
6	50	60	50	60	M	5	6	6	4	3	4
7	50	65	50	65	M	5	6	6	4	4	3
8	51	59	50	58	M	5	6	6	3	3	3
9	56	60	56	60	M	4	6	6	4	2	2
10	46	62	47	61	M	5	6	5	4	3	3
11	55	68	55	68	M	6	6	6	4	4	4
12	62	68	62	68	M	4	6	5	5	5	4
13	48	53	48	53	M	5	6	6	4	4	3
14	59	59	59	59	M	7	6	5	4	3	3
15	65	45	60	43	M	6	6	6	4	3	4
16	61	40	59	52	M	6	6	6	4	3	4
17	52	59	52	59	M	7	6	6	4	4	4
18	51	62	51	62	M	4	6	6	4	4	3
19	42	58	37	57	M	6	6	6	4	3	3
20	51	62	51	62	M	5	6	6	4	3	3
21	39	64	39	63	M	5	6	6	3	3	3
22	49	57	47	59	M	7	6	7	4	3	2
23	53	60	53	60	M	5	6	6	4	4	4
24	40	78	40	78	M	6	6	6	4	4	3
25	44	47	49	48	M	8	6	6	4	3	3

EXHIBIT A.2 ▲

Selected variables from CIRP survey for 170 freshmen (observations 1 to 25)

OBS	SATV	SATM	RSATV	RSATM	SEX	HSGPA	HSENGL	HSMATH	ACDABIL	ACHIEVE	WRITING
26	44	46	44	46	M	5	6	7	4	3	4
27	44	69	44	69	M	3	6	6	3	4	2
28	58	62	55	65	M	3	6	7	4	4	3
29	54	60	55	59	M	4	6	7	5	2	4
30	54	46	54	49	M	5	6	5	3	3	3
31	58	61	58	61	M	5	6	7	4	5	4
32	54	65	54	65	M	7	6	6	5	5	5
33	43	62	44	62	M	5	5	6	4	4	2
34	54	62	54	62	M	5	6	6	4	4	4
35	46	53	39	53	M	5	6	6	4	5	4
36	59	67	59	67	M	7	6	6	5	3	5
37	45	52	45	52	M	4	6	5	4	5	5
38	45	59	45	59	M	8	6	6	4	5	4
39	52	62	53	63	M	6	6	6	4	5	4
40	47	67	47	67	M	7	6	6	5	5	5
41	57	61	57	60	M	7	6	6	4	5	4
42	54	59	54	59	M	6	6	6	4	4	3
43	55	66	49	64	M	5	7	6	4	5	5
44	51	61	51	61	M	7	6	7	4	4	4
45	48	66	48	66	M	3	6	6	3	2	3
46	46	54	43	59	M	6	6	7	3	3	3
47	55	65	57	65	M	8	6	7	4	4	3
48	60	62	62	60	M	7	6	6	4	4	4
49	54	62	53	62	M	8	6	5	5	5	5
50	44	68	44	68	M	7	6	6	5	4	2

EXHIBIT A.3 ▲

Selected variables from CIRP survey for 170 freshmen (observations 26 to 50)

OBS	SATV	SATM	RSATV	RSATM	SEX	HSGPA	HSENGL	HSMATH	ACDABIL	ACHIEVE	WRITING
51	56	65	52	63	M	0	6	6	4	5	4
52	61	56	56	61	M	6	7	0	4	4	4
53	51	64	51	64	M	4	6	6	5	3	4
54	52.5	62.5	63	52	M	6	5	5	0	2	4
55	45	55	43	57	M	5	6	6	4	3	2
56	46	64	46	64	M	5	6	6	4	4	5
57	56	56	52	57	M	6	6	7	4	5	2
58	50	50	54	46	M	5	6	6	4	3	4
59	42	66	48	60	M	7	6	6	4	5	2
60	59	65	59	65	M	7	6	6	3	4	5
61	37	60	41	60	M	6	6	6	3	4	3
62	65	67	61	68	M	4	6	6	4	2	4
63	48	45	45	48	M	6	6	6	4	4	3
64	59	52	51	56	M	5	6	5	4	4	5
65	51	47	54	43	M	4	6	5	3	4	4
66	48	38	48	38	M	4	6	5	3	4	4
67	60	68	60	68	M	5	6	0	5	2	4
68	55	63	52	63	M	7	6	6	4	5	3
69	41	52	41	52	M	5	6	6	4	4	3
70	55	45	50	46	M	6	6	5	3	2	0
71	50	57	54	55	M	3	6	6	3	3	4
72	62	76	64	74	M	5	6	5	4	4	4
73	48	65	48	65	M	6	6	7	4	3	3
74	50	65	50	65	M	5	7	6	4	4	4
75	59	69	59	69	M	5	6	6	5	4	4

EXHIBIT A.4 ◄

Selected variables from CIRP survey for 170 freshmen (observations 51 to 75)

OBS	SATV	SATM	RSATV	RSATM	SEX	HSGPA	HSENGL	HSMATH	ACDABIL	ACHIEVE	WRITING
76	54	62	54	62	M	4	6	6	4	3	3
77	61	73	61	73	M	3	6	6	5	2	4
78	50	60	50	60	M	6	6	6	4	4	4
79	49	51	41	53	M	4	6	5	3	3	3
80	51	76	51	76	M	5	6	6	4	2	3
81	51	59	51	59	F	5	6	6	4	4	2
82	48	54	37	56	F	5	6	6	3	3	4
83	45	58	45	58	F	5	6	6	3	3	2
84	48	52	48	52	F	5	6	6	3	3	2
85	68	70	68	70	F	8	6	6	3	3	3
86	45	45	44	46	F	4	6	5	4	4	3
87	51	57	45	57	F	6	6	6	3	3	2
88	54	56	52	56	F	5	6	6	4	4	3
89	43	63	43	63	F	5	6	6	3	3	3
90	52	46	38	46	F	6	6	5	4	4	2
91	49	48	49	48	F	5	6	5	3	3	4
92	60	57	61	56	F	5	6	6	4	4	2
93	49	51	43	51	F	5	6	6	4	3	5
94	51	54	51	52	F	6	6	5	4	4	3
95	63	61	63	60	F	7	6	6	5	5	4
96	48	59	51	57	F	6	6	6	5	5	5
97	54	56	49	52	F	7	6	5	4	2	3
98	58	58	55	58	F	5	6	6	4	4	2
99	57	53	57	53	F	5	6	6	4	4	4
100	67	61	67	61	F	7	6	6	4	3	5

EXHIBIT A.5 ▲

Selected variables from CIRP survey for 170 freshmen (observations 76 to 100)

OBS	SATV	SATM	RSATV	RSATM	SEX	HSGPA	HSENGL	HSMATH	ACDABIL	ACHIEVE	WRITING
101	55	61	53	61	F	4	7	6	4	4	3
102	47	56	37	56	F	6	6	6	4	5	4
103	50	53	46	57	F	6	6	6	4	5	5
104	42	38	38	52	F	7	6	6	4	4	3
105	54	59	51	59	F	5	6	6	4	4	4
106	44	51	44	51	F	5	6	5	4	4	5
107	39	52	35	50	F	6	6	6	4	4	3
108	64	56	64	56	F	6	6	6	5	5	5
109	56	49	56	49	F	8	6	6	4	4	3
110	43	42	46	49	F	7	7	6	4	5	5
111	48	59	48	59	F	4	6	7	3	4	3
112	42	43	42	43	F	8	6	5	4	5	4
113	53	50	50	53	F	7	7	6	4	5	4
114	53	54	49	58	F	5	7	5	4	4	4
115	37	51	35	52	F	5	6	6	3	4	3
116	48	48	48	48	F	5	6	6	3	3	5
117	70	63	70	63	F	8	5	5	5	4	4
118	58	62	45	58	F	5	6	6	4	3	5
119	47	54	48	55	F	7	6	5	5	5	5
120	54	65	54	65	F	7	0	7	4	4	4
121	57	58	58	57	F	7	6	6	5	5	5
122	47	60	47	60	F	8	6	5	5	5	4
123	60	40	53	47	F	6	6	5	4	3	5
124	51	69	51	69	F	8	6	7	5	4	4
125	63	62	63	62	F	8	6	6	5	4	5

EXHIBIT A.6 ▲

Selected variables from CIRP survey for 170 freshmen (observations 101 to 125)

OBS	SATV	SATM	RSATV	RSATM	SEX	HSGPA	HSENGL	HSMATH	ACDABIL	ACHIEVE	WRITING
126	41	66	41	66	F	7	6	6	5	5	5
127	47	33	43	37	F	5	6	6	4	4	3
128	60	65	58	55	F	8	6	6	5	3	4
129	57	60	55	60	F	8	6	6	4	5	4
130	62	58	62	58	F	5	6	4	4	4	5
131	62	71	62	71	F	8	6	5	5	5	5
132	59	61	54	70	F	5	6	7	4	4	3
133	66	42	60	48	F	6	6	5	5	4	4
134	57	63	57	63	F	8	6	5	5	4	5
135	65	53	61	54	F	6	6	4	5	4	5
136	60	46	60	44	F	8	6	5	4	4	5
137	45	54	45	54	F	6	6	5	4	5	2
138	45	57	45	57	F	5	6	6	4	3	2
139	55	56	56	55	F	8	6	6	4	4	4
140	72	73	72	73	F	8	6	6	5	4	4
141	49	61	48	62	F	8	6	6	3	4	3
142	56	51	55	51	F	7	6	6	4	5	3
143	44	56	47	53	F	5	7	6	4	3	3
144	44	42	37	41	F	4	6	5	3	3	3
145	44	55	44	55	F	7	6	6	4	4	3
146	46	46	46	46	F	7	6	5	4	4	4
147	46	54	46	54	F	5	6	5	4	4	3
148	50	54	46	56	F	6	6	6	3	4	3
149	55	55	54	56	F	7	7	5	5	5	5
150	46	52	44	47	F	6	6	5	4	5	3

EXHIBIT A.7 ▲

Selected variables from CIRP survey for 170 freshmen (observations 126 to 150)

OBS	SATV	SATM	RSATV	RSATM	SEX	HSGPA	HSENGL	HSMATH	ACDABIL	ACHIEVE	WRITING
151	60	55	60	55	F	6	6	5	4	3	4
152	56	55	56	55	F	6	6	5	4	4	5
153	58	63	57	64	F	7	6	6	5	4	4
154	50	60	50	60	F	7	6	6	4	4	3
155	50	56	51	55	F	6	6	6	4	4	3
156	57	55	57	55	F	6	6	5	4	5	4
157	59	54	57	58	F	5	7	6	4	4	4
158	63	57	63	58	F	7	6	6	5	5	4
159	48	47	47	48	F	5	6	5	4	3	4
160	42	53	42	53	F	6	6	5	4	3	5
161	62	58	62	58	F	5	6	6	4	2	5
162	62	63	62	63	F	7	6	6	4	5	4
163	62	62	53	63	F	6	7	6	4	4	4
164	55	50	55	54	F	6	6	5	4	4	5
165	44	64	46	62	F	6	6	6	4	4	3
166	38	54	43	54	F	7	6	6	4	4	4
167	49	50	47	51	F	5	6	5	3	3	3
168	48	43	43	48	F	6	6	6	4	4	3
169	52	62	52	62	F	8	6	5	5	5	4
170	41	45	39	45	F	5	6	6	3	4	2

EXHIBIT A.8 ▲

Selected variables from CIRP survey for 170 freshmen (observations 151 to 170)

The statistical power to detect larger effects ($\eta^2 > .1$), would be even greater, and so we do not need to check them explicitly. However, we ought also to check power for small effects ($\eta^2 = .03$). Exhibit C.5 in Appendix C reveals that power at $\alpha = .05$ would be between about .57 for a very complicated model ($n - PA = 150$) and .70 ($n - PA = 200$).[2] This is certainly adequate but not exceptional power. There is some chance we might miss a theoretically interesting, but small effect.

Also, as described in Chapter 5, we can estimate power by making informed guesses about likely values of relevant parameters. To do so we need to consider specific variables and models. Let's create two difference scores:

SATVDIFF = SATV − RSATV

SATMDIFF = SATM − RSATM

(These and all other variables constructed for the analyses in this appendix are in Exhibit A.9 for easy reference.) An obvious question would be whether these difference scores equal zero, on average. So for SATV we want to compare

MODEL A: $SATVDIFF_i = \beta_0 + \varepsilon_i$

MODEL C: $SATVDIFF_i = 0 + \varepsilon_i$

The power analysis for SATMDIFF is identical, so we will not do it explicitly.

To use the formula for the estimated value of η^2 from Chapter 5, we need to "guestimate" SSE(A) and SSR = SSE(C) − SSE(A). ETS developed the scoring algorithm so that the standard deviation for each SAT scale is approximately 10. Hence, the variance for both SATV and SATM

EXHIBIT A.9 ▶

Names and definitions of computed variables

SATVDIFF = SATV − RSATV
SATMDIFF = SATM − RSATM
RSATVDEV = RSATV − 51.147
RSATV10 = RSATVDEV − 10
AADEV = ACDABIL − 3.99
GENDER = +1 if SEX = "F", = −1 if SEX = "M"
SATTOT = (SATV + SATM)/$\sqrt{2}$
SATDIF = (SATV − SATM)/$\sqrt{2}$
RSATTOT = (RSATV + RSATM)/$\sqrt{2}$
RSATDIF = (RSATV − RSATM)/$\sqrt{2}$

---

[2] $n - PA$ could not, of course, ever equal 200 for the present data. However, using $n - PA = 200$ provides the best upper bound we can obtain, given the coarse resolution of the power table for large numbers of observations.

is approximately 100, and this seems a reasonable value to expect for the variance of RSATV. But we need to estimate the variance of the difference SATVDIFF. From a mathematical statistics book[3] we learn that the variance of a difference is a function of the variances and intercorrelation of the components of the difference, so that

$$\sigma^2_{\text{diff}} = \sigma^2_1 + \sigma^2_2 - 2r_{12}\sigma_1\sigma_2$$

It seems reasonable to assume that r, the correlation between SATV and RSATV (i.e., $r = \sqrt{\text{PRE}}$ when predicting SATV with RSATV) is relatively high, say about .9. Then

$$\sigma^2_{\text{SATVDIFF}} = 100 + 100 - 2(.9)(10)(10) = 200 - 180 = 20$$

So a reasonable estimate of SSE(A) is given by

$$\text{SSE(A)} = n\sigma_2 = 170(20) = 3400$$

A difference of 5 points between self-stated and recorded SATV scores (i.e., $\beta_0 = 5$ in the above MODEL A) would certainly be of interest, so let's ask how much power we would have for detecting such a difference. We can estimate SSR using

$$\text{SSR} = \sum_{i=1}^{n} (\hat{Y}_{iA} - \hat{Y}_{iC})^2$$

$$= \sum_{i=1}^{n} (5 - 0)^2$$

$$= 170(25) = 4250$$

It is then easy to estimate the true proportional reduction in error that we would expect as

$$\text{Expected } \eta^2 = \frac{\text{SSR}}{\text{SSE(A)} + \text{SSR}} = \frac{4250}{3400 + 4250} = .56$$

Consulting Exhibit C.5 of Appendix C with $\eta^2 = .56$ and $n - \text{PA} = 170 - 1 = 169$, we find that power is essentially equal to 1. This means that we are virtually certain to conclude there is a difference if the true difference is 5 points or larger.

Given we have so much power to detect a difference of 5 points, it is interesting to ask how much power we have to detect even smaller differences. For a difference of 1, SSR = 170 so

$$\text{Expected } \eta^2 = \frac{170}{3400 + 170} = .05$$

---

[3]The necessity of such complications illustrates why it is almost always more practical to do the power analysis in terms of sizes of η^2 as we did above, instead of estimating specific paramaters.

Using η^2 and $n - \text{PA} = 169$, we find that power approximately equals .85 for detecting a difference between self-stated and recorded SATV scores of only 1.

In summary, either method for estimating power reveals that with 170 observations we have sufficient statistical power for detecting even very small differences. In fact, we have so much power that we may be concerned about finding differences that are reliable but so small as to be inconsequential in practice.

A.4

Are Self-Stated SAT Scores Accurate?

A.4.1 SATV

Now that we know we have a very good chance of detecting differences, if they exist, between self-stated and officially recorded SAT, we can test for those differences. We begin with SATV. Our question corresponds (see Chapter 5) to comparing the following models:

MODEL A: $\text{SATVDIFF}_i = \beta_0 + \varepsilon_i$

MODEL C: $\text{SATVDIFF}_i = 0 + \varepsilon_i$

The null hypothesis is that there is no difference between stated and recorded SATV scores or, in terms of these models, that $\beta_0 = 0$. Exhibit A.10 displays the relevant output from SAS PROC UNIVARIATE for comparing these models. The prediction equations are

MODEL A: $\widehat{\text{SATVDIFF}}_i = 1.03$ SSE = 1682.13

MODEL C: $\widehat{\text{SATVDIFF}}_i = 0$ SSE = 1861.25

PRE = .096 $F^*_{1,169} = 18.0$ $p < .0001$

Thus, on average self-stated SATV exceeds the officially recorded score by 1.03. Although PRE is only about 10%, the overstating of SATV scores is reliably different from zero. Remember that in terms of the three-digit scores ETS reports to students that this represents an overstating of 10.3 points on a scale of 200 to 800.

Note that SSE(A) = 1682.13 is considerably less than the value of 3400 we guestimated in the power analysis. This illustrates the difficulty of making guestimates; we prefer to do power analyses in terms of η^2.

Exhibit A.11 presents several useful plots for examining the SATVDIFF variable. Note in the histogram that 87 (51%) of the students had scores of zero on the SATVDIFF variable, which means that they

EXHIBIT A.10 ▶

Results from SAS PROC UNIVARIATE for SATVDIFF

UNIVARIATE

VARIABLE=SATVDIFF   SATV − RSATV

MOMENTS

N	170	SUM WGTS	170
MEAN	1.02647	SUM	174.5
STD DEV	3.15491	VARIANCE	9.95344
SKEWNESS	1.01697	KURTOSIS	3.74472
USS	1861.25	CSS	1682.13
CV	307.355	STD MEAN	.24197
T:MEAN=0	4.24213	PROB>|T|	.0001
SGN RANK	922	PROB>|S|	.0001
NUM ^= 0	83		

QUANTILES(DEF=4)   EXTREMES

100% MAX	14	99%	13.29	LOWEST	HIGHEST	
75% Q3	2	95%	7	−10.5	9	
50% MED	0	90%	5	−6	10	
25% Q1	0	10%	−1	−5	11	
0% MIN	−10.5	5%	−3.45	−5	13	
		1%	−7.305	−4	14	

RANGE	24.5
Q3-Q1	2
MODE	0

reported their SATV scores exactly accurately. The other 49% of the students gave inaccurate reports, which tended on average to be in the direction of overstating SATV scores. With so many observations clustered in the very center of the distribution we are bound to have thick tails, as is confirmed by the pattern in the normal quantile plot[4] in Exhibit A.11 and by the box plot. This suggests that we ought to look for outliers.

For the simple model there is no need to examine the levers because they all must equal $1/n = 1/170 = .006$ (see Chapter 9). Exhibit A.12 displays the observations with the highest absolute studentized deleted residuals (RSTUDENT) and, necessarily, the highest values of Cook's D. There are several studentized deleted residuals that appear to be rather large. The four highest are greater than 3.0 and so, according to our informal rule, require a closer look. More formally, we can use the Bonferroni inequality to protect against the dangers of having implicitly conducted 170 statistical tests; that is, we will use $\alpha = .05/170 = .00029$ to evaluate the reliability of the RSTUDENT values.

---

[4]Usually we examine the normal quantile plot of the errors or residuals. However, for the simple model the normal quantile plot of the data will be identical.

EXHIBIT A.11 ▶

Histogram, box plot, and normal quantile plot for SATVDIFF

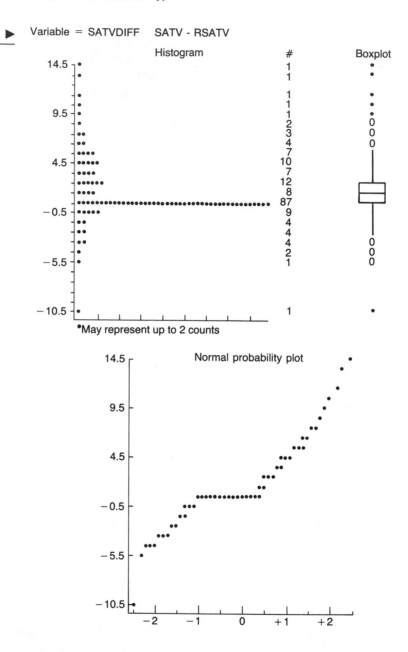

Variable = SATVDIFF   SATV - RSATV

$F_{1,168;.00029} = 13.67$, so the critical value for comparing the RSTUDENT values (remember that they are t^*'s for the outlier model presented in Chapter 9) is $\sqrt{13.67} = 3.70$. Three of the RSTUDENT values exceed, in absolute value, this critical value. However, because none of these extreme observations also has an unusual lever, none of the values for Cook's D are too threatening.

EXHIBIT A.12 ▶

Outlier statistics for the simple model of SATVDIFF

SATV	RSATV	SATVDIFF	RSTUDENT	COOK'S D
52	38	14.0	4.3361	.100651
58	45	13.0	3.9691	.085733
52.5	63	−10.5	−3.8078	.079450
48	37	11.0	3.2597	.059484
47	37	10.0	2.9153	.048154
62	53	9.0	2.5768	.038019
42	48	−6.0	−2.2607	.029524
59	51	8.0	2.2432	.029081
49	41	8.0	2.2432	.029081
44	49	−5.0	−1.9312	.021718

What should we do about the outliers? For the present, nothing. Note that most of the extreme observations are in the direction of presenting a more favorable view of the student with respect to SATV scores. These values of SATVDIFF are what our hypothesis predicted, so we certainly do not want to throw them out. Rather, the challenge is to develop a more complex model that can make conditional predictions of which students will overstate their SATV scores and which ones will not. These observations should not be outliers in a more sophisticated model. If they are, then we will worry a lot more about these outliers. The bottom line is that because of the outliers and because of the thick tails in the normal quantile plot, we do not want to put too much faith in the simple model for SATVDIFF and we certainly do not want to end our analysis here.

One of the outliers deserves a special note. For only one of the five most extreme observations is SATVDIFF negative (−10.5, representing a large *understatement* of SATV). Note also that this student must have reported his SATV score as 525; this is an impossible score because the last digit in the score ETS reports to students is always 0. This student is observation number 54 in Exhibit A.4. Note that he also reported his SATM score with 5 as the last digit. But the biggest surprise is that it appears that he has *reversed* his SATV and SATM scores. This is remarkably similar to the kind of error we used to illustrate outlier problems in Chapter 9. It means that he is a negative outlier on SATVDIFF, but that he is likely to be a positive outlier on SATMDIFF. We cannot just throw out this observation even though the reversal seems obvious, because this reversal may be an interesting twist on a self-serving bias: it may have been psychologically important to this student to see himself doing better on the quantitative than the verbal portion of the SAT. On the other hand, it may have just been a simple mistake by someone who did not read the question carefully. We will keep this observation in the analysis for now, but we will also watch it carefully because it could be a unique observation with devastating consequences when we consider more sophisticated models.

A.4.2 SATM

We now consider whether reports of SATM scores are accurate. This corresponds to comparing the following models:

$$\text{MODEL A:} \quad \text{SATMDIFF}_i = \beta_0 + \varepsilon_i$$

$$\text{MODEL C:} \quad \text{SATMDIFF}_i = 0 + \varepsilon_i$$

The null hypothesis is that there is no difference between stated and recorded SATM scores or, in terms of these models, that $\beta_0 = 0$. We do not have space to reproduce all the computer outputs relevant to the data analyses in this appendix, so we begin a practice of just reporting the summary results. In this case,

$$\text{MODEL A:} \quad \widehat{\text{SATMDIFF}_i} = -.27 \qquad \text{SSE} = 1190.07$$

$$\text{MODEL C:} \quad \widehat{\text{SATMDIFF}_i} = 0 \qquad \text{SSE} = 1202.25$$

$$\text{PRE} = .010 \quad F^*_{1,169} = 1.73 \quad p = .19$$

There is a very slight, but unreliable, tendency to understate SATM scores by $-.27$, on average. A majority (97 or 57%) of the students reported their SATM scores exactly accurately. Thus, there is no suggestion that students overstate their SATM scores.

The normal quantile plot (not shown) displays the same thick-tail pattern as did SATVDIFF, with an especially long negative tail. The outlier statistics are similar to those for SATVDIFF: four observations have RSTUDENT values that exceed the conservative critical value of the Bonferroni inequality, but again none of the values of Cook's D are especially threatening. As expected, Observation 54 appears as a positive outlier with a studentized deleted residual of 4.27. Removing this positive outlier does not make the understating of SATM scores reliable.

A.4.3 Summary

There is a small but very reliable overstating of SATV scores. In terms of the units in which students receive their scores from ETS, the overstatement is about 10.3 points. Most students report their SATV scores accurately. On the other hand, there is no evidence for rejecting the null hypothesis that students report their SATM scores accurately. It is somewhat disturbing that we should find a bias for reporting one SAT score and not the other. This raises the possibility that even though the effect for SATV scores is very reliable, it may be spurious or may be caused by very few students. Before having great confidence in the overstating of SATV scores, we would need to replicate this result with a different group of students, perhaps the students responding to next year's survey. The interested reader may want to estimate the power of detecting a difference of this magnitude in a new group of students of comparable size using the procedures in Chapter 5. Nevertheless, we will continue our analysis in hopes of understanding better which students overstate their SATV scores and why students do not appear to overstate their SATM scores.

A.5

Are Self-Stated SAT Scores Accurate? A More Powerful Test

We noted in Chapter 13 that analyzing difference scores was often not the most powerful method for detecting changes or differences. Instead, using one of the two scores in the difference to predict the other (i.e., use one of the variables as a covariate) will often produce a more powerful test. We hardly need more power for SATV, but we will do the more powerful test anyway both to illustrate the procedure and to gain insights that the slightly more sophisticated model might provide. So we want to make predictions of SATV conditional on RSATV using the simple regression procedures of Chapters 6 and 7. Transforming RSATV to mean deviation form will make interpretation easier because b_0 in the resulting model will equal the mean of SATV. So we create

$$\text{RSATVDEV}_i = \text{RSATV}_i - \overline{\text{RSATV}} = \text{RSATV}_i - 51.147$$

The accuracy question is then equivalent to comparing the following pair of models:

MODEL A: $\text{SATV}_i = \beta_0 + \beta_1 \text{RSATVDEV}_i + \varepsilon_i$

MODEL C: $\text{SATV}_i = 51.147 + \beta_1 \text{RSATVDEV}_i + \varepsilon_i$

The implicit null hypothesis in comparing these two models is that $\beta_0 = 51.147$, but since β_0 corresponds to the mean of SATV this is equivalent to asking whether the mean of SATV equals the mean of RSATV, which is the accuracy question we want to ask.

Before examining the results of fitting these models, it is useful to consider the different models that *could* result. If students were perfectly accurate then in MODEL A we would find $b_0 = 51.147$ and $b_1 = 1.0$. In other words, the regression line would be a diagonal line as depicted in Exhibit A.13. But we already know from our previous analysis that the mean of SATV exceeds the mean of RSATV by 1.03, so the regression

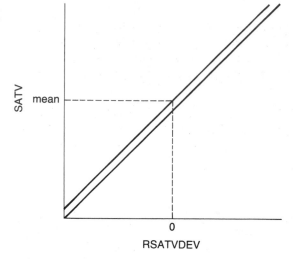

line must be, on average, slightly above the diagonal line representing perfect accuracy. If $b_1 = 1.0$, then we would obtain the regression line depicted as the upper line in Exhibit A.13. (Note that the difference score analysis presumed that $b_1 = 1.0$, so in this case the regression analysis would *not* be more powerful.) This model would indicate that, on average, everyone exaggerates their SATV score a little bit. In particular, this model would imply that students with high SATV scores are just as likely to overstate their SATV scores as those with low scores. This is probably not a reasonable assumption, so we will be surprised if indeed $b_1 = 1.0$.

If instead $b_1 > 1.0$, then we would obtain a model such as the one depicted in Exhibit A.14. This model would imply that students accentuate their scores relative to the mean. That is, students with high scores overstate their SATV scores while students with low scores understate their SATV scores. Such a model is psychologically plausible: students who coded their performance as being good may across time remember those scores as being even better than they were, while students who coded their performance as poor may across time remember their scores as being worse than they were. Such accentuation effects in memory may not be uncommon.

The last possibility, depicted in Exhibit A.15, is that $b_1 < 1.0$. Such a model would imply that students, on average, report their SATV scores as being closer to the mean score than they actually were. This is the classical regression toward the mean effect which often occurs when comparing extreme cases on one measure to their scores on a different

EXHIBIT A.14 ▶

Predicting SATV with RSATVDEV: $b_1 > 1$

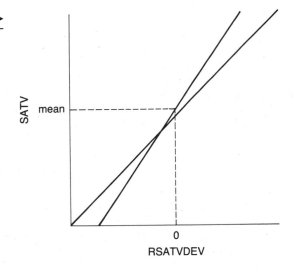

EXHIBIT A.15 ▶

Predicting SATV with RSATVDEV: $b_1 < 1$

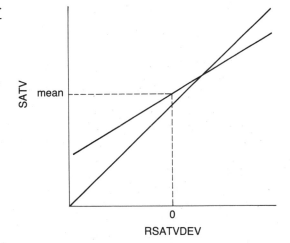

measure. This would imply that students with high scores understate their SATV scores while students with low scores overstate their scores. This model is also psychologically plausible. And there is also an artifactual explanation: it is harder for students with high scores to err in the direction of overstating because there is simply less room between their scores and the ceiling of 800; conversely, it is harder for students with low scores to err in the direction of understating because there is simply less room between their scores and the floor of 200.

Considering the three possibilities for b_1 reveals that not only may the regression analysis be a more powerful test of average accuracy than the analysis of difference scores, but also it might provide insights about which students are overstating and which are understating. With this understanding of what we can learn, we now turn to the results.

MODEL A: $\widehat{SATV}_i = 52.17 + .87\ RSATVDEV_i$ SSE $= 1534.49$

MODEL C: $\widehat{SATV}_i = 51.14 + .87\ RSATVDEV_i$ SSE $= 1713.61$

PRE $= .105$ $F^*_{1,168} = 19.61$ $p < .0001$

As expected, this model comparison reveals, as did the previous analysis of difference scores, that the mean SATV reliably exceeds the mean RSATV by $52.17 - 51.14 = 1.03$. This test is somewhat more powerful than the difference score analysis because both PRE and F^* are higher.

A more important result from this analysis is that $b_1 = .87$ is less than 1.0. We ought to confirm that this difference is reliable by comparing these models:

MODEL A: $\widehat{SATV}_i = 52.17 + .87\ RSATVDEV$ SSE $= 1534.49$

MODEL C: $\widehat{SATV}_i = 52.17 + 1.0\ RSATVDEV$ SSE $= 1682.13$

PRE $= .088$ $F^*_{1,168} = 16.16$ $p < .0001$

Thus, the slope is reliably less than 1.0, which means that the present analysis is truly more powerful and that the model is like the one depicted in Exhibit A.15. That is, according to the model, students with high SATV scores tend to understate while those with low scores tend to overstate. This could be a real bias or it may just be an artifact due to ceiling and floor effects.

With any analysis it is our practice to calculate residual statistics and examine relevant plots to test normality and homogeneity of variance assumptions. However, we simply do not have the space to present those statistics and plots for every analysis in this appendix. Instead, we will only note them when there is something remarkable that ought to be considered. For the present analysis, the outliers and plots are essentially as they were before.

For the comparable models for predicting SATM conditional on RSATMDEV, the slope is not reliably different from 1.0 so this more sophisticated analysis would not be more powerful. Hence, there is still no basis for rejecting the null hypothesis that students report their SATM scores accurately.

A.6

Does the Degree of Over/Understating Depend on RSATV? Polynomial Models of SATV

The previous linear analysis of SATV suggests that students with high RSATV scores tend to understate their true SATV scores while students with low RSATV scores tend to overstate their true SATV scores. However, as Exhibits A.13–A.15 illustrate, the linear model from simple regression is rather constraining. For example, it cannot allow for more complicated ways in which the degree of over/understating might depend on RSATV. One possibility that we ought to consider is that students who score high may report their scores accurately, but students who score low may feel a greater need to overstate their SATV score. We can evaluate such a hypothesis by examining polynomial models as in Chapter 10.

It seems reasonable in this case to consider quadratic and cubic components. Polynomials higher than this are usually difficult to interpret. Unless one has specific hypotheses, examining higher-order polynomials amounts to a fishing expedition. So, we first loosen the constraints of the linear model by comparing the following linear and quadratic models:

MODEL A: $SATV_i = \beta_0 + \beta_1 RSATVDEV_i + \beta_2 RSATVDEV_i^2 + \varepsilon_i$

MODEL C: $SATV_i = \beta_0 + \beta_1 RSATVDEV_i + \varepsilon_i$

The implicit null hypothesis is that $\beta_2 = 0$, or, equivalently, that we do not need the quadratic term $RSATVDEV^2$ in the model. If the null hypothesis is not rejected then there would be no evidence for a complicated dependence of over/understating on RSATV. The following models result when we fit them to the data:

MODEL A: $\widehat{SATV}_i = 51.75 + .87RSATVDEV_i$

$\qquad\qquad + .0077RSATVDEV_i^2$ $\qquad$ SSE = 1484.54

MODEL C: $\widehat{SATV}_i = 52.17 + .87RSATVDEV_i$ $\qquad$ SSE = 1534.49

PRE = .033 $F^*_{1,167} = 5.62$ $p = .0189$

Thus, we can reject the null hypothesis that the simple linear model is adequate. But the quadratic model is itself rather simple. So before interpreting the meaning of our current MODEL A,[5] we first check the need

---

[5]Note that b_0 is no longer the mean of SATV because $RSATVDEV^2$ is not necessarily in mean deviation form even though $\overline{RSATVDEV} = 0$.

for a cubic component in the polynomial model. We obtain the following fits:

MODEL A: $\widehat{\text{SATV}_i} = 51.66 + .963\text{RSATVDEV}_i + .0101\text{RSATVDEV}_i^2$

   $- .000683\text{RSATVDEV}_i^3$ SSE = 1440.44

MODEL C: $\widehat{\text{SATV}_i} = 51.75 + .87\text{RSATVDEV}_i$

   $+ .0077\text{RSATVDEV}_i^2$ SSE = 1484.54

PRE = .030 $F_{1,166}^* = 5.08$ $p = .0255$

Thus, there is a reliable cubic component. For curiosity we can also check for a quartic component. Fortunately (we use this term because polynomial models with many terms are often very difficult to interpret), when we test the quartic component we find that it is not reliable:

   PRE = .013 $F_{1,165}^* = 2.22$ $p = .138$

This does not necessarily imply that all higher-order polynomials are unreliable, but we probably would not be able to interpret them anyway. So, without any hypotheses motivating a look at higher-order interactions, we will stop with the cubic model.

What does the cubic model mean? We can interpret each parameter as we did in Chapter 10. In particular the slope in the SATV-RSATVDEV relationship is not constant but instead depends on RSATVDEV. The expression for the "simple" slope is

   $.963 + .02\text{RSATVDEV} - .002\text{RSATVDEV}^2$

Thus, when RSATVDEV = 0 (i.e., for the average student), the slope is .963, which is remarkably close to the slope of 1.0 that would be consistent with accurate reporting. For an observation 10 points above the mean on RSATV (i.e., RSATVDEV = 10), the slope would be

   $.963 + .02(10) - .002(100) = .963 + .2 - .2 = .963$

which is also very near 1. Thus, for average and better than average students, the slope relating SATV to RSATV is consistent with accurate reporting. What about a worse than average student, say one whose RSATV is 10 points below the mean? That slope would be

   $.963 + .02(-10) - .002(100) = .963 - .2 - .2 = .56$

which for poorer students is consistent with overstating of SATV scores. Thus, the parameters in the cubic model indicate that for average and better than average students there is little or no over- or understating of SATV scores but for worse than average students there is a tendency to overstate SATV scores. The tendency to overstate is more pronounced the worse the true RSATV score. These interpretations are eaiser to see

EXHIBIT A.16 ▶

Predicting SATV with RSATVDEV: cubic model

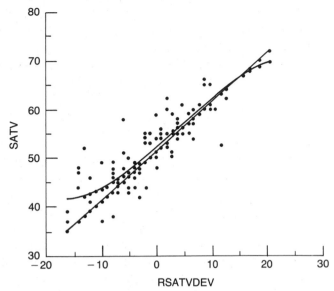

in Exhibit A.16, which plots the cubic model and, for comparison, the diagonal line representing perfect accuracy.

We now have a much more sophisticated understanding of these data. The overstating of scores comes primarily from those students who, in fact, did poorly. Note that this eliminates the artifactual ceiling-floor hypothesis mentioned previously; that hypothesis would not predict a differential effect at the top and bottom of the range. The R^2 (PRE for comparing a model to the simple model) for just the linear model is .8246; for the cubic model with two additional parameters, R^2 only increases to .8353. Although the increase seems tiny, it is a reliable increase (as the above tests of the cubic model demonstrate) and it changes our understanding of the data in important ways. This illustrates that small, but reliable, effects can sometimes be crucial in a model.

A.7

Does Self-Rated Academic Ability Relate to Overstating of SATV?

Now that we are more confident that the overstating of SATV scores is a real effect, we turn our attention to which personal characteristics of the students might predict that effect. A reasonable first step is to consider the three self-rating variables ACDABIL (academic ability),

ACHIEVE (desire to achieve), and WRITING (writing ability). Several plausible hypotheses are readily available. Students might misremember their SATV scores in a direction consistent with their self-image; that is, students who *believe* they are better than average may be more likely to overstate their scores and students who *believe* they are worse than average may be more likely to understate their scores. Another plausible related hypothesis is that students who thought they ought to have scored better than they did may be more likely to overstate their scores.

To answer these questions we want to begin by using multiple regression (Chapter 8) procedures to evaluate this model:

MODEL A: $SATV_i = \beta_0 + \beta_1 RSATVDEV_i + \beta_2 ACDABIL_i$

$+ \beta_3 ACHIEVE_i + \beta_4 WRITING_i + \varepsilon_i$

As is always the case with multiple regression, there are a number of reasonable MODEL C's that might be considered, each one asking a different implicit question about the data. A good first question would be whether, as a group, the three self-ratings predict over- or under-stating of SATV scores. Or, in other words, when controlling for actual performance do self-ratings predict self-stated SATV scores? The appropriate comparison model is

MODEL C: $SATV_i = \beta_0 + \beta_1 RSATVDEV_i + \varepsilon_i$

MODEL C has been estimated above and the SAS output resulting from fitting MODEL A is reproduced in Exhibit A.17. We therefore obtain the following models:

MODEL A: $\widehat{SATV}_i = 49.21 + .840RSATVDEV_i + .735ACDABIL_i$

$- .233ACHIEVE_i + .256WRITING_i \qquad SSE = 1487.04$

MODEL C: $\widehat{SATV}_i = 52.17 + .87RSATVDEV_i \qquad SSE = 1534.49$

$PRE = .031 \quad F^*_{3,165} = 1.75 \quad p = .16$

Thus, there is no evidence that, as a group, the self-ratings predict over/understating of SATV scores.

With multiple degrees of freedom in the numerator of the F^*, we may have the needle-in-the-haystack problem discussed in Chapter 8. When we look more closely at the output in Exhibit A.17 we notice that the test of MODEL A against a MODEL C that just leaves out ACDABIL is close to being reliable ($p = .067$). We also note that the tolerances are less than 1, indicating some redundancy among the self-ratings (as we would expect). This suggests that we just consider the ACDABIL self-rating as a predictor. We do so with some caution because we have no theoretical reason for focusing on this self-rating. To the contrary, it seems more reasonable a priori that WRITING ought to have been the

```
DEP VARIABLE: SATV          Self-reported SAT-Verbal score
                              ANALYSIS OF VARIANCE

                     SUM OF          MEAN
   SOURCE     DF     SQUARES        SQUARE        F VALUE       PROB>F

   MODEL       4    7261.09397    1815.27349      201.421       .0001
   ERROR     165    1487.03691       9.01234492
   C TOTAL   169    8748.13088

        ROOT MSE       3.002057    R-SQUARE       .8300
        DEP MEAN      52.17353     ADJ R-SQ       .8259
        C.V.           5.753984

                          PARAMETER ESTIMATES
                     PARAMETER       STANDARD       T FOR H0:
   VARIABLE   DF     ESTIMATE         ERROR       PARAMETER=0    PROB > |T|

   INTERCEP    1    49.20828586     1.64844699      29.851       .0001
   RSATVDEV    1      .83963032       .03527627     23.802       .0001
   ACDABIL     1      .73547284       .39839571      1.846       .0667
   ACHIEVE     1     −.233249         .30241724      −.771       .4416
   WRITING     1      .25564140       .27863658       .917       .3602

                                                  VARIABLE
   VARIABLE    DF    TOLERANCE                      LABEL

   INTERCEP     1         .                      INTERCEPT
   RSATVDEV     1     .76838036                  MEAN DEV: RSATV − 51.147
   ACDABIL      1     .75714892                  ACADEMIC ABILITY
   ACHIEVE      1     .83992321                  DRIVE TO ACHIEVE
   WRITING      1     .73512848                  WRITING ABILITY
```

EXHIBIT A.17 ▲

Multiple regression analysis of SATV using self-ratings

most useful predictor of verbal skill on the SAT. Our reasons for further consideration of ACDABIL are therefore purely empirical, and we may be guilty of "fishing." However, we will continue our more focused analysis so that we can better illustrate the procedures of Chapters 8 and 10, but we probably would not have much confidence in the analyses in the remainder of this section unless they could be replicated in an independent sample.

With the following models we ask whether the self-rating ACDABIL, by itself, is a useful predictor of over/understating of SATV scores:

MODEL A: $\widehat{SATV}_i = 49.23 + .85RSATVDEV_i$

$\qquad\qquad\qquad + .36ACDABIL_i$ $\qquad$ SSE = 1497.80

MODEL C: $\widehat{SATV}_i = 52.17 + .87RSATVDEV_i$ $\qquad$ SSE = 1534.49

PRE = .024 $F^*_{1,167} = 4.09$ $p = .0447$

Let's think carefully about what this model comparison is telling us. The statistically significant (i.e., surprising) values of PRE and F^* indicate that when controlling for differences in the officially recorded scores (RSATV), there is a reliable relationship between self-rated academic ability (ACDABIL) and stated SATV score. When controlling for recorded scores, predicted stated SATV scores increase by .36 for each unit increase in ACDABIL. Or, in other words, if we had two students with the same recorded scores, MODEL A predicts that their stated SATV scores will differ by .36 for each unit their self-ratings of academic ability differ. Academic ability ratings are on a five-point scale, so the largest difference predicted by the model would be $5 \times .36 = 1.8$.

Note that the size of the ACDABIL effect is small. Of all the error left after using RSATVDEV to predict SATV, ACDABIL reduces only 2.4%. Thus, although ACDABIL provides some understanding of which people are overstating their SATV scores, there is still a lot more that we do not understand.

A fair summary is that students who performed poorly relative to their own assessments of their academic ability tended to overstate their SATV scores. It seems reasonable that there also might be an interaction: students who scored low, especially if they thought they ought to have done better, may be more likely to overstate their scores than students who scored high. To test this interaction we compare, as we did in Chapter 10, a model that includes the product of the two predictors to a model that does not. The following results when we estimate these models:

MODEL A: $\widehat{SATV}_i = 50.65 + .35RSATVDEV_i + .33ACDABIL$

$\qquad\qquad\qquad + .12(RSATVDEV_i)ACDABIL_i \qquad SSE = 1414.08$

MODEL C: $\widehat{SATV}_i = 49.23 + .85RSATVDEV_i$

$\qquad\qquad\qquad + .36ACDABIL_i \qquad\qquad\qquad SSE = 1497.80$

$PRE = .056 \quad F^*_{1,166} = 9.83 \quad p = .002$

Thus, the interaction is reliable: the relationship between SATV and RSATVDEV depends on the level of ACDABIL. To understand the nature of this dependence, we rewrite MODEL A as a "simple" relationship between SATV and RSATVDEV; thus,

$\widehat{SATV}_i = [50.65 + .33ACDABIL_i] + [.35 + .12ACDABIL_i]RSATVDEV_i$

The slope $[.35 + .12ACDABIL_i]$ describes the relationship between SATV and RSATVDEV as a function of ACDABIL. Clearly, as ACDABIL increases, the slope increases and, hence, the relationship between SATV and RSATVDEV becomes stronger. Simply, the recorded score is a better predictor of stated SATV score for those students who rate themselves high on academic ability and is a relatively poor predictor for those who rate themselves low. In particular, the slope for those who give themselves the highest rating on academic ability (ACDABIL = 5) is .35 + .12(5) = .95, very near the slope of 1.0 that we would expect with perfect accuracy. The slope for those who give themselves the lowest rating (ACDABIL = 1) is only .35 + .12(1) = .47, which at the low end of RSATVDEV, where most of them happen to be, indicates considerable overstating of SATV scores. The differential reporting accuracy as a function of self-rated academic ability is easily seen in Exhibit A.18 which plots separate SATV-RSATVDEV regression lines for low, medium, and high values of ACDABIL.

It may be useful to test and interpret the other parameter estimates in the interactive model, particularly those for the two-component predictors of the product by themselves. Remember with products in the model that the coefficient of a single component represents the simple relationship between that variable and Y *when the other component in the product equals zero.* So, the coefficient of .33 for ACDABIL in MODEL A is the slope for predicting SATV when RSATVDEV = 0. RSATVDEV = 0 represents average performance in terms of recorded scores, so we can say for two average students their SATV scores are predicted to differ by .33 times the difference in their self-ratings of ACDABIL. However, the coefficient of .33 is not reliably different from zero (PRE = .005, $F^*_{1,166}$ = .77, p = .38),[6] so there is no evidence that ACDABIL is related to overstating of SATV scores *for average students*.

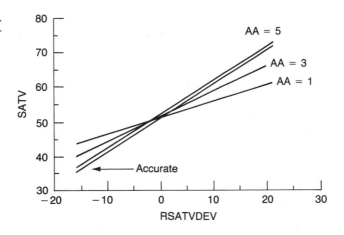

---

[6]We omit the estimates for the appropriate MODEL C for reasons of space and because we do not want to be tempted to interpret the parameters of an interactive model that does not include as separate predictors all the components of product terms.

The coefficient of .35 for RSATVDEV, which is reliably different from zero (PRE = .028, $F^*_{1,166}$ = 4.75, p = .03), is the relationship between SATV and RSATVDEV when ACDABIL is zero; but the lowest possible value for ACDABIL is 1, so this coefficient does not have a meaningful interpretation.

As they stand, the coefficients in the interactive model are not very informative. We can change the focus of the questions addressed by the single-component predictors by making simple transformations to change when the other component equals zero. For example, the action in overstating of SATV scores appears to be among the lower-scoring students so we might focus on those, say, about 10 points below the mean by using

$$RSATV10_i = RSATVDEV_i - 10$$

as the predictor. We also might want to focus on the students who give average ratings of academic ability by using

$$AADEV_i = ACDABIL_i - \overline{ACDABIL} = ACDABIL_i - 3.99$$

as the other predictor. Doing so, we obtain the following model:

$$\widehat{SATV}_i = 60.58 + .86RSATV10_i + 1.60AADEV_i$$
$$+ .12(RSATV10_i)(AADEV_i)$$

This model must make the same predictions as the model using the untransformed predictors, so the SSE must remain the same. Note also that, as it must, the coefficient for the product term has remained the same. However, the coefficients for the single components of the product have changed because they are now focused on different aspects of the data. The coefficient for RSATV10 (b_1 = .86) is now reliably different from zero (PRE = .816, $F^*_{1,166}$ = 736, p < .0001) and represents the relationship between the recorded score and stated score *when* AADEV = 0. Since AADEV = 0 on average, this is equivalent to saying that on average SATV increases by .86 units for each increase in the officially recorded score. Similarly, the coefficient for AADEV (b_2 = 1.60) is also reliably different from zero (PRE = .071, $F^*_{1,166}$ = 12.67, p = .0005) and represents the relationship between self-rated academic ability and stated SATV score *when* RSATV10 = 0. But RSATV10 = 0 for students whose official scores are 10 points below the mean so b_2 = 1.60 implies that such students state SATV scores 1.60 units higher for each unit higher they rate themselves on academic ability. In other words, we might say that students who scored low but who had high self-ratings of their academic ability tended to overstate their SATV scores more.

The analysis based on self-ratings reveals that it is the lower scoring students who are more likely to overstate their SATV scores. This is essentially the same conclusion we reached when we interpreted the cubic model. It may be the case that both analyses are detecting the same aspect of the data. If we were to control for the curvilinear relationship we detected earlier, then ACDABIL and its interaction with RSATV might not be reliable predictors of SATV. We can check this possibility by adding ACDABIL and its product with RSATVDEV to the cubic model reported above. When we do so, we find that the interaction is still reliable (we leave the estimation of the parameters to the reader). Hence, self-ratings of academic ability and its product with recorded SATV score increases predictive ability of the model. Thus, we have even stronger evidence that overstating of SATV scores is concentrated among students who scored low, especially among those who had relatively high estimates of their academic ability.

A.8

Does Gender Predict SATV?

It can be dangerous to look for differences based on demographic variables. The problem is that if we look often enough we will sometimes find apparent differences which are really Type I errors. To avoid this we should have reasoned hypotheses involving any predictor we intend to test in a model. The work of Eccles (1987) and her colleagues suggests that at an early age many girls receive the message from their parents and others that they are supposed to be good at verbal skills and not so good at quantitative skills. It therefore seems reasonable to ask whether males and females differ in their reports of SATV scores. Note that we are not asking yet whether there is a gender difference in over- or underreporting, but just whether there is a gender difference in reported scores.

The gender question is a simple one-way analysis of variance of the kind considered in Chapter 11. We will create a contrast-coded variable GENDER that is equal to $+1$ if the respondent is female and -1 if the respondent is male. Then comparison of the following models asks whether GENDER is a reliable predictor of stated SATV scores:

MODEL A: $\text{SATV}_i = \beta_0 + \beta_1\text{GENDER}_i + \varepsilon_i$

MODEL C: $\text{SATV}_i = \beta_0 + \varepsilon_i$

The null hypothesis is that $\beta_1 = 0$, or, equivalently, that there are no gender differences in self-stated SATV scores. The estimated models are

MODEL A: $\widehat{\text{SATV}}_i = 52.15 + .43\text{GENDER}_i$ SSE $= 8716.88$

MODEL C: $\widehat{\text{SATV}}_i = 52.17$ SSE $= 8748.13$

PRE $= .004$ $F^*_{1,168} = 0.60$ $p = .44$

There is not a reliable reduction in error when making differential predictions of SATV based on GENDER. We therefore have no basis for rejecting the null hypothesis of no gender differences in self-stated SATV scores. Note that, even though we used a contrast code for GENDER, the estimates of b_0 differ slightly in the two models. This is because there are unequal numbers of males (80) and females (90) in this data set. Thus, in MODEL A, $b_0 = 52.15$ represents the unweighted grand mean or, equivalently, the mean of the separate male and female means. In MODEL C, $b_0 = 52.17$ represents the grand mean of all the observations.

A.9

Does Gender Predict Over/Understating of SATV?

The previous analysis did not reveal any differences in stated SATV scores. But it is a very different question, with potentially a very different answer, to ask whether males or females are more likely to over- or understate their SATV scores. Remember that to address over- or understating of scores we need to include RSATV, the officially recorded score, in the model. Thus, we want to compare these models:

MODEL A: $SATV_i = \beta_0 + \beta_1 RSATV_i + \beta_2 GENDER_i + \varepsilon_i$

MODEL C: $SATV_i = \beta_0 + \beta_1 RSATV_i + \varepsilon_i$

Formally, this is an analysis of covariance, which we considered in Chapter 13, because we have at least one categorical predictor and one continuous predictor. The null hypothesis is that $\beta_2 = 0$, or, equivalently, that when controlling for officially recorded score there is no gender difference in stated SATV score. The resulting estimated models are

MODEL A: $\widehat{SATV}_i = 52.14 + .88RSATVDEV_i$

$+ .587GENDER_i$ SSE $= 1476.10$

MODEL C: $\widehat{SATV}_i = 52.15 + .87RSATVDEV_i$ SSE $= 1534.49$

PRE $= .038$ $F^*_{1,167} = 6.60$ $p = .011$

Thus, when controlling for a student's officially recorded score, there is a small (PRE $= 3.8\%$) but statistically reliable effect of gender. This means that were a male and a female student to have the same official score, the female would, on average, report a score $2 \times .587 = 1.174$ higher than the male. We therefore can conclude that females overstate their SATV scores more than males. Note that we cannot determine from this test or either model whether males also overstate, or report accurately, or understate their SATV scores; we just know that females report higher scores than males, given the same official score.

This analysis just asks whether different intercepts are required for separate male and female regressions. The answer is yes. We might also want to ask whether separate slopes are required. That is, is there a different relationship between SATV and RSATVDEV for males and females? This is easily tested by determining whether the interaction product RSATVDEV × GENDER ought to be added to the model. Comparing models with and without the interaction yields PRE = .001, $F^*_{1,166} = .14$, $p = .71$. Thus, there is no evidence for different relationships between SATV and RSATVDEV for males and females.

Given what we know from our previous analyses about the curvilinear relationship between SATV and RSATVDEV and about the relationship between SATV and ACDABIL, we ought also to determine whether GENDER is a useful predictor in those more sophisticated models. Doing so does not introduce any new model types so we do not present those analyses here. However, the interested reader who does conduct those analyses will find that GENDER remains a reliable predictor after controlling for the curvilinear relationship and for self-rated academic ability. Thus, in these data there is a reliable difference between males and females.

Discovering that females slightly overstate their SATV scores relative to males is precisely the kind of surprise with demographic variables that can lead to trouble in the form of unwarranted assertions about group differences. We might not be confident in this conclusion unless we could replicate it in a new sample. To determine our chances of replicating this result—the statistical power—we first calculate an unbiased estimate of η^2, the true proportional reduction in error, using the following equation from Chapter 5.

$$\text{Unbiased Estimate of } \eta^2 = 1 - (1 - \text{PRE})\left[\frac{n - \text{PC}}{n - \text{PA}}\right]$$

$$= 1 - (1 - .038)\left[\frac{168}{167}\right]$$

$$= .032$$

This corresponds to what we termed a small effect in the power analysis above so we know that our chances of replicating this gender difference in a new group of students are good—power equals about .7—but still far from certain. We might well find that the gender difference was a quirk of this group.

We do not presently have another data set which we can check for a gender effect. However, we do have another similar variable in this data set—SATM—for which we have both stated and officially recorded scores. Although it is not as useful as an independent data set, it still is worthwhile to determine whether there is a gender difference in the reporting of SATM. We know from an analysis above that there was no overall tendency to over- or understate SATM scores, but there still might be a gender difference.

However, when considering SATM scores we must deal with the obvious nonindependence problem: stated SATV and SATM scores from the same person are likely to be related. We can test that by predicting SATV with SATM (or vice versa). We obtain (omitting the obvious models) PRE $= .054$, $F^*_{1,168} = 9.57$, $p = .002$. The relationship between SATV and SATM (which corresponds to a correlation of $\sqrt{.054} = .23$) might be weaker than we expected,[7] but it still demonstrates a reliable dependence between the two scores. The errors for a model of SATV would likely be correlated with the errors for a model of SATM. We therefore will want to use the procedures of Chapters 14 and 15 for dealing with nonindependence. We now turn to more sophisticated models involving both SATV and SATM.

A.10

Does Gender Predict SAT Total and Difference?

We begin our joint consideration of SATV and SATM by asking whether there is a gender difference in stated scores. In this analysis we will not be considering whether there is over- or understating of scores. We have two data values for each student so we probably have a nonindependence problem. We therefore need the techniques of Chapter 14. With two data values we need to construct two new data values W_0 and W_1. These correspond to the total and the difference, respectively, of the two SAT scores so we will refer to them as SATTOT and SATDIF. That is,

$$\text{SATTOT}_i = \frac{\text{SATV} + \text{SATM}}{\sqrt{2}}$$

$$\text{SATDIF}_i = \frac{\text{SATV} - \text{SATM}}{\sqrt{2}}$$

---

[7]This might be due to a restriction in the range of the scores. Students with very low scores, especially those with low scores on both SATV and SATM, would not be admitted. And students with exceptionally high scores might have gone to more prestigious universities. It is possible for such restrictions to turn an inherently positive relationship into a negative one.

Remember that we divide by the square root of the sum of the squared contrasts to make the sum of squares appropriate for a traditional summary table; however, if we did not divide by $\sqrt{2}$ in this case, we would still obtain the appropriate PREs and F^*'s.

Comparison of the following two models determines whether there is a gender difference in the total SAT score reported:

MODEL A: $\text{SATTOT}_i = \beta_0 + \beta_1 \text{GENDER}_i + \varepsilon_i$

MODEL C: $\text{SATTOT}_i = \beta_0 + \varepsilon_i$

The null hypothesis is that $\beta_1 = 0$, or equivalently, that males and females report the same average total SAT score. The resulting estimated models are

MODEL A: $\widehat{\text{SATTOT}_i} = 77.68 - 1.51\text{GENDER}_i$ SSE $= 11806.03$

MODEL C: $\widehat{\text{SATTOT}_i} = 77.59$ SSE $= 12193.54$

PRE $= .032$ $F^*_{1,168} = 5.51$ $p = .02$

So there is a reliable difference in stated SAT total scores due to gender. To interpret the parameters we must divide by $\sqrt{2}$ to return to the mean of SATV and SATM or multiply by $\sqrt{2}$ to return to the sum of SATV and SATM; we choose to do the latter. Thus, from MODEL C we obtain that the overall average total SAT score is $77.59\sqrt{2} = 109.73$. However, from MODEL A we find that for males the average total SAT score is $[77.68 - 1.51(-1)]\sqrt{2} = 111.99$, and for females the average total is $[77.68 - 1.51(+1)]\sqrt{2} = 107.72$; this difference of 4.27 is statistically reliable, although it is not a large effect (PRE $= .032$). In summary, males tend to report higher total SAT scores.

We now address the difference between SATV and SATM. Before considering whether there are gender differences in the stated difference between SATV and SATM, we first consider whether there is, on average, a difference between the two component scores. A comparison of the following models compares the difference to zero:

MODEL A: $\text{SATDIF}_i = \beta_0 + \beta_1 \text{GENDER}_i + \varepsilon_i$

MODEL C: $\text{SATDIF}_i = 0 + \beta_1 \text{GENDER}_i + \varepsilon_i$

The null hypothesis is that $\beta_0 = 0$. The estimate b_0, when a contrast-coded predictor is in the model, equals the unweighted grand mean, so an equivalent statement of the null hypothesis is that the unweighted[8]

---

[8]It is the unweighted grand mean because the mean of the predictor GENDER is not zero, even though it is contrast coded, due to the unequal numbers of males and females. If we wanted the estimate b_0 to be the weighted or overall grand mean then we could convert GENDER to mean deviation form by subtracting its mean in the same way we did for continuous predictors.

grand mean for the difference between SATV and SATM stated scores is zero. The resulting fitted[9] models are

MODEL A: $\widehat{\text{SATDIF}_i} = -3.93 + 2.12\text{GENDER}_i$ SSE = 6863.89

MODEL C: $\widehat{\text{SATDIF}_i} = 0 + 1.89\text{GENDER}_i$ SSE = 9486.78

PRE = .276 $F^*_{1,168} = 64.2$ $p < .0001$

Thus, there is strong evidence that the unweighted grand mean is not zero; instead, students state, on average, SATM scores that are $3.93\sqrt{2} = 5.56$ higher than SATV scores.

Now we can ask whether the stated difference between SATV and SATM scores depends on gender by comparing the following models:

MODEL A: $\text{SATDIF}_i = \beta_0 + \beta_1\text{GENDER}_i + \varepsilon_i$

MODEL C: $\text{SATDIF}_i = \beta_0 + \varepsilon_i$

The null hypothesis is that $\beta_1 = 0$, which in this case is equivalent to no difference between males and females in the difference they state between their SATV and SATM scores. The fitted models are

MODEL A: $\widehat{\text{SATDIF}_i} = -3.93 + 2.12\text{GENDER}_i$ SSE = 6863.89

MODEL C: $\widehat{\text{SATDIF}_i} = -3.81$ SSE = 7625.19

PRE = .100 $F^*_{1,168} = 18.63$ $p < .0001$

There is a reliable and moderately large effect of gender on the stated difference between SATV and SATM scores. We obtain the following two mean differences for the two groups:

FEMALES: $\overline{\text{SATDIF}} = (-3.93 + 2.12(+1))\sqrt{2} = -2.56$

MALES: $\overline{\text{SATDIF}} = (-3.93 + 2.12(-1))\sqrt{2} = -8.56$

In other words, both males and females tend to state higher SATM scores than SATV, but this is more so for males. We now turn to the question of whether these reports are accurate.

A.11

Does Gender Predict Over/Understating of SAT Total and Difference?

We now come to the critical question which culminates the analysis of these data: Does gender predict over/understating of total SAT scores

---

[9]The estimates for MODEL C are easily obtained by most regression programs which have an option for not having an intercept or for "forcing the regression through the origin."

and/or the difference in the SAT scores? Before examining the answer to this question, let's consider some plausible hypotheses. We know that in this group of students females tended to overstate their SATV scores relative to males. It is possible that women also overstate their SATM scores in which case there would be a large gender difference in overstating total SAT score, with women overstating more. This hypothesis also suggests that there would be little or no difference in the stated difference in scores. An alternative hypothesis is that women, like many groups who are the victims of stereotypes, may have come to believe the stereotype that they are good, relative to men, at verbal tasks and relatively bad at quantitative tasks. If so, it might be the case that women overstate their SATV scores but understate their SATM scores. If so, then we would expect to find no gender difference in stated total scores and a large difference in the stated difference, with women overstating a larger difference in the two component scores, favoring verbal scores.

With two data variables—SATV and SATM—and two covariates—RSATV and RSATM—for each student, this analysis design corresponds to a repeated-measures-with-repeated-covariates design like the ones we considered in the second half of Chapter 15. To use those procedures we need to code the covariates parallel to the data variables. That is,

$$RSATTOT_i = \frac{RSATV + RSATM}{\sqrt{2}}$$

$$RSATDIF_i = \frac{RSATV - RSATM}{\sqrt{2}}$$

Then by including RSATTOT in a model of SATTOT we will be asking about stated total scores when controlling for officially recorded total scores. Just as when we examined SATV when controlling for RSATV, we will be able to ask whether total scores are over- or understated. Similarly, RSATDIF in a model of SATDIF enables us to ask whether the difference between scores is over- or understated.

A.11.1 SATTOT

We first consider total SAT scores. Without stating the obvious models in terms of β's we turn directly to estimated fits for the relevant models. Exhibit A.19 lists the parameter estimates and SSE's for seven relevant models. We will ask questions by comparing appropriate models from the list in Exhibit A.19.

Do stated SAT scores, when controlling for recorded SAT scores, vary with gender? Comparing model[10] T5 and T3, we find no evidence

---

[10]We will use the convention of listing MODEL A first and MODEL C second.

MODEL T1: Simple Model

$\widehat{\text{SATTOT}} = 77.59$

SSE = 12193.54

MODEL T2: Gender Difference

$\widehat{\text{SATTOT}} = 77.68 - 1.50\text{GENDER}$

SSE = 11806.02

MODEL T3: Controlling for RSATTOT

$\widehat{\text{SATTOT}} = 4.59 + .95\text{RSATTOT}$

SSE = 926.85

MODEL T4: Fixing $b = 1$ for RSATTOT

$\widehat{\text{SATTOT}} = .54 + 1.0\text{RSATTOT}$

SSE = 961.56

MODEL T5: Gender Controlling for RSATTOT

$\widehat{\text{SATTOT}} = 4.25 + .95\text{RSATTOT} + .18\text{GENDER}$

SSE = 921.67

MODEL T6: Gender, Fixing $b = 1$ for RSATTOT

$\widehat{\text{SATTOT}} = .52 + 1.0\text{RSATTOT} + .26\text{GENDER}$

SSE = 949.69

MODEL T7: Gender by RSATTOT Interaction

$\widehat{\text{SATTOT}} = 3.98 + .95\text{RSATTOT} + 1.2\text{GENDER} - .013 \text{ RSATTOT(GENDER)}$

SSE = 919.69

EXHIBIT A.19 ▲

Summary of models, parameter estimates, and SSEs for SATTOT

of a gender difference (PRE $= .006$, $F^*_{1,167} = .94$, $p = .33$). Thus there is no reason not to use model T3 for both males and females. Returning to the accuracy question, we can ask then whether the slope for the recorded score is reliably different from 1.0. Comparing models T3 and T4, we find the difference in slopes for RSATTOT between .95 and 1.0 is reliable (PRE $= .036$, $F^*_{1,168} = 6.29$, $p < .02$). The interpretation of the slope less than 1.0 is the same as for the analysis of SATV above. That is, there is either a slight artifactual regression toward the mean or a slight tendency for students with low scores to overstate and those with high scores to understate.

In summary, the gender difference in overstating we found for SATV does not appear when we analyze SATTOT. Maybe it is obscured by a different relationship between SATTOT and RSATTOT for males and females. We can check this possibility by comparing models T7 (interaction) and T5. There is no evidence for different relationships (PRE $= .002$, $F^*_{1,166} = .36$, $p = .55$). Thus, we can eliminate our hypothesis that women would overstate both their SATV *and* SATM scores. Our alternative hypothesis that women would overstate SATV and understate SATM remains viable. We explore it further in the next set of analyses.

A.11.2 SATDIF

Exhibit A.20 lists the parameter estimates and SSEs for seven relevant models. We will ask questions about stated differences between SATV and SATM scores by comparing appropriate models from the list in Exhibit A.20.

Do stated differences between SATV and SATM scores, when controlling for the difference in the recorded scores, vary with gender? We can answer this basic question by comparing models D5 and D3. The answer is that, when controlling for the officially recorded difference, males and females do differ in the difference they state between their SATV and SATM scores (PRE = .044, $F^*_{1,167}$ = 7.66, p = .006). That is, if a male and a female student had the same actual difference between RSATV and RSATM, model D5 predicts that the female would state a larger difference between SATV and SATM than would the male. In the traditional language of analysis of covariance, if SATV and SATM are treated as two levels of a type-of-test variable, then we say there is an interaction between type of test and gender. Before interpreting this

EXHIBIT A.20 ▼

Summary of models, parameter estimates, and SSEs for SATDIF

MODEL D0:   Zero Model

$\overbrace{\text{SATDIF}} = 0$
SSE = 10093.00

MODEL D1:   Simple Model

$\overbrace{\text{SATDIF}} = -3.81$
SSE = 7625.19

MODEL D2:   Gender Difference

$\overbrace{\text{SATDIF}} = -3.93 + 2.12\text{GENDER}$
SSE = 6863.89

MODEL D3:   Controlling for RSATDIF

$\overbrace{\text{SATDIF}} = .66 + .95\text{RSATDIF}$
SSE = 1892.52

MODEL D4:   Fixing b = 1 for RSATDIF

$\overbrace{\text{SATDIF}} = .92 + 1.0\text{RSATDIF}$
SSE = 1910.65

MODEL D5:   Gender Controlling for RSATDIF

$\overbrace{\text{SATDIF}} = .48 + .92\text{RSATDIF} + .72\text{GENDER}$
SSE = 1809.51

MODEL D6:   Gender, Fixing b = 1 for RSATDIF

$\overbrace{\text{SATDIF}} = .88 + 1.0\text{RSATDIF} + .60\text{GENDER}$
SSE = 1850.24

MODEL D7:   Gender by RSATDIF Interaction

$\overbrace{\text{SATDIF}} = .51 + .92\text{RSATDIF} + .61\text{GENDER} - .023\text{RSATDIF(GENDER)}$
SSE = 1806.25

result we ought to be sure that the relationship between SATDIF and RSATDIF does not depend on gender. Comparing models D7 (interaction) and D5 does not suggest there is a differential relationship between stated and recorded scores in each gender group (PRE = .002, $F^*_{1,166}$ = .30, p = .58).

We now can interpret model D5. One way to do so[11] is to specify the separate regression functions, derived from model D5, for males and females. That is,

$$\text{Males:} \quad \widehat{\text{SATDIF}_i} = .48 + .92\text{RSATDIF}_i + .72(-1)$$

$$= -.24 + .92\text{RSATDIF}_i$$

$$\text{Females:} \quad \widehat{\text{SATDIF}_i} = .48 + .92\text{RSATDIF}_i + .72(+1)$$

$$= 1.20 + .92\text{RSATDIF}_i$$

According to the model, a student for whom RSATDIF = 0 states a difference of −.24 if male and +1.20 if female. To return to the original metric of the SAT scores we need to multiply by $\sqrt{2}$. So, when controlling for the recorded difference in scores, the adjusted mean stated difference between SATV and SATM for males is $(-.22)\sqrt{2} = -.31$, and for females is $(1.22)\sqrt{2} = 1.72$. Thus, the model predicts that for two students with the same recorded difference in SAT scores, the male would, on average, state a difference on the questionnaire that slightly favored his SATM score to his SATV score by .31 point while the female would, on average, state a difference that favored her SATV score to her SATM score by 1.72 points. In terms of the units in which students receive and report their scores, this means that for two students with the same recorded difference, the difference reported by females is, on average in this group, $[1.72 - (-.31)]10 = 20.3$ higher than the difference reported by males. Although this is not a large statistical effect (PRE = .05), a difference of 20.3 points is appreciably large.

Remember that in our very early analyses we encountered an interesting outlier: Student 54 essentially reversed his SATV and SATM scores. The difference for his recorded scores is $63 - 52 = 11$, but the difference in his stated scores is $52.5 - 62.5 = -10$. In the present analysis we used the former difference to predict the latter. Clearly, this case has the possibiltiy of being a large outlier because his error is compounded when we compute the difference. Exhibit A.21 lists the outlier indices for the 15 cases with the highest values of Cook's D. Indeed, in the analysis of SATDIF, the RSTUDENT for student 54 equals −4.6, the lever is .046, and the Cook's D is .30. These values are all large, especially the RSTUDENT, relative to the values for the other observations. The

---

[11]Another way to interpret model D5 is to calculate adjusted means for each group using the formula from Chapter 13.

normal quantile plot (not reproduced here because it is so similar to Exhibit A.11) also indicates that the error for this observation is in the extreme tail of the distribution. These problems with observation 54 suggest that we ought to try the analysis with this observation deleted; he is just so different from the other 169 observations that he ought not to be included in the same analysis. With this case deleted, the GENDER difference for SATDIF when controlling for RSATDIF is still reliable (PRE = .032, $F^*_{1,166}$ = 5.42, p = .02) but reduced in magnitude: the coefficient for GENDER drops from .72 to .58. In terms of the scores reported to students, the difference between females and males is now estimated to be 16.4 instead of 20.3. Thus, our conclusion would remain essentially the same: there is a small but reliable gender difference. Note that the last observation in Exhibit A.21 is a male who also appears to have reversed his SATV and SATM scores. However, his two scores were close so his reversal did not produce a particularly large value of RSTUDENT.

The other cases in the list of potential outliers in Exhibit A.21 do not seem nearly so threatening; note the rapid drop in values of Cook's D. The second largest values of Cook's D and RSTUDENT are for a male who, unlike the other males, overstated his SATV and understated his SATM. It might be worth exploring the effect on the analysis of deleting this observation but we leave that exploration to the interested reader. Note in this list of potential outliers that all of the women but one have SATDIF greater than RSATDIF because they overstated SATV and/or understated SATM. This is precisely the trend that our model comparison revealed so we ought not to consider these cases as outliers in the

EXHIBIT A.21   ▼

Outlier indices for model D5

SEX	SATV	SATM	RSATV	RSATM	SATDIF	RSATDIF	LEVER	RSTUDENT	COOK D
M	52.5	62.5	63	52	−7.07	7.78	.046	−4.60	.30
M	61	40	59	52	14.85	4.95	.034	3.36	.12
F	66	42	60	48	16.97	8.48	.034	2.50	.07
F	42	38	38	52	2.83	−9.90	.018	3.38	.07
F	60	40	53	47	14.14	4.24	.021	2.83	.05
F	48	54	37	56	−4.24	−13.44	.028	2.14	.04
F	59	61	54	70	−1.41	−11.31	.022	2.42	.04
M	42	66	48	60	−16.97	−8.48	.013	−2.79	.03
M	59	52	51	56	4.95	−3.54	.014	2.62	.03
M	50	50	54	46	.00	5.66	.036	−1.54	.03
M	65	45	60	43	14.14	12.02	.069	1.06	.03
F	52	46	38	46	4.24	−5.66	.012	2.56	.03
M	51	47	54	43	2.83	7.78	.046	−1.27	.03
F	60	65	58	55	−3.54	2.12	.016	−2.07	.02
M	61	56	56	61	3.54	−3.54	.014	2.17	.02

usual sense. However, when we remember that the majority of students gave accurate reports of their SAT scores, this suggests that the overall gender effect we observed may be due to a relatively small number of cases. That is, there is an effect of gender because the few women who did not report accurately consistently erred in the direction of overstating SATV and understating SATM. One of the dangers of interpreting differences due to demographic variables is attributing the difference to every member of the group. In this case, it appears that it is unwarranted to make the blanket statement that women, relative to men, overstate a difference in their SAT scores in favor of verbal abilities. Instead, a more accurate statement is that most students report their scores accurately but among those few who do not, women are more likely to exaggerate their SATV scores and understate their SATM scores. Looking at the potential outliers has therefore increased our understanding of the model and the data.

As a final check of model adequacy, we also need to check the plots recommended in Chapter 16. Exhibit A.22 plots the residuals from model D5 against the predicted values. From this graph there do not appear to be any serious problems with assuming homogeneity of variance of the errors for model D5. Note the one very low predicted value of about -25; this student had the unusual pattern of a very low SATV score (40) and a very high SATM score (78). He had the highest lever (.084), but since he stated his scores accurately, he did not have large values of either RSTUDENT or Cook's D. Also note that case 54 appears as an obvious outlier in the lower right corner of Exhibit A.22.

For a check of the normality assumption, we examine Exhibit A.23 which presents the histogram and the box plot of the errors in addition to the normal quantile plot of the residuals. There is still a suggestion of thick tails, but the errors from this model appear much more normal than the errors from the simple model depicted in Exhibit A.11. These apparently thickish tails are because most students reported accurately and so are clumped more tightly in the middle than is expected for a normal distribution. There is no appropriate transformation for this situation; instead, our understanding of these data has simply been increased by considering the normality issue.

A.11.3 Summary

Exhibit A.24 presents the models T5 and D5 in a standard analysis of covariance summary table.[12] Our conclusion is that there is not a reliable gender difference between stated total SAT scores when controlling for

---

[12]To be consistent with Exhibits A.19 and A.20, we report the table for the analysis including the outlier Student 54. The interested reader will find it an interesting exercise to produce the corresponding tables with that observation deleted.

EXHIBIT A.22 ▶

Residuals versus predictions for model D5 (letter indicates gender)

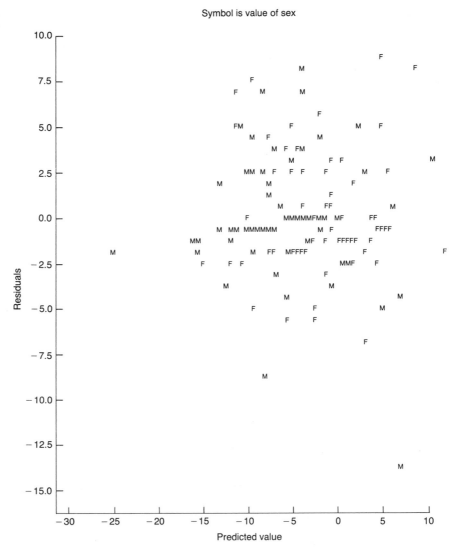

Note: 52 OBS hidden

officially recorded scores. That is, males and females do not differ in the degree to which they over- or understate their total SAT scores. To determine whether the average student was over- or understating total SAT score, we would need to predict SATTOT with RSATTOT transformed to mean deviation form. We leave that analysis to the interested reader. There is, however, a reliable gender difference between stated SATV and SATM scores when controlling for the recorded difference between scores; females report a difference more in favor of SATV than

EXHIBIT A.23 ▶

Histogram, box
plot, and normal
quantile plot for
the errors from
model D5

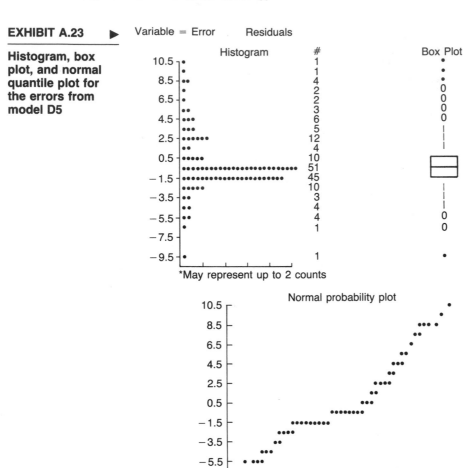

do males. In particular, as the hypothesis we derived from Eccles (1987) suggests, females tend to overstate their SATV scores and understate their SATM scores. If we look separately at over- and understating by females of SATM scores (using the same techniques we used earlier for looking at SATV scores), we find that although it is in the direction of the hypothesis, the understating of SATM scores is not reliable (PRE = .029, $F^*_{1,88}$ = 2.66, p = .11). Thus, most of the gender difference is due to the tendency of females to overstate their SATV scores. An examination of the outliers suggests that much of the apparent overall gender difference is due to a relatively small number of students.

Source	b_j	SS	df	MS	F*	p	PRE
Between (SATTOT)							
RSATTOT	.95	10,884.35	1	10,884.35	1971.8	.0001	.92
GENDER	.13	5.18	1	5.18	.9	.34	.01
Error		921.67	167	5.52			
Total Between		12,193.54	169				
Within (SATDIF)							
TEST	.68	23.92	1	23.92	2.21	.14	.01
TEST × RSATDIF	.92	5,054.38	1	5,054.38	466.27	.0001	.74
TEST × GENDER	1.02	83.01	1	83.01	7.66	.006	.05
Error		1,809.51	167	10.84			
Total Within		10,093.00	170				
Total		22,286.54	339				

EXHIBIT A.24 ▲

Analysis of variance summary table for SATV and SATM

A.12

Summary of All Analyses

There are many other interesting questions that could be asked of these data using the model comparison approach. For example, do we need to consider curvilinear components of RSATTOT and RSATDIF just as we did for RSATVDEV? And, are HSENGL (years of high school English) and HSMATH (years of high school math) useful predictors in this data set? However, we have already served our purpose in this appendix of illustrating all the types of model comparisons used in this book. We encourage the interested reader to answer some of these remaining questions. Nevertheless, it is worthwhile to summarize what we have learned from the analyses presented in this appendix.

By and large, stated SAT scores are fairly accurate. Most people report their scores exactly. Although there is a reliable bias in the reporting of SATV scores, the absolute magnitude of this bias is not large and might not have important practical consequences. Thus, at least in this case, survey respondents are reasonably accurate. We have to temper this conclusion with caution because we were only able to check the accuracy of score reporting for those students who gave their permission. The possibility remains that the more honest students were the ones who gave their permission.

The bias in reporting that does exist was detected, even though it was small, because the large number of observations provided enormous statistical power. Although the bias in SATV score reporting may not have important practical consequences, it does have some interesting theoretical implications. In particular, it is interesting to determine which students are more likely to overstate or enhance their scores. Our model comparisons revealed that overstating was likely to come from students with lower official scores.

The most fascinating but at the same time most tenuous result is that there is no gender difference in the over or understating of combined SAT scores but a reliable gender difference in the over- or understating of the component SAT scores. In particular, males are reasonably accurate with a slight understating of the SATV-SATM difference while those few females who are not accurate tend to overstate their verbal scores and understate their quantitative scores, creating a larger then expected differential between stated SATV and SATM scores.

APPENDIX B

Problems and Exercises

Problem numbers refer to relevant chapters.

Problem 2.1   Using one or more of the computer packages available to you, obtain estimates of the mean and median and the variance and standard deviation for two variables (other than FATRATE) for the state automobile data listed in Exhibit B.1. Write a few sentences describing your results in substantive terms.

Problem 2.2   If your statistical computer package has a capability for generating separate analyses for groups of cases, then use it to obtain separate estimates of the mean fatality rate for each level of the variable for minimum legal drinking age. That is, obtain the mean fatality rate for those states in which 18 is the minimum legal drinking age, obtain the mean rate for those states in which 19 is the minimum legal drinking age, etc. Write a sentence or two describing these results; be sure to indicate whether it appears that it would be useful to make fatality rate predictions conditional on minimum legal drinking age. Note: In SAS use the BY statement within either PROC MEANS or PROC UNIVAR-IATE; in SPSSX and SCSS use BREAKDOWN; in MINITAB use UNSTACK (see pp. 337–339 in Ryan, Joiner, & Ryan, 1985) followed by separate uses of DESCRIBE.

Problem 2.3 Using one or more of the computer packages available to you, calculate estimates of the mean, median, variance, and standard deviation for the DRIVERS variable in Exhibit B.1. Calculate these values both including the state of California and excluding it. Why do some of these estimates differ dramatically as a function of whether California is included or excluded, while other estimates differ much less? In the estimates that include California, what percentage of the total sum of squared errors is due to the sum of squared error for California? What percentage of the total sum of squared errors might we expect to be due to an individual observation chosen at random from this data set?

Problem 3.1 Use the stem-and-leaf and box plot output below from PROC UNIVARIATE in SAS to answer the following questions about the values of 60 WGTGAIN scores (WGTGAIN is the measure of the mother's weight gain in pounds during pregnancy). Dot not calculate the responses to any of the questions, but rather give your best estimate based on the plots.

1. Approximately what is the median score?
2. What is the modal score(s)?
3. Approximately what is the mean?
4. What percentage of the scores are above the top of the box?
5. What percentage of the scores are between the middle line in the box and the bottom of the box?

```
VARIABLE=WGTGAIN        MOM WGT GAIN DURING PREGNANCY

Stem Leaf                     #              Box Plot
  7 5                         1                  *
  7
  6
  6 00                        2                  0
  5
  5 00                        2                  |
  4 5                         1                  |
  4 0                         1                  |
  3 55557                     5                  |
  3 0022224                   7              +-----+
  2 555556778888             12              *--+--*
  2 01122233444              11              |     |
  1 577888899999             12              +-----+
  1 00234                     5                  |
  0 8                         1                  |
    ----+----+----+----+
    Multiply STEM.LEAF by 10**+01
```

State	Fatality Rate	Drinking Age	Gasoline Use	Drivers	Density	January Low Temp
Alabama	4.2	19	2.4	2.2	68	40
Alaska	4.7	19	.2	.2	1	18
Arizona	5.3	19	1.6	1.5	16	38
Arkansas	3.6	21	1.5	1.4	37	29
California	3.4	21	12.6	15.1	128	47
Colorado	3.5	21	1.6	2.0	21	16
Connecticut	2.3	18	1.5	1.9	624	22
Delaware	3.3	20	.3	.4	277	24
Florida	3.2	18	5.0	6.8	125	45
Georgia	3.3	18	3.5	3.4	79	33
Hawaii	4.0	18	.3	.5	120	65
Idaho	4.8	19	.6	.6	9	21
Illinois	3.0	21	5.8	6.9	199	17
Indiana	2.9	21	3.3	3.6	145	20
Iowa	3.0	19	1.9	2.0	51	11
Kansas	3.5	21	1.5	1.8	28	21
Kentucky	3.2	21	2.1	2.0	81	25
Lousiana	4.6	18	2.3	2.3	81	44
Maine	3.1	20	.6	.7	32	12
Maryland	2.5	21	2.2	2.6	397	25
Massachusetts	2.7	20	2.6	3.7	727	23
Michigan	3.2	21	5.3	6.3	156	19
Minnesota	3.3	19	2.3	2.6	48	3
Mississippi	4.8	21	1.6	1.6	47	41
Missouri	3.5	21	3.1	3.2	68	23
Montana	4.0	19	.6	.5	5	8
Nebraska	2.9	19	1.0	1.0	19	12
Nevada	5.6	21	.5	.5	4	16
New Hampshire	2.8	20	.5	.6	82	10
New Jersey	2.2	18	3.6	3.4	953	24
New Mexico	5.8	21	.9	.8	8	24
New York	3.6	18	6.2	9.2	381	26
North Carolina	3.6	21	3.5	3.6	104	32
North Dakota	3.7	21	.4	.4	9	-3
Ohio	2.9	21	6.0	8.7	260	22
Oklahoma	3.5	21	2.0	1.9	37	26
Oregon	3.9	21	1.6	1.8	22	33
Pennsylvania	3.0	21	5.8	7.1	262	23
Rhode Island	1.7	18	.4	.6	906	25
South Carolina	3.8	21	1.9	1.8	86	37
South Dakota	3.4	21	.5	.5	9	2
Tennessee	3.3	20	2.9	2.6	95	29
Texas	4.0	18	9.5	8.5	43	38
Utah	3.9	21	.8	.8	13	19
Vermont	3.4	18	.3	.4	48	8
Virginia	2.7	21	3.1	3.4	117	32
Washington	3.5	21	2.2	2.4	51	25
West Virginia	4.0	18	1.0	1.4	73	24
Wisconsin	3.1	18	2.6	2.9	81	10
Wyoming	5.4	19	.4	.3	3	15

EXHIBIT B.1 ▲ **Automobile fatality rates and other variables for 1978**

6. Are there a greater number of extreme scores above or below the median? How do you know this?

7. Are the scores normally distributed?

8. Do you think that there are any outliers in these data?

Problem 3.2 A researcher asks 10 runners how many miles they train a week. He then times them in a half mile race. The resulting data are

Runner	Miles per week	Time (seconds)
1	20	210
2	55	170
3	80	155
4	60	163
5	10	240
6	42	185
7	45	150
8	30	187
9	62	172
10	20	195

He estimates a model for predicting each runner's time from the number of miles he trains each week. The following prediction function minimizes the sum of the squared errors of prediction:

$$\widehat{TIME_i} = 226.80 - 1.04MILES_i$$

Given this model, derive for each runner the predicted value of time, the residual, and the squared residual. Plot the residuals as a function of Miles. Next, plot the residuals as a function of the predicted Time values. What is the value of the mean squared error from this prediction function?

Problem 4.1 Imagine that we have conducted a study of aggression in pairs of twins. One member of each pair is shown a Road Runner cartoon (high violence), and the other watches Sesame Street (low violence) for the same amount of time. Our dependent measure is the number of times each child hits a Bobo-doll (a large weighted, inflated doll that pops back up after it is knocked over) during a subsequent 15-minute play period. If we were to treat these data as if they came from two different groups of subjects, what assumption or assumptions about errors have we violated? Explain how we have violated it. Is such a violation likely to have serious consequences for our statistical inference?

Problem 4.2 During the Viet Nam War, 19-year olds were inducted into the armed forces according to the day of the year on which they were born. To determine who was drafted in the first year, 365 balls (each with one number written on them between 1 and 365) were placed in a large bingo cage. Those young men born on one of the days indicated by the first 30 balls drawn were inducted. A charge was made that the balls were not stirred up enough and that, as a consequence, the balls drawn did not constitute a random sample. To check this a statistician calculated the mean for the 30 balls drawn and compared it to an expected value. What was that expected value? What assumption about errors was violated? Is such a violation likely to have serious consequences for our statistical inference?

Problem 4.3 A study is designed to test the effects of group discussion on a group of college students who report feeling depressed. A standardized test of mood or affect is given at both the beginning and end of the study. (High scores are better on the mood test.) The score for one student is unusually low (more than 1.5 standard deviations below the next lowest score). Further investigation reveals that this student has been previously hospitalized with a severe case of depression. The investigator includes the data for this student in the analysis. What assumption about errors was violated? Is such a violation likely to have serious consequences for our statistical inference?

Problem 4.4 Answer the following questions by assuming that the variable X has a normal distribution with a mean of 10 and a standard deviation of 5.

1. What percentage of cases have values greater than the mean?
2. What percentage of cases have values less than zero?
3. What percentage of cases have values greater than zero but less than 10?
4. What approximate score separates the bottom 10% of the distribution from the top 90%?
5. Suppose we were interested in describing the sampling distribution of the mean if we repeatedly drew samples of size 25 from this normal distribution. What would be the expected value of these means? What would be the variance of the sampling distribution of the means?
6. Among samples of size 25, what proportion of the samples drawn from the distribution of X would have a mean value greater than 11?

Problem 5.1 We normally will let the computer do all the computational drudgery for us. However, it is so important that we thoroughly understand the basics of statistical inference that we will do this problem by hand. A market researcher wants to know whether people can distinguish the taste between regular and decaffeinated coffee. He performs a taste test with 10 consumers. For each of 10 different coffee blends he prepares two batches: a regular batch and a decaffeinated (Swiss water process) batch. For each blend the consumer is given a sample of each batch in identical, unmarked cups. The consumer is asked to indicate which of the two cups has the caffeine. Each consumer's score is the number of times (out of 10) that the batch with caffeine was correctly identified. Thus, a score of 4 means that for 4 of the 10 pairs the consumer correctly indicated which cup had caffeine and for 6 of the 10 pairs the consumer incorrectly indicated which cup had caffeine. The scores for the 10 consumers were

$$4 \quad 5 \quad 6 \quad 9 \quad 10 \quad 3 \quad 6 \quad 9 \quad 10 \quad 7$$

Should the market researcher conclude that consumers can detect by taste the presence or absence of caffeine? Answer the market researcher's question by specifying appropriate MODELs C and A, estimating the needed parameter(s), calculating the respective SSEs, and then calculating PRE and F^*. (Hint: What would be the average score if no one could tell the difference between regular and decaf coffee and therefore had to guess on each of the 10 trials? That average score you would expect from guessing is the value to use for MODEL C.) Be sure to write a brief summary of your conclusions.

Problem 5.2 An attitude researcher gives an attitude questionnaire to a group of incoming freshmen students and four years later gives the same questionnaire to the same students. She wants to know whether their attitudes have changed during the four years. She calculates a change score for each student; that is, CHANGE = FRESH − SENIOR where FRESH is the student's attitude score as a freshman and SENIOR is his or her attitude score four years later. There are 117 students in the study. Using PROC UNIVARIATE in SAS we obtain the results at the top of page A-53.

Specify a MODEL C and a MODEL A to answer the question of whether attitudes changed over the four years of college. (Hint: If there is no change in attitudes, FRESH = SENIOR so CHANGE = 0.) Calculate PRE and F^* to answer that question. Be sure to write a brief summary of your conclusions and remember that if there is a change we would not know whether it was due to college, aging, or noncollege events that occurred during those four years. (Note: As we will see in Chapter 13, this is not necessarily the most powerful way to analyze pre/post data such as these.)

```
                    UNIVARIATE
        VARIABLE=CHANGE

                     MOMENTS

        N                 117   SUM WGTS         117
        MEAN          -3.7094   SUM             -434
        STD DEV       28.1394   VARIANCE     791.829
        SKEWNESS    .0427386    KURTOSIS    -.703738
        USS             93462   CSS          91852.1
        CV             -758.6   STD MEAN     2.60149
        T:MEAN=0      -1.4259   PROB>|T|      .15659
        SGN RANK        -466    PROB>|S|     .199636
        NUM ^= 0          116
```

Problem 5.3 In a particular year, a graduate department admitted 38 new students. The admissions committee wants to know whether GRE verbal, GRE math, and undergraduate GPA are useful predictors of the students' first-year GPA.

1. The admissions committee compares a MODEL C that just estimates the mean with a MODEL A that estimates the mean and makes conditional adjustments based on GRE verbal, GRE math, and undergraduate GPA. If the true ability of these measures to predict graduate GPA corresponds to what the text refers to as a "moderate" effect in the social sciences, what are the approximate chances that the admissions committee will correctly conclude that MODEL A is better than MODEL C if they use $\alpha = .05$?

2. Given that they cannot admit any additional students (to increase the number of observations), state two things they could do to increase the power of their test.

3. Eight hours of each first-year student's GPA is determined by the grades in statistics, so one member of the admissions committee wants to know whether GRE math by itself is a good predictor of first-year GPA. That is, MODEL C just estimates the mean and MODEL A adds an additional parameter for GRE math. What are the approximate chances of detecting a "moderate" effect in this comparison? Why or why not does it agree with the value obtained above?

Problem 5.4 The administrators of an urban hospital are concerned with the quality of births at their hospital. One variable of interest is whether there are more preterm babies than normal. To check this, data are collected on the gestation period (GESTAT) from a sample of 60 births at the hospital. Normal human gestation is 40 weeks, and the administrators wish to know how the hospital sample compares to the standard gestation period. We have computed a new variable, GEST40 = GESTAT − 40. The PROC MEANS output from SAS is reproduced below for both GESTAT and GEST40.

VARIABLE	N	MEAN	UNCORRECTED SS	CORRECTED SS
GESTAT	60	37.1166667	84371.0000	1712.18333
GEST40	60	−2.8833333	2211.0000	1712.18333

1. Specify the MODELs C and A to answer the administrators' question.

2. What is the null hypothesis?

3. Construct the full ANOVA source table, being sure to include both PRE and F^*.

4. Is MODEL C rejected in favor of MODEL A using $\alpha = .05$? Write a brief substantive interpretation of these results.

5. Construct a 95% confidence interval for the gestation period in this hospital's sample.

6. The historical average gestation period at this hospital has been 38.75. Does the average for the current sample of 60 women differ significantly from the historical average? Use your confidence interval to answer this question.

7. The hospital board is concerned that the gestation period for their patients is so low relative to the normal gestation period. The board decides that if a replication with the next sample of 21 patients has an average gestation significantly below 40, then they will implement a community program emphasizing the importance of prenatal care. Use the results for the first sample of 60 patients to determine whether the null hypothesis of 40 is likely to be rejected for the new sample of 21 patients. What would be the chances of rejecting the null hypothesis if the board waited until there were about 60 women in the second sample?

Problem 6.1 Reconsider Problem 3.2. In that problem the following model was estimated for predicting each runner's time from knowledge of the number of miles he runs each week:

$$\widehat{TIME}_i = 226.80 - 1.04 MILES_i$$

1. Provide short interpretations of this model's two parameter estimates.

2. Suppose that the TIME variable was transformed and reexpressed in terms of minutes to run the half mile race (i.e., dividing each runner's TIME by 60). What would be the values of the two parameter estimates if we then regressed this transformed TIME variable on MILES? (Hint: You do not need to go back to the raw data and recalculate the parameter estimates from those data. Think about the parameter estimates already given and how those would change if TIME were expressed in minutes rather than in seconds.)

3. Assuming TIME is measured in seconds, what would the parameter estimates be if MILES were recorded as tens of miles run per week (i.e., the score on MILES for someone who runs 42 miles a week would be 4.2)?

4. Using the raw data of Problem 3.2, determine what the two parameter estimates would be if we transformed MILES into mean deviation form and then regressed TIME on this transformed MILES. Interpret both of the resulting parameter estimates.

Problem 7.1 The following hypothetical data contain information about fathers' and sons' heights (in inches) in each of 10 families.

Family	Father	Son
1	68	69
2	73	72
3	69	71
4	75	74
5	64	65
6	71	70
7	69	73
8	67	65
9	69	70
10	74	75

Enter these data into whatever statistical package you have available and using the regression procedure answer the following questions:

1. Is there a reliable relationship between sons' and fathers' heights in these data?

2. For every unit increase in fathers' heights, can we conclude that there is on average a one unit increase in sons' heights? (Hint: You will

only be able to answer this question using your regression procedure if that procedure allows you to test hypotheses that parameter values equal values other than zero. For instance, in SAS you will want to use the TEST statement in PROC REG to test whether the value of the slope differs from 1.0. If your regression procedure does not include such an option, you can always answer this question by calculating SSE for augmented and compact models by hand.)

3. Is the average of the sons' heights different from the average of the fathers' heights? Answer this question two different ways. First answer it by using the single-parameter model of Chapter 5, treating sons' height as the dependent variable and asking whether its mean differs from 69.9 (the mean of fathers' heights). Then answer it within the context of a two-parameter model, regressing sons' heights on fathers' heights (Hint: In mean deviation form). Why do these two tests of the same null hypothesis produce different PRE and F^* values?

4. Subtract the value of 69.9 from the values of sons' heights. Regress the resulting values on fathers' heights in mean deviation form. Interpret the resulting parameter estimates.

Problem 7.2   A political scientist believes that income ought to be predictive of political beliefs, with individuals having higher income possessing more conservative political beliefs. He believes that this relationship is a relatively weak one, but wishes nonetheless to collect data from a sufficiently large sample to demonstrate its reliability setting $\alpha = .05$.

1. Assuming that the relationship is in fact a small one, from how many people does he need to collect data in order to achieve power of .90?

2. Let us assume that the standard deviation of income, measured in thousands of dollars, in the United States equals 19. Let us also assume that political beliefs, when measured on a seven-point scale, varying from "very conservative" to "very liberal" have a standard deviation in the United States of 1.6. Still assuming that the relationship between the two variables is a relatively weak one, what is an approximate value of the slope that our researcher would observe if he regressed the political beliefs variable on income?

3. Assuming the researcher gathers data from 300 individuals, what would be the confidence interval for the slope parameter?

Problem 8.1   A psychologist is interested in the ability of an attitude measure to predict political campaign contributions above and beyond the predictions based upon nine sociodemographic variables. She regresses campaign contributions on these 10 variables for a sample of 40 people. The multiple $R^2 = .3$.

1. If she were to apply the parameter estimates to a new sample of people, what value of PRE would she expect?
2. To test her key question of whether the attitude measure (a psychological variable) would be useful after the sociodemographic measures (sociological variables) were already in the prediction equation, she found the PRE for adding the attitude measure to be .25. Is this PRE significantly different from zero for $\alpha = .05$?
3. If she repeats this study with a new sample of 40 people, approximately what are her chances of finding a reliable effect for the attitude measure above and beyond the effect of the sociodemographic variables?

Problem 8.2 A sociologist is interested in examining predictors of job prestige. One hundred men are interviewed and their job prestige, Y_i, is ascertained. The sociologist is interested in estimating the degree to which the job prestige of each respondent's father, F_i, and each respondent's educational level, E_i, are predictive of the respondent's job prestige.

Three regression equations are calculated, regressing Y_i on both E_i and F_i; regressing Y_i on only E_i; and regressing Y_i on F_i. The sum of squared errors for each of these regression equations and for the simple model are given below:

$$Y_i = \beta_0 + \beta_1 E_i + \beta_2 F_i + \varepsilon_i$$

$$\text{SSE} = 178$$

$$Y_i = \beta_0 + \beta_1 E_i + \varepsilon_i$$

$$\text{SSE} = 197$$

$$Y_i = \beta_0 + \beta_1 F_i + \varepsilon_i$$

$$\text{SSE} = 235$$

$$Y_i = \beta_0 + \varepsilon_i$$

$$\text{SSE} = 300$$

The sociologist and her colleague disagree about how to interpret these results. The sociologist argues that the sum of squares explained by E_i equals 103 (i.e., $300 - 197$) and the addition of F_i results in an increase of sum of squares explained of only 19 (i.e., $197 - 178$). Therefore she wants to conclude that respondent's education is a much more potent predictor of occupational prestige than is the occupational prestige of one's father.

The colleague argues that the sum of squares explained by $F_i = 65$ (i.e., $300 - 235$) and the addition of E_i to the model results in an increase of sum of squares explained of only 57 (i.e., $235 - 178$). The colleague thus wants to conclude that the predictive power of father's occupational prestige is at least as large as the predictive power of respondent's education.

1. According to this analysis, the sum of squares total for Y_i can be broken up into four components: A component uniquely explained by E_i; a component uniquely explained by F_i; a component that can be explained by both E_i and F_i; and a component that can be explained by neither. Calculate the sum of squares for each of these four components.

2. Using your answers from above, explain why the sociologist and her colleague disagree. Also give your judgment about which of the two interpretations is correct. How would you interpret the results of these analyses?

Problem 8.3   Throughout most of this book we have defined ERROR to be the sum of squared errors. However, when analyzing nominal or categorical data we sometimes use a much simpler definition of ERROR. The MODEL prediction is the category for each observation and ERROR = 0 if category predicted by the MODEL is the actual category and ERROR = 1 if category predicted by the MODEL is wrong. In other words, ERROR is simply the count of misclassifications. To minimize this ERROR, the best MODEL prediction is simply the modal or most frequent category. We can use this simple definition of ERROR in conjunction with our concept of PRE to develop statistical indices for categorical data.

In a study of voting behavior in a sample of 2843 voters, an investigator found the following results:

Voted for	
Dem	Rep
1527	1316

In the absence of any other information the best guess (i.e., the MODEL's prediction) would be to predict that each person voted for the Democratic candidate. In that case, ERROR = 1316 because we would miscategorize all those who voted for the Republican candidate. This is equivalent in the simple model with SSE to predicting the mean for every observation. As was the case for the regression model, the next question is whether there is any additional information which we could use to improve the prediction?

In this particular study information was also available as to the voter's registered party affiliation and the voter's political attitude as measured by a battery of attitude survey questions. Those data for each additional variable separately are as follows:

Party	Voted for	
	Dem	Rep
Democrat	1103	207
Independent	309	343
Republican	115	766
Total	1527	1316

Attitude	Voted for	
	Dem	Rep
Democrat	722	175
Neutral	570	414
Republican	235	727
Total	1527	1316

Use PRE measures (one for each data table above) to determine which of these variables is the better single predictor of voting behavior for senate candidates. The PRE measure using the above simple definition of ERROR is known as Goodman-Kruskal λ (see Goodman and Kruskal, 1954).

Combining both variables results in the following data table:

Party		Voted for	
Reg	Att	Dem	Rep
D	D	620	80
D	N	367	64
D	R	116	63
I	D	89	40
I	N	151	150
I	R	69	153
R	D	13	55
R	N	52	200
R	R	50	511
Totals		1527	1316

How much additional reduction in ERROR can be obtained by adding ATTITUDE given that PARTY has already been used in the predictions? How much additional reduction in ERROR can be obtained by adding PARTY given that ATTITUDE has already been used in the predictions? PRE's so defined are known as "partial λ's." What is the total PRE for using both variables compared to the simple model in which no conditional predictions are made? (It would be reasonable to call this PRE the "multiple λ," but we know of no previous use of this name.)

Unfortunately, there is no easy analog in this case to "PRE per parameter" and F^* so we will not develop the statistical test for λ here. Assume however that all the λ's calculated above are statistically reliable and write a brief paragraph interpreting your analysis of these data.

Problem 8.4 A psychologist studying Hmong refugees living in the United States believes that Hmong high school students' level of acculturation for various attitudes and behaviors is related to the level of intergenerational conflict they experience within their families and communities. Acculturation is measured using a set of attitude and behavioral items. Each student's total score is recorded in a variable called ACCULT. Each student's total number of conflict items checked on a checklist of typical intergenerational conflict behaviors is recorded in a variable called IGCON. There are additional measures of attitudes toward the elderly (ELDER) and attitudes towards independence (INDEP). For each question below, specify an appropriate MODEL C and MODEL A for answering the question. For each MODEL C/A pair, specify the null hypothesis being tested.

1. Hmong students who are more acculturated are more likely to experience intergenerational conflict.
2. Do boys experience greater intergenerational conflict than do girls?
3. Is the typical level of intergenerational conflict significantly different from 10?
4. Are attitudes toward the elderly useful predictors of intergenerational conflict?
5. Is it useful to make predictions of intergenerational conflict conditional on attitudes toward the elderly if predictions are already conditional on attitudes toward independence?
6. Relative to the simple model, is it useful to make predictions of intergenerational conflict conditional jointly on attitudes toward the elderly and attitudes toward independence?

Problem 10.1 A researcher is interested in the relationship between the number of vehicles on an expressway and the average speed of the vehicles. He takes 16 random samples throughout the day and finds that traffic volumes range from 5.5 (thousands) to 9.9 (thousands) and that average MPH ranges from 2 to 60. The mean number of vehicles is 7.5 (thousands). He fits a quadratic equation to his data and obtains the following prediction equation:

$$\widehat{MPH}_i = 47.9 - 12.4VDEV_i - 3.1VDEV_i^2$$

$VDEV_i$ represents the deviation of the number of vehicles (in units of 1000) from the mean number of vehicles across the 16 samples. All the coefficients are reliably different from zero ($p < .01$).

1. Interpret each coefficient in substantive terms.
2. It is often dangerous to use an equation derived from empirical data to make predictions beyond the ranges of the data. Given that the average speed for 5.5 (thousands) vehicles was 60 mph, does the predicted average speed for 4.0 (thousands) vehicles make sense?
3. To the nearest thousand vehicles, for what number of vehicles does the equation predict that traffic will come to a standstill?

Problem 10.2 A political scientist is interested in factors influencing judgments of political candidates. To explore these issues, he uses some national survey data collected from a randomly drawn sample of 989 voting age citizens. Data on each of the following five variables are available from each of these survey respondents:

CAND The respondent's judgment of the liberalness/conservativeness of a particular candidate. Respondents make their judgments of the candidate on a seven point scale, with 1 defined as "very conservative" and 7 defined as "very liberal."

SELF Respondent's judgment of his or her own liberalness/conservativeness on the same seven point scale as for CAND.

LIKE Respondent's judgment of liking for the candidate. Judgments are on a 100 point scale with 0 indicating the respondent very much does not like the candidate and 100 indicating the respondent very much likes the candidate.

TRUST Respondent's judgment of the candidate's trustworthiness on a seven-point scale where 1 indicates "very untrustworthy" and 7 indicates "very trustworthy."

KNOW A composite measure of the respondent's political knowledge, ranging from 0 to 10, with a score of 10 indicating that the respondent is very knowledgeable about political issues and a score of 0 indicating that the respondent knows nothing about politics.

Based on these data, the researcher wishes to conduct analyses to answer each of the following questions. For each question, indicate the compact and augmented models that should be compared to answer the question and state the null hypothesis being tested. In addition, indicate the degrees of freedom associated with the F^* that would be used to evaluate each hypothesis. Some of these questions may require that you construct new variables out of the five that are measured.

1. Are judgments of liking for the candidate predictable from the respondent's self judgment of liberalness/conservativeness?

2. Are judgments of the candidate's trustworthiness related to candidate evaluation even when controlling for the respondent's own political persuasion?

3. Are judgments of how the candidate is evaluated predictable from trustworthiness judgments less strongly among politically knowledgeable respondents?

4. Do those respondents whose political views are relatively extreme, in either a liberal or conservative direction, like the candidate less well than those who are more moderate, even controlling for the fact that liberals prefer the candidate to those who are more conservative? (Hint: Draw a graph of this hypothesis.)

5. On average, do respondents assimilate judgments of the candidate's position to their own position? That is, the more liberal respondents are, the more they judge the candidate to be liberal. The more conservative respondents are, the more conservative they judge the candidate to be.

6. Does the extent to which respondents assimilate judgments of the candidate's position to their own depend on the degree to which they like or dislike the candidate? Those who relatively like the candidate assimilate the candidate's position to their own more strongly than do those who like the candidate less well.

7. Is liking for the candidate predictable from knowledge of the absolute difference between the respondent's judgment of his or her own political position and his or her judgment of the candidate's political position?

8. Do those who know nothing about politics have perfectly neutral evaluations of the candidate on average (i.e., give a LIKE rating of 50). (Provide the most powerful test of this hypothesis.)

Problem 11.1 An experimental psychologist measures pain sensitivity in rats randomly assigned to three treatment groups. One group is a control group. A second group receives a behavioral treatment known to induce "learned helplessness," a state in which rats have decreased pain sensitivity. A third group receives the same behavioral treatment but also is administered Drug A which is an antagonist of the chemical C, which is suspected of producing the reduced pain sensitivity. If pain sensitivity is not reduced in the drug group then it suggests that the behavioral treatment causes the rats to produce chemical C in greater than normal quantities. Use the following data to decide whether the behavior group has lower pain sensitivity than the control and drug groups and whether the drug group differs from the control group. The standard deviation $s = 3.91$ and is calculated from all scores without regard to group. Higher scores indicate greater sensitivity to pain.

	Control	Behavioral	Drug
Mean	13.2	6.7	10.9
N	10	9	10

Surprisingly, there is adequate information above to complete all entries in a one-way ANOVA source table. Do so. Write a brief paragraph summarizing your conclusions.

Problem 11.2 A drug company wishes to test the side effects of a new drug. They used five groups: A control group which received no medication (C1), a control group which received an inert placebo (C2), a treatment group which received the regular formulation of Drug A (A1), another treatment group which received a buffered version of Drug A (A2), and a final treatment group which received a different Drug B which is presumed to have the same therapeutic effects as Drug A (B). Generate a set of contrast codes for groups C1, C2, A1, A2, and B to answer these questions:

1. Do the drug groups differ from the control groups?
2. Do the two control groups differ from each other?
3. Do the Drug A groups differ from the Drug B group?
4. Do the two formulations of Drug A differ from each other?

Verify that all of your contrast codes are orthogonal to each other.

Problem 11.3 An institutional researcher is interested in how satisfaction with college varies as a function of the amount of time spent in college. She gathers data from 50 freshmen, 50 sophomores, 50 juniors, and 50 seniors at the college where she is employed. Satisfaction is measured by asking students for a rating on a 7 point scale, where 1 indicates very dissatisfied with college and 7 indicates very satisfied with college. The following are the means and standard deviations for each of the four samples:

	Freshmen	Sophomores	Juniors	Seniors
Mean	5.4	4.9	4.5	5.2
S.D.	2.1	1.8	1.7	2.2

1. Generate a set of contrast codes that examine the linear, quadratic, and cubic effects of year in college on satisfaction ratings.
2. Specify the parameter estimates that would result if satisfaction ratings were regressed on the three contrast-coded predictors you defined.
3. What is the value of PRE and F^* for testing the reliability of the quadratic trend in these satisfaction data?

Problem 12.1 A decision researcher is interested in how different choice strategies affect memory for the information used to make the choice. Subjects are told that they will be asked to choose a car from six different hypothetical cars. Each of these six cars will be described in terms of six different attributes. The subjects are told that after they have seen all 36 pieces of information (i.e., where each of the six cars stands on each of the six attributes), they will be asked to make a choice among the cars.

Subjects are randomly assigned to one of four conditions. These conditions differ in how the 36 pieces of information are presented. In one condition, subjects are shown all of the information a single time and the information is organized by car, i.e., they get all six pieces of information about one car before they get any information about the next car. In a second condition, subjects are shown the information a single time and the information is organized by attribute, i.e., they get information about where all six cars stand on a given attribute before they get information about the next attribute. In the third condition, they are exposed to the 36 pieces of information twice and information is organized by car. Finally, in the fourth condition, subjects are exposed to the 36 pieces of information twice and information is organized by attribute.

Following the exposure to the information, subjects are given a cued recall task. They are given the names of the six cars and asked to recall as many of their attributes as they can. The dependent variable is the number of correctly recalled pieces of information (maximum = 36). There are eight subjects in each condition. The following condition means and variances summarize the resulting data:

Conditions	Mean	Variance
Car Organization One Exposure	12	10.5
Attribute Organization One Exposure	25	13.2
Car Organization Two Exposures	20	12.7
Attribute Organization Two Exposures	28	12.5

Conduct a one-way analysis of variance on these data to determine whether memory differs as a function of condition. A particular theory posits that memory ought to improve, on average, from condition to condition in the order in which the conditions are listed above. That is, worst memory is expected with car organization/one exposure and best with attribute organization/two exposures. Test that hypothesis using a complete set of orthogonal contrast codes. Make sure you specify the set of contrast codes you use, the resulting augmented model, and the full source table, including the test of each of the contrasts.

Problem 12.2 Derive a new set of contrasts that permit a two-way analysis of variance of the data in Problem 12.1, treating one factor as organization and the second factor as number of exposures. Conduct the two-way analysis of variance, providing a complete source table and an interpretation of each of the tests included in the table.

Problem 13.1 As a statistical expert, you have been approached by a student in the athletic department who conducted a study comparing two training methods for runners. Five runners were trained under method A, and five under method B. The student used a contrast-coded variable X_1, to represent training method, coding method A as 1 and method B as -1. When the student regressed posttest running times on the contrast-coded predictor variable, she was disappointed to find a value of F^* that did not quite reach statistical significance using $\alpha = .05$ level. The results from this initial regression run are reproduced as the first regression model below.

You find out that the student also has pretest running times (PRET), so you suggest that she run two additional regression models, one including both the pretest and X_1 as predictors and one including PRET, X_1, and their product (PRETX$_1$). These regression results are also given below.

Based on these regression models, answer the following questions:

1. What are the mean posttest running times for method A and for method B?

2. The regression coefficient for X1 in the first equation equals 2.0. In the second equation, this coefficient equals 6.0. In the final equation it equals 22.0. Interpret each one of these coefficients. Why do they differ from each other? Which one would you prefer if you wanted to get an estimate of the difference in the posttest due to training method?

3. Assuming the grand mean on the pretest equals 52.5, what are the pretest means for runners in method A and for runners in method B?

4. Interpret each of the coefficients in the final model that includes the interaction. (Obviously you need not interpret the coefficient for X_1 since you already did that in 2 above.) On the basis of this final model, what substantive conclusions should be drawn by the student who has sought your advice?

MODEL 1

Dep variable: POST

SOURCE	DF	SS	MS	F	PROB>F
MODEL	1	40.0	40.0	4.0	.08
ERROR	8	80.0	10.0		
TOTAL	9	120.0			

PARAMETER ESTIMATES

VARIABLE	PARAMETER ESTIMATE	T	PROB>T
INTERCEPT	40.00	40.0	.000
X1	2.0	2.0	.081

MODEL 2

Dep variable: POST

SOURCE	DF	SS	MS	F	PROB>F
MODEL	2	116.8	58.4	127.7	.00
ERROR	7	3.2	.5		
TOTAL	9	120.0			

PARAMETER ESTIMATES

VARIABLE	PARAMETER ESTIMATE	T	PROB>T
INTERCEPT	−44.00	6.8	.000
X1	6.00	16.0	.000
PRET	1.6	13.0	.000

MODEL 3

Dep variable: POST

SOURCE	DF	SS	MS	F	PROB>F
MODEL	3	119.2	39.7	298.0	.00
ERROR	6	.8	.1		
TOTAL	9	120.0			

PARAMETER ESTIMATES

VARIABLE	PARAMETER ESTIMATE	T	PROB>T
INTERCEPT	−50.0	13.2	.000
X1	22.0	5.8	.001
PRET	1.7	24.0	.000
PRETX1	−.3	4.2	.005

Problem 14.1 Four researchers are interested in exploring the same phenomenon: The ability of proofreaders to detect typographical errors. There are two factors that they believe affect this ability. The first is whether the text is read aloud or silently. The second is whether the text is read backward or forward.

The first researcher designs a study in which each subject reads one text backward and one text forward. Each subject reads both texts either aloud or silently.

The second researcher designs a study in which each subject reads four texts, one aloud and backward, one aloud and forward, one silently and backward, and one silently and forward.

The third researcher designs a study in which each subject only reads one text. Some subjects read their text silently; others read it aloud. Some subjects read it backward; others read it forward.

The fourth researcher designs a study in which each subject reads one text aloud and one text silently. Each subject reads both texts either forward or backward.

For each of these designs, write the rows of the full source table for the appropriate analysis of variance. Obviously, you can't fill in the values of the sums of squares and mean squares. Assume, however, that each researcher runs a total of 32 subjects and that there are equal n's in the various experimental conditions. Indicate the degrees of freedom for all rows in each source table.

Problem 14.2 Two drugs designed to alleviate pain are to be tested. All subjects are hospital patients experiencing chronic pain. Subjects are assigned to one of three drug conditions. Either they receive Drug A, or they receive Drug B, or they receive a Placebo. After taking the drug or placebo to which they were assigned, they give pain ratings at three times, each spaced one hour apart. Thus, each subject gives a pain rating one hour after getting the drug or placebo, two hours after, and finally three hours after. Pain ratings are done on 7 point scales, with higher numbers indicating more pain. The following are the resulting data:

		Hour		
Drug	*Subj*	*1*	*2*	*3*
A	1	2	3	5
	2	3	3	6
	3	1	3	4

(continued)

Drug	Subj	Hour		
		1	2	3
B	4	5	3	3
	5	4	3	2
	6	6	4	3
Placebo	7	5	7	7
	8	6	6	6
	9	4	6	7

Do a full analysis on these data to answer the following questions: Is there a drug versus placebo difference? Does drug A differ from drug B? Do subjects on average show more or less pain over time? Is there any evidence to suggest that the drugs have different effects over time?

Problem 14.3   An environmental engineer is interested in determining whether house exposure reliably affects heating bills. He believes that houses exposed to the north ought to have higher heating bills than houses with a southern exposure. To test this hypothesis he randomly selects two houses from each of five city blocks, one house in each block having a northern exposure and one house in each block having a southern exposure. For each of the resulting 10 houses, he consults the public utility's records for the cost of their December heating bill. The values of these heating bills are as follows:

Exposure	Block				
	1	2	3	4	5
Northern	66	100	78	87	90
Southern	59	103	66	80	97

1. Analyze these data to see if exposure does affect heating bills as the engineer predicted. Present a full source table for this analysis and write a sentence or two to summarize the results.

2. Calculate the intraclass correlation for these data, estimating the degree of nonindependence due to block. From this correlation, indicate whether an analysis that ignored the possible nonindependence in these data would have produced too large an F^* or too small an F^*.

Problem 14.4   A researcher is interested in replicating a result of Park and Rothbart (1982). They found that one tends to see outgroup members as relatively more homogeneous or similar to each other than one sees ingroup members. This result has come to be known as the outgroup homogeneity effect.

   Our researcher gathers data from 24 subjects, half of them black and half of them white. Crossed with subject's race is whether or not they come from a segregated or integrated neighborhood. Thus, there are six black subjects from an integrated neighborhood, six white subjects from an integrated neighborhood, six black subjects from a segregated neighborhood, and six white subjects from a segregated neighborhood. The researcher is interested in examining whether whites will see whites as less homogeneous than they see blacks and whether blacks will see blacks as less homogeneous than they see whites. In addition, she wonders whether the magnitude of this outgroup homogeneity effect depends on whether one has had a lot of contact with outgroup members or only a little contact (i.e., whether it depends on having lived in a segregated versus integrated neighborhood).

   She asks each subject to estimate the percentage of blacks who are very athletic, somewhat athletic, somewhat unathletic, and very unathletic. She asks subjects to provide the same percentage estimates for whites. From these percentage estimates she computes for each subject how variable that subject sees blacks along this dimension and how variable the subject sees whites along this dimension. In the data of Exhibit B.2, the first measure is labeled BSD (for black standard deviation) and the second is labeled WSD (for white standard deviation). Subject's own race is indicated by w or b and whether they come from an integrated or segregated neighborhood is indicated by s or i. Using a regression package available to you, analyze these data to determine whether there is an outgroup homogeneity effect and whether its magnitude depends on the type of neighborhood one comes from. (Hint: The outgroup homogeneity effect should be considered as the interaction between subject's own race and the within-subject factor of racial group.) Provide a complete source table for these data and summarize the substantive conclusions.

Problem 15.1   A political pollster is interested in differences in how three candidates are evaluated. He asks each of 12 respondents to evaluate three different political candidates on a 1 to 7 scale where 1 indicates disliking and 7 indicates liking. Since each respondent rates all three

EXHIBIT B.2 ▶

Data for Problem 14.4

S's Race	Neighborhood	WSD	BSD
w	s	3.2	2.8
w	s	2.8	3.0
w	s	3.6	3.3
w	s	2.8	2.7
w	s	4.6	4.2
w	s	3.7	3.2
b	s	3.2	3.5
b	s	3.7	3.9
b	s	2.6	2.6
b	s	4.3	4.6
b	s	2.8	2.7
b	s	3.2	3.9
w	i	2.8	2.7
w	i	3.4	3.2
w	i	4.2	4.1
w	i	3.7	3.7
w	i	2.9	2.9
w	i	3.6	3.8
b	i	2.6	2.7
b	i	2.3	2.5
b	i	3.4	3.2
b	i	2.9	3.2
b	i	3.6	3.5
b	i	2.7	2.6

candidates, the pollster is worried that the order in which they are rated may affect the ratings given. Hence, he decides to use a latin square design to unconfound order and candidate. He uses the following latin square design, where the letter in the cells refer to which candidate is rated and the columns indicate the order in which each is rated:

Sequence	Order		
	1	2	3
1	A	B	C
2	B	C	A
3	C	A	B

Four respondents are randomly assigned to each of the three sequences. The resulting data are given in Exhibit B.3. Using a regression procedure available to you, analyze these data as a function of the between-subject variable of sequence and the within-subject variables of candidate and order. You will need to first treat candidate as the within-subject variable of interest, regressing the within-subject contrasts that code candidate on between-subject contrasts that code sequence. Then you need to rearrange the data to treat order as the within-subject variable. Then, assuming you are willing to make the appropriate assumptions, you can combine the pooled terms into a single composite source table.

EXHIBIT B.3 ▶

Data for Problem 15.1

	Candidates		
Respondent	A	B	C
Sequence 1			
1	6	6	4
2	7	5	1
3	5	2	5
4	4	1	6
Sequence 2			
5	5	7	4
6	5	6	3
7	3	3	6
8	4	3	7
Sequence 3			
9	5	4	4
10	6	5	5
11	5	1	7
12	4	1	7

Problem 15.2   To establish comparative gas consumption figures for three types of automobiles, each of four test drivers drives each of the three cars for 20 miles. The mileage per gallon of each car when driven by each driver is recorded. These data are given below:

Driver	Car A	Car B	Car C
1	20	26	18
2	24	27	23
3	21	24	18
4	18	27	20

Analyze these data to determine whether the mean differences between the three cars are reliable. Use the procedures of Chapter 14 to remove nonindependence due to driver.

In addition to miles per gallon, the average speed at which each car was driven by each driver was recorded. These speeds (miles per hour) are given below:

Driver	Car A	Car B	Car C
1	45	48	55
2	42	45	52
3	44	52	55
4	52	53	57

Using these data, reanalyze the mileage per gallon data to determine whether the differences among the cars are due in part to differences among the cars in the speed at which they are driven. In other words, we want to know whether the cars would differ in their mileage when we control statistically for differences among them in the speed at which they were driven.

B.1

Answers to Selected Problems

Answer 5.1 Appropriate models are

MODEL C: $Y_i = 5 + \varepsilon_i$

MODEL A: $Y_i = \beta_0 + \varepsilon_i$

For MODEL A the best estimate of β_0 would be $b_0 = \overline{Y} = 6.9$. The necessary SSE calculations are as follows:

Y_i	MODEL C			MODEL A		
	$\hat{Y}$	e_i	e_i^2	$\hat{Y}$	e_i	e_i^2
4	5	−1	1	6.9	−2.9	8.41
5	5	0	0	6.9	−1.9	3.61
6	5	1	1	6.9	−.9	.81
9	5	4	16	6.9	2.1	4.41
10	5	5	25	6.9	3.1	9.61
3	5	−2	4	6.9	−3.9	5.21
6	5	1	1	6.9	−.9	.81
9	5	4	16	6.9	2.1	4.41
10	5	5	25	6.9	3.1	9.61
7	5	2	4	6.9	.1	.01
SSE			93			56.90

Source	SS	df	MS	F*	PRE	p
Reduced	36.1	1	36.1	5.71	.388	<.05
Error Model A	56.9	9	6.3			
Total	93	10				

Since both F^* and PRE exceed their respective critical values, we reject model C in favor of model A. We therefore conclude that subjects' scores reliably depart from the value of 5, predicted by a model suggesting that subjects are unable to discriminate the presence or absence of caffeine. We therefore conclude that subjects are able to perform at better than chance levels.

Answer 5.2 The appropriate models are

MODEL C: $Y_i = 0 + \varepsilon_i$

MODEL A: $Y_i = \beta_0 + \varepsilon_i$

The best estimate of β_0 would be $b_0 = \overline{Y} = -3.71$. The necessary sum of squares are:

SSE(C) = 93462

SSE(A) = 91852.1

Source	SS	df	MS	F*	PRE	p
Reduced	1,609.9	1	1,609.9	2.03	.017	>.05
Error (A)	91,852.1	116	791.8			
Total	93,462	117				

Based on the fact that F^* and PRE do not exceed their respective critical values, we are unable to reject MODEL C in favor of MODEL A. Substantively, this means that we cannot conclude that there has been a change in attitudes during the four years of college based on the present data.

Answer 10.2

1. MODEL A: $\text{LIKE}_i = \beta_0 + \beta_1\text{SELF}_i + \varepsilon_i$

    MODEL C: $\text{LIKE}_i = \beta_0 + \varepsilon_i$

    $F^*_{1,987}$ $H_0: \beta_1 = 0$

2. MODEL A: $\text{LIKE}_i = \beta_0 + \beta_1\text{SELF}_i + \beta_2\text{TRUST}_i + \varepsilon_i$

    MODEL C: $\text{LIKE}_i = \beta_0 + \beta_1\text{SELF}_i + \varepsilon_i$

    $F^*_{1,986}$ $H_0: \beta_2 = 0$

3. MODEL A: $\text{LIKE}_i = \beta_0 + \beta_1\text{TRUST}_i + \beta_2\text{KNOW}_i$
    $$+ \beta_3(\text{TRUST}_i)(\text{KNOW}_i) + \varepsilon_i$$

    MODEL C: $\text{LIKE}_i = \beta_0 + \beta_1\text{TRUST}_i + \beta_2\text{KNOW}_i + \varepsilon_i$

    $F^*_{1,985}$ $H_0: \beta_3 = 0$

4. MODEL A: $\text{LIKE}_i = \beta_0 + \beta_1\text{SELF}_i + \beta_2\text{SELF}_i^2 + \varepsilon_i$

    MODEL C: $\text{LIKE}_i = \beta_0 + \beta_1\text{SELF}_i + \varepsilon_i$

    $F^*_{1,986}$ $H_0: \beta_2 = 0$

5. MODEL A: $\text{CAND}_i = \beta_0 + \beta_1\text{SELF}_i + \varepsilon_i$

    MODEL C: $\text{CAND}_i = \beta_0 + \varepsilon_i$

    $F^*_{1,987}$ $H_0: \beta_1 = 0$

6. MODEL A: $\text{CAND}_i = \beta_0 + \beta_1\text{SELF}_i + \beta_2\text{LIKE}_i$
    $$+ \beta_3(\text{SELF}_i)(\text{LIKE}_i) + \varepsilon_i$$

    MODEL C: $\text{CAND}_i = \beta_0 + \beta_1\text{SELF}_i + \beta_2\text{LIKE}_i + \varepsilon_i$

    $F^*_{1,985}$ $H_0: \beta_3 = 0$

7. Create a new variable $\text{DIFF}_i = |\text{SELF}_i - \text{CAND}_i|$.

    MODEL A: $\text{LIKE}_i = \beta_0 + \beta_1\text{DIFF}_i + \varepsilon_i$

    MODEL C: $\text{LIKE}_i = \beta_0 + \varepsilon_i$

    $F^*_{1,987}$ $H_0: \beta_1 = 0$

Answer 11.1 There are two keys to solving this problem. First, note that the standard deviation $s = 3.91$ so that the variance $s^2 = 3.91^2 = 15.29$. Then remember that the variance is the MSE for the simple model. Since SSE = MSE/$(n - PC)$, it is easy to calculate SSE = $(15.29)28 = 428.12$ which is SSE(C), or SST in the traditional one-way table. Second, generate appropriate contrast codes to answer the two questions (e.g., $[1 -2\ \ 1]$ and $[-1\,0\,1]$) and use the contrast-code formulas for calculating b_j and SSR. It is then easy to get SSE(A) by subtraction.

Source	SS	df	MS	F	PRE	p
B vs. C, D	177.66	1	177.66	20.62	.41	<.001
C vs. D	26.45	1	26.45	3.07	.06	.06
Error	224.01	26	8.62			
Total	428.12	28	15.29			

The pain sensitivity of the behavior treatment group is reliably different from that of the control and drug treatment groups (Means 6.7 versus 12.1, $F^*_{1,26} = 20.6$, PRE = .41, $p < .001$). This suggests that the drug counteracted the behavioral effects on pain sensitivity. The pain sensitivity of the drug treatment group is not reliably different from the control group (Means 10.9 versus 13.2, $F^*_{1,26} = 3.07$, PRE = .06). Thus, with the additional drug treatment, pain sensitivity returned almost to the level of the control group. However, as always caution must be exercised in accepting the null hypothesis, especially in this case because the difference between the drug and control groups is almost significant ($p < .10$).

Answer 13.1

1. From the first model, substituting values of 1 and -1 for X_1, we get a posttest mean of 42 for method A and a mean of 38 for method B.
2. **2.00**: Half the difference in the posttest means between method A and method B.

   6.00: Half the difference in the adjusted posttest mean, adjusting for or removing differences on the pretest.

22.0: Half the difference on the posttest between method A and method B when pretest equals zero.

These values differ from each other because they are estimating different things. We prefer the value of 6.00, because apparently runners were not randomly assigned to method and thus it makes sense to control for pretest differences in estimating the effect of method. Other choices could be supported, however.

3. The value of the regression coefficient for the X_1 contrast codes equals 6.0 when the pretest covariate is included. We know that this regression coefficient equals the regression coefficient for X_1 in the model that does not include the pretest (i.e., 2.0) adjusted for the difference between the two methods on their pretest means. In other words,

$$6.0 = 2.0 - 1.6\left(\frac{\text{PRET}_A - \text{PRET}_B}{2}\right)$$

From this equation, we can solve for $\text{PRET}_A - \text{PRET}_B$. It equals -5.0. Since the grand mean on the pretest equals 52.5, the mean pretest score for method A equals 50 and the mean pretest score for method B equals 55.

4. Intercept: The predicted value on the posttest for a runner who had a time of zero on the pretest on average collapsing across the two training methods.

Coefficient for X_1: See above.

Coefficient for PRET: As pretest times go up by one unit, our prediction of posttest times changes by 1.7 units when $X_1 = 0$ (or on average collapsing across the two training methods).

Coefficient for PRETX1: As Pretest times increase by one unit, the difference between the predicted posttest times for the two training methods decreases by twice the value of this regression coefficient.

The substantive conclusion that ought to be reached based on this model is that the effect of training methods, while reliable on average across runners (based on model 2) tends to be smaller with runners who had higher pretest times than with runners who had lower pretest times.

Answer 14.1   We will use the label DIR to refer to the forward versus backward factor and the label ALO to refer to the aloud versus silent factor.

Researcher 1: Source	df
Between Ss	
ALO	1
Error between	30
Total between	31
Within Ss	
DIR	1
DIR by ALO	1
DIR by Ss within ALO	30
Total within	32
Total	63

Researcher 2: Source	df
Between Ss	
Total between	31
Within Ss	
DIR	1
DIR by Ss	31
ALO	1
ALO by Ss	31
DIR by ALO	1
DIR by ALO by Ss	31
Total within	96
Total	127

Researcher 3: Source	df
Between Ss	
DIR	1
ALO	1
DIR by ALO	1
Error between	28
Total between	31

Researcher 4: Source	df
Between Ss	
DIR	1
Error between	30
Total between	31
Within Ss	
ALO	1
ALO by DIR	1
ALO by Ss within DIR	30
Total within	32
Total	63

Answer 14.2 The following source table results from this analysis:

Source	SS	df	MS	F*
Between Ss				
A+B vs. Placebo	37.50	1	37.50	37.50
A vs. B	.50	1	.50	.50
Error between	6.00	6	1.00	
Total between	44.00	8		
Within Ss				
Linear Time	2.72	1	2.72	6.13
Linear by (A+B vs. Placebo)	1.78	1	1.78	4.00
Linear by A vs. B	21.33	1	21.33	48.00
Linear by Ss within Drug	2.67	6	.44	
Quadratic Time	.17	1	.17	.50
Quad by (A+B vs. Placebo)	1.33	1	1.33	4.00
Quad by A vs. B	0	1	0	0
Quad by Ss within Drug	2.00	6	.33	
Total Within	32.00	18		

This analysis is consistent with the following conclusions:

1. There is a reliable Drug effect, with Drugs A and B producing lower scores on the dependent variable than the Placebo.

2. There is a linear trend in the dependent variable over time, with lower scores during the first hour on average than during the last one.

3. The linear trend over time is, however, dependent on which drug one took. For Drug A the linear trend results in higher scores at hour 3 than at hour 1. For Drug B the linear trend results in lower scores at hour 3 than at hour 1.

No other effects are reliable.

Answer 15.1 First, we analyze the data as they are arranged in the problem, treating candidate as the within-subject variable of interest. The two within-subject candidate contrasts compare candidates A with C and compare candidate B with the average of A and C. The between-subject variable of sequence defines two contrast codes comparing sequence 3 with 1 and sequence 2 with the average of sequences 1 and 3. The following source table results:

Source	SS	df	MS	F*
Between Ss				
Sequence 1	.17	1	.17	.15
Sequence 2	.50	1	.50	.45
Error between	10.35	9	1.15	
Within Ss				
Candidate 1	.00	1	.00	.00
C1 × S1	5.08	1	5.08	1.33
C1 × S2	1.69	1	1.69	.44
C1 × Ss within Seq.	34.35	9	3.82	
Candidate 2	12.60	1	12.60	2.93
C2 × S1	2.54	1	2.54	.59
C2 × S2	7.62	1	7.62	1.77
C2 × Ss within Seq.	38.72	9	4.30	
Pooled Candidate	12.60	2	6.30	1.55
Pooled C × S	16.93	4	4.23	1.04
Pooled Error	73.07	18	4.06	

When Order is treated as the within-subject variable of interest, the following source table results:

Source	SS	df	MS	F*
Between Ss				
Sequence 1	.17	1	.17	.15
Sequence 2	.50	1	.50	.45
Error between	10.35	9	1.15	

(continued)

Within Ss				
Order 1	16.73	1	16.73	3.95
O1 × S1	2.26	1	2.26	.53
O1 × S2	4.10	1	4.10	.97
O1 × Ss within Seq.	38.12	9	4.24	
Order 2	.00	1	.00	.00
O2 × S1	5.38	1	5.38	1.59
O2 × S2	1.01	1	1.01	.26
O2 × Ss within Seq.	34.95	9	3.88	
Pooled Order	16.73	2	8.37	2.06
Pooled O × S	12.75	4	3.19	.78
Pooled Error	73.07	18	4.06	

We can combine the two pooled sections of these source tables into one, making the assumptions that part of the order by sequence interaction is really due to candidate and that part of the candidate by sequence interaction is really due to order.

Source	SS	df	MS	F*
Pooled Candidate	12.60	2	6.30	1.55
Pooled Order	16.73	2	8.37	2.06
Pooled Residual				
C × S or O × S	.18	2	.09	
Pooled Error	73.07	18	4.06	

APPENDIX C

Critical Value and Power Tables

The entries in all tables were generated using functions in the SAS statistical programming language. The program code for each table is presented at the end of this appendix. These codes can be easily modified to produce tables for other values of α, PA − PC, and n − PA.

EXHIBIT C.1   Critical Values of PRE for PA − PC = 1

n − PA	.5	.2	.1	.05	α .025	.01	.005	.001
1	.500	.905	.976	.994	.998	1.000	1.000	1.000
2	.250	.640	.810	.902	.951	.980	.990	.998
3	.163	.472	.649	.771	.853	.919	.949	.982
4	.121	.370	.532	.658	.753	.841	.887	.949
5	.096	.303	.448	.569	.667	.765	.820	.904
6	.079	.257	.386	.499	.595	.696	.756	.855
7	.067	.222	.339	.444	.536	.636	.699	.807
8	.059	.196	.302	.399	.486	.585	.647	.761
9	.052	.175	.272	.362	.445	.540	.602	.717
10	.047	.158	.247	.332	.410	.501	.562	.678
11	.042	.145	.227	.306	.379	.467	.526	.642
12	.039	.133	.209	.283	.353	.437	.495	.608
13	.036	.123	.194	.264	.330	.411	.467	.578
14	.033	.114	.181	.247	.310	.388	.441	.550
15	.031	.107	.170	.232	.292	.367	.419	.525
16	.029	.100	.160	.219	.277	.348	.398	.502
17	.027	.095	.151	.208	.262	.331	.379	.480
18	.026	.090	.143	.197	.249	.315	.362	.461
19	.024	.085	.136	.187	.238	.301	.346	.443
20	.023	.081	.129	.179	.227	.288	.332	.426
22	.021	.074	.118	.164	.208	.265	.307	.395
24	.019	.067	.109	.151	.192	.246	.285	.369
26	.018	.062	.101	.140	.179	.229	.266	.346
28	.016	.058	.094	.130	.167	.214	.249	.325
30	.015	.054	.088	.122	.157	.201	.234	.307
35	.013	.046	.075	.105	.135	.175	.204	.269
40	.011	.041	.066	.093	.119	.155	.181	.240
45	.010	.036	.059	.083	.107	.138	.162	.216
50	.009	.033	.053	.075	.096	.125	.147	.196
55	.008	.030	.048	.068	.088	.115	.135	.180
60	.008	.027	.044	.063	.081	.106	.124	.166
80	.006	.020	.033	.047	.061	.080	.094	.127
100	.005	.016	.027	.038	.049	.065	.076	.103
150	.003	.011	.018	.025	.033	.043	.051	.070
200	.002	.008	.013	.019	.025	.033	.039	.053
500	.001	.003	.005	.008	.010	.013	.016	.021

Generated using SAS function BETAINV.

EXHIBIT C.2   Critical Values of PRE for $\alpha = .05$

	PA – PC								
n – PA	1	2	3	4	5	6	7	8	9
1	.994	.997	.998	.999	.999	.999	.999	.999	1.000
2	.902	.950	.966	.975	.980	.983	.985	.987	.989
3	.771	.864	.903	.924	.938	.947	.954	.959	.964
4	.658	.776	.832	.865	.887	.902	.914	.924	.931
5	.569	.698	.764	.806	.835	.856	.872	.885	.896
6	.499	.632	.704	.751	.785	.811	.831	.847	.860
7	.444	.575	.651	.702	.739	.768	.791	.810	.825
8	.399	.527	.604	.657	.697	.729	.754	.775	.792
9	.362	.486	.563	.618	.659	.692	.719	.742	.761
10	.332	.451	.527	.582	.624	.659	.687	.711	.731
11	.306	.420	.495	.550	.593	.628	.657	.682	.703
12	.283	.393	.466	.521	.564	.600	.630	.655	.677
13	.264	.369	.440	.494	.538	.574	.604	.630	.653
14	.247	.348	.417	.471	.514	.550	.580	.607	.630
15	.232	.329	.397	.449	.492	.527	.558	.585	.608
16	.219	.312	.378	.429	.471	.507	.538	.564	.588
17	.208	.297	.361	.411	.452	.488	.518	.545	.569
18	.197	.283	.345	.394	.435	.470	.501	.527	.551
19	.187	.270	.331	.379	.419	.454	.484	.510	.534
20	.179	.259	.317	.364	.404	.438	.468	.495	.518
22	.164	.238	.294	.339	.377	.410	.439	.466	.489
24	.151	.221	.273	.316	.353	.385	.414	.440	.463
26	.140	.206	.256	.297	.332	.363	.391	.417	.440
28	.130	.193	.240	.279	.314	.344	.371	.396	.418
30	.122	.181	.226	.264	.297	.326	.353	.377	.399
35	.105	.157	.198	.232	.262	.289	.314	.336	.357
40	.093	.139	.176	.207	.234	.259	.282	.304	.323
45	.083	.125	.158	.186	.212	.235	.257	.277	.295
50	.075	.113	.143	.170	.194	.215	.235	.254	.272
55	.068	.103	.131	.156	.178	.198	.217	.235	.252
60	.063	.095	.121	.144	.165	.184	.202	.219	.234
80	.047	.072	.093	.111	.127	.142	.157	.171	.184
100	.038	.058	.075	.090	.103	.116	.128	.140	.151
150	.025	.039	.051	.061	.070	.080	.088	.096	.104
200	.019	.030	.038	.046	.053	.060	.067	.074	.080
500	.008	.012	.015	.019	.022	.025	.028	.030	.033

Generated using SAS function BETAINV.

EXHIBIT C.2   (Continued)

n − PA					PA − PC				
	10	12	15	20	25	30	40	60	120
1	1.000	1.000	1.000	1.000	1.000	1.000	1.000	1.000	1.000
2	.990	.991	.993	.995	.996	.997	.997	.998	.999
3	.967	.972	.978	.983	.986	.989	.991	.994	.997
4	.937	.947	.956	.967	.973	.977	.983	.988	.994
5	.904	.918	.933	.948	.958	.964	.973	.982	.991
6	.871	.889	.908	.928	.941	.950	.962	.974	.987
7	.839	.860	.883	.908	.924	.935	.950	.966	.982
8	.807	.831	.858	.887	.907	.920	.938	.958	.978
9	.777	.804	.834	.867	.889	.905	.926	.949	.973
10	.749	.778	.810	.847	.872	.890	.914	.940	.969
11	.722	.753	.788	.828	.855	.875	.902	.931	.964
12	.696	.729	.766	.809	.839	.860	.890	.923	.959
13	.673	.706	.745	.791	.823	.846	.878	.914	.954
14	.650	.685	.725	.773	.807	.832	.866	.905	.949
15	.629	.664	.706	.756	.792	.818	.855	.896	.944
16	.609	.645	.688	.740	.777	.804	.843	.888	.939
17	.590	.627	.671	.724	.762	.791	.832	.879	.934
18	.573	.610	.654	.709	.748	.778	.821	.871	.929
19	.556	.593	.638	.694	.735	.766	.810	.862	.924
20	.540	.577	.623	.680	.722	.754	.800	.854	.919
22	.511	.548	.595	.653	.697	.730	.779	.837	.909
24	.484	.522	.568	.628	.673	.708	.759	.822	.899
26	.461	.498	.544	.605	.651	.687	.740	.806	.890
28	.439	.476	.522	.583	.630	.667	.722	.791	.880
30	.419	.456	.502	.563	.610	.648	.705	.777	.871
35	.377	.412	.457	.518	.566	.605	.665	.742	.848
40	.342	.375	.419	.479	.527	.567	.629	.711	.825
45	.313	.345	.387	.446	.493	.533	.596	.681	.804
50	.288	.319	.360	.416	.463	.503	.567	.654	.784
55	.267	.297	.336	.391	.437	.476	.540	.629	.764
60	.249	.277	.315	.368	.413	.452	.515	.605	.746
80	.196	.220	.252	.299	.339	.375	.436	.526	.679
100	.162	.182	.210	.251	.288	.321	.377	.465	.623
150	.112	.127	.148	.180	.208	.235	.282	.360	.515
200	.086	.098	.114	.140	.163	.185	.225	.294	.439
500	.036	.041	.048	.060	.071	.082	.102	.139	.231

Generated using SAS function BETAINV.

EXHIBIT C.3   Critical Values of F for PA − PC = 1

$n - PA$	.5	.2	.1	.05	α .025	.01	.005	.001
1	1.00	9.47	39.86	161.45	647.79	4052.2	16211	405284
2	.67	3.56	8.53	18.51	38.51	98.50	198.50	998.50
3	.59	2.68	5.54	10.13	17.44	34.12	55.55	167.03
4	.55	2.35	4.54	7.71	12.22	21.20	31.33	74.14
5	.53	2.18	4.06	6.61	10.01	16.26	22.78	47.18
6	.51	2.07	3.78	5.99	8.81	13.75	18.63	35.51
7	.51	2.00	3.59	5.59	8.07	12.25	16.24	29.25
8	.50	1.95	3.46	5.32	7.57	11.26	14.69	25.41
9	.49	1.91	3.36	5.12	7.21	10.56	13.61	22.86
10	.49	1.88	3.29	4.96	6.94	10.04	12.83	21.04
11	.49	1.86	3.23	4.84	6.72	9.65	12.23	19.69
12	.48	1.84	3.18	4.75	6.55	9.33	11.75	18.64
13	.48	1.82	3.14	4.67	6.41	9.07	11.37	17.82
14	.48	1.81	3.10	4.60	6.30	8.86	11.06	17.14
15	.48	1.80	3.07	4.54	6.20	8.68	10.80	16.59
16	.48	1.79	3.05	4.49	6.12	8.53	10.58	16.12
17	.47	1.78	3.03	4.45	6.04	8.40	10.38	15.72
18	.47	1.77	3.01	4.41	5.98	8.29	10.22	15.38
19	.47	1.76	2.99	4.38	5.92	8.18	10.07	15.08
20	.47	1.76	2.97	4.35	5.87	8.10	9.94	14.82
22	.47	1.75	2.95	4.30	5.79	7.95	9.73	14.38
24	.47	1.74	2.93	4.26	5.72	7.82	9.55	14.03
26	.47	1.73	2.91	4.23	5.66	7.72	9.41	13.74
28	.47	1.72	2.89	4.20	5.61	7.64	9.28	13.50
30	.47	1.72	2.88	4.17	5.57	7.56	9.18	13.29
35	.46	1.71	2.85	4.12	5.48	7.42	8.98	12.90
40	.46	1.70	2.84	4.08	5.42	7.31	8.83	12.61
45	.46	1.69	2.82	4.06	5.38	7.23	8.71	12.39
50	.46	1.69	2.81	4.03	5.34	7.17	8.63	12.22
55	.46	1.68	2.80	4.02	5.31	7.12	8.55	12.09
60	.46	1.68	2.79	4.00	5.29	7.08	8.49	11.97
80	.46	1.67	2.77	3.96	5.22	6.96	8.33	11.67
100	.46	1.66	2.76	3.94	5.18	6.90	8.24	11.50
150	.46	1.66	2.74	3.90	5.13	6.81	8.12	11.27
200	.46	1.65	2.73	3.89	5.10	6.76	8.06	11.15
500	.46	1.65	2.72	3.86	5.05	6.69	7.95	10.96

Generated using SAS function FINV.

EXHIBIT C.4 Critical Values of F for $\alpha = .05$

$n - PA$	1	2	3	4	PA − PC 5	6	7	8	9
1	161.45	199.50	215.71	224.58	230.16	233.99	236.77	238.88	240.54
2	18.51	19.00	19.16	19.25	19.30	19.33	19.35	19.37	19.38
3	10.13	9.55	9.28	9.12	9.01	8.94	8.89	8.85	8.81
4	7.71	6.94	6.59	6.39	6.26	6.16	6.09	6.04	6.00
5	6.61	5.79	5.41	5.19	5.05	4.95	4.88	4.82	4.77
6	5.99	5.14	4.76	4.53	4.39	4.28	4.21	4.15	4.10
7	5.59	4.74	4.35	4.12	3.97	3.87	3.79	3.73	3.68
8	5.32	4.46	4.07	3.84	3.69	3.58	3.50	3.44	3.39
9	5.12	4.26	3.86	3.63	3.48	3.37	3.29	3.23	3.18
10	4.96	4.10	3.71	3.48	3.33	3.22	3.14	3.07	3.02
11	4.84	3.98	3.59	3.36	3.20	3.09	3.01	2.95	2.90
12	4.75	3.89	3.49	3.26	3.11	3.00	2.91	2.85	2.80
13	4.67	3.81	3.41	3.18	3.03	2.92	2.83	2.77	2.71
14	4.60	3.74	3.34	3.11	2.96	2.85	2.76	2.70	2.65
15	4.54	3.68	3.29	3.06	2.90	2.79	2.71	2.64	2.59
16	4.49	3.63	3.24	3.01	2.85	2.74	2.66	2.59	2.54
17	4.45	3.59	3.20	2.96	2.81	2.70	2.61	2.55	2.49
18	4.41	3.55	3.16	2.93	2.77	2.66	2.58	2.51	2.46
19	4.38	3.52	3.13	2.90	2.74	2.63	2.54	2.48	2.42
20	4.35	3.49	3.10	2.87	2.71	2.60	2.51	2.45	2.39
22	4.30	3.44	3.05	2.82	2.66	2.55	2.46	2.40	2.34
24	4.26	3.40	3.01	2.78	2.62	2.51	2.42	2.36	2.30
26	4.23	3.37	2.98	2.74	2.59	2.47	2.39	2.32	2.27
28	4.20	3.34	2.95	2.71	2.56	2.45	2.36	2.29	2.24
30	4.17	3.32	2.92	2.69	2.53	2.42	2.33	2.27	2.21
35	4.12	3.27	2.87	2.64	2.49	2.37	2.29	2.22	2.16
40	4.08	3.23	2.84	2.61	2.45	2.34	2.25	2.18	2.12
45	4.06	3.20	2.81	2.58	2.42	2.31	2.22	2.15	2.10
50	4.03	3.18	2.79	2.56	2.40	2.29	2.20	2.13	2.07
55	4.02	3.16	2.77	2.54	2.38	2.27	2.18	2.11	2.06
60	4.00	3.15	2.76	2.53	2.37	2.25	2.17	2.10	2.04
80	3.96	3.11	2.72	2.49	2.33	2.21	2.13	2.06	2.00
100	3.94	3.09	2.70	2.46	2.31	2.19	2.10	2.03	1.97
150	3.90	3.06	2.66	2.43	2.27	2.16	2.07	2.00	1.94
200	3.89	3.04	2.65	2.42	2.26	2.14	2.06	1.98	1.93
500	3.86	3.01	2.62	2.39	2.23	2.12	2.03	1.96	1.90

EXHIBIT C.4   (Continued)

					PA − PC				
n − PA	10	12	15	20	25	30	40	60	120
1	241.88	243.91	245.95	248.01	249.26	250.10	251.14	252.20	253.25
2	19.40	19.41	19.43	19.45	19.46	19.46	19.47	19.48	19.49
3	8.79	8.74	8.70	8.66	8.63	8.62	8.59	8.57	8.55
4	5.96	5.91	5.86	5.80	5.77	5.75	5.72	5.69	5.66
5	4.74	4.68	4.62	4.56	4.52	4.50	4.46	4.43	4.40
6	4.06	4.00	3.94	3.87	3.83	3.81	3.77	3.74	3.70
7	3.64	3.57	3.51	3.44	3.40	3.38	3.34	3.30	3.27
8	3.35	3.28	3.22	3.15	3.11	3.08	3.04	3.01	2.97
9	3.14	3.07	3.01	2.94	2.89	2.86	2.83	2.79	2.75
10	2.98	2.91	2.85	2.77	2.73	2.70	2.66	2.62	2.58
11	2.85	2.79	2.72	2.65	2.60	2.57	2.53	2.49	2.45
12	2.75	2.69	2.62	2.54	2.50	2.47	2.43	2.38	2.34
13	2.67	2.60	2.53	2.46	2.41	2.38	2.34	2.30	2.25
14	2.60	2.53	2.46	2.39	2.34	2.31	2.27	2.22	2.18
15	2.54	2.48	2.40	2.33	2.28	2.25	2.20	2.16	2.11
16	2.49	2.42	2.35	2.28	2.23	2.19	2.15	2.11	2.06
17	2.45	2.38	2.31	2.23	2.18	2.15	2.10	2.06	2.01
18	2.41	2.34	2.27	2.19	2.14	2.11	2.06	2.02	1.97
19	2.38	2.31	2.23	2.16	2.11	2.07	2.03	1.98	1.93
20	2.35	2.28	2.20	2.12	2.07	2.04	1.99	1.95	1.90
22	2.30	2.23	2.15	2.07	2.02	1.98	1.94	1.89	1.84
24	2.25	2.18	2.11	2.03	1.97	1.94	1.89	1.84	1.79
26	2.22	2.15	2.07	1.99	1.94	1.90	1.85	1.80	1.75
28	2.19	2.12	2.04	1.96	1.91	1.87	1.82	1.77	1.71
30	2.16	2.09	2.01	1.93	1.88	1.84	1.79	1.74	1.68
35	2.11	2.04	1.96	1.88	1.82	1.79	1.74	1.68	1.62
40	2.08	2.00	1.92	1.84	1.78	1.74	1.69	1.64	1.58
45	2.05	1.97	1.89	1.81	1.75	1.71	1.66	1.60	1.54
50	2.03	1.95	1.87	1.78	1.73	1.69	1.63	1.58	1.51
55	2.01	1.93	1.85	1.76	1.71	1.67	1.61	1.55	1.49
60	1.99	1.92	1.84	1.75	1.69	1.65	1.59	1.53	1.47
80	1.95	1.88	1.79	1.70	1.64	1.60	1.54	1.48	1.41
100	1.93	1.85	1.77	1.68	1.62	1.57	1.52	1.45	1.38
150	1.89	1.82	1.73	1.64	1.58	1.54	1.48	1.41	1.33
200	1.88	1.80	1.72	1.62	1.56	1.52	1.46	1.39	1.30
500	1.85	1.77	1.69	1.59	1.53	1.48	1.42	1.35	1.26

Generated using SAS function FINV.

EXHIBIT C.5   Power of PRE and F for $\alpha = .05$ and PA $-$ PC $= 1$

	Crit Values		Prob(PRE > Critical Value of PRE)							
			TRUE PRE η^2							
$n - PA$	F	PRE	0	.01	.03	.05	.075	.1	.2	.3
1	161.45	.994	.05	.05	.05	.05	.05	.05	.06	.06
2	18.51	.902	.05	.05	.05	.05	.06	.06	.07	.09
3	10.13	.771	.05	.05	.06	.06	.06	.07	.10	.13
4	7.71	.658	.05	.05	.06	.07	.07	.08	.12	.17
5	6.61	.569	.05	.05	.06	.07	.08	.09	.15	.22
6	5.99	.499	.05	.06	.07	.08	.09	.11	.18	.27
7	5.59	.444	.05	.06	.07	.08	.10	.12	.21	.32
8	5.32	.399	.05	.06	.07	.09	.11	.13	.24	.37
9	5.12	.362	.05	.06	.08	.09	.12	.15	.27	.42
10	4.96	.332	.05	.06	.08	.10	.13	.16	.30	.46
11	4.84	.306	.05	.06	.08	.11	.14	.17	.33	.51
12	4.75	.283	.05	.06	.09	.11	.15	.19	.36	.55
13	4.67	.264	.05	.06	.09	.12	.16	.20	.39	.59
14	4.60	.247	.05	.06	.09	.13	.17	.21	.41	.63
15	4.54	.232	.05	.07	.10	.13	.18	.23	.44	.66
16	4.49	.219	.05	.07	.10	.14	.19	.24	.47	.69
17	4.45	.208	.05	.07	.11	.15	.20	.25	.49	.72
18	4.41	.197	.05	.07	.11	.15	.21	.27	.52	.75
19	4.38	.187	.05	.07	.11	.16	.22	.28	.54	.77
20	4.35	.179	.05	.07	.12	.16	.23	.29	.57	.80
22	4.30	.164	.05	.07	.12	.18	.25	.32	.61	.84
24	4.26	.151	.05	.08	.13	.19	.27	.35	.65	.87
26	4.23	.140	.05	.08	.14	.20	.29	.37	.69	.89
28	4.20	.130	.05	.08	.15	.22	.31	.40	.72	.92
30	4.17	.122	.05	.08	.15	.23	.33	.42	.75	.93
35	4.12	.105	.05	.09	.17	.26	.37	.48	.82	.96
40	4.08	.093	.05	.10	.19	.29	.42	.54	.87	.98
45	4.06	.083	.05	.10	.21	.33	.46	.59	.91	.99
50	4.03	.075	.05	.11	.23	.36	.51	.64	.93	*
55	4.02	.068	.05	.11	.25	.39	.55	.68	.95	*
60	4.00	.063	.05	.12	.27	.42	.58	.72	.97	*
80	3.96	.047	.05	.14	.34	.53	.71	.84	.99	*
100	3.94	.038	.05	.17	.41	.62	.81	.91	*	*
150	3.90	.025	.05	.23	.57	.80	.93	.98	*	*
200	3.89	.019	.05	.29	.70	.90	.98	*	*	*
500	3.86	.008	.05	.61	.98	*	*	*	*	*

* Power > .995.
Generated using SAS function PROBF.

EXHIBIT C.6   Power of PRE and *F* for α = .05 and PA − PC > 1 for Small (.03), Medium (.1), and Large (.3) η^2

n − PA	η^2	1	2	3	4	5	7	10	15	20
					PA − PC					
5	.03	.06	.06	.05	.05	.05	.05	.05	.05	.05
	.1	.09	.07	.07	.06	.06	.06	.06	.05	.05
	.3	.22	.15	.12	.11	.09	.08	.07	.07	.06
10	.03	.08	.07	.06	.06	.06	.06	.05	.05	.05
	.1	.16	.12	.10	.09	.08	.07	.07	.06	.06
	.3	.46	.34	.27	.23	.20	.16	.13	.10	.09
15	.03	.10	.08	.07	.07	.07	.06	.06	.06	.05
	.1	.23	.17	.14	.12	.11	.10	.08	.07	.07
	.3	.66	.52	.44	.38	.33	.27	.21	.16	.13
20	.03	.12	.09	.08	.08	.07	.07	.06	.06	.06
	.1	.29	.22	.18	.16	.14	.12	.10	.09	.08
	.3	.80	.68	.59	.53	.47	.39	.31	.23	.19
35	.03	.17	.13	.11	.10	.09	.09	.08	.07	.07
	.1	.48	.38	.32	.27	.25	.21	.17	.14	.12
	.3	.96	.92	.88	.84	.80	.73	.63	.51	.42
50	.03	.23	.17	.15	.13	.12	.11	.09	.08	.08
	.1	.64	.52	.45	.40	.36	.31	.25	.20	.17
	.3	*	.99	.97	.96	.94	.91	.85	.75	.66
75	.03	.32	.25	.21	.18	.17	.14	.12	.10	.09
	.1	.81	.72	.65	.59	.55	.48	.40	.32	.27
	.3	*	*	*	*	*	.99	.98	.95	.91
100	.03	.41	.32	.27	.24	.22	.19	.16	.13	.12
	.1	.91	.85	.79	.74	.70	.63	.55	.45	.38
	.3	*	*	*	*	*	*	*	.99	.98
150	.03	.57	.46	.40	.36	.33	.28	.23	.19	.16
	.1	.98	.96	.94	.91	.89	.85	.78	.69	.61
	.3	*	*	*	*	*	*	*	*	*
200	.03	.70	.59	.52	.47	.43	.38	.32	.26	.22
	.1	*	.99	.98	.98	.97	.95	.91	.85	.79
	.3	*	*	*	*	*	*	*	*	*
500	.03	.98	.95	.92	.90	.87	.83	.77	.68	.61
	.1	*	*	*	*	*	*	*	*	*
	.3	*	*	*	*	*	*	*	*	*

* Power > .995
Generated using SAS function PROBF.

SAS Code for Exhibit C.1

```
options ls=79 ps=66;
/* Table of Critical Values of PRE */
/* PRE with PA−PC and n−PA degrees of freedom has a beta
   distribution with parameters a=(PA−PC)/2 and b=(n−PA)/2
   see Abramowitz & Stegun, p. 944 */
data pretab;
  df1 = 1; /* all with PA−PC = 1 */
  a = df1/2;
  do alpha = .5, .2, .1, .05, .025, .01, .005, .001;
  do df2 = 1 to 20 by 1, 22 to 30 by 2, 35 to 60 by 5, 80, 100,
     150, 200, 500;
    b = df2/2;
    precrit = betainv(1−alpha,a,b);
    output;
  end; end;
run;
proc tabulate formchar='                              ' format=6.3 noseps order=data;
  class df2 alpha;
  var precrit;
  label precrit='Critical Values of PRE for PA−PC = 1';
  label df2='n−PA';
  label alpha='Alpha';
  keylabel sum=' ';
  table df2, precrit*alpha /rts=7;
    run;
```

SAS Code for Exhibit C.2

```
options ls=79 ps=66;
/* Table of Critical Values of PRE */
/* PRE with PA-PC and n-PA degrees of freedom has a beta
   distribution with parameters a=(PA - PC)/2 and b=(n-PA)/2
   see Abramowitz & Stegun, p. 944 */
data pretab;
  alpha = .05; /* do all this at alpha = .05*/
  do df1 = 1,2,3,4,5,6,7,8,9;
/* do df1 = 10,12,15,20,25,30,40,60,120   for 2nd half of table */
  a = df1/2;
  do df2 = 1 to 20 by 1, 22 to 30 by 2, 35 to 60 by 5, 80, 100,
    150, 200, 500;
    b = df2/2;
    precrit = betainv(1-alpha,a,b);
    output;
  end; end; run;
proc tabulate formchar='                        ' format=6.2 noseps order=data;
  class df1 df2;
  var fcrit;
  footnote 'Generated using SAS Function BETAINV';
  label fcrit='Critical Values of PRE for Alpha = .05'
        df2='n-PA'     df1='PA-PC';
  keylabel sum=' ';
  table df2,fcrit*df1/rts=7;
    run;
```

SAS Code for Exhibit C.3

```
options ls=79 ps=66;
/* Table of Critical Values of F */
    /* F = PRE/df1/(1-PRE)/df2 */
data ftab;
  df1 = 1; /* all with PA-PC = 1 */
  do alpha = .5, .2, .1, .05, .025, .01, .005, .001;
  do df2 = 1 to 20 by 1, 22 to 30 by 2, 35 to 60 by 5, 80, 100,
    150, 200, 500;      /* df2 = n-PA */

    fcrit = finv(1-alpha,df1,df2);
    output;
  end; end;
run;

proc tabulate formchar='                              ' format=6.2 noseps order=data;
  class df2 alpha;
  var fcrit;
  footnote 'Generated using SAS Function BETAINV';
  label fcrit='Critical Values of F for PA-PC = 1';
  label df2='n-PA';
  label alpha='Alpha';
  keylabel sum=' ';
  table df2, fcrit*alpha /rts=7;
    run;
```

SAS Code for Exhibit C.4

```
options ls=79 ps=66;
/* Table of Critical Values of PRE */
    /* F = PRE/df1/(1-PRE)/df2 */
data ftab;
  alpha = .05;   /* do all at this alpha */
  do df1 = 1,2,3,4,5,6,7,8,9;
 /* do df1 = 10,12,15,20,25,30,40,60,120 for 2nd half of table */

  do df2 = 1 to 20 by 1, 22 to 30 by 2, 35 to 60 by 5, 80, 100,
    150, 200, 500;

    fcrit = finv(1-alpha,df1,df2);
    output;
  end; end; run;
proc tabulate formchar='                              ' format=6.2 noseps order=data;
  class df1 df2;
  var fcrit;
  footnote 'Generated using SAS Function BETAINV';
  label fcrit='Critical Values of F for Alpha = .05'
        df2='n-PA'      df1='PA-PC';
  keylabel sum=' ';
  table df2,fcrit*df1/rts=7;
    run;
```

SAS Code for Exhibit C.5

```
options ls=79 ps=66;
data power;
k = 1;      /* dummy variable to trick proc tabulate */
df1 = 1;      /* df1 = PA-PC */
alpha = .05;   /* for fixed alpha */
do df2 = 1 to 20 by 1, 22 to 30 by 2, 35 to 60 by 5, 80, 100,
         150, 200, 500;
   fcrit = finv(1-alpha,df1,df2);   /* find critical F */
   precrit = betainv(1-alpha,df1/2,df2/2); /* and critical PRE */
   do pre = 0, .01, .03, .05, .075, .1, .2, .3;
      nc = pre*df2/(1-pre);   /* non-centrality parameter */
      if (nc > 100) then power=1;   /* power too big to calculate */
      else
      power = 1-probf(fcrit,df1,df2,nc);

      output;
   end;
end;
     run;
proc tabulate formchar='                            ' format=5.2 noseps order=data;
  class df2 k pre;
  var fcrit precrit power;
  footnote 'Generated using SAS Function PROBF';
  label power='Prob(PRE > PRECRIT)';
  label df2='n-PA';
  label pre='TRUE PRE';
  keylabel sum=' ';
  table df2, k*fcrit*mean*F=6.2 k*precrit*mean*F=5.3 power*pre/rts=6;
     run;
```

SAS Code for Exhibit C.6

```
options nocenter ps=66;
/* generates power table for small, medium, and large effects for
   numerator df > 1    */
data power;
alpha = .05;  /* for fixed alpha */
do df1 = 1, 2, 3, 4, 5, 7, 10, 15, 20;
do df2 = 5, 10, 15, 20, 35, 50, 75, 100, 150, 200, 500;
  fcrit = finv(1−alpha,df1,df2);
  precrit = betainv(1−alpha,df1/2,df2/2);
    nc = .03*df2/(1−.03);  /* for small effect */
    small = 1−probf(fcrit,df1,df2,nc);
    nc = .1*df2/(1−.1);  /* for medium effect    */
    medium = 1−probf(fcrit,df1,df2,nc);
    nc = .3*df2/(1−.3);  /* for large effect    */
    large = 1-probf(fcrit,df1,df2,nc);

    output;
  end;
end;
    run;
proc tabulate formchar='                               ' format=5.2 noseps order=data;
  class df1 df2;
  var small medium large;
  table df2*(small medium large), df1;
  label small='.03';
  label medium='.1 ';
  label large='.3 ';
  keylabel sum=' ';
  label df2='n−PA';
  label df1='PA−PA';
  footnote 'Generated using SAS Function PROBF';
        run;
```

REFERENCES

Abrahams, D. M., and Rizzardi, F. (1988). *The Berkeley Interactive Statistical System.* New York: W. W. Norton.

Anderson, N. H. (1982). *Methods of Information Integration Theory.* New York: Academic Press.

Anscombe, F. J. (1961). Examination of residuals. *Proceedings of Fourth Berkeley Symposium in Mathematical Statistics and Probability, 1,* 1–36.

Anscombe, F. J. (1973). Graphs in statistical analysis. *American Statistician, 27,* 17–21.

Becker, R. A., and Chambers, J. M. (1984). *S: An Interactive Environment for Data Analysis and Graphics.* Belmont, CA: Wadsworth.

Belsley, D. A., Kuh, E., and Welsch, R. E. (1980). *Regression Diagnostics: Identifying Influential Data and Sources of Collinearity.* New York: Wiley.

Bernoulli, D. (1738/1954). Exposition of a new theory on the measurement of risk. Translated by L. Sommer. *Econometrika, 22,* 23–36.

Bradley, J. V. (1978). Robustness? *British Journal of Mathematical and Statistical Psychology, 31,* 144–152.

Box, G. E. P., and Cox, D. R. (1964). An analysis of transformations (with discussion). *Journal of Royal Statistical Society, Series B, 26,* 211–246.

Campbell, D. T., and Stanley, J. C. (1963). Experimental and quasi-experimental designs for research on teaching. In N. L. Gage (Ed.), *Handbook of Research on Teaching*. Chicago: Rand McNally, 1963. (Also published as *Experimental and Quasi-Experimental Designs for Research*. Chicago: Rand McNally, 1966.)

Cochran, W. G., and Cox, G. M. (1957). *Experimental Designs*. New York: Wiley.

Cohen, J. (1977). *Statistical Power Analysis for the Behavioral Sciences*, rev. ed. New York: Academic Press.

Cohen, J. (1978). Partialed products are interactions; Partialed powers are curve components. *Psychological Bulletin, 85*, 858–866.

Conover, W. J., and Iman, R. L. (1981). Rank transformations as a bridge between parametric and nonparametric statistics. *American Statistician, 35*, 124–129.

Cook, R. D. (1977). Detection of influential observations in linear regression. *Technometrics, 19*, 15–18.

Cook, R. D. (1979). Influential observations in linear regression. *Journal of the American Statistical Association, 74*, 169–174.

Cook, T. D., and Campbell, D. T. (1979). *Quasi-Experimentation: Design and Analysis Issues for Field Settings*. Chicago: Rand McNally.

Dixon, W. J. (1983). *BMDP Statistical Software (1985 Printing)*. Berkeley, CA: University of California Press.

Draper, N. R., and Smith, H. (1981). *Applied Regression Analysis*. 2nd ed. New York: Wiley.

Eccles, J. S. (1987). Gender roles and women's achievement-related decisions. *Psychology of Women Quarterly, 11*, 135–172.

Edwards, A. L. (1960). *Experimental Design in Psychological Research*. New York: Holt, Rinehart and Winston.

Freund, R. J., and Littel, R. C. (1986). *SAS System for Regression*. Cary, NC: SAS Institute Inc.

Freund, R. J., Littell, R. C., and Spector, P. C. (1986). *SAS System for Linear Models*. Cary, NC: SAS Institute Inc.

Glass, G. V., Peckham, P. D., and Sanders, J. R. (1972). Consequences of failure to meet assumptions underlying the fixed effects analyses of variance and covariance. *Review of Educational Research, 42*, 237–288.

Goodman, L. A., and Kruskal, W. H. (1954). Measures of association for cross-classifications. *Journal of the American Statistical Association, 49*, 732–764.

Gottman, J. M. (1981). *Time Series Analysis for the Behavioral Sciences*. New York: Cambridge University Press.

Henderson, H., and Velleman, P. F. (1981). Building multiple regression models interactively. *Biometrics, 37,* 391–411.

Hogg, R. V., and Craig, A. T. (1978). *Introduction to Mathematical Statistics.* 4th ed. New York: Macmillan.

Huber, P. (1981). *Robust Statistics.* New York: Wiley.

Judd, C. M., and Kenny, D. A. (1981). *Estimating the Effects of Social Interventions.* Cambridge: Cambridge University Press.

Kenny, D. A., and Judd, C. M. (1986). Consequences of violating the independence assumption in analysis of variance. *Psychological Bulletin, 99,* 422–431.

Keppel, G. (1982). *Design and Analysis: A Researcher's Handbook,* 2nd ed. Englewood Cliffs, NJ: Prentice-Hall.

Kidder, L. H., and Judd, C. M. (1986). *Research Methods in Social Relations.* New York: Holt, Rinehart, and Winston.

Krantz, D. H., Luce, R. D., Suppes, P., and Tversky, A. (1971). *Foundations of Measurement.* New York: Academic Press.

McClearly, R., and Hay, R. A. (1980). *Applied Time Series Analysis.* Beverly Hills, CA: Sage.

Mosteller, F., and Tukey, J. W. (1977). *Data Analysis and Regression: A Second Course in Statistics.* Reading, MA: Addison-Wesley.

Nie, N. H., Hull, C. H., Franklin, M. N., Jenkins, J. G., Sours, K. J., Norušis, M. J., and Beadle, V. (1980). *SCSS: A User's Guide to the SCSS Conversational System.* New York: McGraw-Hill.

Norušis, M. J., (1985). *SPSS-X Advanced Statistics Guide.* New York: McGraw-Hill.

Park, B. and Rothbart, M. (1982). Perception of out-group homogeneity and levels of social categorization: Memory for the subordinate attributes of in-group and out-group members. *Journal of Personality and Social Psychology, 42,* 1051–1068.

Rosenthal, R., and Rosnow, R. L. (1985). *Contrast Analysis: Focused Comparisons in the Analysis of Variance.* Cambridge: Cambridge University Press.

Ryan, B. F., Joiner, B. L., and Ryan, T. A., Jr. (1985). *Minitab Handbook.* 2nd ed. Boston: Duxbury Press.

SAS Institute Inc. (1985). *SAS User's Guide: Statistics,* Version 5 Edition. Cary, NC: SAS Institute Inc..

Scheffé, H. A. (1959). *The Analysis of Variance.* New York: Wiley.

Seber, G. A. F. (1984). *Multivariate Observations.* New York: Wiley.

Steel, R. G. D., and Torrie, J. H. (1980). *Principles and Procedures of Statistics: A Biometric Approach,* 2nd ed. New York: McGraw-Hill.

Stevens, S. S. (1951). Mathematics, measurement and psychophysics. In S. S. Stevens (Ed.), *Handbook of Experimental Psychology.* New York: Wiley.

Stevens, S. S. (1961). To honor Fechner and repeal his law. *Science, 133,* 80–86.

SPSS Inc. (1987). *SPSS-X User's Guide,* 3rd ed. New York: McGraw-Hill.

Tukey, J. W. (1977). *Exploratory Data Analysis.* Reading, MA: Addison-Wesley.

Velleman, P. F., and Welsch, R. E. (1981). Efficient computing of regression diagnostics. *American Statistician, 35,* 234–242.

Wilcox, R. R. (1987). New designs in analysis of variance. *Annual Review of Psychology, 38,* 29–60.

INDEX